History of
The Theological Seminary
in Virginia
and
Its Historical Background

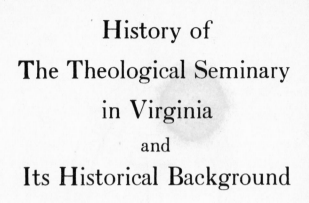

Rev. Wm. A. R. Goodwin, D. D.

Editor and Author

Centennial Edition

1923

Edwin S. Gorham, Publisher and Bookseller
11 West 45th Street, New York

The Du Bois Press
Complete Printing Service
ROCHESTER, N. Y.

The Ascension

"Go ye into all the world, and preach the gospel to every creature."

INTRODUCTION

RT. REV. DR. WILLIAM CABELL BROWN

Bishop of Virginia
and
President of Board of Trustees

IT has often seemed to me quite unaccountable that until now no history of the Virginia Theological Seminary has ever been attempted. And this is all the more remarkable when one remembers the large number of distinguished alumni who have gone forth from the "old Hill", and the conspicuous part the Seminary has played in the life of the Church both at home and abroad.

At last this reproach is to be removed, for the Rev. W. A. R. Goodwin, D. D., accepted several years ago the urgent invitation of the Alumni Association and the Board of Trustees and agreed to undertake the preparation of a history of the Seminary which should be ready, if possible, for distribution in time for the centennial celebration which is to be observed in June, 1923.

Among the many devoted sons of the Seminary none could be found better fitted for this work than Dr. Goodwin. While he was rector of old Bruton Parish, Williamsburg, he determined to undertake the complete restoration of the old Church. To do this it was necessary to devote much time to original research among old documents, and the information thus acquired not only enabled him to write the History of Bruton Parish and carry out admirably his plans for the restoration of the old Court Church of Colonial Virginia, but it has doubtless been of great value to him in the preparation of the history of the Seminary.

Dr. Goodwin, as an alumnus of the Seminary and for many years now a diligent student of its history, was not only peculiarly fitted for this work himself, but as a cursory examination of the table of contents will also show, he has succeeded in enlisting the cooperation of a very able body of assistants, who have prepared at his request many most interesting and valuable papers on the different phases of the life and work of the Seminary.

The many friends and alumni of the Seminary will rejoice at the completion of this monumental work, and no one, I venture to think, will be able to read its pages without a juster appreciation of the splendid services the Seminary has rendered to the Church through the labors of its alumni in our own country and in lands beyond the seas.

WILLIAM CABELL BROWN

Richmond, Virginia—1923.

PREFACE

THE writing of the History of the Theological Seminary in Virginia covering the first one hundred years of its life and work was first suggested to the editor and author by the Rev. Dr. Angus Crawford, then dean of the Seminary. This request of Dr. Crawford was formally seconded by the Alumni Association, and was subsequently endorsed by the Board of Trustees of the Seminary. Dr. Crawford had previously prevailed upon the Rev. Dr. Cornelius Walker, then senior professor of the Seminary, to prepare a manuscript record of the chief historical facts concerning the birth and development of this School of the Prophets. Dr. Walker finished his record after he had retired from the Seminary on account of extreme age and infirmity. His manuscript, and "The Recollections of a Long Life", by the Rev. Dr. Joseph Packard, have been freely used and have been among the most valuable sources of information.

Fortunately the minutes of the Education Society, out of which the Seminary grew, and which was indeed for a while the Seminary itself, together with the minutes of the Board of Trustees and of the Alumni Association, have been preserved in almost unbroken continuity. These have all been carefully read and used as authoritative sources. In order to guarantee the preservation of the most important part of the documentary history of the Seminary, the early minutes of the Education Society and of the Board of Trustees have been carefully copied and are reproduced in the appendix to the second volume. The complete file of "The Theological Repertory" was consulted and "The Southern Churchman", covering almost the whole period of the life of the Seminary, has been carefully examined, as have been selected volumes of other Church magazines and newspapers including the various magazines and publications of the Seminary itself.

We have been fortunate in having had access to the diaries and letters of some of the early graduates.

The plan of the book calls for a word of explanation. It is more than a History of the Seminary. These volumes include a great deal of historical material which finds its rightful place here because it is related to the Seminary or because the Seminary is vitally related to the times and conditions dealt with in these sections of the book. The Theological Seminary in Virginia grew naturally and inevitably out of its environment and was largely the product of conditions precedent and also compelling in their influence. It is for this reason that the treatment of the current history of the Seminary has been preceded by two sections, one dealing with the historical background of the Institution, and the other with the life and influence of some of its founders. These sections stand like the long avenue and pillared portico leading up to a temple.

The chapters written by the Rev. Dr. Edward L. Goodwin and the Rev. Dr. C. Braxton Bryan, included in the first section, constitute a most valuable contribution to the History of the American Church. They show the conditions and the need out of which grew the consciousness in the Virginia Church that a Theological Seminary was necessary. These chapters, also, reveal the social conditions and the atmosphere into which many of the early graduates of this Institution passed in the exercise of their ministry.

It was also fitting that the men most conspicuous as founders of the Education Society and the Seminary should be given place in the forefront. It was upon them that the influences which came out of the background produced their compelling effect. In them were found the faith and the prophetic vision which, wedded to strong courage and consecrated zeal, set in motion the forces which culminated in the creation of the Theological Seminary in Virginia.

The sections devoted to the portrayal of various aspects of the Seminary life in the form of monographs, the biographical sketches of the Seminary professors and of the Bishops of Virginia, who have served as presidents of the Board of Trustees, will prove of interest to all who know and love the Institution. To this section of the book many of the distinguished sons of the Seminary, and other writers, friends of the Seminary, have made valuable contribution. Some of them, speaking out of memories lit by affection, throw a hallowed glow around the history of our Alma Mater.

Special appreciation is felt and expressed for the valuable articles written by the Rev. Dr. Carl E. Grammer, sometime professor of History in the Seminary. Volume I has been greatly enriched by the several contributions made by him. His long connection with the Institution and still longer and more intimate association with some of the older members of the faculty, whose biographical sketches he has written, enabled him to write not only with the clearness of historical insight and literary charm which characterizes this gifted scholar, but also with the glow of personal reminiscence and affection. The Rev. Dr. Samuel A. Wallis, professor emeritus of the Institution, has made a valuable contribution to the work in the chapters on the Library and Seminary Mission Stations and in the biographical sketches of some of the early professors.

Under the supervision of the Rev. Dr. Wallace E. Rollins, professor of History in the Virginia Seminary, the section devoted to the contributions made by this Institution to the domestic and foreign missionary work of the Church has been prepared. This section constitutes an invaluable contribution to the history of the missionary life and endeavor of the Church. It would have been worth all the time and energy which the preparation of this book has demanded to have secured the writing of this section alone.

The reason for inserting the History of the Episcopal High School and the Bishop Payne Divinity School at first may not be apparent. When, however, it is remembered that both of these Institutions were established and fostered by the Board of Trustees of the Seminary, valid reason for the insertion of these chapters becomes evident. The life of the High School and the life of the Seminary have always been inseparably associated. From the Seminary have gone influences to enrich the life of the High School, while from the High School there has come to the Seminary a perennial stream of young life, consecrated to the purpose of giving itself through the sacred ministry to make glad the City of God. The History of the High School contained in the second volume of this History was written by an alumnus of the High School, the Rev. Dr. Arthur B. Kinsolving, who has expanded what he has written for this book into a separate volume, "The Story of a Southern School", giving in full the history of the High School.

The Bishop Payne Divinity School was established as a recognized annex of the Virginia Seminary, and its history is therefore a part of the history of this Institution. This chapter has been written by the Rev. Frederick G. Ribble, D. D., for many years professor in, and now dean of the Bishop Payne Divinity School.

To the Rev. Dr. Edward L. Goodwin special gratitude and appreciation is expressed by the editor in behalf of the alumni for his arduous and valuable work in the preparation of the data contained in Volume II concerning the Alumni of the Seminary.

The responsibility of acting as editor and author has at times been a difficult one. We are fully conscious of the fact that from a critical point of view, the result has not always been satisfactory. The current history and the monograph chapters at times overlap, and there has necessarily been some duplication of subject matter. This repetition has been observed, and, for good reasons, allowed to remain. We have intentionally included a number of repetitions in the memories of some of the older alumni. Many similar rays of light are allowed to fall upon the garden where the flowers grow, but we do not feel that the sunlight's rays are wasted as they combine to make beautiful the flowers in the garden.

The conditions under which this work has been prepared for the press have been, in many respects, far from ideal. For the work of research and writing, time has had to be found amid the many and exacting duties of parochial and diocesan responsibility while rector of St. Paul's Church, Rochester, New York, and later while Professor in the College of William and Mary. Had we not had the co-operation of some in no way connected with the Seminary who have been willing to make exceptional sacrifices of time and energy in giving assistance, the work could not have been brought to completion.

Grateful recognition is made of the generous kindness of several friends of the Seminary, not all alumni, who contributed the funds necessary to defray the preliminary expenses incident to the preparation of the History. The Board of Trustees is under sincere obligation to the Rev. A. E. Clattenburg of Hazleton, Pennsylvania, for his generous and devoted work in conducting without cost to the Seminary the entire campaign of publicity in connection with the distribution of these volumes, and also to the Rev. Henry J. Pulver of Washington, for his kind assistance in securing many of the photographs used in making the illustrations.

To Dr. John R. Slater, professor of English in the University of Rochester, to Dr. Walter A. Montgomery, professor of Latin in the College of William and Mary, and to the Rev. Dr. Edward L. Goodwin, historiographer of the Diocese of Virginia, gratitude is expressed for their patient and scholarly work in reading the manuscripts and helping to correct the proof sheets of these volumes, to Mr. Claude Bragdon of Rochester, New York, for designing the title page and for other advice kindly given, and to the Rt. Rev. Dr. William Cabell Brown, President of the Board of Trustees, for his gracious Introduction.

The book goes forth as a gift of devotion from all those

who have shared in its making. It is hoped that the reading of these records of the History of the Seminary and of the lives of those who have ministered to the making of its greatness will deepen the devotion of the sons of the Seminary for their Alma Mater, and help win for her the friendship and devotion of others.

"From earth's wide bounds, from ocean's farthest coast", there are those who look with fond memory and grateful affection to the old Seminary, and perhaps it will delight those who will come after us to this School of the Prophets for their training for the sacred ministry to read the record of the things which were done in the old times before them.

What has been written is an imperfect offering of love to those especially who love the Seminary. We trust that this History of one hundred years of faith and struggle and achievement in the life of the Theological Seminary in Virginia may minister to make the lamp of memory burn more brightly upon the altars of affection, and that the record given may prompt many to offer more constant and more earnest intercessions for God's continued blessing upon this School of the Prophets.

WM. A. R. GOODWIN

The College of William and Mary
Williamsburg, Virginia—Ascension Day, 1923.

CONTENTS

VOLUME I

xi

SECTION V—*Continued.*

CONTENTS

Volume II *

Section VI

Brief Biographical Sketches of the Later Bishops of Virginia, Presidents of the Board of Trustees, of Bishop Peterkin, Cassius F. Lee, and Francis Scott Key

Section VII

The Alumni Association and the Alumni

* For Page numbers of articles in Volume II, see Table of Contents repeated in Volume II.

ILLUSTRATIONS

VOLUME I

Illustrations—*Continued.*

SECTION I

The Historical Background

INTRODUCTION

REV. W. A. R. GOODWIN, D. D.

TO

SECTION I

THE HISTORICAL BACKGROUND

The Theological Seminary in Virginia is rooted deeply in the past. It was not imposed upon the Church. As a living organism it grew into being through creative forces and vital needs which had long been present in the life of the Church in Virginia. The need for native clergymen trained in the Colony had been felt from the very beginning of the Virginia settlement. This need was voiced in connection with the efforts made in 1619 to establish the University of Henricopolis. This endeavor was brought to naught by the Indian Massacre which occurred on the 22nd of March, 1622.

When the effort to establish a College was renewed by the Grand Assembly held in James City on March 23rd, 1660, the act passed, entitled "A Provision for a College," opens with the words: "Whereas the want of able and faithful ministers in this country deprives us of those great blessings and mercies that alwais attend upon the service of God; which want, by reason of our great distance from our native Country, can not in probability be alwais supplyed from thence; Be it enacted, that for the advance of learning, education of youth, supply of the ministry, and promotion of piety, there be land taken upon purchases for a College and free schoole, and that there be, with as much speede as may be convenient, houseing erected thereon for entertainment of students and scholers."

When in 1693 the College of William and Mary was established in Williamsburg, provision was made for supplying this need through the establishment of a course of Divinity in the College. Bishop Meade in his "Old Churches, Ministers and Families in Virginia" bears witness as to the contribution made by the College of William and Mary, in this respect, to the Church in Virginia, in the following words: "One thing is set forth in praise of William and Mary which we delight to record, viz: that the hopes and designs of its founders and early benefactors, in relation to its being a nursery of pious ministers, were not entirely disappointed. It is positively affirmed, by those most competent to speak, that the best ministers in Virginia were those educated at the College and sent over to England for ordination."

The extent to which this need for a godly and well trained ministry existed in Virginia; the deplorable conditions into which the Church had fallen in the Colony, subsequent to the Revolution, due to this and other causes; the social, moral, political and ecclesiastical condition of the Colonial and Post-Revolutionary period, and the efforts made by the Church to live through them and to better them are told in the chapters to which this section is devoted. It was out of these conditions that the Theological Seminary in Virginia grew, and it was into this environment that her early graduates passed to bear their witness and to do their work of reconstruction.

THE JAMESTOWN CHURCH TOWER

SECTION I

CHAPTER I

THE COLONIAL CHURCH AND CLERGY IN VIRGINIA

REV. E. L. GOODWIN, D. D.

Historiographer of the Diocese of Virginia

The Nature of the Jamestown Settlement 1607—Rev. Robert Hunt—Rev. Richard Buck—Rev. Alexander Whitaker—Henricopolis—Pocahontas—Later Jamestown Clergymen—The House of Burgesses the Governing Body of the Church —Types of Colonial Churches—Parish Vestries—The Position of the Commissary—Salaries of the Colonial Clergy—The Induction Controversy—The Character of the Colonial Clergy—Prominent Colonial Clergymen in Virginia —Commissary Blair—Dissenters in Virginia—Presbyterians—Baptists— The Parsons' Case and Patrick Henry—The Growth of Democratic Principles and the Revolution—Post-Revolution Problems and Difficulties.

The Episcopal Church in Virginia has an unbroken history dating from the first permanent English settlement in America, which was made at Jamestown, Virginia, May 24, 1607. Unlike certain colonies of a later date, founded by emigrants who were seeking to escape conditions at home with which they were dissatisfied, the Colony of Virginia was founded with the distinct purpose of transplanting and establishing English life and institutions, civil and religious, intact in the new world. It was the product of a great national movement, representing the best of English statesmanship and Churchmanship at the beginning of the seventeenth century.

For a long and critical period England had been in conflict with Spain, then the most powerful and the representative Catholic state of Europe. More than an hundred years before, a Papal bull, emanating from that Rome which still assumed to be the mistress of the world, had granted to Spain the yet almost unknown Continent of America. From her exploitation of these possessions Spain had drawn her boundless wealth, wasted in her efforts for universal domination and for the religious supremacy of the Papal power. England meanwhile had become the champion and defender of the Protestant faith, and her own liberties were bound up in the maintenance of that cause. If she would

1

retain the mastery of the seas, so lately wrested from her ancient enemy, and the position she coveted among the nations, and if the political, intellectual and religious freedom which she was learning to claim for herself and to defend for mankind was to be triumphant in the end, it was felt that the power of her still dangerous rival should be offset in the new world by the planting there of English dominions closely united with the mother country. Such was the intention signalized by the formation of the Virginia Company of London, by which this colony was planted and for many years nourished and guided.

A complete list of the members and promoters of this Company, if it had been preserved to us, would contain many thousand names. Government officials, nobility and gentry, the learned professions, the great trades guilds or city companies of London, and not least, Churchmen and divines of the first distinction, were actively interested in a venture the objects of which were more clearly apprehended than its difficulties. But in every enumeration of these objects the planting of the English Protestant Church and religion on these shores was emphasized as among the first, and a distinctly missionary character was stamped upon the enterprise. In the royal Letters Patent commendation is given "Of so noble a work, which may, by the providence of Almighty God, hereafter tend to the glory of His Divine Majesty, in propagating the Christian religion to such people as yet live in darkness and miserable ignorance of the true knowledge and worship of God, and may in time bring the infidels and savages, living in those parts, to human civility, and to a quiet and settled government." And in the "Articles, Instructions and Orders" for the government of the Colonies of Virginia, wherever planted, of which that at Jamestown alone survived, we read:—"And wee doe specially ordaine, charge, and require, the said president and councells, and the ministers of the said several colonies respectively, within their several limits and precincts, that they, with all diligence, care and respect, doe provide, that the true word and service of God and Christian faith be preached, planted, and used, not only within every of the said several colonies and plantations, but alsoe as much as they may amongst the savage people which doe or shall adjoine unto them, or border upon them, according to the doctrine, rights, and religion now professed and established within our realms of England." That these instructions were accepted literally and sincerely by the early settlers, and were never quite forgotten by their successors, can be sufficiently shown. The established Church and religion of England were guarded and perpetuated in the Colony of Virginia until near the close of its history with a zeal and carefulness quite equal to that of the home country. The Acts of Supremacy and of Uniformity were never less inviolate in Jamestown or Williamsburg than in London, and during the period of the Commonwealth, when the Church was nominally disestablished in the Colony as at home, there was no wavering in the allegiance of the people to its forms or teachings.

The pioneer adventurers, numbering one hundred and twenty, who came under Captain Newport in the good ships the *Sarah Constant*, the *Goodspeed* and the *Discovery* and settled at Jamestown, had for their chaplain the Rev. Robert Hunt, M. A., a name which American Churchmen must ever hold in honor. He was a Cambridge scholar and had held for eight years or more the vicarage of Reculver, in Kent, before he was nominated by Archbishop Bancroft and gladly accepted by the Company for this arduous duty. "Truly, in my opinion," said Captain Wingfield, first President of the Colony, "a man not any waie to be touched with the rebellious humors of a papist Spirit, nor blemished with ye least suspition of a factious scismatick, whereof I had a special care." During the six weeks that the ships were storm-bound off the Kentish coasts he was extremely ill, yet he refused to "leave the business," though but ten or twelve miles from his home. Both on the voyage and after the landing he was the peacemaker of the expedition, and by precept and example upheld the courage of the company under all vicissitudes. "Many were the mischiefs," said one of their early chroniclers, "that daily sprung from their ignorant, but ambitious spirits; but the good doctrine and exhortation of our Preacher, Mr. Hunt, reconciled them." In the fire which destroyed the greater part of the rude settlement during its first winter, "good Mr. Hunt lost all his library and all that he had but the clothes on his back, yet (did) none ever see him repine at his loss." The notices which remain of this first Virginian clergyman come from many sources, but agree without exception in ascribing to him a character of rare courage, strength and consistency and in witnessing to the esteem and affection of his little flock.

From the first landing the services of the Church with sermons were regularly held. The first celebration of the Holy Communion of which record is made was on July 1, the Third Sunday after Trinity, on the eve of Captain Newport's return to England. The description given by Captain Smith of the beginnings of Church worship at Jamestown is as follows:—"When we first went to Virginia I well remember we did hang an awning (which is an old saile) to three or four trees, to shadow us from the sunne; our walles were rales of wood; our seats unhewed trees till we cut plankes; our Pulpit a bar of wood nailed to two neighbouring trees. In foule weather we shifted into an old rotten tent, for we had few better, and this came by way of adventure for new.

"This was our church till we built a homely thing like a barne, set upon cratchets, covered with rafts, sedge and earth; so was the walls. The best of our houses of like curiosity; but for the most part of far much worse workmanship, that neither could well defend wind or raine. We had daily Common Prayer, morning and evening; every Sunday two sermons; and every three months the Holy Communion, till our minister died; but our prayers daily with an Homily on Sundaies we continued two or three years after till our other preachers came."

So early did the Colonial Church become dependent upon the services of lay readers, of whom so large use was subsequently made. The primitive building described by Smith was the first Protestant church erected in America. It was destroyed in the fire of the following January, just three days after Newport's return with additional supplies. Newport and his sailors rebuilt the church, and it was doubtless a great improvement on the first, for, with considerable repairs made two or three years later, it lasted for nearly ten years. After the repairs mentioned it was sixty by twenty-four feet in size "with a chancell in it of cedar, with faire broad windows to shut and open as the weather shall occasion, of the same wood, a pulpit of the same, with a font hewen hollow like a canoe, with two bells at the west end." The "good Master Hunt" died early in 1609, and for about two years there was no minister in the Colony. These were years of direful distress, covering the period known as the starving time. The settlers were unseasoned and ignorant of the simplest precautions necessary to protect themselves from disease. The lassitude of malaria sapped their strength both of body and spirit, and they were reduced to a handful. Then came Sir Thomas Gates, June 2, 1610, bringing with him the Rev. Richard Buck, their second minister, but little temporal relief since his expedition had suffered shipwreck on the voyage. The arrival of Lord De la Ware a little later barely averted the abandonment of the Colony.

Mr. Buck was educated at Oxford and received his appointment on the recommendation of the Bishop of London. He was rector of the congregation at Jamestown for twelve or thirteen years. He married in Virginia and left a family. He was, by all accounts, a worthy successor of Hunt and maintained the standard of godly character and faithful ministrations established by his predecessor. Crashaw, the English divine who so earnestly advocated the interests of the infant colony, declared him to be "an able and painfull preacher," and Rolfe bore the same testimony in less ambiguous terms. Another minister came with De la Ware, and several more during the year or two following and from this time onward the Jamestown pulpit was well supplied. Stringent regulations obtained requiring attendance upon the daily prayers and Sunday services unless prevented by sickness or guard duty, and probably at no time since has divine worship filled so large a place in the life of our people.

With Sir Thomas Dale, in May, 1611, came the Rev. Alexander Whitaker, M. A., who has been called the "Apostle of Virginia." He was a son of the distinguished Puritan divine, the Rev. Dr. William Whitaker, Master of St. John's College and Regius Professor of Divinity at Cambridge, and was himself in the way of desirable preferment in the Church at home when he was led by an earnest missionary spirit to proffer three years service to the colony; at the expiration of which time, however, he avowed his purpose to "abide in my vocation here, where God was mindeinge nowe (as we hope) to fulfill His purpose and sett up the Kingdome of His Sonne." A new settlement was established by Dale at Henricopolis in the fall of 1611, and a church built, of which Whitaker became the minister and so the first rector of Henrico parish which included also the plantation at Bermuda Hundred. He was greatly interested in the conversion of the Indians, and his labors to that end were not wholly fruitless. It was doubtless he who instructed and received into the Church by baptism the native princess Pocahontas. He was drowned in crossing James river in the spring of 1617.

The godly clergymen whom we have mentioned were followed by others of like character and zeal, chosen and appointed by the Company in England with a special view to their fitness for the arduous work before them. Among those whose names have come down to us are the Rev. Mr. Glover, "reverenced and respected, in easy circumstances and already somewhat advanced in years," who lived but a few months after his arrival; William Mease, who ministered at Kecoughtan, now Hampton, which contests with Henrico the claim of being the second parish in America; William Wickham, a deacon as we suppose, assistant and successor to Whitaker; George Keith, Thomas Bargrave, brother of the Dean of Canterbury; Robert Paulett, physican and surgeon as well as clergyman, David Sandys or Sands, William Bennett, Hawte Wyatt, brother of Governor Wyatt, Francis Bolton, Thomas White, Jonas Stockton, William Leate, Greville Pooley, and several more, all of whom came before the year 1624. It was purposed that each of the four boroughs, James City, Henrico, Charles City and Elizabeth City, should have at least one minister supported at the expense of the Company, while each particular plantation was urged to maintain one at its own expense. Normally one hundred acres of land, with tenants to cultivate it, was set apart for the minister; but at best they lived in scant comfort, sharing all the privations and dangers of their flocks. Nor did they escape the mortality which was so marked among the early colonists, and several of them survived but a year or two. Some, perhaps most, of these early ministers were classed as Puritans, but they were not dissenters and there is no indication that the entire conformity to the Church of England, prescribed both by the injunctions of the Company and the laws enacted by the legislature of the Colony itself, was either objected to or evaded.

In 1625 the government of the Colony was taken out of the hands of the Virginia Company of London and resumed by the Crown. This event was unfavorable to the interests of religion and of the infant Church in Virginia, which, under the Company, had been particularly cared for but under the Commissioners of the King were almost wholly neglected. The Company, as we have seen, had been very solicitous in regard to the ministers sent by them to serve the adventurers and to lay the foundations of a great missionary enterprise. Doubtless there were those who continued privately to interest themselves in this matter and to urge the emigration of faithful and efficient clergymen to Virginia; but for the most part the colonists were left to their own efforts and devices for securing a needed supply of pastors and generally in maintaining and guiding the destinies of their Church. Fortunately the General Assembly of the Colony, instituted under the liberal policy of the Company in 1619, though suspended for a few years, was allowed by royal favor to survive; and henceforth this became practically the governing body of the Church. Composed of the Governor and his Council and a representative House of Burgesses freely elected by the people, it legislated for their religious as well as their secular interests with but little interference from the King's Commissioners. At its earlier sessions the Assembly contented itself with enacting formally the rigid regulations enjoined upon successive governors and councils in the interest of religion and morality, giving them the sanction of statute law. But as the settlements multiplied and grew it became evident that the canons and customs of the Church in the old land needed to be supplemented to meet conditions never conceived of before. A new parochial system had to

be devised and new expedients adopted for the establishment, support and control of local congregations in scattered
and rudely organized communities which were making a
struggle for life in an unfriendly wilderness. Gradually this
was accomplished, and within two or three decades a series
of enactments had been evolved, tested by practical application, revised and perfected as found necessary, and finally
codified for the local government of the Church. As closely
as possible the canon law of England was followed in this
code, which, however, became practically a part of the canon
law of the Church of Virginia and so continued for more
than a century.

Under these regulations territorial parishes were established as the settlement of the country extended along the
shores of the great rivers, across the bay and then towards
the mountains of the west, at first by the Governor and
Council or the county courts or commissioners, and later
solely by the General Assembly. With few exceptions these
remain to this day with their ancient boundaries unchanged.
There were from one to four parishes to a county, and in
each parish from one to three or four churches or chapels,
according to its size and the needs of the people. These
churches would at first be rude and temporary buildings
such as a few pioneers could erect for themselves, to be supplanted later by larger structures of wood or brick, and later
still, as the community became able to command the means,
by massive and commodious buildings of brick designed to
continue, like the parish churches of England, for long generations.

The parish government was committed to a select Vestry, to be composed of "twelve of the most able and sufficient men," elected by the freeholders on the foundation of
a parish but thereafter continuing as a self-perpetuating
body, unless dissolved by act of the Assembly, in which case
a new election was ordered. As in England, many duties
devolved upon the Vestry which would now be considered of
a purely civil nature, such as the care of the poor, the present-
ment to the courts of evil doers, the processioning of plantations and other lands, and preserving landmarks. All parochial expenses were met by the parish levy, laid year by

year, and collected as other taxes, consisting of so many pounds of tobacco, the money commodity of the Colony, upon the poll of every man and boy of working age, and servant or slave, male or female. This tax fell most heavily, of course, upon the gentlemen of large landed estates with their many dependents, and for this reason, among others, the office of vestryman was generally sought and held by these. Being also men of education and trained in public affairs, they were best fitted for the position. Thus, the parish, as well as the county and the Colony as a whole, was virtually governed by an aristocracy. In the early days it was not only the best but the only practicable system of local government. With the growing spirit of democracy that preceded the Revolution, however, it became increasingly unpopular and was one of the prime causes of the loss of the Church's prestige at that period.

The most difficult problem which the vestries had to solve was that of obtaining proper ministers for their parishes. The Church in England was almost the one source of supply, though occasionally a minister was brought in from another Colony, and for a long time there was no authorized or official agency through whose mediation ministers could be obtained. The vestry of a vacant parish had frequently to engage the good offices of personal friends in England, or of some gentleman returning to that country, or even of the captains of merchant vessels, to present their cause and induce a clergyman to accept their living, unless, indeed, some adventurous and needy parson should emigrate from England to the Colony on the chance of securing a parish. Afterwards, when the Bishop of London appointed a Commissary to represent his nominal authority over this distant part of his diocese, the case was little better. The Commissary could only represent conditions by letter to his diocesan, who too often manifested little interest or intelligence in the matter, and recommend to the vestries those who applied to him for ministerial employment. It is not surprising that not a few inefficient and unworthy clergymen were thus introduced into Virginia, to the great detriment of the Church and injury to the cause of religion. For lack of a better supply the vestries not infrequently induced some educated man known to them, a schoolmaster or attorney perhaps, to secure the recommendation of the Governor or Commissary and voyage to England for preparatory study and to receive Holy Orders, returning after a year or two to take the rectorship which had been kept open for him.

The living and perquisites of a minister were at first very uncertain. For a time they were a small modicum of corn and of the increase of live stock which his parish produced, with his glebe land if he were able to cultivate it. Later his salary was fixed by act of Assembly at sixteen thousand pounds of tobacco annually, with an additional five per cent for shrinkage, and five per cent more for "cask" if necessary. In addition he was to be provided with a glebe, with the necessary buildings thereon, which he had to keep in repair at his own charges. The value of his living, therefore depended chiefly on the price of tobacco, which was subject to wide fluctuations. It also depended on the quality of the weed which his county produced, and a "Sweet-scented" parish was a far more valuable living than an "Oronoko" parish. As a rule, however, the Parson could live as well as, and probably better than, the majority of his parishioners exclusive of the wealthy landowners.

The law of the Colony as well as the canon law prescribed that a minister should be "inducted" into his parish by a formal presentation of the living by the vestry, thus insuring his possession for life or at his pleasure. The Governors, and afterwards the Commissary, were inclined to insist upon induction because of the greater dignity it gave to the clergy and also because of the difficulty of securing ministers from England unless the permanent tenure of a parish could be assured them. On the other hand the vestries, early taught by experience, objected strenuously to being forced to commit their parishes for his lifetime to a minister of whose character or capacities they knew nothing. The result was a frequent contest between the authorities, but in the end the vestries won. Having secured an amendment to the law providing that induction might be deferred for one year after the minister's services were engaged, they frequently adopted the simple expedient of renewing their engagement with him annually. Thus they retained the power of ridding themselves of an unworthy minister, which was very necessary in view of the fact that there was no authority in the Colony by which clerical discipline could be administered other than this.   In practice, however, a minister who was tolerably acceptable in his character and ministrations was secure in his position, and, being known by reputation, not infrequently had opportunity to exchange his parish for a better.   The lack of a formal induction would be felt more in a sense of a loss of independence and a seeming necessity of subserviency to his vestrymen than in any material disadvantage, and this would be but a test of his own strength of character. *

The social position accorded to the clergy, again, depended largely upon their personal qualities.   The old English traditions which lingered long among the aristocracy did not concede to the cloth the respect which is now granted without question, nor, indeed, was it always deserved.   But men of education were then, as now, at an advantage, and the minister easily won the place in the social scale for which he was fitted by culture and habits.

The minister's work was physically, rather than intellectually, arduous.   It involved constant journeyings through a parish of perhaps forty or fifty miles in extent, where roads and accommodations were of the most primitive sort.   If a neighboring parish was vacant he frequently doubled his labors by engaging to preach therein on week-days, receiving a stated sum for each sermon.   He was the sole minister of religion in his parish, and, even if his sense of duty was weak, the law of the land required that he should visit the sick and perform all the customary functions of his office whenever called upon.   A duty specially prescribed was that of catechising the children, which exercises took place, during the favorable seasons of the year, before or after service or in the afternoon of each Sunday.   The sparse evidences which have come down to us indicate faithful efforts on the part of the clergy in general to fulfil their obligations in the face of many difficulties.

* An interesting instance of this "induction" controversy is recorded in "The Historical Sketch of Bruton Parish Church" by Rev. W. A. R. Goodwin, the correspondence having been copied in full from the ancient Vestry book of the parish.

Much has been said and believed about the character of the colonial clergy which was untrue and unjust. After the downfall of the established Church at the Revolution, and when a new ideal of ministerial efficiency had been established under new and better conditions, much blame was attached to them as a class, which was undeserved. An evil tradition, originating largely with the Church's enemies, was thoughtlessly received, and the delinquencies of the few were ascribed to the many with little regard to fairness or to fact. This prejudice was furthered by Bishop Meade, whose high standards of excellence accorded ill with the popular report which had come down to him, and whose almost wholesale condemnation was long accepted as a just estimate of the clergy of our primitive Church. The truth seems to be that throughout its history they were much on a par with the rank and file of clergy of the English Church during the same period, with the exception of a few notorious characters among them whose evil lives brought also an undeserved reproach upon their contemporaries. The latter part of the seventeenth and the first half of the eighteenth centuries were, as is well known, a time of religious depression, when the mother Church was generally benumbed by worldliness and almost wholly lacking in spirituality and evangelical fervor. It is not surprising that the same conditions should exist in the daughter Church which was dependent upon her for her ministerial supply and for that "nursing care and protection" which the Prayer Book acknowledges but which was, in truth, so sparingly and indifferently bestowed. The clergymen who came to Virginia were not greatly below the average of those trained in the English Christianity of their day. In some cases we suppose they were far above that average. The succession seems to have deteriorated in quality with each decade, however, until at the time immediately preceding the Revolution they reflected the religious conditions in the Church of England just before the evangelical revival. At that time, moreover, the most worthy and efficient ministers in Virginia and those most sought after were native Virginians, educated at home and only visiting England to receive their ordination.

BRUTON PARISH CHURCH

The Court Church of Colonial Virginia, Williamsburg

We have the names of about four hundred and seventy-five ministers of the Colonial Church of Virginia. The roster is doubtless incomplete. Many of these are but names, recorded perhaps as having received the "King's Bounty" of twenty or thirty pounds to pay for their passage, or discovered among the musty records of ancient county courts, of whose lives and labors no account remains. Of others we only know the parishes which they served for a few years and the fact of their deaths, so frequently before reaching middle age. But of not a few we have evidences, interwoven with the history of the Colony or gathered from tradition or from old parish records proving them to have been strong in leadership, diligent in their vocation, honored of their contemporaries, and with the interests of religion, the upbuilding of the state and the spiritual welfare of their people warmly at heart. Some of them, at least, were men of learning, bearing University degrees and possessed of good libraries, exponents of the best culture of their day. They kept in close touch with political and ecclesiastical conditions, not only in the Colony but in England as well, were staunch in maintaining the principles which they espoused, which were usually conservative, and jealous of the prescriptive rights of the clergy and the Establishment.

During the period of the Commonwealth the Rev. Philip Mallory and the Rev. John Green were appointed to examine each minister coming to Virginia and certify their abilities to the Governor and Council, nominally that they might be freed from public levies, but also, we suspect, to vouch for their Episcopal ordination. These were our first Examining Chaplains. After the Restoration, Mr. Mallory was appointed to "undertake the soliciting of our Church affaires in England," the General Assembly testifying that he had been "eminently faithful in the ministry and very diligent in endeavouring the advancement of all those meanes that might conduce to the advancement of religion in this country." Among other clergymen dating from the seventeenth century who were prominent in the Colony were Rowland Jones, "Pastor primus et delectissimus" of Bruton Parish; James Sclater of York, and John Gwynne and James Clack of Gloucester; William Cotton and Thomas Teackle of the Eastern Shore, militant for their rights but faithful in their work; Benjamin Doggett and David Lindsey of the Northern Neck; John Farnifold and Stephen Fouace, original trustees of the College; Emmanuel Jones and Robert Yates, the former of whom gave a son, the latter a son and three grandsons to the ministry in Virginia, all men of high distinction and virtue.   John Clayton, minister at Jamestown for several years, was a member of the Royal Society and a writer of no mean attainments, and John Banister, another trustee of the College, was a naturalist of considerable note whose name is still known in the world of science.   And most prominent of all, the stalwart and zealous James Blair, missionary, reformer, educator and statesman, for forty-four years Commissary of the Bishop of London, Founder and President of William and Mary College, Rector of Bruton Parish, Williamsburg, Virginia, Councillor and Acting Governor, who in spite of all opposition never faltered in his devotion to the highest interests of the Church and Colony.

Of only a few of these seventeenth century clergymen is there any record fairly derogatory of their moral or ministerial character.   As Virginia grew in wealth and importance and in attractiveness as a place of residence, as the demand for ministers to supply her multiplying parishes increased as well as the facilities for making the voyage, and as it became understood that there was no Episcopal or other authority here to exercise an efficient discipline, it is not surprising that unworthy men should have crept in unawares.   Some were weak and vacillating and merely unfit for their high office.   A few there were who were utterly lacking in moral character and who by gross intemperance and hardly concealed immorality fell into open disgrace.   These could not tarry long in any cure but were driven by the whip of scorn if not of public prosecution from place to place, leaving a trail of ill repute in the memory of cavillers and on the records of court or parish which presently hardened into popular tradition involving the good name of the whole body of the clergy.   But to suppose that these notoriously evil men were suffered willingly, or were representative of the average clergy of their day, shows little discernment or knowledge of the facts.   For the most part the ministers lived and

labored quietly in their remote and isolated parishes, keeping
out of court and escaping notoriety, and left little record
which has survived, save the fact that they usually spent
their whole ministerial life in a single charge, presumably
honored and respected, and without a breath of scandal
attaching to their names.   Nor were there wanting during
the later years of the Established Church clergymen of
conspicuous standing and ability among those whose names
have come down to us unsullied by reproach.   Among them
may be mentioned David Currie of Lancaster and Archibald Campbell of Westmoreland; David and William Stuart,
father and son, of King George County; John Moncure of
Stafford; Alexander and James Scott, brothers, of Stafford
and Prince William counties; John Skaife and Chicherley
Thacker of King and Queen and New Kent respectively;
Peter Fontaine of Charles City, and James M. Fontaine of
Gloucester; James Marye and James Marye, Junior, of
Spotsylvania; James and Matthew Maury, father and son,
of Albemarle; Lewis Latané of Essex, Patrick Henry of Hanover and Lee Massey of Fairfax; William Stith, scholar and
historian, and Miles Selden of Henrico; William Dawson
and William Robinson, successors of Blair as Commissaries
to the Bishop of London.

Throughout our colonial history there were a very few
dissenters, chiefly Congregationalists and Quakers, in Virginia.   The English Act of Toleration of 1689 was at once
recognized in the Dominion, and attendance upon dissenting chapels was accepted as a compliance with the law demanding church attendance.   A license was required, however, for both chapel and preacher, and the latter had to
take the oath prescribed for all religious teachers as well as
civil officers, which debarred only Roman Catholics.   It
was not until nearly the middle of the eighteenth century
that dissent arose in active opposition to the established
Church.   In 1743 Presbyterianism was planted in Hanover
county, and soon after began to spread rapidly in other sections of the state.   It drew adherents from the upper classes
in larger numbers and before the Revolution had attained a
wide influence.   The Presbyterians insisted upon a more
liberal interpretation of the Act of Toleration than the author-

ities were disposed to grant, or than the neighboring clergy of the Establishment could view with complacency as they saw their congregations drawn from them by these earnest and evangelical preachers. The Baptists, however, were the avowed and inveterate enemies of the Church. Between 1750 and 1760 adherents of the more aggressive branch of that sect, known as Separates, drifted in from the more northern colonies in large numbers. Their ministers courted persecution, and violated every provision of the law regulating assemblies for religious worship in order to compel the unwilling civil authorities to yield them the crown of martyrdom by putting them in jail for contempt.

The clergy of the Establishment, with their formal services, fixed habits and outworn traditions, were ill fitted to cope with these vigorous assaults upon the authority and supremacy of the Church. They were as a rule not without sympathy with the democratic ideals which were taking possession of the popular mind, as is shown by their opposition to the scheme for an English Episcopate for America in 1771 as well as by the loyalty of the great majority of them to the new Commonwealth during the Revolution. But when their own position or prerogatives were assailed they were naturally quick to appeal to the law for defence rather than to fall in with a public sentiment which was setting strongly against old-country precedents.

During the sixth decade of the eighteenth century the tobacco crop was again and again almost a failure and the price of tobacco rose to a high figure. This was, of course, greatly to the pecuniary advantage of the clergy and a corresponding hardship upon their parishioners who were compelled to pay them the usual salary of 16,000 pounds out of their scanty supply. For the relief of the people the General Assembly in 1755 passed an Act allowing all dues payable in tobacco, which included the salary of the ministers, to be compounded at the rate of sixteen shillings and eight pence per hundred. This measure popularly known as the "Two penny Act," was re-enacted three years later. The clergy, who had protested mildly in 1755, now resisted more strenuously. They sent the Rev. Dr. John Camm, one of the ablest of their number, to England to appeal the case to the

King's Council, and with the aid of the Bishop of London the Council was induced to "disallow" or veto the obnoxious act.

Such interference by the crown in the internal affairs of the dominion had grown to be unusual and in the minds of many Virginians was unconstitutional. It was met with a storm of indignation which was not lessened by the animadversions of His Grace of London upon the Governor and Assembly. The Governor published a "repeal" of the Act, but the clergy insisted that a repeal was not a "disallowance" and claimed restitution to the amount of their full salaries for the years that the Act was in force. Many suits were brought to establish their claim and recover damages. The most celebrated of these, and one that was considered a test case, was that of the Rev. James Maury of Albemarle against the vestry of Fredericksville parish, which was tried at Hanover Court House in 1763. The Court declared the Act of 1758 to be invalid. It remained for a jury to assess the amount of damages to be recovered. For the vestry appeared an unknown country lawyer, Patrick Henry, who delivered before an electrified audience the speech that established his fame as an orator and a tribune of the people. Ignoring the law in the case he appealed to the prejudices no less than to the patriotic sentiments of the jury, openly charged a disregard on the part of the King toward the necessities of the people which left them at liberty to consult their own safety and maintain their own laws, and urged that the clergy, by appealing to the crown, had forfeited all claim to consideration. The delighted jury brought in a verdict for one penny damages, and a new trial was refused by the court. It was not the end but it was the doom of "the parsons' cause" in the Dominion. The clergy had justice on their side and the law as construed by the English authorities; but prudence, and a just regard for a fixed public conviction, would have dictated a less persistent opposition to the popular will. Neither they nor the established Church ever recovered the prestige lost by this unfortunate contention.

Even had the clergy been men of greater zeal and more conciliatory temper they would doubtless have been powerless to stem the rising tide of prejudice and resentment against the establishment and the system with which it was identified in the mind of the less educated classes. The over-lordship of England was fast being repudiated in political affairs and was no longer to be brooked in spiritual and ecclesiastical matters. The Established Church was part of a system which the new Commonwealth had outgrown, and it was powerless to adapt itself to new conditions or to free itself from the old. Bound hand and foot by its subord-ination to the civil power, the ties which had been its sup-port and stay in the infancy of the colony were now strang-ling it to death. The clergy were frequently assembled in convention in Williamsburg, but their meetings were but sparsely attended and they contented themselves with attempting to influence legislation and to protect their pre-rogatives rather than devising methods of meeting the spirit-ual needs of a new era. Meanwhile a flood of irreligion and infidelity was rising, which a little later inundated the state and swept many from their professed allegiance to the Church. Her fast friends were among the conservative upper classes, especially in the older parts of the state. But the wisest of these saw wherein her weakness lay under the new order of democratic rule, and when the Revolution came they wrote into their Declaration of Rights and the fundamental law of the commonwealth the principle that "all men are equally entitled to the free exercise of religion, according to the dic-tates of conscience." It was the death knell of the Establish-ment as such; yet for nine years during and after the Revolu-tion it continued to exist, though in name only, the Church remaining absolutely under the control and subject to the dictation and laws of the state, while no longer receiving its support. All levies for the maintenance of the clergy were suspended and they were left with nothing but their old glebes, which were frequently not worth cultivating. A few returned to England. Some turned to teaching, or to more secular pursuits, for a living. Others were overtaken by age or infirmity or fell into hopeless poverty, and disappeared from view. A number, however, continued to exercise their ministry in the face of every difficulty. The vestries, now embracing in many instances men indifferent if not inimical to the interests of the Church, confined themselves chiefly to their civil functions. In the weaker parishes the churches fell into disrepair and were abandoned, their congregations in part drifting away to the new religious teachers, in part abandoning all religious faith, but in part clinging to the Church of their fathers in hope of her rebuilding in better times. The Church, meanwhile, with no power of initative, no form of organization, and, it must be confessed, with little sense of mission, was left stranded and uncared for while her sons and supporters were busy in field and forum with the absorbing concerns of the newly born state.

When the stress of war was ended the Legislature turned to the discussion of religious affairs with much perplexity and wide divergencies of opinion. Churchmen were still in the majority in that body, but by their own act they were wisely committed to the principle of religious freedom and there was no thought of restoring to the Church its ancient exclusive privileges. The question was, how was religion and common morality to be maintained under a new and untried form of popular government which was pledged to non-interference in religious affairs? To many of them it seemed impossible for a Church or Churches to exist without state patronage. There was no precedent for such a thing, and the experiment seemed to them foredoomed to disastrous failure. The proposition was, therefore, urged that levies should be laid as aforetime for the support of religious teachers, with the proviso that every taxpayer should designate the denomination for whose support his payment should be applied. This plan, which for awhile seemed sure of adoption, was finally defeated, and the Churches were left to the hazards of self-support. The old Establishment, however, was confirmed in the possession of her churches and glebes. An act was then passed providing for the incorporation of every religious denomination which would accept the privilege. Under this act, upon the petition of a convention of the Episcopal clergy which met in June 1784, "An Act for the Incorporation of the Protestant Episcopal Church" was passed in December of that year. Thus finally the Church was freed from the bondage of state control and allowed the right of organization and self-government. Under the persistent attacks of her enemies, who were now avowedly bent, not upon her disestablishment but upon her destruction, this act was repealed two years later.   But in the meantime the Diocese of Virginia was organized in Convention, in May 1785, and was looking forward hopefully to a new era of prosperity.   Canons for her government and discipline were adopted, deputies were chosen to represent her in the newly formed union of the dioceses in General Convention, and the next year the Rev. David Griffith, D. D., was elected Bishop. Despairing, however, of reaching England for consecration or of obtaining it in this country, as the Convention had hoped, and in declining health, Dr. Griffith resigned the position two years later; and it was not until 1790 that Dr. Madison was elected and consecrated, and the Church in Virginia, after one hundred and eighty-four years, was given a Bishop.

It was still, however, essentially the old Colonial Church, with its narrow outlook and inherent defects, projected into a new era and an uncongenial environment.   For fifteen years a fruitless struggle was kept up to retain possession of the old parish glebes which had been assured to her by legislative enactment.   With these as the nucleus of an endowment, supplemented by such contributions as could be raised among an impoverished people utterly unaccustomed to voluntary giving for the support of the Church, it was hoped that the country parishes would survive to see better days.   But even this poor remnant of their former prosperity was denied to them.   It was claimed that the glebes, and the churches and their furnishings as well, having been built or purchased with the proceeds of public taxation, should be sequestrated to public uses.   The fact alleged was true only nominally. Some of the Church's property had come to her by gift.   For the rest, the parish levies of colonial days had been assessed by Churchmen against themselves and their fellow-parishioners for this specific purpose, and while apportioned under the forms of taxation they were practically voluntarily imposed contributions to the then established Church.   Such had been the view of the Legislature of 1784 and 1786 and for many years thereafter.   But again the popular will triumphed, though not until after fifteen years of assault upon the old Church which seemed tottering to her final ruin. A decision by the courts, which Bishop Madison and the Convention demanded, was refused, and in 1801 the act was finally passed which allowed the glebes, whenever they became vacant, to be appropriated by the county overseers of the poor for public uses, and extending the same principle in regard to the church buildings, though usually public sentiment refrained from enforcing it.

The property loss in the glebes themselves was not large, for as a rule they had deteriorated in value and were sold for a song, the proceeds being squandered without public advantage. But the loss of prestige, and the triumphant exhibition of a spirit of ruthless vindictiveness avowedly intending her total extinction, disheartened the friends of the Church and combined with other causes to render her case apparently hopeless. In the lower counties, where her strength had formerly lain, many of the old families, which had been her active supporters, were reduced to comparative poverty, while a constant stream of emigration to the west and south depleted the thinning ranks of her adherents. The few efficient clergy that remained, after the Revolution, passed away and left but indifferent successors. There were, it is true, a number of ordinations and accessions from neighboring dioceses, but they added little strength to the Church. As the ministers in the country parishes died, and their glebes, becoming vacant, were confiscated, little effort was made to fill their places. Only in the few towns of the state, and in a few isolated rural communities, did the Church manifest a semblance of vitality. The annual Conventions were sparsely attended, and though the number required to form a quorum was again and again reduced, only two Conventions appear to have been held between 1797 and 1805.

In the latter year Bishop Madison, on account of failing health and the imperative character of his duties in connection with the College, asked for an Assistant Bishop. The matter was deferred until the next Convention, but we have no record of any further Conventions being held until after the death of Bishop Madison. He himself seems to have grown hopeless of a present restoration of the Church. There were at this time probably thirty or forty clergymen in the state. They included a few survivors of the pre-

Revolutionary period, the younger of whom were now old and feeble men; while others were, we suppose, former parish clerks and schoolmasters who had accepted ordination for the usufruct of a wornout glebe and the scant returns for the meagre services they were called upon to render. Their habits of thought and life were conformed to an old order which was moribund and must needs pass away to make room for the revival of spiritual life and consecrated labor that was to follow.

But the Church still lived amid her desolations in the hearts and the homes of an unreckoned multitude of her children. Her traditions were honored, her teachings observed and her Prayer Book used as a treasury of devotion in many godly households to whom her public ministrations were denied. When the hour of her awakening struck, and the apostolic Bishop Moore and his evangelical co-workers moved forward to recover the ground lost in the long period of her decay, there was found in every place a remnant of the faithful to whom the memories of the old Colonial Church were a precious heritage and in whose children her life was perpetuated to become strong and fruitful in the day of her visitation.

THE ANCIENT COLLEGE OF WILLIAM AND MARY

Brafferton Building—1723   Old Main Building—1697   President's House—1732

SECTION I

CHAPTER II

THE INDIAN COLLEGE AND THE COLLEGE OF WILLIAM AND MARY

REV. E. L. GOODWIN, D. D.

The Educational Policy of the Colony of Virginia relative to the Indians—The Indian Boy "Chanco"—The Massacre of 1622—Brafferton Indian School—College of William and Mary—Early Theological Education at William and Mary.

The College of William and Mary, the second collegiate foundation established in America, was the third that was attempted in the Colony of Virginia. It was the outgrowth of a purpose which for eighty years had persisted in the minds of Virginians, inherited from the nursing fathers of the infant Colony, the Virginia Company of London. We have briefly noticed how, in all their instructions to their early adventurers, the Company emphasized the religious character of the enterprise of colonization and the expectation of extending the blessings of Christianity and civilization to the native peoples among whom they should settle. Hardly had a foothold been gained in the new land when plans were laid on a liberal scale to further the latter design by means of Christian education. In 1617 or earlier, royal letters were issued to the Archbishops, doubtless at the solicitation of the Company, directing that contributions and subscriptions be taken throughout the kingdom to assist in the undertaking then in hand of "erecting Churches and Schools for ye education of ye children of those Barbarians." Fifteen hundred pounds were thus secured, more than half being in cash. Over ten thousand acres of land, lying on both sides of James river from Henrico to the falls, were set apart for the endowment of a College, designed primarily for the education of Indian youths but also intended to furnish like advantages for the planters' sons. A few settlers were placed upon these lands for their improvement and the monies collected were carefully invested. The first General

23

Assembly of the Colony, in 1619, petitioned the Company to send, as soon as convenient, "workmen of all sortes, fitt for that purpose," for erecting the necessary buildings. The Company appointed George Thorp, a gentleman in every way qualified for so important a task, to come over and have charge of the affairs of the institution, and preparations for building were begun at Henrico. Meantime further gifts were made, both for the College and for secondary schools for the preparation of students to enjoy its benefits. The first project for such a free school was designed for the benefit of the Indians, an anonymous donor contributing a large sum for this purpose. This money, with additional funds contributed by the Colony, was invested in building the first iron furnace in America, at Falling Creek, Chesterfield County, the proceeds of which were to go to the support of the school. Plans for the East India School for white children, so-called because the beginnings of its endowment were contributed by officers and mariners of the East India Company, more nearly approached realization. The Rev. Mr. Copeland was appointed rector and Mr. Dike, master, and a competent architect and builder was sent from England to erect the school building at City Point.

Efforts for the education of Indian children did not wait, however, upon the actual building for them of school or college. Among the first acts passed by that first American General Assembly was the following:

"Be it enacted by this present assembly that for laying a surer foundation for the conversion of the Indians to Christian Religion, each towne, city, Burrough, and particular plantation do obtaine unto themselves by just means a certine number of the natives' children to be educated by them in true religion and civile course of life—of which children the most towardly boyes in witt and graces of nature to be brought up by them in the first elements of litterature, so to be fitted for the College intended for them that from thence they may be sente to that worke of conversion."

How many Indian children were thus adopted by the colonists we do not know, but it was to one of them, the young Christian convert Chanco, that the inhabitants of Jamestown and the lower plantations owed the warning which enabled them to save themselves in the great massacre of 1622. The children desired could only be obtained, the Governor announced, by treaty with the chieftain Opechancanough, and that wily savage, as was discovered later, had other plans in his head which he was preparing to consummate with singular astuteness. While his plot was ripening for execution he professed the greatest friendliness for the whites, and especially for Mr. Thorp, from whom he received substantial favors, and confirmed his treaties by every assurance which could be devised. Lulled by such a fair show of amity the English freely admitted the red men into their settlements and even into their homes, and were doubtless congratulating themselves that these wild sons of the forest were being easily won to the blessings of civilized life.

On the morning of Good Friday, March 22, 1622, the blow fell. Within a few hours upwards of four hundred English people, or about one-third of the entire population of the colony, lay dead at the hands of those for whose salvation, temporal and spiritual, they were so hopefully laboring. The third who died, moreover, were largely the older colonists who were acclimated and settled upon their improved plantations, and were those chiefly engaged in these educational enterprises. The corporations of Henrico and the upper part of Charles City were literally wiped out, and the results of years of labor, including what had been accomplished on schools and college, were completely destroyed.

Thenceforward for a long season the benevolent designs for Christianizing the Indians gave way perforce to determined efforts to terrorize if not to exterminate them. The project for the College, however, was not abandoned and the Comppany immediately took steps to save what they might from such a disaster and to re-establish its foundation. But a more blighting disaster fell within a year or two in the revocation of the Company's charter and the taking over of the affairs of the Colony by the King and Council. No material aid for such enterprises could then be looked for from England, and the College lands and possessions were gradually absorbed by other interests while the Colony passed through a long period of depression and ill-management.

In the year 1660-61, at the close of the period of uncertainty and unrest in Virginia which marked the era of the Commonwealth in England, the design for a seat of higher learning in the Colony was revived in the General Assembly. Three separate acts or orders were passed during that session of which the first was in these words:

"Whereas the want of able and faithful ministers in this country deprives us of these great blessings and mercies that allwaies attend upon the service of God which want by reason of our great distance from our native country cannot in probability be allwaies supplyed from thence. *Bee itt enacted* that for the advance of learning, education of youth, supply of the ministry and promotion of piety, there be land taken upon purchases for a colledge and free-schoole, and that there be with as much speede as may be convenient houseing erected thereon for the entertainment of students and schollers."

The second act ordered that a petition be sent to the King for letters-patent authorizing collections to be made in England in aid of the undertaking, and a later order recites that considerable amounts in money and tobacco had been subscribed by the Governor and Council and the Burgesses and directs that further subscriptions be received in each county and parish. It will be noted that the education of a native ministry was the special purpose in view in this attempted enterprise, the failure of which at that time may be ascribed in part to the political disturbances culminating in the so-called Bacon's Rebellion in 1676. But it is far from improbable that the chief blame would be found to lie at the door of Governor Sir William Berkeley and his complaisant Council and Burgesses, who ruled with a high hand for many years thereafter and would be likely to do little for the cause of education to which the Governor was confessedly unfriendly.

Twenty years later, however, conditions were more favorable for the fulfilment of the persistent hopes of patriotic Virginians for a College. The demoralizing domination of the Stuarts was happily over. The disturbed state of affairs in England had induced an increased emigration to Virginia of families of position and culture. A new Lieutenant-

Governor, Colonel Francis Nicholson, courting popularity among a distrustful people, was quick to see that a revival of this project would be welcomed with hearty appreciation. Accordingly a popular subscription for a free school and college was again ordered and was promoted with energy and success by the Governor and a Commission appointed for the purpose.

But of more practical consequence was the presence in Virginia of a man ready and qualified to press the design to its accomplishment. The Rev. James Blair was born in Scotland in 1655, received his Master's degree at Edinburgh at the age of eighteen, and was ordained to the Episcopal ministry in that country. Removing to England he attracted the attention of Bishop Compton of London, by whose advice, it is said, he came to Virginia in 1685 and became rector of Henrico parish. His church and glebe were at Varina, the county seat, but little more than a mile from the site of Henrico and the ill-fated Indian College. The story of that early enterprise he must have learned with a quick sympathy, and it is not too much to suppose that it had its influence in stimulating his efforts for reviving such a sacred undertaking. In 1689 he was appointed Commissary of the Bishop of London for Virginia, and in the following year he called and presided over the first regular convention of the clergy in the church at Jamestown. This convention endorsed his scheme for a college and recommended it to the Governor and General Assembly. The Assembly entered heartily into the plan. Trustees were appointed to receive a charter, an address to the King and Queen was adopted outlining the objects, urging the needs and proposing the means for the support of the institution, and Blair was commissioned to proceed to England to obtain the royal decree, solicit further subscriptions, and even to secure the beginnings of a suitable faculty.

This important mission was performed by Dr. Blair with such energy and wisdom that it was crowned with complete success. Their Majesties and the ecclesiastical authorities met his pleas with sympathy and substantial assistance. Grants of money and lands and of a stated revenue from quit-rents were conferred by the government, and almost

every request of the General Assembly was conceded. On
the first of September, 1693, Blair placed in the hands of the
Governor and Council the royal Charter of the College of
William and Mary, bearing date of the eighth of February
of that year.

The objects proposed in the charter were "that the
Church of Virginia may be furnished with a seminary of
ministers of the gospel, and that the youth may be piously
educated in good letters and manners, and that the Christian
faith may be propagated amongst the Western Indians, to
the glory of Almighty God." Dr. Blair was appointed
president, and the gentlemen nominated by the Assembly
were confirmed as visitors, four of them being clergymen.
The General Assembly fixed upon the Middle Plantation,
afterwards known as Williamsburg, as the site of the College,
and made further provision for its maintenance.   The corner stone was laid with ceremony on the eighth of August,
1695, and two years later the buildings, designed by Sir
Christopher Wren, were so far completed that the grammar
school was opened.

In 1705 the College was burned but was rebuilt after a
few years.   In this and other fires which have visited it the
early records have been lost and we do not know how many
of the clergy of the Church in the eighteenth century were
educated within its walls.   But it is known that not a few
of the most exemplary and useful clergymen of the later
colonial Church were alumni of the College, and all the testimony coming down from those days indicates their general
superiority to those imported from England.   The scanty
lists of its alumni during the first century of its existence
which have been collated from various sources, contain the
names of the leading citizens of the dominion in their day
and of a notable number of patriots of the American Revolution.   Nor were the hopes of its founders that its benefits
would be extended to the Indians wholly disappointed.   A
building, which still stands, was erected for their use, and for
three quarters of a century Indian boys were maintained
and educated at the College.   The Indian School Building
known as "Brafferton Hall" still stands on the campus of

The College President's House—1732

Home of Rev. Commissary Blair, D. D., Rev. Doctors Dawson, Stith, Yates, Horrocks, Camm,
Madison (first Bishop of Virginia), Bracken, Wilmer, Empie, and Bishop Johns,
Presidents of the College of William and Mary

Brafferton Indian School Building

College of William and Mary—1723

the College of William and Mary. It was erected through a gift made by Sir Robert Boyle of Brafferton Manor, Yorkshire, England.

Dr. Blair continued as President of the College and Commissary for fifty years, until his death in 1743 at the age of eighty-seven. He was also minister of the church at Jamestown and afterwards at Williamsburg, was a member of the Governor's Council and acted for a time as Governor. He was a man of great ability, of pure motives and of strong and determined character. He was unpopular with the clergy and with successive Governors whose will he contested but he was seldom worsted by his adversaries. Hampered as he was by personal enmities and with his authority disputed on all sides, he stood always for the purity and integrity of Church and Commonwealth and made his influence felt. He was succeeded as President in turn by the Rev. Doctors William Dawson, William Stith, the historian, Thomas Dawson, William Yates, James Horrocks, John Camm, and Bishop James Madison. Since the death of the latter in 1812 the Presidency has been held for ten years by the Rev. Doctors William H. Wilmer and Adam P. Empie and for five years by Bishop John Johns. The names of only a few of the early professors are known, but in 1729 the Rev. Bartholomew Yates and many years later the Rev. John Dixon filled the chair of Divinity, and doubtless throughout the first century of the existence of the College sufficient provision was made for theological education.

The first layman who filled the office of President of the College was the excellent Dr. John Augustine Smith, in 1814. In the year following he addressed a letter to the Convention of the Diocese of Virginia through Bishop Moore, advocating the establishment again of a chair of theology in that institution, a proposition which was welcomed by the Convention. The slow fruition of this movement, resulting after seven years in the appointment of the Rev. Dr. Keith to the chair of Divinity and his subsequent removal to Alexandria, is detailed elsewhere in this book.

Surviving the losses and vicissitudes of a checkered career of two and a quarter centuries the venerable College of William and Mary continues its work for the education of

the youth of Virginia, serving a larger number of students
than ever before. After long decades of neglect it again
enjoys the patronage of the state, while the Church retains
in it only that hereditary interest which its history and traditions no less than its present career of usefulness will
alway ensure.

SECTION I

CHAPTER III

THE CHURCH IN VIRGINIA DURING THE REVOLUTIONARY PERIOD

REV. C. BRAXTON BRYAN, D. D.

Historiographer of the Diocese of Southern Virginia

Relation Between the Colonial Government and the Church—The Power of the Laity in the Church—The Revolutionary Spirit in Politics and in the Church —Character of Colonial Clergy—Controversy concerning Clerical Salaries —Opposition to an American Episcopate—Dissenters—Slavery—Failure of the Church to reach the Middle and Lower Classes—Parishes of Montgomery, Washington and Kentucky—Devereux Jarratt's Testimony—The Bill of Rights—Religious Fanaticism and Lawlessness—The Charge of Persecution —The Baptists—Legislative Controversy—Question of Taxation for the support of Religion—Prevalence of Skepticism, with the breaking up of the old System—Methodist Consecrations—First Convention in Virginia—The Darkest Days—The Glebes and the Legal Controversy concerning them—Legal Battles concerning Church Property.

The political revolution of 1776-1782 involved a revolution in the church, and in this revolution the Church was the greatest sufferer.

In 1774 there were in Virginia ninety-five parishes with more than an hundred churches, and between ninety and an hundred clergymen, a larger number than ever before. The parish system, dating from the beginning of the Colony, still lay, in idea, at least, at the base of the domestic life of each community. The intimate connection between the Church and the State extended from the parish, with its Rector, Vestry and Wardens, up to the Commissary, who represented the Bishop of London and the Governor, who represented the King. The control of the parish was practically in the hands of the Vestry, generally composed of twelve men representing the best intelligence, social standing and wealth of the community, and was self-perpetuating, unless dissolved by an Act of the General Assembly.

The parishes varied in size, from an hundred square miles, or less, to vast areas as large as, or much larger than a modern county. They varied in material and social

31

conditions from wealthy and highly cultivated communities to poor and sparsely settled sections or crude and undeveloped regions. The Vestries naturally represented the same ruling class from which the justices of the county courts, the Burgesses and members of the Governor's Council were elected. The General Assembly, which consisted of the House of Burgesses and the Governor and his Council, had from its first meeting in 1619 taken account of the affairs of the church, and made laws accordingly, subject to the General Canon of the Church of England. The Governor and his Council also had an important part in the government of the church, especially when they acted in their capacity of the General Court, the highest in the Colony, and as such gave orders which were sometimes of a disciplinary character, or made decisions in ecclesiastical matters. The Governor had also his own official authority in connection with the Church, but his powers were not well defined and were quite limited. In addition to these sources of authority, the Governor and the Council, the General Assembly and the Vestries, all laymen, there remained only the Commissary of the Bishop of London, a clergyman, whose powers like those of the Governor, were neither well defined nor well sustained. The Commissary served as a rallying point for the clergy, but until 1690 there was no Commissary. Never was there an ecclesiastical institution which was supposed to be Episcopal in its nature so largely in the power of the laity.

Under these conditions the power of the clergy was extremely limited. They could be called together in convention by the Commissary, and express their views and make protests and appeals either to the government in Virginia or to the Bishop of London or the King, and all this they did from time to time, but they had no regular share in legislation, and labored under many disadvantages in their efforts to influence the real powers either in Virginia or beyond the sea; and when all was done each minister had to deal directly with his Vestry, and the Vestries generally had their way. For indeed the ruling classes in Virginia had been cultivating independence for generations until it had become a fixed habit with them to have their way in whatever concerned the Colony. They looked to their own General Assembly

as the supreme legislative authority for Virginia, and staunchly maintained that "Taxes ought not to be laid on the
inhabitants and proprietors of the Colony but by the common
consent of the General Assembly." And now the time was
at hand when the principles of independence and self government, which for years had been developing, were to bring
forth their ultimate and lasting fruit in separation from the
mother country and the establishment of a democratic form
of government. This necessitated a revolution in religious
affairs quite as radical as in the civil government, a revolution in the course of which the Church suffered more than
any other part of the community.

Several causes other than political ones contributed to
this suffering and loss. Yet these dominating Virginians
sincerely loved their church. Was it not theirs? Had not
they and their fathers been brought up in it, built the churches
and managed the affairs of the churches and of their
neighbourhoods and parishes for more than a century and a
half? But now for these liberty-loving, independent, self-
governing Virginians a revolution was at hand, a revolution
in Church and State, and the churchmen themselves would
lead it and accomplish it. In the revolution of the Church
they would be influenced by others, for bitter enemies to
the church had sprung up in Virginia, but after all the churchmen were in control, the decisions were in their hands. If
all the clergy in Virginia had been Virginians, and if all the
people had been churchmen, this revolution would still have
had to be worked out. It was inherent in the principles which
the churchmen themselves laid down in 1776 in their great
Bill of Rights and their democratic Constitution. The
revolution in the Church might have been accomplished more
justly, less harshly, less hastily, but in its essential principles
it had to come.

The least prepared to meet this revolution and the pecul-
iar victims in the sacrifices that followed were the clergy.
Of necessity they had been ordained in England, and though
a number of them were Virginians educated at William and
Mary, the majority were foreign born, English, Scotch and
Irish, and every one was under his ordination vows to an
English bishop and under his personal oath of allegiance,

supremacy and uniformity, to the King. They could not as a rule feel toward Virginia as the native laymen of Virginia felt, and that was especially true when the period of revolution approached, and the spirit of independence and jealousy for their rights increased among the people who were becoming more and more Virginian and American in their feelings. The clergy had little share in public affairs; on the other hand they often had just cause of complaint, and did complain especially with regard to their hold on their parishes; for nearly all of them were at the mercy of the Vestries and were employed from year to year. It was a question whether the Governor did not have the right of inducting the clergy into their parishes; but whatever right he may have had, the Vestries had long ago got the actual power into their own hands, and almost universally declined to have the clergy inducted. Thus the clergy were kept in an unsettled and dissatisfied condition; with the further effect that the colonial system operated seriously against the increase and maintenance of a high quality of clergy in the Colony.

A great deal has been said against the quality and character of the colonial clergy, but an impartial examination proves that much of this was exaggeration and the result of prejudice. There were bad examples from time to time among the clergy, and the weakness of the system, especially in discipline, made the correction and removal of such cases difficult. But in 1776 the clergy were as good as they had been at any time within an hundred years; some of them were eminent for ability, piety and faithfulness. After all, a Church is best judged by its fruits, and there is no denying that the leading men and women in Virginia at the time of the Revolution were a noble type and those leaders were, by a large majority, churchmen. One can not condemn wholesale the clergy of the Church which produced that generation of men and women. The clergy appear quite distinctly to have been, with rare exceptions one way or another, a body of men of average ability, character and attainments who were doing their part as parsons and teachers in the routine of the parishes. An extraordinary man would not be very apt to go over to Virginia or, being in Virginia, to

enter the ministry. When they got together in their convocations there is not lacking evidence that there were
among them men of unusual brightness, force and originality.
But remarkable originality in thought or action was not
encouraged and would soon have felt the check of the Vestries or the Council, and the extent of the parishes generally
would have taxed the activity of any parson even if confined
to the most ordinary duties.

Unfortunately for these men, they had fallen upon
times when the current of events was separating them from
their chief supporters and constituents. They in their
limited sphere were tied to the establishment; the people
and their rulers were unconsciously drifting towards revolution in which the establishment itself would be broken up
under them. In the outset no one was looking for revolution, least of all the clergy, who, unconscious of their danger,
were sometimes unwisely intent upon their grievances and
on the assertion of their rights. An occasion which illus-
trates this, and also the determination of the General Assembly to manage the Church in Virginia as they saw fit, arose
as early as 1755, and was repeated until it became of cru-
cial and far-reaching influence. The clergyman's salary
had long been fixed at 16,000 pounds of tobacco per annum,
and this and other acts for the maintenance of the establishment, particularly the act of 1748, had been sanctioned by
the King. But as the Colony extended westward and southward, tobacco became less and less available as a medium
of exchange, while it varied so much in quality and value
that great inconvenience came of its use as a standard of
value. This bore particularly but not exclusively hard, upon
the clergy. To meet this difficulty in extreme cases,
payment of such dues were, by especial enactment, authorized to be made in money instead of tobacco, and this was
done in some cases in 1753 and 1754, and again in the year
1755, the year of Braddock's defeat, when the Colony
was at unusual expense on account of the French War, and
when there was a short tobacco crop. Under this pressure,
the Assembly authorized the discharge of tobacco debts in
money, at the rate of two pence a pound for tobacco. The
law was plainly in violation of the law of 1748 which had been

sanctioned by the King.   The clergy protested, but without avail.   At this rate they received compensation when tobacco was cheap and were denied the advantage when it was high.   They complained bitterly and justly to the Bishop of London.   "What clergyman can be expected to come hither from Great Britain, or will here design their sons for holy orders, when the clergy will not be paid in one certain commodity, but in tobacco or money or something else, as any of these shall happen to be least profitable?"   The protest was in vain.   Three years later, in 1758, when a short crop was expected, the Assembly in anticipation again passed a bill compounding tobacco at two pence a pound.   The crop turned out to be short, and tobacco rose to six pence a pound; but by the new law the planter was able to pay in money debts due to be paid in tobacco, at the rate of two pence a pound, and the clergy were losers of two-thirds of the value of their salaries.   Long and hot discussions arose between the clergy and the laymen, and this time the clergy sent a representative to plead their cause before the Privy Council of the King, with the result that the law was disallowed by the King and declared null and void.   This triumph of the clergy was followed by more hot discussions, besides a number of suits for damages in which the clergy met with varying success according to the temper of the courts and the juries.   But whatever their gains in the suits, they were constantly losing in influence with all classes in Virginia, on account of their appeal to the King against the will of the people of Virginia, as expressed in the Act of Assembly, and through the irritation that the disallowance by the King of the Act of Assembly occasioned.

The crisis of this question, which got the name of the "Parsons' Cause," came in December 1763 when the suit of the Reverend James Maury was tried at Hanover Court House as described in a previous chapter.

Henry's speech at Hanover Court House in the Parsons' Case led to his election to the General Assembly which met in the spring of 1765, when the Stamp Act, recently enacted by Parliament, came before the House.   That issue Henry met with the ringing words which made his name immortal. The country was all unconsciously drifting toward revolution.

How little the condition of affairs was realized by the clergy even seven years later was shown when, in June 1771, in response to a proposal emanating from New York and New Jersey, a convention of clergy met in Williamsburg and adopted a resolution to address the King in behalf of an American Episcopate. The number that attended was small, only twelve, and of those, two opposed the resolution. The Burgesses soon replied with an unanimous resolution of thanks to those who opposed the proposition, which they called "the pernicious project of a few mistaken clergymen for introducing an American Episcopate; a measure by which much disturbance, great anxiety, and apprehension would certainly take place among His Majesty's faithful American subjects." This was the end of all talk of a Colonial Bishop.

Some account must now be taken of another potent force in the disestablishment of the Church, the dissenters.

During the first hundred and twenty years of her history there was no considerable number of dissenters in Virginia. No act of toleration was passed until 1699, when the act, passed in England ten years before, was recognized by the General Assembly, and made applicable in Virginia; but it was given a narrower application in Virginia than in England, there being, indeed, as yet, but little occasion for such a provision.

At this time a few Presbyterians were living in Eastern Virginia and on the Eastern Shore, but only a few came until the Scotch-Irish began to drift down through Pennsylvania into the Valley west of the Blue Ridge in 1730. The next appearance of Presbyterians was in Hanover County 1743. Their great leader, Doctor Samuel Davies, writing from Hanover in 1750 to Doctor Doddridge, says, "There were not above four or five dissenters that I know of within a hundred miles of this until about six years ago." Under his lead they complained of, but conformed to, the law of toleration, quietly held their own, and by their natural conservatism and cultured preaching they appealed to and gathered recruits from a higher class of people than did any other dissenters.

Of the Methodists, Devereux Jarratt says that it was in 1772 or 1773 that he first saw a Methodist preacher in

Virginia, and that he preached the doctrine that "He that left the Church left the Methodists." They considered themselves not as dissenters from the Church but a society within it.

A few Baptists came into Virginia about 1714, and in 1762 there was a congregation of them in Pungo, Princess Anne County. Other Baptists, known as Regular Baptists, came into Virginia from Maryland about 1743, settled first in Berkeley County, and in 1755 established themselves in Loudon County and spread into Fauquier, Stafford and Orange Counties. These regular Baptists took out licenses to preach in particular places under the Act of Toleration, and while they did not always confine themselves to the stated places, and so incurred occasional opposition from the magistrates and the people, yet, as their licenses often went unchallenged and as their chief preacher and leader, Mr. David Thomas, was an educated man, they met with far less opposition, and in the long run with less success, than did the Baptists of another type called Separate Baptists, who had little or no regard for either licenses or education. The Separate Baptists came from New England, and they also first appeared in Berkeley County in 1755, but soon passed on and settled in North Carolina, from whence they spread back into Virginia, and established the first Separate Baptist Church in Virginia on the Dan River in Pittsylvania County in 1760. In this then remote section of Virginia the Separate Baptists took a strong hold, and from Pittsylvania they sent preachers in 1765-66 to Culpeper and Orange, where the Regular Baptists had churches. In 1767 the first Separate Baptist Church north of James river was organized in Spottsylvania County.

The dissenters all complained, and justly, of the restrictions of the law of toleration, which were not so liberal in Virginia as in England; and from 1769 to 1774 persistent efforts were made by the Baptists and Presbyterians to have these restrictions on times and places of meeting removed or relieved. In response to these appeals, ameliorating changes in the law were undertaken by the committee on religion in the General Assembly; but in the midst of the pressure of civil affairs preceding the Revolution, nothing satisfactory was arrived at in changing the law until the sweeping actions of 1776 altered everything.

In the meantime, and in spite of the difficulties, the increase in the number of dissenters and especially of the Baptists during the eight years preceding the Revolution was astonishing. In 1768 according to the Baptist historian Benedict there were but ten Baptist churches in Virginia, while in 1776 there were ninety with more than five thousand members. Various causes contributed to the rapid increase of dissent in Virginia, not all of them religious causes by any means. Social, political and religious conditions conspired to create a vast and practically unoccupied field ready to receive the appeals of the dissenting preachers. We have only to look back upon the earlier days to see how naturally this condition developed. The lines were closely drawn between the lower and upper classes; the Church was almost wholly managed and closely identified with the upper, ruling class, who occupied the rich and accessible lands on the great river fronts, while back of these plantations lay the boundless "back woods" or the poorer lands on the ridge between the rivers. On these poorer lands, or interspersed between the larger plantations, or serving on them, the poorer people would be found. Slavery complicated the case. In 1782, according to Mr. Jefferson, nearly half the population consisted of slaves. The ratio was about twenty-seven slaves to thirty free, of all conditions. Few slaves were owned by the lower classes, and this separated the classes still more. At an earlier period, when indentured servants were constantly brought into Virginia from England and were depended upon for labor, the relations between the higher and lower classes of white people were more natural, and the influence of the higher upon the lower was much greater than when the African came between.

But the great possibility for the white man in Virginia was that he could in time betake himself westward and southward, where rich lands were yet open to him, and there drink in the spirit of the new-world liberty and learn independence in a hard school. Unfortunately, he did not learn much more. Ignorance and immorality were common. The old field schools were poor at best, and this class had the poorest of them. The Church rarely followed them effectively. The services and the usual style of preaching were poorly adapted to the lower classes in any part of the Colony, and in the newly settled parts, the establishment of a parish, generally limitless in extent on the farther side, was necessarily not very effective as a religious force. Such a parish was part of the system of Colonial extension by which a new county in the wilds was designated by name and by vast bounds, and equipped with a crude court house with jail, stocks and pillory after the good old English fashion. A Vestry was elected, a glebe might be laid out, parsonage built, and, if he could be had, a clergyman appointed; but to expect him, with the limitations which the establishment laid upon him and with the weapons she put in his hands, to evangelize the scattered people in such a parish was to expect the impossible. This system was followed until 1776, in which year three notable counties and parishes were formed; the county and parish of Washington, the county and parish of Montgomery, and the county and parish of Kentucky. The first two covered the area now covered by about twenty counties in southwestern Virginia, while the county and parish of Kentucky lay still further afield. From the nature of the case, from the spirit of the times and from the character and condition of the people, the parish system had in many cases become impracticable. The result was that all over Virginia there was an increasing number among the lower classes of those who had no attachment for England and little active interest or part in the public affairs even of Virginia and still less in the Church. Devereux Jarratt, who in 1763 began his ministry as a zealous clergyman of the established Church, devoted to the interest of the plainer people, had himself grown up among that class, and gives a vivid picture of their ignorant and irreligious condition, and of the sharp distinction between the upper and lower classes. "We were accustomed to look on what we called *gentlefolk* as beings of a superior order. For my part I was quite shy of them, and kept off at a humble distance. A *periwig*, in those days, was a distinguishing badge of *gentlefolk* and when I saw a man riding the road near our house with a wig on, it would so alarm my fears, and give me such a disagreeable feeling, that I dare say I would run off as for my life. Such ideas of the difference between *gentle* and *simple*, were, I believe, universal among all my rank and age. But I have lived to see a vast alteration in this respect, and the contrary extreme prevail." He adds that the parson in his neighbourhood was a poor preacher, very unapt to teach, and that he himself went not to Church once a year; yet, when a child, his parents had been very careful to teach the children of the family the Church Catechism.

As the Revolution approached there was developed in this neglected part of the population, as well as in the higher classes more and more of the spirit of liberty and independence. In the quiet and well established communities the decorous and familiar service of the Prayer Book, even with a dull preacher, was the accepted order to such earnest churchmen and patriots as Pendleton, Mason, Nicholas, Nelson, Washington and others whose names would presently become famous. To them the Church was identified with Virginia in all her history and was dear and sacred. But even they were pondering the grave questions and difficulties of the times, which were soon to be resolved by them into the principles which would shape the future of both state and church. Hitherto, in the conservative and self-controlled life of Virginia there had been no considerable disturbance, either civil or religious, except in 1676 at the time of Bacon's Rebellion; and whereas the settlement of New England was directly due to dissatisfaction with the religious system of England, the troubles of the Cromwellian period only served to increase, by an addition of royalists and churchmen from the Old Country the conservative element in state and Church in Virginia. But now the double question of civil and religious liberty was being agitated in Virginia; and would not be settled, until in the great Bill of Rights (written by a Virginian, the cavalier and churchman, George Mason) the foundation principles of both civil and religious liberty were laid down more clearly than had yet been done in either Old England or New.

Among the lower classes in Virginia these questions came to be taken as represented by, and in large measure identified with, the new phases of religion introduced by the dissenters, especially by the Separate Baptists already referred to.

Doctor McGuffey of the University of Virginia used to say that the brains of the working people needed to be excited to enable them to think, and he gave that as the explanation of the great influence of Baptist and Methodist preachers over the working people. Certainly the uncultured Baptist preachers managed to excite the common people of Virginia and to make them think as they had not done before. Even their excesses and peculiarities served to attract the masses. Their drear tones, their plainness of speech, their vehement, almost fierce, earnestness, their contempt for opposition, their manifest sincerity, moved the people and brought their message home. Their organization was of the simplest order and gave ample opportunity to the plainest members of their congregations; their preaching was crude and narrow in the extreme, and they were often divided in their opinions among themselves, but they reached the people and brought to many a careless one a consciousness of God and of his own soul, a realization of sin and of his own sinfulness.

The peculiar force of their message was a direct appeal to the individual personality in each man. They woke up the individual. Over against the institutional systems, whether of Church or state, they set the individual man and his individual responsibilities and rights. Beginning as we have seen in the remoter counties south and north where there was less opposition, they spread gradually into the old and well established communities and everywhere with the same general results, a ready response on the part of some, and a contemptuous opposition sometimes breaking out into mob violence, on the part of others. The effects of this vehement preaching, with its materialistic and lurid threatenings, were always startling and frequently altogether out of the ordinary. The people were moved until some even lost physical and rational control of themselves, and fell into muscular contortions, were seized with jerking motions, barked, roared, rolled on the ground, uttered ecstatic shouts or sank into profound unconsciousness. Quiet people were alarmed and troubled. Men protested against members of their families becoming identified with a system which beside

all this recognized no baptism but immersion and utterly
repudiated infant baptism, and which constantly opposed
the Church that had existed in Virginia from the beginning. The mob element, ever ready, sometimes turned the
meeting into uproars and violently abused and assailed the
preachers. The preachers seemed almost to invite opposition, for they for the most part steadfastly refused to submit
to the provisions of the law of toleration, and took the extraordinary effects of their preaching and the outrages of
the mob as a like evidence of their increasing influence. That
their influence increased is certain, but that the preachers did
persist in violating the law, and that their methods did pro-
voke and frequently resulted in breaches of the peace, there
was no denying, and the magistrates issued peace warrants
against them and treated them accordingly. Between 1768
and 1775 inclusive, about thirty preachers were thus imprisoned, which increased the sympathy felt for them and
added to their influence with their adherents. In quite a
number of cases those who had been leaders of the mob
against them became active and effective preachers of the
"new light" religion.

It was commonly maintained by the Baptists at the time
and by their historians afterwards, that the harsh treatment
they received was due to persecution by the Colonial clergy.
The clergy were doubtless opposed to the dissenting preachers,
but it is giving the clergy credit for more influence than they
had, to suppose that they were responsible for the persecution, the arrest and imprisonment of the preachers. The
record shows that the persecution generally arose among
some of the rude classes with whom the dissenting preachers
as yet had no influence, and with whom the regular clergy
had little or none. And as the disturbances were the result
both of the persistent violation by the preachers of the law
of toleration and also of their ways and methods in conducting their meetings, the justice of the peace held them responsible and arrested them. But in fact it was but another
expression by the Virginian authorities of their determination to maintain their own laws. As the law had been maintained in the Parsons' Cause at the expense of the regular
clergy, so now it was maintained against the dissenting

preachers, and it continued to be until the law was changed in 1776. Even after the law was changed, when a petition was made to the House of Delegates as late as 1778 by one of the most influential Baptist preachers, with the hope of recovering the amount of prison charges incurred by him four or five years before in Chesterfield county, the appeal was, after due consideration by the House, rejected on the ground that the offender had been guilty of a breach of the peace. Nevertheless the Baptists persisted in their disregard of the law, and their sufferings, like their crude methods, continued to appeal to the sympathy of the common people; so they boldly set the law at defiance, demanding why *their* preaching should be a matter of toleration? Why should there be time and places when *they* could or could not preach any more than in the case of other people?

In like manner the inequalities in the existing social system were taken advantage of to arouse class hatred and opposition to the Church. Why should dissenters be taxed, they urged with good reason, to support a church for which they had no use and from which they received no benefit? The fact also that the legislative, the taxing and the administrative power was almost wholly in the hands of the representatives of the Church, and had its application to the people directly through the parish system, was constantly dwelt upon and presented as conclusive reason for opposing the Church and especially the clergy, as if the Church and the clergy were wholly responsible for the political system. Influenced by these motives as well as by the preaching, large numbers of the common people flocked into the Baptist congregations. Between the year 1770 and the close of 1774 that denomination increased about six fold, and before 1775 it numbered about five thousand. With this increase in numbers came an increase in political power which was unhesitatingly used, their leaders making every edge cut that shaped things in accord with their interests. And now a change in the constituency of the Baptist congregations began to appear. Some men of larger means were added to them, and here and there a captain of militia or a magistrate was seen in congregations which had begun with people of no such eminence, while political and social motives prevailed with them in a degree undreamed of by the simple pioneers who a few years ago had been urged on by a thirst for souls and a passionate purpose of preaching the gospel. With these changes the established Church became more than ever the object of their fixed hatred, and "so favorable did their prospects appear" says Semple, the Baptist historian, "that towards the end of 1774 they began to entertain serious hopes, not only of obtaining liberty of conscience, but of actually overturning the Church establishment from which all their oppression had arisen. Petitions for this purpose were accordingly drawn and circulated with great industry. Vast numbers readily and indeed eagerly subscribed them." The Presbyterians also continued to circulate petitions to be presented to the General Assembly asking relief, especially in regard to the law of toleration, but their efforts were not marked by the disposition to arouse class hatred or by the intense bitterness towards the Church which characterized the feelings and actions of the Baptists.

There was now a decided disposition on the part of the Burgesses to relax the law of toleration, and a committee was appointed to draw up a bill to that end, and in the meantime the law was more leniently applied; but the bill proved unacceptable to the dissenters, who saw the advantages in their position daily increasing as the Revolution drew nearer, and the result was that no definite change was effected.

In the midst of this state of affairs the year 1775 brought the events which precipitated the Revolution in Virginia. In March 1775 a convention of the first men in the state met in St. John's Church, Richmond; Patrick Henry delivered his epoch-making speech, and his resolutions for embodying, arming and disciplining the militia were adopted. In June the historic House of Burgesses held in Williamsburg what was to be its last meeting, for during the session of that General Assembly, Lord Dunmore forsook his capital and left the colony without an Executive. The convention therefore met again in Richmond in July 1775, and proceeded to embody and organize the militia for the defense of the colony, appointed the famous Committee of Safety to which was intrusted very wide executive powers, elected delegates to the Continental Congress and adjourned until December, when it met again to provide for a more perfect organization of the militia.

The resolution of the Convention in July for raising and embodying the militia provided for a chaplain for each of the regiments to be raised. The chaplains would of course be taken from the clergy of the Church, and it was in connection with this that the Baptists, who were quick to take advantage of the political occasion, made application to the Convention to be allowed to appoint some of the ministers who might, without molestation, preach to the soldiers at convenient times, declaring that "their brethren were left at discretion to enlist without incurring the censure of their religious community," and that many of them had enlisted and more were ready to enlist, but earnestly desired that their ministers should preach to them during the campaign. In response the Convention gave instructions to the commanding officers of the regiments to be raised "that they permit the dissenting clergymen to celebrate divine worship, and to preach to the soldiers, or exhort, from time to time, as the various operations of the military service may permit, for the ease of such scrupulous consciences as may not choose to attend divine services as celebrated by the chaplain." At the same time dissenting ministers or teachers were exempted, along with the ministers of the Church, from enlistment, and both were declared incapable of being elected as delegates to the Convention. This restriction, the Baptists, in spite of their opposition to any official connection between representatives of the Church and state, resented. The number of ministers and teachers who took advantage of the exemption appears to have been too large, for the Convention which met in December restricted the exemption to those who were duly licensed by the general Court or the Society to which they belonged.

These instances in which the dissenting ministers were classed with the clergy of the Church, and the permission given them to preach before the troops, mark the decided advance in their influence on the breaking out of the Revolution. On the 6th of May 1776 the last of these great Conventions, in which the real work of the Revolution was accomplished, met in the Capitol at Williamsburg, and the decisive action was taken by which Virginia ceased to be a colony and became an independent, sovereign, and organized State. These steps were three, and were in advance of the whole country. First, resolutions were adopted on May 15th directing the delegates from Virginia in the Continental Congress to propose to that body to "declare the united colonies free and independent states;" next, her own declaration of independence was made in the form of "The Bill of Rights" which was adopted on the 12th of June; and last, a constitution for the government of Virginia was adopted on July 4th, 1776. The Bill of Rights and the Constitution of Virginia were both written by George Mason of Gunston, in Fairfax County, an earnest churchman and a thorough revolutionist, and are the most remarkable papers produced during the Revolution. From the Bill of Rights, Jefferson drew much of the substance and often the very expressions embodied in the Declaration of Independence; and the Constitution of Virginia was the "first Republican Constitution ever adopted in America" and on it were based the Constitutions of many other states and of the National Government.

During these troubled years while the sons of the Church were directing and effecting the most important actions both in Virginia and in the Continental Congress, the Church and the parochial system in Virginia continued to do their work as they had done for about one hundred and fifty years. With the adoption of the Bill of Rights and especially the 16th Article of that great declaration, all was changed. The 16th Article reads as follows:

"That religion, or the duty which we owe to our Creator, and the manner of discharging it, can be directed only by reason and conviction, not by force or violence, and therefore all men are equally entitled to the free exercise of religion, according to the dictates of conscience; and that it is the mutual duty of all to practice Christian forbearance and charity towards each other."

This 16th article was hailed by the dissenters as the charter of religious freedom, and such indeed it was; and while it is certain that its far-reaching effects were not at first realized by those who adopted it, the extremists among the' dissenters regarded it as not only the declaration of a great principle but as nothing less than an enactment which put an immediate end to the establishment. They therefore took great courage and began preparations, against the meeting of the first General Assembly under the Constitution, for such an assault on the Church as would destroy it. "Having" as Semple says, "started the decaying edifice, every dissenter put to his shoulder to push it into irretrievable ruin." With this object as their first exhibition of the "Christian forbearance, love and charity," commended in the Bill of Rights, the dissenters, who were almost exclusively Baptists and Presbyterians, prepared a number of petitions which were presented to the first General Assembly which met in Williamsburg on October 7th, 1776.

That Assembly was perhaps the most distinguished that ever met in Virginia, but while it heartily supported the principle of the 16th article of the Bill of Rights, there were wide differences of opinion as to the mode of its application. The practical difficulties also were many and obvious; for the Church, apart from the sincere and affectionate attachment in which it was held by a majority of the members of the Assembly, was too intimately connected with the fabric of the State for that connection to be summarily dissolved without carrying confusion into every community. The dissenters, however, were ready for this at all hazards. Their many petitions, in varying terms, aimed at one object, the speedy dissolution and the practical destruction of the Established Church. In these destructive efforts, while the Baptists were much more numerous, the Presbyterians who represented a far more influential constituency, were more active and effective before the Assembly. But all alike appealed to the principle of the Bill of Rights already adopted, and petitioned for the free exercise of religion according to the dictates of conscience. Whatever other differences might exist among the dissenters, all agreed in demanding the abolition of an enforced tax for the support of the establishment. "The Presbyterians, Baptists, Quakers, deists and the covetous," says Leland, "all prayed for this." The Methodists still regarded themselves as members of the Church, and in a united petition representing their whole body of "near if not altogether three thousand members" they made a warm plea in behalf of the Church. "We do all in our power" said they, "to strengthen the said Church, and as we conceive that very bad consequences would arise from the abolishment of the establishment, we therefore pray that as the Church of England ever hath been, so it may still continue to be established." The German congregations, which had existed in Culpeper ever since the days of Governor Spotswood, asked exemption from parochial taxes because they were supporting their own minister and paying the war taxes, but protested that they were "not breaking from the Established Church as do the common dissenters."

The interests of the Church were represented in the Assembly by some of the most patriotic and prominent members of the body, led by Edmund Pendleton and Robert Carter Nicholas. Pendleton had been chairman of the Committee of Safety and President of the Convention which declared the Bill of Rights. He was constitutionally a conservative and a devoted Churchman, but he had held the most dangerous positions in the Revolution and his patriotism was of the highest order. Later he was made President of the Supreme Court of Virginia. The clergy of the Church also sent in their petition; very carefully and moderately expressed, pleading their position as a class prepared for an especial and necessary work, and already called and employed by the State to do it. The good work done by the Church in Virginia during the hundred and fifty years of its life was pointed out, and also the fact that its charity and mildness towards dissenters had in times past been acknowledged "by those very dissenters who now aim at its ruin, many of whom emigrated from other countries to settle in this from motives we may reasonably suppose, of Interest and Happiness."

The question of the establishment was before the General Assembly for nearly two months. Jefferson represents the struggle, in which he opposed the establishment, as being the severest in which he was ever engaged. At length on December the 9th a Bill which had been long and earnestly discussed and frequently amended was adopted. It was the second act passed by the new Assembly, and it enacted that:

1. All laws which rendered criminal the maintaining any

opinion in matters of religion, or forbearing to repair to Church, or exercising any mode of worship whatever, or which prescribe punishment for the same, were repealed.

2. All "dissenters from the Church established by law" were freed and exempted from all levies and taxes towards maintaining the said Church.

3. But the Vestries of the several parishes were required to levy and assess on all tithables within their respective parishes, as well dissenters as others, all salaries and arrears of salaries due to the ministers of their parishes for services up to January 1st, 1777, and to make assessments also to meet their legal engagements already entered into, and to provide for the poor as formerly.

4. For the protection of the Church it was enacted "That there shall in all time coming be saved and reserved to the use of the Church by law established "the Glebe lands already contracted for, all books, plate and ornaments belonging to the said Church, all arrears of money or tobacco due the said Church, and all private donations for the better support of the said Church and its members.

5. The question of the propriety of a general assessment for the support of ministers of the gospel, or whether every society should be left to make voluntary contributions for the support of the several ministers, was discussed and finally left for future consideration, without prejudice of the question.

6. But "whereas by the exemptions allowed dissenters it may be too burdensome in some parishes to the members of the established Church if they are still compelled to support the clergy by certain fixed salaries," it was judged best that this should be done for the present by voluntary contributions.

It will be observed that in this enactment, which cut the very root of the establishment, the vestries and the clergy were left in office, and the Church is still referred to as "the Church established by law;" but forces were put in operation by this very act which would inevitably disestablish it. That this act should have been passed in spite of the regard in which the establishment was held by a majority of that Assembly is truly remarkable, for although Mr. Jefferson claimed that by this time a majority of the inhabitants of Virginia were dissenters, which may be doubted, there is no doubt that not only a majority of the Assembly but a majority of the planters and others of the upper classes were Churchmen. But in this distinguished Assembly the majority were not only Churchmen, they were also broadminded and most liberal statesmen in the midst of a perilous revolution. The great principles of liberty and the inherent rights of men were uppermost in their minds, and Edmund Randolph expressed their motive when in his narrative he described them as "Patriots who dreaded nothing so much as a schism among the people; and thought the American principle too pure to be adulterated by religious dissension. They therefore did in very truth cast the establishment at the feet of its enemies."

The ecclesiastical revolution in Virginia knew no reversal. The plan of a general assessment for the support of the ministers of all Protestant denominations was repeatedly staved off by the dissenters. The act of 1776 suspending levies for the support of the clergy after January 1st, 1777, leaving them after that date dependent upon voluntary contributions, was renewed in 1777 and again in 1778. During these years a number of petitions came up to the Assembly in behalf of the establishment protesting against this law and asking for a renewal of levies for the support of the clergy, while other petitioners asked for a general assessment for the support of all Protestant ministers. None received favorable action. Two elaborate bills were presented in the last session of 1779, one from Accomac, proposing a very broad plan of a general assessment, and the other, prepared and presented by George Mason (the author of the Constitution of Virginia and of the Bill of Rights), "for saving the property of the Church hitherto by law established to the members of the said Church forever," but neither was passed. At last in December 1779, all acts for providing salaries for the clergy were repealed.

Nevertheless, the clergy were left in possession of the glebes and churches, held their official positions and were still responsible for the services, preaching, the administra-

tion of the sacraments and the performance of the marriage
ceremony which still was their exclusive function. Against
this restricted marriage law the dissenters with reason protested and frequently disregarded it. Nevertheless the law
remained unchanged until the fall of 1780 when a more liberal law was provided which was again amended in 1784. By
the help of the glebes and by teaching, some of the clergy
were able to hold their places and to keep the churches
open. An honest effort was also made by some parishes to
provide a support for the clergy by subscription, but the
people were wholly untrained for this, and so uncertain was
the whole situation and so often did these efforts fail that
many of the clergy were utterly discouraged. It became
difficult in many cases to secure a clergyman where one was
really desired, and, in those parishes where dissent largely
prevailed subscriptions were not even attempted.

Since not a few of the clergymen were native born Englishmen, it is not surprising that the question of allegiance became acute and at times most difficult. The act of May
1777 opened with a warning note "Whereas allegiance and
protection are reciprocal, and those who will not bear the
former are not entitled to the latter," the bill required all
free-born males above sixteen years, except imported servants
during their time of service, to renounce allegiance to George
III and to swear allegiance to the Commonwealth of Virginia,
and it was made the duty of the clergy and all ministers and
readers not only to take the oath but announce it in their
churches and meeting houses. The clergy as a class had
long been held under an undue suspicion of disloyalty by the
enemies of the Church, and now the time had come when it
was hard indeed for the man who, for whatever reason,
would not take the oath. Fortunately, the number of such
among the clergy is found upon careful and impartial examination to have been small. Some of these left their churches
and got out of the country or retired to such obscurity as
they were allowed; but a very few bold spirits held their
ground and bravely stood by their first allegiance to the
King. The lot of these non-juring clergymen, or of any who
were even suspected of not sympathizing with the Revolution, was very hard. One of them, the Reverend Christo-

pher Macrae of Littleton parish, Cumberland County, a man of high character and great piety, was threatened, petitioned against, and at last assaulted and almost killed, because he was suspected of being a Tory. But the best of the people stood by him, Patrick Henry himself defended him before the legislature, and his persecutors were punished. He remained in Virginia all during the Revolution and in 1785 represented his old parish in the convention which re-organized the Church. Indeed a careful examination shows that of the more than ninety-five clergy who were in Virginia during the Revolution, only nine can justly be accounted Tories, while nineteen held the conspicuously patriotic position of being members of the county committees of safety, twelve were chaplains in the Continental Army, and four served in that army, one as a major-general and one as a colonel.

The years of inconsistent action which held the Church in unsupported and ineffective connection with the state reduced the parochial system to the utmost disorder. In 1780 the Vestries in the great frontier counties beyond the mountains were dissolved, and civil officers appointed to care for the poor. Petitions for the dissolution of the vestries in eastern counties steadily increased. The deaths of vestrymen and wardens, the neglect and inefficiency of many who remained, the diminished number of tithables, the depreciation of currency, the breaking up of old estates, incident to the abolition of the law of entail, all operated against the old system. The Church as an institution was almost extinct.

On April 19, 1783, Washington announced to the army that peace had been proclaimed by Congress, and the men began to return home. The political revolution was accomplished, but the Church in its broken and discredited condition was, in spite of the Bill of Rights, still in a measure subject to the legislature. What was to be done with it? One thing was apparent to all; along with the practical abolition of the old system, irreligion, skepticism and immorality had alarmingly increased. Dissenters as well as churchmen felt and lamented it. Semple confesses that "the war, though very propitious to the liberty of the Baptists, had an opposite effect upon the life of religion among them. As if persecution was more favorable to vital piety than unrestrained liberty, they seem to have abated in their zeal upon being unshackled from their manacles." Devereux Jarratt says that "the state of religion is gloomy and distressing, and the Church of Christ seems to be sunk very low." For support he received for some time not so much money as would buy him a shirt, and he had been a favorite with his people.

In the midst of this disorder, the Methodists, who had stood by the Church during the Revolution, now became disaffected. Pleading the lack of regular clergymen to administer the sacraments,—"Some of the lay preachers undertook to ordain themselves, and make priests of one another."* Francis Asbury who was himself one of Mr. Wesley's most zealous lay preachers, disapproved of this extraordinary innovation, came from Delaware to Virginia bringing Mr. Wesley's twelve "Reasons Against Separating from the Church of England," and reclaimed some of these self-ordained preachers to the Church. This was in 1784. But in that very year Mr. Wesley determined to send Dr. Thomas Coke (a presbyter of the Church of England who had joined in Mr. Wesley's work) and two other preachers to America. Dr. Coke urged Wesley, in a letter, to ordain him a bishop, and early in September, 1784, at Bristol, England, Wesley ordained two of his preachers to be presbyters, and at the same time ordained Dr. Coke superintendent, and gave him letters of ordination, an abridged copy of the Prayer Book, and a plan for the organization of the Methodists in America. Dr. Coke and his companions arrived in New York on November 3rd, and at a general conference of the Methodists in Baltimore at Christmas 1784, he ordained Francis Asbury a deacon, on December 25th, and elder, on December 26th. Asbury, having been elected superintendent by the conference, was then ordained superintendent by Dr. Coke on December 27th. Dr. Coke and Mr. Asbury then proceeded to ordain other

* Devereux Jarratt.

deacons and elders.   Thus the Methodists were organized, and the whole body began to withdraw from the Church. Mr. Wesley took no counsel with the conference in England before this action, nor even with his devoted brother Charles Wesley, who writing of the event said "I can scarcely yet believe that in his eighty-second year, my brother, my old intimate friend and companion, should have assumed the episcopal character, ordained elders, consecrated a bishop, and sent him to ordain the lay preachers in America.   I was then in Bristol, at his elbow; yet he never gave me the least hint of his intention.   How was he surprised into so rash an act?   He certainly persuaded himself that he was right."   The effect of this action was immediately and very injuriously felt in the Church in Virginia.   The title, superintendent, was later dropped and that of bishop assumed.

Bad as the outlook was, it was not to be expected that the friends of the Church, many of them among the most prominent leaders of the Revolution and the most influential people in the state, would abandon the Church to utter ruin and disorder; especially since it was evident that the reaction following the removal of almost all legal restraint upon forms and obligations of religion, together with the skeptical ideas introduced by the French allies, were producing a recklessness in opinions, manners and morals which threatened society.   When, therefore, the matters touching the reestablishment of peace had been disposed of by the General Assembly of 1783, the two sessions of 1784 were largely taken up with the consideration of these problems by the very men who had led in the Revolution.   The acts of that Assembly show how fixed the idea still remained in the mind of a majority of the representatives that the legislature had the right to make laws concerning Church government and economy.   And indeed in spite of the passage of the Bill of Rights, the statutes of past years made further action necessary.

Ever since 1776, a considerable element in the state had favored a general assessment in support of the Christian religion.   The question had been successfully staved off from time to time by the dissenters, but now it came up more strongly supported than ever; for it became known that Henry, who, though he had been the very genius of the Revolution, was at heart a conservative, and in favor of the plan, and Richard Henry Lee was also pronounced in his support. The combined influence of Henry and Lee, backed by the conservative leaders, together with the wretched effects of the old assessment plan, left little doubt of its being adopted. Even the Hanover Presbytery, yielding to what appeared inevitable (not to mention the prospect of the material advantages of the assessment) presented a memorial to the Assembly in October 1784 approving a liberal form of assessment. The Baptists seem to have considered the adoption of the plan as foregone and said nothing. The plan took the form of a Bill presented in December, "Establishing a provision for teachers of the Christian religion." For this purpose a small tax was to be laid on all taxable property, and the person taxed was to name the Church or society to the support of which his tax was to be devoted, or, if he preferred, it could be devoted to the support of schools in his county.

Another matter touching religion which was before the Assembly at this time, was the further amendment of the marriage law. This long vexed question was finally disposed of by a bill passed in December 1784 which removed the last vestige of difference between the Episcopal clergy and other ministers as to their rights in performing the marriage ceremony. All were put on the same level, and especial provision was made to meet the peculiarities of the Quakers, Mennonites and similar sects.

The clergy of the Protestant Episcopal Church, as the Church was now called, had already asked the Assembly for an Act of Incorporation to enable them to regulate all the spiritual concerns of the Church, alter its forms of worship and enact such rules of government as were suited to their religious principles. In general, they asked that the legislature would aid and patronize the Christian religion. This request had been favorably received by the Assembly, which in committee of the whole resolved in November that "Acts ought to pass for the incorporation of all Societies of the Christian religion which may apply for the same." The

Act of Incorporation was passed December 22, 1784, incorporating the Church by the name of "The Minister and Vestry of the Protestant Episcopal Church," in the parish where they respectively resided. The Act secured to the Church its property, repealed all existing laws for the government of the Church, dissolved all existing vestries on the following Easter, 1785, and effectually disestablished the Church. The passing of this act at once excited the jealous enmity of the dissenters and also quickened opposition to the assessment plan. The whole act of incorporation, the securing of her property to the Church, and the asking by the Church at the hands of the state authority to regulate her own affairs, though this was nothing more than asking for the necessary changes in existing laws, all was regarded by the dissenters as so many steps toward the reestablishment of the Church as a state institution. Protests were uttered that they for their part would accept no incorporation at the hands of the state; and since the Act incorporating the Church was already passed, their opposition took the form of renewed opposition to the assessment plan which seemed on the point of being adopted. This opposition was rendered more effective by the election of Mr. Henry in November to be Governor (for the second time) of the state, in view of which he withdrew from the House, thus depriving the conservatives of his support, which if continued would almost certainly have resulted in the passage and permanence of both of these acts. As it was, the Assessment Bill was now postponed until the year 1785. In the meantime Mr. Madison, relieved of the presence of Mr. Henry, prepared and circulated broadcast a "Remonstrance" against the whole idea and plan of Assessment, which had such effect that, when the Assembly met in October 1785, and the Assessment Bill was referred to the Committee on Religion, active opposition was renewed, and so many adverse petitions were laid before the Committee that the Bill was not reported back to the House but lost in the Committee.

Looking abroad for a moment at the work of Episcopalians in other states, an important fact must be noted. On the 13th and 14th of May 1784, a few clergymen of New York, New Jersey and Pennsylvania had met at Brunswick in New Jersey to consider "in what way to renew a society for the support of widows and children of deceased clergymen." Their consultations led them to consider further "some general principles of a union of the Episcopal Church throughout the states" and to this end, they procured a larger meeting which was held in New York on the 5th of October 1784. At that meeting, certain general principles of union were agreed upon and referred to the Episcopalians in the other states, with the recommendation that a meeting of representatives of the Church, clerical and lay, be held in Philadelphia on the 27th of September, 1785, for the consideration of the whole subject.

Much encouraged by the Act of Incorporation, and having in mind the important meeting to be held in Philadelphia in the following September, the Episcopal Church in Virginia held its first Convention on May 18th, 1785 in Richmond. Forty-eight counties and the city of Williamsburg, comprising in all sixty-nine parishes, were represented by seventy-one laymen and thirty-six clergymen. Twenty-nine of the clergy had been in Virginia during the Revolution, and all but one, the Reverend Christopher Macrae, already referred to, had been patriots, faithful to the cause of the Revolution. It was the first ecclesiastical convention in Virginia in which laymen had representation, and among them were some of the most distinguished and influential men in the state, including that staunch friend of the Church, Edmund Pendleton. The Reverend Dr. James Madison, President of William and Mary College, who was to become later the first Bishop of Virginia, presided. His cousin, James Madison, destined to become President of the United States, was by his "Remonstrance" even then working the undoing of the fond scheme of Assessment.

There being as yet no union of the churches in the various states, the Church in Virginia was acting for itself as an independent Protestant Episcopal Church, and this Convention was the first really independent and constructive work done by the Church during this protracted period of revolution.

Among the first acts of the Convention, after it was organized for business, was the election of delegates to the

General Convention which was to meet in Philadelphia in the following September, to whom written instructions were given. The laity were largely in the majority and the proceedings bear the mark of the dominant mind of those masterful men who had brought the country through the Revolution. The very phraseology of the resolutions and rules is in the familiar style of the General Assembly, and the powers and functions of the Standing Committee, the executive committee of the Church, seem based upon those of the old revolutionary committees of "Correspondence" and "of Safety". There is small evidence of ecclesiasticism. The lay mind was in the ascendant.

The Canons of the Church of England were declared to be of no obligation in the Protestant Episcopal Church in Virginia, but the Liturgy of the Church of England was to be used in the Church with such changes as the revolution made necessary. Being an Episcopal Church, they proposed to have a Bishop, but they "conceive that the office of a Bishop, according to the true apostolic institution, differs in nothing from that of other ministers of God's Word except in the power of ordination and confirmation." They require him to be a Rector of a Parish as well as Bishop of the Diocese. He must visit the churches at least once in three years, and when he does so he "shall confirm such as choose to receive confirmation." The "Bishop shall be amenable to the convention, which shall be a court to try them from which there shall be no appeal." "Accusations against a Bishop, as such, shall come from the Vestries," but no such accusations were to be received unless they came from three vestries. Complaints against a minister were likewise to be from the Vestry of his parish "and from no other person or persons whatever." They were to be directed to the Bishop or to such person as the Convention appointed to receive such complaints, and to direct courts of examination. Each vestry had power to choose and appoint its own minister. But no minister could be received until he produced satisfactory evidence that he had received Episcopal ordination and had taken the oath of allegiance to the Commonwealth, and subscribed to be conformable to the doctrine, discipline and worship of the Protestant Episcopal Church. The Bishop also was required to swear allegiance to the Commonwealth. Here was ecclesiastical democracy still holding the reins, and with a shrewd eye on the clergy.

Among the forty-three Rules of Government and Discipline, the eighth made special provision for the over-sight of the clergy. It provided that the State should be divided into districts, of which twenty-four were appointed, corresponding in lines with the senatorial districts of the State, each district containing not less than three, nor more than ten, parishes. The clergy of each district were to meet annually in presbytery in April, and be presided over by one of their own number chosen by themselves and called the Visitor, and it was the duty of the Visitor to visit each parish in his district annually, and "attend to and inspect the morals and conduct of the clergy, see that the canons and rules of the Church are observed, and that no abuses were practised, to admonish and reprove privately those clergymen who are negligent or act in an unbecoming manner, and report yearly to the Bishop" or, in his absence, to the next convention, noting down offenders and offences. Thus the clergy were to be carefully looked after, but among all the forty-three rules, in which discipline is given prominence, there was no special provision for safe-guarding the morals and conduct of the laity.

The Convention could hardly be expected to be enthusiastic, and there was a note of sadness in the address which was sent out to the members of the Church throughout the State. But both the clergy and laymen were in a measure hopeful. The act of incorporation already passed secured its property to the Church, including the rectories and glebes, while the Assessment Act, of the passage of which they still had good hope, would put the support of the clergy on something like the familiar system of taxation, the only system which the laity as yet regarded as dependable. Both clergy and laity were doomed to disappointment.

The opposition had no idea of allowing either of these plans to prevail. The broadcast dissemination of Mr. Madison's Remonstrance and the activity of the pronounced enemies of the Church did their work, and when the next General Assembly met in October 1785, such a flood of appeals and memorials were sent up against assessment plan that, as has been noted, the bill was not even reported from the committee to which it had been referred, and was hopelessly lost.

This same General Assembly of October 1785 passed a bill directing overseers of the poor to be appointed in every parish, or district, as the political territory was called, who should perform those functions with reference to the poor which had hitherto been performed by the church wardens, and the church wardens were called upon to make a settlement of their parochial accounts. On January 16, 1786 of this notable session, Mr. Jefferson's famous bill, "An Act for establishing religious freedom," was, after various amendments, passed; and just a year later, in January 1787, the Act incorporating the Episcopal Church was repealed. With this Act the last trace of connection between the Church and the state disappeared. This Act was so formed that it preserved to all "religious societies" "the property to them respectively belonging," and also authorized the appointment by such societies of trustees to hold and apply such property to the uses of the society.

As the management of Church property had hitherto been transacted by the Vestries, and as, although the Church was now no longer incorporated, the Vestries still existed, some doubts arose as to whether the trustees appointed under the act repealing the act of incorporation had the power to act as successors to the former Vestries in the management of the property vested in them. It was accordingly enacted in December 1788 "that the said trustees and their successors, shall, to all intents and purposes, be considered as successors to the former Vestries, and shall have the same power of holding and managing all the property formerly vested in them, whether for charitable purposes by private donation, or in trust for the use of individuals." Thus the management of Church property was by this law taken out of the hands of the Vestry and put into the hands of the trustees. Nevertheless Vestries continued to be elected in the parishes and continued, albeit through the trustees, to manage the Church property. This awkward arrangement still applies to the management of Church property by the ruling bodies of all religious denominations in Virginia. In most other states there is no more difficulty as to the incorporation of a congregation or parish than the incorporation of a theological seminary.

The depressing effect of these several acts of legislation upon the Church was indicated in the attendance on the next three Episcopal Conventions in which the clerical and lay attendance fell off to less than half of what it had been in 1785. Darker days were yet to come, and more than fifty years passed before an Episcopal Convention met in which the lay and clerical deputation was as large as in the first Convention which assembled in 1785.

The separation of Church and state was now as complete as legislative enactment could make it. Those intricacies which during the long years of the colonial period had united the Church and state, and which had extended throughout the entire body politic, had been cut out to the last fiber; and in this operation, perilous to both religion and the state, the Church was brought well nigh to that condition which the Baptist historian Semple describes as aimed at when "every dissenter put his shoulder to push it to irretrievable ruin." But the Church still lived, and was still the object of active and determined opposition. The thing that now provoked her enemies was that the Church owned property. Ever since 1607 when the first minister, Robert Hunt, had brought the English Bible, Prayer Book and Sacramental vessels to Virginia, when the colonist built up that humble little log church in the stockade at Jamestown, the Church had owned property. The Virginians had proceeded on the natural and sound principle that, however connected with the state, and whatever functions the Church performed on account of that connection, still the Church had its own separate and essential existence and character as a Church, and the fact that it performed duties for the state was recognized as a reason for its receiving property from the state. In an agricultural settlement such as Virginia was, land was a necessity to the ministers of the Church, and, as nothing was so plentiful as land, much of the Church property was in real estate, land bestowed by action of the colonial government or by individuals. The glebe, the Church building and graveyard, the Communion vessels, and other property were a recognized provision made by the state, or by individuals, for the Church and were Church property. The glebe generally consisted of about two hundred acres, and was for the benefit of the minister and also of the parish, but it was not the property of the minister. He only had the use of it while he remained in charge of the parish. If he gave up the parish he gave up the glebe, and he was obliged by the law to leave it and its furnishings in as good condition as he received it. Nor did the glebe belong to the Vestry. If for any reason it became necessary or expedient to sell the glebe, an Act of the General Assembly had to be enacted by which the Vestry for the time being was put in trust of the glebe, and so enabled to sell it and give legal title for it, and the proceeds of the sale remained Church property and had to be invested in another glebe or in some other way for the benefit of the Church. Thus the General Assembly itself recognized and guarded the property-rights of the Church, and these property rights were guaranteed by the great Bill of Rights of 1776, by the act incorporating the Church in 1784, and by the act which repealed the act of incorporation in 1787. In spite of these repeated enactments and of the whole history of Virginia, there was a strong determination on the part of many dissenters to deprive the Church, if possible, of its glebes and Church buildings; but how doubtful the right to do so appeared, even to themselves, was shown when the question whether the glebes should be regarded as public property or not was discussed in a meeting of the General Committee of the Baptist Church on August 10, 1787. On being put, it was decided in the affirmative by only one vote. That vote decided the fate of the glebes. The Presbyterians also met in Convention later in the same month and drafted a memorial to the General Assembly asking that the glebes be sold and the money divided among the different denominations of Christians in each parish according to the number of their tithes, to be applied by them to religious uses, and that the Churches with their furniture be used in common for religious worship. This memorial resulted in a resolution being presented to the General Assembly which met in October 1787 "That the glebe lands in the several parishes throughout this state, derived from the contributions of the people thereof, and in which there is no Episcopalian minister, be disposed of for public purposes, provided a majority of the parishioners shall consent thereto." The resolution was lost by a vote of 45 to 62, the most influential men in the Assembly voting against it. The question was not pressed again for two years, but in August 1789 the General Committee of the Baptists memorialized the Assembly for the sale of the glebes and the use of the Churches in common. The memorial was referred to the Committee for Religion of which Patrick Henry and Edmund Randolph were members, and the Committee reported a resolution that the memorial "involves in it one of the greatest rights of the people," and therefore provided that copies of the memorial and of the committee's resolution be printed and distributed as was done with the assessment bill in 1785. They referred to the origin of the glebes and to the Act of 1776 guaranteeing the Church's property, and maintained "that the Protestant Episcopal Church was the same in rights as the former Church." The Committee further reported that "In order, therefore, to put an end to these disputes, it is declared and resolved by the General Assembly:

"1. That they will forever adhere to the act concerning religious freedom.

"2. That the contest for the Glebes, Churches and chapels is not of a religious nature, but is to be decided by the rules of private property.

"3. That the grants aforesaid from the treasurer and company, and from the King of England, were to the followers of the Church in each parish, forming one society, exclusively of all other persons whatsoever.

"4. That the transferring of the private donations, or any part of them, from the support of the Protestant Episcopal Church, to that of any other religious order, would be an unconstitutional invasion of right, and would in effect oblige the donors to contribute to the maintenance of tenets which they either did not foresee, or foreseeing, might not have approved.

"5. That the Glebes, Churches and chapels, whether purchased or given, being vested in bodies which were capable in law of taking and holding them to their own use, and which actually did take and hold them to their own use, it is against reason and practice of every sect, that those who voluntarily depart from communion with them, should demand a share of their possessions.

"6. That it would be usurpation in the Legislature to convert the money arising from the sale of Glebes, Churches or chapels, to public necessities.

"7. That the Legislative sanction for such a sale would soon grow into a precedent for the constant intrusion of the State into all things which concern religion.

"8. That the stipulation and guarantee aforesaid, ought to be inviolably preserved."

With this strong statement of the rights of the Church and with a view to giving the people generally, time to consider the matter, the further consideration of the Baptist memorial was postponed until 1790. In that year the Baptists came again before the Assembly with a petition for the sale of the glebes. The motion to sell them was lost by a vote of 52 to 89, Patrick Henry, Henry Lee, Richard Lee and John Marshall voting against the confiscation of the Church property. But the influence of the most eminent patriotism, public service and legal talent went for nothing against the determination to despoil the Church.

It would be neither pleasant nor profitable to follow in detail the various forms in which the dissenters and especially the Baptists presented and pressed year after year their memorials for the confiscation of the Church property. Suffice it to say that the attempt failed in 1791 by a vote of 48 to 77; in 1792 a similar bill failed of a second reading and so was lost; in 1793 the question was not discussed; in 1794 an act to repeal so much of the act of 1776 as guaranteed its property to the Church failed by a vote of 52 to 80. In 1795 the attempt again failed by a vote of 63 to 70. In 1796 the annual attack of the Baptists was repeated and now the Episcopal Church also presented a petition in its own defense. Both were referred to the Committee of Courts of Justice, which brought in a carefully prepared report practically repeating the argument in favor of the right of the Church to hold its property so fully set forth by the Committee on religion in 1789. To this the radical element made a long and labored reply, and the House, as if to indicate its weariness of the whole question, laid both petitions on the table.

The General Assembly was weary of the question of the glebes, so often decided by them in vain. It began to be felt that the question could not be decided by the legislature but only in the courts. With this in mind Bishop Madison called a convention of the Episcopal Church which met in Richmond on December 6th, 1797. The question of the rights of the Church to its property was referred to a Committee consisting of Bushrod Washington, Edmund Randolph and John Wickham. The Committee agreed in their opinion as to the right of the Church to its property "on the same grounds with the rights of private property, which

have been recognized and secured by the principles of the
revolution and by the constitution." They were of the
opinion also that the question "must be decided constitutionally by the judiciary and by the judiciary alone."

The vexed question of Church property had now been
before the people of Virginia for twenty years, during which
time much of the glebe land and many of the Church buildings had suffered from neglect or been practically deserted
by the discouraged ministers and Vestries. But the principle of the Church's rights remained, and had been constantly defended by a majority of the leading representatives
in the General Assembly, the men who had led and effected
the Revolution and framed the Bill of Rights and the Constitution. Among them were George Mason, Edmund Pendleton, Patrick Henry, Henry Lee, Richard Lee, John Marshall,
James Monroe, Wilson Cary Nicholas, Carter Braxton,
William Giles, Richard Bland, Edmund Randolph, Benjamin Harrison and many others. Some of these great men
were decidedly progressive statesmen who opposed the act
incorporating the Church and the plan of a general assessment for the support of religious teachers, but they were
steadfast in maintaining the right of the Church to its property. If this group of men did not know the mind of the
framers of the Bill of Rights and the Constitution, it would
be difficult to find true interpreters of those great papers.

But another influence was now coming actively into play.
Radical ideas had advanced in Virginia far beyond those held in
the early days of the Revolution. Stimulated by the progress
and success of democratic principles in politics, religion and
social life, the spirit of the age was now coming under the influence of the still more radical ideas absorbed from the French
Revolution. They prevailed more or less in all the States and
their influence was felt in the colleges and in politics, and was
generally inimical to religion in any shape. This was sadly
true in Virginia. Conservatism of all sorts was at a discount, and of all conservatism, conservatism in religion was
least regarded. The length to which this radical spirit was
ready to go and its impatience with religious matters, was
shown in the General Assembly in 1797 and 1798 when the
Baptists sent up their yearly memorial against the property

rights of the Episcopal Church, and when the Church itself had expressed its readiness to submit the question to the decision of the Courts. The radical element was found to be so far in the ascendant that early in January, 1798, the House in the Committee of the whole, going back to the Bill of Rights, and taking the most radical interpretation of that great Bill, brought in a resolution to the effect that since by the Constitution of Virginia the government of the King of England was totally dissolved, and since by the Bill of Rights the subject of religion was referred to conscience, and the power to revive any species of ecclesiastical or Church government was excepted from the powers of the substituted government, therefore the several laws touching religion, exempting dissenters from supporting the establishment; repealing the act for the support of the clergy; the incorporation act; the act authorizing the election of Vestries, the act repealing the incorporation act; the act giving power to trustees; "ought to be repealed as violating the principles of the Constitution and being inconsistent with religious freedom." This was saying plainly that the men who made the Constitution did not know what they had meant by it or what it meant, and that they were guilty of ignorance and inconsistency when they went on to enact laws under it.

EDITOR'S NOTE:—Illness made it necessary for Dr. Bryan, at this point, to suspend his writing. He sent the unfinished manuscript and expressed the hope that the last few pages would soon follow. He was, however, soon called to the peace of Paradise. The Editor, therefore, brings this chapter to its conclusion by copying from his Historical Sketch of Bruton Parish Church the account of the final issues of this long and bitter controversy.

"On the 24th day of January, 1799, an act was passed, 'whereby every act which had been passed since the Revolution, touching the Church and its property, was repealed.' †.

"The enemies of the Church, having influenced the Legislature to pass the law of 1799, now found it easy to strike the final blow. This was done through an act passed on January 12th, 1802, 'by virtue of which the glebe lands were ordered to be sold for the benefit of the public.'*

"The Convention of Virginia authorized Bishop Madison to take the case into the Court of Appeals. This was

†Laws of Virginia, edition 1803, p. 338. Hawks, p. 233.
*Hawks, p. 233.

done in 1804. This case was decided by a vote of three against one in favor of the Episcopal Church. But on the night preceding the day when the opinion was to have been pronounced, Judge Pendleton died.

"Judge Tucker was appointed to succeed him, and the case was again argued. Upon the second hearing the court was equally divided, Judge Fleming, who favored the Church, having in each instance refused to sit on the case because he considered himself interested in the decision. The decree of Chancellor Wythe, from which the appeal had been taken was thus affirmed, ‡ and the glebe lands of Bruton Church, with those of many other Virginia Churches, were sold".§

In one notable case, however, the title of a parish to its glebe was successfully defended. Fairfax parish lay chiefly in Fairfax county, but the parish church and the glebe were situated in that part of the county which had been ceded to the general government and formed part of the District of Columbia. This fact gave to the Church-wardens the right of appeal to the Supreme Court of the United States when the state Court had upheld the Overseers of the Poor in selling the glebe and appropriating the proceeds. The Opinion and Judgment of the Supreme Court was prepared and delivered by Justice Story (9 Cranch, 43), and may be found, in part, in Meade's Old Churches, etc. Vol. II, p. 452 ff. It was a complete vindication of the position taken by the friends of the Church, following somewhat the opinion of Judges Carrington and Lyons of the Virginia Court of Appeals, and declaring that "the statutes of 1798, ch. 9, and of 1801, ch. 5, are not, in our judgment, operative so far as to divest the Episcopal Church of the property acquired, previous to the Revolution, by purchase or by donation." The previous Acts of the Legislature, from 1776 down, confirming to the Church the title to its property, were declared to be, not inconsistent with the Constitution or Bill of Rights but rather "a contemporaneous exposition the Constitution" on the part of its very framers. Thus the *only* judgment ever delivered by a Court of Appeal on this question was in favor of the Church.

‡Hawks. Ecclesiastical History, Virginia, pp. 237-239.
§Historical Sketch of Bruton Parish Church. Goodwin, p. 50.

THE RIGHT REVEREND DOCTOR JAMES MADISON

First Bishop of Virginia

SECTION I

CHAPTER IV

BISHOP MADISON

REV. E. L. GOODWIN, D. D.

James Madison, first Bishop of Virginia, was the eldest son of John and Agatha (Strother) Madison, and was born at Madison Hall, the seat of his father, near Port Republic, Augusta county, now Rockingham county, Virginia, August 27, 1749. Of his youth little is known. He attended an academy in Maryland, and in 1768 entered William and Mary College, graduating with high honors in 1772. He studied law under Chancellor Wythe and was admitted to the bar but never practiced. In 1773 he was chosen Professor of Natural Philosophy and Mathematics in the College. In May, 1775, he went to England for Holy Orders, and doubtless pursued his studies there, returning about the outbreak of the Revolution in Priests' Orders. He resumed his professorship, and in 1777, at the age of twenty-eight, he succeeded the Rev. James Camm, D. D. as President of the College of William and Mary, the highest position open to a clergyman in Virginia, and, indeed, in America. He held this office until his death thirty-five years later.

He was a fine classical scholar and was well versed in the humanities also, but his tastes ran strongly to scientific studies. The map of Virginia engraved from his surveys, and known as Madison's map, was remarkable for its accuracy of detail and was long the standard map of the state. In the summer of 1779 he and his colleague, the Rev. Professor Robert Andrews, were appointed commissioners on the part of the state of Virginia to meet a similar commission from Pennsylvania to determine the boundary line between these states. After prolonged conference the *termini* of Mason and Dixon Line extended were agreed upon, the line surveyed, and the south-west corner of the state of Pennsylvania was fixed "with great astronomical precision."

Almost immediately after his ordination Dr. Madison became the rector of James City parish, embracing Jamestown Island and a portion of the county lying on the mainland. The church on the island, however, the fifth Jamestown church, had been abandoned, owing to the small population remaining there, and a new parish church built "on the main." Dr. Madison held this rectorship, at least nominally, until his death, and so was the last rector of the first parish established in America. The parish was thereafter merged with Bruton parish, Williamsburg. No record of his pastoral work remains.

On May 18, 1785, the first Convention of the Diocese of Virginia, now happily freed from state control, met in Richmond. Over this Convention, the largest, and in the personnel of the laity attending, the most distinguished, which assembled during the first sixty years of our diocesan history, Dr. Madison was chosen to preside. He was active during the following years in the affairs of the Diocese. Dr. Griffith, the first choice for bishop, being in failing health and despairing of reaching England for consecration or of receiving it in this country, relinquished his appointment and died soon after. At the Convention of May, 1790, Dr. Madison was elected Bishop, receiving forty-three of the fifty-two votes cast. An appropriation of two hundred pounds was made for his expenses in securing episcopal orders.

Almost the only word from his own pen which we have found touching upon his election is a meagre mention of it in a letter to his cousin, the Hon. James Madison, afterwards President and then a member of the first United States Congress. He inclosed two letters to Bishop Seabury which he desired to have forwarded through the courtesy of some member of the Congress from New England, and added: "A late Convention of our Church thought proper to elect me to ye Episcopal office, and I have consented, whether wisely or not I cannot say, to undertake it."

During that summer Dr. Madison voyaged to England seeking consecration. He found none of the difficulties awaiting him which had harassed and delayed his predecessors who had gone thither on the same errand, and was consecrated at Lambeth on the 19th of September, 1790, by Archbishop Moore of Canterbury, assisted by the Bishops of London and Rochester.

Returning to Virginia the new bishop entered upon his untried duties without acclaim or ostentation but with unmistakable zeal and purpose. He was then forty-one years of age, and was among the youngest of the clergy of his diocese. He was tall and slender in figure with refined and scholarly features, gentle in manner, graceful and courteous in bearing, and benevolent in disposition. He was peculiarly gifted as a reader, having a voice of singular sweetness and distinctness. He was also regarded as an eloquent preacher. "His style" says President John Tyler, one of his pupils, "was copious and Ciceronian, and his manner strikingly impressive. His discourses were not so much of a doctrinal as a moral cast. He addressed himself to the moral sense and enforced the importance of observing the high moral duties." This was in accord with the religious fashion of the day. But Bishop Madison was firm in his grasp upon the fundamentals of our holy religion, and he was intensely eager in his desire that they should be truly preached and followed by his clergy and people, though doubtless his emphasis was laid on other than those distinctly evangelical truths so faithfully and fruitfully preached by his successors, to which the revival of the Church in Virginia was due. His Episcopal addresses are almost the only remains of his public deliverances which have come down to us. The first of these after his consecration, read before the Convention of 1791, was, we make bold to say, one of the most comprehensive and convincing charges ever delivered in the American Church. It was a fearless and searching inquiry into the causes of the weakness of the Church in those days of her depression and an exhortation, instinct with feeling, to renewed zeal and greater fidelity. And this was followed through a series of years by others of equal fervor and urgency.

For his support the new Bishop was dependent entirely upon the College, since the Convention undertook only to pay the expenses of his visitations and it is doubtful whether this was always done. His duties as president and professor were as imperative as they were engrossing. William and Mary had lost heavily on account of the war, and the work of a university devolved upon four or five professors. Yet

this was the only seat of higher learning in the Commonwealth and the only source to which the Church could look
for men qualified for the ministerial office or for social leadership. Bishop Madison, while his health permitted, taught
from four to six hours each day on Natural Philosophy, Moral Philosophy, Political Economy and International Law,
besides performing his administrative and other public
duties. His visitations, therefore, had to be performed
during the short vacations of the College, and these periods
seem to have been devoted to diocesan ministrations. He
expressed to the Convention his purpose to visit each parish
triennially. His reports of his visitations made to the Convention were usually not published in its journals, but we
learn that in the second year of his episcopate he visited
fourteen parishes in widely separated parts of the state, and
in five of them he confirmed upwards of six hundred persons.
His journeyings, we know, were extensive and laborious.
The Bishop was strong in his belief that the Church of Virginia would recover something of her prestige and be restored
to a measure of her former influence and dignity. He inscribed as the motto upon his episcopal seal the single word
"Resurgam" and in the faith thus expressed he labored
diligently until his hopes had vanished one by one. He interested himself actively in the vain attempt to preserve for
the Church her property in the parish glebes, the sole remnant of her ancient vested rights, which had been assured to
her by repeated enactments of the legislature of the state,
since upon these depended largely the maintenance of the
clergy. In this contest Bishop Madison's legal training
showed itself in his clear presentation of the principles involved. In another matter he was, perhaps, not so wise.
Long after the proposition for the support of religious teachers of all denominations by public assessment or taxation,
which had been so strongly urged by leading statesmen after
the disestablishment of the Church, had been defeated
through the influence of his kinsman, James Madison, the
statesman, he continued to defend and even to advocate the
principle as a sound political doctrine. His democracy,
however, and his patriotism, were unimpugned, and it is

said of him that he uniformly represented the Kingdom of Heaven as a republic.

The first proposition ever made in the American Church looking toward Church unity was made by Bishop Madison in the General Convention of 1792 and was directed towards winning the Methodists back to their mother Church. It was a purpose dear to his heart and was also in agreement with the earnestly expressed sentiment of the first Convention of his Diocese in 1785. But his proposal, though indifferently assented to by the Bishops, was refused consideration by the House of Deputies.

Owing to the long distances to be traveled and the difficulties in communication, the poverty of the clergy and their rapidly diminishing numbers, the Conventions of the Diocese grew smaller year by year until it was increasingly difficult and finally seemed impossible to get a quorum together, and the Bishop was left to struggle on without the advice or cooperation of that body. For ten years before his death only two Conventions appear to have been held, and of one of these no journal seems to have been published. In 1805, however, a Convention met, probably at the Bishop's special solicitation, and he proposed to it the election of an assistant Bishop on account of his inability, because of failing bodily strength and the pressure of other obligations, to discharge all the duties of his office. The matter was, however, deferred until the next Convention, and none other was held during his lifetime. Of the last years of Bishop Madison's life little or no record remains. We only know that he continued to exercise his episcopal functions as occasion offered until his end. His physical health, never robust, was failing slowly for several years. In a letter to President Madison, dated February 1, 1812, he writes: "My health, I fear is gone. I am laboring under dropsy. Medical aid seems of little avail though I have sought for it among our most skillful physicians. Digitalis has had some effect, but it produces a weakness which could not long be supported."

Bishop Madison died on March 6, 1812, and was buried under the chapel of the College which he had served so faithfully and so long.

SECTION II

Some of the Founders of the Seminary

SECTION II

SOME OF THE FOUNDERS OF THE SEMINARY

PREFATORY NOTE BY THE EDITOR

I

REV. DR. WILLIAM H. WILMER

Rev. P. P. Phillips, D. D.

II

RT. REV. DR. WILLIAM MEADE

Rev. E. L. Goodwin, D. D.

III

RT. REV. DR. RICHARD CHANNING MOORE

Rev. W. A. R. Goodwin, D. D.

Prefatory Note by the Editor

History finds its most vital interpretation in the biographies of epoch-making men. In them we see the forces of the past and the conditions of their contemporaneous life finding culmination. Into the crucible of their thought enter facts and forces, the ideas and ideals hitherto vague and uncorrelated; and under the influence of the divine creative Spirit there is born a new vision, a new purpose and a more divine order in human society. Thus the spirit of the past flowing through the present, and meeting there the Eternal Spirit, incarnate in chosen personalities, makes the enriched and more beautiful future. The great epochs of history have thus been created by epoch-making men. Light has come out of thick darkness as "the Light of the world" has become incarnate in the consecrated lives of men, who, with faith and courage, arise to be the torch-bearers of truth and the heralds of a new order.

Thus, too, institutions are born. Conditions which need correction press through human thought into a formulated purpose. The solution of a need becomes apparent. The seer, the prophet, communicates his vision and purpose to a kindred spirit, and these find others who enter into fellowship, binding themselves together in thought and love and in the determination to serve that their vision and hope may find realization. The institution which results is thus the outward and visible outcome of the divine thought and purpose, invisibly incarnated, by the Holy Spirit, in the hearts and minds of men.

The Theological Seminary in Virginia came into being in just this way. It is, therefore, most fitting that we should introduce the reader to the history of the Seminary through some of those creative spirits who stand at its portals. They saw the needs of their day and generation. They sought to find the way out of darkness into light. They interceded with God, and through prayer rose to the mount of vision. In them a divine thought became incarnate. Of this thought and vision they became the prophets and the heralds. Through them the Church was roused from its long lethargy and awakened to action. The need for trained and well equipped leaders, seen at first by a few, came to be felt by the Church at large and the Seminary came into being. It was born of God. It came into existence because He called men whom He had fitted to know and to fulfil His purpose.

The question, "Who founded the Virginia Seminary?" has been often raised and debated. Incomplete answers have been written on paper and inscribed in marble. For no one man can this honor be claimed. It does not belong exclusively to even all of those whose biographical sketches follow. They stand preeminent among the many who prayed and labored in laying the foundations, and because in them the thoughts and purposes out of which the Seminary grew find their clearest exposition, they are given prominent place at the outset of the History of the Seminary as interpreters of the spirit in which this Institution was born and as the prophets of its purpose and destiny.

SECTION II

CHAPTER I

REV. DR. WILLIAM H. WILMER

REV. P. P. PHILLIPS, D. D.

In the custody of the writer of this article are two books; one, the records of the standing committee of Virginia from its reorganization in 1813; the other, the records of the Education Society of Virginia from its organization in 1818. Both of these books are still in use. They contain much of the early unpublished History of the Episcopal Church in Virginia. From them the writer has drawn much of the material of this paper, showing the part Dr. Wilmer took in the founding of the Seminary; for, unfortunately, no life of Dr. Wilmer was ever written; and as he died ninety years ago, no personal memory of him exists.

The late Rev. Dr. Cornelius Walker, for many years a beloved professor in our Seminary, was often heard to say that due credit had never, in his time, been given Dr. Wilmer for his part in the founding of this Seminary. Dr. Walker was in the position to know, for he had not only heard the traditions in the matter, but had studied them, and was nearer their source than we of today.

In 1815, at a meeting of the Virginia Council, a letter was received from Dr. John Augustine Smith, president of William and Mary College, on the advisability of establishing a Professorship of Theology in that institution. The Committee on the State of the Church, to whom this communication was referred, reported back: "That the Bishop and Standing Committee be requested to ascertain what practical mode can be devised to that effect, and that they be authorized to adopt measures for the promotion of an object of so great magnitude, and which may, under the blessing of God, be productive of the most beneficial consequences."

The Rev. Dr. Packard, a professor in the Seminary from an early period, and in personal touch with its history, said

76

that this resolution was written by Dr. Wilmer, though presented by the chairman of the Committee on the State of the Church, the Rev. William Meade, afterwards the great Bishop of Virginia.

This was the beginning of the movement to found a Theological Seminary. Several years after a theological class was started at William and Mary College with the Rev. Dr. Keith as professor. It never had more than one student. It began in 1821, and ended in 1823.

In June, 1818, a meeting of certain clergymen and laymen of Washington and Georgetown, in the District of Columbia, and of Alexandria, Virginia, was held in Washington. It was for the purpose of founding a society to be called "The Society for the Education of Pious Young Men for the Ministry of the Protestant Episcopal Church." The Rev. Dr. Wilmer was elected President, and held that office until his removal from Alexandria in 1826.

With Dr. Wilmer as editor, a publication was commenced called "The Theological Repertory" as the organ of the Society. Dr. Wilmer was its editor till 1826. The Society needed funds. Its clerical members went from time to time, to Churches in Maryland and Virginia to present its claims. Contributions were acknowledged in the Repertory. In 1822 Dr. Wilmer reported to the Council that $10,000 had been raised for a Theological Department.

The effort having failed at William and Mary College to start anything like a Theological Seminary, another effort was made by Dr. Wilmer in Alexandria. In 1823 a class of fourteen young men met in the Parish Building of St. Paul's Church, of which Dr. Wilmer was the Rector. He took the Chair of Systematic Divinity, Church History, and Ecclesiastical Polity. Dr. Reuel Keith, who had taught the one student at William and Mary, had the Chair of Old and New Testament Biblical Criticism and Evidence.

The undertaking was a success. There was a steady increase in students. There were twenty-three in the Seminary when Dr. Wilmer left Alexandria three years after. Since the class formed in Alexandria in 1823, the Seminary has had a continuous existence.

At first the Education Society, of which Dr. Wilmer was the first President, and the Seminary practically were one and the same institution. For many years the Education Society paid the salaries of the Professors in the Seminary. As late as 1842 it is recorded in the minutes that the salary of Rev. Professor Packard be increased. How long after this the Education Society paid the Professors, we are not told.

Dr. Wilmer was not the only one who labored to make the Seminary more than a vision. It cannot claim to be the result of any one man's work. Others labored hard, with loving zeal. But Dr. Wilmer was the recognized leader. He was made the head of the Education Society at a time when it needed a brave, earnest and spiritual man of intellectual power. This recognition of his character and ability was not confined to those associated with him in Virginia, it was acknowledged by the Church at large.

Dr. Wilmer was born in Maryland in 1782. He was one of three brothers, all of whom entered the ministry of the Protestant Episcopal Church. He was educated at Washington College on the eastern shore of Maryland, and ordained deacon in 1808 by Bishop Claggett. In 1812 he came to Alexandria to take the rectorship of St. Paul's Church. He held this office for fourteen years, and here the large part of his ministerial work was done. The congregation had just been formed, demanding the time and strength of a new rector, but Dr. Wilmer soon found another burden upon his shoulders. St. John's Church in Washington, a short distance from the President's House, had been lately organized, and Dr. Wilmer was asked to be its first rector, a position he occupied for one year, the Rev. William Hawley being his assistant. At the end of the year he was asked to give all his time to St. John's, but he refused, and resigned, in order to retain the rectorship of St. Paul's in Alexandria. He must have seen the greater possibilities of St. John's Church, situated in the center of the social and diplomatic life of Washington, but it may be that the possibility of helping to found a theological school decided him to remain in Alexandria. The Council of Virginia had passed resolutions to that effect, and looked to him to help carry them out.

He was thirty years old when he cast his lot with the Virginia Church. During his rectorship in Alexandria, he worked hard to resuscitate the church in the neighboring counties. He would drive a fast horse far and wide, stopping with the families of those who by birth were Church people, having services for them and encouraging them to cling to the Church of their fathers. He never seemed to tire. He was a faithful pastor among his own people in Alexandria. He was professor in the Theological School. He was busy with his work as head of the Education Society, and he was a voluntary missionary over a large section of Virginia.

His diocese recognized Dr. Wilmer's value. He was the president of the Standing Committee from its reorganization in 1813 to 1826, when he left Alexandria. Its records show how indefatigable he was in advising and sympathizing with Bishop Moore, who would come to Alexandria to consult with the committee in those critical days of the resuscitation of the Church.

Dr. Wilmer presided over the Council which elected Dr. Richard Channing Moore of New York, Bishop of Virginia. Dr. George T. Wilmer, his son, a professor in William and Mary College, stated that his father was sounded as to accepting the Bishopric, which could be his if he expressed a willingness. Dr. Wilmer refused. He preferred to do the work to which he had given himself, and he was anxious to see Dr. Moore elected Bishop of Virginia. He wrote many letters to the Bishop elect, urging his acceptance of the office. An extract from one of these letters gives us some insight of Dr. Wilmer's spiritual character. He wrote "We want a Bishop who will watch over his clergy with tears and tenderness. Who will be an example as well as teacher to his flock. Who will know nothing among us 'save Jesus Christ and Him Crucified,' and who, while he inculcates a due reverence for our venerable form of doctrine, discipline and worship as being of Apostolic authority, will at the same time direct his best energies towards the end of all religious institutions, namely, the deliverance of immortal souls from hell. Such a Bishop will have our cooperation, our love, and our prayers."

Dr. Wilmer was earnest, sound in the accepted doctrines of the Church, and deeply spiritual. The impress of his spirituality was felt by his scholars in the theological classes. It has, we believe, been the heritage of the Seminary, an influence running from class to class, through nearly a century of existence.

The General Convention gave recognition to Dr. Wilmer's wisdom, worth and intellectual power by electing him four times president of the General Convention. Some of the strongest papers sent out to the Church were from his pen. He was influential, in a rare degree, both in Virginia and in the Church at large.

In 1826 he accepted the presidency of William and Mary College, removing from Alexandria to Williamsburg. While there he was also the rector of old Bruton Parish Church. All the time he could spare from his college and parish duties he used in going about the surrounding country, looking up the straying and lost sheep of the Church.

As far as results show, Dr. William H. Wilmer lived a much longer life than most men. He might be said to have done the work of four-score years. His family were a long-lived race. Dr. Wilmer had done a great work. He received again and again the highest honors the Church can give. He was the Priest of a large Church. He was President of the Standing Committee. He was President of the Education Society, from which grew the Virginia Seminary. He was President of the Virginia Church Council. He presided over four General Conventions. He was President of William and Mary College and all the time a sort of general missionary of the Diocese of Virginia. Yet he was only forty-five years old when he died. He died in the harness, died, we may think, of over work; died at the age when many have not much more than commenced their work.

Many labored in the founding of our Seminary; they labored in thought and with prayer, with body and soul, but the most commanding figure, certainly the hardest worker and the strongest personality in laying the foundation, was the Rev. William Holland Wilmer, D. D. In a rare degree he had the mental equipment, the true spirit and the unflagging energy to lead in the work of founding our Seminary. He had a vision of the Church in Virginia in the years to come, and planned and worked accordingly. When we consider the positions he occupied in the Church, when we think of his more than ordinary mental gifts, his devoted zeal, and consecration to his work, we can perhaps appreciate his relation to the Seminary, which began in Alexandria in his own study, and was continued in a building belonging to the Church of which he was rector.

In learning the character of any one, we must not only have the light of great deeds to shine upon him, but we are fortunate if we have also the light of the small things that make up so much of life.

Bishop Richard H. Wilmer of Alabama, called the Confederate Bishop, because consecrated during the Civil War, was the son of the Rev. Dr. W. H. Wilmer. He was accustomed to pass a part of the summer in Berryville, Virginia, where he had charge of a Church of which, years after, the writer was the rector, and recalls the first time he saw him, venerable and erect, walking in the grove surrounding the rectory. He stated he had come to visit the grave of an old dog he had buried there forty years before. He said that when he left Berryville, he gave his dog to the Rev. Joshua Peterkin, his successor, and a year after returned for a visit to the Rectory. When he started to go he could not find his hat on the hall chair where he had left it. He went out on the porch, and there saw his old dog, blind, deaf, with his paws around the hat, and his nose upon it. He had recognized his master's hat, taken it out, and was waiting for its beloved owner. It is a simple story, but it throws light upon the gentle heart of a great man.

He told the writer a story of his cousin, Bishop Pere Wilmer. On a visit to New Orleans, the Bishop of Louisiana asked him to go with him to see an old colored man, who had been a slave of his father. The old man was dying. After praying with him Bishop Pere Wilmer said "Joe, is there anything more I can do for you, because we shall never meet again on earth." The old colored man answered: "Massa Pere, you know, when we were little boys, how we used to play under the old tree in the garden, and how, when we were tired, we would sleep in each other's arms? I think if you would lie by me and hold me in your arms again, I will die more easily." Without a moment's hesitation, the Bishop lay down by the old colored man and held him in his arms till his soul departed. It was an act of tender, gracious consideration. This spirit came to the Wilmers as a natural inheritance from the saintly scholar and devoted Churchman, William H. Wilmer.*

On the wall of old Bruton Parish Church, Williamsburg, Virginia, is a tablet inscribed:

IN

MEMORY

OF

THE REV.D WILLIAM H. WILMER D. D.

WHOSE EMINENT TALENTS AND EXEMPLARY PIETY

ENABLED HIM TO FILL, WITH DIGNITY

AND USEFULNESS,

THE IMPORTANT STATIONS OF

RECTOR OF THIS CHURCH:

PRESIDENT OF WILLIAM AND MARY COLLEGE:

PRESIDENT OF THE HOUSE OF CLERICAL

AND LAY DEPUTIES OF THE PROTESTANT

EPISCOPAL CHURCH.

HE WAS BELOVED IN PRIVATE,

RESPECTED AND HONORED IN PUBLIC LIFE:

A SOUND DIVINE,

A FAITHFUL PASTOR,

A SINCERE AND PRACTICAL CHRISTIAN.

BORN AT CHESTER-TOWN, MARYLAND,

MARCH 9TH. 1784:

DIED JULY 24TH. 1827.

THIS MONUMENT IS ERECTED BY THE CONGREGATION,

AND CHRISTIANS OF OTHER DENOMINATIONS,

IN TESTIMONY OF THEIR PROFOUND RESPECT,

AND ARDENT AFFECTION

FOR THE DECEASED.

* *Editor's Note:*—Further mention is made of the character and influence of Dr. Wilmer in the Chapter entitled "Wilmer Hall." This building which was formerly the Seminary Library was, on June 8th, 1922, set apart as the refectory and formally dedicated "Wilmer Hall" in grateful recognition of Dr. Wilmer's devotion to the cause of establishing the Theological Seminary in Virginia.

THE RIGHT REVEREND DOCTOR WILLIAM MEADE

Third Bishop of Virginia

SECTION II
CHAPTER II
RT. REV. DR. WILLIAM MEADE
REV. E. L. GOODWIN, D. D.

By his later contemporaries the title of Founder of the Theological Seminary of Virginia was ascribed to Bishop William Meade, and it is so inscribed upon his tomb. This honor, however, he never claimed for himself, and he was ever prompt to attribute to others the full meed of praise as the first movers in this sacred enterprise. But its nursing father he was from its inception, consecrating his every energy to its welfare and serving it in every capacity with enthusiastic devotion; so that none contributed more than he to its upbuilding and its prestige or impressed upon it more strongly the principles and ideals which shone resplendent in his own personality.

Bishop Meade was a Virginian of the Virginians and dwelt among his own people. His immigrant ancestor was Andrew Meade, of County Kerry, Ireland, who came to America near the close of the seventeenth century, married a Quakeress of Flushing, New York, and finally settled in Nansemond county in Virginia. His son, David Meade, married Susanna, daughter of Sir Richard Everard, Governor of North Carolina, and Susanna, his wife, who was a daughter of Richard Kidder, Bishop of Bath and Wells. Seven children sprang from this union, of whom the fourth was Richard Kidder Meade, who married first, Jane Randolph of Curles, who died without issue, and second, Mary, daughter of Benjmain and Bettie (Fitzhugh) Grymes and widow of William Randolph of Chatsworth. Their fifth child was William Meade, born in Frederick county, Virginia, November 11, 1789.

Colonel Richard K. Meade, the Bishop's father, was educated in England. At the outbreak of the Revolution he sold his plantation in Prince George county and divided the greater part of the proceeds among his relatives, but intrusted $3000 to a friend to be invested in the fertile lands of the Shenandoah Valley, where he afterwards made his home. He was in active service throughout the war and rose to the rank of Colonel on the personal staff of General Washington, whose close friendship he enjoyed until the death of the latter. After the war Colonel Meade settled upon his new estate, "Lucky Hit," in Frederick, now Clarke, county, where he built a plain house of logs and lived the simple life of a frontier farmer. He died when his son William was fifteen years of age, leaving his children to the care of a devoted and godly mother whose moulding influence upon his character the future Bishop ever remembered and acknowledged with filial gratitude.

The Church in Virginia will never know the debt she owes to those steadfast and devout women who, in the days of her humiliation and threatened extinction, kept the fires of piety and devotion aglow on many a household altar. At a time when her sanctuaries were deserted and her few remaining clergymen were benumbed in hopeless discouragement, when her claims were flouted alike by popular dissent and fashionable infidelity and her most loyal sons were almost in despair, these Mothers in Israel, like Lois and Eunice of old, kept the Church of their fathers alive in a multitude of humble homes and trained their children to hold fast her faith and walk in her ways. In these old Virginian households, where culture and piety oftentimes dwelt undismayed with poverty and broken fortunes, the best traditions of the ancient commonwealth were sacredly guarded and the seed-corn of the Church was nourished against the day of restoration.

After receiving the rudiments of his education from his mother young Meade attended an excellent private school in his neighborhood until, at the age of seventeen, he entered Princeton College, where he graduated with honors two years later. His purpose of devoting himself to the sacred ministry was already formed, and through the advice of his kinswoman, Mrs. George Washington Custis of Arlington, he entered the home of the Rev. Walter Addison of Maryland to pursue his theological studies under the guidance of that godly man from whose example he so largely derived his high ideals of the worthy and consistent ministerial character. After some months his eyesight gave him so much trouble that he was obliged to return home. Later he repaired again to Princeton as a graduate student to read divinity there, but a well nigh fatal illness once more compelled him to relinquish his studies for the restoration of his health. His mother set apart for him a small farm, as farms went in those days, from the patrimonial estate, upon which he built a small house, largely by his own labors. A larger house was afterwards erected and this estate, "Mountain View," became his seat for life, being famed for its high state of cultivation and the beauty of the trees and shrubbery with which he adorned it. At the age of twenty years and a few months he married Miss Mary Nelson, who lived but seven years thereafter. His second wife was her cousin, Miss Thomasia Nelson of Hanover county. Late in life the Bishop published brief memoirs of these "Two Beloved Wives" as worthy examples of the highest type of Christian womanhood.

Mr. Meade's purpose of seeking Holy Orders was never relinquished and he pursued his studies with such diligence as circumstances would permit. But now a new perplexity arose in view of the canon of the Church, adapted from a corresponding canon of the Church of England, which forbade manual labor on the part of the clergy as incompatible with the sacredness of their office. Depending for the support of himself and his family upon his labor as a working farmer, as, indeed, he did during a great part of his ministry, he was doubtful whether this fact would not debar him from taking orders. He laid the question, with others upon which he wished advice, before Bishop Madison, and received from him a frank and sympathetic letter which set his scruples at rest. In midwinter, at the age of twenty-two years and three months, clad in a rough suit of homespun, he journeyed on horseback to Williamsburg and presented himself to his Bishop. He was examined by the Bishop and Dr. Bracken before breakfast on Sunday, February 24, 1811, and was ordained deacon the same morning at Bruton Parish Church. The circumstances must have been depressing in the extreme. More than forty years afterwards Bishop Meade recalled them with painful exactness, being chiefly impressed with the almost utter disregard of the Church and her services in this See city of the Diocese. The church was gloomy and comfortless. "The congregation which assembled consisted of two ladies and about fifteen gentlemen, nearly all of whom were relatives or acquaintances. The morning service being over, the ordination and communion were administered, and then I was put into the pulpit to preach, there being no ordination sermon."

This was probably the last ordination administered by Bishop Madison. No actor in that simple service realized its dramatic significance. The old Post-Revolutionary Church, itself little more than a relic of Colonial days, in the person of the aged Madison passed the torch from her palsied hands to those of the ardent young Meade, the herald and forerunner of her revival to a new and more vigorous life. It marked a turning point in the fortunes of the Church in Virginia. That a young Virginian whose capacities and high social position were widely known through his prominent family connections should consecrate himself to the ministry of this Church which was popularly supposed to be moribund beyond the hope of resuscitation was esteemed by many, as the Bishop himself states, as a mark of extreme eccentricity or a lack of good common sense. To others, however, it appeared as a harbinger of better things, and from the first the eyes of the godly remnant were fixed hopefully upon this young deacon as one destined to a great work. "Certain it is," the Bishop wrote long afterwards, "that my ministry was received with a favor which neither my imperfect theological education nor my most unfinished sermons nor anything else about me was entitled to."

Mr. Meade returned at once to his Valley home to minister among his neighbors and kinspeople as opportunity might offer. The only other clergyman in that part of the state was the aged Dr. Alexander Balmaine at Winchester, titular rector of Frederick parish, who welcomed the young deacon as unofficially his assistant and assigned to him the services at the "Old Chapel," a small church built of stone a few miles from his home. During the next fall he was induced to take temporary charge of Christ Church, Alexandria, which had just passed through a disastrous experience with a most unworthy minister, dividing his time between that place and his charge in the Valley where his family remained. The journey of about sixty miles between them was made on horseback almost weekly without regard to weather conditions, and the traditions connected with his frequent visits to the homes of the people along the way remained for several generations. This arrangement continued for eighteen months, when he relinquished the congregation in Alexandria, in a flourishing condition, to the Rev. Oliver Norris. Meanwhile Mr. Meade himself had become most favorably known not only in that city but in Washington. This experiment of taking temporary charge of a congregation in distress he afterwards repeated in Christ Church, Norfolk, and St. Paul's, Petersburg, with the happiest results in every case. With these exceptions his entire parochial ministry was spent in Frederick parish, covering Frederick and Clarke counties. After the death of Dr. Balmaine he succeeded to the rectorship of Christ Church, Winchester, in connection with his chapel congregation, for several years, and after securing for that church another rector he founded the churches at Berryville and Middletown. Meantime, however, his occasional ministrations were extended over six or seven neighboring counties where there were no ministers to shepherd our scattered flocks. During his ministry in Alexandria he reached the canonical age and was ordained to the priesthood in Christ Church by Bishop Claggett of Maryland.

Bishop Madison died in March, 1812, and in May of that year and again in May, 1813, small Conventions of the Diocese were held in Richmond. They did little more than emphasize the incompetence of the older generation of her clergy for her revival. An erroneous impression has long been prevalent, due to a mistaken reading of a passage in Bishop Meade's "Recollections," as to the number of ministers remaining in the Diocese at this time. It has been frequently stated that there were but from four to six or seven. There were, in fact, at least seventeen clergymen in more or less active service, and the whole number was probably between twenty-five and thirty. For the most part, however, they were old men and were chiefly dependent for their support upon their own exertions either as farmers of the wornout glebe lands remaining to them or as school teachers. They were scattered far and wide from the Atlantic to the Alleghanies. Even if the call for a Convention reached them, they were too poor or too feeble to undertake the journey of from two to four days to Convention, while the experience of fifteen years gave them little confidence that a quorum could be assembled or, if so, that anything of value would be accomplished. They were good men and faithful who, in their poverty and isolation, continued to minister to their scattered flocks under the most depressing conditions, and some of them lived to take an honorable part in the revival of the Church which followed the coming of Bishop Moore.

After the Convention of 1813 Mr. Meade himself was for a time a confessed victim of that despair with which he, and others after him, have somewhat harshly charged Bishop Madison and the clergy of his day. "There was nothing," he wrote forty years afterwards, "to encourage us to meet again. I well remember that, as I took my solitary way homeward on horseback I found myself continually saying in relation to the Church in Virginia,—'Lost—lost—lost!' and never expected to cross the mountains again on such an errand." But he did, in the May following; preaching the opening sermon in the new Monumental Church in Richmond and taking part in the election of the Rev. Richard Channing Moore, D. D. as the second Bishop of Virginia, an event which he had aided in bringing about in co-operation with the new Standing Committee of the Diocese.

From this moment the prospects of the Church in the Old Dominion began to brighten and Mr. Meade, as one born to leadership, threw himself with unrestrained vigor into the work of arousing her from her spiritual lethargy to a renewed life. For this task he was fitted above any of his contemporaries. The new Bishop and the great majority of the other clergy, then and for twenty years afterwards, were not native but adopted sons of the old state. They were received with the utmost regard and were reckoned among her most devoted and loyal citizens, while their ministry was gratefully accepted of men and signally blest of God.

But the ruling classes of Virginians have never taken kindly to admonition or dictation in regard to their personal affairs or opinions from those who were from without, and Bishops and ministers from beyond her borders have sometimes been conscious of that handicap, however relieved by courtesy, respect and genuine affection. But Meade was one of themselves and to the last syllable spoke the language of the tribe. In his family and social connections and in that inbred knowledge of and loyalty to the history, the traditions, the customs and habits of thought of the true aristocracy of Virginia he was native and to the manner born. He possessed in a high degree those qualities which were admired among his people, the broad intelligence, the persuasive eloquence, the attractive presence and social graces, coupled with the simplicity, sincerity and firmness of purpose which marked the Virginia gentleman at his best estate. Even his somewhat peremptory and dominating manner was an accepted characteristic of his class. Thoroughly democratic in principle and teaching, and a puritan in practice, he was essentially an aristocrat to the end of his days.

His love and godly jealousy for the Church of his fathers was the key to Bishop Meade's ministry and whole ecclesiastical attitude, which has not always been sympathetically understood. He knew the history of the Church in Virginia from within outward, and understood, as perhaps none of his contemporaries did, wherein lay the hurt of God's people and that it was not to be "healed slightly." For more than a century and a quarter the religious interests of the growing commonwealth in Virginia, the most favored of all the American colonies, lay wholly in the hands of this Church. She planted and kept the religion of the Church of England of that day alive in this physical and spiritual wilderness throughout that period and brought forth much fruit unto righteousness. But in the end she proved unequal to her task and, in a measure perhaps unduly magnified in his mind, was faithless to her trust, so that her candlestick was almost removed from its place. The Evangelical Revival which, during the latter part of the eighteenth century, was re-leavening the Church of England and arousing it from its deadly torpor of formalism and spiritual lethargy, had not reached the neglected daughter-Church before the period of the Revolution and her disestablishment. The "common people" multiplied in the land and their spiritual and social needs were overlooked by the Church, while unauthorized teachers arose to minister at once to their religious cravings and their mutinous discontent. A score of Devereux Jarretts could have saved these to the Church and guided a spontaneous and sincere, but untaught and unregulated religious movement in her orderly ways. But no other was found among the hundred or more clergy of the Establishment. Practically without ecclesiastical headship or spiritual stimulus, they clung to the ossified traditions of their caste, preaching a cold and formal morality in the stilted language of a past generation, jealously defending their accustomed privileges and relying upon the prestige and authority of the established Church for the maintenance of its influence and power. The majority of them were men of high personal character and of no little, though frequently misdirected, zeal, while there were not a few whose moral delinquencies and disregard of their sacred profession brought the Church into great discredit. Meanwhile a flood of skepticism and practical infidelity inundated the state and found its exponents chiefly among those who professed to be of her children. The vices of an era of social disturbance and revolution flourished almost unrebuked by her voice, and the lives of many of her lay people, as well as of some of her ministers, failed to disprove the too hasty charge of her enemies that the Church was utterly lacking in true religion or the power of moral reformation. For fifty years she grew more and more impotent, to all outward seeming, until her ultimate extinction appeared inevitable.

Such was the condition of the Church in Virginia when William Meade and his contemporaries came upon the scene. Within her bosom, cold and sterile as it was, there yet dwelt saintly men and women whose unfailing piety and devotion kept her soul alive; but her outward estate was utterly decayed, her influence had almost vanished, her power of mission, and even of self-perpetuation, had wasted away. The young prophet saw clearly and with a burning indignation wherein her failure had lain. Her watchmen had too often slumbered upon her walls and their trumpet had given but an uncertain sound. She had greatly failed in the day of her opportunity to call men to repentance and to present to them the gospel of salvation in its simplicity and power, and so the day of her calamity had come and found her powerless and unmindful of where her strength lay.

For this condition, with his strong evangelical principles he could conceive of but one remedy—a return to the fundamental precepts of the gospel, "repentance toward God and faith toward our Lord Jesus Christ," and the bringing forth of fruits, meet for repentance in a godly life. A phrase which is full of real significance to one generation sometimes becomes little more than an empty catch-word to the next. To Meade and his fellow workers "preaching the gospel" meant something very definite and very radical. It meant the strong, imperative call of God to a careless and godless people, awakening in each soul a sense of its accountability to God, its need of personal salvation through a heartfelt acceptance of the redemption that is in Christ Jesus, its obligation to lead a godly and consistent life in full view of a judgment to come. The test of religion was a conscious, personal experience of its power to change the heart and create newness of life. Their preaching was not without a strong touch of Calvinistic severity and the course of Christian living enjoined was almost puritanical in its exactness. But it was suited to the conditions of their day and was blest of God to the revival and reformation of the Church, which regained the confidence and won back the allegiance of multitudes long estranged from her fold.

The scarcity of faithful ministers was much felt, and to supply in part this deficiency there was borrowed from Maryland the expedient of holding "Associations," or parochial missions as they would now be called, which was long a feature in the progressive work of the Diocese. Two or three, or even more, ministers would gather in a parish destitute of regular services and continue often for several weeks, preaching and teaching "publicly and from house to house." In this work Mr. Meade delighted and his services were in great demand, his unusual power as a preacher and his zeal in pastoral ministrations fitting him for it in a peculiar measure.

Family worship and religious instruction in the home were strongly urged upon Christian parents as a paramount duty. Among the works recommended by Bishop Madison to Mr. Meade for his study were those of the saintly Bishop Wilson of Sodor and Man, whose "Sacra Privata" has long been a devotional classic. During his ministry in Alexandria he was delighted to discover in the library at Arlington a folio copy of Bishop Wilson's works which had been presented to General Washington by a son of the author. From these he compiled and edited a small volume of prayers, meditations and devotional exercises for private and family use, which he published at his own expense. Its excellence has hardly been surpassed by any modern work of the same character. It passed through several editions and, being widely circulated through the Diocese, was largely instrumental in kindling the fires on countless family altars where Virginia Churchmen of succeeding generations received their first religious impressions.

The duty of affording adequate religious instruction for the slave population of the state was one which Mr. Meade particularly stressed by word and pen, himself setting an example by devoting a considerable part of his own ministry to this class. The problems presented by the institution of slavery weighed heavily upon him as they did upon every thinking man of the South. He emancipated his own slaves, but experience and a wide observation afterwards convinced him that this was a mistaken kindness. He was a liberal and active supporter of, and for a time an agent for, the old Colonization Society, which founded the Republic of Liberia as a home for emancipated slaves; until the futility as well as the unwisdom of this patriotic scheme became manifest. In its behalf he undertook at least one long journey through the South. He was also active in furthering the work of the Bible Society and Tract Societies, in the formation of parochial missionary and benevolent associations and Sunday-schools, and in the development of every agency through which the religious interests of his people and state might be advanced.

The Institution, however, upon which his hopes and endeavors were chiefly centered was the Theological Sem-

inary. He knew that the revival of the Church in Virginia
and Maryland, and its extension in the newer states west
and south, depended solely, under the blessing of God, upon
a due supply of faithful ministers trained in her ways and
filled with that earnestness of spirit which was characteristic
of her new life. He realized also, in the language of the
second report ever made to the Convention on this subject,
"the importance of retaining among ourselves, for education,
those young men who may be disposed to devote themselves
to the sacred office of the ministry." The wisdom of this
remark will be readily recognized by any one familiar with
the conditions, social, political and ecclesiastical, existing at
that time. None was more assured of its soundness than
Mr. Meade, who knew so thoroughly his own people and their
problems; and the effort afterward made to confine the
education of candidates for orders to a single institution only
confirmed him, as well as the other friends of the Alexandria
Seminary, in their convictions as to the necessity for this
School also. Mr. Meade was a member of the Committee
on the State of the Church which brought before the Convention of 1821 the report from which we have quoted, and
was one of the Trustees appointed by the Convention for the
establishment of a school of theology in connection with the
College of William and Mary at Williamsburg. He acquiesced
in this proposed measure as the best that seemed possible at
the moment, though he wisely doubted whether Williamsburg was the best place for a permanent institution of this
character or whether its connection with the College was
advisable. The failure and abandonment of this project
and the steps taken leading to the foundation of the Seminary
in Alexandria are detailed elsewhere in this volume. With
the new plan Mr. Meade found himself in the most hearty
accord, and both as a trustee and individually he devoted
himself to its advancement with a well directed zeal which
knew no abatement. Year by year he stood before the
Diocesan Convention as the spokesman of the Trustees, reading their reports, which came from his own pen, and urging
the paramount claims of the Seminary upon the liberality of
the Church. He personally canvassed the Diocese for funds
to erect the first buildings on Seminary Hill, raising the largest

sums secured for that purpose; and allowed no other object, not even the endowment of the episcopate, to take precedence of this in its appeal to the generosity of the Churchmen of Virginia and elsewhere. His own contributions to its endowment were large, exceedingly generous, indeed, considering his meagre resources. "To build up this Institution," said Dr. Gibson, a fellow Trustee, "Bishop Meade gave all the energies of his mind and body, and much of his estate." And Dr. Packard testifies: "To this Seminary the heart, the cares, the thoughts of Bishop Meade were given. He watched over it with a father's care, yea, and with a mother's tenderness. When straitened for funds, as was often the case, he relieved its necessities by means obtained through his great personal influence. He conducted its affairs with the greatest economy, and saved it from making shipwreck on the rock on which so many institutions have split." He kept in close touch not only with the faculty but with the student body, and for many years gave instruction to the Senior Class in Pastoral Theology, preparing for the purpose a rather ponderous course of lectures which he published at his own expense and which long served as the textbook on this subject. Bishop Moore spoke of him as "the individual through whose instrumentality the School was first set in motion;" and Bishop Johns said that he was "truly the father of this Seminary, one to whose instrumentality in founding and cherishing this Institution the Church at large, and especially the Church in Virginia, owes a debt of gratitude which no epitaph can adequately express."

Nor was he less earnest in securing proper students to enjoy its benefits and fulfil its purpose in supplying well equipped men for the sacred ministry. It was the custom of the wealthier gentlemen of the Shenandoah Valley, as was usual throughout the state, to employ tutors in their families for the education of their children and those of their neighbors. They were obtained principally from New England, or were graduates of her many colleges, and were for the most part strangers to the Episcopal Church. Mr. Meade was prompt to cultivate the friendship of these young gentlemen, to encourage them to visit him, to engage them in Sunday-school work or in cottage services for the colored people under his supervision and generally to "try them out." When, with that almost uncanny gift of reading character which he possessed (Bishop Johns once humorously ascribed it to an extraordinary development of the sense of smell) he detected the qualities which he sought, he would so impress upon their possessor a love for this Church and a desire to take part in her ministry that he would soon have another candidate for Holy Orders. Probably no less than half a score of men whose ministries proved of the utmost value to the Church were thus gained in as many years. In several instances these were prevented by circumstances from attending the Seminary and read theology under his own direction, sometimes in his own home; among whom may be mentioned that stalwart Churchman and long-time Trustee of the Seminary, the Rev. Dr. C. W. Andrews.

Mr. Meade was elected a deputy to the General Convention while yet a deacon, and to every succeeding Convention but one, until his elevation to the episcopate. In 1826 he received a majority of one vote of the clergy cast in an election for an Assistant to the venerable Bishop White of Pennsylvania. The question having been raised, however, as to the right of a certain clergyman to a vote the Convention adjourned in a deadlock, and before another was held Mr. Meade very positively declined to have his name again presented. In 1827 he received the degree of Doctor of Divinity from the College of William and Mary.

At the Convention of May, 1828, Bishop Moore requested that the constitution of the Diocese of Virginia, which then provided that there should be but one Bishop in the Diocese, should be so amended as to allow the election of an Assistant Bishop, since his duties were becoming too onerous for his strength. "It is my sincere desire," he said, "that such a bishop shall be appointed during my life; and as such an appointment can now be made with perfect unanimity it is expedient that it should be done." The necessary amendment to the organic law was promptly proposed and adopted, subject to confirmation by the succeeding Convention. The next May the change was finally approved, though not without some opposition, and the Convention voted to proceed to the election of an Assistant Bishop, who was, however, "not to be considered as entitled to the succession, but it shall be the right and duty of the Convention of the Diocese of Virginia, on the demise of our venerated bishop, to proceed to the election of a principal bishop, as a successor to the said deceased bishop." It is impossible now to determine what motive prompted the adoption of the above provision, and that by a vote of nearly four to one in the Convention. Doubtless it was accepted as a concession to a minority who did not approve of the office, which was almost a new one in the American Church and with its authority and limitations as yet wholly undefined by canon. Certainly no reflection on Dr. Meade was intended, since his election followed by a vote of twenty-five of the clergy out of twenty-seven, there being two blank ballots, and the unanimous vote of the thirty-six lay delegates. When the election came up for confirmation at the General Convention of the following August this provision was declared to be "highly inexpedient and wholly inadmissible," and the House of Bishops took order for the consecration only because they "entertained no doubt of Dr. Meade's succeeding to the diocesan episcopacy in the event of his surviving the present bishop." The consecration accordingly took place in St. James Church, Philadelphia, on Wednesday, August 19, 1829, Bishop White being both preacher and consecrator, assisted by the entire House of Bishops, then numbering eight, with the exception of Bishop Ravenscroft, who was absent. At the next Convention of the Diocese the restriction in regard to the succession was rescinded in view of the new canon on the subject and in testimony to "its confidence in the Assistant Bishop of this Diocese."

From this time forward the new Bishop was occupied usually about eight months in each year in his visitations throughout the Diocese. He was then endowed with unusual health and strength and was accustomed to an active out-of-doors life. "When a minister was given to complaining of fatigue from his professional services and to being economical of ·himself in his ministrations," says Bishop Johns, "he was apt to think the infirmity more moral than physical." With a disregard of possible physical limitations for which he afterwards paid heavily, he gave himself without stint to the most engrossing performance of his duties. On horseback or in his own carriage, or in such rude public conveyances as the limited facilities for travel in those days afforded, he traversed the length and breadth of the state from the Atlantic to the Ohio over and over again, doing the work of an evangelist and a pastor *in partibus* as well as that of a Bishop, and sharing all the missionary labors of his devoted clergy. He also undertook several prolonged journeys through the south, ministering in Dioceses still without episcopal supervision. While at home he conducted an enormous correspondence and exerted an ever widening influence through his pen. This continued for more than ten years, by which time such unremitting labors had told very seriously upon his health. He became subject to nervous troubles, the existence of which he had previously considered imaginary, to serious impairment of his voice, to distressing headaches and an affection of the heart which he expected would eventually terminate his life. Bishop Moore died in the fall of 1841, and at the Convention in May, 1842, Bishop Meade asked for an Assistant, who was at once given him in the person of the Rev. Dr. John Johns of Maryland. But even with such a coadjutor his own labors were but slightly lessened. He continued his visitations with but little cessation, though for many years he did not preach on these occasions but contented himself with an address from the chancel. He was also much more largely occupied with the affairs of the general Church, in which his ever widening influence and acknowledged leadership compelled him to take a large part.

Bishop Meade never wavered in his adherence to that system of evangelical teaching and practice to which his earliest religious convictions were due, and under the preaching of which he had seen the Church in Virginia rise as though from the dead. He knew its power to arouse the hearts and consciences of men and he considered it truly representative of the teachings of the Prayer Book as well as faithful to the doctrines of God's word, and therefore the true interpretation of the genius of the Anglican Church and her daughter in America to which he was so devotedly loyal. With all the intensity of his nature he opposed the Tractarian movement in the Church, the peculiar teachings of which he deprecated and the tendencies of which he clearly foresaw. To offset its active propaganda he was among the founders, and was always an earnest supporter, of the "Evangelical Societies," and he was ever ready, in the face, oftentimes, of misrepresentation and calumny, to advocate and uphold the principles in which he believed and for which he was always prepared to give a reason. He became a recognized leader of the "Low Church" or Evangelical school of thought in the Church, and by his superior talents, his singleness of purpose and purity of character he commanded the respect and admiration of his opponents and also a due recognition of the principles which he maintained, which remain today as inalienable factors in that heritage of truth and liberty which we have received from our fathers.

One must have more than a superficial understanding of the conditions existing in those days, and of the significance of those differences which gave rise to such sharp contentions between men equally zealous for truth and righteousness, to judge rightly of their motives and actions. Each generation is prone to boast itself upon its superior attitude and broader outlook, forgetting that these may be due less to a sudden accession of wisdom than to a gradual change of circumstance. Bishop Meade and his contemporaries held convictions that were the fruit of the deepest religious experience fortified by honest and laborious study and applicable to the conditions and needs of their own time. Fundamentally they are true today, though new times have taught new duties and new aspects of the truth have come to the light. But the travail by which their convictions were gained, the sacredness in which they were held, and the courage and constancy with which they were maintained deserve a recognition and honor not always accorded them in these times of intellectual luxury and moral complacency.

Second only to his zeal for purity of doctrine was Bishop Meade's intense earnestness in restoring and maintaining the godly discipline of the Church. Here again the instinctive bent of his own mind was stimulated by the conditions of his times. His own life was marked by simplicity and rigid self-denial. "I once visited him," says Dr. Packard, "and there was not a soft chair in the house." The world, the flesh and the devil were to him stern realities, the enemies of God and of his own soul, to be constantly resisted and completely overcome. He had little patience with self-indulgence and still less with wilful inconsistency of life and a minimizing of the responsibilities attaching to a Christian profession. His standard of unworldliness was strict and unbending. He had seen how the Church of his love had fallen from her high estate and become a by-word among men through her failure in this regard, and believed that no external prosperity or restoration of her wonted respectability would avail for the fulfillment of her high mission without a thorough reformation in the daily life and conversation of her members. For twenty years he fought for an amendment to the constitution of the Diocese requiring that delegates to the Convention should be communicants, on the self-evident ground that those who legislated for the Church should themselves conform to her teachings and be in full communion with her life. Sternly he "reasoned of righteousness, temperance and judgment to come," reproving, rebuking, exhorting, both publicly and privately, with apostolic faithfulness and authority, and saw the Church grow in strength and influence as it grew in consistency and purity of life.

His zeal and vigilance in this regard gave to the Bishop a reputation for sternness and austerity, and doubtless, indeed, fostered those qualities in his character. But to those who knew him his native gentleness and sweetness of disposition could not be hid. He could neither be flattered nor easily befooled, and, as so wise an admirer as Dr. Sparrow has admitted, "he did not always make due allowance for the difference of training, temperament and manners of different persons and classes." But a loving heart beat under his grave exterior, and the sincere admiration and warm, personal love of his people throughout his Diocese testified to his own affectionate nature. An anecdote will illustrate these phases of his character. On one occasion two young ladies, at whose homes he was a frequent visitor, were guests in the house of the Rev. Dr. W— and were exchanging their impressions of the Bishop. One of them confessed that she was a little afraid of him, he seemed so stern and severe. But the other would not have it so. "When he comes to our house," she said, "he loves to have my sister or myself stand behind his chair and comb his beautiful white hair. He thanks us so affectionately, and says it soothes him and cures his headache. Don't you think," she continued, appealing to their host, "that the Bishop is just the dearest, sweetest old man in the world?" "Yes, my dear," said the Doctor with judicial gravity, "I think so, on the whole; though it does make some difference whether you happen to be combing his head or he is combing yours."

Intensely patriotic, Bishop Meade loved his native state with a rare devotion. He knew her history and also her people, their virtues and their failings, as did few of his contemporaries. Almost the last of his many publications, and that by which alone he will be remembered as author, were the two lengthy volumes on the "Old Churches, Ministers and Families of Virginia," bearing on every page the impress of his own personality. Begun as a short series of "Recollections" published in the Protestant Episcopal Quarterly Review in 1855, and continued in occasional contributions to the Southern Churchman, its material was gathered largely from old parochial records which he had himself rescued from oblivion, from correspondence and chance memoranda, or from data stored in his memory during a period of fifty years. The work is ill arranged, and is by no means free from error or bias, but it will always remain an invaluable source-book for Virginian Church history and a monument to the good Bishop's care for the preservation of her ancient landmarks.

At the General Convention of 1859, held in Richmond, Bishop Meade presided in the House Bishops as next in seniority to the Presiding Bishop who was unable to be present. Thirty-eight bishops constituted the House, in place of the eight at the time of his consecration, five being added during its session. His own influence was never greater, and his heart must have rejoiced at the growing prosperity of the Church, not only in his own beloved Diocese but throughout the country. But already the skies were darkened by the clouds of approaching war. With Bishop Meade, love for the Union was an inbred characteristic, and no one entertained the thought of its dismemberment with more anguish of spirit. In common with the great majority of the thinking men of his state he deprecated and opposed secession until the immediate prospect of invasion by hostile forces necessitated that action as a measure of self defence. Thenceforward there was no question in his mind as to the righteousness or the propriety of her course. The change of civil government necessitated a corresponding change in the ecclesiastical relations of the southern dioceses; and Virginia sent her deputies to, and Bishop Meade as the Senior Bishop, presided over, an adjourned Convention which met at Columbia, South Carolina, in October, 1861, to formulate the Constitution of the General Council of the Protestant Episcopal Church in the Confederate States. After its adjournment his first duty as Presiding Bishop was to take order for the consecration of one of his own clergy, the Rev. Dr. Richard H. Wilmer, to be Bishop of Alabama. In the disturbed state of the country it was found impossible to secure the presence of three Bishops unless he could himself attend. Suffering from illness, and in the midst of most inclement weather, he left his Valley home when it was threatened by invasion and journeyed to Richmond. On the appointed day he was able only to take part in the act of consecration, being supported by his brother bishops while delivering the apostolic commission. It proved to be his last public service.

"These Evangelicals die well," was a remark often quoted in England and America in the olden days. It was never more strikingly exemplified than in the passing of Bishop Meade. He lingered for eight days, often in great pain, and thoroughly conscious of his approaching end. "Few things impressed me more during the last days of his life," said Bishop Johns, "than his perfect naturalness. In health he habitually thought and acted as if there was but a step between him and death, judgment and eternity; and when he knew and said that the ensuing night or the following day would end his connection with earth, the welfare of his country and the interests of his friends were as near his heart, and as emphatically on his lips, as if he expected to share their portion here for many years. He was on his death bed precisely what we all saw him to be in life, except his sufferings." Dr. Gibson, who was present, describes his last interview with General Robert E. Lee, who had just been called to Richmond to receive his appointment as Commander in Chief of the Confederate armies. Though visitors were forbidden he demanded to be allowed to see the General when he learned that he had called to enquire for him. "Bishop, how do you feel?" said the General as he grasped the feebly outstretched hand. "I am almost gone, but I wanted to see you once more," was the Bishop's reply, and he asked affectionately about the members of his family and put several earnest, eager questions in regard to public affairs and the state of the army. He then said, "God bless you! God bless you, Robert, and fit you for your high and responsible position. I can't call you General, I have heard you say your catechism so often." "Yes, Bishop, very often," said the General as he stooped tenderly over him and pressed his hand; "and I think I saw a tear drop," adds the narrator. On the day before he died he gave to Bishop Johns his "testimony on some things of importance," and asked to have it committed to writing. The opening sentence was this: "The views of evangelical truth and order which I have held and advocated for fifty years, I approve, and exhort my brethren, North and South, to promote more than ever." The rest was an expression of approval of the political course of his state and country, of his readiness to depart, his unshaken hope in Christ alone and repudiation of any worth or merit of his own deserving, and his charity towards all men, "even our bitterest enemies;" closing with a prayer commending his brethren and especially the Church in Virginia to the tender mercies of Christ. Just before passing into unconsciousness he was asked whether he suffered much. "Yes," he said, "I suffer a good deal; but I have a blessed Redeemer!" So he passed beyond, in the seventy-third year of his age, the fifty-first year of his ministry and the thirty-third of his episcopate.

He was buried in Hollywood cemetery; but fifteen years later his remains were removed to the little God's acre on the Seminary grounds and rest almost under the shadow of this School of the Prophets which he so devotedly loved and served.

THE RIGHT REVEREND DOCTOR RICHARD CHANNING MOORE

Second Bishop of Virginia

SECTION II

CHAPTER III

RT. REV. DR. RICHARD CHANNING MOORE

REV. W. A. R. GOODWIN, D. D.

The Rt. Rev. Dr. Richard Channing Moore was very closely connected with the Theological Seminary in Virginia in many ways.

In the fall of 1814 Rev. Dr. John Augustine Smith, President of the College of William and Mary, met Bishop Moore on the street in New York, and suggested to him that a Chair of Theology be established in the College at Williamsburg. This suggestion marks the beginning of the Theological Seminary in Virginia.

When in 1815 a communication was received from the President of the College of William and Mary, suggesting the expediency of establishing a theological professorship in that institution, Bishop Moore gave the suggestion enthusiastic support in his address to the Convention.

Bishop Moore presided at the Conventions of the Church in Virginia when in 1821 it was determined to establish a Theological Department at the College of William and Mary; when in 1822 a Constitution for a Theological School was adopted; when in 1823 it was determined to move the Seminary to Alexandria and to retain Rev. Dr. Reuel Keith as Professor, the experiment in Williamsburg having failed. He was presiding over the Council when in 1825 the Board reported a detailed course of Theological study; and when, in 1827, the Trustees reported that they had "determined to purchase or erect in some healthy situation near Alexandria, but in the State of Virginia, a house, or houses, sufficiently large to accommodate two Professors and twenty students" and also, when, in 1828, they reported the present property purchased.

When the proposition to establish the Virginia Seminary was first discussed Bishop Moore was reluctant to give his assent and for some time seems not to have been very enthusiastic with reference to the endeavor. He felt that it might seem disloyal to the mind and intention of the General Church expressed in General Convention in establishing the General Seminary. When, however, Bishop Hobart became an advocate of Diocesan Seminaries, and the issue in controversy was settled, Bishop Moore became an ardent and devoted friend of the endeavor to found and upbuild the Virginia Seminary. In seeking to evaluate the special contribution made by Bishop Moore to the Seminary, it is clearly evident that his successful efforts to rebuild the fallen Virginia Church created the need, which the Seminary was called to supply, for a large increase in the ministry. When he came to Virginia most of the Churches were closed and many of them had been abandoned. His zeal, his indefatigable energy, the eloquence of his preaching, and the potency of his prayers roused the dormant Church to life and made the need for well trained ministers everywhere clearly apparent.

The recognition of this need quickened the disposition of the people to contribute to the building and support of the Seminary and above all helped to turn the attention of many young men to the consideration of Holy Orders.

Then, too, the earnestness and unstinted devotion with which he gave himself to his stupendous task, the eloquence of his preaching and the enthusiasm and optimism with which he faced dark days and made them bright and beautiful days in the life of the Virginia Church, could but stimulate the minds and hearts of the students in the Seminary, many of whom were looking forward to their ministry under his Episcopal supervision.

For these, and other reasons a sketch of his life finds rightful place in the History of the Seminary, which was founded during his Episcopate and of whose Board of Trustees he was long the faithful and devoted President.

The Convention called in 1812 to elect a Bishop to fill the vacancy, chose the Rev. Dr. Bracken, who in 1813 declined the election. In counting a quorum the clerical and lay-delegates were numbered together and not counted as of two orders. This fact is here mentioned because it appears that there were only seven clergymen present at the Con-

vention of 1814. There were, however, present nineteen
lay-delegates. The clerical delegates present at this memorable Council which met in the Capitol, in the City of Richmond, on May 4th, 1814, were the Rev. Oliver Norris and
the Rev. W. H. Wilmer, of Alexandria, the Rev. Wm. H.
Meade, of Frederick Parish, the Rev. J. Cameron, D. D., of
Cumberland, the Rev. John Dunn, of Shelburne, the Rev.
J. Buchanan, D. D., of Henrico Parish, and the Rev. Andrew
Syme, of Bristol Parish. The names of most of the nineteen lay-delegates present in this Council are nearly all
familiar in the Church in Virginia today. Among them we
find the name of the Hon. John Marshall as a lay-deputy
from Monumental Church.

"It was "Resolved that the appointment of a Bishop for
this Diocese is highly expedient and necessary for the maintenance and support of the Church."

"It was next "Resolved that the Convention proceed
immediately to the election of a person to fill the Episcopate
in the same." Dr. James McClurg then presented a certified
extract from the Vestry book of Monumental Church in
Richmond showing the appointment of the Rev. Richard
Channing Moore, D. D., of the City of New York, to the
Rectorship of that Church.

"On motion, Ordered that the Secretary read sundry
letters, exhibited by members of the Standing Committee
from Dr. Moore and the Rt. Rev. Bishop Hobart.

"Dr. Moore was nominated to fill the office of Bishop in
this State.

"No other person being in nomination, the Convention
proceeded to ballot for a Bishop.

"The Hon. John Marshall and Mr. Edmund Lee were
appointed to count the ballots, who reported that there were
twenty-three votes for Dr. Moore and one for Dr. John Buchanan, whereupon Reverend Richard Channing Moore was
declared to be duly elected to the Episcopate in the Diocese
of Virginia, and the members of the Convention proceeded
to subscribe to the testimonials required by the Constitution
of the General Church in the United States."†

†Hawks' Journals, p. 92.

Bishop Moore was nearly fifty-two years old when made Bishop of Virginia, having been born in the City of New York on the twenty-first day of August, 1762. His father, Thomas Moore, was the son of the Hon. John Moore, who had served as one of his Majesty's Council for the province of New York. At eight years of age he was placed under the care of Mr. Alexander Leslie, Professor of Languages in King's College, now Columbia College. At sixteen he began the study of medicine under Doctor Richard Bayley, a distinguished physician and surgeon of New York City, and having completed his professional studies he began the practice of medicine and built up a large and lucrative practice, which he continued until 1787.

Bishop Moore was prone to recognize an overruling providence in the common occurrences and coincidences of his daily life. He attributed the turning of his life to Christ with full and serious purpose to the chance reading of the passage of Scripture containing the question of Saul the persecutor, "Lord, what wilt thou have me to do?" upon which he chanced to fall while waiting one day for his turn in a barber shop. His was a nature which gave itself with enthusiasm to the convictions of his mind and to the devotions of his heart, and it is not surprising that, having found the more abundant life, he should have consecrated himself to the purpose of making the way of salvation known to others. Having read for orders while continuing his medical practice, he was ordained deacon in July, 1787, by the Rt. Rev. Dr. Provost, in St. George's Church, New York City, being the first person to receive ordination at his hands. In September he was advanced to the priesthood and took charge of Grace Church, Rye, in the County of Westchester, New York. In 1788 he accepted a call to St. Andrew's Church, Staten Island, where he ministered for twenty-one years with fidelity and devotion.

While noted for his fidelity as a pastor, Dr. Moore was best known as a convincing and eloquent preacher. His intense spiritual conviction, his earnest piety, his charm and grace of manner, his tenderness of feeling, his sincere devotion to his Master, and absolute dependence upon the inspiration and power of the Spirit, Whom he invoked in constant and earnest prayer, to which was added a voice of melodious sweetness whose tender and pleading tones won the sympathy and engaged the attention of his hearers, combined to create for him a reputation as a preacher which attracted crowded congregations to hear him proclaim the message of salvation from the great gospel of redemption. It is stated that upon one occasion, having preached and concluded the service with the benediction, to his great surprise he observed that no one present seemed disposed to leave the Church. After a short interval one of the congregation arose and requested him to preach to them the second time. After singing a hymn a second discourse was delivered, when again the congregation refused to leave and a request was made that he should continue to speak. Having responded to this second request, he concluded the service, and announcing that he was too exhausted to speak any longer, he again dismissed the people with the blessing and urged them to return to their homes. Some time since a young English clergyman, having read this incident, said, "Well, really that is very remarkable; you know I never had anything like that occur during my ministry."

In 1809 Doctor Moore became rector of St. Stephen's Church in New York City, composed, at the time of his acceptance of the call, of not more than thirty families; when, five years later, he resigned this Church to come to Virginia, he left in the Church about four hundred communicants.

The call extended Dr. Moore to come to Virginia was preceded by a number of interesting letters in which, on the one hand, he was urged by the Rev. W. H. Wilmer, the Rev. William Meade, the Rev. Mr. Norris, and by a joint letter signed by Bushrod Washington and Edmund L. Lee, to come to Richmond and preach. In these letters assurance was given that if the people could hear him preach, his reputation would be established by the evidence which his presence would give of his power, and that there would be no question that he would be called to the rectorship of Monumental Church, and soon afterwards to become Bishop of the Diocese of Virginia. Some of these letters Doctor Moore seems not to have answered at all. To others he sent belated replies. In all of them he decidedly but courteously declined to act upon the suggestion that he should visit Richmond in furtherance of the proposition of securing the call to the Church and the election to the Episcopate.

Finally the call was extended to Dr. Moore to become the rector of the Monumental Church in Richmond and was accepted, it would seem, some time during April, 1814. Notice of his acceptance of this call having been certified to the Convention of the Diocese, which met on May 4, 1814, Dr. Moore was, as we have seen, elected without opposition to be Bishop of Virginia.

Bishop Hobart, with whom Dr. Moore had had a serious controversy while they were both serving churches in New York City, as to the expediency of conducting informal prayer meetings and services in the homes of the people, seems, in after years, to have become convinced of the supreme loyalty of Dr. Moore to the Prayer Book, and of his devotion to the use of the Liturgy unaltered and unimpaired in the service of the Church, and while at the time of the controversy he looked with scant respect upon the informal devotional services conducted with such marked success by Dr. Moore, he became convinced, when the heat of controversy had subsided, of his supreme loyalty to the Church, to her teachings and to her ancient liturgy, and sent to Virginia the following letter endorsing, as Bishop of New York, his life and ministry:

"New York, April 25th, 1814.

My Dear Sir,—I have furnished the Rev. Dr. Moore with the testimonial required by the canons in the case of a removal from one diocese to another. I deem it, however, an act of justice to him, further to state to you, that Dr. Moore's ministrations have been uniformly respectable, popular, and useful. He evinces sincere attachment to the doctrines, the order, and the worship of the venerable Church in which he has been educated, and in which he has been for many years a zealous labourer. And such is the confidence placed in his fidelity to his principles, and in his prudent and zealous efforts to advance her interests, should the order of Providence remove him to Virginia, that I believe he will go there with the good wishes and the prayers of his brethren generally in this quarter. I very sincerely declare that Dr. Moore's intercourse with me is so frank, respectful, and friendly, and he appears so heartily disposed to co-operate with me in advancing the common interest of our Zion, that I shall regret his removal from this diocese, at the same time that I trust and believe that his ministrations and labours, by the blessing of God, will be advantageous to the cause of religion and the Church in Virginia.

I remain, dear sir,

Very sincerely and respectfully,

Your obedient friend and brother,

J. H. HOBART.

Edmund I. Lee, Esq."

Rev. Dr. Richard Channing Moore was consecrated Bishop of Virginia in St. James' Church, Philadelphia, on the 18th of May, 1814, by Bishops White, Hobart, Griswold and Dehon. It is distinctly interesting to note that this event, so significant and vital to the Church in Virginia, took place almost exactly one hundred years prior to the day when the Church in Virginia, on the 20th day of May, 1914, elected the Rev. Dr. William Cabell Brown, now President of the Board of Trustees of the Seminary, to serve as a Bishop in the Church of God in this Diocese.

As a pastor Bishop Moore won the esteem and affection not only of his own congregation, but of all in the community where he lived. While devoted and loyal to the doctrines and worship of his own Church, he was entirely free from the bigotry which so often makes churchmen narrowminded and sectarian. Christians of every name loved him for his exceeding goodness. A striking testimonial of this high regard and affection was given when on the first of January, 1835, he was presented with a beautiful copy of the New Testament printed in golden letters on porcelain paper, which bore the following inscription: "Presented to the Right Reverend R. C. Moore by the Citizens of Richmond, members of the different religious denominations, as a tribute of their affectionate regard and esteem for one who has so long and so carefully devoted his life to the great cause of Christianity." The cost of the book was fifty dollars, but that many might be privileged to join in the gift, no individual was allowed to contribute more than fifty cents.

His truly catholic views were strikingly exhibited in connection with his cooperation in the extension of the work of the American Bible Society. There were those in the Church who interpreted their ordination vows in terms of narrow exclusiveness, and by means of a process of reasoning, ecclesiastically logical, but spiritually obtuse, concluded that loyalty to the Church required them to refrain from any cooperation with those who were not in organic union with the Church. Bishop Hobart in 1816 issued a pastoral letter reiterating the views of Bishop Marsh and some others in England advising Episcopalians to withhold their patronage and support from the Bible Society upon the ground that cooperation with other Christians in this matter would be a virtual recognition of their defective ecclesiastical organizations and compromise their position as loyal Churchmen.

With a full knowledge of the arguments advanced in this controversy against cooperation with the American Bible Society, Bishop Moore cordially accepted the position as the first President of the Virginia Branch of the American Bible Society, as the venerable Bishop White had previously done in Pennsylvania, and gave the society his cordial support until the time of his death.

This position taken by Bishop Moore is in harmony with the catholic sympathy and thought of the Church as we find it expressed by the Lambeth Conference of 1908 (p. 185), "The Committee believe that few things tend more directly to godly union and concord than cooperation between members of different communions in all matters pertaining to the social and moral welfare of the people. It is in the common service of humanity, in the name of Him Who is its Lord, that the ties of friendly relationship are most readily created and most surely strengthened."

To infer from these exhibitions of his spirit of co-operation that Bishop Moore was lax in his loyalty to the Church would be to draw an unwarranted inference which is refuted by the many evidences of his supreme devotion to the

Church, and by numerous letters which he addressed to his clergy enjoining upon them the necessity of using the liturgy of the Church unimpaired in the public services. To one of his clergy he writes: "What assurance, I would ask, can our vestries have in our integrity other than that they derive from our promises of fidelity? If they see us violate our ordination vows, will that violation exalt us in their estimation? The Church boasts of her uniformity. I know if I were engaged as a private worshipper in the services of the Church, the devotional feelings of my heart would be distressed to perceive the officiating minister violating order, and thus depriving me of a service to which I have a legitimate claim, and which he is bound to perform." To another clergyman he writes: "As I know from experience the temptations to aberrate from the Liturgy with which you will be assailed; you must pardon me, in requesting that you resist them all. We have solemnly promised to conform to the discipline and worship of the Church upon all public occasions; and however agreeable a departure from our obligation may be to some, still men of principle will venerate and respect us for our fidelity, and be pleased to see in us a scrupulous regard to our ordination vows."

To his clergy he also wrote letters dealing with the practical and parochial side of their ministerial life. To one of restless mind and of a roving disposition he wrote: "Before you conclude to settle in any place, reflect deeply upon the subject, and, when your mind is made up, enter upon the discharge of your duties with spirit; never expect to fix yourself in any parish in which everything will be agreeable, but endeavoring to meet your difficulties with fortitude, enduring hardness as a good servant of Jesus Christ. A frequent change of residence will operate to the disadvantage of any man. Endeavor to be stationary in your habits, and in so doing Providence will take care of you and promote you in due time; but should you be found frequently on the wing, depend upon it such a disposition will prove a disadvantage to you through life. I have dropped the above remarks from motives of a sincere and fatherly regard, they are such as I should present to my son, and endeavor to impress on his mind in indelible characters."

A letter addressed to another clergyman of the Diocese urging fidelity in pastoral visiting and giving practical instruction as to how such visits can be made effective is most interesting. "Take your horse and go to every family in your parish; breakfast with one and pass an hour in suitable religious conversation with the family; dine with a second and pursue the same course; take a cup of tea or coffee with a third, and read, converse and pray with them all. When you have finished, devote a few weeks to your studies and begin again, and never think the work finished so long as you possess health and strength and life."

The devotion of Bishop Moore to the Liturgy of the Church and his insistence upon its use without alteration in the regular services of the Church, did not preclude him from taking a vital interest in establishing and frequenting the more informal meeting of what was known as the "Associations," where a number of clergy gathered together for conference and prayer and series of services for the good of the community. Of an association held in Alexandria in 1831 he thus spoke in his address to the Convention of 1832: "I embarked for Alexandria at which place we held an association. On that occasion we were joined by a number of the clergy of this Diocese and of Maryland, and were assisted in our labours by the Rev. Dr. Henshaw, and the Rev. Mr. Johns, of Baltimore, and Rev. Dr. Bedell, of Philadelphia. To say that our meeting at that time was instructive and agreeable, would be expressing myself in language too faint for the occasion. A spirit of great zeal and fervour and devotion appeared to animate every bosom, the congregations were deeply solemn and attentive, and overflowing; many were awakened to the consideration of eternal things and openly avowed their love and gratitude to the Almighty. It would rejoice my heart, brethren, to witness a similar evidence of divine influence in every parish in the Diocese. As a proof of the devotional feeling which prevailed, more especially among the young, I with pleasure announce to the Convention, that I confirmed, during my visit, upwards of ninety persons."

In addition to the services rendered in his own Diocese Bishop Moore made Episcopal visitations in North Carolina from 1819 to 1823, and in other Dioceses during periods of vacancy, besides continuing to serve as Rector of Monumental Church.

In 1823 he expresses the hope of soon having an assistant in Monumental Church, and offers to contribute personally five hundred dollars a year for his support. This hope was realized through the co-operation of the Conventions of 1824 and 1825.

In 1829 the Convention met in Charlottesville. The Bishop was now in his sixty-seventh year. At the Convention of the previous year he had asked that the constitution and canons of the Church should be so revised as to make the election of an assistant Bishop possible. This having been done, it was now "Resolved that this Convention deem it expedient, considering the age and bodily infirmity of our most venerated Bishop, to proceed to the election of an assistant, who is not to be considered as entitled to the succession, but that it shall be the right and duty of the Convention of the diocese of Virginia, on the demise of our venerated Bishop, to proceed to the election of a principal Bishop as a successor to the said deceased Bishop."

The Convention, upon the passage of this resolution proceeded to an election, and the Rev. Dr. William Meade received every vote, excepting two blank votes, cast by the members of the Convention. This election proved a great satisfaction and relief to Bishop Moore, who ever spoke of Dr. Meade in terms of deep appreciation and affection. The General Convention, while consenting to the consecration of Bishop Meade, in spite of what it considered the unwise and unprecedented restriction relative to the succession, passed a canon giving all future assistant bishops who should be elected the right of succession, whereupon the next Virginia Convention repealed the restriction imposed upon the election of Bishop, and gave him the right of succession. The labors of Bishop Moore were, however, unabated, and at every Convention he had the satisfaction of reporting the progress and development of his diocese. In one of his addresses he reported that of the fifty-six clergymen belonging to the Diocese in 1833 not less than forty-four had been ordained by him.

During his Episcopate of twenty-seven years he had the satisfaction of seeing a number of Diocesan institutions and organizations established which have continued to help and bless the Church which he so deeply loved and so faithfully served.

In 1816 a society was formed for the distribution of Prayer Books and religious tracts.

At this Convention a fund was established for the support of the Episcopate.

In 1818 the Education Society was organized in Georgetown, D.C., subsequently transferred to Virginia, and nourished and fostered by his interest and unfaltering co-operation.

In 1823 the Theological Seminary, which is the chief memorial of his Episcopate, was formally opened in Alexandria.

In 1829 the Diocesan Missionary Society was established, and its constitution adopted. This action was the culmination of efforts which had been made for the support of diocesan missionaries dating back as far as the Convention of 1813.*

At this Convention a Committee was also appointed to take into consideration the laws and regulations for the government of the society for the relief of distressed widows and orphans of deceased clergymen.

The Bishop had also given his support to the establishment of the Southern Churchman, which he cordially endorsed and commended in his Convention address of 1835.

His last addresses to his Convention glow with the fervor of matured affection, and with the devotion to the evangelical faith which constituted the unfailing theme of his preaching. In tender tones he urged his clergy to "Labour with diligence in the vineyard of your Master and be not weary in well doing. Be faithful unto death and God will give you a crown of life."

These old Conventions of the Diocese of Virginia were unique in the history of our Church in America. Thither came the people from far and near, as the tribes came up to Jerusalem to the great feasts of the Temple. Writing to invite Bishop Ravenscroft, of North Carolina, to endeavor to be present at the Convention soon to meet in Petersburg,

* Hawks' Journals, p. 90.

he mentions the fact that there had been at least twelve hundred visitors at the Convention which met the previous year in Fredericksburg. Of these old Virginia Conventions a contemporaneous historian writes as follows:

"A Virginia Convention! There is something to animate and warm the heart in the very title! When we speak of most other Diocesan Conventions, we think of assemblages of the clergy and lay delegates, with the Bishop at their head, convened chiefly for the purpose of attending to ecclesiastical business, of regulating the fiscal and other ordinary interests of the diocese. But how different the impression made upon the mind when a *Virginia* Convention is spoken of! The annual ecclesiastical meetings of that diocese have but little of a secular character connected with them! Business is but a secondary and subordinate matter. The assembly is not limited to the elected members, but is a gathering together of the devoted friends of the Church, clerical and lay, from all parts of the state, not excepting the more distant and remote parishes. Persons of all ranks and ages, 'young men and maidens, old men and children,' are gathered together for the purpose of religious improvement and spiritual edification. It is such a scene as was exhibited among God's people of old, at their solemn festivals, as described in the words of the Psalmist, 'I was glad when they said unto me, we will go into the house of the Lord. Our feet shall stand in thy gates, O Jerusalem. Jerusalem is built as a city that is at unity in itself. For thither the tribes go up, even the tribes of the Lord, to testify unto Israel, to give thanks unto the name of the Lord.'

"In the midst of the hallowed and interesting scenes of that annual festival, the Bishop moved as the presiding genius. He was the centre of attraction and unity to the numerous family of devoted and affectionate children by which he was surrounded. He was a leader or participator in the numerous devotional services which took place day after day, and night after night. His heart glowed with the kindled fervours of faith and love; his eyes sparkled under the inspiration of hope and joy; and his tongue flowed with melting eloquence, as now he urged his ministers to greater zeal and faithfulness, and then exhorted the people to repentance and a holy life. These annual Conventions were to him sources of unaffected pleasure and delight. As, amidst these times of refreshing, he beheld the word of God taking effect upon the hearts and consciences of the people, and witnessed answers to prayer in the conversion of sinners, he rose to higher and higher degrees of enjoyment, till, as the end drew near, it seemed as if he were in a rapture or ecstacy; just ready, like Elijah, to go up in a chariot of fire to heaven! Never have we witnessed a spectacle which so nearly answered to our idea of the purity, and joy, and love of the primitive Church, as the closing scene of a Virginia Convention. When the body of weeping clergy gathered around the altar, while, in the presence of a crowded but praying assembly, their Right Reverend Father in God, with shaking hands and whitened locks, stood before them as an appropriate representative and successor of the Apostles, and, with streaming eyes, and a voice tremulous with emotion, gave them his parting counsels, and pronounced over them his affectionate farewell, a scene was presented upon which attending angels might gaze with rapture."

In 1840 the Bishop journeyed to Baltimore to assist in the Consecration of the Rev. Dr. Whittingham to the Episcopate in Maryland, and also went to Philadelphia to ordain his kinsman, Rev. G. T. Bedell, to the Diaconate. Responding to an urgent invitation he went to Westchester, New York, in August, 1841, to ordain Mr. Bedell to the Priesthood, and was assisted in the service by two of his own sons. It is interesting to note that though the Bishop was seventy-nine years of age, he took an active part in an Association which Rev. Mr. Bedell had planned in his Parish co-incident with his ordination, and spoke with great earnestness and spiritual power four times in addition to conducting the examination for orders, celebrating the Holy Communion and taking the ordination service. Following the sermon by Dr. Tyng at the evening service, Bishop Moore made a touching appeal for personal consecration. "I shall never forget," wrote Rev. Mr. Bedell, "how the old man eloquent, stood that evening on the border of the grave, his white locks, and his uplifted, trembling finger, telling of experienced age, but in the cause of Christ forgetting every weakness of the flesh, one finger only resting on the chancel rail, his whole frame roused by the energy of his mind and active under the influence of his feelings. How impressively he told us of the Savior whom he had served for fifty years and so bade us hear an old man's testimony. The tears of not a few persons in the audience showed the power of his eloquence, among them being an old soldier of the revolution who said afterwards that he had not shed a tear before for many years."

While in New York Bishop Moore attended the session of the General Convention and lent his voice and influence to the project of appointing two bishops, one for Texas and the other for West Africa. This was his last service to the General Church. Leaving New York before the adjournment of the Convention he returned to Richmond, and two days after commenced, in his eightieth year, a journey of a hundred and fifty miles to Lynchburg, arriving there on the 5th of November, where, after speaking at an evening service previous to a confirmation service which was to take place on the following day, he was taken ill and died of pneumonia in the home of Rev. Thomas Atkinson, Rector of St. Paul's, on the 11th day of November, 1841. His death was mourned throughout the whole Church. His body was carried back to Richmond, where the last tributes of devotion were paid to his hallowed memory, not alone by the bereaved members of his Church, but by the whole community.

The Southern Churchman, which appeared on November 19, 1841, in deep mourning, says that when the news of Bishop Moore's death reached the Seminary "A meeting of the Faculty and Students was holden in Prayer Hall on November 16th, 1841 and the following preamble and resolutions were adopted:—

"WHEREAS, It has pleased Almighty God to remove by death the Rt. Rev. Richard Channing Moore, D. D., Bishop of this diocese and president of this Seminary

"RESOLVED—That we deplore with deepest sorrow his loss and shall ever cherish the memory of his apostolic zeal in the discharge of the holy functions. The fervor and unction with which he dwelt upon the things which concerned the Lord Jesus Christ, which, together with his many private virtues, greatly endeared him to our hearts.

"RESOLVED—That as members of this Institution, we have reason to feel especially his loss in as much as from the foundation of this Seminary to the time of his death, he was its constant and devoted friend and patron, and always manifested the warmest interest in its prosperity."

Over his grave the Vestry of Monumental Church erected a monument which bears the following inscription:

"RICHARD CHANNING MOORE, D. D.

WAS BORN IN THE CITY OF NEW YORK,
AUGUST 21ST, 1762."
"HE LABOURED FAITHFULLY AND SUCCESSFULLY IN
THE MINISTRY OF THE
PROTESTANT-EPISCOPAL CHURCH 54 YEARS."
"HE WAS RECTOR OF THE MONUMENTAL CHURCH
IN RICHMOND,
AND BISHOP OF THE DIOCESE OF VIRGINIA,
27 YEARS."
"IN THE CONVENTION THAT CALLED HIM TO THE
EPISCOPATE,
THERE WERE ONLY 7 MEMBERS."
"AT THE TIME OF HIS DEATH THERE WERE 95
CLERGY IN THE DIOCESE OF VA."
"HE DIED IN LYNCHBURG, VIRGINIA,
NOV. 11TH, 1841,
AT THE AGE OF 79."

Of this monument Rev. Dr. Henshaw gives this description:

"On the opposite side of this monument is an inscription commemorative of Mrs. Moore. At the base of the pyramid, on the east side, is sculptured in bas-relief, a cross, over a portion of which some drapery is hung, and on the opposite side an altar; on the northern side there is a representation of a Bible with the following inscription engraved thereon:

"DANIEL, CHAPTER XII."

"THEY THAT BE WISE SHALL SHINE AS THE BRIGHTNESS OF THE

FIRMAMENT, AND THEY THAT TURN MANY TO

RIGHTEOUSNESS

AS THE STARS FOR EVER AND EVER."

"And on the opposite side a Prayer-Book is represented with this inscription:

'IN THE MIDST OF LIFE, WE ARE IN DEATH.'"

SECTION III

The History of the Seminary

I. The Education Society and the Genesis of the Seminary.

II. The Subsequent History of the Seminary.

SECTION III

THE HISTORY OF THE SEMINARY

CHAPTER I

The Education Society and the Genesis of the Seminary

1818-1827

REV. W. A. R. GOODWIN, D. D.

The Teaching Mission of the Church—First Step taken after Revolution for Ministerial Education—The Devastated Virginia Church—The Founding of the Education Society—Chief Founders—Theological Repertory—Increasing Scarcity of Clergy—Original Constitution of Education Society—Dr. Thomas Henderson—Dr. J. P. K. Henshaw—Statement by Dr. William H. Wilmer—Opposition to Diocesan Seminaries—Theological Professorship at College of William and Mary—Rev. John Augustine Smith—Virginia Council Resolutions Relative to Establishing the Seminary—Unique Circular—Maryland Seminary Project—Reasons for Establishing the Seminary Set Forth—Beginning of the Seminary in Alexandria—Rev. Dr. Reuel Keith—Other Professors—Womens' Auxiliary to the Education Society—The Leadership of Bishop Meade—The Education Society Continues the Indispensable Ally of the Seminary—Invaluable Contributions Made by the Society to the Seminary—The Real Date of the Founding of the Seminary—The Location of the Seminary in Alexandria—The Faculty of the Alexandria Period—Dr. Keith and Christ Church, Georgetown—Rev. Dr. William H. Wilmer—Rev. Oliver Norris—Rev. Edward R. Lippitt—Rev. Dr. Clemson's Description of the Early Days of the Seminary—Dr. Packard's Account of the Courses of Study Provided, and Other Incidents—The Removal from Alexandria to "The Hill."

Religious Education has ever been recognized as a fundamental and vital necessity in the Christian Church. Upon it the very existence of the Church depends. The Founder of our most holy religion was preëminently a Teacher. He went about doing good. He worked miracles. "But this I do," He said, "that ye may know that the Son of man hath power on earth to forgive sins." By the seaside, upon the mountain top, in the market place, by the wayside as well as in the temple, He taught men the things concerning the Kingdom of God; but all His teaching was related to His supreme purpose, to give to men the revelation of God Incarnate, that they might come to know their Father and reveal Him to those who knew Him not. His call to men was, "Come unto me" and "learn." His command to them was, "Go, teach." In Him, through perfect love, perfect truth was revealed. He made the love of God the motive power of the will to serve, and made the knowledge of His Father's will, revealed to men, the program of the Church's mission. Ephemeral and evanescent emotion, unrelated to abiding truth, does not tend to produce abiding results either in the life of man or in the life of the Church; but emotion, when it impassions truth, gives to it glow and beauty and a contagious power. Those who have wisely thought and labored for the upbuilding of the Kingdom of God have ever recognized that neither the Church nor society could be reformed and reconstructed unless a knowledge of the truth was wedded with the love for the God of truth in the souls of men. The master-builders in God's Kingdom have ever seen that a program of education closely related to a life of devotion could alone rescue human endeavor from failure, and give to man's purpose the power to produce abiding results.

It was because the voice of truth had been hushed by the din of war and by the clamor of greed and passion and the pursuit of pleasure that the knowledge and love of God had so largely vanished in Virginia and elsewhere during the closing years of the eighteenth and the early years of the nineteenth centuries. These facts were clearly recognized by those who undertook in the early days of the nineteenth century to upbuild a devastated Church and to restore religious conviction and the religious life to their rightful place. It was this conviction which led to the formation of the Education Society of Maryland and Virginia, which was first designated as "The Society for the Education of Pious Young Men for the Ministry of the Protestant Episcopal Church."

The Southern Churchman of September 13, 1839, contains one of the series of articles by the Rev. Philip Slaughter on the history of the Church in Virginia in which the statement is made that in 1783 the Convention of the Church in Virginia passed a resolution looking to the raising of a fund for the education of two young men from their early years for the ministry of the Church. "To the honor of Virginia," says Dr. Hawks, "this was the first step taken by the Church after the Revolution for ministerial education."

The founding of the Education Society in 1818, however, marks the real beginning of the Theological Seminary in Virginia. This Society was indeed the Seminary in embryo; and those who were responsible for its organization and its accomplishments were, in reality, the founders of the Theological Seminary in Virginia, which grew out of and for many years was fostered by this endeavor.

Of this organization the Rev. Dr. William H. Wilmer was the first president. Associated with him in this enterprise were a number of devoted clergymen and laymen resident principally in Washington and Alexandria.

William E. Gladstone said that perhaps never in history had there been gathered at one time and in one place a group of men so able and distinguished as those found in America at the time of the Revolution and during the years immediately following. It may likewise be said that during no period in the history of the American Church was there ever gathered at one time and in one vicinity any band of men more fitted for the fulfillment of the divine purpose than those who were ministering in Washington and Alexandria at the time of the founding of the Education Society. The Rev. William Meade, in 1811, had become rector of Christ Church, Alexandria, and in 1812 the Rev. William H. Wilmer, D. D., became rector of St. Paul's, Alexandria. In Washington the Rev. Dr. Hawley was rector of St. John's, and in 1817 the Rev. Dr. Reuel Keith had become rector of Christ Church, Georgetown. The Rev. John Johns was ministering in Frederick-City, Maryland. The Rev. Stephen H. Tyng, who was in Prince George County, Virginia, soon became rector of St. John's Church, Georgetown. The Rev. Dr. Addison was in St. John's, Georgetown, prior to the election of Dr. Tyng. And nearby, in the city of Baltimore, was the Rev. Dr. J. P. K. Henshaw, subsequently Bishop of Rhode Island, and Rev. Dr. Charles P. McIlvaine.

Together with them were two devoted laymen, Dr. Thomas Henderson and Francis Scott Key, the author of "The Star Spangled Banner", both of whom were vestrymen of Christ Church, Georgetown.

Almost coincident with the establishment of the Education Society was the publication in Washington, beginning in 1818, of "The Theological Repertory." Its editors were also founders of the Education Society, the chief editor being Rev. Dr. William H. Wilmer.

Primarily a theological review, its pages express the theological and religious convictions which the Education Society and subsequently the Seminary were designed to express and propagate through a well-trained ministry. It is interesting to note that Dr. Muhlenberg's hymn "I would not live always" first appeaied in this magazine, and also the hymn "Lord, with glowing heart I'd praise Thee," by Francis Scott Key. This hymn was published in 1823, the year of the founding of the Seminary in Alexandria. The profits of this magazine were devoted to the Education Society.*

On page 157 of Volume I of this magazine the reasons for the formation of the Education Society are strongly set forth. It is stated that "since the year 1799, or during the last twenty years, the actual number of Episcopal clergymen in Maryland and Virginia has diminished more than one-third; in the state of Virginia within that short period, nearly one-half. The diminution in the states south of Virginia is still greater. Within the above named period the population of the United States was nearly doubled. In 1799 the whole number of clergymen reported to the General Convention was 220 and in 1817, 263, giving an increase of only forty-three."

"In consequence of this state of things, which no Christian can survey without emotion, many of our once flourishing parishes are disorganized, decayed, and fast hastening to utter dissolution and extinction. Churches that once resounded on every Sabbath and solemn festivals with the voice of prayer and thanksgiving uttered by a numerous concourse of worshippers, are now literally deserted and des-

---

* "The Theological Repertory". Vol. V. page 26.

olate, and either actually fallen or fast sinking into ruins. Infidelity and ungodliness abound. The simplest and most essential doctrines of salvation are either unknown or obscure and perverted by many, very many, who on almost every other subject are deservedly regarded as intelligent, and hold a distinguished rank in the community. The importance of a regular and qualified order of Evangelical instructors is less and less felt, and a growing indisposition to obtain and support them is in many places but too apparent."

A short time before, in the year 1811, the following minute had been entered on the journal of the General Convention of the Church held at New Haven:

"They fear, indeed, that the Church in Virginia is from various causes so depressed that there is danger of her total ruin, unless great exertions, favored by the blessing of Providence are employed to raise her."

We are fortunate in the fact that the original minute book of the Education Society is still in existence. From this book and from the minutes of the Standing Committee of the Education Society and the minute book of the Vestry of Christ Church Parish, Georgetown, D. C., and from the early Journals of the Convention of the Church in Virginia, together with the addresses and appeals issued by the Society and published in the "Theological Repertory", we are enabled to write the record of the founding and achievements of this Society.

The minute book of the Society under date June 1818 contains the following record of its organization: "CONSTITUTION of the SOCIETY FOR THE EDUCATION OF PIOUS YOUNG MEN FOR THE MINISTRY OF THE PROTESTANT EPISCOPAL CHURCH.   June 1818.*

WHEREAS The Conventions of the Protestant Episcopal Church in Maryland and Virginia, have, by various resolutions, recommended measures for educating young men for the ministry; and

WHEREAS Societies have been formed in Baltimore and other places, for promoting this laudable object, several of the clergy and laity from the two Dioceses above named,

---

* Date of organization meeting taken from Theological Repertory, Vol. I. p. 158

met in the city of Washington, and resolved themselves into a Society, with a view of imitating their brethren in this zeal and labour of love, and adopted the following Constitution:

I.   This Society shall be called the Society for the Education of Pious Young Men for the Ministry of the Protestant Episcopal Church.

II.   The officers of the Society shall consist of a President, two Vice-Presidents, selected from among the clergy, a secretary and treasurer, together with a Board of Managers, consisting of six clergymen and six laymen, to be chosen annually by ballot; whose duty it shall be to manage all the concerns of the Society not otherwise provided for.

III.   The annual meeting of the Society shall be held on the last Thursday in October, in each year, in the cities of Washington, Alexandria, and Georgetown, in regular rotation.

IV.   The President shall have power to call a meeting of the Society and in case of his death or absence, either of the Vice-Presidents, at the request of any two of the Managers, at such time and place as may be most convenient, in the District of Columbia; five of whom shall constitute a quorum for the transaction of business.

V.   The managers shall appoint by ballot, at their annual meeting, a standing committee, consisting of three clerical and three lay members to be chosen out of the Board of Managers, whose duty it shall be to select and recommend to the Board of Managers such candidates as they may deem proper; and if approved of by a majority of the Board, the committee shall proceed to appropriate the necessary assistance for the prosecution of their studies.   The President of the Society shall be ex-officio President of the committees.

VI.   Annual subscribers to this Society, of one dollar or more, shall be considered as members thereof; and those who pay fifty dollars, or upwards, at one time, shall be considered as members for life.

VII.   This Constitution shall be unalterable unless at an annual meeting of the Society, and with the concurrence of two-thirds of the members present.

The Following Officers were then elected:—President, Rev. William H. Wilmer; 1st. Vice-President, Rev. Walter D. Addison; 2nd. Vice-President, Rev. William Hawley; Secretary, Rev. Enoch M. Lowe; Treasurer, Mr. C. Page.

Managers

Rev. Oliver Norris, Rev. William Meade, Rev. Edward C. McGuire, Rev. George Lemmon, Rev. Reuel Keith, Rev. Charles Mann, Francis Scott Key, Esq., Daniel Murray, Richard W. West, William A. Knox, Edmund I. Lee, Esq., Philip Nelson, Esq."

The Constitution, as above recorded, was altered and amended at a meeting of the Society held on October 30th, 1823.*

The biographical sketches of Rev. Dr. Wilmer, Bishop Meade, Rev. Dr. Keith, Rev. Dr. Norris, and Francis Scott Key, prominent among the founders of this Society, are given elsewhere in this book. Thomas Henderson, M. D., appears in 1820 as one of the managers and, with Francis Scott Key, as a member of the Standing Committee of the Society. The Southern Churchman of December 7th, 1854 contains an interesting sketch of the life of Dr. Henderson and also a six column reprint from the Theological Repertory of August 1823, giving an account of the founding of the Society.

"Dr. Thomas Henderson was born in Dumfries, Prince William county, Virginia, on the 6th of January, 1789, being the youngest son of Alexander Henderson, Esq.

"After completing his professional studies in Philadelphia, he settled for the practice of medicine in Warrenton, Virginia.

"In 1816 he moved to Georgetown and thence to Washington City, in 1826. In 1833 he received the appointment of assistant surgeon, United States Army, and was assigned to duty at the United States Military Academy at West Point. As a professional man few enjoyed higher reputation. To intellectual qualities of highest order, were added the judgment, the watchfulness and the tenderness which gave so much value to the services which he rendered as a physi-

* See Appendix Education Society Minutes.

cian. For many years he was the professor of theory and practice of medicine in Columbian College, D. C., and while in this chair, published a translation of Bichat's Work on Human Pathology.

"He was appointed by the Surgeon-General, to special duty on the Board of Medical Examiners for candidates for admission into the Medical Staff of the Army. While attending one of these Board meetings, he presented a project for regulating the standard of proficiency in these examinations which was unanimously adopted by the Board and has since constituted the basis upon which the medical corps of the United States Army has been organized since 1834. He urged the establishment of a naval academy, and it is believed that the force of these letters had influence in calling public attention to the necessity of establishing the United States Naval Academy at Annapolis.

"Dr. Henderson was confirmed by Bishop Moore in Warrenton, Virginia, shortly after having been converted at a Presbyterian revival in 1813. He was appointed by the Bishop lay reader of the Church at Warrenton, and served so acceptably that the congregation protested against the necessity of calling a minister, saying 'that they did not think they could get a better preacher than Dr. Henderson.'

"He discussed with Bishop Meade his thought of entering the Christian ministry, but so valuable were his services as a physician and so strong was the influence of his professional life upon the community that the Bishop replied 'that although the Church is in great need of ministers, it is also in need of active and pious laymen, and that if the doctor would bring his Christian character into prominent existence through his professional life, he might do as much good to the cause of the Redeemer as a clergyman.'

"Upon his removal to Georgetown in 1816, he joined with Francis Scott Key and others in the organization of Christ Church.

"It was during his residence in Georgetown that measures were taken for the establishment of the Theological Seminary near Alexandria. His part in the matter is given in his own words conveyed in a letter in response to an inquiry from the Rev. Robert Nelson, missionary in China. Dr. Henderson writes as follows: 'By the time Dr. Keith left Williamsburg, Dr. Carnahan left Georgetown for Princeton College. I wanted to have a good school in Georgetown and to lay such a foundation as would be extended into a protestant College, somewhere in the district. Dr. Keith passed through Georgetown for Vermont and I set out in pursuit of him; went as far as Philadelphia where the General Convention was sitting; could not overtake him, returned to Georgetown, wrote to him to come down and take the Academy. He came down soon after. We met Messrs. Key, Meade, Wilmer and Hawley; the whole matter was talked over at my house in repeated interviews, which resulted in the determination to open a 'School of the Prophets' in Alexandria. I was directed to prepare an address, did so, took it up into Mr. Meade's room at my house; he read it; gave one of his sweet smiles; said I might make a preacher. I had it printed; paid the piper; and further your deponent saith not, except, that the Address was printed afterwards in the Theological Repertory where it may now be found. *Quorum pars fui.* This is all I know of the incipiency of the matter. Now I don't mean to say in this connection that I originated the Theological Seminary; far from it. The clergy did that, and took Mr. Keith away from my good College scheme.'"

In 1820, Rev. Dr. J. P. K. Henshaw is recorded as a member of the Society. "Dr. Henshaw was born in Middletown, Connecticut, in June 1792. He was a graduate of Middlebury College, from which he received the degree of A. B. at the age of sixteen. He spent a year at Harvard as a resident graduate. During his residence at Harvard he officiated as lay-reader in the Church at Cambridge. He likewise founded two congregations in the northern part of Vermont, and all of this was accomplished before he reached his nineteenth year. He was ordained on the day of his twenty-first anniversary. For a short time he held the rectorship of the Church at Marblehead, Massachusetts. Thence he removed to Brooklyn, New York and officiated there as rector of St. Anne's Church for three years.

"In 1817 he came to Baltimore to St. Peter's Church. He was an eloquent and forceful preacher. He was conspicuous in the state and General Conventions of the Episcopal

Church. Dr. Henshaw wrote many pamphlets and books, among them being a minister's "Instruction to his People on the Subject of Confirmation"; a "Communicant's Guide"; "Directions for Reading the Church Service"; and "Theological Guide for the People". He was also the biographer of Bishop Moore. Dr. Henshaw afterwards became the Bishop of Rhode Island."*

Under date February 13th, 1819, the Rev. Dr. Wilmer writes a circular letter from Alexandria in which he says: "There are many pious young men desirous of devoting themselves to the ministry; some of whom have talents to render them useful, but who are deficient in the necessary education; others who have the advantages of talents and education, but who are destitute of the means of supporting themselves long enough to finish their theological studies. With some of these, the want of pecuniary means is total; with others it is only partial and requiring a small assistance. The plan proposed is, to place them in the family of some respectable clergymen, and to raise a fund, out of which a small annual stipend may be allowed them, which, with the assistance that the clergyman with whom they live may be able to afford them, and the means they may possess in themselves, will be sufficient to defray their necessary expenses. By this means the same amount of funds will embrace a larger number of students than by any other mode whatever, and hereby also they will enjoy the great benefit of learning practical as well as theoretical divinity, and of acquiring the important routine of parochial duty under the example of the minister with whom they reside. In this view it will be perceived that the society does not design to supersede or to interfere with the General Seminary intended to be established by the Church; but to reach those local cases to which the nature of the General Institution would not be adapted."†

This reference to the General Seminary grew out of the fact that at this time there was considerable opposition throughout the Church to the idea of establishing diocesan seminaries, which opposition was urged on the ground that

* From The *Southern Churchman* November 25th, 1842.
† From "The Theological Repertory" March, 1820.

they would involve unnecessary expense and that the endeavor would be disloyal to the will of the Church as expressed in General Convention in the establishment of the General Seminary. The objection was finally disposed of by the General Seminary authorities themselves. The issue had been raised in connection with a legacy given to the General Seminary upon certain conditions. To adjust these difficulties Bishop Hobart of New York issued a publication in defence of diocesan seminaries and opposition to them soon ceased. The General Seminary was transferred from New Haven, where it was first located, to the city of New York, under terms which put its control largely under the diocese of New York, thus removing the ground of opposition to diocesan seminaries.

At a meeting of the Education Society of Maryland and Virginia held on the 26th of October 1820, the following resolutions were adopted:

RESOLVED—That it is expedient to establish a Theological Professorship to be located at William and Mary College, or elsewhere, as the Society may from time to time order or direct, and

RESOLVED—That the President, Rev. Dr. Wilmer, be, and is hereby requested, to prepare a circular explanatory of the object of the Society and urging the support of the Church for this desirable and useful establishment.

The address which under this resolution the President was requested to issue was sent out from Alexandria under date November 8, 1820, and is in part as follows:

"The managers deem it their duty to take advantage of the peculiar circumstances which in this case present themselves in favor of the attempt to establish a local Seminary in the southern country.

1. The College of William and Mary has offered to Theological Students certain privileges which will render the resources that may be obtained in this section of the country more effective and useful in their appropriation in that way than in any other.

2. It is ascertained that the public will give more liberally and cheerfully to an object thus brought home to

them, and identified with their local interests and associations, than to the remote though equally important institution at New Haven.

"The plan proposed is, to provide funds for a Theological Professor who will probably be located at William and Mary College. That institution is now supplied with able professors and with all the securities for procuring a complete education. The faculty, with one exception, have offered a gratuitous course of instruction to all *bona fide* students of Theology. An excellent theological library is attached to the College, and, in the event of our succeeding in the professorship, a very valuable private library belonging to a clergyman of our Church will be added by that worthy person. The living at Williamsburg is cheap, and the climate healthy, except during the months of vacation when the professor and students might easily and to advantage of their health, remove into the upper country."*

In the fall of 1814 Rev. Dr. John Augustine Smith, president of the College of William and Mary, met Bishop Moore on the street in New York and suggested to him that a chair of Theology be established in the College at Williamsburg. In the Seminary Library there is a copy of the recollections of Rev. Dr. Smith, published in 1852 with the following inscription by him on the fly leaf, "For the Theological Seminary from its author, to whom the idea of establishing the institution first occurred, as Bishop Moore bears witness." Bishop Moore had then only recently, on the 18th of May, 1814, been consecrated Bishop of Virginia. In 1815 Dr. Smith sent one of the faculty of the College of William and Mary to the Virginia Convention to urge the expediency of establishing a Theological professorship at this College. The Bishop gave the suggestion enthusiastic support in his address to the Convention.

The Rev. Dr. William H. Wilmer, chairman of the Committee on the State of the Church reported a resolution which was adopted: "That the Bishop and Standing Committee be authorized to adopt measures for the promotion of an object of such magnitude, and which may, under the

* From "The Theological Repertory" December, 1820.

blessing of God, be productive of the most beneficial consequences." In 1820 Dr. Wilmer, in his report as chairman of the Committee on the State of the Church, recommended the appointment of a clerical professor at the College of William and Mary; and in 1821 Dr. Wilmer, as chairman of the same committee, recommended the establishment of a Theological School in Williamsburg. He further recommended that a board of Trustees be appointed to select one or more professors, to raise funds for this object, and to correspond with the Standing Committees of Maryland and North Carolina to ascertain if they were disposed to cooperate. Later this purpose was carried into effect, and funds deemed sufficient having been secured, the Rev. Dr. Reuel Keith was invited to assume the duties of this professorship. In January 1820 he resigned the rectorship at Christ Church Parish, Georgetown, to accept the professorship of History and Humanities and the chair of Theology at William and Mary College and to become Rector of Bruton Parish Church. The experiment of maintaining a theological chair at William and Mary proved a complete failure, and it is reported that during the continuance of the effort only one student presented himself for instruction.

At a meeting of the Board of Managers of the Education Society held in Alexandria, May 15, 1821, after deliberating on the subject of the establishment of a Theological Professorship and other concerns of the Society, "the Board adjourned to the 26th of June for the purpose of affording the Conventions of Virginia and Maryland an opportunity of expressing their opinions on the subject before the Society should take any active measures for the accomplishment of this object."

Immediately following this meeting of the managers of the Education Society held on May 15, 1821, the Virginia Diocesan Convention assembled in Norfolk on the 17th and 18th of May, 1821. The question of appointing Trustees for a Theological School was brought to the attention of the Convention in the following report of the Committee on the State of the Church, the adoption of which authorized the appointment of Trustees for a Theological School in Virginia and the appointment of Mr. John Nelson to solicit subscriptions for its establishment:

"The Committee on the State of the Church, taking into consideration the deficient condition of the diocese as respects the means of Theological Instruction, and the importance of retaining among ourselves for Education, those young men who may be disposed to devote themselves to the sacred office of the ministry, recommend to this convention, the establishment of a Theological School in Williamsburg; it being understood that the society of the College in that place is willing that such a step should be taken, and that the faculty have generously offered to afford gratuitously, to all *bona fide* students of theology, a course of lectures, for the support of such school.

"It is therefore recommended, that a Board of Trustees, consisting of clergymen and laymen, any three of whom shall constitute a quorum, be appointed to adopt the most efficient means for establishing the same, by raising funds and selecting one or more professors; the proceedings of which board, shall be subject to the decision of the next convention.

"It is also recommended, that the Board of Trustees enter into a correspondence with the standing committees of the dioceses of Maryland and North Carolina, in order to ascertain whether the members of our church in those states are disposed to cooperate with us in this important measure.

"In recommending these resolutions, the Committee think proper to declare, that they do not intend any opposition to the General Seminary established by the general convention. On the contrary, we cordially desire to see the prosperity of an institution so vitally connected, as that is, with the reputation and interest of our Church. But as there are peculiar circumstances which render it necessary to cherish a seminary in the southern district, we consider the duty of attempting it, as coming within the scope of the resolution made by the house of bishops, which declares its intention, 'not to interfere with any plan now contemplated or that may be hereafter contemplated in any diocese or dioceses for the establishment of theological institutions or professorships.'"

"Therefore, Resolved, That Mr. John Nelson, Junior, delegate from St. James's Parish, Mecklenburg county, be appointed to solicit subscriptions throughout the diocese for the above purpose.

"Resolved further, That the Board of Trustees be authorized, in case of death or resignation of the above collector to appoint another for the said purpose; and generally to give such instructions and directions as shall, in their judgment be proper."

This report and the accompanying resolutions were agreed to by the Convention.*

The Rev. Mr. Wilmer, from the Trustees of the Theological School, reported "that during the last year a committee was appointed to draft an address to the members and friends of the Church, which was printed and circulated very generally throughout the diocese." He also reported "that Mr. John Nelson, the agent appointed to solicit subscriptions, had obtained contributions to the amount of $10,268.33." *

"The Trustees express their sanguine hope that the future applications which will continue to be made will enable them at an early date to put in operation so desirable an institution. The delay of another year, however, is inevitable, because the subscriptions were taken payable in three installments, the first only is now due; a measure judged prudent from the very depressed state of the country in its money concerns. A correspondence was entered into with the dioceses of Maryland and North Carolina, which resulted in some difference of opinion on the part of the Diocese of Maryland, as to the usefulness of the contemplated school, and its location at Williamsburg, but was deferred as to any definite step until the meeting of the Convention in the present year. From North Carolina no reply had been received." †

Bishop Meade gives the following account of the result of this correspondence: "From North Carolina we received no answer. From Bishop Kemp of Maryland we received a prompt and decided refusal, accompanied with such severe strictures on the religion and morals of Virginia that we did not present it to the Convention, but only reported our fail-

* From "The Theological Repertory." Vol. II. Page 381.

† From "The Theological Repertory" July 1822.

ure. Williamsburg, especially, was objected to, on account
of the infidelity, as altogether unfit for such an institution.
Those of us who were engaged in the resuscitation of the
Church were also said to be extravagant in some of our
notions, as is apt to be the case with those who, in flying
from one extreme run into another. Manifestly, there was
no prospect of help or cooperation from that direction."

A constitution of the Theological School was also reported,
and, being slightly amended, was adopted by the Convention. This Convention was held in Charlottesville, Virginia,
on May 16th, 1822.

The Theological Repertory of January 1823, beginning
on page 171, contains a thirteen-column notice of a circular
issued by the trustees of the Theological School in Virginia
at a meeting of the board held in Fredericksburg, Virginia.
This circular reviews the lamentable state into which religion
had fallen throughout the entire country, and points to the
fact that the only hope of revival lies in the establishment
of institutions for the training of a native ministry. It
cites as an example the Seminary at Andover, Massachusetts,
"where nearly $400,000 has been spent on buildings and
equipment, and where more than one hundred pious youths
are continually preparing themselves for the sacred office."

The appeal of this circular set forth by the Board of
Trustees is for an institution where not only religious truth
may be taught but where the widest and deepest culture may
also be given to the students. "It is worthy of observation,"
says this report, "that when the Almighty thought proper
to separate the Jewish nation from all others delivering his
laws and ordinances to them and constituting them the
depository of his revealed will; He selected for the achievement a man 'even Moses who was learned in all the wisdom
of the Egyptians' which was, in truth, all the wisdom of the
then-known world. With him was associated Aaron because
he was an eloquent man."

The circular then reviews the work of the School of the
Prophets established in Israel "where retired from the world,
and devoted to prayer and study and every pious exercise,
they prepared themselves for the instruction of the people."
In answer to the objection sometimes raised that the Evan-

gelists of our Lord were unlearned and ignorant men, the
Trustees answer that it should be remembered that they were
the companions of the Christ Himself and that "in a super-
natural manner He endued them with the knowledge of
languages, that all men might be addressed in their own
tongues." They next call attention to the fact that St.
Paul "had been brought up at the feet of Gamaliel a learned
doctor among the Jews. He studied the wisdom of this
world and of the princes and wise men thereof, and therefore,
the better knew that it was foolishness with God and would
come to naught. He it was who stood in the midst of Mars
Hill, in Athens itself, the great seat of learning and politeness;
and there, before the most renowned assembly in the world,
preached the faith of Jesus, charged their nation with super-
stition, and quoted their own poets and mythology against
them. He it was that reasoned so nobly on righteousness,
temperance, and judgment to come, that a profligate governor, seated on his throne, trembled as he spoke; and he it
was who so sublimely displayed the wonderful doctrines of
the Cross before the noble Festus, as to make him exclaim,
'Paul! Thou art beside thyself. Much learning doth make
thee mad.' But so surely were they the words of truth and
soberness which he spoke, that ere the apostle's argument
was over, the unbeliever was forced to say 'Almost thou
persuadest me to be a Christian.'

"Thus in every age, have learned and eloquent defenders
of the faith, by the irresistible force of their reasoning, by the
wisdom of their councils, by their solemn appeals to the
conscience, and pathetic addresses to the heart obtained an
homage for religion."

"Who were those martyrs and confessors that lived and
died only for Christ? Who were Ireneus, Clemens, Tertul-
lian, Cyprian, Eusebius, Jerome, Chrysostom and Augustin?
Who but men, the most learned of their age, acquainted, as
all their writings evince, with all the Greek and Roman lore
and able to show that all their religion was vain conceit or
proud rebellion against God? When Europe later was
covered with the shadow of night, and both ministers and
people were sunk in ignorance, who were they who fanned
the dying spark into a flame, and relumed and warmed the

Church into new life? Who were Wycliffe, Jerome, Luther, Melancthon, Calvin, Latimer, Ridley, Cranmer, Knox, and others who might be mentioned, but the most learned and most eloquent men of their age, whose writings are even now read with profit and delight? Lastly let us ask, who are those who have continued the work so nobly begun by the first reformers? Who the men that have contributed by their labors and writings to preserve true doctrines and recommend the true practice of religion to succeeding generations, and who are now quoted by all denominations as the standards of holiness and orthodoxy? Who but Tillotson, Chillingworth, Hooker, Hammond, Baxter, Doddridge, Watts, Horseley, Porteus, Buchanan, Faber and Chalmers, —men skilled in all the departments of science which could throw one ray of light, or even one argument towards the great truths of revelation. These are the men whom God has in every age raised up for the defence of that faith which he hath determined to preserve by the instrumentality of man.

"In His infinite mercy He hath vouchsafed the blessing of Christianity to us through the pious affection of our forefathers. Shall we not faithfully guard it, and religiously bequeath it to our children by the means of his own appointment? That is the question before the American churches."

Subjoined to this interesting circular is a list of the subscriptions obtained by the single exertions of Mr. John Nelson of Mecklenburg County, amounting to about $11,000 to be paid in three annual installments. The circular is signed by the following board of managers:—

Right Rev. Richard C. Moore, D. D., Bishop of Virginia, President; William Meade, Vice-President; Edward C. M'Guire, Secretary; William H. Wilmer, D. D.; John S. Ravenscroft; Oliver Norris; Enoch M. Lowe; Burwell Bassett, Esq.; William Mayo, Esq.; John Gray, Esq.; Hugh Mercer, Esq.; Dr. Carter Berkley, Esq.; John Nelson, Esq.

This eloquent statement and appeal, which has been quoted only in small part, shows the ideals which dominated the minds of this first Board of Trustees of the Theological Seminary in Virginia. It is significant that it is an appeal primarily for a School of the Prophets. The reason for this is to be found partially in the conditions of the times, and partially, also, in the fact that most of the clergy who composed the Board, and indeed most of those who in the early years of the Seminary served as its professors, were trained under the Puritan influences of the North, having, in many instances, attended Andover Theological Seminary or having graduated at Princeton Theological Seminary.

This appeal and many others of similar nature, issued by the Education Society and the Board of Trustees, succeeded in awakening the dormant Church to the necessity of establishing a Theological Seminary in Virginia.

It is interesting to note that just at this time an effort was being made in the diocese of Maryland to establish there also a Theological Seminary. The Theological Repertory of October 1822, page 95, reports "the second meeting of the Board of Trustees of the Theological Seminary of the Protestant Episcopal Church in the diocese of Maryland, located in the District of Columbia, which meeting was held in Georgetown on the third of October." Agents were appointed for the collection of funds and the Rev. William H. Wilmer, D. D. was nominated as the professor of this Seminary, and a financial committee was appointed to regulate the fiscal concerns of the Institution. The Board of Trustees of this proposed Seminary consisted of: The Right Rev. James Kemp, D. D., President; Rev. John P. K. Henshaw, Vice-President; Rev. Henry D. Davis, D. D., Annapolis; Rev. William E. Wyatt, D. D., Baltimore; Rev. George Weller, Cambridge; Rev. William Hawley, Washington; Rev. John Johns, Frederickstown; Rev. Charles P. McIlvaine, Georgetown; Rev. Stephen H. Tyng, Georgetown; Hon. John C. Herbert, Prince George County; Francis Scott Key, Esq., Georgetown; Clement Smith, Esq., Georgetown; Elisha De Butts, M. D., Baltimore; Thomas Henderson, M. D., Georgetown.

The Maryland Convention which met in Baltimore on the 28th of May, 1823, adopted a resolution by which all further proceedings on the part of this Board of Trustees were suspended, and further resolved that "their proceedings shall not be renewed except the proposition to that effect be made at one Convention, published on its journals, and passed at the next Convention."*   This resolution brought to an end the Maryland Theological Seminary, the establishment of which was strongly opposed by Bishop Kemp.

On the 2nd of July, 1823, the Education Society rescinded the resolution to establish a Theological Professorship at the College of William and Mary, and it was "Resolved that the said Professorship be established in Alexandria, in the District of Columbia."

In 1823 an address was issued by the Board of Managers of the Society and signed by Dr. William H. Wilmer and all the officers of the Society, which expresses the convictions of the Education Society relative to the need for a Theological Seminary in the South.   The reasons actuating those who were primarily responsible for founding the Theological Seminary in Virginia can best be recorded in the words of this forceful and official statement, whch is as follows:

ADDRESS OF THE BOARD OF MANAGERS OF THE EDUCATION SOCIETY. †

"Until the year 1817 no Seminary for theological instruction under the patronage of our Church existed in this country. At that time measures were taken in General Convention for the establishment of a General Seminary to be located in the city of New York.   At the following Convention, in 1820, measures were instituted in furtherance of this object, and the location of the Seminary was transferred to New Haven.   At a subsequent special Convention in 1821, it was again removed to New York.   In reference to this Institution it is proper to observe that whilst we admit the obvious advantages which may be connected with the General Seminary and whilst it is our earnest desire that the Seminary now formed under the auspices of the Church may be so sustained and conducted as to prove of the most extensive benefit; it must also be confessed, that there are many important exigencies which a general Institution can never meet.   The remoteness of some parts of our extended country from the city of New York; the necessary expenses

---

* From "The Theological Repertory" 1823.   Vol. IV, page 348.

† From "The Theological Repertory" August 1823.

of a residence there, already felt and complained of by some who have gone thither for instruction, must certainly preclude very many from sharing the benefits of the Seminary established in that place. Peculiarly must this consideration operate upon the measures of our Society and ever prevent us, if there were no other reason, from enabling our beneficiaries to enjoy the instruction of that Seminary, since we are obliged by so many pressing applications to manage our funds with the most rigid economy. Besides this, there seems a peculiar fitness that candidates should be trained upon the theatre on which they are hereafter to act, and thus become assimilated in habits and manners with the people among whom they are destined to officiate.

"On these accounts diocesan schools, not only have not been considered as hostile to the General Seminary, but seem to have been contemplated in its provision for establishment of branches as necessary auxiliaries and adjuncts to that Institution.

"Accordingly, when the House of Bishops gave their consent to the removal of the General Seminary from New York to New Haven, they declared "that in concurring in the resolutions relative to the Theological Seminary they did not mean by this concurrence to interfere with any plan now contemplated or that may hereafter be contemplated in any diocese or dioceses for the establishment of Theological Institutions or Professorships." *

"The Society to which we belong in accordance with these principles and views was formed in the year 1818, consisting of members of the dioceses of Maryland and Virginia for the purpose of affording the means of education for the ministry of the Episcopal Church. It was resolved in the year 1820 'To establish a Professorship to be located at the College of William and Mary, or elsewhere, as the Society from time to time directs,' and an address was published setting forth this object and calling for the friends of the Church to aid in its promotion."

At a meeting of the Board of Managers in Georgetown, on the 2nd of July, 1823, the resolution to establish a Theolog-

---

* Journals of General Convention.

ical Professorship in Williamsburg having been rescinded, the following resolution was unanimously adopted:—

"Whereas the Convention of the Diocese of Virginia has established a Theological Seminary which it is expected will ere long go into operation, be it Resolved that the beneficiaries of this Society, who are students of Theology, be placed under the care of that Institution, when it shall have commenced operations; and, that in the meantime, the Rev. Dr. Keith, who is to reside in the city of Alexandria, be appointed to take charge of them, and any other students that may be disposed to place themselves under his instruction in that place. Be it also Resolved that the sum of six hundred dollars be paid the Rev. Dr. Keith as a salary for one year to commence from the 1st of July, 1823."

"Alexandria is recommended as a place for carrying into effect the views of the Board by several considerations. Access may be had there to an excellent Library, and lodging and board can be obtained upon the most reasonable terms. The District of Columbia, from its being the resort of a great share of the intelligence of our country and the emporium of its jurisprudence and oratory, presents a school which in these particulars is certainly unrivalled in the United States. Nowhere in the Southern Country, nowhere south of Philadelphia, is the Episcopal interest so concentrated and powerful as in Alexandria, and its neighborhood. Six Episcopal Churches in the district with as many ministers, closely united in plans and feeling, possessing opportunities of easy and constant intercourse, offering their libraries and every assistance in their power to candidates for orders in Alexandria, present considerations too important to be disregarded.

"The Rev. Dr. Keith, a clergyman well-known, and very highly prized for his talents and learning and piety, will begin his instructions in Alexandria on the 15th of October next (1823).

"It seems unnecessary to prove to you the need of such an Institution, for you must be well aware of the lamentable deficiency of our ministry in the southern country, when compared with the widespread devastation and incessant entreaties of our Churches for those that can break to them the bread of life.   A calculation made with great care some two or three years ago, furnishes the following results:

"Forty-six counties in Virginia have no Presbyterian minister; the whole state has not one Congregational minister; forty-six counties containing a population of more than three-hundred thousand, have neither Episcopalian nor Presbyterian ministers.

"The state, according to the census of 1810, contains nine-hundred seventy-four thousand inhabitants, and but ninety-two Episcopal and Presbyterian ministers, leaving upward of eight-hundred eighty-two thousand souls destitute of such ministers.

"Virginia is peculiarly the state of Episcopalians.   Originally established there and liberally endowed, the scattered congregations of our Church are discovered over all its regions and very numerous and most deplorable are the crumbling remains of our once excellent temples, constantly reminding us that ministers, zealous and well-qualified, and not materials and people, are especially needed to build up the waste places of Zion."

This address is signed by the Rev. William H. Wilmer, D. D., as President, and all the other officers and managers of the Education Society.

At a meeting of the Education Society held in Alexandria, D. C., on October 30th, 1823 "The report of the Board of Managers contains the statement that in connection with the Seminary just opened in Alexandria, in addition to the course of lectures to be given by Professor Keith, provision is also made for a course on Systematic Theology, Ecclesiastical Polity, and Church History." *

This meeting of the Education Society was held two weeks after the Seminary opened in Alexandria on October 15th, 1823.   "The Rev. Dr. Keith" says Dr. Packard, "gave his entire time to teaching the Old and New Testament, Biblical Criticism and Evidences.   Rev. Dr. Wilmer, rector of St. Paul's, taught Systematic Divinity, Church History, and Polity, without compensation.   In the spring of 1825, the Rev. Mr. Norris, rector of Christ Church, Alexandria, was

---

* From "The Theological Repertory" October 30th, 1823.

chosen Professor of Pastoral Theology, but was soon after seized with fever and died."

During this period and for many subsequent years the Education Society was the unfailing and indispensable ally of the Seminary. The establishment of the Seminary in Alexandria stimulated its endeavors and widened the circle of its influence. The pressing need of larger resources spurred the Society on to more earnest endeavor to enlist a new and enlarged clientele. In 1824, we find the names of Rev. Dr. Milner of New York City, Mr. Nathan B. Crocker of Providence, Rhode Island, Mr. John Boyd of Philadelphia, and Mr. Steven W. Prestman of New Castle, Delaware, among the members of the Board of Managers.

The larger need for support enlisted the cooperation of the women of the Church, and in 1824, and subsequently, frequent mention is made, in the newspapers of the Church, of Female Societies auxiliary to the Education Society. The "Theological Repertory" of January 1824 contains the constitution of the auxiliary society formed in the city of Baltimore under the title "The Constitution of the First Sewing Society of the Protestant Episcopal Church, Baltimore." This constitution, which served as a model for many similar organizations auxiliary to the Education Society, has been included in the appendix of this book, following the minutes of the Education Society.

The Rev. Dr. Walker makes record of the fact that in 1832 a list of these auxiliary societies was published, showing that there were then twenty-seven in existence. In addition to those in Virginia and Maryland branches were then in existence in Brooklyn, New York, and Beaufort, South Carolina. Bishop Meade had, from the organization of this society, of which he was a charter member, been its firm and constant advocate. After his consecration to the episcopate in 1829 in his visitations throughout Virginia he gave his support to these organizations and lent the strong influence of his personality and of his office to the appeal for increased support for the Education Society and the Seminary.

"This organization was," says Dr. Walker, "the first of its kind in the Episcopal Church in this country, and for thirty years was the only one in existence."

Its name in the light of its early history is misleading. Popularly designated at first as "the Education Society of Maryland and Virginia" and subsequently as the "Education Society of Virginia," it was in reality distinctly general both as to the scope of its appeal and as to the extent of its benefactions. Its sympathy and its interest knew no sectional bounds. This is shown by the fact that its first beneficiary was a student from Vermont, the second from Virginia, the third from New York, and the fourth from Philadelphia. The records show that its assistance was extended to students from practically every diocese in the American Church.

We refrain from giving here in detail and at length the names of the subscribers to the Education Society. In the current numbers of the "Theological Repertory," beginning with 1818 and extending through many years, and later in "the Southern Churchman," are to be found lists of the subscribers to this organization and the acknowledgment of the amounts contributed. (See special chapter on Contributions to the Seminary). These lists include the names of practically every family prominent in the life of the Church in Virginia during the early years of the existence of this organization, and also the names of devoted Churchmen in many other parts of the United States. It is of interest to note that the first contribution was made in connection with the meeting of October 1818, held in St. John's Church, Georgetown. Bishop Meade reports $50 as the life-membership of Dr. Alexander Balmaine, $50 from the Church at Winchester, and $5 from a Sacramental offering.

Among the early donors are found the names of Mrs. Mary Custis, who makes an annual subscription of $10, and a contribution of $20 from the Hon. John Randolph of Roanoke through Bishop Meade.

The Minute book of the Standing Committee of the Education Society is still in existence and is in the Seminary Library. As first organized Rev. Dr. William H. Wilmer was Chairman and Rev. Ethan Allen, Secretary, the other members being the Rev. Mr. Hawley and Rev. Dr. Keith.

The minute book contains the record of the proceedings of the Committee from June, 1825 to May, 1844. It makes record chiefly of the action of the committee with reference to the applications of those seeking the aid of the Society while at the Seminary or while at college preparatory to entering the Seminary. It contains also many other notes of interest. It shows that the Education Society was, during this period, and for many subsequent years, the commissary and treasury department of the Seminary. It would appear, indeed, that this organization was an indispensable factor to the very existence of the Seminary. It not only contributed from $60 to $112 to cover the cost of the students' board, but it helped to maintain the boarding department, paid the salaries of the Seminary matrons and the wages of the servants, bought brooms, fuel, and milk, whitewashed and repaired the buildings, and paid the salary of the negro janitor. The Society subsequently paid for the erection of houses for the professors when the Seminary moved to "The Hill," and also for many years paid the salaries in whole or in part of the professors who lived in them. Dr. Keith, Dr. Lippitt, Dr. Packard, Dr. Sparrow and Dr. May are all mentioned in the records as receiving salary payments from the Society.

A number of notes copied from the minute book of this Committee have been appended to the early minutes of the Education Society printed in the appendix.

The subsequent activities of the Education Society and its Standing Committee, as they relate to the life of the Seminary, will be noted as we trace the progress and development of the Institution.

When it is borne in mind that the Education Society, since its establishment in 1818, has helped between nine hundred and a thousand young men in their preparation for the ministry of the Church, training a number of them before the Seminary was formally and fully established; and when its further and invaluable aid to the Institution, as hitherto mentioned, is recalled, most cordial assent can be given to the opinion expressed in the Episcopal Recorder of April 1825, namely, that "The facts detailed relative to the Education Society and its connection with the Theological Seminary of Virginia prove conclusively, I think, that that important Institution owes its existence and present flourishing state mainly to this Society, and had all its funds been expended in rearing up this school of the prophets, it would richly deserve the confidence and support of the Church which has sustained it."

In 1835 it was reported by the Secretary of the Society that "nearly one-tenth of the clergy in the Protestant Episcopal Church in the United States have in whole or in part been assisted by this society. One-sixth of the present clergy of Ohio, one-eighth of those of Pennsylvania, one-fifth of those of Maryland, and a large proportion of those in Virginia have derived aid from its funds, while it is now affording assistance to about one-seventh of all the students in the several theological schools of the Church in the United States." In addition to all this, the Education Society contributed from its funds money to aid in purchasing the present site of the Theological Seminary in Virginia, and paid in full the salary of the Rev. Dr. Lippitt, who was appointed to the Chair of Systematic Theology in 1826.

THE DATE OF THE FOUNDING OF THE SEMINARY

In the light of the records which have been quoted, it is clearly evident that the Education Society, from the time of its organization in 1818 up to the time of the formal establishment of the Theological Seminary in Virginia by action of the Virginia Convention and its location in Alexandria in 1823, had been doing real pioneer Seminary work.

This endeavor constituted in purpose and fulfilled in reality the object for which a Seminary exists. This organization selected learned and devoted clergymen of the Church, and commissioned them to teach those who sought entrance into the ministry of the Church. It examined the qualifications and gave its sanction of approval to those who desired to study for holy orders, and it solicited funds and provided the means for their support during the prosecution of their studies. If this endeavor and its fulfillment constitutes the existence of a Seminary, then the Seminary of Virginia began with the formation of this Society in June, 1818. If the formal establishment of a theological professor-

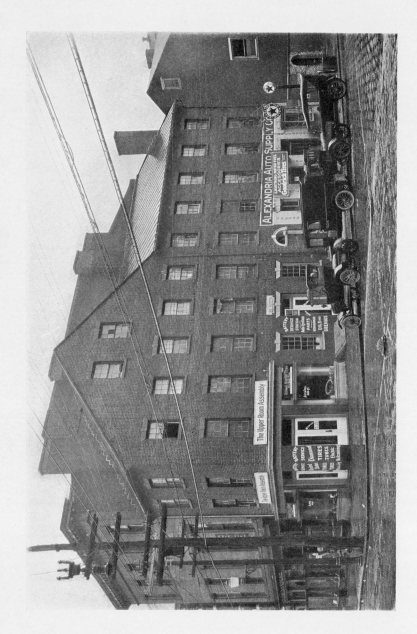

THE FIRST HOME OF THE SEMINARY—1823

Corner of King and Washington Streets, Alexandria, Virginia

ship in an incorporated institution under the sanction of the
president and Trustees of such institution constitutes the
founding of a school of Theology, then the Seminary in
Virginia dates from the establisment of a chair of Theology
in the College of William and Mary in Williamsburg, Virginia in 1820, under the professorship of the Rev. Dr. Reuel
Keith.   If, however, the recognized existence and distinctive
character of an institution dates from the authorized action
of the Board of Trustees, not only in selecting the professors,
but also in renting a building in which the classes are to be
taught by a faculty of more than one man, then the Theological Seminary in Virginia dates from October 15th, 1823,
when the work of training men for the ministry in Virginia,
which had been going on under other conditions above mentioned since 1818, was begun in the town of Alexandria.
While it would seem that a rightful claim to the year
1818 might be made and maintained as the date of
the origin of the Virginia Seminary, the Board of
Trustees, by their action in 1873 in designating that year for
the Semi-Centennial Celebration of this Institution, gave
their sanction, at least, to the year 1823 as the year in which
the Seminary was founded.   The Trustees rented the building in Alexandria at the corner of King and Washington
Streets which constituted the first formally recognized abiding place of the Theological Seminary in Virginia.

The Seminary in Alexandria

The year 1823 found the Rev. William H. Wilmer, D. D.
Rector of St. Paul's Church, Alexandria.   Associated with
Dr. Wilmer, as a teacher of a school, which was held in the
Sunday School room of St. Paul's Church, was Mr. John
Thomas Wheat, who subsequently graduated from the Sem-
inary in the class of 1825.   "That little schoolhouse" says
Rev. Dr. Packard, "was the birth place of the present Sem-
inary."

The necessity for another and larger building was, however, immediately felt.   It was therefore determined to rent
a brick building which stood on the south-east corner of
King Street and Washington Street in Alexandria.   "This
house," says Dr. Packard, "was the home of Miss Sally

Griffith, the daughter of the Rev. Dr. David Griffith, who
was elected first Bishop of Virginia in 1786 but was unable
to find means to go to England for his consecration, his
salary being then only $250 a year and his friends being un-
able to raise the money to send him to England. In her
house Professor Keith and four of the students lived, and all
of his recitations were in that building. How many pass it,
even of our alumni, on the streets of Alexandria, without
any recognition or knowledge of its existence or associations.
Judging from the various signs on its walls, it has now a
variety of uses. 'Ah Moy Laundry' is one of the most prominent, the corner room facing both streets, on the lower floor.
A 'heathen Chinee' in the room of Dr. Keith! 'W. E. Dienelt,
Ophthalmic Optician, Eyes Examined Free,' is another sign in
a line with the former, towards Duke Street. Beyond this
are two others of a plumber and gas-fitter. On the second
floor, fronting King Street, is another. 'Rooms of the Business League of Alexandria'; and on the same floor, fronting
Washington street, there is another, of 'a school of short-
hand and typewriting.' Thus the original Seminary still
has its hive of workers. But of what different nature and
for what different purposes!" *

This building is still standing. The same Chinaman, or
a Chinese successor, still occupies the laundry establishment
in the room on the corner, but the "Alexandria Auto Supply
Company" has supplanted some of the tenants mentioned
by Dr. Packard.

Before the close of the Alexandria period of the Seminary
history, certain changes took place with reference to the
accommodations provided for the students, although Dr.
Keith and a number of the students continued to use the
original building on King Street. "Dr. Keith," says the
Rev. George A. Smith, "and a few students who entered the
opening of the Seminary, were domiciled in the house of
Miss Sally Griffith at the corner of King and Washington
Streets, except Mr. Cook and myself who had been previously boarding with Dr. Wilmer. At a later period Mr. (afterwards Dr.) May boarded at Mrs. Page's at the corner of

* "Recollections of a Long Life" by Dr. Packard. page 81.

Prince and Alfred Streets.   All of Dr. Keith's recitations
were held in this building.   Dr. Wilmer's, I think, were
held in the Vestry Room of St. Paul's Church.   I found also
students living in the house at the corner of Washington and
Duke Street, kept by Miss Peggy Ashton, who was a kind of
mother to the students.   This arrangement was continued
until the removal of the Seminary to its present site."

With the abandonment of the William and Mary Theological Professorship the Rev. Dr. Reuel Keith was called to be
the head professor in the Seminary opened in Alexandria on
October 15, 1823.   The circumstances leading to the first
finding of Dr. Keith and his selection for this teaching work
are told in an address by Mr. J. Holdsworth Gordon, Vestryman of Christ Church, Georgetown, D. C., delivered at the
Seminary on the occasion of the celebration of the one hundredth anniversary of the Education Society held in the
Seminary Chapel on June 6th, 1918.   We quote from Mr.
Gordon's address, which is to be found in full in The Southern Churchman of June 29th and July 6th, 1918, as follows:

"In November, 1817, Christ Church Parish, Georgetown,
D. C., was organized.   After much deliberation and careful
survey of the field the rector selected to lead the new parish
was the Rev. Reuel Keith.   As showing the very high esteem
in which Mr. Keith was held, I quote from the letter of the
vestry calling him to the rectorship.   This letter, found
amongst the records of our parish, is dated December 1817:

'The most prominent, important and interesting duty
devolved on us is the selection of a minister in whose devotion to the religion of Christ, and the doctrines and forms of
the Episcopal Church, the utmost confidence can be placed.
We are very happy in assuring you that we have reason to
expect from you a conscientious discharge of the duties
attached to the ministerial character, and therefore take
unfeigned pleasure in asking you to take charge of the
congregation.'

"This shows the very high esteem in which Mr. Keith was
held as a churchman, a man of undoubted devotion to the
religion of Christ and loyal to the doctrines and ritual of our
own church.   Mr. Keith accepted the call thus made and
continued in charge of the parish until January, 1820, when

he was called to take the Theological Chair at William and Mary College. Our minutes also contain the letter addressed by the rector on his retirement to accept the duties he was to assume. It shows the pious and fervent character of the man selected for the chair as well as his loving and affectionate disposition. The letter bears date January 20, 1820, and in it the writer says:

'It is with emotions more painful than I can recollect to have felt on any occasion that I sit down to communicate to you the determination of my mind respecting the Williamsburg professorship. With my present situation I have ever been and am still not merely pleased, but highly delighted. My prospect of usefulness is certainly all that could be reasonably expected in any congregation....No town that I have ever seen appeals to me preferably, as a place of residence, to this healthy, beautiful and flourishing city. The tokens of friendship and affection which I have received from that portion of its inhabitants which constitute the congregation of Christ Church are such as I despair of ever experiencing from any other people. The thought, therefore, of separating from a people for whom I cherish a devoted attachment (the full force of which I never felt till now), for whose eternal welfare I have through the grace of God long felt the deepest concern, with whom I confidently hoped to close my labors, and to finish my course on earth, is inexpressibly distressing. But after having three times positively declined leaving here, at length in defiance of the influence of my attachment to my congregation, over the decision of my understanding and wholly against my will, I am brought to the conclusion that it is my indispensable duty to go. I cannot but consider the situation of William and Mary College in connection with the state of religion in Virginia and the adjacent States, such as to render me altogether inexcusable before God, were I to decline the invitation given me to become one of its officers.'

"Comfort, and loved surroundings, all that could contribute to human happiness, are cast aside and counted as nothing worth at the call of duty; a duty entailing hard labor, mental anguish and promising disheartening disappointments. Of such mould was Reuel Keith.

"Dr. Keith" says Mr. Gordon, "is described as being tall and slender. His visage, complexion, eyes and hair, dark. His memory retentive, quick and active. He ranked high as a preacher and had a very melodious voice. Another, speaking of him, said that while in the pulpit the subject of his discourse 'seemed to absorb his whole inner man, and control his outer. In mind and body he seemed magnetized, charged with gospel sentiment and emotion, love of Christ, benevolence towards men, zeal for religion and deep humility before God.'"

Such was the first rector of Christ Church Parish, and the head teacher of this Seminary in the days of its infancy.

Upon the removal of the Seminary to Alexandria, Dr. Keith became head professor and gave his entire time to the work of teaching, his course being the Old and New Testament, Biblical Criticism, and Evidences.

Following the minute recording the acceptance of Mr. Keith's resignation, we find evidence of the deep interest of the parish in the work he was about to undertake, for the following appears:

"Resolved—That it is expedient to form a Society for the Education of pious young men for the ministry of the Episcopal Church, auxiliary to that now in existence, for the Dioceses of Maryland and Virginia."

Dr. Keith had been trained under Moses Stuart at Andover Seminary. In connection with his work as Professor in the Virginia Seminary, he translated Hengstenberg's Christology from the German in 1836, and used it as a text book in his course. It was said of this book that it was one of the best translations that had ever been made into English.

The Rev. Dr. William H. Wilmer, who, before the Seminary was started had, without compensation, given himself to the work of training men for the ministry, became professor of Systematic Divinity, Church History, and Church Polity in the newly organized Seminary in Alexandria. He served in this capacity without compensation, while still rector of St. Paul's Church, until 1826, when he resigned to accept the position of President of the College of William and Mary and the rectorship of Bruton Parish Church. His work in Williamsburg lasted only one year, his death occuring on July 14th, 1827, in the forty-third year of his age.

The failure on the part of those in years gone by to recognize the interlaced relationship of the Education Society with the early history of the Seminary; the non-recognition of the fact that this Society actually did the initial work of the Seminary, and was the chief spring from which the ever-widening stream of the life of the Seminary flowed—this failure has led, until more recent years, to the belated recognition of the place of honor which the Rev. Dr. William H. Wilmer held as the prime moving spirit in these pioneer days in bringing the Seminary into existence. The careful reading of the records of the Education Society and of the proceedings of the Virginia Church Conventions gives convincing evidence that to him, under the blessing of God, this Institution owes a debt of gratitude and appreciation of which the lately dedicated "Wilmer Hall" will bear perennial witness.

In the spring of 1825 the Rev. Oliver Norris, rector of Christ Church, Alexandria, was elected Professor of Pastoral Theology, but shortly afterwards, in August, became the victim of fever and died. "He was a man," says Dr. Packard, "of gentle, persuasive manners, and deep piety, a tender and faithful pastor and preacher."

In 1826 the Rev. E. R. Lippitt was appointed Professor of Systematic Divinity. "He was," says Dr. Packard, "of a distinguished family in Rhode Island and had been in the Diocese, a few years before, as rector of Norborne parish, Berkeley county. He was a graduate of Brown University, and had been master of the Latin school there. He was highly recommended for the position of professor and was here until 1842, when he resigned. Dr. Sparrow said that his mind was highly cultivated, but that his extreme modesty repressed the exhibition of his powers. He was the only man I ever knew overburdened with modesty."

We have this account written in 1873 by Dr. Clemson of Delaware, who was graduated in 1826: "There were but few students in my time, and they had happy homes in the families of Miss Peggy Ashton and Miss Sally Griffith. The professors then were the Rev. Dr. Keith, Dr. Wilmer, and Mr. Norris. The Rev. Mr. Norris was a lovely man, of the greatest piety; and he always reminded me of the Apostle John. The Rev. Dr. Keith was the main professor. He was a man of fine intellect and attainments, but rather severe in his piety. All respected and revered him. He was remarkable for his very solemn and impressive manner in prayer, and in his extempore addresses. The Rev. Dr. Wilmer was a bland, cheerful, companionable man. The students found him very accessible and affectionate, his manner inviting confidence. He was a very popular and beloved pastor. He and the Rev. Mr. Norris had services, in the evenings of the week, which were of social character, and in which the students were invited to exercise their gifts. They were, all three, men who honored their calling, as Ministers and as Teachers. I revere their memory, and revert with sad pleasure to those early days. The opening years of the Seminary were very auspicious. They were wise and true men who made choice of such fit instruments, for laying the foundation, as it has been reared, of so grand a superstructure to the glory of God."

The Rev. Dr. Joseph Packard who continued his work at the Seminary until the time of his death in 1902, speaks out of personal knowledge of these early days. "The session of 1824 opened with twenty-one students. The course of study was good. The four Gospels and the Acts of the Apostles were critically studied in Greek, and eighteen chapters of Genesis and thirty Psalms in Hebrew by the Junior Class, besides the usual English studies. The Senior Class studied all the Epistles, and twenty chapters of Isaiah in Hebrew, with Systematic Divinity and Church History, etc. Each member of this class, as now, had in his turn to prepare a thesis, a sermon, and to read the service. On these occasions the students were permitted to offer their criticisms and remarks on the performances, which must have made things lively and interesting, and the next week each of the professors criticised them. In the class of 1824 was the Rev. Caleb J. Good, with whom I was associated at Bristol College as colleague, and with whom I was very intimate, for he was my dearest friend there. He was afterwards professor at Trinity College, Connecticut. He was a man of earnest piety, and faithful in every sphere—as preacher, as teacher, and as friend. He was for some time in Caroline county, Virginia." Dr. Packard further speaks with affectionate memory of the Rev. John T. Wheat, D. D. of the class of 1826 and of the Rev. Dr. John T. Brooke, also of the class of 1826, father of the Rt. Rev. Francis Key Brooke, Bishop of Oklahoma, and of other members of the classes from 1826 to 1828. *

These were the men whose lives and teachings are associated with the Alexandria period of the life of the Seminary, which extended from October 15th, 1823, to the fall of 1827, when the Seminary was removed to its present location on "The Hill."

"As an item of interest," says Dr. Walker in his manuscript History of the Seminary, "we may note the number of students in attendance while the Seminary was located in Alexandria. In 1823-4, with Dr. Keith and Dr. Wilmer, there were from twelve to fourteen students, and three graduates: Rev. George A. Smith graduating in 1823. In 1824-5, with Dr. Keith, Dr. Wilmer and Mr. Norris, there were twenty-one students and seven graduates. In 1825-6, with Dr. Keith, Dr. Wilmer, and Professor Lippitt, there were twenty students and nine graduates. In 1826-7, with Dr. Keith and Professor Lippitt, there were ten students and four graduates. In 1827-'28, the year of the removal, with Dr. Keith and Professor Lippitt, there were seventeen students and seven graduates.

"In this list mention may be made of George A. Smith, the first graduate, at one time rector of Christ Church, Norfolk, later on editor of the Episcopal Recorder, and later still of the Southern Churchman, and still later head of the Clarens School near the Seminary; of John T. Brooke, who did a large work in Maryland and Ohio; of William F. Lee, who began with missionary work in Virginia, was afterwards rector of St. John's and Christ Church, Richmond, and who later on, when in failing health, was the first editor of the Southern Churchman; of John P. McGuire, who did a great missionary work in the Northern Neck, and afterwards was rector of the Episcopal High School; of John T. Wheat,

* "Recollections of a Long Life" by Dr. Packard. pages 84-88.

first in pastoral and later in educational work; of James May, with his pastorate in Wilkes-Barre and Philadelphia, and his twenty years of teaching for the Seminary. To these may be added John Grammer and Leonard H. Johns, and Mr. M. T. C. Wing, eminent and effective in their work of pastoral effort, and Mr. Wing in his special work of teaching."

A hundred years have elapsed since 1823 when the Theological Seminary in Virginia found its first abiding place and a welcome in Alexandria. We are sure from the way they look today that the old cobblestones must have paved the streets as they do now, and doubtless then, as now, the grass grew between the stones, somewhat softening their appearance though in no way deadening the sound of traffic. Dr. Keith and Dr. Wilmer must often have had to raise their voices, as Demosthenese did on the shore of the sea, to overcome the roar of sound as the stage-coach rolled by, or as gigs and carts rattled over the streets. Yet it would hardly occur to the historian of today that the Seminary deserted Alexandria in a quest for quiet. The voice from the hills was, however, heard, and the call of the woods responded to, and the Seminary, baptized and named down by the waters of the Potomac, passed, in 1827, into the Wilderness and found amid the silence and beauty of "The Hill" its permanent home.

SECTION III

THE SUBSEQUENT HISTORY OF THE SEMINARY

REV. W. A. R. GOODWIN, D. D.

BIBLIOGRAPHY

Recollections of a Long Life, Rev. Dr. Joseph Packard—Manuscript History of the Seminary, Rev. Dr. Cornelius Walker—Old Churches and Families in Virginia, Bishop Meade—Diary of a Refugee, McGuire—Memories of General William Pendleton, Susan Pendleton Lee—Life of Phillips Brooks, Allen—Semi-Centennial Reports and Addresses, 1873—Life of Bishop Meade, Bishop Johns—Life of Bishop Moore—Complete file of Virginia Seminary Magazines—Theological Repertory, First six volumes.—Bound volumes of the Southern Churchman, 1835 to 1902.—Original Minute Books, Board of Trustees—Four Volumes, 1821 to 1922, (Minutes from 1840—1861 in volume lost)—Episcopal Recorder 1835—Complete Minutes of the Education Society from 1818 to 1922—Minute Book of the Standing Committee of Education Society from 1825 to 1844—Complete Minutes of the Alumni Association from 1836 to 1922, Three volumes—Manuscript Diary of Rev. F. D. Goodwin, Class of 1831—Journals of the Council of the Diocese of Virginia—Hening's Statutes—Hawk's History of Episcopal Church in Virginia—Pamphlets published by Alumni Association—Sermons and addresses by Dr. Wilmer, Bishop Moore, Bishop Meade, and Dr. Sparrow.   Virginia Seminary Magazines.
This Bibliography does not include reference material used by the writers of the special articles contained in this volume.

CHAPTER II

1827-1837

The Ministry of Poverty in the Beginning of the Seminary—The Removal to Seminary Hill—Description of Property Purchased—Early Buildings of the Seminary—Bishop Meade's Invaluable Assistance—The Pessimism of Chief Justice Marshall—Mr. John Gray, Treasurer of the Board—Miss Mary Dobson, Matron—Opening Session on "The Hill," 1827—Rev. Dr. Reuel Keith as a Teacher—Dr. Lippitt—First Seminary Chapel—Girls' School on Seminary Hill—Presentation of Organ and Communion Silver—New Professorship Proposed—Prayers for the Increase of the Ministry—Dr. Packard elected Professor—Conditions on "The Hill" in 1836—Length of Dr. Packard's Service—Activities of the Alumni Association.

God has ever been wont to call men into the wilderness and there, in the deep stillness of the woodland or beneath the silent stars, has made them conscious of His presence and brought them into fellowship with His purpose.   The solitary place has ever been the best viewpoint for the vision of God.   The hours of deepest need and the days when the clouds hung darkest have ever been the times when men have sought most earnestly and found most really the Divine presence and help.

The Old Seminary Building and Chapel

Into the virgin forests and into the wild ways of the wilderness of Fairfax County came the Theological Seminary in Virginia in the days of its infancy.   The scene, the situation, and the circumstances connected with its permanent establishment upon "The Hill" near Alexandria were all significant and of far-reaching importance in the history of the Institution.

The Master had long ago said to his disciples, "Come ye yourselves apart into a solitary place".   He had called them up into the Mount that he might give to them there the revelation of the Kingdom of God.   Into the wilderness He Himself had gone and, looking down upon the glare and glitter of the world below, had chosen the way of the Cross, the way to the more abundant life.

And now, once again, those appointed by Him to teach chose the wilderness and the solitary place as the situation for their Seminary.   They came almost empty-handed. This was fortunate, for it rooted the Seminary in faith and in prayer.   This Institution was born out of an unfaltering trust in the love and providence of God.   The early teachers had no guarantee whatsoever of continued support, except their faith.   That they found in the silence close communion with God and used it to bring their thought into fellowship with His thought there is ample evidence in the spiritual tone, the depth and reality of their teaching.   That they lived in conscious dependence upon God for guidance and continued support is shown by the tone of the appeals set forth by the Education Society and the Board of Trustees.

It is significant that the appeals of these early days were not primarily for money, but rather for the constant and unfailing intercessions of the Church.   Convinced that they were in the path of duty and were standing where they had been called of God to serve, these early founders faced their responsibilities with an unfaltering trust.   As we shall see in the further following of the History of this Institution, the need which was most vitally and constantly felt and voiced was that the Church should ceaselessly invoke the Divine blessing upon their endeavor.   There is good reason for the Church to render heartfelt thanks to God that this Institution started without munificent endowment and passed along the path of poverty in prayer, to the days of sure progress and the years of larger prosperity.

As we have gone through many "quaint and curious volumes of forgotten lore" in search for contemporaneous records of the founding and upbuilding of this Institution; as we have read the addresses of the saintly and scholarly men who taught in this Seminary in the early days of its history; and, as we have heard out of the past the voices of Wilmer, Meade, Moore, and others, pleading with the Church for loyalty to the Seminary just because of the love which the Church should show for her crucified and risen Lord, we have felt all along the glow of the faith illuminating the day-dawn of the history of this Seminary, which has done so much to build up the fallen and desolate Church in Virginia and to carry the light of the Gospel into the darker places of the earth.

This is not by way of further introduction to the current history of the Virginia Seminary. It is the most important part of its history. The revelations of the divine purpose and the manifestations of God's providence, which give assurance of His guidance and help in human endeavor, are the most vital and important aspects of human history. If the Seminary were the result of man's endeavor alone, its history might well begin with a date in time and with the record of the names and achievements of its founders. The history of spiritual endeavor must, however, look back of human records and human achievements and find its beginnings in the thought and purpose of God, revealed through faith and love to the mind and will of man. The Virginia Seminary was a thought of God. It lingered in the divine mind and purpose until human conditions and human need brought the minds and hearts of men, upon whom the divine spirit was working, into an attitude of receptivity. Then the divine thought became incarnate and was born out of eternity into time. When the divine purpose became thus incarnate the Seminary became a visible token in God's visible kingdom of the invisible and eternal thought and love out of which it was sent "to give knowledge of salvation unto his people" that "*His* way might be known upon earth: *His* saving health among all nations".

The disadvantages of having the Seminary located in the town of Alexandria led the Board of Trustees, at the meeting in May 1827, to the determination to remove the Institution to some suitable place out in the country and near Alexandria. In June 1827 a committee of the Board of Trustees went to Alexandria and after thorough examination selected the site where the Seminary is now located. The situation was chosen, it was stated, "on account of the healthiness of the atmosphere, the beauty of its prospect and its many conveniences." The property then purchased contained about sixty-two acres of land. It was well enclosed, about half cleared, and covered with forest trees and meadow grass. Upon the land purchased was a new brick dwelling house with out-buildings.

In the Minute Book of the Board of Trustees containing the records of the Board from May, 1866, to February, 1893, there is a written record pasted on the inside binding descriptive of the deeds under which the Seminary property was secured. The record is as follows:—

"Jonah Thompson and wife by deed dated 28 Sept. 1827, conveyed to Richard Channing Moore and others as Trustees the property upon which the Seminary buildings stand including Dr. Walker's (house next to Refectory) Dr. Nelson's (house next to Chapel) and Dr. McElhinney's (house known as "Wilderness") houses, describing them by metes and bounds, containing two lots for the use of the Protestant Episcopal Theological School in Virginia.

"One Tract, twenty-four acres; Second Tract, thirty-five and one-quarter acres; Together fifty-nine and one-quarter acres.

"Augusta Lockwood, by deed dated the 28th day of May, 1838, conveyed to Richard Channing Moore and others, for the use and benefit of the Theological School of the Protestant Episcopal Church in Virginia, for the sum of $3500.00, the land upon which Dr. Packard's house stands, (house near the new Library to left of road entering Seminary grounds, now occupied by Dean Green) containing ten acres, two rods and thirty poles.

"William F. Alexander and wife, by deed dated the 26th day of June, 1839, conveyed to Richard Channing Moore and others, as Trustees for the use of the Theological School of the Protestant Episcopal Church in the diocese of Virginia, the land upon which the High School buildings are erected, "Howard", containing one hundred acres more or less, for the consideration of $5000.00.

"The whole property is as follows: Seminary Tract, fifty-nine and one-quarter acres; Dr. Packard's house, ten acres; High School, one hundred acres; total one hundred sixty-nine and one-quarter acres."

The original deed can not be found, but official copies are with other papers in the First National Bank, Alexandria, Virginia.

The money for the purchase of the property was advanced by Mr. John Gray, of Traveler's Rest, Virginia, the treasurer and liberal benefactor of the Seminary.

The site chosen is two hundred and twenty-five feet above the Potomac and is about three miles from Alexandria. From the Hill on which the Seminary stands, the city of Washington, seven miles distant, is clearly seen. The dome of the Capitol, the gilded dome of the Congressional Library, and the pure whiteness of the Washington monument rise clear against the distant sky line. Until recent years the ancient city of Alexandria slept day and night in the valley below. It has waked to a vision of its possibilities and has since gone out to meet and mingle with the out-reachings of Washington, stretching down the river. At the foot of the hills and far in the distance can be traced the winding course of the majestic Potomac. A few miles below, the lawns of Mt. Vernon slope to the river's brink and the tomb of Washington gives silent benediction to the stately river as it flows on to the sea. The country now thickly populated or intensely cultivated was then clothed with the virgin forest. "When I came to the Seminary," says Dr. Packard, "it was embosomed deep in lofty woods, which stretched nearly all the way from Alexandria, with paths and roads running through them. Twenty years later Phillips Brooks lost his way in these woods in search of the Seminary and speaks of having come at last to a fence which enclosed the forest on the Hill in which he found the Seminary buildings."

Upon this property the Board of Trustees erected, at the cost of $3000, a brick house of three stories containing twelve rooms beside the basement, which was used for a dining room and kitchen.

This building was the south wing of the old Seminary. In 1832 a north wing was added, the building being of the same size and costing the same amount as the one previously erected. Afterwards, in 1835, a central building connecting these two wings was erected, at a cost of $5000, containing thirty-six rooms, a prayer hall, and a refectory.

In 1827 $8000 was collected, entirely in Virginia, to make payment for the property purchased and for the erection of the first building. The "Theological Repertory", of 1828 (p. 427) contains four closely printed pages giving the names of the contributors, according to locality, with the amounts given. This number of the "Theological Repertory" also contains a list of books presented to the Seminary Library by Mr. William Harrison of Brandon, Prince George County, Virginia. A list of the subscribers to the Seminary fund is contained in the Virginia Council Journal of 1829. The permanent fund of the Seminary in 1829 had reached the sum of about $11,000.

It would often seem, as we review the history of great institutions and human enterprises of a vital and far-reaching nature, that God in His gracious and merciful providence has raised up and prepared especially gifted men as the chosen instruments of His purpose. They appear upon the scene of action at the moment of greatest need, prepared and thoroughly furnished for the good work in which they show themselves indispensable. These men who tower above their fellows come variously endowed; for there are diversities of gifts suited to the diversity of need. To one, God's gift is the large-hearted and generous spirit of the philanthropist, deeply conscious of his sense of responsibility for the stewardship of the material possessions of which God has made him a trustee. Upon another, there has been bestowed the spirit of wisdom and a sound mind, endowing him with the ability to guide wisely his fellows by his exercise of good judgment in all things. To another still, God gives of His own nature the spirit of a boundless patience and indomitable persever-

ance; while to others, He gives the gifts of teaching, the
capacity rightly to divide the word of truth, and a genius
for unfolding the mysteries of God, bringing to light the
latent and hidden beauty of eternal truth.   To one man there
is divinely given the creative spirit.   He appears among
his brethren as Joseph did, a dreamer of dreams and a seer
of visions.   His dreams are discounted and his visions repudiated, but he dreams on until some other man differently
endowed finds fellowship with him, and comes to share his
faith and provides the means, of which the dreamer was
destitute, for the fulfillment of the vision.   In the early life
of the Seminary these different types of men, so differently
endowed by God, met for the fulfillment of the divine purpose in the upbuilding of the Seminary.

The versatile and talented Wilmer was now dead, and
from this time on, one who had been a co-laborer with him in
the establishment of the Education Society and in founding
the Seminary now takes a place of unquestioned and dominant leadership in promoting the welfare of the Seminary.   In
the councils of the Board of Trustees, in the Church conventions of Virginia, in the pulpits of Churches all over the state
which he visited first as a missionary presbyter (because he
would not have wished us to call him priest,) and subsequently as a missionary bishop, and constantly in his private
conversations, William Meade was ever the devoted and
undaunted friend of the Seminary.   There were everywhere
reasons for discouragement.   When he applied to Chief
Justice Marshall for aid, the great jurist, distinguished for
liberality as he was for sagacity and judgment, declared his
hearty good will for the enterprise, but said that in his opinion "the Episcopal Church was so hopelessly prostrate in
Virginia that it would be wrong to encourage young men to
enter the ministry in a communion in which all their talents
and energies, however exerted, must be without fruit."

In spite, however, of such opinions,—and the opinion of
Chief Justice Marshall was generally held throughout the
state,—the Bishop had from the beginning persisted in his
untiring endeavors, and at this period and for many years
after he was preeminent as the friend and advocate of the
Seminary.

The next man of this period of whom mention should be made was Mr. John Gray, who was treasurer of the Board of Trustees of the Seminary from the time of its organization until the time of his death, when he was succeeded in office by his son-in-law, Mr. William Pollock. Mr. Gray and Mr. Pollock gave their services gratuitously to the Seminary for a period of thirty-one years. Mr. Gray not only invested and guarded the trust funds of the Institution with such watchful care that none of its funds were lost through unwise investment, but gave from his personal funds to help tide over periods of financial difficulty, and at other times lent large amounts to the Institution pending the time when funds would be available from subscriptions. He also made in his will a generous bequest to the Seminary.

Among those who filled with fidelity an important place in the life of the Seminary at this period was Miss Mary Dobson, who for many years, until 1843, discharged the duties of Matron.

The first session on "The Hill" opened in the fall of 1827 with the Rev. Dr. Reuel Keith and Professor Edward R. Lippitt resident upon the Seminary grounds, they being the only professors in the Institution until the coming of the Rev. Dr. Joseph Packard in 1836. Dr. Keith, it will be recalled, had been giving his entire time to teaching in the Institution since the Seminary opened in Alexandria in 1823, and the Rev. Dr. Edward R. Lippitt had been appointed professor of systematic divinity in 1826.

In the sections of this book devoted to the biography of the professors of this Institution, the life and life work of the Rev. Dr. Reuel Keith have been reviewed. He was the first among the six early professors of the Virginia Seminary who came to us from the North, having been born in Vermont and educated at Middlebury College and Andover Theological Seminary. He was a masterful teacher and a man of austere piety. Devoted to books from his youth, he was an accurate scholar and a proficient linguist, having thoroughly mastered the Hebrew, Greek and Latin languages, and, as has been said, being in need of a text book for one of his courses, he learned German in order to translate "Hengstenberg's Christology". In his theology he was a moderate Calvinist, and like all the early professors of the Institution, was a pronounced Evangelical. In his classroom the eloquence which he possessed, and which made him the leading preacher of his day in Virginia gave to his teaching a compelling force. Socrates was accustomed to say that all men are sufficiently eloquent in that which they know. With due deference to the opinion of Socrates, it may nevertheless be said that not all men who know the truth and who deserve the highest rank as investigators and scholars possess the ability to teach the truth to others. On the other hand, many men who are accorded the reputation of being eloquent are not sufficiently versed in the subject matter of truth to make their eloquence produce an abiding impression upon the lives of men. In Dr. Keith scholarship and eloquence were so wedded that he won the attention and the admiration of his pupils, impressed his learning and his scholarship deeply upon their minds, and roused in them an abiding sense both of gratitude and appreciation. To these facts the testimony of his early students bears abundant witness.

Dr. Keith continued to teach in the Institution until shortly before his death, which occurred in 1842.

His home on "The Hill" was the house next to the Seminary Chapel, subsequently occupied by the Rev. Dr. Sparrow, Dr. Nelson, and Dr. Wallis, and is now the home of the Rev. Dr. B. D. Tucker. This was one of the original buildings on the property purchased by the Seminary.

The Rev. Dr. Edward R. Lippitt was appointed professor of systematic divinity in 1826. He was of a distinguished Rhode Island family and a graduate of Brown University, where for a time he served as master of the Latin School. He remained professor in the Institution until 1842, when he resigned and became editor of the "Southern Churchman." Dr. Sparrow speaks of him as having possessed a mind highly cultivated, and Bishop Smith, his life-long friend, refers to him as a refined gentleman and an accurate scholar. He first occupied the house on "The Hill" which was subsequently the home of Dr. Packard and which is now occupied by the Rev. Dr. Berryman Green, Dean of the Seminary. This house, which was known as "Melrose," was also a part

"Melrose" or "The Abbey"

*The Home of Reverend Doctor Berryman Green, Dean
Former Home of Reverend Doctors Lippitt and Packard*

"Oakwood"

*The Home of Reverend Doctor Beverley D. Tucker
Former Home of Reverend Doctors Keith, Sparrow, Nelson and Wallis*

of the original Seminary purchase. Subsequently Dr. Lippitt lived in the house next to the old Library now used as a refectory and designated as Wilmer Hall. This home was afterwards occupied by Dr. May, Dr. Walker and Dr. Massie, and is now the home of Dr. Rollins.

The Southern Churchman of June 15, 1835, reports: "that a Bible Society has been formed in the Institution and a Charity School for the benefit of the neighboring poor: and that during the past year thirty-two students have been connected with the Seminary, and that the invested funds of the Institution amounted to $20,000."

In 1836 a notice appeared in the Southern Churchman relative to the Seminary Chapel. This notice also makes mention of an effort which was then being made to secure funds for an additional professorship, and announces that Mrs. Jane C. Washington, of Mt. Vernon, had presented a fine organ to the Chapel and that John Tappan, Esq., of Boston, Massachusetts, who was not an Episcopalian, had presented the Chapel, with a large and beautiful set of Communion silver, consisting of four chalices, two plates, two tankards, and a baptismal bowl. Mrs. Washington is also mentioned as an annual contributor to the fund for the establishment of a new professorship.

"There was no Chapel on 'The Hill', says Rev. Dr. Walker, "until as late as 1838-'39. Prior to this time the students attended services at Alexandria and many of them acted as teachers in the Sunday Schools of Christ Church and St. Paul's. With the erection of the middle building in 1835, with Prayer Hall in its basement, Sunday services began to be held in the Seminary." *

The increase of the population on "The Hill", the presence of from forty to fifty pupils from the School of the Rev. George A. Smith, at Clarens, located on Seminary Hill, and the establishment of the Episcopal High School adjacent to the Seminary in 1839, made the need of an adequate Chapel imperative. The first Seminary Chapel was begun in 1839 and was ready for use during the session of 1840-'41. The services were conducted by the Seminary professors and by the Rev. Dr. Pendleton, principal of the High School.

* Dr. Walker's "Manuscript"

"The Southern Churchman" of February 14, 1840, published an appeal from the Seminary professors for funds with which to complete the Chapel. This appeal says "the room in which we are compelled to worship is entirely inadequate, it is neither plastered nor has any ceiling. In its present condition the Chapel can not be occupied. Shall the thirty-two students of the Theological Seminary be left destitute of a place where they can worship Almighty God in decency and order, and shall the pupils of the High School, who by next session will number one hundred, be excluded from public worship and therefore many parents be disappointed and the hopes of the founders frustrated?" (Signed) Reuel Keith, Edward R. Lippitt, Joseph Packard.

By July the Chapel was so nearly completed that it was consecrated. In the Southern Churchman of July 17th, 1840, mention is made of the consecration service, and it adds that "a beautiful cupola has been erected in the Seminary building in which a bell has been placed of excellent tone, the gift of a few friends of the Seminary residing at the Seminary and in its neighborhood."

A communication signed by Charles Mann, Reuel Keith and E. R. Lippitt appeared in the Southern Churchman of January 29, 1835, setting forth the advantages which would follow the establishment of a "Female Boarding School" on Seminary Hill, which Mrs. Wilmer, widow of the late Dr. William H. Wilmer, was planning to open, and on April 1, 1835 announcement was made that this school was prepared to receive pupils, the terms being $130 a year, if bedding and towels were furnished by parents, and $140 if furnished by Mrs. Wilmer, payable quarterly in advance.

It is interesting to note that at this time the students of the Seminary agreed among themselves to "select some young man of piety and good talents and make him the subject of persevering prayer, and also to bring to bear upon him such means as may be lawfully used in leading an individual to enter the ministry of the gospel of Christ." The students extended the suggestion still further and proposed to every minister and student of theology throughout the country to select some young man of suitable qualifications among the communicants of the Church for intercessory prayer. *

The report of the ordination which took place in St. Paul's Church, Alexandria, on July 13, 1837, is of interest as showing the wide distribution throughout the country of the students graduating that year from the Seminary.   On this occasion Bishop Moore ordained to the diaconate Charles Goodrich, of Louisiana, David M. Fackler, William Hodges and Thomas E. Locke, of Virginia, Alcott Buckley, William J. Clark, and William Harris of Pennsylvania, and Joshua Peterkin of Maryland, and Samuel T. Carpenter of New Jersey.

At the same time the Rev. F. B. McGuire was ordained to the priesthood.   The sermon was preached by Bishop Meade from I Tim. 4:16.

In 1836 the Rev. Dr. Joseph Packard was elected Professor of Sacred Literature in the Seminary.   Dr. Packard was born in Wiscasset, Maine, on December 23rd, 1812.   He studied at Phillips Academy, Andover, and in 1827 entered the freshman class of Bowdoin College, Maine, where his brother Alpheus Packard was professor of Latin and Greek. Among his professors was Henry W. Longfellow, who in 1829 had been elected to the chair of Modern Languages and Librarian of the College.   From this institution Dr. Packard graduated with highest honors, and was one of the four in a class of twenty-one elected to the Phi Beta Kappa Society. From Bowdoin he went to Andover Theological Seminary, graduating there in 1831.   While there, although he had only recently become acquainted with the Episcopal Church, he was one of the few who met in an upper room and established the first Episcopal Church in Andover.   Among the professors at Andover while he was a student there was Moses Stuart, who taught Biblical Literature, and "exerted", says Dr. Packard, "a greater influence upon my life than any man I ever knew."

Shortly after graduating from Andover, Dr. Packard went to Bristol College, Pennsylvania, as Professor of Latin, Hebrew "and other branches of learning."   While teaching

* From "The Episcopal Recorder." January 23rd, 1836.

there, he was elected, in April 1836, Professor of Sacred Literature in the Theological Seminary in Virginia. "The election", says Dr. Packard, "was due to the influence of Professor William N. Pendleton, my colleague there, and through the influence of the Virginia students at Bristol College who at that time were twenty-five in number." It was doubtless largely through Dr. Packard that in 1839 Professor Pendleton was called to be the first Principal of the Episcopal High School.

Dr. Packard's coming to the Seminary and his first impressions of the Institution were recalled by him in his address delivered at the Semi-Centennial of the Seminary;

"When, on a crisp October afternoon in 1836 I reached the Seminary for the first time, I found it embosomed in woods. It is no wonder, as Phillips Brooks told me, that he lost his way going to the Seminary and that the road seemed to end at no place, for it was hidden in the depth of forest. The Seminary, which had been moved from Alexandria nine years before and the buildings put up in different portions after an unrecognizable order of architecture, was destitute of ornaments. The basement was low, the halls narrow, the windows with small panes. Two rooms thrown into one contained the Library of 1500 volumes.

"There were twenty-nine students in the Seminary when I came, of whom thirteen are now living. There were but two professors on "The Hill", Dr. Keith and Dr. Lippitt. The students had a common woodpile where each sawed his own wood which he carried to his room. They did not fare sumptuously every day on a board bill of $75 a year. The students took the management of the refectory pretty much into their own hands and constituted themselves an *imperium in imperio*. There would be occasionally a bread and butter rebellion when the faculty would meet the students for consultation. I remember on one occasion the difficulty was settled by resolution that the students should not be limited in their demands for fried apples.

"No carpets covered the floors. The age of luxury had not yet come. It was the iron age of the Seminary. The Post Office was in Alexandria and each student in turn walked in and brought out the daily mail. The three professors were

considered amply sufficient for instruction and all these had
to attend the weekly sermon by a student and criticize it.
The generation of clergy now on the stage is not perhaps
aware of the changes in the customs and practices of the
Church. They have silently taken place in the last fifty
years. The black gown was then worn both in the desk and
in the pulpit, and this was not peculiar to Virginia. It was
customary then at the administration of the Communion
to sing a stanza of a hymn between the different sets of communicants and the congregation repeated the General Confession and the Creed after the minister in the manner of a response. It was not uncommon for extempore prayer to be
offered after the sermon, and Bishop Eastburn advocated
the practice.

"The last fifty years have been marked not only in the
world by discoveries and inventions, but also in the Church
by its government. When I was ordained in 1836 by Bishop
Griswold, as it happened on the very day that Bishop White
died, there were about eight hundred ministers in the Episcopal Church. Since then their number has increased five-fold
and the number of communicants ten-fold." *

Dr. Packard was ordained to the Priesthood in the basement of the Seminary by Bishop Meade on September
29, 1837. ** He served as Professor in the Institution
sixty-five years, from 1836 until 1902. In 1874 he was
made Dean of the Seminary and held the position twenty-
one years, when he resigned, continuing, however, to teach
in the Seminary. It may be truly said that he taught up
to the hour of his death, which occurred on May 3, 1902;
for, though at the very last the infirmities of old age and illness
made it impossible for him to attend his classes, the presence
and power of his influence was felt by every one on "The
Hill". His life and his example were "living epistles seen
and read of all men."

The faculty of this period consisted of the Rt. Rev. Rich-
ard Channing Moore, D. D., *ex officio* President; the Rev.
Reuel Keith, D. D., Professor of Systematic Theology and
Instructor of Pulpit Eloquence; the Rev. Edward R. Lippitt,

* "Reminiscences of a Long Life" by Dr. Packard (page 73)
** From "The Southern Churchman." July 8th, 1886.

A. M., Professor of Pastoral Theology and Instructor of Ecclesiastical History; and the Rev. Joseph Packard, A. M., Professor of Sacred Literature.

The Alumni Association, at the annual meeting of the Society and through circular appeals, kept constantly before the graduates of the Seminary the dominant object of the Society at this period, which was to raise funds to pay the salary of Dr. Packard, the Professor of Sacred Literature. The Southern Churchman of July 28th, 1837, reports the action of the Alumni Association in raising funds for the salary of the professor of Sacred Literature. It is ordered that if more than $500 be secured for the salary of the Professor, the balance will be used for purchasing new books for the Library. A further resolution requests each alumnus to contribute $10 annually for the purposes indicated.

It would be quite impossible for any one fully and vividly to portray the life of the Seminary during the early years of its history after its removal to "The Hill". The historian of today and of the future can record the facts in their chronological sequence, but life is more than chronological sequence. It is linked and fused into the continuity of a creative process. In the Biblical record of the genesis of the natural and spiritual order into time, there is something more than the recital of the events with which began and ended the successive creative days. The Spirit of God is felt and witnessed to as moving over and within the void and darkness and shaping events to the fulfillment of the Divine purpose. God speaks His creative word. An atmosphere of mystic beauty and of rich and varied hue gathers about bald mountain peaks and settles over sea and vale and woodland. Harmonies which defy delineation breathe through creative processes and poems which are felt, but which defy translation, proceed from the souls of personality, and come to us out of the far past as music from sources invisible.

SECTION III

CHAPTER III

1830-1840

The Missionary Character of the Seminary—Dr. Hill and the Greek Mission—
The China Mission—The African Mission and the Seminary Chancel Rail—
Contributions made by Foreign Missions to the Church at Home—The Sem-
inary Mission Stations—The Episcopal High School—Faculty Meetings.

The chief glory of the Theological Seminary in Virginia
has been her loyalty and devotion to the mission of the
Church. This devotion was a necessary consequence of the
emphasis which she was led from the beginning by God's
Spirit to place upon the distinctive truths of the great gospel
of redemption. Teaching, as she has always done, that
the individual man is personally related to God, personally
dependent upon him for redeeming grace and the guidance
and help of the Holy Spirit, and also personally responsible
as a steward of the manifold gifts of His providence; teaching, as she has ever done, the catholic nature of the gospel
with its necessary implications as to the catholic mission
of the Church; seeing in the Cross the revelation of the
unbounded love of a Father revealed in the life and lifting up
of His Son; giving the revelation that "whosoever believeth
in Him should not perish but have everlasting life", she
has ever felt that she was a debtor, and has always taught
her sons that they were also debtors to proclaim, out of
gratitude, the message of God's love and to

> "Hasten the time appointed,
> By prophets long foretold.
> When all shall dwell together,
> One Shepherd and one Fold,"

and become partakers, through the Christ, of the blessings
of His Kingdom.

It was out of this conviction, born of truth and inspired
by love, that when the Seminary came to choose the text
to be inscribed on the chancel wall over the Communion
Table, the one selected was taken from our blessed Lord's
commission to His disciples: "Go ye into all the world and
preach the Gospel to every creature."

In recognition of the contributions made by this Seminary to the endeavor to fulfil the mission of the Church, a whole section of this book has been devoted to the recital of the part and privilege which this Institution has had in the extension of the Kingdom of Christ. It is, therefore, unnecessary to make detailed record in the current history of the Seminary of the going forth of the men who here received the inspiration which sent them into far places as heralds of the Cross and of the risen Christ. On the other hand, the history of the Seminary would cease to be current and become stagnant if the perennial flow of missionary spirit were entirely diverted from the channel of her life and endeavor. Then, again, there was a return current,—a constant inflow of inspiration which came back to the Seminary from the men who had gone into the mission field. The river of Life which makes glad the city of God makes the desert also to bloom and blossom as a rose, and flowing back again it comes with a greater depth and a richer fulness brought from the far lands whither it has gone.

The first manifestation of the missionary spirit in the life of the Seminary is to be seen in the disposition which led the first students to come to the Institution when it opened its doors to receive them. Outside of a few centers where the Church was comparatively well established, the whole territory of the United States was practically a field for missionary endeavor. The impulse which led these early students to the Seminary was, therefore, distinctly the missionary impulse, for they came with the desire either to restore the deserted temples of their forefathers, or to extend the Church and her message where neither were known. It is difficult for us in these days of easy transportation, with the country bound together by closely knit means of communication, to realize how very remote and isolated were the scattered points of light set burning by these pioneers who went out from the Seminary during the early years of its history. No part of the Church's mission is foreign to the heart and mind of God. His love knows no geographical bounds. For the sake of convenience we designate the different aspects of the mission of the Church as "Foreign" and "Domestic".

The first far-flung expression of the missionary spirit of the Seminary resulted in the establishment of the Church's mission in Greece. To us, at first glance, this seems most surprising. When we follow the unique course of this mission endeavor, it is distinctly remarkable. The Rev. Dr. John H. Hill graduated in the class of 1830. He sailed, with his wife, that same year for Greece. They established themselves in the Island of Tenos, but, finding that this was not the right field for their labors, after employing themselves in acquiring a knowledge of the language, character, and habits of the modern Greeks, they went to Athens in 1831, and in 1832, for the sum of $600, purchased a lot twenty-four feet from the beautiful Doric columns of the ancient Agora on which to erect a schoolhouse for the work of the Mission. The fact that this Mission was subsequently abandoned by the Church has tended to obscure its far-reaching importance from attention and consideration in recent years. Another reason why it is not more widely known is the fact that Dr. Hill intentionally refrained from setting up an independent or separate ecclesiastical organization in conflict with the Greek Orthodox Church. It is doubtful, however, if any missionary enterprise ever undertaken and conducted by the Church produced, in the same length of time and with the same limited expenditure of means, results so important and far-reaching as were attained through Dr. Hill's unique and exceptional work in Greece. His statesmanlike vision, his catholic charity, and the genius with which he devised and carried forward his plan, won for him the confidence and support of the Greek State and the Greek Church. Stevens, in his book entitled "Travels in Egypt, Greece, etc." speaks in the highest terms of Dr. Hill and the mission under his direction. He says, "The Greeks were warmly prepossessed in favor of our country, and the conduct of the missionaries themselves was so judicious that they were received with the greatest respect and the warmest welcome by the public authorities and the whole population of Athens."

While Dr. Hill ministered in several languages to the foreign populations resident in Athens, his chief work consisted in founding schools in which he and Mrs. Hill, Miss Baldwin, and others, taught the youth of Greece. Young women carefully selected from the various provinces were brought to the Hill School and thoroughly instructed and sent out to organize and conduct schools in every part of the country. The influence of Dr. Hill's work upon the Greek Church itself, was most far-reaching, as many of the Greek youth who afterwards entered the priesthood of the orthodox Church received their early education at the Hill Schools. The Greek King gave to Dr. Hill's work his cordial approval and expressed his interest by frequent visits to the School, and a picture in the royal palace at Athens represents King Otho, sitting upon his horse, surrounded by the children of the School on the occasion of one of his visits.

The work of Dr. Hill was strongly opposed by many in this country who did not understand the conditions under which he worked and who were not in sympathy with the purpose which he had in mind. Among these critics was the Rev. Dr. Andrews of the Seminary Board of Trustees. It is interesting to note, however, that a Presbyterian Missionary, who pursued a different course and undertook to set up an independent organization, was attacked by a mob, which destroyed his house and threatened his life. Upon the death of Dr. Hill, the whole of Greece paid him homage, and the Greeks themselves have borne testimony to the fact that his work lay at the foundation of the whole system of modern education in Greece.

The Rev. Dr. Rollins, in his chapter on the Mission in Greece, has done the Church an invaluable service in writing for the Seminary history the detailed account of this unique and exceptional endeavor of the Rev. Dr. Hill and his co-laborers.

The year 1835 stands conspicuous in the annals of the Missionary life of the Seminary. In that year the Rev. Francis R. Hanson sailed from New York to inaugurate a Mission of the Church in China. While waiting to gain entrance into the country he was joined by William J. Boone of the class of 1835, who went out from the Seminary shortly after and became the first American Bishop of the Church in China. The history of the influence of the Virginia Seminary in founding and helping to sustain the China mission is recited in full in the missionary section of this volume.

The chancel rail in the Seminary Chapel, where successive classes of students kneel to commemorate the supreme sacrifice of the Son of God, and to receive Him who gave Himself for us and gives Himself to us, is a visible memorial to another event memorable in the history of the Mission life of the Seminary. This rail was brought by Bishop Penick from the forests of Africa, where, in 1838, Payne and Savage and Minor of the class of 1836 went to inaugurate the Mission of the Church in Liberia. In the soil out of which the tree grew which furnished this communion rail to the Seminary, lie the mortal remains of Launcelot B. Minor, C. Colden Hoffman, Robert Smith, H. H. Holcomb, and E. J. P. Messenger, who were prepared for their work in this Seminary. In the graveyard at Cape Palmas, near where the waters of the Atlantic wash the sunlit sands of Africa, sleep these five martyrs of the Christian faith. Concerning one of these the London Christian Observer said: "We do not commit ourselves to terms of excessive commendation in declaring our belief that the annals of Missionary excellence do not furnish a brighter example than that of Colden Hoffman."

The Mission of the Church to Japan, inaugurated by the Rev. John Liggins of the class of 1855, and fostered through many years by another son of the Seminary, the Rt. Rev. Dr. Channing Moore Williams, and the Mission to Brazil, belong to a later date.

The Virginia Seminary would be disloyal to the faith and devotion of her sons if she did not feel just pride in the fact that through them were inaugurated the first Missionary endeavors of the American Episcopal Church in Greece, in Africa, in China, in Japan, and in Brazil.

The old Seminary building in which Boone and Payne and Savage met to offer themselves to God in the prayers of consecration and to implore His guidance in helping them to choose the way in which He would have them go, has long since vanished, but it has been replaced by other buildings where other men, through successive years, have offered like prayers and in response to the heavenly vision have answered "Here am I, send me."

"I have asked," said Rev. Dr. Slaughter, "my old classmate, Bishop Payne, the battle-scarred veteran of thirty years war in Africa, what was the cause of this uprise of the Missionary spirit, at this time in the Seminary. He replied in a late letter, that there was a general rise of the Missionary spirit in the world, occasioned by the circulation of the memoirs of Martyn, Brainard, Buchanan and others. This, he added, in connection with the earnest piety, illustrated by the lives and teachings of our professors, induced a high standard of ministerial character; but, more than to any one cause, were we indebted for this Missionary spirit, to William Boone. This view is doubtless just; but it may be that our good professors were the conductors, piercing the heavens, that attracted and concentrated this Missionary spirit which was in the air, brought it down to earth, and distributed it through these halls. There must have been something peculiar in the atmosphere which invested the Seminary Hill. I remember, too, a prayer meeting in Boone's room, conducted chiefly by Boone, Payne, Minor and Savage. I cannot but regard that prayer meeting as one of the chief motives which sent that burning light, William Boone, on his grand mission to China. It was this influence too, which helped to fire the hearts, and nerve the arms of Payne, and Minor, and Savage, to invade the entrenched camp of Satan in Africa, and plant within this camp, the banner of the Cross, which still waves as a rallying point for Missionaries, in that benighted land. I can not but devoutly thank God that it was my good fortune to be the classmate of these men. And here you will pardon me, if, in the intoxication of these memories, I invoke from all your hearts and voices everlasting honor to this little band of martyrs, and pray that the mantle of these ascended prophets may fall on us all."

From these men frequent letters came back addressed to the "Seminary Society of Inquiry concerning Missions," founded in 1824. The Church press of this period gave extensive space to the publication of the communications and appeals from these newly opened fields of Church endeavor and contained many letters from Dr. Hill, Bishop Payne,

Bishop Boone and other missionaries, especially from those who were laboring in the African mission in Liberia.

The debt of gratitude which the whole Church owes to these men is incalculable. The Virginia Seminary has given to the Church many men of distinction and some whose influence and fame have been felt and known through the whole civilized world, but her chief contribution to the Church at home has been the men whom she sent abroad. Their heroism, their devotion, their appeals, quickened the pulse of the life of the whole Church. They infused into the mind of the Church the consciousness of her mission and inspired her heart with devotion to the will and purpose of her Lord and Master.   Mention is made of Rev. Mr. Boone using the time during which the ship on which he had embarked to China was detained in Boston, in arousing deep interest in the China Mission, by preaching and making addresses in many places in Boston. The Southern Churchman of February 10, 1837, contained the following notice of the service rendered the home Church by the missionaries about to embark for the coast of Africa:

"The missionaries now waiting for the spring expedition to embark for Cape Palmas, have been diligently employed in visiting many of the parishes in Maryland and Virginia in order personally to present the subject of African Missions and when it is recollected that much of their course has hitherto been through the smaller parishes, the receipt of about $2000 by Mr. Minor in Virginia and more than $900 by Mr. Payne in Maryland, it is most encouraging evidence that the cause of Africa is coming near to many hearts and that the Church will be sustained and her Missionaries encouraged in this Mission. We especially call attention to a Sewing Circle of young ladies in Trinity Parish, upper Marlborough, Maryland, who intend to support one Missionary."

The Spirit of Missions in 1837 reports a most cordial reception given by the Bishop and clergy of South Carolina to the Rev. Mr. Minor, who had stopped at Charleston in the interest of the African mission.

As showing one way by which the Mission endeavor established bonds of fellowship, the following letter, written

by Dr. Savage, is of interest. It was dated from Mount
Vaughan, Cape Palmas, Africa, April 10th, 1837, and in
part is as follows: "I have just returned from a very
pleasant excursion in the dominions of two of the most powerful and influential kings of this region. We had a son of
each of these kings in our school. The country of King
Barrahkiddy, the mighty old chief, is very extensive, and
his good will, as well as that of Baphro, the other king, is
highly essential to our operation in this region. During
this excursion, which was performed almost wholly on foot,
we have obtained from each of the kings of the interior,
another son, for the purpose of education. I have called
the name of one of these boys 'Charles P. McIlvaine' " (it
is to Bishop McIlvaine that this letter is addressed) "and the
name of another 'J. H. Hobart' (after Bishop Hobart of New
York)." The letter concludes with an earnest appeal for
the support of the Mission.

Parishes and dioceses which might otherwise have become
as stagnant as the Dead Sea found life in giving the water of
life to the desert places in response to the appeals of these
men who gave their lives, as the Christ gave His, that others
might "have life and have it more abundantly".

From the very outset the students found opportunity
for Christian service in connection with their work
in the Seminary. In Alexandria they taught in the
Sunday School of St. Paul's Church and Christ Church and
did religious work among the fishermen, who at that time
were very numerous in and around Alexandria. When the
Seminary moved out on "The Hill", gradually Mission
Stations were established in the neighborhood, where Sunday
Schools were conducted and the Church services held by the
students who were also given license to make exhortation.
The work was done under the supervision of one of the Faculty, and members of the Faculty regularly administered the
Sacraments of the Church. The people were appreciative
and very generally gave to the students loyal and devoted
cooperation. Sometimes, however, they would make the
extra effort needed to come the longer distance to attend the
service in the Seminary Chapel, because, as one of them said
one Sunday morning, they "got tired of having the students

The Episcopal High School

practise on their souls." The history of the Seminary Mission Stations is told in a separate chapter written by the Rev. Dr. Samuel A. Wallis, who for many years while professor at the Seminary, was the devoted and beloved Pastor of the Mission Stations, assigning the students to their respective stations, supervising the work, and serving as Rector and Pastor to these scattered flocks to which the students ministered.

THE EPISCOPAL HIGH SCHOOL

The establishment in 1839 of the Episcopal High School in connection with and adjacent to the Seminary was an event of vital and far-reaching importance in the history of this Institution. The close relationship which has ever existed between these two schools under one Board of Trustees, the fact that the High School for a time served as the recognized Preparatory Department of the Seminary, and has ever since its establishment served as an introduction to so many of its students into the Seminary and ministry of the Church, warrants the giving of large space in the history of the Seminary to the history of the High School. The section of this volume given to the history of the High School has been prepared through the devotion of the Rev. Dr. Arthur B. Kinsolving, an alumnus of that Institution.

The Southern Churchman of July 19th, 1839, contained the following brief notice of the opening of the School:

"A committee appointed by the Board of Trustees and consisting of Bishop Meade, Rev. Edward C. McGuire, Rev. George Adie, the Rev. Mr. Dana, and Mr. Cassius F. Lee, met in Alexandria on the 12th of July, and made arrangements for the commencement of the Episcopal High School early in October, 1839, under Professor Pendleton and such assistants as may be required. No more than twenty-five or thirty students can be received this fall. Bishop Meade is about to visit some of the most approved institutions of this kind in the Northern states, in order to derive every useful lesson from their example."

The Convention of the Church in Virginia held in May, 1839, gave cordial endorsement to the School and commended it to the patronage and generous support of all the members of the Church.

The Southern Churchman of June 24, 1839, contains a three column article relative to the Episcopal High School of Virginia describing the location, telling of the election of the Rev. Mr. Pendleton, first a professor at West Point and afterwards at Bristol and Newark Colleges, as principal, and setting forth at length the reasons for the establishment of the school and the purposes which it is designed to serve. This article states that the Church in Virginia had indeed in two previous Conventions recommended the establishment of one or more high schools for the education of youth, and some steps had been taken towards the accomplishment of the object. The friends of the Theological Seminary had for many years recognized the great advantage of having such a school in connection with it, and had appointed a committee to devise ways and means for its execution.

This subject has, however, been so completely and so exquisitely treated by Dr. Kinsolving in his chapter on the High School and "The History of a Southern School" into which he has expanded this chapter, that we refrain from entering upon the details of the High School history, except to make brief record of a somewhat humorous incident in connection with Dr. Pendleton's dealing with his boys as recorded by Mrs. Susan Pendleton Lee, daughter of General Pendleton, in her "Memoirs" of her father.

"At the outbreak of the Civil War, Professor Pendleton enlisted in the Confederate Army where he served with distinction and became Brigadier General and Chief of Artillery of the Army of Northern Virginia." In speaking of his administration while Principal of the High School, Mrs. Lee says, "Gentleness and firmness were combined in his government. Some of his modes of punishment had a touch of the comical connected with them. A truant fishing expedition brought as punishment a long day's angling from an upper window by the boys who had engaged in it. A mock duel, gotten up to terrify the challenged party, was deprived of all dignity and amusement by the principals and seconds having to stand up in the presence of the assembled school and drench each other with water discharged from huge tin squirts.

Baseball was not known in those days and 'bandy' was the favorite game, in which Colonel Pendleton took an active part."

It is interesting also to note and worth while to record two quotations made by the "Southern Churchman" at the time when the proposition of establishing the High School was under discussion. They give evidence of the dominating thought which was in the minds of the founders of the School, and are interesting as expressions of the conviction which was then so firmly held that religion must constitute the foundation of education if education is to minister to the enrichment of civilization. The article, giving support to the High School, quotes the opinion of Dr. Benjamin Rush, writing a defense of the Bible as a school book. This editorial is of interest not alone because the argument made and the quotations cited reveal the convictions which moved the minds of those who founded the High School, but also because they are still vital and valid reasons for insisting upon the association of religious education with secular education. Today as then, as Roger Babson says, "Secular Education without Religious Education is a menace to Society."

"In contemplating the political institutions of the United States, I lament," says Dr. Benjamin Rush, "that we waste so much time and money in punishing crimes and take so little pains to prevent them.

"We profess to be republicans, and yet we neglect the only means of establishing and perpetuating our republican forms of government, that is, the universal education of our youth in the principles of Christianity by means of the Bible; for this divine book, above all others, favors that equality among mankind, that respect for just laws, and all those sober and fundamental virtues which constitute the soul of republicanism.

"The present fashionable practice of rejecting the Bible from our schools, I suspect has originated with the Deists. They discover great ingenuity in this new mode of attacking Christianity. If they proceed in it they will do more in a half century in extirpating our religion than Bolingbrooke and Voltaire could have effected in a thousand years."

The editorial then quotes as follows from the distinguished French philosopher, Victor Cousin:

"Thank God, sir, you are too enlightened a statesman to think that true popular instruction can exist without moral education, popular morality without religion or popular religion without a Church. Christianity ought to be the basis of the instruction of the people. We must not flinch from an open profession of this maxim, for, it is no less polite than it is honest.

FACULTY MEETINGS

Reverting to the missionary spirit which has ever characterized the life of the Seminary, the results of which were mentioned in the first part of this chapter, it is doubtless true that the "Faculty Meetings" contributed largely to develop and keep alive this vital interest in the Mission of the Church. These meetings were held every Thursday night. After an informal service, the students were addressed on some aspect of ministerial life and responsibility or upon some other topic of a personal and spiritual nature by one or more of the Professors. A chapter in this book has been devoted to an attempt to give some conception of these meetings so potent in the life of the Seminary. The Rev. Dr. Walker, out of his long experiences as a student, a member of the Board of Trustees, and for many years as a Professor, speaks with authority when he says, "The Faculty Meetings contributed most to the Missionary Spirit in the Seminary, as to all spiritual life and effort here." These meetings have continued to the present time.

Every living alumnus of the Institution shares Dr. Walker's assurance as to the creative and inspirational power of these Faculty Meetings, and also the hope that they may ever continue a means of blessing to the life of the Seminary. The Spirit of Missions will be abiding in the Institution and in the life of the students as long as the Faculty Meetings continue to develop and keep alive the spirit of fellowship between the faculty and students, and between the Seminary and its students, and the Divine purpose.

SOME MEMBERS OF THE CLASS OF 1857

SECTION III
CHAPTER IV
1840-1860

The Death of Bishop Moore—Large Increase in Number of Seminaries—The Coming of Dr. William Sparrow—Phillips Brooks' opinion of Dr. Sparrow—Dr. James May—Aspinwall Hall—Dining Room Experiences—Some Distinguished Students of this Period—Senior Preaching—Social Life on "The Hill"—Consecration of Bishop Payne and Volunteers for the Mission Field—The Seminary Graduates at this time in the Episcopate—The Beginning of the Preparatory Department—Mrs. Keith—The Death of Dr. Keith—The Death of Francis Scott Key—The Examinations before the Board of Trustees—Warning to the Seminary not to Become a Monastery—Invaluable work done by Rev. John Cole—Answer to Letter of Inquiry from Rev. Dr. William B. Stevens, rector of St. Andrew's Church, Baltimore—Ordination of Bishop Brooks—Dr. Packard's Summary of Qualifications Essential for the Ministry—Ordination Address by Dr. Packard—Daniel Webster on "Preaching"—The Seminary and the Oxford Movement.

The Theological Seminary had now become surely and strongly established not only on "The Hill", but also in the thought and devotion of the Church. The experimental stage had been passed. The wisdom of the Trustees in the choice of the professors had been amply justified by the success with which they were discharging their responsibilities. The removal of the Institution out from Alexandria had, from the first, proved advantageous in every respect, and "The Hill" had now become the congenial home of those who were associated in the fellowship of the Seminary life. The distinctive character and emphasis of the teaching given by the Virginia Seminary had become well known throughout the Church; and the Bishops who sent their postulants to the Institution and the students who came of their own volition made deliberate choice, and sought the Seminary for what they knew the Seminary was prepared to give in spiritual training and in doctrinal teaching.

The Southern Churchman which appeared on November 19, 1841, was marked with deep lines of mourning running between every column of the paper. The Rt. Rev. Richard Channing Moore, D. D., Bishop of Virginia and president of the Board of Trustees, was dead. Bishop Moore, it will be recalled, had been elected Bishop of Virginia in 1814 and so had been with the Seminary from its very beginning. The enthusiasm which characterized his nature was somewhat restrained with reference to the Virginia Seminary during the time when the question of establishing this Institution was under consideration. He had come to Virginia from New York. Unlike the early professors in the Seminary, his education and training for the ministry had not been colored so decidedly by the Puritan influence. He had been associated closely with Bishop Hobart of New York, though he differed from him radically upon many questions of churchmanship (which differences tended to make him acceptable in the Virginia Convention when it assembled to elect him Bishop). Bishop Moore, nevertheless, had high regard for the opinions of Bishop Hobart in his administrative capacity, and somewhat hesitated at first to give his enthusiastic support to the proposition of founding a Seminary in Virginia which might appear to be a rival of the General Seminary established under enactment of the General Convention. When this question was, however, finally decided, Bishop Moore gave to the endeavor to establish the Seminary, and to the welfare of the Institution after it had been founded, his enthusiastic and cordial support. His contagious devotion and compelling eloquence had done much to revive the Church in Virginia and to create the need for a larger number of men to officiate in churches restored and newly opened throughout the diocese. When, therefore, it was announced in 1841 that the old Bishop had died, the faculty and the students of the Seminary met in Prayer Hall and passed resolutions expressive of the sorrow and loss felt because of the death of their "constant and devoted friend and patron."

The need for Seminaries, not only in our own communion but among the Christian people of the country in general, had come to be widely felt, and the disposition to establish them seems to have found general and ample expression, as the following statistics taken from the American Quarterly Register and copied in the Southern Churchman of February 15, 1839, will clearly show. The report is as follows:

"Theological Seminary, Andover, Mass., Rev. Justin Edwards, D. D. Founded 1808. Senior Class 27, Middle Class 34, Junior Class 50—Total 111.

Theological Seminary, Princeton, N. J., Rev. Archibald Alexander, D. D. Founded 1813. Senior Class 29, Middle 34, Junior 29—Total 92.

Theological Seminary, Bangor, Me., Rev. Enoch Pond, D. D. Founded 1816. Senior Class 18, Middle 15, Junior 10—Total 43.

Theological Seminary (Episcopal) New York City, Rt. Rev. Benjamin Onderdonk, D. D. Founded 1819. Senior Class 18, Middle 24, Junior 24—Total 66.

Theological Seminary, Auburn, N. Y., Rev. James Richards, D. D. Founded 1821. Senior Class 8, Middle 20, Junior 20—Total 48.

Theological Seminary, New Haven, Conn., Rev. Nathaniel W. Taylor. Founded 1822. Senior Class 15, Middle 24, Junior 15—Total 64.

Theological Seminary, Fairfax Co., Va., Rev. Reuel Keith, D. D. Founded 1823. Senior Class 7, Middle 8, Junior 5—Total 20.

Theological Seminary, Cambridge, Mass., Rev. Henry Ware, D. D. Founded 1824. Senior Class 8, Middle 6, Junior 5—Total 19.

Theological Seminary, Newton, Mass., Rev. Ira Chase, M. A. Founded 1825. Senior Class 10, Middle 13, Junior 11—Total 34.

Theological Seminary, Mercersburg, Penn., Rev. Lewis Mayer. Founded 1825. Students all in the Junior Class and number 9.

Theological Seminary, Gettysburg, Penn., Rev. Samuel S. Schmucker, D. D. Founded 1826. Senior Class 4, Middle 8, Junior 8—Total 20.

Theological Seminary, Allegany, Penn., Rev. David Elliot, D. D. Founded 1827. Senior Class 11, Middle 19, Junior 11—Total 41.

Theological Seminary, East Windsor, Conn., Rev. Bennett Tyler, D. D. Founded 1834. Senior Class 10, Middle 7, Junior 6—Total 23.

Theological Seminary, Gilmantown, N. H., Rev. Aaron Warner, M. A. Founded 1835. Senior Class 10, Middle 6, Junior 10—Total 26.

Theological Seminary, New Hampton, N. H., Rev. Ely B. Smith, M. A. Founded 1836. Senior Class 8, Middle 9, Junior 8—Total 25.

Theological Seminary (Presbyterian) New York City, Rev. Thomas M'Auley, D. D., LL.D. Founded 1836. Senior Class 23, Middle 22, Junior 32—Total 77.

Theological Seminary, Hudson, Ohio, Rev. George E. Pierce, D. D. Students in all classes 15.

NOTE: With the exception of Rev. Justin Edwards of Andover, and Rev. Thomas M'Auley of the Presbyterian Seminary in New York, who were presidents of their Seminaries, all the other names mentioned are Senior Professors."

The Southern Churchman of March 1st, 1839, contains a list of the principal colleges in the United States with attendance in each. This list makes mention of nineteen students in the Divinity School of Harvard University, and seventy-four in the Theological School at Yale College.

The development of theological learning and the further specialization in theological teaching which naturally resulted from this great increase in the number of theological institutions, led the Board of Trustees to the recognition of the need of increasing the courses of instruction in the Seminary through the enlargement of the faculty.

The wisdom of no action of the Board of Trustees has perhaps ever been more thoroughly vindicated than this choice, in 1841, of the Rev. Dr. William Sparrow as professor in the Virginia Seminary. Dr. Sparrow was born in Massachusetts. He was educated until sixteen years of age in Ireland, graduated from Kenyon College, Ohio, and at the time of his election by the Board of Trustees to the faculty of the Seminary he was serving as the president of Gambier College, Ohio. He was then forty years of age. He was a finished scholar and was doubtless the most profound thinker and theologian in the American Church at the time of his election to the faculty. He loved the truth with a supreme passion of devotion. To know the truth and to teach it clearly and cogently he consecrated every faculty of his richly endowed heart and mind. He saw in truth transcendent beauty and a compelling and dominating power. He scorned to circumscribe his vision by sectarian limitations or even within the confines of the logic of human reason. Profoundly metaphysical and sound in his logical processes of thought, he visioned truth so profoundly and so vastly that his mind swept beyond the limitations of ordinary human thought into realms of speculation where convictions were born in the clear vision of God and in the light of a transcendent faith. His influence upon his students was dominating, but never domineering. He stimulated thought, but ever treated with reverence the thought processes of the students who came under his influence. He seemed to prefer that men for a time should think wrongly rather than they should not think at all, and yet he so wisely guarded and guided the awakened minds of his pupils that in the end they were led to perceive the fallacy of false thinking and found themselves either possessed of a certainty of conviction or else certain that conclusions must be held in abeyance until truth had been further pursued.

Seldom has any teacher in college, university or seminary received in after years such unqualified recognition of his ability from the students whom he had taught and such tributes of gratitude and devotion, as have been accorded to the Rev. Dr. William Sparrow by the students who came under his instruction in the Virginia Seminary.

Dr. Packard says of Dr. Sparrow, "His teacher's chair was to him a very throne from which he ruled the hearts and minds of men. So absorbed would he become in his subject that rarely the bell that rang at the close of the hour was heard by him, and I had to go in and tell him that it had rung, in order to get my class, even fifteen minutes late. In appearance he was the picture of a teacher and scholar. Tall, erect and spare, with a lofty brow, and piercing eye, one could see that he was a man of intellectual force. When you met him, the charm of his conversation, his ripe scholarship, his wide and varied learning, rich with the spoils of ancient and modern times, his sympathetic and loving heart, his countenance lighting up with a beautiful smile, all combined to make a deep impression. His love of the truth, 'come whence it may, lead where it will, cost what it may,' his sturdy independence of all authority save that of the Word of God, his intolerance of error, his clearness of thought and felicity of expression, are characteristics well known to all his pupils. Sometimes in the class room he was kindled by his subject, his eye flashed, his face became radiant, his utterance strong, and there would be a burst of eloquence."

Phillips Brooks says of Dr. Sparrow, "It is easy to say of men who have not much accurate knowledge to impart, that they are men of suggestion and inspiration. But with the Doctor clear thought and real learning only made the suggestion and inspiration of his teaching more vivid. I have never looked at Knapp since he taught us out of it; my impression of it is that it is a very dull and dreary book, but it served as a glass for Dr. Sparrow's spirit to shine through, and perhaps from its own insignificance I remember him in connection with it more than in connection with Butler. His simplicity and ignorance of the world seemed always to let me get directly at the clearness of his abstract thought, and while I have always felt that he had not comprehended the importance of the speculative questions which were just rising in those days and which have since then occupied men's minds, he unconsciously did much to prepare his students' minds to meet them. His intellectual and spiritual life seem to me, as I look back upon him, to have been mingled in singular harmony and to have made but one nature as they do in few men. The best result of his work in influence on any student's life and ministry must have been to save him from the hardness on the one hand, or the weakness on the other, which purely intellectual or purely spiritual training would have produced. His very presence on 'The Hill' was rich and salutary. He held his opinions and was not held by them. His personality impressed young men who were just at that point of life when a thinker is more to them than the results of thought, because it is of most importance that they should learn to think, and not that they should merely fortify their adherence to their inherited creed.

"With all his great influence I fancy that he did not make young men his imitators. There has been no crop of little Dr. Sparrows. That shows, I think, the reality and healthiness of his power. The Church since his day has had its host of little dogmatists, who thought that God had given

His truth to them to keep, and of little ritualists, who thought that God had bidden them save the world by drill. Certainly Dr. Sparrow is not responsible for any of them. He did all he could to enlarge and enlighten both. He loved ideas and he did all he could to make his students love them. As to his preaching, I have not very clear impressions. I remember that his sermons sometimes seemed to us remarkable, but I imagine that a theological student is one of the poorest judges of sermons, and that the Doctor had preached too much to students to allow him to be the most successful preacher to men. On the whole, he is one of the three or four men whom I have known whom I look upon with perpetual gratitude for the help and direction which they have given to my life, and whose power I feel in forms of action and kinds of thought very different from those in which I had specifically to do with them. I am sure that very many students would say the same of Dr. Sparrow."

The Rev. Dr. James May entered the faculty of the Virginia Seminary in 1842. He was then thirty-seven years of age. He was born and educated in Pennsylvania. Having graduated at Jefferson College, he first studied law with his uncle, ex-Governor Stevens of Maryland but having decided to become a minister, he entered the middle class of the Virginia Seminary in 1825. He was ordained by Bishop White on December 24, 1826. He first served in Wilkes-Barre, Pennsylvania, and in 1836 was called to St. Paul's Church, Philadelphia. His health becoming impaired, he traveled in Europe, and while there became proficient in Italian and French and pursued his historical studies. In Athens he visited the Rev. Dr. Hill, who had only recently gone from the Seminary to begin his work in Greece, then continued his journey into Egypt, intending to go into Palestine, but was prevented from doing so by the plague, which led him to return to Europe. There he visited Austria, Prussia, Bohemia, Italy, Switzerland, France and Holland. In July 1842 he accepted the chair of Church History in the Virginia Seminary.

Dr. Packard speaks of Dr. May as possessed of sound scholarship and clear views which especially fitted him for instruction. "As Professor of Pastoral Theology he was a

model to his class in the subject matter of his preaching,
which was always Christ and His Cross. He was the most
perfect Christian character I have ever known, and after
long and intimate intercourse with him, I count my knowledge
of him among the greatest blessings of my life." Dr.
Sparrow, also, speaks of him as exceedingly acceptable as
a Professor.

After leaving the Seminary in 1861, upon the outbreak
of the War he wrote, "Shall we ever reassemble? You can
imagine nothing so sweet and lovely as everything looks.
The new buildings have all just been completed. The yard
beautifully green in young leaf, with numberless flowers and
blossoms. The woods have been raked over and trimmed.
The birds seem wild with life and fill the air with song. Who
knows how soon everything will be destroyed? If the tears
shed on this hill, this week, were gathered, how many there
would be! And yet, is not this beauty the beginning of
sorrows?" He went away with a heavy heart, never to
return, for he entered the rest of Paradise in 1863. When
the Seminary reassembled in 1865, Dr. Sparrow wrote, "As
long as I am connected with it, the Seminary shall always be
what it was when dear May was of our number."

In 1843, Cornelius Walker entered the Seminary as a
student in the Junior Class. From this time until his death,
he was closely in touch with the life of the Institution, serving as member of the Board of Trustees, and for many years
upon the faculty. His memory of this period of the History
of the Seminary is so vivid that we feel that it can best be
portrayed by quoting at length from his personal reminiscences. Dr. Walker, writing near the close of his long and
useful life, says:

"This period of the life of the Seminary is well known to
the writer, as he became a student at its beginning. Dr.
Sparrow, coming from the presidency of Gambier, had been
giving instruction in the Seminary and High School during
the session preceding, 1841-42. The instruction at High
School was in Mental and Moral Science, given to the eldest
and most advanced of the pupils, and was highly appreciated.
As his tall, upright form moved across the field to his place
of recitation, the boys would speak of him as 'Captain Spar-

row,' and in spite of the length of his sermons they listened to him with interest and attention.

"Bishop Moore's last visit to the Seminary and his first to the High School was in the spring of 1841. Sitting out on the front porch of the High School, he asked Dr. Pendleton if any of the boys were in the habit of smoking. The reply was that if they had such a habit they had to indulge it secretly, as, by the rules of the school, smoking was not allowed. Dr. Pendleton then inquired whether the Bishop would like a cigar. The Bishop declined, saying that he did not smoke himself, but added that it was sometimes pleasant to be near someone who was smoking. Doubtless a boy could have been found who would have been glad to gratify him in this.

"Dr. Sparrow, as Professor of Systematic Divinity and Evidences, had his Junior Class begin with Butler's Analogy and his own questions on Christian Evidence. The Middle Class took up Knapp's 'Theology' with its meaning brought out by the inferences and applications of the teacher, and by profitable suggestion. * Dr. Sparrow's teaching was a combination of the question and lecture method, demanding specific knowledge on his part, a method which taught the students to do their own thinking. This might also be said of his Junior work on Butler and Christian Evidences, and of his Senior course in Burnet and Pearson, with his written questions on the Thirty-nine Articles, especially at that time with reference to the new issues of the Oxford movement. Dr. Sparrow was at this time in his forty-first year, in the prime of life, and though in delicate health had daily strength for daily needs.

"As with Dr. Keith, the importance of his work was shown in a threefold way: in the pulpit, in the recitation room, and in the Faculty meetings. In each he was peerless. His published sermons, while showing his ability, give no conception of their power as they were delivered. Unlike Dr. Keith, Dr. Sparrow always depended upon his manuscript, and it is doubtful whether he ever preached a sermon without having it before him. At the same time he had the most

* Editor's Note: As Professor of Systematic Divinity, Dr. Walker continued to use Knapp's Theology as a text book.

extravagant admiration for the gift of extemporaneous speaking in others. It may be said of him, however, that when called upon to speak unexpectedly, no one could do so more effectively. His impromptu speech on 'Missions' in the old Prayer Hall, following an appeal of Bishop Boone for sympathy and helpers, was one that those present could never forget. He was most effective in his addresses at Faculty Meetings. In the class room, he was no less happy and effective, enlarging upon his subject and making proper applications of the points covered. These recitations, which were then held in the old North Building and afterwards in Aspinwall, have been so often described by his pupils, that it is scarcely necessary to dwell upon them. Few students— real students, ever took this course without a quickening of their intellectual and moral life. Butler and Knapp and Burnet were not dry under his teaching.

"Dr. Packard continued his work with little or no change after the coming of Dr. Sparrow. In the Faculty Meetings he was very happy in what he said. Not having Dr. Sparrow's dread of speaking without a manuscript, he extemporized easily and was very practical in his applications. In his recitation room, which was in the old Prayer Hall (in the basement of the Middle Building), we had narrative Hebrew and Greek the first year, with Jahn's introduction. During the Middle year we had Hengstenberg's Christology, translated by Dr. Keith, and the prophecies and poetical books of the Bible in the Hebrew, continuing the latter the first year when we also took up the interpretation of the Old and New Testament in the original. The favorite reference books were those of Moses Stuart, while those of Olshausen were used in New Testament interpretation. The great works of English scholars in these departments had not then been written.

"In his study course Dr. May seems, with slight modification, to have followed Professor Lippitt, who preceded him. His text book in General Church History was Moseheim, long since superseded by others; in the History of the Church of England he used the work of Bishop Short, who, like Moseheim, is hardly known today. He was also professor of Homiletics. There was no text book covering this subject in those days, so Dr. May gave personal instruction and criticism. Hooker was his text book in Church Polity, and the Articles and Literature of the English and American Church were used for reference. In the pulpit, as in the Faculty Meeting, he always spoke extemporaneously and with remarkable facility. Had these sermons been reported verbatim, there would scarcely have been need for anything like correction or revision. 'Semper paratus' might have been truly said of him, for not alone was he always careful in his choice of language, but he never failed to have his subject well thought out. Bishop Meade, with the year 1845, began the delivery of his lectures on Pastoral Theology to the Senior Class. This he continued for some years following.

"Of course with these three the Faculty meetings went on and lost none of their significance in the life of the Institution. These devoted men, by their talks in the Faculty Meetings, created an intellectual and life-giving atmosphere, which was a benefit to teachers and pupils alike.

"Some of the outward changes of this time have their interest. The old Chapel, as already mentioned, had been built and put in condition for regular use. The Library was in the North Building until about 1856, when the present one (now, in 1923, the refectory) was erected, and enlarged at a later period. A new house for Dr. Sparrow, sometimes playfully referred to as 'Sparrow Roost', though generally called 'The Wilderness,' being surrounded by the forest, was erected during the session 1840-41. This house was subsequently occupied by Dr. Crawford and is now the home of Dr. Bell. When the forest was thinned out, Dr. Sparrow marked the best trees to be left and the others to be cut down. The workmen cut down the good trees and left the imperfect and indifferent ones standing. Within a year Dr. Sparrow moved over to Dr. Keith's residence, (the house next to the Chapel), and the 'Wilderness' was occupied by students, the increased number making this change necessary. Between this and the Seminary the ground was covered with huckleberry bushes, abounding in seed ticks, with occasionally a terrapin or a moccasin crawling about. Gradually they were cleaned away. Dudley Tyng occupied what is now the

'Wilderness' parlor, Albert Duy was in the apartment above him, and Eli Canfield and John Stearns were in two other rooms above, and the writer was in what is now the dining room. St. George's Hall, a gift of St. George's congregation, New York City, was erected about the same time as was the Library, and in 1859 the old Seminary, with its North, South, and Middle buildings, was taken down and replaced by Aspinwall Hall, the gift of Messrs. William A. and John L. Aspinwall made through the suggestion of Bishop Bedell. Bohlen Hall, the gift of John Bohlen of Philadelphia and members of his family, and Meade Hall, made possible by contributions from Virginia, were erected within the next eighteen months, just before the abandonment of the buildings in 1861.

"The consecration of Aspinwall Hall was of a deeply interesting character. It took place a few days before the meeting of the General Convention in Richmond in 1859, thus affording an opportunity for many friends and alumni to be present. Bishops Hopkins, Polk, Smith, Bedell, Lay, Meade and Johns, with about fifteen of the clergy, were present. Addresses were made by Bishops Meade, Johns and Bedell. Bishop Bedell said in his address that his heart overflowed with emotion at the remembrance of early days of Seminary life, which by their influence on his ministry had become inexpressibly precious. 'What,' said he, in speaking of the Seminary, 'do we not owe to its faithful theological training, and to the atmosphere of true spiritual religion which is here generated and kept surcharged with the Christ life?' *

"As the old Seminary building gave place to the new Aspinwall Hall, Rev. Dr. Packard tenderly recalled the associations by which through many years the old building had been hallowed. 'Well do many of us remember the old Seminary building,' he says, 'in its unadorned simplicity, destitute of all architectural ornament. Its basement was low, its halls narrow, its windows with small panes; but the

* It is interesting to know upon the authority of The Southern Churchman of 1856 that the style of architecture of Aspinwall Hall is "Elizabethan" and that the building *then* was considered very beautiful and imposing.—Editor.

memory of many old students fondly turns to it, as to no other place. In that humble basement for thirty years they had assembled, morning and evening, to unite their voices in the hymn, which rose and fell upon the ear of the passer-by, and in the accents of prayer. There had they often kneeled together before the Table of Him who bore His own Cross to Calvary, and there had they drunk of the cup of the Communion of the blood of Christ, which, like the Eleven, they were to administer to others. There had they tasted, from Sunday to Sunday, the good Word of God. There had been the Faculty Meeting, at which the tongues of Doctors Keith and May had 'dropped manna,' and of which Bishop Bedell said: 'With still deeper reverential feelings, do I recall the Thursday evening Faculty Meetings, when our Professors met us in the basement to pray with and for us, and to remind us, week by week, to seek for higher attainments in the Christian life. They were greatly profitable hours.' There had been farewell missionary meetings, not without tears, and there had been not a few ordinations. Loving hearts were turned toward the old building by those far away, who loved its very walls, for they had found it a refreshing place from the presence of the Lord. Could those walls have spoken, what could they not have told, of struggles at the foot of the Cross against besetting sins, of strivings after a clearer and fuller understanding of the Gospel, of hours of spiritual wrestling, in deciding the question where they could best labor, so as to glorify Him who had bought them with a price. And as a vision appeared to Paul in the night, of a man of Macedonia praying him, 'Come over into Macedonia and help us,' so a man of Africa prayed Bishop Payne to come over and help them, and a man of China stood before Bishop Boone, till prostrating themselves before the Master, they cried: 'Here, Lord, are we. Send us!'

"The old buildings at this time were still standing, so as to enable the student work of the previous year to go on. They were last used for a lunch in the old basement dining room and Prayer Hall, and very shortly afterward were removed. The building of Bohlen and Meade Halls immediately followed.

"Coming back to the interior life of this interval, we may note some of the particulars of the religious services. Services morning and evening were conducted by students of the Senior Class, opening with a hymn and followed by prayers, without regard to the regular morning and evening order of service. Sunday services were of course held in the Chapel, the Clarens boys and those from the High School attending. Besides these, there was the regular monthly Missionary Prayer Meeting, with its address, collection, and report of the missionary work going on in the neighborhood, and also the class prayer meetings on Saturday evening after supper.

"Up to an early time during this period the mail had been taken in and brought out by the Junior Class in alphabetical order. Now, however, an innovation took place in the establishment of a post office, which was made possible through one of the students having some acquaintances in Congress; and Cleveland, with the 'Lightning Express', as his 'one horse shay' was called, became an indispensable part of the Seminary life.

"About the same time a change tending to greater comfort took place in the old dining room which was in the basement of the South Building. The dining table was a single one, extending the entire length of the room, inconvenient for both students and servants. As is the case with all matrons, Miss Mary Dobson had her favorites, and they grouped themselves towards her end of the table so as to carry on conversation with her. One of these was a great talker. As this brother talked on at the table and Miss Mary listened, the serving of tea was greatly hindered. One of our reformers, William Duval, managed to bring about a change, which consisted in breaking the long table up into three or four smaller ones, and placing a student at the head of each. The convenience of this plan was at once recognized.

"Duval was the originator of the ten o'clock bell at night, which was to remind visiting students from the neighborhood that their hosts might be a-weary of waiting for them to take their departure. Duval's mission work in Alexandria during his student life, as afterwards in Richmond, was a noble one, full of blessing to those for whom he labored.

"This special allusion to one of the students is a reminder of others who were with him at this time. The number of students in attendance then was as large as, if not larger than, at any other earlier or subsequent period. Bishop Griswold of Massachusetts, for instance, who was in full sympathy with the teaching of the Seminary, was a visitor there in 1843 and commended it to his candidates. So it was with his successor, Bishop Eastburn. The same was true of Pennsylvania after the election of Bishop Alonzo Potter. In this disposition he was encouraged by the influence of the strong evangelical element in his diocese. Maryland and the southern dioceses, also, sent many students to the Seminary. There were, however, in other dioceses among those not of the Evangelical school of thought, strong opposition expressed against sending candidates to the Virginia Seminary. The canon which gave the Bishop the prerogative of designating the Seminary where his candidates should prosecute their studies, had not been enacted, and even when there was such a lack of sympathy with the Virginia Seminary as that just alluded to, there was no interference with those seeking its instruction. In many cases convenience as to distance, etc., was also considered. The only seminaries prior to 1861 were the General Seminary in New York, Gambier in Ohio, and Nashotah in Wisconsin.

"Among those of this time whose names are well known because of their later work and influence are Milo Mahan, catalogued with the Class of 1842, but really belonging to the Class of 1844, known as the author of several works, later as Professor of Church History in the General Seminary, later still as Rector of St. Paul's, Baltimore, and delegate to the General Convention; Edwin A. Dalrymple, Rector of the High School, and later teaching and doing pastoral work in Baltimore; Eli H. Canfield, Rector for several years of St. Ann's, Brooklyn; Henry M. Dennison, Rector in Louisville, Kentucky, and afterwards in Charleston, South Carolina, where he fell a martyr under the yellow fever; Richardson Graham, Henry W. Woods and Edward W. Syle, missionaries to China, Edmund Hening and Erasmus J. P. Messenger to Africa; John Freeman Young, first Bishop of Florida; George Wildes, George Packard, Lewis Walke, Andrew Fisher,

Henry C. Lay, Bishop of Arkansas, and later of Easton; Edmund J. Perkins, Francis M. Whittle, Francis Sprigg, George H. Norton, Samuel A. Clark, J. Monroe Banister, Albert W. Duy and Dudley A. Tyng. To these others might be added.

"Each class had its assigned duties. As already mentioned, the Juniors were the mail carriers, with the Post Office as the final outcome. From the Middle Class were selected those who delivered the monthly missionary addresses. The Seniors held their services on Wednesday evening, at which they did the preaching, for a long time under the competent supervision of Dr. May, who kindly filled this office through a long period, discharging his duties most efficiently. * Later on the presiding officer was elected from among the students. As Professor of Homiletics Dr. May was with the Middle and Junior classes during the Senior exercises of the Wednesday evening service and sermon, and gave a criticism immediately at the close of the service, but at a later period, in order to make the service more devotional and practical, he deferred the criticism until the recitation of the next day. There was a monthly election, at which a moderator was chosen from the entire student body. His work was to assist the Matron in her household offices, as she might indicate. Miss Mary Dobson, already mentioned, gave up her charge during the session 1842-43. After a short interval she was succeeded by Mrs. Stewart, the widow of an English officer, who proved very capable and continued during a long period of service. As she did not need the assistance of a moderator, that office ceased.

"The Rhetorical Society had by this time come into existence and effective operation. Dr. May was the presiding officer, the meetings being held in Prayer Hall.

"There was special opportunity for cultivating the social side of Seminary life. The students were cordially welcomed

---

* This duty was subsequently performed by Dr. Cornelius Walker in connection with his course in Homiletics. The Editor can well remember the kindly and yet always candid criticism of the old Doctor, especially on an occasion when a senior undertook to preach from a manuscript, the pages of which had not been numbered and were not arranged in order of sequence. Subsequent to the time mentioned by Dr. Walker, Senior Preaching was held in the afternoon and the Literary Society met on an evening during the week.—Editor.

in each one of the professors' houses. Dr. Packard's hospitality was proverbial, and a supper and evening there, after a
hard day's work, remained a bright spot in the memory.
The Doctor's repeated invitation to a bashful student to
'take another biscuit, take another, take two, take three,'
was in its substance and spirit often repeated. Equally
attractive and cordial in its welcome was the home of Dr.
May, and many of the students of that time will remember
the delightful evenings spent in Mrs. May's parlor, and the
charm of her conversation. The student long remembered
Dr. Sparrow's family circle, consisting of his wife and daughters. With Dr. Sparrow intercourse was delightful, whether
the conversation dealt with ordinary topics or was on an
intellectual plane, and Mrs. Sparrow's maternal presence
gave a home feeling that made a deep impression.

"In those days athletics had not yet come into fashion,
but the old games of Bandy, Chummy, or 'Cat', as it was
called, and Prisoner's Base afforded abundant opportunity
for exercise. Walking was frequently resorted to, and Alexandria was the objective point. As these walks sometimes
ended in a visit, it was important that the students should
be neat and presentable in appearance. On one occasion,
as soon as one of these students got into town, he was asked
by a couple of young ladies to take off his hat and brush his
clothes, and it was found that he had a looking glass in his
hat for such purposes.

"Thus life among the students, whether they were studying or working, had its relaxations, and pleasant was the
intercourse in the dining room and out on the porches. Edwin A. Dalrymple, who later had the title of 'Doctor',
was among the story tellers, and this story comes to mind.
A stage office clerk came out to verify his list of passengers
who had paid their fares, and finding that there was an extra
man, he made an announcement of that fact. But there
was no reply. Then, in a more positive tone, he said 'Gentlemen, I insist that you let me know how this is.' Then,
from one of the corners of the stage came a little squeaking
voice, 'I am a pious young man studying for the ministry.
Do I have to pay?' One or two of the listeners were curious
to know whether the stage clerk let him go free. His reply

was: 'No, he tumbled him out in spite of his piety and good intentions.'

"An event of deep interest to all occurred about the middle of this period, in 1851, in the consecration of Rev. John Payne, who was to have Episcopal supervision of the African Mission, for which field he was one of the first volunteers. The consecration took place in Alexandria on the tenth of July, 1851, the day after the ordination of the graduating students at the Seminary. The earlier custom of having the ordinations and special services during the closing week of the session, and the missionary sermon, etc., in Alexandria, had by this time been changed. This year there was an alumni address in the Seminary Chapel by Rev. Mr. Pendleton, followed by Bishop Payne's touching account of his labors and the trials he had experienced in his Mission. This was followed by the ordination service for the graduates, with a sermon by Rev. Dr. Bedell. These were preparatory to the consecration of Dr. Payne on the following day.

"This took place in St. Paul's Church, Bishops Eastburn, Meade, and Johns officiating. Bishop Eastburn preached in the morning, and Dr. Tyng in the afternoon. It was an occasion of deep interest to the Seminary, and few who were present will be apt to forget it. The attendance of the colored population was very large, one of the side galleries being filled. Musu, the African, who had been living with Dr. May, and one or two other native Africans, were with him.

"During this period there were the following volunteers for the Mission field: Hazelhurst of the class of 1842, for Africa; Edmund Hening of 1844, for Africa, and Richardson Graham, Henry W. Woods, Edward W. Syle, for China; E. J. P. Messenger of 1845, for Africa, and Robert Nelson for China; Jacob Rambo of 1848 and C. Colden Hoffman, for Africa; Cleveland Keith of 1850, for China; Hugh Roy Scott of 1852, for Africa; Robert Smith and William Wright of 1853, for Africa; H. H. Holcomb of 1855, for Africa; John Liggins for China and Japan, and Channing Moore Williams for Japan; Elliott H. Thomson, Thomas S. Yocum, James T. Doyen, Henry M. Parker, Henry Purdon and Dudley D.

Smith of 1859 for China. Some of these on account of ill
health and for other causes, were obliged to return home,
but the larger portion were able to continue and did their
work effectively and successfully. One of these volunteers,
Cleveland Keith, a son of Dr. Keith, the first professor, was
lost in the burning of the ship 'The Golden Gate' while
returning to China, and another, Henry M. Parker, was
murdered in China by the natives. Edmund Hening,
after seven years work in Africa, came back in a state of
total blindness. He was able, however, in a very striking
and eloquent manner, to present his Mission work and cause
to the Church in this country, and thus was able to help this
cause to which his life had been devoted. 'The History
of the African Mission' by his wife, is a noble record of
loving and self-denying exertion, in which they persisted
in spite of the discouraging effects of a malarious climate and
the frequent deaths of their fellow-workers.

"Among those of this period in the Episcopate may be
mentioned John Freeman Young, Bishop of Florida; Henry C.
Lay, missionary Bishop of Arkansas and afterwards of Easton;
Francis M. Whittle, Bishop of Virginia; Channing Moore
Williams, Bishop of Japan; William S. Perry, Bishop of Iowa;
John H. D. Wingfield, Bishop of California; Henry C. Potter,
Bishop of New York; Alfred M. Randolph, Bishop of South-
ern Virginia; and Phillips Brooks, Bishop of Massachusetts.
The eminence and work of some of these men will be imme-
diately recognized. The character of the Seminary, like
that of the mother of the Gracchi, is reflected in her sons.

"Before closing the record of this period a most interesting and important change is to be noted in the introduction
of the Preparatory Department. Phillips Brooks was its
first teacher. Prior to this, opportunity for such preparatory
work was given in the High School, Dr. Sparrow and Dr.
May assisting in giving the instruction needed. This ended
with the close of the session 1844, and subsequent to that,
under Dr. Dalrymple and Mr. McGuire, no such provision
was made. In exceptional cases some one was prepared by
one of the Seminary students, and this suggested the idea of
a preparatory department which was put through successfully. This was continued until the break-up in 1861, was

renewed in 1866, and continued until 1896. During its continuance Dr. Walker gave instruction in Mental and Moral Science, as did Dr. Nelson and Dr. Grammer for a short time. Its place in the Seminary was at that time a needed one, and its pupils have proved some of our most effective workers in the ministry."

The Southern Churchman of January 1, 1841, contains the notice of the death of the beloved wife of the Rev. Dr. Keith. It makes mention of her culture and scholarship, and says, "that she participated in all the doctor's studies, being able to read in all the languages in which they were conducted. She had won the confidence and commanded the respect and lived in the affection of the students. Her society was a most important benefit to them, and few have gone thence, who have not carried away an indelible impression of her wisdom and her excellence."

On the 3rd of September, 1842, the Seminary and the Church were called to mourn the loss of the Rev. Dr. Reuel Keith, the first professor in the Seminary. During the closing years of his life, his mind had been shadowed by persistent spells of depression which merged into melancholia, and when deprived of the companionship of his devoted wife, he rapidly passed into decline, and lingered only a little while before the merciful hand of death released him, opening to him the doors of a cloudless and eternal life.

In January 1843, announcement was made of the death of Francis Scott Key, one of the founders of the Education Society and a constant and devoted friend of the Seminary.

Mention has been made in the chapter on the Alumni Association of the deep and continuous interest of the Association in the welfare of the Seminary. During the period which we are now considering, persistent efforts, crowned with large measure of success, were made by the Association in raising funds for the permanent endowment of the professorship of Sacred Literature in the Seminary.

The examinations conducted at the Seminary by the faculty and chaplains have always been and will doubtless continue to be regarded with some degree of apprehension by the majority of the students. The students of today, however, may congratulate themselves that one custom of the by-gone days no longer adds terror to the anxiety which came with the approach of examinations. The following notice which appeared in the Churchman of July 23, 1847, is only a sample of similar notices which appeared in the Church press preceding and following the annual examinations of the Institution:

"The annual examinations of the Seminary of Virginia, took place in the Chapel on Tuesday and the two succeeding days in the presence of the Bishop of the diocese and the Board of Trustees and indicated very commendable industry and successful application on the part of the students."

The following article appeared in the Southern Churchman on June 4, 1846, being copied from the Witness. The writer gives evidence of an intimate acquaintance with the inner life of the Seminary, and yet one wonders what could have happened to give rise to the forebodings which he expresses in conclusion, for, whatever else might have been dreamed of in connection with the Virginia Seminary, the thought of the Institution becoming a monastery is, to say the least, somewhat startling. It may have been conceived in some prophetic anticipation and is therefore inserted as an admonition to the present and future faculties of the Seminary:

"The Seminary of Virginia has peculiar advantages for training up men for the ministry. Each department of theological learning is well filled with competent and efficient professors. The situation is one which is very favorable to habits and study. Standing apart from a city, there is very little to divert the attention of the student from the great objects to which he has devoted himself. There is a harmony and unity of effect in all the influences, and environment in the midst of which he lives. Everything about him tells him that he has withdrawn from the busy world for a season, that he may prepare himself to go down into the midst of it as an ambassador for God. Thus, with little distraction, he devotes himself to study. Nor are the circumstances under which he finds himself less favorable for his growth in grace. In this respect the Institution is most highly favored. I speak from my own long knowledge of the internal arrangements of the Institution when I express my conviction that in no institution in the land can the theological student find more incitements to quickening and keeping alive the spirit of earnest and living piety. None of the branches of theological instruction is taught in a dry and scholastic style dissevered from subjective and practical results. Exegesis, systematic divinity, ecclesiastical history, are all taught with a special reference to furnishing the mind of the student with the best methods of bringing truth to bear upon the souls of men and upon their own souls for their sanctification. In addition to these constant and daily influences, the senior class have the benefit of a series of lectures on the duties of the pastoral office by the Rt. Rev. Bishop Meade."

The article proceeds to call attention to the necessity of keeping the Seminary in touch with modern life and also of keeping the professors sound in the faith.

The writer points out that the greatest revolutions in religious opinion have commenced in the seats of theological learning, citing the instance of Luther in Germany, the movement in theology originating with the recluse professors at Oxford and the controversy which then agitated the Dutch Reformed Church raised by the teaching of professors Schaff and Nevins.

"The influence of theological Seminaries," says this writer, "must of necessity be very permanent and powerful and far-spreading. It is, therefore, most essential that they should be kept firm in the faith. It is a question which many are beginning to ask, 'Is there not something in the retired and secluded life devoted wholly to study and with little opportunity to observe the practical effect of certain doctrines on the mass—is there not something in this mode of life to which professors in the Seminary are consigned which tends to give play to speculative, to one-sided and to partial views of things? Is there not something in these circumstances to foster a love for what is peculiar to a few, rather than a sympathy with the feelings and understanding of the wants of the many?'"

He urges, therefore, that theological professors should frequently seek human contact and keep their thought in touch with the currents of modern life in order that they may resist "the attempts which seem now to be made in some places to introduce the monastic element into institutions of theological instruction."

Among those who stand conspicuous "in labors more abundant" for the Seminary, whose efforts contributed richly in securing means for the establishment of new professorships and placing the Institution, through an increased endowment fund, upon a secure foundation, was the Rev. John Cole. He was graduated with the class of 1828 and was ordered deacon by Bishop Moore. He is remembered among other things as introducing the custom of singing "The voice of free grace" at the close of the Virginia Conventions. He was possessed of indefatigable energy and winsome personality and was well fitted for the task committed to him by the Board of Trustees of being their agent in soliciting funds for the Seminary. In 1853, he became representative of the Alumni Association in the efforts which the Society was also making to strengthen the financial condition of the Institution. His reports submitted to successive meetings of the Association show not only signal success in the effort to raise funds, over $40,000 having been secured, but they also show the spirit with which he went about doing his work. He regarded money, as it should always be regarded by the Church, as simply a symbol and token of Christian devotion. His prayers were constant that God's Holy Spirit would inspire the hearts of His people with the love and disposition which would make the giving of their means an instinctive act of devotion. Employed at a salary of $1000 a year and his expenses, he kept his expenses down to the minimum and at the end of the year refused to receive more than $500 in compensation for the work he had done.

In 1854 a letter was addressed to Mr. Cole by the Rev. Dr. William B. Stevens, Rector of St. Andrew's Church, Philadelphia, making inquiry relative to the Seminary. His purpose was doubtless to gain information to use in aiding Mr. Cole in his work. To this letter Mr. Cole replied:

"Reverend and Dear Sir:

"It affords me very great pleasure to reply to the inquiries which you make of me, as one of the committee of the alumni in reference to the Theological Seminary of Virginia, not only because the questions are proper in themselves, and that it is due to you to answer them on account of the well-known interest which you have ever felt in the prosperity and usefulness of that beloved Institution; but also, because it gives me the opportunity of furnishing such information in relation to its history and character as will place it before the Church in general and its friends, in such a light as must compel all right minded members of our communion to say in earnestness of spirit, "May the blessing of God attend upon the efforts now being made by its alumni to secure its complete and efficient endowment."

"I will, therefore, without any further preliminary remark, say in reply to the inquiries which you have made:

"First: "*How far can it be called a local Institution?*" That it is no farther local than that it is in Virginia, is under the direction of a Board of Trustees incorporated by the legislature of Virginia, and members of the Protestant Episcopal Church in Virginia, and that from the beginning of its existence (more than thirty years) down to the present time, it has been altogether supported by the Church in Virginia.* In all other respects it has always been even more general than the General Seminary itself, inasmuch as no influences, so far as I have ever known or heard, have ever been used by the Bishop of the diocese or the Trustees of the Institution to keep our graduates from going wherever the Lord of the Harvest calls them to his work. On the contrary, the blessing of God has always been prayed for to attend them wherever they have gone, whether to the heathen, or to the destitute poor of our own land. But your second question will enable me to reply more fully to this point.

"Second: "*Of the graduates, how many are in other dioceses and in foreign lands?*" It is not difficult to answer this second inquiry in such a way as to illustrate, in the most striking manner, the general (practical) character of our school. I find on referring to the published catalogue of the students for 1853-54 that there have been educated in our

---

* Mr. Cole is not entirely correct in this statement, as contributions for the support of the Seminary during the years mentioned were received from Maryland and other dioceses of the Church.—Editor.

Seminary in all about three hundred clergymen, that of that number seventy-nine were Virginians by birth; seventy-five Pennsylvanians; twenty-six from Massachusetts; twenty-five from Maryland, and the rest from almost every state in the Union; and that at the present time, my impression is (though I am not able to speak with certainty as to this point) there are more young men pursuing their education from Pennsylvania than from Virginia herself. Of the seventy-nine Virginia graduates, forty-nine only are now in the diocese, and only sixty out of the whole three-hundred, two of them being from Pennsylvania and the others from other states. Of the seventy-five Pennsylvania graduates, forty-six are now laboring in their native state, eight are dead, and with the exception of two who are in Virginia, the rest are either in foreign fields or are laboring in the waste places of our own land, or are filling important positions in other dioceses. Twenty-six graduates (as I have said) were from Massachusetts, and are rendering good service to the cause of the Master either in their own or in other dioceses. Twenty-five of our alumni, as remarked, are from Maryland, the remainder of the three hundred (about ninety-five) are from almost every state in our Union.

"In reply to the second branch of your question: *"How many are in foreign fields?"* the answer is full and complete, when it is said that all our foreign missionaries in Africa, China, and Greece, are graduates of our school—that the Bishops of China, and Africa are numbered among our alumni. Bishop Polk, of Louisiana is also one of our graduates.

"Third: *"What support do the Professors receive?"* This question is one of great importance. Its answer is full of instruction in regard to the self-denial of our professors, and the noble Christian spirit which controls them. Two of them until very lately, (one of them having a very large family) have received but $1200. Now they are promised (contingent upon the success of the present effort of the alumni) $1500. The other receives (having also a large family) $2000. The trustees of the Seminary, as one of them informs me, are able to pay him only $1600. The remainder is made up from educational or private sources.

Let it be observed in this connection, that the professors of our Seminary are differently situated from regular pastors in regard to fees and presents, (which often serve to swell their means of support)—not having regular congregations, though constantly preaching; and that from their ability as preachers, they have been much sought after by wealthy congregations, that were willing to give them almost anything in the way of salary and comfort which they would ask, provided they would accept the calls which they made them. There is perhaps no more trying field of labor than the one which they occupy. While it is one of the most importance, it is at the same time one that requires more faith and self-denial and more looking to God for sustaining and comforting Grace than almost any other to which the Christian ministry can be called; they have no parochial sympathies such as are manifested in a thousand ways to the regular clergy, by presents and tokens of kindness and expressions of gratitude (from those who are brought to the Saviour through their instrumentality) always so comforting and encouraging to the heart of a pastor. The professors preach regularly in the Seminary Chapel to the students and the families on Seminary Hill and the neighborhood. In the way of preaching they do the work of regular pastors. It is difficult for clergymen, not so circumstanced, to enter fully into the trials and the way of parochial sympathies of such a position. Let us, as brethren, however, and let the Church not be wanting in efforts to make them as comfortable as their position will allow and to cheer their hearts with such tokens of sympathy and affection as we are able to bestow.

"Fourth: *"What are the present aspects and most pressing needs of the Seminary?"* It will be seen that this question has in part been answered by the reply which I have just given to the third question. Its chief and great pressing present need is an adequate support for its able and laborious professors. It is a reproach to the Church that for an Institution which has done and is doing so much for her, she has done so little. Our great need is the very endowment which the alumni, out of gratitude to God and their Alma Mater, are now seeking to procure. Next there is needed at once a fire-proof library building and lecture room. Our library is in constant jeopardy from fire, and great inconvenience is constantly felt for want of a suitable hall for lectures and recitations.

The present aspect of the Seminary, when we consider that it has students from almost every part of our widespread country, going through a regular course of preparation for the ministry, in our own and foreign lands, is such as must excite the gratitude and encourage the heart of every true friend of the Protestant Episcopal Church, and of all who love the Lord Jesus in sincerity and truth.

"Fifth: In reply to the question, *"What guarantee does its charter and constitution give that the pure doctrine of Evangelical Truth shall ever be taught within its walls?"* I have only to say that they give all, and no more than can be secured by care and watchfulness on the part of truth-loving Christian men and a constant looking to God in prayer, by its friends for his guardian care and daily blessing upon its professors and students. Our professors are true men, full of faith and prayer, loving and teaching the truth as it is in Jesus, to all the students who resort to our school for instruction and guidance in their preparation for the ministry.

"Sixth: *"What amount of money is required to put the Seminary on a permanent basis?"* A reply to your sixth question touches the present effort of the alumni. Our proposal was to raise $50,000. Of this we consider secure $30,000. There is money enough among the members of our Church, consecrated to God, that only needs the proper direction to be given to it to cause it to flow towards the Seminary and fill up to the full, all our present and future need.

"Seventh: In regard to your last and seventh inquiry, *"whether there is anything sectional in the teaching of the professors,"* I have only to say that the only qualifications which the Bishop, the Trustees, and the Church in Virginia have ever looked to as fitting the professors for this responsible trust, are that they hold and teach the great Evangelical doctrines of our articles of religion and the Reformation— that, in other words, they hold and teach "the truth as it is in Jesus." That these great and blessed truths have ever been taught within our walls ever since their foundation, will not, I suppose, be questioned by any who are in the least acquainted with the history of our school.

Very truly and respectfully yours.

John Cole

One of the Committee of the Alumni."*

In connection with this we give the following interesting extract from a letter to Mr. Cole from Dr. May.

"There are now here (within the walls of the Seminary) thirty-nine students, eighteen of whom were matriculated this year. They are from Massachusetts, six—Rhode Island, one—Connecticut, one—New York, five—Pennsylvania, nine—Delaware, two—Virginia, nine—Maryland, thirty-one—Indiana, one—Arkansas, one. The catalogue for this term is not yet printed. Many students who come to this Seminary, become candidates in Virginia, merely that they may be ordained with the class. In the catalogue, they, in many instances, are printed as belonging to Virginia, though they are from other dioceses and intend to leave Virginia, and go back immediately after ordination. Last year out of ten ordained here, only two remained in Virginia. The year before, only one out of five. The year preceding that, only four out of fourteen remained in Virginia. Besides this, a demand is made on this diocese to give up some of her best pastors for poor churches, though that occurs in all dioceses. Virginia gains few, almost none to her clergy from other dioceses on account of her Seminary.

"Bishop Meade has avoided persuasion to induce young men to remain in this diocese who belong to others, even though they may be candidates here and as deacons subject to his direction. Since I have been here, nearly three-fourths of the students graduated have been from other dioceses and have returned thither (the proportion of forty to one hundred thirty-one). Of these forty, sixteen have been drawn since ordination from this diocese to other stations, a due proportion to the African and Chinese dioceses. The Education Society has aided beneficiaries from all dioceses in the Union. When one applies for aid it is not asked whence he comes nor where he proposes to labor. The

* The Committee of the Alumni was a Committee of "One." It therefore accomplished results.—Editor.

Society has not, in any case, reduced or put off an application properly recommended. Even want of ready money has not been made the cause of refusal, for, if funds were not in the treasury, steps were taken to get them. This I know to be true. The Society has been at times sorely pressed, but faith has prevailed." *

The Virginia Seminary is indebted to the indefatigable perseverance of the Rev. Mr. Cole for the granting by the Virginia Legislature in 1854 of a charter to the Institution. Denominational prejudice, together with suspicion with reference to the Church which had continued to linger since the days when the Church of England was established in the colony under law, had defeated all previous efforts to get a charter. Again and again the Legislature had been applied to, but every effort had been in vain. Although Bishop Meade was exceedingly anxious that the Institution should be chartered, he gave reluctant consent to Mr. Cole's request that he be allowed to make still another effort. The Bishop's consent having been secured, Mr. Cole for a time gave himself entirely to this endeavor. He secured the good will of the Speaker of the House, whom he personally knew, and in tactful interviews brought arguments to bear upon the members of the Legislature, and, although opposition to his effort was exceedingly strong, the justice and propriety of the application were at last made manifest and the act of incorporation was granted in a thoroughly satisfactory form. The granting of the charter put the financial affairs of the Seminary upon a firm foundation and gave to the endowment funds legal security.

"An interesting break in the routine of Seminary life was occasioned by the visit to the Seminary of Rev. Robert Smith, missionary to Cape Palmas, Africa, and the Rev. Mr. Hening, of the African Mission, both of whom spoke to the Seminary missionary society. The description given of this meeting reminds one of the farewell given by the Church at Ephesus to St. Paul." †

* From "The Episcopal Recorder", and quoted in "The Southern Churchman" of November 9th, 1854.

† "The Southern Churchman", May 25th, 1854.

Mention is also made of the meeting of the Auxiliary branch at the Seminary of the Evangelical Knowledge Society, with addresses by Dr. May, Dr. Sparrow, and Mr. McGuire of the High School, and also by the Rev. R. T. Brown, agent of the American Sunday School Union.

In 1856, the Southern Churchman reports: "that the professors and students of the Seminary, together with some of the neighbors were highly gratified and delighted with three lectures delivered there last week by F. Wharton, Esquire, of Philadelphia, one of the editors of the Recorder and professor of law in Kenyon College. After an introductory lecture, the subject commented upon was "French Religious Immigration in America." In the account of the commencement held on Tuesday morning, June 28th, 1859, note is made of the fact that among the orations pronounced by the senior class, one was delivered by Mr. Phillips Brooks of the diocese of Massachusetts. Subject, "The Centralizing Power of the Gospel".

On Friday morning at eleven o'clock, Phillips Brooks was mentioned among those admitted to the order of deacons by the Rt. Rev. Bishop Meade. The communion on this occasion was administered by the Rt. Rev. Bishop Payne, missionary Bishop of Cape Palmas, Africa.

Bishop Payne is also recorded as having made the address on June 29th of this year to the Alumni Association.

Prior to the ordination of the class which graduated from the Seminary in June 1854 of this year, there was delivered to the class an address by the Rev. Dr. Packard which appears in the Southern Churchman of August 17, 1854. The address is entitled "On the Training of the Christian Ministry", and was, in part as follows:

"The peculiar tendencies of the present day, the necessity of the ministry adapted to them, and how such a ministry may best be trained," said the doctor, "furnishes the topic suitable for the present occasion.

"While there are tendencies which Lord Bacon called 'fallacies of the race' which are not of one age but are found at all times, and which are natural to men, yet every age has its peculiar tendencies. By a study of the characteristics of each age we may learn lessons from the past experience of the Church and thus enlarge the narrow sphere of our own observations.

"There is need at the present day, for the most thorough and comprehensive training in the ministry. The people will not be satisfied with what was even sufficient fifty years ago. The full power of the word of God must be brought to bear upon the age. In all its individual and local application to our own ways of life and habits of thought and action. The ministry must be conversant with those languages in which the superscription upon the Cross was written. They must be well acquainted with the histories and controversies of the Church, the wide field of Christian evidence, and not unread in history and science. In fact every kind of human knowledge may be employed for the illustration of divine truth and commended with great importance to the minds and hearts of men.

"The clergy in some periods have been sustained by the religious reverence paid to their office. This has fallen off, and now can only be secured by their life and doctrine, or men will despise them. The unbelief of the world can only be cast out by faith in the ministry, by prayer and separation from the world. It will be an evil day for the Church when she lowers the qualifications of her ministry and admits to it unlearned and ignorant men of neglected and unbalanced minds."

The address proceeds to discuss the comparative value of training men under private tutorship and the training given in the Theological Seminary. "Theological students do not," says the doctor, "want so much odds and ends of miscellaneous knowledge, as a frame in which they may put in its proper place everything valuable they meet. They want a solid foundation which can sustain a super-structure of the greatest height.

"Among the advantages of Seminary training, is the intercourse which the students have with each other. The fellowship of kindred minds and hearts, associated in the study of the same divine truth is animating; it generates enthusiasm and awakens active thought. Men who have been educated by private study are often one-sided, pragmatical, and conceited. They are not aware how insignificant they are and how many are superior to them. Nor of the best sources of information. Now in the society of the Theological Seminary, faults of character are corrected, rough points are worn off, and the student is prepared to enter the ministry with a formed clerical character, with far greater breadth of view than if he had not thus measured himself with his fellows.

"Then, too, there are always among the students in the Seminary, men of eminent piety, rare examples of the transforming efficiency of divine grace. We have seen the influence of such men in raising the standards of piety in this holy Institution. As we have witnessed the deep and lasting effect of their example, we have thought that such men have done a work here for the Church whose power can not be estimated in exerting an influence over their fellow students and through them over the whole Church.

"There is, too, in such a place as this, not only society, but that retirement which has ever been loved by the great minds and hearts of the Church.

> 'And Wisdom's self
> Oft seeks to sweet retired solitude,
> Where with her best nurse Contemplation
> She plumes her feathers and lets grow her wings.'

Those who have most blessed the Church have, in some spot like this, garnered up those treasures of wisdom and knowledge which they have poured forth for the welfare of mankind. Nor are there wanting here opportunities of practical usefulness in visiting the sick and destitute, and instructing the ignorant. These are among the safeguards of the Christian life, and keep alive the soul of piety.

"There are associations of peculiar interest connected with the Theological Seminary. With what a loving spirit do many turn to this spot as a place of refreshment where they sat down for awhile with great delight and then went on their way rejoicing. This is the case with many on earth, with some now among the saints in heaven. Prayer is made, we believe, for this place, in China, Africa, and Greece, in the ends of the earth, and far-off upon the sea. There are associations with this chapel, with its cup of communion, from which a band of those who are to minister this cup to others have, year after year, drunk; with its pulpit, from which the sweet word of God has been heard; with the Prayer Hall, where voices are blended of those united by a common faith and hope and work; with these walks and groves, dear to many a heart now far from us. These are among the most sacred associations of life, and can never die, for they are associated with divine truths which can never die. Here the voice from the heathen 'Come over and help us' was heard, as when St. Paul heard it at night, and the resolution has been formed to preach unto them the Gospel of salvation. May such a spirit ever dwell in this Institution. May its motto be, "Light, Love, Life," as we gain the more light, may we grow in love, and both together will work out the truest life.

"We have journeyed, dear brethren, in pleasant fellowship for the space of three years, and now you must prepare to leave this place, while it is good to be here, it is better to descend to the untried labors and responsibilities of the ministry. We need not say that our hearts go with you, that we shall follow, while life lasts, your ministry with our prayers, that 'the God of all grace, who has called us into his eternal glory, make you perfect, stablish, strengthen, settle you,' and bring us all at the last to an abundant entrance into the everlasting Kingdom of our Lord and Saviour, Jesus Christ."

Daniel Webster, than whom no man was more competent to speak concerning oratory, once said: "If clergymen in our day would return to the simplicity of the Gospel and preach more to individuals and less to the crowd, there would not be so much complaint of decline of true religion. Many of the ministers of the present day take their texts from St. Paul, and preach from the newspapers. When they do so, I prefer to enjoy my own thoughts, rather than to listen. I want my pastor to come to me in the spirit of the Gospel, saying, 'You are mortal. Your probation is brief; your work must be done speedily. You are immortal, too. You are hastening to the bar of God! The judge standeth before the door.' When I am thus admonished, I have no disposition to muse or to sleep. These topics," said Webster, "have often occupied my thoughts; and if I had time, I would write upon them myself." *

* Quoted in "The Southern Churchman," March 10th, 1853.

It was not alone the emphasis which was placed at the
Virginia Seminary on the vital importance of preaching the
Gospel of Christ as a means of Grace, but also the theological
and ecclesiastical convictions of the faculty and the traditions
of the Seminary which caused the Institution to view with
alarm and grave suspicion the pronouncements and trend of
the Oxford movement. This movement came up for consideration in the Virginia Diocesan Convention in May, 1841. The
intention of the Oxford movement was to find in the primitive
Church teaching and practice, a "Via Media" between Roman and Protestant teaching and to restore to the Church its
ancient heritage. To Bishop Meade, Bishop Griswold, and
others, it seemed a sinister movement designed rather, in
the name of primitive teaching, to lead the Church back to
the material bondage of medievalism. There can be no
question but that this movement in its ultimate effect upon
the American Church has influenced the Seminary in the
direction of a fuller recognition of the value of the sacramental system of the Church and has led to stronger emphasis
in her teaching upon the heritage of the Church in her apostolic Order and unbroken continuity of life. It is, however,
well for the Church that the Seminary and her sons and men
of like mind in England and America should have viewed
the movement in its ultimate tendencies with grave mis-
giving and positive opposition, otherwise what it contained
for the enrichment of the life of the Church would have been
given at the cost of impoverishing the Church by repudiating
the heritage secured to Christendom through the Reformation.
The prevalent conception of the Oxford movement held in
the Seminary at the time when the tempestuous waves of
agitated thought lashed but failed to inundate the Seminary
Hill was in effect the same as that expressed by the Rev.
Dr. Carl E. Grammer in his article on Newman and the
"Via Media" published in the Virginia Seminary Magazine
while he was a professor in the Institution; his position
being that Newman's deflection into the Roman Church
was the natural and logical result of his system and teaching.
With this as the destination of the Oxford movement, as
seen from the Seminary point of view of that period, it was
natural that it should have been viewed with grave appre-

hension and that it should have met with a positive protestant opposition.

The later movement, led by Maurice, Kingsley, and others in the Church of England, met with a more welcome reception in the Seminary, though extreme caution was always taken to guard against the radical tendencies of the Broad Church school of thought as they in anyway detracted from the supreme and unique divinity of Christ or the integrity and authority of Scripture. In this realm of thought and action, the Virginia Seminary Professors were to be found in General Convention voting with the old-fashioned high Churchmen of Connecticut and elsewhere.

Movements and battles of mind in the realms of ecclesiastical and theological controversy were soon, however, to give place to events which were destined to disrupt the Seminary and suspend its operations. In the distance Washington still looked calm and peaceful in the upper valley of the Potomac, but the halls of Congress were in turmoil. Bitter sectional debates and factional fights were hastening the days of disaster, and already the dark shadows of gathering war clouds were beginning to fall upon "Seminary Hill".

SECTION III
CHAPTER V
1860-1870

Forebodings of Civil War reach Seminary Hill—Letter from Dr. Sparrow upon the
Outbreak of the War—The Outbreak of the War—The Closing of the Seminary—The Departure of Dr. May—The Occupations of the Professors during
the War—Students Taught in Private Homes—The Death of Bishop Meade—
Military Occupation of the Seminary during the War Period—Seminary
Buildings used as a Hospital—The Re-opening of the Seminary—The Scant
Funds Available—Student Reminiscences of the Civil War Period—Binding
up the Ties Broken by War—The Election of Dr. Walker—Contributions
from the Seminary to the Episcopate—Rev. Randolph H. McKim, D. D.

The session of 1861-62 opened most auspiciously with
seventy-three students present, a larger number than had
ever before been in attendance at the Institution. About
thirty of these students had come to the Seminary from the
North, little knowing how short their stay would be. Fortunately, through the recent completion of Meade Hall, accommodations had been provided for all who had enrolled.

The Southern Churchman of July 1860 had made announcement of the fact that contributions amounting to
$4644.29 for the completion of Meade Hall had been received,
and in October 1860 it further stated that the Hall had been
completed and fully furnished.

The work during the fall of 1860 and the winter months
of 1861 was inaugurated and progressed under conditions
which were almost normal, so far as the life upon "The
Hill" was concerned. The conflicting sentiments and convictions prevailing in the North and in the South met in the
mail bag, brought each day from Alexandria out to "The
Hill", and the newspapers which the bag contained reported
the rising tide of turmoil. The debates in Congress were
becoming acrimonious. The issues involved were discussed
among the students with the earnestness of convictions
widely different. It is interesting, however, to know upon
the testimony given by Dr. Sparrow and Dr. Packard that
no deep lines of cleavage and no rancor of bitterness entered
the life of the Seminary as the outgrowth of sectional
and political differences of opinion. The hope held on "The

THE SEMINARY BUILDINGS

Bohlen Hall—Aspinwall Hall—Meade Hall—The Chapel—Porch of the New Library

Hill" up to the very last, was that the earnest contention of Virginia for the preservation of the Union would prevail in the halls of legislation.   The question of prime consideration was not as to the right or the wrong of slavery, but as to the right of the states, under the Constitution, to secede from the Union, and also as to the expediency of exercising this right under the pressure of the conditions which then existed.   In Virginia there was little difference of opinion as to the right of secession.   She shared with some of her sister states in New England the conviction, which they had previously expressed, as to the sanction given in the Constitution to this right.   Virginia, however, had contributed largely through the influence of Washington and the genius of Chief Justice Marshall and others to the establishment of the Federal Constitution.   These statesmen, while recognizing the inherent right of the states, federated under the Constitution, knew full well that local self-interest would always tend to exert a dominating influence in legislative deliberations.   They, therefore, intentionally endeavored to safeguard the Union by making as strong as possible the bonds of federation.   Their hope was that the Union would prove perpetual and that in this Union the states would secure the largest measure of individual prosperity.

When, therefore, the debates preceding the outbreak of the War between the States were in progress, the voice of Virginia was strongly raised not against the right of secession, but against its advisability.   In her own halls of legislation the sentiment was predominately in favor of preserving the Union, if this result could be obtained through any reasonable measure of compromise or of concession.   In the Halls of Congress, and in the influence which she sought to bring to bear upon those with whom rested the responsibility of decision, her appeal continued to be voiced in the interest of preserving the peace and maintaining the Union.   It was not until the crisis arose in South Carolina which led to a declaration of war and necessitated the passing of Union troops through Virginia to coerce a sister southern state, that Virginia finally reached the conclusion that the issue having been forced, her duty called her to secede in the defense of her rights under the Constitution.   She finally took the step with deep regret and yet with full conviction of duty, and with the sure consciousness that her soil would be the great battlefield of the conflict and that it would be drenched with the blood of her sons and their confederates.

It was doubtless this persistent hope that, through compromise or through concession, some way out would be found other than the way of war, that led the Northern and Southern men dwelling together in the life of the Seminary to hold on to the very last.

In the spring of '61, it became evident that these hopes could be no longer held. Virginia had seceded. The War had begun. The clash of conflict had taken place in the streets of Alexandria. The Seminary must, of necessity, be disrupted. The Northern men could, of course, no longer remain within the Southern lines. To the Southern men of good health who were not sufficiently near the end of their course in the Seminary to pursue it with a view of serving as chaplains there came the call to the ranks of the Confederate Army.

The Southern Churchman makes mention of the withdrawal of the Northern students and of the feeling existing in the Seminary at that time in the following notice which appeared in the issue of April 26, 1861:

"About thirty of the students of the Theological Seminary of Virginia who resided at the North, have left the Seminary on account of the troubles of the country. It was pleasing to know that the young brethren there parted from each other with true Christian feeling and brotherly kindness. If the feeling there exhibited on a small scale could only now be seen in our country at large, what little need there would be of War."

Among the documents of this period there is one of exceptional historic interest. It had become the sad duty of Dr. Sparrow, as Dean of the Seminary, to report to the Board of Trustees the reasons which had necessitated the closing of the Seminary. In this report his master mind penetrates through the transient turmoils of the time into the deep and beautiful and abiding realities of that spirit life which constitutes the enduring bonds of human fellowship. To the Board of Trustees he writes:

"Gentlemen:

"I commence this report with a sad heart. The causes are already known to you through the public press. We commenced this term under more favorable auspices than any other in the history of the Seminary, with the most abundant accommodations, either in possession or immediate prospect. We had on our roll all totaled seventy-three students, fifteen of these being in the preparatory department. In point of talent and promise they stood high. As to their industry, it seemed stimulated by their numbers. It was very cheering also to observe as long as the term lasted a large and growing measure of seriousness among the students generally, and some of them made very observable progress in personal religion.

"In the midst of this encouraging state of things, it has pleased God in his providence to bring our proceedings to a premature and sudden close. The students from the North, about three weeks ago, were either called home by their parents, or began to depart from their own sense of expediency, as soon as the preliminary steps towards Secession were taken in this state. The Southern students also began to return to their homes, owing to the unsettled state of affairs in this neighborhood disqualifying them for study.

"You may, possibly, have seen statements in the papers that our Northern students were driven away, being waited upon and warned by committees, etc. These reports are without foundation. No committee waited on these students. No committee was appointed. No threats were used to my knowledge or belief, and from the nature of my position, I must have known it if it had been so. Indeed, if it had been so at all here, it would, from the necessity of the case, have been known to everybody. Allow me to add, as I am aware how unhappy you would feel if you thought there was any just ground for these reports, that while of course the Northern students generally were the first to leave, some three or four were the very last, which would not have been if these reports were true. The Institution has from the beginning embraced students from all sections of this northern continent, and when differences of opinion began to

arise in the country on sectional questions, as was of course
to be expected, the sons for the most part partook of the
sentiment of their fathers, and did not fail also of course occasionally to express them. Nevertheless through the
moderating influence which was studiously exercised over
them, and by a strict and exclusive adherence to the teachings of scripture on points involved, as well as by their own
sense of Christian duty and propriety, a remarkable degree
of forebearance and good feeling was preserved among them,
considering all the peculiar circumstances of the case. It
gives me great comfort to be able to add that never was this
remark so fully verified as during the several months of the
term now suddenly closed. This fact was a subject of remark and mutual congratulation among the professors.
Oft times during the fall and winter as the crisis approached,
instead of increasing in excitement, the students gradually
seemed saddened and solemninized, and rendered more
forebearing and considerate towards one another. The
closeness of their intercourse was in conformity with this
statement. No one could have witnessed the separation of
the students as they returned to their homes without being
impressed by the scene, and it was not merely the tenderness
of youthful friendships that was evidenced. There seemed
to be something more solemn and elevated. A universal
feeling of distress that the ties which bound them together
as men of one blood and language and religion and ecclesiastical relations,—ties strengthened by the happy intercourse of daily life for one, two, or three years, should thus
be rent asunder. So strongly did the Southern students
feel this painful disruption, that they held a meeting and by
resolutions unanimously passed, expressed their feeling of
affection for their Northern brethren, departing from their
midst, and their deep regret at the separation.

"To conclude this topic, in reviewing the history of
this Institution for the last twenty years in relation to the
difficulties that now beset our country, it is a great satisfaction to those in any way connected with its management,
to reflect that like the Church to which we belong, it has
had neither part nor lot in inducing or precipitating these
troubles, but, on the contrary, has ever exerted within its

humble sphere, a conservative influence, moderating human passion, correcting extravagances of human opinion, and encouraging forbearance as a Christian duty for nations and individuals alike.

"So much for the past; if I might be permitted to say a word in regard to the future of the Seminary it would be this—Its hope of recovery from the tremendous blow which it has received lies, with God's blessing, in the preparatory department. It is only through this instrumentality that a sufficient number of indigeneous students can be raised up to justify men in devoting their lives to their instruction in theology.

"What I thus have written is on my own responsibility alone. The absence of my colleagues has prevented me from conferring with them."

"Respectfully submitted.

W. Sparrow.

Dean of the Faculty." *

The session of 1860-61 was brought to an early close. The ordination took place in the Chapel on the 7th of May, 1861, and immediately afterwards the Bishop and Professors and the Principal of the High School left "The Hill" with their families.

"The mayor of Alexandria," says Dr. Packard, "sent out word that there might be firing and they had better move away. Little did we think that the storm of war would sweep over our homes for more than four years, and our houses be despoiled of their contents. We went away leaving everything, thinking a lock and key sufficient to protect our household goods. We left everything in the house, linen, pictures, books, china, furniture; and silver in a box in the Library. Never did my home look fairer than when I left it in May, 1861, my family having gone before. It seemed to put on all its loveliness as I was about to leave it. Some natural tears I shed.

"We expected, ignorant as we were, that we should soon return and find our goods in peace. When, after four years I returned, my house was dilapidated, few panes of glass left

---

* From "The Southern Churchman" May 24th, 1861.

in it, and books, furniture, and cherished memorials were all
gone.   A friend at the North thought I spoke with severity
of my loss, since he had seen my books carefully packed away.
His remark was repeated to me by a friend, and I simply
said: 'Packed up! yes; but they did not send them to me.'
My large family Bible with records was carried off, and
twenty years after, the postmaster at Alexandria received a
letter asking of me, and the writer said that he would send
it to me if I would forward stamps, which I did.

"Some neighbors had kindly come in and saved a picture
or two.   A beautiful portrait of Anne Lee, my wife's grandmother, by Sully, copied from Stuart, was ruthlessly ripped
up by a bayonet.

"I carried Dr. May to town in my carriage as he was
going to Philadelphia, and he looked like Jeremiah, the
weeping prophet; we were both very sad at parting."

Dr. May, after a brief term of service as Professor in the
Philadelphia Seminary, died in December, 1863.

Bishop Johns, who had been living at "Malvern" on
"The Hill", moved to the neighborhood of Richmond.   Dr.
Sparrow went to Staunton, and Dr. Packard to the Plains
in Fauquier County, and later to Staunton in December
1861, where he remained until May, 1862, when he returned
to Fauquier.   Between this time and the close of the War,
he spent his time in Washington and Alexandria.   In Alexandria he was dislodged from the parsonage of Christ Church
by military authority, but was able for a time to carry on
religious services in the old Odd Fellow's Hall, and later in
Liberty Hall, alternating his services with the services conducted by the Baptists.   Dr. Sparrow, with the few students
who had followed him to Staunton, continued to carry on his
work of teaching.   In 1862, they were compelled to leave
Staunton for military reasons and found an abiding place
in the home of the Rev. John T. Clark and one of his neighbors in Halifax County.   "During our sojourn in Staunton,"
says the Rev. William H. Meade, "the students did duty
in the Parish Sunday School and also in the Mission Schools
of the neighborhood.   The Rector, the Rev. Mr. Latané,
instituted a weekly informal prayer service in behalf of the
soldiers.   On these occasions Dr. Sparrow used to make

tender and solemn extemporaneous prayers, and gave some of the most impressive impromptu addresses which I have ever heard from him." '

Henry Tucker Conrad, one of the middle class of the Theological Seminary, was killed with his brother in the first battle of Manassas.

Mr. T. C. Hutcheson, who was the only theological student whom Dr. Sparrow had left in his class, died of pneumonia during the March following, his delicate health having evidently made it impossible for him to enter the service.

Added to the gloom which shadowed the hearts of the professors as the result of war, and the disruption of the Seminary and the severing of cherished friendships, dark shadows fell upon them through the breaking of tender earthly ties by the hand of death. As the year 1860 was drawing to its close Dr. May was called to mourn the death of his beloved wife. The Rev. Dr. Packard, who, it will be remembered, had been born in Maine and educated in the North, sent three of his sons into the Confederate Army. His son Walter died in Hanover County during the summer of 1862, and his son William in 1863 at Point Lookout, where he was a prisoner of war; and in October of 1862 his little daughter Kate died of scarlet fever. Dr. Sparrow was called to mourn the death of two of his daughters, Mrs. Dashiell of Richmond and Mrs. Dudley A. Smith, who had gone as a missionary to China. Besides these, there were other sorrows which came to them from without. In 1864 news was received that Bishop Boone, of China, who had been through his influence, a missionary teacher in the Seminary, had ended his earthly labors. Then came the news that on Friday, March 14, 1865, the beloved Bishop Meade had died. From the first he had been the constant friend of the Seminary, being conspicuous among its founders and preeminent afterwards as its foster father. Whatever opinion may be held as to precedence in zeal and priority in position among the founders of this Institution, (which was a point its founders never paused to consider) there can be no question that after the establishment of the Seminary, William Meade, upon the death of Dr. William H. Wilmer, his friend and co-laborer in the Education Society and the Seminary endeavor, became its chief advocate and its most constant and valuable leader and its chief master builder.

Meanwhile death, wholesale death, and dire destruction, had been going on upon Seminary Hill. The departure of the professors and their families had left the buildings and homes of the professors deserted save for the presence of a few students who lingered for a while, and of Mr. Cassius F. Lee, who remained upon the scene as the official representative of the Board of Trustees. They were all finally compelled to leave, and the circumstances of their leaving and the events following can best be described through the record left by Rev. Dr. Sparrow:

"Within a few weeks following the occupation of Alexandria, squads, sometimes of stragglers from the army, sometimes of vicious persons from the neighborhood, began to make depredations upon unprotected property. Particularly was this the case with unoccupied houses. One of the outer buildings of the Seminary had been broken open during the night, and a request was made to the officer commanding in the neighborhood to furnish a guard for the protection of the property and its inmates. I went out with Mr. Lee to the Seminary, to meet the guard that Col. Heintzelman had promised for its protection. It was a bright afternoon in June, and everything was looking very fresh and beautiful. But for the closed houses of the professors, it might have been taken for the time of vacation. We found the six or seven students in possession, apparently anxious in regard to the protection which had been requested, and we endeavored to reassure them. In less than twenty minutes the guard made its appearance, too large, as I thought, for the purpose—some twenty or twenty-five men, under the command of a lieutenant. We received them at the front door, and after a few words, they marched into Prayer Hall and stacked their muskets. I mentioned to the lieutenant that this was the place of prayer for the students, morning and evening; and that arrangements would be made for the accommodation of his command in other parts of the building, and we soon took our departure. We had hardly got back to Mr. Lee's house before we received a message from the students, that a line of sentinels had been drawn around the buildings, and that no one was allowed to pass through it. On our return to remonstrate, we found that Dr. May's and Dr. Sparrow's residences had been broken open, so as to be searched; that the rooms of the Seminary, not already opened, had been subjected to the same operation, and that the guard, which had been asked for protection, had actually taken possession. The inmates, of course, got away as soon as they could, and within the next four months the buildings were appropriated for hospital purposes."

During the time when the Seminary property was occupied by military authorities, the Seminary, including St. George's Hall and the "Wilderness", and also the High School buildings, were occupied as hospitals. The home of Dr. May, now the residence of Dr. Rollins, was used by the Medical Department and occupied by some of the surgeons. Dr. May's books and furniture all disappeared. Fortunately for Dr. Sparrow his home was occupied by Mr. Jerome, the Federal chaplain who was his son-in-law, and he saw to it that Dr. Sparrow's books were saved from destruction. Dr. Packard's home, "Melrose," was converted into a bakery and entirely dispoiled. "Malvern," the home of Bishop Johns, was occupied by the Federal officers. His books were sent to the Smithsonian Institute in Washington by some of his friends, but unfortunately with the burning of some of the buildings of the Institute most of his books were destroyed.

In 1861 the Library of the Seminary was broken into soon after the Federal troops took possession and a number of the books were either destroyed or stolen and sent away. Mr. Cassius F. Lee applied to General McClellan for permission to remove the remaining books of the library of the Seminary to his warehouse in Alexandria. Fortunately this building was spared, and in 1865 the Seminary Library was restored to "The Hill". A large number of temporary buildings were erected upon the grounds of the Seminary, especially between the fields and the present buildings and Alexandria. The country was denuded of trees and of fences and of grass.

In the Southern Churchman the following description of the Seminary as seen by a visitor appeared under date of July

4, 1862: "Having recently made a visit to the Theological Seminary, I thought it would interest many of your readers to know its present condition.

"Approaching the Seminary in the rear, we found the country so much altered that we could scarcely recognize it. All the trees for miles in the rear of the Seminary have been cut down. A grove has been left around St. George's, and a few trees in front of the Seminary and those around Dr. Sparrow's and Dr. May's houses have been mostly spared. We observed in the rear of the Seminary several stockades and sheds for horses. At Howard (The High School property), all the trees had been cut down with the exception of those in front of the building. No fences have been left upon the grounds.

"We first visited Dr. Packard's house. We found a tent in the yard and a squad of soldiers playing quoits. The house was occupied by a surgeon and his family and several officers. We found it less misused than we expected. The study has been turned into a kitchen, and the book shelves used for kitchen utensils. The kitchen has been enlarged into a bakery. The furniture with the exception of two or three large pieces has been taken away. Not a relic could be found to be brought away with us. The books that we saved were deposited in the Seminary Library by Mr. Lee. Dr. Sparrow's house is used as a hospital. We understand that his library has been locked up and was uninjured with the exception of a few books in another room. We found the Seminary building used as a hospital; more than two hundred sick were in it. Dr. Sparrow's recitation room was the dispensary. The furniture was nearly all destroyed. The books of the Library were mostly packed up in boxes, so that we could not tell how many were missing. This was done by Rev. Dr. Butler and Mr. Carver to be placed in the Treasury Building at Washington for safe keeping as was alleged, but Mr. Lee obtained an injunction from General McClellan staying the proceedings and a safeguard for the Library that it should be used for no other purpose. Dr. May's house was given up to contrabands, with which it seemed swarming. We were told that Bishop Johns' house and grounds had been but little injured, through the strictness of General Kearny who makes it his headquarters.   Major Herbert's house has been demolished, and a fort with tents occupies the hill on which it stood.   We may, with deepest sadness, say 'our holy and beautiful house has been desecrated and our pleasant places laid waste.'

"In the hall once dedicated to God and which resounded with prayer and praise are now heard horrible blasphemies. 'Open Thine Eyes, Oh Lord, and behold our desolation.'   In Alexandria we heard that St. Paul's Church was used as a hospital."

The "Alexandria News", as quoted by the Southern Churchman of November 6, 1863, also describes the Seminary under military occupation.   This article is of interest as showing that the Institution at this time was still in some measure being used for religious purposes. Some question may be raised as to the entire accuracy of the closing part of the first paragraph of this article, which is as follows:

"It must be a source of great gratification to the numerous friends of the Episcopal Theological Seminary and the High School, residing north and south, that notwithstanding the large number of troops all the time quartered in this vicinity or passing through, and that it has been and still is occupied as an hospital, everything is in handsome order, and when the time arrives for the professors and teachers to take up their places again, or new ones are called, they will find matters in good condition.

"The Rev. Mr. Jerome, son-in-law of one of the former professors, Dr. Sparrow, labors as a chaplain with great earnestness to do good to the souls of the large family committed to his care.   Service is held in the chapel every Sabbath at ten-thirty in the morning, and every night in the week except two.   His labors are incessant in bringing souls to the Master.   He has no sinecure office at this Seminary, but is instant in and out of season to do good to the souls as well as the bodies of men.

"Should Virginia be returned to the Union, which God in his mercy grant, and that right speedily, may we not hope that this school of the prophets may once more be made an instrument of great good to the Church in Virginia as well as throughout our whole country, and the world, as in the days gone by, and that its numerous friends, North and South, may once more meet together as friends, not as enemies, having one common object—the building up of the Redeemer's Kingdom upon the earth. Both North and South have done nobly for this Seminary in days gone by. Let them still cherish the hope that the day is not far distant when they will meet again on a common platform. Peace on earth and good will to men."

In 1865 the work of restoration at the Seminary began. With the exception of Dr. Sparrow's home, there was no furniture left in any building on "The Hill" except such as had been used and abandoned by the Federal Army. It was almost like making a new beginning. With the exception of $6,000 which remained in a Baltimore bank unpaid from the John Johns' legacy of $15,000, and which was immediately available, there were no funds at their disposal. Such furniture as could be secured was gotten together, and in the fall of 1865 the Seminary was opened again with eleven students, Dr. Sparrow and Dr. Packard returning to take up their work of teaching. The students wore their old Confederate uniforms, stained and battle-worn, and often in their conversation addressed each other under military title, for among them was Major Dudley, and Colonel Hullihen, and others who had won distinction upon the field of battle.

"Our great difficulty," writes Dr. Sparrow, "is to find means to support the men, and to furnish their rooms. Should you," he says to his correspondent, "come across any monied or liberal soul who would probably be willing to help a young man in the preparation for the ministry by a scholarship of $200, at his pleasure, you will render a great service to that needy young man, and also to our Seminary."

The conditions of life in the Seminary during this period can best be pictured in the words of some of those who were among the students returning. Among these were the Rev. David Barr, the Rev. Horace E. Hayden, Bishop Dudley, and the Rev. Dr. John S. Lindsay. From all of these, reminiscences were secured by the Rev. Dr. Walker and are inserted here as a valuable part of the historical record of the Institution.

"It would be difficult," says the Rev. David Barr, "to find a much more desolate place than the Seminary and its surroundings in the chilly and bleak November evening of my first acquaintance with it. It stood in the centre of a desolate region, in which a fence could not be seen for miles, excepting around a house, here and there, and upon which the sod had not been turned, seemingly, for years, saving now and then a small patch for a garden. In striking contrast with this was the cordial greeting given me by the good Doctor upon my arrival. He had reestablished himself in his long deserted home, and was working and praying for the bright days to come for his beloved Seminary."

"I found five students present, Horace E. Hayden, James H. Williams, Benjamin E. Reed, Edward W. Hubard, and Nicholas H. Lewis. I was the sixth. In a few weeks William H. Laird arrived, and before many weeks had passed, came the lamented Bruce Davis, then George Fitzhugh, then young Davidson of Missouri, who remained only a few weeks, then Thomas U. Dudley, and Walter Q. Hullihen, and lastly a Mr. Phelps, who like Davidson, stayed only a few weeks. I never heard what became of them.

"It would be impossible to describe the spirit of the little flock gathered there from different quarters; and, in connection with them, the few returned inhabitants of "The Hill," during that never-to-be-forgotten year, after the resuscitation of the Seminary. What prayerful diligence on the part of the students. What unity, what love, and sweet Christian fellowship among them. What joy, such a state of things, must have afforded to our teachers.

"As to the work of the Seminary, the Theological classes at Dr. Sparrow's lectures recited at first, if I rightly remember, in either Dr. Sparrow's study, or in one of the students' rooms. Dr. Packard's recited in his study, or in the Prayer Hall. The preparatory classes, in Greek and the Sciences, recited to Dr. Sparrow in his study. His fondness for Greek made him a painstaking teacher of it. I think of those Greek days with Dr. Sparrow in his study, as the most pleasant and instructive spent at the Seminary. Dr. Packard taught the Latin class. The Faculty Meetings were not restored at once; not indeed, I think, until towards the end of the session. Lewis had been at the Seminary before in the class of 1861, and retained deepest impressions of the Faculty meetings, in which the lowly minded May had participated, and he aroused my desires for their speedy beginning. Upon their renewal I found that the half had not been told me concerning them. The remembrance of them is refreshing and edifying.

"During the first half of the session, we used one of the second story rooms in Aspinwall Hall as our dining room, our number being too small, and our arrangements too simple, to require so large a room as the dining room in Bohlen Hall. We 'messed,' as it is called, each man paying about twelve dollars and a half a month, and had one of our number as caterer. In the spring of 1866, we were favored with the services of Miss Jones as our matron, a change decidedly for the better in many respects; and this change was followed by our removal to the dining room of Bohlen Hall."

"Our fare," says Rev. H. E. Hayden, "for some weeks, during the first months of the session, was very little better than the rations we had received in the field. We had, however, been soldiers and had learned to endure hardness. We discovered, after a time, that the cook boiled the potatoes in the coffee pot, and made the coffee afterwards. The peculiar flavor thus imparted to the coffee, led to the discovery, and caused a change in our household arrangements. The butcher failed one day to bring out our supply, and we sent to borrow from Dr. Sparrow. Mr. Hayden said to Dr. Sparrow, "It just occurred to me, to ask Mrs. Sparrow if she had any fresh beef." Her reply was, "Yes, but it is in the oven for tomorrow. She sends some of it, with the smell of fire upon its skirts, hoping it may nevertheless answer.""

"We were scattered," says Mr. Barr, "as regarded our accommodations, in the three principal Halls, Aspinwall, Meade, and Bohlen, one or more sleeping in each. Aspinwall was principally occupied, however, as affording better rooms, and rendering things more cheerful and homelike. Prayer Hall was used for public services till the early spring of 1866; the Chapel, I think, being out of repairs perhaps,

and certainly very cold without stoves.   As those were days
of poverty, we used what we had."

"It was," says Bishop Dudley, "as I remember, a cold
gloomy evening in January, 1866, that I arrived upon 'The
Hill' to begin my career as a student for the Ministry.   I
received cordial welcome at 'Melrose', the hospitable home
of dear Dr. Packard, whom I had known for several years.
And as I recall it, that same evening I went with him by a
muddy path to the Prayer Hall in Aspinwall to attend my
first 'Faculty Meeting.'   According to custom, after one
of them had said some prayers, and a hymn had been sung
by the little company of students present, the two Professors,
Dr. Sparrow and Dr. Packard, sitting in their chairs, talked
to us briefly, simply, and earnestly, about the spiritual life,
and specially about the temptations and trials of a Clergyman.   I remember that I went away from this first meeting
disheartened and afraid.   The ideal which had been set
before us was so high, that I felt unequal to even attempt
its attainment.   And I cannot forget the sweet and comforting words of Dr. Packard, which he spake to me on our way
to his home, in response to my expression of fear that I could
not go forward to the work of the Ministry.   This was my
initiation to the Seminary.   At that meeting in Prayer Hall
there were present as I recall them, Hayden, Lewis and Hullihen of the Middle Class, (there was no Senior Class that
year) Williams and Reed, and Hubard were of the Junior
Class, and Laird and Barr in the Preparatory Department.
I think there were no more and that I was the ninth student
to enter.   It was, indeed, a day of small things.   The buildings which had been occupied as a Hospital by the Federal
troops bore very evident marks of such use.   The furniture
in the students' rooms was but the wreckage saved from the
military provision.   I cannot forbear to mention the building of a plank walk out of boards picked up on the grounds
from the Seminary to 'Melrose' by two students who shall
be nameless.

"The months passed by, filled up with blessed toil, inspired by the Christian enthusiasm of the Professors.   Two
men came to join us, Davis of South Carolina, and Alrich,
a Presbyterian minister who had, as the Canon then required,

to spend but six months of probation before his ordination. We were happy—happy in our work, happy in all our surroundings. For be it remembered though buildings were damaged and endowment all gone, though poverty was the marked characteristic of the old Institution, and even the clerical vestments of divine service had disappeared, that the teachers were there as aforetime, rich in spiritual experience and theological learning, clad always in the shining vestments of Christian righteousness.

"Somebody said once that his idea of a University was a student on one end of a log and Mark Hopkins on the other. Surely Dr. Sparrow with one student or an hundred would have made a Theological Seminary.   And Dr. Sparrow was there in the very prime and vigor of his strength.   I have been accustomed to say, and I trust that my language will not be esteemed intemperate, that his was the greatest intellect with which I have come in contact in any department of life.   He was the hardest man to differ from I have ever met, and when in obstinate maintenance of a contrary opinion I have once or twice refused consent to his conclusion, it has been, as I said to him once, only because he had taught me 'the right and the duty of private judgment.'   This was his great gift to his pupils that he taught them to think and in all humility to seek 'seek the truth, come whence it may, cost what it will.'   And joined to this colossal intelligence was a humility, a self depreciation, that a man who knew him not well, could with difficulty believe to be genuine.   A teacher of such luminous thought and expression as I have seen nowhere else, a preacher of tremendous eloquence, if true eloquence be matter of thought, and not of mere expression, he yet was timid as a girl when called upon to address an audience without his manuscript, and made some of his boys laugh as he complimented them upon the excellence of their extemporaneous effusions, to which he had listened outside a Chapel window, and said that he was envious of their gift of utterance.

"The truth, the truth, this he sought and this he taught, even the truth as it is in Jesus, for his diligent search had found it nowhere else.

"And what may I say of his colleague, dear Dr. Packard, save that he was worthy to be such a colleague. *Par nobile fratrum* they were, albeit almost contradictory in their modes of thought and methods of instruction. Dr. Packard was preëminently the student, and the student of the Bible. His knowledge of the Scripture was minute and accurate, his knowledge of the commentators almost equally so, and I can hear now the very tone in which he was wont to express his contempt for one whose writings had been most popular, and whose views he considered most heretical, as he answered the student's quotation of them with, 'Oh, Barnes!' But for me his life was more than his learning, and the privilege of daily intimate communion with him, more valuable than his lectures. His presence was a benediction, and his reading of the lessons from Holy Scripture in the Chapel, was itself an illuminating comment. These were our teachers for whom we, now grown to be old men, do unceasingly praise God.

"But they did not make us Churchmen, it has been complained. No, if Churchmanship be a matter of colours and postures, of lights and Leviticus, of arrogant exclusiveness and contemptuous disdain, let it be granted that the charge is true. These men did not seek to make what Dr. Washburn used to call 'chanting Levites'. But if Churchmanship means an intelligent, rational, loyal devotion to the Historic Church, her Orders, her Doctrine, her Prayer Book, her Spirit of Missions, then I can assert their faithful endeavour and their good success. Their men went forth accepting the teaching of Hooker as to Orders, of Pearson as to Doctrine. They had been taught that the Prayer Book was made for man and not man for the Prayer Book, and that the blessed book is dishonored by its attempted use under impossible conditions. And all their men were taught the liberty wherewith Christ hath made us free, and that for this Christian liberty the Church is appointed to stand. Best proof of all of their true Churchmanship was the missionary spirit by them evolved to be the very atmosphere of 'The Hill.' They taught that true Apostolicity is the eager obedience to fulfil the great commandment, 'Go preach'; and the graves in Western Africa and in Asia, and the living men who today are serving in China and Japan, Africa, Brazil, these all testify to the Churchmanship made at the Virginia Seminary. There is no reason why we, her sons, should be ashamed of her record; there is all reason why we should thank God that we sat at the feet of these men.

"A second year I passed at the Seminary, but of that period I need not speak, for the conditions were then become almost normal. Dr. Walker, a distinguished graduate of the Seminary, came to be the Professor of Ecclesiastical History, the financial burden was measurably eased by the gifts of new friends, and a goodly class entered that year. The old Seminary passed through the fire, but she has come forth mightier for good and for God, than ever before. *Esto perpetua!*"

Dr. John S. Lindsay adds to this the following:

"One cold and dreary day, of the last week of November in 1868, I arrived at the Seminary of Virginia, and attended Evening Prayer at night, conducted by a member of the Senior class, in one of the lecture rooms. The small congregation consisted of students only, and the service was simple, warm, and hearty. The scene was in contrast with that of the outside world, and was most grateful to one who had passed through the storm of severe mental trials. I shall never forget it.

"My life at the Seminary was very brief, covering less than a single session. But it was keenly enjoyed, and has been followed by a constant observation of the Institution, and a close and continuous acquaintance with its professors and students.

"As I had but recently left the University of Virginia, I was not indifferent to the personnel of the Faculty, and to their methods of instruction. It seemed to me, then, as it does now, that the teaching was abreast of the times, and fruitful of good results. In Greek I was well taught by Dr. Packard, in Church History and Homiletics by Dr. Walker, and in Theology and Apologetics by Dr. Sparrow.

"While in the University of Virginia, I had much to do in public and in private with Dr. W. H. McGuffey, the Professor of Metaphysics and Moral Science. For clearness of exposition, power of catching and holding the attention, and for capacity for inspiring the student with a love of learning, he seemed to me while I was under him, the greatest teacher that I had ever known.   After entering the Seminary I soon came to see that Dr. Sparrow was every whit the equal of Dr. McGuffey.   To this day, these two men stand out in my life as the most powerful promoters of my own mental development.

"I was profoundly affected by my fellow students. Many of them had passed through the war as soldiers of the South. They were sobered and matured by their experiences.   They came largely from the fine old Virginia homes, in which religion and refinement were united, and where inherited manliness distinguished the youth of the households.   Unpretending, virile, and yet gentle, thoroughly religious, but without severity and without sentimentality, they furnished an environment for a new-comer that was most useful. Some of the dearest friends I have ever had were found in this body of men.   Alas, many of them have crossed over the river; but enough remain to recall those days of preparation for Holy Orders.

"The Seminary cannot be thought of by an old student without his remembering the families of the neighborhood, —those of the Bishop and the Professors and the masters of the High School and others, whom we visited often, and knew well.   In the formative period of a young man's life, such social advantages, as were afforded the students of the Seminary, are far more useful than the pretentious society that one often finds in the city where sometimes wealth counts for too much.

"A spirit of piety that was most invigorating pervaded the community.   The teaching in the Seminary was evangelical, but it was not Calvinistic; and so the tone of professors, students, and neighbors was in no sense Puritanical, but altogether cheerful, and entirely free from cant and asceticism.

"How clearly after the lapse of years do I recall the plain, dignified services in the Chapel, with those strong sermons, (all of the professors were good preachers), the Faculty Meetings with those glimpses of a deeper, higher world that we caught through the uplifting addresses of the men who were our teachers, the fervid worship of our class prayer meetings. Through all of the religious life there was that note of foreign missions ever sounding, drawing many men to the foreign field, and raising the standard of consecration in the lives of many men who felt that their duty was at home.

"We were not left to ourselves to work out alone our theological opinions, and to shape our characters. It is always unsafe for that to be done in a Theological School. In addition to the practical public instruction that the students received, they were under the personal, spiritual direction of the Dean and other members of the Faculty. The Dean's relation to the students was truly pastoral. He knew their intellectual difficulties, and their short-comings, and spiritual dangers. Many a time since I left the Seminary have I heard of students who had been guided into safe and smooth waters by the spiritual insight and the faithful care of Dr. Sparrow. I emphasize this phase of the Virginia Seminary's influence because I think it is in this one respect prominent among the Theological Schools of our Church. As I try to sum up the results that were likely to be attained at the Theological Seminary in Virginia by its students generally, when I was one of them, my memory constructs this group: clear, conservative convictions of Christian truth, loyalty to this Church, a high conception of the Christian ministry, a genuine consecration to its work, —all permeated by manly piety.

"Other Seminaries may have produced better scholars, but this unpretending school made men,—men who could fill the positions to which they were called, and fit themselves to new conditions, in which the mere scholar or ecclesiastic would have been found wanting.

"Not long ago I chanced to be talking with a distinguished member of the United States Senate from one of the Northern States, and who had been a general in the Union Army during the Civil War, who spoke to me somewhat in this way: 'For years past the rectors of my parish have been graduates of the Virginia Seminary, and I have been profoundly impressed, through my acquaintance with them, with the influence of that school; its alumni, whom I have known, were singularly high-minded, true-hearted gentlemen, and unusually capable in dealing with men from the pulpit and in the private relations of life.' This was the judgment of an impartial witness, whose intellectual ability and wide acquaintance with the world, invest his opinion with the highest value."

In order to secure funds necessary to carry on the work of the Seminary, the Board of Trustees requested the Rev. Dr. Sparrow to devote himself to the work of raising funds among the friends of the Seminary in Virginia and in the North. In compliance with this request, Dr. Sparrow, from friends in Washington, Baltimore, Philadelphia, New York, and elsewhere, succeeded in raising $5000, and in addition to this, collected a large part of the amount needed to pay the salary of an additional professor.

In 1866 the Rev. Dr. Cornelius Walker was elected to the Faculty in the place of the Rev. Dr. May, whose death has been mentioned as having taken place soon after the outbreak of the war. Dr. Walker continued his work as professor in the Seminary for thirty years. His first course was Church History, and after the death of the Rev. Dr. Sparrow, he was made professor of Systematic Divinity. Gentle, courteous, and deeply spiritual, Dr. Walker exerted a profound influence upon the Seminary and its students. He was a devoted pastor, and a conscientious and earnest teacher. We are fortunate in having as the writer of the biographical sketch of this beloved professor, his friend, his pupil, and his associate in the faculty, the Rev. Dr. Carl E. Grammer.

Gradually life in the Seminary became normal. The Faculty Meeting, the Missionary Meeting, and the Rhetorical Society were resumed. Very soon students from the North again began to enter the Institution. And, on one occasion, when a Confederate soldier student was relating the incident which had occurred in a certain battle, a student on the other side of the table responded, "Yes, I was there, and saw what you speak of from the other side of the battle line."

A rumor unfortunately gained circulation that a Ku Klux Klan had been organized in the neighborhood and that

one of its objects was to assault and even kill the Northern
students, and one of them became alarmed and left the
Institution.   There was absolutely no foundation in fact
for this rumor, and from the day when the Seminary re-
opened, a cordial invitation was extended to Northern men
to return, and a cordial welcome was given them at the Seminary, where there was no trace of sectional feeling, and no
disposition to introduce the animosities or bitterness of the
past.

The class room work went on much as usual, Dr. Walker,
taking in addition to Church History, the Old and New
Testament, Homiletics, and the History and Interpretation
of the Book of Common Prayer, beside Mental and Moral
Philosophy in the Preparatory Department.   The Junior
Preparatory students were taught by college graduates
among the theological students; the first one after the War
charged with this responsibility was Thomas U. Dudley,
afterwards Bishop of Kentucky.

At the meeting of the Board of Trustees held in 1867,
the salaries of the professors were fixed at $2,000 annually.
In 1869 the treasurer was ordered to pay the professors an
additional $500 a year, as long as the funds of the Seminary
would permit.

By action of the Board of Trustees in 1868, Dr. Sparrow
was appointed Dean of the Faculty, and Bishop Johns was
elected professor of Pastoral Theology.

In 1867 there was held the first meeting of the Alumni
Association since the outbreak of the War.   A large number
of the former students both from the North and from the
South were present, and the peculiar circumstances under
which they met seemed to draw them closer together than
ever before.

From among the students of this period, Charles Clifton
Penick entered the African Mission, and was subsequently
made Bishop of Cape Palmas, and William J. Boone followed
his father to China and succeeded him as Bishop there.   This
period in the History of the Seminary furnished to the Episcopate Thomas U. Dudley, Bishop of Kentucky, and George
W. Peterkin, Bishop of West Virginia.   From the Preparatory class, Bishop Beckwith of Alabama, he having taken his

theological work elsewhere; Robert A. Gibson, Bishop of Virginia; Isaac L. Nicholson, Bishop of Milwaukee; H. Melville Jackson, Bishop of Alabama; and George H. Kinsolving, Bishop of Texas. To this period also belongs the Rev. John S. Lindsay of St. Paul's, Boston, known throughout the Church as the distinguished president of the House of Clerical and Lay Deputies of the General Convention.

Another student of this period was the honored and distinguished alumnus of the Seminary, the Rev. Dr. Randolph H. McKim, rector of Epiphany, Washington. Ever loyal to the traditions of the Seminary, he lent the strength of his personality to every effort designed to promote the welfare of the Institution, and was for many years the Alumni representative upon the Board of Trustees. Perhaps no man among the Alumni of the Seminary in Virginia was better known throughout the American Church. With the pen of a ready and yet scholarly writer, he was ever zealous to defend the truth as he had learned and cherished it. His writings as well as his pulpit utterances gave evidence of long and continuous scholarship, and in General Convention and elsewhere, men learned to know that in debating a question with Dr. McKim a thorough knowledge of the facts of History was essential on the part of his antagonist, if he wished to hold his own in debate. Upon the floors of Convention, as in his controversal papers in the Church press, and in pamphlet literature, Dr. McKim never let the strength and passion of his conviction lead him into any word of discourtesy. He recognized what many forget, that no man in contending for Christian truth, is justified in doing violence to elemental Christian virtues. It was our good fortune to secure from Dr. McKim, before his death, the fulfillment of his promise to write a chapter for this book on "The Seminary During the War Between the States." No man was more competent for this service than this gallant soldier and devoted son of the Seminary.

The Seminary emerged from these days of darkness and trial, more strongly equipped in faith and devotion for the work to which she was committed. Again, as in the beginning of her life, she faced heavy responsibilities, impoverished in material possessions and impotent except for her conquering faith in God and in her Mission. These experiences, which led her in supplication to the throne of Grace, contributed as all such experiences do to the strengthening of her spiritual life, and to the development of her faith. Out of the deep she had called unto God, and God answered her, and she passed on her way having seen and known in her days of trial, Him to Whom she was ordained and consecrated to bear witness.

THE OLD FACULTY

Rev. Dr. Angus Crawford.　　　Rev. Dr. Carl E. Grammer.
Rev. Dr. Cornelius Walker.　Rev. Dr. Joseph Packard.　Rev. Dr. John J. McElhinney.
Rev. Dr. Kinloch Nelson.

SECTION III

CHAPTER VI

1870-1886

Bequests from S. G. Wyman of Baltimore, Mr. Anson Phelps Dodge, and Others —The Reinicker Lecture Fund—Election of Dr. McElhinney—The Ritualistic Emphasis of the Virginia Seminary—Meeting of Evangelical Alliance—An Optional Course, ever Popular in the Seminary—The Semi-Centennial Celebration—Death of Dr. Sparrow—Death of Bishop Payne—Dr. Slaughter's Tribute to the Missionary Spirit of the Seminary—Tribute to Dr. Andrews— Election of Dr. Kinloch Nelson—Introduction of Examining Chaplains and the Temporary Confusion Following—Incorporation of the Education Society —The Board of Trustees takes active interest in Teaching and Text Books— Death of Bishop Johns—Dr. Hodge of Princeton and Bishop Johns—Brief Sketch of life of Bishop Johns—Preparatory Department—Bishop Payne Divinity School Established—The Salaries of the Professors—Difficulties Attending Effort to Secure Christmas Holidays—Committee to Erect New Chapel—The relation of the Seminary to the Southern Churchman—Memorial Window Given by Bishop Pinckney of Maryland—Tablet from the Dean of the Virginia Military Institute—A Chapel for Colored People—The Colored Servants of the Seminary—Resignation of Dr. McElhinney—Semi-Centennial of Dr. Packard's Professorship—The Mellow Glow of Light which Falls upon the Closing Years of this Period.

As in the ordered sequence of the Christian year the shadows of the Cross are dispelled by the light of the resurrection morn, so in the life of the Seminary the gloom which shrouded the Institution during the dark years of Civil War was soon succeeded by the brightness of a better day and by the songs of triumph and the year of jubilee in the life of our Alma Mater.

Through the untiring efforts of Dr. Sparrow and Dr. Packard generous contributions were secured for the Seminary. From Mr. S. G. Wyman of Baltimore $5,000 was received which partly paid for the erection of Wyman Hall, used for a gymnasium. Anson Phelps Dodge gave to Dr. Packard his check for $1,700, and his note for $10,000, and Mr. Cleveland Dodge of New York made contributions amounting to $33,000. From Miss Anne Jones of New York, through Dr. Packard, $20,000 was received at different times, and in her will she left $64,000 to the Seminary. Mr. George A. Reinicker founded a lectureship and an annual prize for elocution. The Rev. John S. Wallace gave $2,000 to found two annual prizes for extemporaneous discourse,

and from Mrs. George Zabriskie Gray, of New York, a generous gift was received in loving memory of her husband.

In 1871 the Rev. Dr. John J. McElhinney was elected to
the faculty as Professor of Hebrew and Apologetics. This
election made the faculty consist of Rev. Dr. Packard, Rev.
Dr. Sparrow, Rev. Dr. Walker and Rev. Dr. McElhinney.

"In the Seminary at this time," says Dr. Walker, "the
ritualistic results of the Oxford movement began to seek
entrance through genuflections made down in the pews."
They never seemed to have reached the chancel save when
some student entering there followed some ritualistic practice
which he had been taught to observe in his home parish.
This went unnoticed or was passed without comment and
generally soon ceased.

As one reads the records of these days and marks the
emphasis negatively placed in Virginia and in the Virginia
Seminary on ritual and ritualism, one is inclined to the
conviction that perhaps Virginia and the Virginia Seminary
were, next to Fond du Lac and Nashotah, the most ritualistc
centers in the American Church. For ritual, while it is a
matter of outward form and practice, is also an attitude of
mind and a matter of emphasis, and it is quite possible for
the mind to be as thoroughly obsessed with a prejudice
against as with a prejudice in favor of ritual practice, and
to be as much distracted from spiritual contemplation and
contact by constantly watching for as by indulging in ritual
observance. In their protest against ritual some of the sons
of our Seminary have at times indulged in ritual acts of
protest which were outward and visible tokens of dissent
just as conspicuous and equally distracting to the mind as
some of the practices which they sought to discount. Irreverent protest against irreverent ritualism is as unchurchly
and as unspiritual as the practice protested against, and fails
to minister either to edification or to decency in the conduct
of the service of the Church. The long withholding of the early
Communion on Sunday morning from a place in the Seminary,
and the refusal for many years by those in authority to provide for a Communion celebration at the opening of the Virginia Church Conventions, were tokens of this fearful attitude of the protesting mind. It will be remembered by some

that when the question of providing an early Communion in the Seminary Chapel came before the Board of Trustees the point was made, in defense of introducing this service, that the Seminary stood in danger of making her graduates feel that they had proven disloyal to the Seminary and become extreme high Churchmen, when upon going as curates to parishes, or as rectors to Churches where the Communion was more frequently offered, they immediately and naturally began to do what was not allowed in the Seminary. This and other arguments prevailed, and the early Communion was provided in later years. Surely no one will think that the Seminary is any less spiritual or less loyal to the real purpose and intent of its founders in providing spiritual food for those who come to her with a cultivated hunger for the more frequent feeding upon the Bread of Life.

Historical judgment must needs be ever discriminating. Past practices and by-gone attitudes of heart and mind must be judged in the light of the day and generation in which they found their place and performed their function. Issues which, in the past, dominated the foreground of thought, called for certain emphasis and a distinct expression of pronounced conviction in order that among contending thoughts the balance of truth might be maintained. The resultant at length is found among the contrary forces contending for mastery. New issues arise and consistency no longer demands the same emphasis upon old restraints or the use of the same iron-clad armor in the battle for truth. Truth, as it is progressively revealed to man, can not be standardized, neither can the Church, without peril to herself, allow herself to be standardized. The progressive revelation of the mind of Christ demands a progressive development in the organism which He has ordained to be the means for giving the revelation, and this organism is His Body, the Church.

The Evangelical Alliance, representing the various bodies of Protestant Christianity throughout the world, met in the city of Washington shortly before the Seminary Semi-Centennial. The faculty and students, being in thorough sympathy with the aims of this organization, attended the meetings, some of which were held in Trinity Church. Among the distinguished visitors present was Dr. Payne

Smith, dean of Canterbury, who, by invitation, visited the Seminary and made an address. In this address he greatly surprised both faculty and students by calling attention to the fact that more was required of them in the way of theological preparation than was required from the students of Oxford and Cambridge.

Some of the students at the Seminary at this time, and subsequently, were beneficiaries of the Education Society, of which the Rev. Dr. Robert C. Matlack, a graduate of the Virginia Seminary, was for many years the efficient secretary, and of which Phillips Brooks was a devoted patron.

One of the courses frequently pursued in the Seminary, but not mentioned in the catalogue, was commented upon in an editorial in The Southern Churchman to the effect that "the Christian religion is one especially favoring love and marriage, its business being the cultivation of gentle affections and its most beautiful figure being the marriage of Christ and the Church. For such reasons we need not wonder at the energy with which our young theological students enter upon matrimony, nor complain a great deal that courting and marriage should seem to be a part of our Seminary course."

At a meeting of the Board of Trustees held on May 20, 1873, a committee consisting of the Rev. Dr. George H. Norton and Mr. Cassius F. Lee was appointed to make suitable arrangements for celebrating the Semi-Centennial anniversary of the Seminary, in conference with the Faculty and Alumni, and the treasurer was authorized to pay the expenses of the Celebration. Bishop Johns was made chairman of the Committee, and at a meeting of the Trustees, held on June 24th, he reported that the Committee had deemed it best to have the Celebration on the 24th and 25th of September. At the time appointed there assembled to take part in the Semi-Centennial, representatives of thirty-four classes out of the fifty which had graduated since 1823, one hundred and one former graduates of the Seminary coming from almost every diocese in the Church. In addition to these there were twenty-two clerical visitors from various dioceses.

The Semi-Centennial Celebration began with the devotional meeting held at seven o'clock on the morning of September 25th, followed at ten o'clock by a meeting of the Alumni in Prayer Hall. At eleven o'clock an opening address was made in the Chapel by the Rt. Rev. Dr. Johns, and Dr. Joseph Packard read an account of the history of the Seminary, with special emphasis on the life and work of its teachers and Alumni. There followed an address by the Rev. Dr. Andrews in memory of Bishop Meade, and one from Bishop Lee of Delaware on "The Spiritual Work of the Seminary". In the afternoon, the Alumni met to deliberate on the best methods to promote the welfare of the Institution.

"On Thursday, at ten A. M., the Holy Communion was administered to more than one hundred and fifty persons. Then followed an address by Dr. Tyng and one by Rev. Philip Slaughter in commemoration of the deceased professors. After an interval of one hour the audience again assembled to hear an address by Dr. Dalrymple on 'The Necrology of the Alumni.' Bishop Wilmer of Louisiana followed with a brief address. Bishop Johns, presiding, made the closing as well as the opening address. The weather was all that could be desired, and the attendance exceeded all expectations. The deepest interest was manifested by all present from the beginning to the end."

In the account published at the time are the names of the Alumni present and their respective classes, also the names of the visiting clergy and friends who took part in the services and exercises. Following is the full program of the proceedings:

"THE ORDER OF EXERCISES"

"The Trustees, Professors, Alumni of the Seminary, invited guests and other friends assembled in Prayer Hall, at 10 o'clock A. M., where a Procession was formed, under the direction of the Rev. Arthur S. Johns which moved, at 10:30 A. M., to the Chapel of the Seminary.

EXERCISES IN THE CHAPEL

Wednesday Morning

Address of Welcome.
    By the Rt. Rev. John Johns, D. D., Bishop of Virginia.
Prayer.
    By the Rt. Rev. John Johns, D. D., of Virginia

Singing of the 25th Hymn of the Prayer Book.

The first Address, which was assigned to the Rev. Alexander H. Vinton, D. D., of Boston, was not delivered, the Rev. Speaker having been prevented, by a domestic affliction, from being present.

The Bishop then introduced the Rev. Joseph Packard, D. D., Professor of Biblical Literature in the Seminary, who delivered an Historical Address on the origin of the Seminary, its purpose, and what it had accomplished.

The next Address was delivered by the Rev. Charles W. Andrews, D. D., of Shepherdstown, West Virginia, being an eulogy upon the character of the late Rt. Rev. William Meade, D. D., Bishop of Virginia.

The Bishop then called on Rt. Rev. Alfred Lee, D. D., Bishop of Delaware, who delivered an extemporaneous Address.

After a brief intermission, the Alumni and Friends of the Seminary reassembled in the Chapel, where a meeting was held to deliberate upon the interests of the Seminary.

Thursday Morning

"The exercises were commenced by the administration of the Holy Communion at 10 A.M., the Rt. Rev. John Johns, D. D., the Rt. Rev. Alfred Lee, D. D., and the Rt. Rev. Francis M. Whittle, D. D., officiating.

After a brief intermission, the Rt. Rev. Bishop Johns introduced the Rev. Stephen H. Tyng, D. D., of New York City, who delivered an address "on the Maryland side of the History of the Seminary."

After singing the Hymn, "Lo, what a cloud of witnesses," Bishop Johns introduced the Rev. Philip Slaughter, of Culpeper Co., Virginia, who delivered an Address, commemorative of the deceased Professors of the Seminary.

After an intermission of an hour, the Services were resumed in the Chapel by the Bishop introducing the Rev. E. A. Dalrymple, D. D., of Baltimore, who delivered an Address in memory of the deceased Alumni.

At the close of the Address, there was held the final meeting of the Alumni and Friends of the Seminary.

The business meetings of the Alumni, on Wednesday and Thursday have their interest, and we briefly indicate the substance of their proceedings. The Rev. George A. Smith, the first graduate of the class of 1823, presided, and the Rev. E. A. Dalrymple of the class of 1843 was secretary. These positions, we may add, they held until the time of their decease.

After addresses by Rev. Joshua Morsell, Rev. Charles H. Page, and Rev. George D. Wildes, a motion was made by Rev. Dr. Norton, that a committee of six clergymen and four laymen be appointed, to consider and report to the meeting, some plan for the financial benefit of the Seminary.

This committee reported the following resolution.

First, in view of the necessity of the case, that effort he made within the next twelve months, to add $100,000 to the vested funds of the Seminary.

Second, that their belief is that this amount can be secured.

Thirdly, their suggestion, as to the names of the Clergy and Laity, who can successfully secure the desired result.

The meeting closed with the adoption of a resolution offered by Dr. Julius Grammer of Maryland.

"Resolved that we, the Alumni, and friends of the Theological Seminary in Virginia, acknowledge, with devout gratitude to the Almighty God, His protecting Providence, which has been over our beloved Seminary, during the past fifty years; and that we pledge ourselves, in future years, to love her more, and serve her better, and that we renew our devotion to her distinctive Protestant Evangelical teaching".

The meeting, next day, Thursday, opened with an address from Bishop Wilmer of Louisiana, followed by a motion of the Rev. T. U. Dudley, Jr., of Maryland, for the appointment of the Local Committee, referred to in the third resolution of the day before. This was adopted, and the Committee appointed.

On motion of Dr. Walter W. Williams, resolution was adopted, securing the publication of the addresses which had been made.

The closing resolution was by Cassius F. Lee, Esq., which was unanimously adopted.
Resolved that the Rev. Thomas U. Dudley, Jr., of Maryland, be, and he is hereby
  requested, with the consent of his Vestry, to act as special Agent of the Alumni
  and friends of the Seminary, here present, at this Semi-Centennial meeting, to
  solicit funds for the Seminary; and the Trustees of the Seminary are requested
  to provide for a supply for his pulpit, while he is thus occupied, and to pay his
  necessary traveling expenses.
After appropriate devotional exercises, the meeting adjourned *sine die.*"

The addresses given on this occasion, together with the
minutes of the meeting of the Alumni Association, were
subsequently published in pamphlet form and widely distributed. We have refrained from publishing these addresses
in full because of the fact that they are accessible in pamphlet
form, and also because the events referred to by the speakers
have already been included elsewhere in this History.

In order to give effect to the resolutions adopted by the
Alumni at the Semi-Centennial meeting, the Board of Trustees requested Dr. Sparrow to undertake for three years the
work of soliciting contributions. He had, however, hardly
entered upon this duty, when his death occurred on January
17, 1874. His funeral services took place in the chapel of
the Seminary on Tuesday morning, January 20th, at eleven
o'clock. A large congregation was present, among which
were many clergy from a distance. Bishop Johns and Bishop
Whittle took part in the service and Rev. Dr. Andrews made
a brief address, followed by an address by Bishop Johns.
The interment took place in the cemetery near the Chapel.
Soon after his death, a mural tablet was placed in the Seminary Chapel in loving memory of their teacher, by the
students of the Seminary.

In 1874 news was received of the death of Bishop Payne.
From the time when he had reached his decision to give his
life to help brighten the darkness of darkest Africa, his influence had been felt as an inspiration in the life of the Seminary. His letters written from Liberia and his visits to
the Seminary when on furlough, had contributed largely to
keep brightly burning in the Seminary the flame of devotion
to the Church's Mission to those lying in darkness and the
shadow of death. Declining health had made it necessary
for him to spend the closing years of his ministry in his old
home parish in Westmoreland, where he had done his first
missionary work. He resumed this work and carried it on

until his death in October 1874. During his whole missionary career he kept a Journal which opens with a graphic
description of his experiences, of the prayer services held
in the Seminary under the leadership of William Boone, and
in association with Thomas Savage and Launcelot Minor.
"Among my most vivid recollections of the Seminary,"
writes Dr. Philip Slaughter a few weeks before his death,
"is the Prayer Meeting held before the dormant day in
Boone's room, conducted chiefly by Boone, Savage, Payne
and Minor. I have often said since, that the incense ascending from that upper room was one of the chief conductors
which, piercing the heavens, drew down the missionary
spirit and diffused it through the Seminary, sending Boone
to China, Payne, Minor and Savage, to Africa, at whose
gates pestilence had so long stood sentinel. Everlasting
honor be to this high band of martyrs!"

An appeal signed by Edward Wall, Edward W. Wroth,
John K. Mason, and L. W. Saltonstall, a committee of
students, was sent in 1874 to each alumnus of the Seminary
asking for a contribution toward a fund of $250 for the pur-
chase of a new organ for the Seminary Chapel.

The minutes of the meeting of the Board of Trustees
held in June 1876, make mention of the death of the Rev.
Charles Wesley Andrews, D. D., who for many years had
been a member of the Board and a faithful friend of the
Seminary. Dr. Andrews |was a staunch Evangelical and
exerted great influence in the General Conventions, where he
was considered one of the ablest debaters in the Church.

At this meeting of the Board, the Rev. Kinloch Nelson
was elected to the Chair of Church History. He began his
work as professor in the Seminary in the fall of 1876. Dr.
Nelson had been prominent in the councils of Virginia, and
had exerted great influence in the life of the Church. He
was sent three times by the diocese of Virginia to General Convention. Born on the 2nd of November, 1839, he
received his education at the Episcopal High School and
at the University of Virginia. He served throughout the
entire Civil War, and was among the students who entered
the Seminary when it reopened in 1865, graduating in 1868.
Before his election as professor in the Seminary he had served

as rector of Leeds Parish in Fauquier County, and in Richmond, Virginia. Dr. Nelson was a strong and winsome personality, and from the very outset won the confidence, esteem and affection of the students. He was their pastor, their comrade, and their constant friend. Books never separated him from men, and study did not isolate him from constant companionship with the students. The writer can see him now, standing near the side-lines of the tennis court in the grove between the Seminary and St. George's Hall, watching with keen interest the game, and giving his applause to any brilliant play which he witnessed. We can see him in the quadrangle, watching with interest the impromptu ball play of the students, even though he knew, as we did, that ball played just at that place did not meet with the approval of good Dr. Suter. In the class room he did his work with earnestness and with fidelity. He made no pretense to profound learning. He was preeminently a practical theologian. He first asked us what Ellicott had to say in his commentary on the text, and then proceeded to tell us how to apply what Ellicott said, or what was said in the text, to the practical work of the pastor, and to the practical and common sense preaching of the Gospel. He served as professor in the Seminary until October 1894, when he fell asleep, honored, beloved, and lamented by all who knew him.

Upon the election of Dr. Nelson a rearrangement of the course of study was made among the members of the faculty. Dr. Packard continued to teach his old course, assisted by Dr. McElhinney. Dr. Nelson was appointed to the Chair of Church History and Ecclesiastical Polity and Dr. Walker became professor of Systematic Divinity, including Butler's Analogy, and was also appointed professor of Homiletics. Dr. Nelson was placed in charge of the Seminary Mission Stations. He was preeminently fitted for this work by reason of his exceptional pastoral gifts and was most acceptable to the students in charge of the mission stations and to the people to whom they ministered. He also served as chief pastor to the Episcopal High School, where he endeared himself to the teachers and the students by his cordial manner and his kindly and gracious personality.

A change of some moment was introduced into the life of the Seminary at this time through the appointment under the new canons of the general Church of Diocesan Examining Chaplains. As a result of this innovation no little confusion and trouble was at first occasioned. It happened that in many instances those who were appointed as chaplains were not of the Alumni of the Seminary and based their examination questions upon text books different from those taught by the faculty of the Seminary. Until this condition was altered by subsequent appointment of chaplains from among the Alumni, frequent friction arose between the chaplains and the faculty and something worse than friction resulted in the disastrous experiences suffered by the students at the hands of some of the examiners.

The Education Society which, since 1818, had been rendering invaluable service to the Church and the Seminary, was incorporated by an act passed by the Virginia Legislature under date January 8, 1875.

The minutes of the Board of Trustees of this period in the history of the Seminary give evidence of a very close and critical interest on the part of the Board in the class room work of the professors. The secretary is authorized to call the attention of the Rev. Dr. Walker to the fact that he has mentioned in his report the use of the text book which has not received the sanction of the Board. It was resolved, "That in case of any proposed change in the text book or course of study in the Seminary, the proposal for such change be made at one annual meeting of the Board of Trustees to be acted upon at the next annual meeting, except there should be an unanimous vote of the quorum of the Board to take action at the time when the proposal was first made."

In 1876, the Board resolved that the "Professor of Systematic Divinity be requested to require his students to commit to memory the Thirty-nine articles of Religion, and also the proof texts in Knapp's Theology, and that the other Professors be requested to require their students to commit portions of the Gospel and Epistles to memory."

Dr. Sprigg is requested, under resolution offered in 1878, to confer with the Rev. Dr. McElhinney and ascertain why he does not teach the first and second books of Hooker's

Ecclesiastical Polity. Later the minutes record that Dr. McElhinney replied, "that he did not teach these two books because they were being taught by Professor Nelson."

In the spring of 1876 grief and distress were brought into the life of the Seminary by the death of the Rt. Rev. Dr. John Johns, Bishop of Virginia, and president of the Board of Trustees. Bishop Johns had been educated, as was Bishop Meade, at Princeton University, and was through his entire life a close and devoted friend to the Rev. Dr. Charles Hodge of Princeton. "He was," says Dr. Hodge, "only eighteen months my senior, but yet his feeling towards me was always somewhat paternal. He used to say that he brought me up and that if I did not behave he would bring me down." When Dr. Archibald Alexander was appointed professor in Princeton he found the work assigned to him so burdensome that he determined to select some young man to whom he might assign the work in the Hebrew Department. He selected John Johns, but when Johns decided to enter the Episcopal Church, he transferred this work to Dr. Hodge. Johns was a brilliant student at Princeton, graduating in 1815. He entered the Theological Seminary at Princeton, where he remained only two years, having decided to enter the ministry of the Episcopal Church. He studied for orders at Princeton, under Dr. Alexander and Dr. Miller. He was ordered deacon by Bishop White in St. Peter's Church, Philadelphia, on May 6, 1819, and served in Frederick, Maryland, until 1829. In Baltimore he had charge of old Christ Church until a new Church was built for him. At the Virginia Convention at Staunton, in 1842, he was elected assistant to Bishop Meade, by a vote of forty-three out of forty-nine of the clergy and was consecrated in St. Paul's Church, Richmond, in 1842, by Bishops Meade, Griswold, Ives and Whittingham. In 1849 he was elected president of the College of William and Mary, where he remained for five years. Feeling, however, that Alexandria was a more convenient center from which to work, he built a house on Seminary Hill, which he named "Malvern," where he removed with his family in 1854.

His coming to Seminary Hill proved a great blessing to the Institution. His family added a rich contribution to the social life of "The Hill". The Bishop was not alone valuable to the Seminary by reason of the executive duties which he performed, but as professor of Pastoral Theology, he rendered a most valuable service in training the students for the work of their ministry. As a preacher he was noted for his eloquence, and for the soundness of his theology, his sermons being rooted and grounded in the truth which he had mastered through his long years of scholarship. He was a man of delightful and contagious humor, and was beloved on "The Hill" for his genial companionship, as well as for his fatherly counsel and interest in every department of the work of the Institution.

His burial took place on April 17, 1876, and after his death a cemetery was made on the slope of Seminary Hill, facing "Malvern" and there he was buried. "Thither," says Dr. Packard, "were removed later on the remains of Bishops Meade and Payne, of Dr. Sparrow, and last of all, we buried Dr. Kinloch Nelson there." *

In 1877 the vested funds of the Seminary are reported as totaling $196,350, and in June of this same year, Mr. Cassius Lee is authorized to secure a seal for the Seminary.

In 1878 the Board makes provision for the election of a teacher of elocution.

The minutes of the Board of Trustees of 1878 are of special interest. They record at length the contract made with Mr. L. M. Blackford, principal of the Episcopal High School, relative to the erection of certain buildings upon the High School property, and also the report of a committee appointed to examine into the conduct of the Preparatory Department, together with their recommendations, which report is mentioned in the chapter in this volume on the Preparatory Department.

Of special interest is the record in the minutes of this year of the establishment of the Bishop Payne Divinity School in Petersburg, Virginia, under the care of the Rev. Thomas Spencer and under the direction of a committee of the Board of Trustees. The details of the action of the Board in this matter are recorded in the chapter on the Bishop Payne Divinity School in this History. It is of interest, however,

---

* "Recollections of a Long Life," by Dr. Packard. (page 206)

to note here the fact that this school was established by action of the Board of Trustees of the Virginia Seminary and for many years continued to do its work under the supervision and direction of the Board and with funds appropriated for the purpose from the funds of the Seminary. The Bishop Payne Divinity School thus became, in deed and fact, a special department of the Virginia Seminary, and its history, therefore, finds its proper place in the History of this Institution. For the reasons stated in the separate chapter devoted to this school, it was quite impossible as well as entirely inexpedient that colored men seeking to enter the ministry of the Church should have been brought for their training into the Virginia Seminary. They were in no way prepared to do the work then provided either in the Preparatory Department or in the Seminary, and as pointed out elsewhere, it would have been disastrous to them as well as to the Seminary to have admitted them as students here. It was for these and other cogent reasons that the Board established this department of the Virginia Seminary in the city of Petersburg, under the direction of wise and faithful men. The Bishop Payne Divinity School has been doing, since the year of its foundation, an invaluable work in training colored men for the sacred ministry of the Church, and the Church's Mission to these people has been more largely furthered through this Institution than through any other means provided by this Church for training and helping these worthy people.

The faculty of the Seminary during this period suffered constant anxiety by reason of uncertainty as to the amount of salary which they could expect from the Board of Trustees. The contract salary was kept at $2,000, but from time to time, the Board would vote from $250 to $500 increase, subject to the ability of the treasurer to pay the extra amount from the funds available, and there is evidence which leads to the belief that the professors often justly felt that if the Board and its members were as zealous in raising funds for this purpose as the faculty had been in raising money, at the request of the Board, for other purposes, the increase voted by the Board to the Professors of the Seminary could have been easily maintained. There is no question but that the faculty were fully justified in this feeling, in view of the exceptional zeal which they had repeatedly shown in the efforts to raise funds for the Institution in which they were teaching, which was clearly outside their stated duty. Many thousands of dollars had been raised by Dr. Sparrow and Dr. Packard for the general funds of the Institution, without which effort on their part the Seminary would not have been able to continue its work. The faculty could not, however, solicit funds for the payment of their own salaries, and it would seem that this should have been clearly recognized by the Board and that from their own membership, those might have been appointed who could have relieved the faculty of the responsibility of raising funds for the Institution in general and could also have raised an amount adequate to pay the salaries of the faculty.

An incident in the life of the Seminary is revealed by certain entries in the minutes of the Board of Trustees at this period relative to the Christmas holidays. To the meeting of the trustees held in June 1879, a petition was presented signed by the students of the Seminary and Preparatory Department, asking for a week's vacation at Christmas time, to which the Board paid no attention. In 1881 the Rev. Dr. Packard came to the help of the students and submitted a report to the Board in which he said, "I take the opportunity to suggest to the Trustees the propriety of restoring the Christmas recess. It is as far as I know universal in theological seminaries. Dr. Green of Princeton expressed to me his surprise that we had none. 'For', said he, 'We got it from your Church.' It would, too, in a great measure prevent application for leave of absence during a long season of nine months." To this request no reply was made by the Board. Finally, in 1882, Bishop Peterkin offered the following resolution: "Resolved that until it be otherwise ordered, a recess of one week at Christmas be allowed, to begin on such day as the faculty may determine." This resolution, originating within the Board, was unanimously adopted.

In 1879 the Board of Trustees at their meeting held on June 29, adopted a resolution appointing a committee "consisting of the Rev. Dr. Kinloch Nelson, and Messrs. Arthur Herbert, Cassius F. Lee and C. R. Hooff to erect a new Chapel on the site of the present Chapel at a cost not to exceed $5,000." The committee was given power to select plans subject to the approval of the Bishop. This action was taken by reason of the unsafe condition of the Chapel, Dr. Walker and Dr. Nelson having refused to hold services any longer in the old building. The subsequent action of this committee and the result obtained in the erection of the new Chapel are set forth in the article written on this subject by the Rev. Dr. Packard. Dr. Packard says that the Chapel was erected at the cost of $11,000 of which $8,000 was contributed by the Alumni and their friends in all parts of the country. The chancel rail of the new Chapel was made of rosewood brought by Bishop Penick from Africa for this purpose.

We have not been able to determine just what vested interest the Seminary had in the property of "The Southern Churchman." It will be recalled that this paper had been for many years edited by the Rev. Dr. Lippitt, who had been professor in the Seminary, and it is quite evident that the closest relationship existed between this publication and the Theological Seminary. At a meeting of the Board of Trustees held on June 22, 1880, the Trustees while declaring that they had no material property in "The Southern Churchman," agreed for the sum of $600 to transfer the name and good will of said paper to the Rev. Dr. D. F. Sprigg.

The president of the Board of Trustees announced to the Board at its meeting of 1882, that the Rt. Rev. William Pinckney, D. D., Bishop of the diocese of Maryland, had offered a stained glass window at a cost of $150 to be placed in the eastern end of the Seminary Chapel to correspond with the window in the chancel. Whereupon it was resolved "That the Trustees hereby return their warmest thanks to the Rt. Rev. Brother for his generous kindness and express the hope that this manifestation of his interest in our Theological Seminary may tend to bind together the dioceses of Maryland, West Virginia, and Virginia in close and enduring bonds of faith, sympathy, and love."

A communication was read to the Board of Trustees at its meeting in June, 1879, from Colonel F. H. Smith of the Virginia Military Institute, a son-in-law of Dr. Henderson, conveying the offer to erect a mural tablet in the Seminary Chapel to the founders of the Theological Seminary in Virginia. The tablet offered was gratefully received and ordered erected under the supervision of the executive committee of the Board. This tablet, presented by Colonel Smith, was made memorial to the Rev. William H. Wilmer, D. D., Rev. William Hawley, the Rev. William Meade, Francis Scott Key, Esq., and Thomas Henderson, M. D., who were among the earliest friends and founders of the Seminary.

Permission was given by the Board in 1882, upon request of Rev. Benjamin Dennis, to erect upon the south-east corner of the Seminary grounds a chapel for the colored people, where a Sunday School could be conducted and Church services held by the students of the Seminary for these people, many of whom were serving the Seminary in various capacities.

This note recalls to memory those who through successive years were familiar to the students,—the servants of the Seminary. In an humbler station they ministered, some of them with devotion and fidelity for many years, in ways indispensable to the necessities and comforts of student life on "The Hill". From the kitchen at times would rise the melody of their voices as they chanted together in rhythmic cadence some hymn or familiar plantation song. In the dining room Archie, James, and others cheerfully moved among us, often with a welcome smile and always sure as they came to us with fried chicken, ginger-bread and ice-cream, of a welcome smile in return. Nor do we forget the good cheer of Rachel and Matilda, climbing the steps with a basket filled with laundry deftly poised and balanced on their red bandana coiffured heads, or the kind indulgence with which they waited sometimes for their money when we did not have any ourselves. It was good that a Chapel should be built for them, and their friends upon Seminary Hill. We owe more to these kindly folk than we realize until they vanish away and their place knows neither them nor their like any more.

The Rev. Dr. J. J. McElhinney, because of old age and infirmity, resigned from the faculty on the 7th of June, 1887. A committee of students of the Theological Seminary waited

on him at his residence and presented him with a gold headed
ebony cane.   They also read a series of suitable resolutions
adopted by the students regretting his retirement from the
Seminary, to which the Doctor feelingly replied.   The resolutions were as follows:

"Whereas in the providence of God our venerated and
beloved Professor John Joyce McElhinney, D. D., is about
to retire from his professorship, therefore resolved by the
students assembled:

"First: That we place on record our high appreciation
of his rare personal worth as a man of God and of his superior
qualities as a wise counselor, a clear thinker, an able and faithful teacher and preacher.

"Second: We gratefully record God's goodness to the
Church in sparing him so long to occupy so responsible a
position and to be for a third of a century the instructor of
so many of her ministers and we feel thankful to the great
head of the Church that for so long a period the Church has
shared the labors of a life of so great usefullness.

"Third: That we extend to him our heart-felt love and
express our appreciation of his patience with us, and of his
many kindnesses to us, and that we present the accompanying token in further evidence of our esteem, affection and
regret at parting.

James W. Morris, secretary of the meeting."

In the account of the Theological Seminary commencement, which appeared in "The Southern Churchman" of July
1, 1886, mention is made of its being the Semi-Centennial
of Dr. Packard's professorship.

"Upon the entrance of the venerable Dean at the Alumni
Meeting, the whole assembly rose spontaneously to their
feet.   Eloquent and feeling addresses were then made by
Rev. George A. Smith, and Rev. Julius E. Grammer and
Rev. George H. Kinsolving, followed in like affectionate
strain on behalf of the post-bellum generation of the students.
After which Bishop Dudley, with that rare eloquence of
which he stands unrivalled master, told with a depth of
feeling that brought tears to many an eye, of the many

expressions of tender affection for the honored teacher that had come to him as chairman of the committee to receive the contributions of the alumni.

"The response of Dr. Packard, delivered in full, strong tones, was most happy. Those who have heard him at his best in Faculty Meetings will form some idea of it when we say that it excelled even his Faculty Meeting talks. It was full of instruction, humor and pathos, and he evoked alternately smiles and tears. He held the unflagging attention of his audience for nearly an hour while he spoke of the men and manners of former days of the Seminary, and of the changes in customs that had come over the Church since in 1836, he had, at the age of twenty-three, entered upon his duties of professor here. He concluded by saying that the great fear for the future of the Seminary was lest the rationalistic tendencies of the age should creep in here as elsewhere, and by invoking God's blessing upon the Seminary to preserve her from this, as from all evil."

The period which has just been under review in the History of the Seminary was a period void, except for the Semi-Centennial, of major events of extraordinary interest. Most of the things which happened occurred in the normal carrying on of the routine work and established policies of the Institution. News is always abnormal. As long as the days and years come and go bringing the ordinary duties and accustomed benedictions and men and institutions naturally and unostentatiously grow in wisdom and stature and in favor with God and man, the pen of the historian remains poised in mid-air waiting for something strange and new and abnormal to happen. Yet these deep quiet years furnish the time when the roots, undisturbed by turmoil, strike deep into the soils, and silently the tendrils of ivy weave mantles of green over the red bricks and bare stone walls and clothe the symbols of the Institution's life with the green garment of beauty, and mellow the years of experiment and trial with the lichens and close clinging vines which tell of enduring success approved and sealed by the mellowing touch of time.

A new era is about to dawn. From the American point of view, condescendingly smiled upon by our trans-Atlantic friends, the Seminary already has in 1886 a somewhat ancient history. Among the marks of its antiquity are the Seminary grounds and the venerable Dean. The cows browse upon the lawns or take refuge from pestilential flies amid the undergrowth and blackberry bushes flourishing undisturbed under the protecting shade of the Seminary grove. In the spring the arbutus and the wild violets carpet the ground and the birds nest in the wild wilderness between the Seminary and the High School. Old Dr. McElhinney lingers among the books of the Library and moves about the solitary places of the Seminary like an ancient monk queerly garbed, but all unmindful of the changing fashions of a fickle world. The old Dean, who for fifty-one years already has lived and taught on "The Hill" now moves through grounds and buildings "with feeble step and slow." How we loved and revered the dear old "Rab," and yet our love for him was as the starlight is to the sunshine compared to his love for his boys. His sleeve hangs empty of its arm; his tall form is bent with the weight of years and his hair is silvered; but still his heart is young, and he moves about, a living witness to Butler's argument for the immortality of the soul, for in him, amid the decay and dissolution of the body, love and the other gentle graces of character retain their immortal youth. He has now come to where the shadows of life are lengthening in the sunset glow of eventide. Yet to him the shadows are all tinged and lined with light from realms invisible. As he moves about "The Hill" his memory lingers upon vanished scenes and faces "loved long since and lost awhile", and he writes, "The early light of the morning rests upon the picture which the lights and shadows of the intervening years have not dimmed."

Amid his memories and anticipations of the glory which will soon be revealed, Dr. Packard lingers on. Soon a new professor of Hebrew will come, and one of his old students, and the grandson of his beloved comrade and friend, Dr. Sparrow, will arrive, called to "The Hill" and the Seminary which the old Dean so deeply loves, to be a teacher and also to be to him as a loving son. The Doctor waits to welcome them, and lingers awhile to inspire them, and then turns again home and passes peacefully into Paradise.

SECTION III

CHAPTER VII

1887-1902

Election of Dr. Grammer and Dr. Crawford in 1887—Claim for Damages Done to the Seminary during the Civil War—Virginia Seminary Magazine—Theological Repertory—Improvements to Seminary Grounds and Buildings under Dr. Crawford's Administration—Meeting of International Students' Alliance —The Beginning of the Brazil Mission—Volunteers for other Fields—Class of 1891—Rev. George A. Smith—Cassius F. Lee—Dr. Suter—Dr. Norton—Dr. Slaughter—First Death to Occur in the Seminary—Building of Whittle Hall—Joshua Peterkin—Visits from Returned Missionaries—The Seminary and Phillips Brooks—Dr. Kinloch Nelson—Dr. Samuel A. Wallis elected Professor—Abolition of the Preparatory Department—Establishment of Reinicker Lectures—The Resignation of Dr. Packard as Dean of the Seminary —Sixtieth Anniversary of Dr. Packard's Professorship—The Ely Professorship—Bachelor of Divinity Degree—Election of Dr. Berryman Green and the Rev. Robert K. Massie—Election of Dr. R. W. Micou—Dr. Crawford Elected Dean in 1900—Conference of Representatives of the Faculties of all Seminaries at the Seminary—Establishment of Sparrow Fellowship—Death of Dr. Packard—Death of Bishop Whittle.

The election to the Faculty of the Rev. Dr. Angus Crawford and the Rev. Dr. Carl E. Grammer in the spring of 1887 inaugurated a new era in the life of the Seminary. With them came the beginning of the modern history of the Institution. New ideas began to make themselves evident in the outward appearance of "The Hill" and new ideals began to stir and quicken the currents of Seminary life.

A committee of the Board, of which Rt. Rev. Dr. A. M. Randolph was chairman, after making extensive search and diligent inquiry, succeeded even beyond their own expectations in finding a very up-to-date man to teach the very ancient language of Hebrew. Bishop Randolph of the committee appointed to nominate a professor for the chair of Hebrew reported as follows:

"Various names have been presented to the committee by correspondence and otherwise from sources entitled to respect. The committee has been impressed with the difficulty of securing a scholar of the requisite qualifications in the Episcopal Church in this country. Scholarship in the Hebrew and cognate languages, such as are requisite and

THE FACULTY (1902)

Rev. Dr. Robert K. Massie   Rev. Dr. Berryman Green
Rev. Dr. Richard H. Micou. Rev. Dr. Angus Crawford. Rev. Dr. Samuel A. Wallis.

necessary to afford the students of our Seminary the best advantages in the critical study of the Holy Bible, is very rare among our clergy. The demand created by modern investigations in oriental literature, in archaeology, and in historic science, as it bears upon the Old Testament, for a higher grade of scholarship in these special lines in the Seminary professor, seems to forbid the selection of an ordinary general scholar for this special work. With these considerations in view the effort of the committee has been to find a scholar read in the Hebrew and Semitic languages which are necessary to a scientific understanding of the Old Testament. In their opinion the Rev. Angus Crawford of Mount Holly, New Jersey, has the qualifications for a successful teacher in this department and they would present his name as a suitable person to fill the chair."

Upon resolution, the Rev. Angus Crawford, was elected Professor of Hebrew and Oriental Languages. At the time of his election to the faculty of the Virginia Seminary, Dr. Crawford was rector of Trinity Church, Mount Holly, New Jersey. He was recommended for election to the faculty by Professor William R. Harper, of Yale University, afterwards president of the University of Chicago.

The Rev. Dr. Grammer was assigned to the Chair of Church History and incidentally supplemented the work done in the department of Greek by requiring the students of his Church History class to read the first book of Christian Church History, the Acts of the Apostles, in Greek, translating it in his class room. Dr. Grammer's versatile and brilliant mind refused to remain within the confines of the traditional limits of his department. The study of the Acts in Greek gave him opportunity to express certain convictions relative to the vital worth and necessity for accurate and thorough scholarship, and also opened a direct way for his mind into the realm of Church Polity. The responsibility which his course in history placed upon him to teach the origin and development of Christian institutions stimulated the controversial tendencies of his thought to express very pronounced convictions on the origin and nature of the orders of the ministry. A thin partition alone separated Dr. Grammer's class room from that of Dr. Kinloch

Nelson, the officially delegated teacher of Church Polity, but there were wide stretches between the views and convictions of the two teachers as to orders in their succession and consequent authority. There was official Greek and officially taught Church Polity, with strong emphasis placed on *"Episcopos"* and the succession on Dr. Nelson's side of the partition, and *subrosa* Greek and interrogatively taught Church Polity with the major emphasis on *"Presbuteros"* taught on Dr. Grammer's side of the partition. The situation was stimulating to the students and we could but wonder, at times, if it did not have a certain disciplinary value in its effect upon the temper and good nature of Dr. Nelson, who strongly believed in "the Church as the seamless robe of Christ."

Then, too, the arrival of the ancient heresies upon the scene of action in Dr. Grammer's class room and the looming up of some ancient theologian who had views and taught convictions which had to be known and rightly measured, naturally led Dr. Grammer's mind into the field of speculative theology. His conclusions and convictions were, however, not always found authenticated in Dr. Walker's beloved Knapp, whom neither Phillips Brooks nor Dr. Grammer regarded as containing the final word in theology. It fortunately happened that Dr. Walker's profound love for truth and his recognition of its vastness, together with Dr. Grammer's respect for the cogent clearness of Dr. Walker's thought, enabled them to dwell and teach together in unity without falling out by the way. The only course upon which Dr. Grammer's mind did not throw vivid and richly colored side-lights was Dr. Crawford's course in Hebrew. Here there was but one gardener assiduously working to cultivate Hebrew roots and he alone sought to graft the minds of the students into the ancient Israelitish olive tree.

At this time Dr. Packard's health made his attendance upon his class room work necessarily infrequent, and Dr. Walker's voice was growing faint with the approaching feebleness of old age. The coming of Dr. Grammer and Dr. Crawford was most opportune and most welcome. Their election made the Faculty of this period consist of the Rev. Dr. Joseph Packard, professor of Biblical Literature, the Rev.

Dr. Cornelius Walker, professor of Systematic Divinity, the Rev. Dr. Kinloch Nelson, professor of Greek, Church Polity, and Liturgics, the Rev. Dr. Carl E. Grammer, professor of Church History and Canon Law and the Rev. Dr. Angus Crawford, professor of Hebrew and Old Testament Interpretation.

In view of the destruction wrought by the occupation of the Seminary grounds and buildings by the Federal Troops, the Board of Trustees felt that they were amply justified in laying before Congress a claim for $20,000 damages.   The petition, however, addressed to Congress, asked that the government pay what seemed a reasonable amount for the rent of the Seminary buildings while used by the Northern Army for hospital purposes.   The responsibility for pressing this claim was placed in the hands of Mr. Cassius F. Lee. To the Board of Trustees which met in May, 1889, Mr. Lee was able to report that the justice of the claim had been admitted, and that a part of the amount had been paid over to the Board of Trustees.

When the proposition to pay rent for the Virginia Seminary buildings was reported to the House from the committee of the whole on March 9th, General W. H. F. Lee, member of Congress from the eighth Virginia district, made an eloquent and effective speech in advocacy of it, from which we take the following abstract as reported by the correspondent of the Richmond Dispatch.—"As to the question of loyalty—I do not propose to go into that.   It is said that these professors were not 'loyal'.   They were, not to an earthly but to a celestial power.   They did not go forth to fight the battles of their great chieftain with the red banners of terrestrial war, but they carried the white flag of peace uplifted by their great captain almost two thousand years ago.   It was said by one of the great soldiers of modern times in the zenith of his power, that a million men would spring to arms at his command and rush joyfully to death at his bidding.   Yet, sir, barely more than half a century has passed, and today the followers of his dynasty would hardly dare unfurl his banners in the capitol of his country. The great Founder of Christianity has been dead nearly twenty centuries, yet you can know His followers by millions;

and today, like their forefathers, these faithful followers of
the Cross would go fearlessly amidst storm and shell of
battle, or to the stake, for the principles they maintain.
Even in the barbarous days of early history we have found
the Church to be the refuge for the humblest citizens and
even for the culprit and I had hoped that in this 19th century,
this question would have received at the hands of this house,
more generous treatment than some gentlemen on the other
side seem disposed to give."

The claim was passed by a vote of 130 ayes, to 96 nays. *

The Board of Trustees on June 25, 1889, ordered the
building of a residence on the site of the old High School
garden for the Rev. Professor Grammer. This home was
subsequently occupied by the Rev. Dr. Micou, the Rev.
Dr. Bell, and is now the residence of the Rev. Dr. Nelson.

Brief note may be made of the appearance in 1887 of
the "Virginia Seminary Magazine," which succeeded a paper
published for some years by the Seminary students, known
as the "Seminarian". The Faculty finally decided to accept
the offer of the students to take over the "Seminarian"
and to enlarge it into a magazine of from forty-five to fifty
pages, to be published nine times a year. It served a most
valuable purpose as a means of communication between the
thought of the Seminary and its friends, and the general
public, upon questions of vital importance in the realm of
theology, church history, missionary endeavor and the current life of the Church. This magazine, together with other
publications of the Seminary, has been reviewed in the article
in this volume entitled "Seminary Publications."

At the beginning of the life of the Seminary, the "Theological Repertory," which began its publication in 1819,
while not owned or controlled by the Education Society or
the Seminary, was published by the founders of the Education Society and the early friends of the Seminary, and was
the means of publicity through which the Society and the
Seminary expressed their thought and made their needs
known to the Church.

During the time of publication of the Seminary magazine
and "The Protestant Episcopal Review" which succeeded it

* From "The Southern Churchman." March 15th, 1888.

some of the best known thinkers in the Church made contributions to its pages. It was a distinct loss to the Seminary, and also to the Church, when, for financial and other reasons, it was decided that it was not best to continue the publication.

Very soon after Dr. Crawford's arrival on "The Hill" the Seminary began to feel the impress of his highly developed sense of order and conception of the eternal fitness of things. The condition of the grounds and buildings as they were before his coming has been spoken of. There was no responsibility resting upon the newly elected professor to add to his duties as professor in the Institution the care and oversight of the physical side of the life of the Seminary. He, however, soon began to exercise his energies to beautify and modernize "The Hill." The unkept wilderness of long neglected growth first claimed attention. It was upon this wild undergrowth that he looked out from his home "The Wilderness." The briar bushes and underbrush soon vanished. The trees were trimmed and the dead timber cut from the grove. The grass, which had hitherto only cows for lawn-mowers, began to receive more expert and scientific treatment. The walks of mud and cinders in which successive generations and classes had been mired in the pursuit of duty and pleasure, gave place to concrete. Soon electric lights began to replace the dingy lamps which sputtered and smoked at the intersections of the Seminary by-paths and in the Seminary buildings. It is true, as Dr. Grammer says, that we missed the blue-eyed forget-me-nots which vanished from the grove, and it is true also that the stars seemed to lose some of the dim radiance of their mystic beauty as their light fell upon the stillness of the grove by reason of the new and brilliant lights which were hung about the grounds, but there is no question but that the Seminary soon came to be a more comfortable, a more habitable place in which to dwell. The many other improvements inaugurated through the untiring interest of Dr. Crawford while professor and subsequently dean of the Seminary, are mentioned in other parts of this volume, where, also, are reported the lists of contributions which he received from those whom he interested in his endeavor. He was the originator of the Class Contribution Plan, through which many thousands of dollars were received from the Alumni and their friends for the further execution of the plans and improvements which seemed to constantly emerge from Dr. Crawford's fertile mind.

"The Rev. Dr. Crawford," says Dr. Packard in his "Recollections," "Soon after coming here, raised about $20,000 which was most wisely expended under his supervision, in making great improvements in our grounds and buildings. He had the roads laid off, and graded, the trees planted, water works built, and St. George's Hall enlarged." In addition to these improvements mentioned by Dr. Packard, Dr. Crawford also had the grounds in the front of the Seminary fenced in, and improved. Until this time they had been regarded by the neighborhood as public property, and were often used for hunting grounds, when frequently the professors in the classes would be startled by the firing of shotguns, within a few hundred yards of the recitation room. Rows of trees were planted down an avenue opened in front of Aspinwall Hall, and many improvements and conveniences were added to the homes of professors and to the buildings of the Seminary. Through Dr. Crawford's interest first steps were taken looking to the erection of a new and fireproof library, and for the first time in the History of the Institution, the salaries of the Faculty were placed upon a reasonably sure foundation.

The International Students' Alliance met at the Virginia Seminary in 1887. Most careful preparations had been made for this meeting by Mr. Foreman, of the Union Theological Seminary and Mr. Wilder, of Princeton. "During the previous session they stirred up," says one of the students of that time, "an enthusiasm on the subject of missions such as had not been known in the Seminary since the days of the elder Bishop Boone. They not only had meetings in Prayer Hall, delivering strong spiritual and inspiring addresses, but they also had prayer services with the men in the rooms of those especially interested. Their earnestness was phenomenal. No hour of the night was too late for talking with the men, and urging upon them the claims of the heathen world. As the result of these meetings, at least a dozen of the students signed a paper, signifying their willingness to go to the foreign field if God, in His providence, would open the way." "Few will ever forget," says Dr. Walker, "the services held in the Chapel in connection with the meeting of the International Students' Alliance. Among those who soon after volunteered for the foreign mission of the Church were J. Poyntz Tyler, John C. Ambler, Perry Nugent, J. Lindsay Patton, F. P. Clark, and Richard A. Roderick. Unfortunately Mr. Tyler, Mr. Nugent, Mr. Clark and Mr. Roderick were unable to pass the medical examination, and were rejected by the Board of Missions."

The Rev. Dr. Carl E. Grammer and the Rev. Dr. James Morris have told, in the chapter devoted to the Mission in Brazil, of the steps which led to the origin of the Brazilian Mission. The interest aroused which resulted in the establishment of this mission followed immediately upon the meeting of the Students' Alliance. The story of the disappointment of Clark and Roderick, of the resignation of James Morris from his appointment to the China Mission that he might step in and take the place of one of those who had been prevented from going to Brazil, the timely and somewhat sudden decision of Lucien Lee Kinsolving to accompany Morris, the almost spectacular way in which John Meem won the recognition and support of the Church in his determination to go also, in spite of the fact that no funds were available, the organization at the Seminary of the "Fairfax Brazilian Missionary Society," the brilliant presentation by Dr. Grammer of the Brazilian Mission project before the American Church Missionary Society, and the final decision of this Society to undertake the work, furnishes one of the most interesting chapters in the missionary annals of the Church. The decision of the American Church to take over the Brazil mission was arrived at largely as a result of the sudden appearance in their meeting of one of the volunteers who had been sent by the Seminary to this meeting to plead their cause, while the men at the Seminary were earnestly praying for God's blessing upon this endeavor.

Following an appeal from the venerable Archdeacon Elliot Thomson of the China Mission, H. C. Collins, James Addison Ingle, and Robert K. Massie volunteered to go to China, and soon afterwards Arthur H. Mellen was sent to the Mission in Cuba, going subsequently, because of the Revolution in Cuba, to take up work in Mexico. Within the next two years William Cabell Brown, John C. Meem, Miss Mary Packard, daughter of the Rev. Dr. Packard, Dean of the Seminary, sailed for the Brazilian Mission. They were accompanied to the ship which sailed from Newport News by Dr. Packard, Dr. Walker and Dr. Grammer, who went to bid them "God Speed" in their endeavor.

It was the writer's privilege to be a member of the Junior Class of the Seminary during the year when the Senior Class had among its membership, James Addison Ingle, William Cabell Brown, John G. Meem, Robert K. Massie, William D. Smith, all of whom volunteered for the Foreign Mission work of the Church. Another member of this class was Ernest M. Stires, who, while not going into the Foreign Missionary work, has, as a member of the Board of Missions, in General Convention, and in the National Church Council, ever been a firm and constant advocate of the Church's mission and has, through St. Thomas' Church in New York, of which he is rector, made substantial contributions in furtherance of the work to which so many of his classmates devoted their lives. The influence of this class in the life of the Seminary was most pronounced, and it may be said without invidious distinction that no class since the one in 1836, which had among its members Payne and Savage and Minor, who entered the African Mission, has contributed so largely to the Foreign Missionary endeavor of the Church.

In 1889 the oldest alumnus of the Seminary, the Rev. George A. Smith, who is listed in the catalogue of the College of William and Mary in the Class of 1824-25* who was then living in Alexandria, reached the close of his earthly life. He was well known upon the Seminary Hill. For many years he was the principal of the boys' school which he organized at Clarens, near the Seminary, where he had among his teachers Edwin A. Dalrymple and Francis M. Whittle. He was for a long term of years the honored president of the Alumni Association.

---

* Mr. Smith is listed in the Seminary Catalogue as graduating in 1823. Either one or the other of these dates must, therefore, be wrong.

In 1890 Mr. Cassius F. Lee, because of old age and impaired health, tendered his resignation as treasurer of the Board of Trustees and also of the Education Society. He had been a manager of the Education Society since 1831 and had served as its secretary and general agent from 1837 to 1890. He had been a member of the Board of Trustees from 1842 to 1890, and treasurer from 1865 to the time of his resignation. His death, which followed soon after, deprived the Institution of one of its most faithful and devoted officers. Most of his work was done without remuneration. It was he who saved the Seminary Library from destruction during the War by interceding with General McClellan and securing permission for the removal of the books, and as long as it was possible for him to remain, he lingered at the Seminary after the military occupation, seeking to safeguard and preserve its buildings and other property. Bishop Meade said of him that "to no individual in the diocese are we indebted for so large a share of labor and anxiety on our behalf as we are to Cassius F. Lee."

Upon his resignation, the Rev. Dr. Henderson Suter, of Alexandria, was appointed to be the supervisor of the grounds and buildings of the Seminary, and Colonel Arthur Herbert was elected treasurer of the Board of Trustees, which duty he performed with signal devotion and fidelity until the time of his death.

In 1893 the Rev. Dr. George H. Norton, who had been for many years a member of the Board of Trustees, who had declined an Episcopal election and who had been the constant and devoted friend of the Seminary, died in the rectory of St. Paul's Church, Alexandria.

On June 19, 1890, the following note of the death of the Rev. Philip Slaughter is made. "On Thursday, June 12, Rev. Dr. Philip Slaughter died at his home in Culpeper County, near which he was born in or about 1813, being the son of Captain Philip Slaughter, an officer in the Revolutionary War. He was educated at the University of Virginia for the law, graduated at the Theological Seminary of Virginia in 1834 and was ordained May the 25th of that year by Bishop Meade in the Church at Staunton. His first charge was in Prince William County. Soon afterwards he removed to the diocese of Maryland and his name does not appear in the Journals of Virginia until 1840, when he was rector of Meade Parish, Loudon County. In 1844 he became rector of St. Paul's Church, Petersburg, Virginia, where his health became so broken down that he was forced to make a voyage to Europe. On his return home he became an agent of the Virginia Colonization Society. Unable to preach regularly, as opportunity offered he took charge of one or two small parishes in or near Culpeper. At one time he made a chapel in his own dwelling house. He afterwards built a church nearby, but poor health caused him to resign even this.

"Some years ago he was appointed historiographer of the diocese. The last historical paper of his was read at the Council in Fredericksburg by his friend Colonel Skinner of Staunton. Listening to it, no one could have supposed it was written by a man eighty years of age. His leisure time was occupied in writing histories of several parishes in the diocese, St. George's, Fredericksburg; Bristol, Dinwiddie; St. Mark's, Culpeper; etc. 'Man and Woman' and 'Memorial of Randolph Fairfax'. His last publication was an historical sermon preached in old Pohick Church on the 'Religious Character of Washington' which drew from those at home and from those at a distance, the highest encomiums. His mental vigor was unabated to the last. He was a close and devoted friend of Dr. Keith, of Dr. Packard, and of Dr. Sparrow, and was among those who spoke at the Semi-Centennial of the Seminary".*

On the morning of Christmas Day, 1890, there occurred at the Seminary the death of young Michael Pannetti. It is interesting to note that, from the foundation of the Institution, this was the first death which had occurred at the Seminary of any student matriculated.

In 1891, through the interest of one of the students, Robert S. Carter, aided by a number of ladies on "The Hill" and other friends of the Institution, Whittle Hall was built on the grounds of the Seminary near the entrance gate, next to the home now occupied by Dr. Green. It was used for many years for public lectures and for the services con-

* From "The Southern Churchman." June 19th, 1890.

ducted for the children resident in the neighborhood, and served a most useful purpose until it was later destroyed by fire.

In 1892, the Rev. Dr. Joshua Peterkin, long a devoted friend of the Seminary and a member of the Board of Trustees, ended his earthly ministry. Pastor, preacher and saint, he had endeared himself to the Church in Virginia and was widely known in the Church general. He was the father of the Rt. Rev. Dr. George W. Peterkin, Bishop of West Virginia. At the time of his death he was rector of St. James' Church, Richmond, Virginia. The proverbial gentleness and charity of his nature were widely known. The story is told that on one occasion, two gentlemen in Richmond wagered each other that Dr. Peterkin could not be gotten to say a disparaging word about anything. The one who believed he could be trapped into doing so, went to him one day and began to abuse the devil, feeling assured that he would in this way get the good Doctor to say something uncomplimentary about Satan at least. Dr. Peterkin listened to the tirade of abuse and then quietly remarked, "Yes, but we can but admire the perseverance of the devil."

In 1893, and also in subsequent years, delegations of students from the Seminary were sent to the University of Virginia, the College of William and Mary, Washington and Lee University, and to the Virginia Military Institute for the purpose of presenting to the students of these Institutions, the claims of the Christian ministry. There are men, today, serving with distinction in the Church and some in the far mission fields of the Church's endeavor, whose decision to enter the ministry or whose first thoughts looking to this decision resulted under the blessing of God from these visits.

It is interesting to observe in the various historical notes relating to the history of the Seminary, how gratefully the returned missionaries were received upon "The Hill". Appreciative mention is made of the coming of the Rev. John Ambler, with Mr. Tai, a Japanese convert, and of the return of the Rev. J. Thompson Cole, and of a visit of the Rev. Dr. Pott, president of St. John's College, Shanghai, of addresses made by the Rev. Mr. Tyng and the Rev. Henry D. Page of Japan, and of the welcome visit and stirring addresses from

William Cabell Brown and Lucien Lee Kinsolving, and
almost invariably following these visits, we find students
making response to the appeals which have been given in
the dedication of their lives to the foreign missionary service
of the Church.   This, and other influences, led to the offering in 1899 of James J. Chapman to Japan, of Cameron F.
McRae to China, of George Wallace Ribble to Brazil and
of Henry St. George Tucker and John Armistead Welbourn
to Japan.   From the class of 1900, Edmund J. Lee volunteered for China and Nathan Mathews for Africa, and from
the class of 1902, the Rev. Robb White went as a missionary to the Philippine Islands.   In 1904, William M. M.
Thomas volunteered for Brazil and Robert Atkinson Walke
for China.

During 1891 the missionary life of the Seminary was
greatly quickened by a visit from the venerable Bishop
Whipple, and an address by Dr. John D. Paton, Presbyterian
missionary from the New Hebrides.   To these influences
was added the stimulus derived from the meeting of the
Missionary Convention held on "The Hill" in 1893, at
which addresses were made by the Rev. Dr. Langford, secretary of the Board of Missions, and the Rev. Dr. Arthur
Brooks.   In connection with this Convention, addresses
were made by missionaries from China, Japan and some of
the Bishops engaged in the domestic missionary work of the
Church.

We have sometimes wondered what motive restrained
the biographer of Phillips Brooks from giving due recognition
to the place and part which the Virginia Seminary was privileged to have as an influence in his life.   Possessed of the
wisdom and talent and massive mind to which his biographer
bears abundant witness, it would seem that his judgment
in leaving Massachusetts and passing through New York
and searching around in the woods where he got lost in his
effort to find the Virginia Seminary, sufficiently indicated
his appreciation of what the Institution had to offer to make
his choice in this matter worthy of appreciative record and
most generous comment.   That, having come, he should
have returned during the two successive sessions and remained at the Seminary until his graduation, is indicative of

THE RIGHT REVEREND DOCTOR PHILLIPS BROOKS

Bishop of Massachusetts

his belief that the Seminary afforded the best opportunities which were then available in the Church for giving to him that which his master mind so deeply craved in its search for truth. That he returned so often to his Alma Mater, and reverted in affectionate memory to the days spent on "The Hill" and to the influences which helped to shape his life, surely furnishes sufficient ground and reason for a more generous recognition of the influences brought to bear upon his life by the Virginia Seminary than has been given by his scholarly biographer.

It was natural, in view of the recognition which Phillips Brooks himself made of his own debt of gratitude to the Seminary, that the Seminary should cherish with pride the fact that he, the greatest preacher in the American Church and doubtless the greatest preacher of his generation, should have been one of her honored sons.

When, therefore, in January, 1893, news was received upon "The Hill" that his earthly ministry had come to an untimely end, his Alma Mater mourned his loss with a sorrow as deep as that felt in the diocese which he served.

Phillips Brooks was born in Boston in 1835, and graduated from Harvard in 1855. In 1856 he entered the Theological Seminary in Virginia and graduated with the class of 1859. He was ordered deacon in 1859, and began his ministerial work in the Church of the Advent, Philadelphia, from which he was soon after called to the Rectorship of Holy Trinity, Philadelphia. In 1869 he moved to Boston and became the rector of Trinity Church, and in October 1891, he was consecrated Bishop of the diocese of Massachusetts.

His death occurred in Boston on January 19, 1893. Not very long prior to his death, he had made a visit to the Seminary, where he had been entertained with a few friends who accompanied him. In the dining room he addressed the Faculty and students and while on "The Hill" went over to see his old room in St. George's Hall. This was the last of several visits which he had made to the Seminary. He had come in 1878 to deliver the address before the Alumni Association, and had returned to the Seminary for another visit prior to 1892.

While a student at the Seminary he worked in the Mission Station at Sharon, and to his brother he wrote with reference to his work among the people to whom he ministered there. "I feel that I am better for the work, more and deeper in sympathy with simple, honest men, and have a clearer light into what common men's minds are doing, and how they may be taught to do better and nobler things."

"He visited our Seminary several times," says Dr. Packard, "and on both of his later visits I walked with him down to the little burying ground, to see Dr. Sparrow's monument, on which is the inscription 'Seek the truth, come whence it may, cost what it will.' He always attended the Seminary Alumni reunions at General Conventions, and spoke very warmly at Philadelphia and Baltimore of his Seminary life. At the latter place, in 1892, he playfully offered me a cigar. I was called on by Bishop Randolph to ask the blessing, though nine Bishops were present, more worthy than myself. I heard Dr. Brooks preach in his own Church in Boston and I went up and spoke to him, and he said, 'I saw you.'"

Rev. Dr. Arthur Brooks wrote to the Seminary professors, January 3, 1893, for himself and his brothers: "We know how constantly and lovingly his mind reverted to his Seminary days, and how strong was the sense of the value of the preparation for his great work that he there received. The hearty fellowship, the deep religious spirit, the large views of the Church's life, which were marks of his action, he was always ready to ascribe to the influence of the Seminary, whose work is thus identified with his."

Phillips Brooks on one occasion said, "It is the five years after college which are the most decisive in a man's career. The years which come before are too fluid; and the years which come after are too solid." In view of the fact that the larger part of his five years after leaving college were spent at the Virginia Seminary, it is interesting to note some of the impressions which he himself recorded of his life on "The Hill", even though some of his reflections were not at all complimentary to the Seminary as he found it.

In a letter written home on the night of his arrival, he says, "My lordly apartment is a garret in an old building called 'The Wilderness'. Its furniture consists of a bedstead and a washstand. I looked in for a moment, threw down my carpet bag, and ran. I have seen the head, Dr. Sparrow, who is a thin, tall gentleman, with not much to say. The South is a mean and wretched country at best as far as I have seen it."

On the next morning he added the following postscript, "I have slept overnight in my cheerful hole, and am rejoicing this morning in a cold and cramp. They have the least idea of New England comfort down here of any place I ever saw. I am in the room with a son of Bishop Potter. 'Tis an awkward thing, this living in a garret."

It was doubtless due to the fact that Phillips Brooks found that he could not stand up in this garret, that led him soon after to remove his headquarters to St. George's Hall where the ceiling is higher.

Later he wrote, "I shall never forget my first experience in a Divinity School. I had come from a college where men studied hard, and said nothing about faith. I had never been at a prayer meeting in my life. The first place I was taken to at the Seminary was the prayer meeting; and never shall I lose the impression of the devoutness with which these men prayed and exhorted one another. Their whole souls seemed exalted and their natures were on fire." Elsewhere in this book the comments of Phillips Brooks on the failure of the students to be as zealous in study as they were in prayer are also recorded.

On the 9th of October, 1858, he wrote the following letter from the Seminary telling his family of his election as teacher in the Preparatory Department: "I have time for only a word today to tell you about 'The School'. I have made an engagement to teach Latin and Greek two or three hours per diem, and shall begin on Monday. I am to have $300 and board, equal to $400 in all. Not very large pay, but all they can afford to give, and as much, I suppose, as I had any right to expect. At any rate it will be enough to cover my expenses through this year. I am at my first sermon."

On one occasion at the meeting of the Virginia Seminary Alumni at General Convention, when Bishop Brooks spoke of the influence of Dr. Sparrow upon his life as he had done on several occasions, doubtless leaving the impression that in his mind Dr. Sparrow was not only the chief, but also the departed glory of the Seminary, leaving the Institution a somewhat drear and desolate place without him and his influence, Dr. Kinloch Nelson in the speech immediately following, reminded Dr. Brooks that Seminaries, like Bishops, sometimes grew with the passing of the years, and with humorous reference to the gigantic figure of the great and eloquent speaker, reminded Dr. Brooks that he, himself was a bigger man than when he preached at Sharon Mission and that the Seminary, also, had been growing through the years into a larger life and a wider influence.

While at the Seminary Phillips Brooks was impressed, as others have been, with the lack of intellectual earnestness on the part of some of his fellow students, who seemed willing to substitute costless emotion and inherited or acquired personal piety for genuine and persistent intellectual application. He later commented upon this fact and spoke, as the Rev. Dr. Carl E. Grammer has spoken also, of the regret felt that men, who had consecrated themselves to the ministry of the Christ, should view with such measure of unconcern the responsibilities which rested upon them to fit their minds through diligent application clearly to apprehend and rightly divide the great revelation of eternal truth. It is interesting to note that these convictions, so cogently expressed by Phillips Brooks and Dr. Grammer relative to the intellectual side of the Seminary work are now accepted not alone by the Faculty as a whole, but by the students of the Seminary also. It would doubtless be a source of deep gratification to this honored alumnus of the Seminary to note the advance which he would be quick to recognize in the scholastic ideals which now dominate and control the students of the Seminary.

In 1894 the Seminary suffered the loss by death of the beloved Dr. Kinloch Nelson, professor in and chief pastor of the Seminary and its mission stations. Dr. Nelson was elected Bishop of Easton, but decided that his best work could be done at the Seminary, declined the offer tendered him, and remained at his post until the close of his career.

The illness of Dr. Grammer and the ill-health of Dr. Crawford made it necessary, shortly after the death of Dr. Nelson for the Board of Trustees to make special arrangements by which the Rev. Dr. William Meade Clark was engaged temporarily to teach in the Seminary, and later the Rev. Dr. W. H. Neilson was secured as a substitute teacher for the class in the English Bible.

In 1894 the Rev. Dr. Samuel A. Wallis was elected by the Board and assigned to the work formerly done by the Rev. Dr. Nelson, as professor of Greek, New Testament Interpretation and Liturgics.   Dr. Wallis also succeeded Dr. Nelson in the care of the Seminary Missions.   He did his work as professor with recognized fidelity, was honored and beloved by the students, and by the congregations of the Mission Stations of which he was pastor.   From his home, where he and Mrs. Wallis ever extended to the students cordial welcome and the most genuine hospitality, there radiated an influence which was felt throughout the life of the Institution.   In 1920 Dr. Wallis became professor emeritus of the Seminary and is now doing faithful ministerial work in the suburbs of Alexandria.

The abolition of the Preparatory Department, reasons for which are set forth in the special chapter devoted to this branch of the Seminary work, took place in 1894.   There can be no question but that the wisdom of the Board in abolishing this Department has been amply justified.   The temporary result, however, was to decrease largely the number of students upon "The Hill" and to create for a time a certain sense of depression.

It became evident that many students were using it as a short cut into the ministry, and were being deprived of the broader culture and fuller training which a university or college education would afford. For many years the students aided in their preparation were sent, and others advised to go, to Roanoke College in Salem, Virginia. Subsequently William and Mary was chosen partly because of the regularity of the Church's ministrations in Bruton Parish.

Very soon after the death of the Rev. Dr. Henderson Suter, which occurred in 1895, Mr. Joseph Wilmer was elected by the Board of Trustees proctor of the Seminary and High

School and served in this position most acceptably, until 1901, when he was succeeded in office by Mr. George Stuart, of King George County, who has continued in office up to the present time. Mr. Stuart married Miss Annie Hoxton, daughter of Col. Llewellyn Hoxton of the High School, and the charm and hospitality of their home has added greatly to the social life of "The Hill."

The Reinicker Lectureship was established in 1895 through a gift of $5,600 received from Mr. Reinicker of Baltimore, which was secured through the interest of Mr. Charles Gauss, assisted by Rev. Dr. Julius E. Grammer, to whose congregation the donor belonged.   Under the foundation noted speakers have given lectures on various subjects at the Seminary.   Many of the addresses were subsequently published in the Virginia Seminary Magazine.

At the Board of Trustees meeting held on June 25, 1895, a resolution was adopted expressing regret at the death of Mr. Henry H. Houston of Philadelphia and expressing the appreciation of the Board for his friendship and liberality to the Seminary.

At the same meeting the resignation of the Rev. Dr. Packard as Dean of the Seminary was accepted, with expressions of deep regret and appreciation, and the Rev. Dr. Cornelius Walker was elected Dean for one year.   It was also ordered that morning and evening prayer should be said every day in the Chapel of the Seminary during the session.

In October, 1896, the sixtieth anniversary of the Rev. Dr. Packard's professorship in the Seminary was observed on "The Hill."   The professors and students went over to "Melrose" in a body, and Dr. Cornelius Walker in a few gracious words expressed their good wishes and congratulations.   To these greetings the Doctor made a fitting and affectionate response, expressing his love of the Seminary, his gratitude to God, and his continual interest in the welfare of the students.

The Board of Trustees at its meeting on June 22, 1897, received a communication from the American Church Missionary Society conveying notice of the legacy left by David J. Ely to be used for a professorship in the Virginia Seminary, upon certain conditions, one of them being that the American

Church Missionary Society should be allowed to nominate the professor elected under the terms of the gift. The Board of Trustees accepted the offer with appreciation and also accepted the conditions as to the election of the professor, with the proviso that the nomination made by the executive committee of the American Church Missionary Society should meet with the entire approval of the Board of Trustees.

The degree of Bachelor of Divinity was established by the Board of Trustees at its meeting held on June 22, 1897, and in February, 1898, an Act was passed by the Virginia Assembly authorizing the Trustees at their discretion to confer the degree. In 1911 it was provided that the Trustees could confer the degree of Doctor of Divinity.

It is an interesting fact that the origin of the title of Doctor of Divinity, and also the titled Learned Doctor of Laws, dates back to the Twelfth Century, and were then held in exceedingly high esteem.

Upon the resignation of the Rev. Dr. Grammer in 1898 the Rev. Dr. William Meade Clark, rector of St. James' Church, Richmond, Virginia, was elected to succeed him, but declined to accept. Until this vacancy was filled by the election of the Rev. Robert K. Massie, the Rev. Thomas J. Packard of Rockville, Maryland, was employed to give special instruction in the department of Church History, and the Rev. A. M. Hilliker, assistant to Dr. McKim in Epiphany Church, Washington, was secured as instructor in the English Bible and Liturgics, which position he filled until the election of Dr. Green. The Rev. Dr. Berryman Green was invited to become temporary instructor in the English Bible and Liturgics in connection with his work as rector of Christ Church, Alexandria, and continued to perform this double duty until he was elected in June 1902 to full professorship in the Institution.

In January 1898, the Seminary suffered the loss of two of her honored professors. On account of the infirmities resulting from old age, the Rev. Dr. Walker, professor of Systematic Divinity, retired, and the Rev. Dr. Carl E. Grammer resigned his position as professor of Church History, which he had filled with such brilliant ability, to become

rector of Christ Church, Norfolk, Virginia. The Rev.
Robert K. Massie was elected professor of Church History
in the Seminary in succession to Rev. Dr. Carl E. Grammer,
at the meeting of the Board held in 1898. Professor Massie
had gone upon his graduation, as a missionary to China and
had there done a successful and devoted work from 1891 to
1895, which he had, however, been compelled to relinquish
on account of illness in his family. Professor Massie was
graduated from the University of Virginia in 1888. While
Professor in the Seminary he received the degree of Doctor
of Divinity from Washington and Lee University. Dr.
Massie was a forceful and able teacher, but, unfortunately remained at the Seminary a comparatively short
time, resigning in 1912 to take up parochial work again.

At the meeting of the Board held on the following May,
the Rev. Dr. R. W. Micou was elected Professor of Systematic
Divinity. Dr. Micou was recognized as one of the foremost
thinkers of the Church and brought to his work at the Seminary exceptional talent, and ability as a teacher. He was a
distinctly advanced thinker and succeeded in bringing his
course of instruction in the Seminary abreast with the best
modern thought of the age. Dr. Micou's term of service
was comparatively short, as his death occurred in 1912.

Several efforts were made prior to 1900 by the Board of
Trustees to secure a permanent Dean in view of Dr. Packard's resignation of this office. The Board first elected the
Rev. Dr. Beverley D. Tucker, rector of St. Paul's Church,
Norfolk. The appointment was, however, declined by Dr.
Tucker, and the Board next elected the Rev. Dr. Randolph H.
McKim, rector of Epiphany Church, Washington, certain
special conditions being attached to the offer with the hope
that he would be able to accept it. Dr. McKim also declined the election. The Board next extended an invitation
to the Rev. Dr. J. H. Eccleston of Emanuel Church, Baltimore. He visited the Seminary and inquired as to the nature of the work, and his specific duties, but after careful
consideration he also declined to accept the election. The
Rev. Dr. Walker, therefore, continued to perform the duties
of this office until his retirement from his professorship at
the close of the session of 1897-98, when the Rev. Dr. Craw-

ford, the senior professor, was requested to act as Dean until a specific election should be made.   Eventually, in 1900, Dr. Crawford was formally elected Dean of the Seminary, which position he held with honor to himself and profit to the Institution, performing the duties of Dean in connection with his work as professor of Hebrew. The election of Dr. Crawford gave great satisfaction to the students and Faculty. At the meeting of the Board in May 1900, a resolution was adopted extending the thanks of the Board to the Rev. Dr. Crawford for his successful efforts in securing the gift of a new organ for the Chapel.

The interest of the Seminary in the Alaskan Mission was quickened by a visit of Bishop Rowe to the Seminary in 1901.   He had been preceded by Rev. Mr. Provost and the Rev. John W. Chapman, who had also addressed the students on the work of the Alaskan Mission.

The Rev. Dr. Walker makes mention of a meeting of representatives of the faculties of all the Seminaries of the Episcopal Church held at the Seminary during this period. He says that one of the conclusions arrived at as a result of this conference was that it sometimes happened that the shortest cut into the ministry of the Church was for a student to be dismissed from the Seminary for incompetence, or because he was an incurable crank, and then to go to his Bishop with a sorrowful tale of persecution or of martyrdom for his convictions, rouse the unsuspecting sympathy of the Bishop and secure hasty ordination. Mention is made of one young man who secured ordination within a year when re- fused admission to the Junior Preparatory Department because of his lack of qualifications for entrance. Against such practice those present expressed most decided and earnest protest.

The Sparrow Fellowship Foundation was established at a meeting of the Alumni held at the Seminary in 1902, the funds for this foundation having been secured through the efforts of the Rev. Charles J. Holt.

Perhaps never since its foundation was the Virginia Seminary more deeply affected and brought more fully under the solemn hush of reverent and yet glorified grief than when, in May, 1902, the beloved Dr. Packard passed into the fellowship of those whom he had taught and loved who had gone before him into the life eternal. Dr. Packard had been associated with all the professors of the Seminary from Dr. Keith, who was on "The Hill" when Dr. Packard arrived in 1836 to begin his duties, up to and including Dr. Massie and Dr. Green. He had served as Dean of the Institution from the death of Dr. Sparrow in 1874 until he resigned in 1895. Thirty-six Bishops of the Church sat under his instruction and came under his influence in the Seminary. Among them were: Bishop Payne of Africa, from the class of 1836; Bishop Richard H. Wilmer of Alabama, from the class of 1839; Bishop Gregory T. Bedell, third Bishop of Ohio, class of 1840; Bishop J. Freeman Young, second Bishop of Florida, class of 1845; Bishop Henry C. Lay, third Bishop of Arkansas, and first Bishop of Easton, class of 1846; Bishop Francis M. Whittle, fifth Bishop of Virginia, class of 1847; Bishop Channing Moore Williams, Bishop of China and second Missionary Bishop of Yedo, Japan, class of 1855; Bishop William S. Perry, second Bishop of Iowa, class of 1855; Bishop John H. D. Wingfield, first Missionary Bishop of Northern California, class of 1856; Bishop Henry C. Potter, seventh Bishop of New York, class of 1857; Bishop Alfred M. Randolph, first Bishop of Southern Virginia, class of 1858; Bishop Phillips Brooks, fifth Bishop of Massachusetts, class of 1859; Bishop Thomas U. Dudley, second Bishop of Kentucky, class of 1867; Bishop George W. Peterkin, first Bishop of West Virginia, class of 1868; Bishop William J. Boone, fourth Missionary Bishop of China, class of 1868; Bishop Charles Clifton Penick, third Bishop of West Africa, class of 1869; Bishop Isaac L. Nicholson, fourth Bishop of Milwaukee, class of 1871; Bishop H. Melville Jackson, Bishop-Coadjutor of Alabama, class of 1873; Bishop Beverley D. Tucker, second Bishop of Southern Virginia, class of 1873; Bishop George Herbert Kinsolving, second Bishop of Texas, class of 1874; Bishop James Winchester, Bishop of Arkansas, class of 1877; Bishop Arthur Selden Lloyd, President of the Board of Missions and Suffragan Bishop of New York, class of 1880; Bishop James B. Funsten, first Missionary Bishop of Idaho, class of 1882; Bishop William Loyall Gravatt, second Bishop of

West Virginia, class of 1884; Bishop John Poyntz Tyler, Bishop of the Missionary District of North Dakota, class of 1888; Bishop Robert Carter Jett, first Bishop of Southwest Virginia, class of 1889; Bishop Lucien Lee Kinsolving, first Bishop of Southern Brazil, class of 1889; Bishop William Cabell Brown, Bishop of Virginia, class of 1891; Bishop James Addison Ingle, first Bishop of Missionary District of Hankow, China, class of 1891; Bishop Arthur C. Thomson, Bishop-Coadjutor of Southern Virginia, class of 1893; Bishop William T. Capers, Bishop of West Texas, class of 1894; Bishop John D. La Mothe, Missionary Bishop of Honolulu, class of 1894; Bishop Edward Arthur Temple, first Missionary Bishop of North Texas, class of 1895; Bishop George C. Hunting, fourth Missionary Bishop of Nevada, class of 1895; Bishop Henry St. George Tucker, second Missionary Bishop of Kyoto, Japan, class of 1899; and Bishop Thomas C. Darst, third Bishop of East Carolina, class of 1902.

He had taught every missionary who had gone out from the Seminary since 1836 until the time of his death, and he knew Dr. Hill, of the class of 1830, who had gone to Greece, and Bishop Boone of the class of 1835, who was the first Missionary Bishop to China. In the first class which Dr. Packard taught in the Seminary were Payne, Minor, and Savage of the African Mission.

Dr. Packard had been for twenty-eight years the honored president of the standing committee of the diocese of Virginia, and was also a member of the Education Society and president of its Executive Committee. He had been honored by being appointed a member of the American Committee for the revision of the English Bible, and perhaps was known and loved by more of the clergy of the American Church than any other man who had ever lived and served in the ministry of the Church.

If the student of the History of the Theological Seminary in Virginia would catch these undertones and feel this atmosphere, he should read in leisure moments, the "Recollections of a Long Life" by Dr. Packard. It is not alone a history of events told out of the memory of life's long and varied experiences but is the autobiography of a rich and saintly soul. The memories of the old Professor and Dean are mellowed by an exquisite tenderness and hallowed by the mystic spirit of fellowship with God and with the men whom he knew and loved. He had been associated with all the professors of the Seminary from Reuel Keith up to the faculty which he left in 1902, when he passed into Paradise. Professors Cornelius Walker, Kinloch Nelson, Carl E. Grammer, Samuel A. Wallis, Robert K. Massie, and Berryman Green, had been students under him.

When in 1836 Dr. Packard came to the Seminary, Payne, Savage, and Minor were preparing to leave for Africa, Launcelot Minor, Hening and Colden Hoffman were his students as were the younger Boone, Bishop of China; Channing Moore Williams, first Bishop of Japan; Liggins and Cleveland Keith of China; and Kinsolving of Brazil, together with Morris, Meem and Brown. Besides these all the men who went from the Seminary to Africa and China, Japan, Cuba and Brazil from 1836 to 1902 carried with them the impress of his personality and teaching, and in their going as in their years of labor and loneliness, they felt ever assured that each day their old professor was calling down upon them the blessings of heaven because they remembered that "the fervent effectual prayer of a righteous man availeth much", they knew that Dr. Packard prayed for them daily and that he was "a good man, full of the Holy Ghost and of faith."

With tender touch the old Dean delighted to recall to memory the students of the early years of the Seminary. He personally knew men who had graduated in every class from the beginning of the Institution in Alexandria and makes mention of George A. Smith of the class of 1823, of Mackenheimer, Wheat, Brooke, John Grammer, Wing, May, and Boyden of the earliest graduating classes. He loved to linger among these memories. They cheered him along the way and illumined the vistas of faith down which he looked with assurance, seeing the hand of God guiding the Seminary in the further fulfillment of her mission to upbuild and extend the Kingdom of God.

His funeral took place from the Seminary Chapel. "As we laid," says a writer in "The Southern Churchman," "our beloved and venerated professor to rest on our eastward Hill, the beautiful words written by Dean Alford, on the funeral of Canon Chesshyre of St. Martin's, Canterbury, occurred to us as most appropriate.

'We stood, his brothers, o'er him, in the sacred garb he
wore;
We thought of all we owed him, and of all we hoped
for more;
Our Zion's desolation on every heart felt chill,
As we left him, slowly winding down that ancient eastward hill.

'To our places in the vineyard of our God return we now,
With kindled eye, with onward step, with hand upon
the plough;
Our hearts are safely anchored; our hopes have richer
store;
One treasure more in heaven is ours, one bright example
more.' "

The commencement exercises of the Seminary were going on when on June 8, 1902, the news of the death of Bishop Francis M. Whittle was received on "The Hill." Bishop Whittle was born in Mecklenburg County, Virginia, July 7, 1823. This year would be, therefore, the one hundredth anniversary of his birth as it is also of the birth of the Seminary which he loved and served in varied capacities. He entered the Episcopal High School in its first session in 1839. After teaching awhile in the School of Rev. Mr. Smith at Clarens, he entered the Seminary, graduating in 1847. His service in the Church is recorded in the biographical sketch written by the Rt. Rev. Dr. Beverley D. Tucker. As Bishop of the Church of God, to which responsibility he was called in May, 1867, when he was elected assistant Bishop of Virginia, his connection with the Seminary was constant and close. He was made a member of the Board of Trustees in 1867 and was the President from the death of Bishop Johns to the time of his death. For many years he lectured to the students of the Seminary on the Book of Common Prayer.

There is no record of his having followed the example of Bishop Meade in sawing crosses off any part of the Seminary, but no one doubts but that he would have sawed them off or knocked them down with axes and hammers, assured that he was doing God's service, had any unnecessary ones appeared on Seminary Hill while he was in authority.

One sometimes wonders whether it is really possible for any one to be temperamentally and personally as radically anti-ritualistic as was Bishop Whittle in his official capacity. Like Bishop Meade, he doubtless felt that vital issues were at stake. He sometimes spoke of the ritualistic wedge. He feared the small break in the dyke as he saw the rising stream of extreme ritualistic practice in the Church. Virginia lay between two such streams. The Bishop, therefore, protested against some practices concerning which he probably possessed no personal prejudice. He was determined to save his diocese from inundation. He did some things and said some things which his most devoted friends and admirers regretted, but his strongest opponents knew that he did and said these things out of the depth of a sincere and honest and uncompromising conviction. During the closing years of his life he was partially blind.

As out of the rugged granite cliff there flows the gentle spring of clear crystal water, so from the depth of his nature there flowed streams of beautiful and glowing affection. He drew men to him by cords of love strong and enduring. In his retirement he welcomed the comings of his clergy and gave to them his fatherly benediction, with a tone and tenderness long cherished in memory. "I cannot read them any more," he would say as he handed some of his books to the clergy who called. In his solitude he touched, through prayer, heaven's potent powers and released them that they might flow to bless and strengthen the clergy of the Church, especially those who had gone to the far off mission fields. "Remember," he said to a returned missionary, "remember in your loneliness and labor that I am praying for you by name every day." And so the Seminary paused in the midst of its commencement in 1902, to mourn for him and to rejoice that God had given him to bear through the years of his strong and faithful ministry witness to truth eternal.

We have said a new era began with the coming of Dr. Crawford and Dr. Grammer to the Seminary. With the passing of Dr. Packard and Bishop Whittle the old era, which had merged into and mellowed the new, was brought to its close. Yet, somehow, it will never be an era separate and apart from the new days that have since come and are yet to be. As the sunset glow lingers upon the landscape, so lingers the radiance, soft and beautiful, of those by-gone days and departed men. This glow will never depart from the Seminary. It remains as the vision of God remained radiant in the face of Moses when he came down from the Mount. It remains and will remain here always as the light of glory lingered in the face of the Master after He had communed with Moses and Elijah and with God upon the Mount of Transfiguration.

SECTION III

CHAPTER VIII

1902-1923

The Expression of Appreciation which Awaits the Present Faculty—Dr. Green Elected to Full Professorship—Dr. Crawford Reports Generous Subscriptions to the Seminary—Provision made for Alumni Trustees—Meeting of the Church Students' Missionary Society—Devotion of Bishop Potter to his Alma Mater —Memorial Gifts to the Chapel—Contributions from Mr. Black of Baltimore and Mr. Houston of Philadelphia—Visit of the Lord Bishop of London—Election of Dr. Kennedy—Class Memorials—Minutes Incident to the Death of Bishop Potter—Temporary Friction and Misunderstandings Healed by the Abiding Spirit of Loyalty and Devotion—The Long and Honorable Service of Colonel Arthur Herbert—Provision made for Special Students—Election of Dr. Bell—Death of Dr. Micou—Achievements in the Life of the Seminary during Dr. Crawford's Administration—Election of Dr. Rollins—Election of Mr. Hoxton, Principal of the High School—Gifts to the Seminary—The Skinner Legacy—Substitute Courses for Hebrew Provided—Other Bequests—Resignation of Dr. Crawford as Dean of the Seminary—Death of Bishop Peterkin— Memorial Pew at the University of Virginia—Cross placed on the Holy Table —The Branch Memorial Scholarship—The John Black Legacy—The Packard Memorial Library—Weekly Celebration of the Holy Communion begun at the Seminary—Resignation of Colonel Arthur Herbert—Death of Bishop Randolph—The Seminary and the World War—The Dean of the Seminary and the Principal of the High School Invited to Make Reports in Person to the Board—Retirement Allowance for Professors—Election of Dr. Tucker and Dr. Nelson—Death of Bishop Gibson and Colonel Herbert—The Death of Dr. Randolph H. McKim—His Devotion to the Seminary—The Question of Limiting the Enrollment of the Seminary—Proposition to Constitute Separate Boards of Trustees for the Seminary and High School Presented—Missionary Day at the Seminary—Program of Centennial Celebration—In Conclusion.

The last chapter of the Current History of the Seminary is the hardest chapter to write. It covers a period which will be an inspiration to the historian of the future. The old professors in the faculty and many of the members of the Board of Trustees, who, for long years, had been associated with the Seminary, have vanished from the scene. At commencement time and on other occasions when the Alumni gather, the spirits of Dr. Packard and of Dr. Walker are invisibly present amid the scenes and associations hallowed by their memory. To the Alumni of a later day there come memories of Dr. Nelson, Dr. Micou, and others who have also passed into realms invisible. New and potent personalities have come upon the scene. In place of the old "Rab" and Dr. Walker, affectionately known as the "Centurion",

young and vigorous men, with minds keenly alert to modern
thought, but no less loyal to ancient truth, occupy the chairs
left vacant by their honored predecessors, or fill chairs
created in recent years.

With the passing of time it will be possible to speak of
these men and of their work in terms of unreserved appreciation. The force of affection, the mystic and indefinable
radiance of their rich and cultured personalities is, during
these years with which we are now concerned, passing from
the present faculty into the hearts and minds of a new generation of students. Out of it all the halos which will surround
these men in the affection of the future will grow. Out of
the fellowship of this period will come the enriched associations in which the Seminary of the future will be enshrined.

The minutes of the Board of Trustees covering these
years are crowded with numberless details which reveal
the growth and expansion of the life both of the Seminary
and the High School. The record of these details does not
lend itself either to smoothness of literary style or as a stimulus to thought and imagination. The record, however, dry
as it may be, is essential as a part of the history of the Institution. Much of the Spartan simplicity of other years has
disappeared. This was inevitable. There is surely no
justifiable reason why the inconveniences incident to the
life of one generation should be imposed upon the life of
the generation following when no reason for the imposition
exists other than the wish to make the new generation un-
comfortable. The Board of Trustees is, therefore, to be
commended, and the Alumni to be congratulated, upon the
improvements made during this period upon the grounds
and buildings of the Institution; and experience has shown
that the students are not only working as hard by electric
lights as they ever did by oil lamps and tallow candles, but
there is good reason to believe that they are working much
harder. While no foot prints are being left in cindered and
sandy walks or in mud unfathomably deep, through which
the students of olden days trudged from St. George's Hall
to the Chapel for purposes of devotion, there is every reason
to believe that the men who are using the new concrete walks
and other modern conveniences of the Seminary are leaving

an impress which it will be easy for others to find and an inspiration for them to follow.

At the meeting of the Board of Trustees held on June 16, 1903, Rt. Rev. Robert A. Gibson, D. D., Bishop of Virginia, was unanimously elected president in succession to Bishop Whittle.

At this meeting of the Board the Rev. Dr. Berryman Green, elected in 1902 to full professorship in the Seminary, was formally assigned to the chair of English Bible, Homiletics, Christian Ethics and Sociology. At this same meeting a committee consisting of Bishop Randolph and Mr. Joseph Bryan was appointed to apply to the Legislature to change the charter of the Seminary and High School so as to enable the Board of Trustees to confer the degrees of Doctor of Systematic Theology and Doctor of Divinity.

Dr. Crawford, as Dean, reported on November 11, 1903, subscriptions received from various sources amounting to $10,480.30 of which $5000 was received from Mr. John Black of Baltimore and $1000 each from Mr. P. H. Mayo of Richmond, Virginia, and Mr. W. H. Baker of Winchester, Virginia. Dr. Crawford further reported that $1000 had been received for the Library Fund and $1200 for the Fellowship Fund of the Seminary, and urged the establishment of a publication fund for the purpose of printing the Reinicker Lectures and the Reports of the Meetings of the Alumni Association.

The Board of Trustees at its meeting held on June 14, 1904, amended By-law Seven of the Board so as to provide for the election of two members to the Board of Trustees, to be selected from the Alumni of the Seminary under such rules and regulations as the Board from time to time may make, such Alumni trustees to serve for five years. It was provided that the Trustees should nominate three members of the Alumni Association and that such nominations should be sent by the secretary of the Board to each alumnus, being a clergyman of this Church in good standing, with request that he vote upon the nominations within three months, returning his vote to the secretary of the Board; it being understood that three alumni should be nominated for each

THE RIGHT REVEREND DOCTOR HENRY CODMAN POTTER
Bishop of New York

alumnus to be elected. Rev. Dr. Randolph H. McKim was the first Alumni trustee elected under this plan.

The Board of Trustees at its meeting held on November 9, 1904, voted to pay the expenses of entertaining from sixty to seventy-five delegates of the Church Students' Missionary Society convention, to be held at the Seminary in December 1904.

Among the Alumni of the Virginia Seminary who have won distinction in the Church, the Rt. Rev. Dr. Henry Codman Potter, D. D., Bishop of New York, stands conspicuous for his loyalty and devotion to the Seminary in after years. He constantly reverted in his public utterances to his affection for and gratitude to the Institution. In 1905 the Bishop of New York gave tangible expression to his feeling of affection for the Seminary by making a generous gift for the enlargement of the Seminary Chapel. The Chapel enlargement consisted of the building of a chancel at the west end of the Chapel at a cost of $7,586.70. Bishop Potter increased the amount of his gift to enable the Board to carry out the plans of the architect. Mrs. S. F. Houston of Philadelphia donated the stained glass window to be placed in the new chancel.

While the Chapel was being enlarged, it was decided by the committee to make certain other improvements in the building. A vesting room was added and new furniture secured for the chancel and the choir, the committee soliciting additional funds for this purpose. A carved oak pulpit was given by the descendants of the Rev. Anson B. Hard, an alumnus of the Seminary of the Class of 1829. An oak lectern was presented by the family of Rev. Theodore Sill Rumney of St. Peter's Church, Germantown, a graduate of the class of 1849.

From the gift made by Bishop Potter, a sufficient amount was left after paying for the chancel addition, to provide three stalls for the professors, which were erected as memorials to the three professors, Dr. Sparrow, Dr. Packard and Dr. May, who taught Bishop Potter while a student at the Seminary. Another stall was erected as a memorial to Bishop Johns by Miss Mary Coles of Philadelphia, and a stall was added as a memorial to Bishop Whittle of Virginia, for many years president of the Board of Trustees. The window presented by Mrs. Houston was designed and executed in Munich, the subject portrayed being Christ's last Commission to the Apostles before His Ascension. A new Bible for the lecturn was presented by Bishop Potter. Five sets of Prayer Books and hymnals were given by Mr. George C. Thomas of Philadelphia, and one set by Mr. Thomas Whittaker of New York. In 1907 Bishop Potter made an additional gift to the Seminary for the purpose of placing on the further side of the chancel stained glass windows, one in memory of Bishop Boone, First Bishop of China, and the other in memory of Bishop Johns of Virginia.

Grateful mention is also made in the Trustee minutes of 1906 of the generous donations of Mr. John Black of Baltimore for the increase of the salaries of the professors of the Seminary, and also for the contribution of $1000 a year from Mr. S. F. Houston of Philadelphia. The Board at its meeting held on November 14, 1906, authorized the building of a frame house for the use of the Proctor of the Seminary.

In 1907 the Board took action providing for the appropriation of funds for the reception at the Seminary of the Lord Bishop of London at the time of his visit to the United States in connection with the celebration of the Three Hundredth Anniversary of the permanent establishment of the English Church and English civilization in America.

In 1907 the Board placed at the disposal of the Committee on the Church Exhibit at the Jamestown Exposition such books and other objects of interest in possession of the Seminary as would add to the interest of the exhibit.

At the meeting of the Board held October 23, 1907, the Rev. Paca Kennedy was elected to the position of Professor of Greek and New Testament Literature, in the Seminary. At a subsequent meeting of the Board, in the readjustment of the course of study, the teaching of Pastoral Theology and Church Polity were assigned to Dr. Wallis, who was also elected chaplain of the Institution. A course of study in Sunday School Pedagogy was added to the curriculum of the Seminary and substitute studies were provided for students having dispensation from either Hebrew or Greek, or both of these languages. The minutes of this period mention the making of many long needed improvements upon the grounds and buildings of the Seminary, including concrete walks, electric lights and a new and up-to-date water system.

In 1907 the Board gave permission for the placing of three small windows in the choir, one memorial to the Rev. Robert Hunt, chaplain at Jamestown of the Colony of 1607, presented by the class of 1907, one to Bishop James Addison Ingle of China, presented by his classmates, and one in memory of Miss Rhett, for many years matron of the Seminary, presented by the older alumni of the Institution.   At this meeting the Board authorized the selection of a hood in connection with the degrees conferred by the Board of Trustees of the Seminary, the colors selected being white and black, with the border of red.

Mention is made in the minutes of the Board of 1908 of a gift of $100 made by the class of 1902 in memory of the Rev. John E. Huhn, a member of this class, who died while a missionary at Rampart, Alaska, the interest from the gift to be used by the Professor of Missions for the purchase of Missionary Books for the Seminary Library.   Mention is also made of the bequest of $1000 in the will of Winslow W. Sever, the income from which was to be used for the purchase of books for the Seminary Library.

Record is made in 1908 of the gift of a Baptismal Font for the Seminary Chapel by the daughter of Mr. Cassius F. Lee in memory of her father.   The class of 1902 presented a brass book rest for the Communion Table, the class of 1903 a Communion service book.   The class of 1904 gave a brass alms basin.   The class of 1905 made a gift of a pulpit lamp, and the class of 1906, a stone gable cross for the Chapel.

The Board in 1908 approved the seal to be used on the diplomas of the Seminary.   On June 5, 1909, the time for the opening of the Seminary was fixed by the Trustees as the fourth Wednesday in September instead of the third Wednesday, as had hitherto been the custom.   The purpose of this change being to bring the examinations one week later and thus secure the attendance of the students at the commencement exercises of the Seminary.   At this meeting resolutions were passed incident to the death of the Rt. Rev.

Henry Codman Potter, D. D., LL. D., D. C. L., Bishop of New York. The resolutions expressed the profound sense of gratitude felt by the Board for the long continued and devoted interest of Bishop Potter in the welfare of the Seminary and of the generous financial contributions made by him to the Institution.

At the meeting of the Board held on November 10, 1909, steps were taken to enlarge the power of the Seminary to confer academic and theological degrees upon such persons as they should select. At the meeting held in June 1910, it was reported to the Board that this matter had been brought to a satisfactory conclusion and that all the legal and other requirements to give the Board this enlarged power had been fulfilled.

Mention is made in the report of Dean Crawford submitted to the meeting of the Board held in June 1910, of the fact that the percentage of men from the dioceses in the two Virginias attending the Seminary as compared with men from the other dioceses was very small, and that difficulty was being felt in holding the student body to the fundamental traditions of the Institution by reason of the many-colored ideals and aspirations expressed in connection with worship in the Seminary Chapel. Suggestions were frequently being made by students from other dioceses who were in large majority in the student body, asking for changes and alterations in the services in the Seminary Chapel looking to more elaborate ritual. The faculty and the Board, while fully understanding the background out of which such requests arose, determined to adhere to the simple form of service which had always characterized the worship of the Seminary Chapel, introducing only such innovations as tended to contribute to the enrichment and dignity of the service without destroying its traditional simplicity.

The minutes of the Board of Trustees covering the early part of the period with which this chapter deals give evidence at times of a certain amount of friction between those in whom authority was vested in the conduct of the Seminary, between the student body and the faculty, the student body and the Board of Trustees, and also at times between those in authority in the Seminary and in the High

School. It is clearly evident that in every instance this friction occurred as a result of the effort on the part of the different parties concerned to promote the best interests of the Institution. It was a period of rapid progress in the development of the material as well as the intellectual life of the Seminary, when new plans and new ideals, introduced by new men, came into conflict with traditional habits and clashed with long entrenched convictions and customs. Misunderstandings at times arose between the Dean and the Board and between the Dean and the Faculty, and between the Faculty and the Board, which called for the exercise of wise judgment, good temper and a generous portion of patience. It is to the credit of all concerned that these differences in every instance found an amicable adjustment, and while rightful independence was in no instance sacrificed, the spirit of courtesy and of conciliation constantly characterized the conduct of the conferences through which ultimate adjustments were determined. The Board of Trustees, recognizing its ultimate responsibility in the management of the Institution, in no single instance sacrificed its prerogative or responsibility, and yet in every instance maintained its authority with the restraint and dignity which won the confidence, the cooperation and the respect of all concerned. The harmony which characterized the latter portion of this period gives evidence that the friction to which reference has been made, had vanished and that the edges by which it had been caused had worn off, leaving the Seminary in a stronger and more coherent condition than would have been possible had these differences and difficulties never occurred.

Conspicuous among those who have served the Seminary, have been the Treasurers of the Board of Trustees. Mention has already been made of the long and faithful service of Mr. John Gray, first treasurer of the Board, and the Seminary will always hold in grateful remembrance the self-sacrificing and faithful devotion of Mr. Cassius F. Lee, who also served the Board in this capacity through a long and continuous term of years. His successor in office was Colonel Arthur Herbert, a gentleman of courtly manners and possessed of a character refined and beautified through long years of close companionship with the Christ Whom he honored and served with loyal devotion. It was, therefore, with sincere regret that the Board in November 15, 1911, accepted Colonel Herbert's resignation as treasurer, which resignation he was led to tender by reason of the increasing infirmities of old age. It is characteristic of old age to be tenacious of prerogative and oblivious of the limitations which come with advancing years. It is notable that in his resignation Colonel Herbert wrote to the Board that he was taking this step by reason of his recognition of the limitations growing out of advanced age and that he hoped he was resigning before these limitations became too apparent to others. The Board accepted the resignation of Colonel Herbert with regret and appointed a committee to convey to him their sincere appreciation for the long and faithful service which he had rendered to the Institution.

Mr. Julian T. Burke of Alexandria, Virginia, was elected to succeed Colonel Herbert as Treasurer of the Board, and continued to serve until his death, which was reported to the Board in June, 1916.

At the meeting held on November 15, 1911, the Board made provision for courses of study to be pursued by special students entering the Institution, who for good reason, were not in a position to take the full course looking to graduation. These provisions deal especially with the substitute branches of study to be pursued in lieu of the study of the Greek and Hebrew languages.

The Rev. W. C. Bell was elected full professor in the Seminary at the meeting of the Board held December 1911. On June 18, 1912, resolutions were passed by the Board incident to the death of the Rev. Dr. Micou, professor of Systematic Divinity, and also expressing the gratification of the Board upon hearing that steps were being taken to publish a volume on Apologetics, based on the classroom notes of Dr. Micou. This book has since been published and is a valuable contribution to Christian literature.

At the meeting of the Board of Trustees held June 18, 1912, Dr. Crawford presented a report in which he called attention to the fact that he had been for twenty-five years in the service of the Seminary and that during this period three hundred and fifty-six men had been trained for the ministry, twenty-seven of whom had entered the Foreign Missionary Field, and six of whom had been elected to the Episcopate. During this time the chair of English Bible had been established in the Seminary, the Reinicker Foundation secured, and the Wallace Prize had been given, and the Brazil Mission had been founded largely as a result of the interest and activity of the Seminary. The Library had grown from seventeen thousand to thirty thousand volumes, and he had been able to secure about $80,000 for the Seminary and Education Society. The corpus of the Seminary had grown during this period from three hundred and thirty thousand to nearly a half million. Dr. Crawford further expressed the conviction that the failure of the Seminary to receive larger bequests was perhaps due to the ambiguous title of the Institution and suggested that steps should be taken by which the Seminary and High School might be separated in so far as title to receive and hold property was concerned. The Dean further called attention to the fact that the small number of men studying Latin and Greek in the universities of the land suggested the importance of providing, in the Seminary, a preparatory course in these languages to enable such students to qualify under the canons for entrance upon a course of theological study.

At the meeting of the Board held on November 21, 1912, authority was given for the borrowing of an amount not to exceed $75,000 for improvement of the Episcopal High School provided the Alumni and friends of the School would raise at least $25,000 additional and that a subscription of $10,000 would entitle the subscriber to a scholarship in the school for ten years.

At the meeting held January 8, 1913, Rev. Dr. Wallace E. Rollins was elected Professor of History, being assigned to teach Ecclesiastical History and Christian Missions and Canon Law in place of Rev. Dr. Massie, who had resigned to accept a call to Lexington, Kentucky. On June 17, 1913, Mr. Archibald R. Hoxton was elected principal of the High School. The service which Mr. Hoxton has rendered not only to the Church in Virginia, but to the Church at large, by his self-denying devotion and conspicuously able discharge of his duties is recognized by the Board and other friends of the High School. It is only because, as was said of Washington, "his modesty alone exceeded his ability," that we refrain from making further record in recognition of the signal success which has marked his masterful administration.

Mention is made in the minutes of the Board of a legacy from Mr. James M. Moelick of Pulaski, Virginia, of $300.00 cash and $1000.00 in bonds, and a legacy of $5000.00 to the Episcopal High School from Miss Alice Leigh. The Board at this meeting expressed appreciation of a portrait of the Rt. Rev. Dr. A. M. Randolph, Bishop of Southern Virginia, presented by Mr. and Mrs. J. Preston Carson of Forrest Hill, Richmond.

To the Board of Trustees the Treasurer reported on November 11, 1914, the receipt of $29,793.13, in part payment of the legacy of Miss Fanny Skinner of Staunton, Virginia, the interest to be devoted to the work of the Education Society. In June, 1915, the Board received notice of a bequest from Captain T. Skelton Jones of Atlanta, Georgia, of $500.00

Provision was made at this meeting of the Board for offering substitute courses as an equivalent to the study of Hebrew, the courses provided being "The Contemporary History of the Old and New Testament" with a special course in Ecclesiastical History culminating in a study of the Religious Conditions of the Present Day, and a course in Historical and Comparative Religions introductory to the study of "Christian Theology and Missions."

On November 10, 1915, the Board received the notice of a bequest of $5000.00 from Miss Nannie J. Thomas of Smithfield, Virginia, to be designated as the "Julius O. Thomas Endowment Fund", the income from which was to be devoted to scholarships.

A bequest was also received from Miss Alice Leigh of $3750.00 and a legacy of $1000.00 from Miss Nannie Jacobs, former matron of the Seminary.

On June 6, 1916, after many years of devoted service, the Rev. Dr. Crawford tendered his resignation as Dean of the Seminary, which was accepted with the expression of sincere appreciation on the part of the Board for the valuable services which he had rendered to the Institution. The Board placed on record its high appreciation of the great value both to the Seminary and to the Church at large of Dr. Crawford's services during his term of office as Dean of this Institution. "His service," declared the Board, "has been marked by a spirit of loyalty to the best traditions of the Institution, and by faithful and unswerving devotion to its highest interests." Satisfaction was expressed by the Board that the resignation of Dr. Crawford as Dean would not cause a severance of his relation to the Seminary, in view of the fact that he would continue to occupy the Chair of Hebrew.

To the Board, at this meeting, the Rev. Dr. Phillips reported the death of the Treasurer, Mr. Julian T. Burke, and nominated as his successor Mr. Arthur Herbert, Jr., who for sometime had served as assistant to the Treasurer. In the election of Mr. Herbert, the Board added to the list of faithful and efficient treasurers another who has already won for himself the esteem of his colleagues. His fidelity and skill mark him as well qualified to take an honored place in the list of the devoted men who, in this capacity, have rendered such conspicuous service to the Seminary.

The Rev. Dr. Berryman Green was elected Dean of the Seminary to assume the duties of the office after July 1, 1916.

Among those who, in later years, gave to the interest of the Seminary their untiring devotion, none stands more conspicuous than the beloved Bishop Peterkin of West Virginia, whose death was announced to the Board at its meeting held in June 1916. Bishop Peterkin was among the students connected with the War-between-the-States period of the Seminary and upon his election to be Bishop of West Virginia he entered the Board of Trustees with the knowledge of the Seminary and a loyalty to her traditions which made him, from the first, a wise counselor and a loyal and devoted friend. Besides serving as a member of the Board of Trustees, he was for many years the honored president of the Alumni Association, and his death removed one of the most valuable friends that this Institution has ever possessed.

In order to establish a link between the High School and Seminary and the University of Virginia, to which many students go from the High School and return to the Seminary, an appropriation of $500 was made by the Board of Trustees for a memorial pew in St. Paul's Church, at the University of Virginia, to be known as the "Episcopal High School Pew."

The question of allowing a Cross to be placed on the Holy Table in the Seminary Chapel had for some years been under consideration by the Board of Trustees. Finally in 1916, the offer of the class of 1908 to present to the Seminary a memorial Cross, was accepted with the thanks and appreciation of the Board of Trustees.

The Board was notified at this meeting of a cablegram received from Mr. Blythe W. Branch, formerly of Richmond, then living in Paris, of a donation of $5000 for the purpose of establishing the Branch Memorial Scholarship, the income to be devoted to the education of a boy at the Episcopal High School.

A minute incident to the death of Mr. Julian T. Burke and appreciative of his valued and devoted service on the Board of Trustees, appears in the minutes of the Board in 1916, and also a note of the legacy of Mr. John Black of Baltimore, amounting to $175,000.

The minutes of the Board during this period contain lengthy correspondence between the officers and the Board, and Mr. W. W. Laird, of Baltimore, relative to a gift of $10,000 to the Seminary as a contribution to a fund for building a Library as a memorial to the Rev. Joseph Packard. It is not necessary in this place to give a detailed record of this correspondence, as all the facts of interest are set forth in the chapter on the Library by the Rev. Dr. Wallis. It is interesting, however, to note that the final cost of the Library as reported on November 9th, 1921, was $71,059.70.

At a meeting of the Board of Trustees held in June, 1917, the love of Bishop Peterkin for the Seminary was evidenced by the announcement of the bequest of $500 made in his will to the Board of Trustees of the Seminary and High School. The minutes of this meeting make mention of the institution for the first time of the weekly celebration of the Holy Communion in the Seminary.

Colonel Arthur Herbert, having in 1917, reached the fiftieth anniversary of his membership upon the Board of Trustees, resolutions of the sincere appreciation of the Board for his long and valued service, were adopted. These resolutions recite the conviction of the Board that, "No man has done more for the welfare of this Institution than Colonel Herbert. As one of the executive committee of the Board for many years, as a member of its Finance Committee during the time that Mr. Cassius F. Lee was treasurer, and through those years the chief financial advisor of the Board, as treasurer in succession to Mr. Lee; he has always had the closest association with, and kept the most watchful eye upon our business affairs, and much of the present prosperous condition of the Seminary is due to his careful management. The Board has always found him a wise counsellor; faithful in service; loyal in spirit; versed in the best traditions of this Institution; and devoted to their preservation. He has shown himself a kind and courteous and considerate friend, not only to this Board as a whole, but to each and all of its members individually."

In expressing his appreciation of the action of the Board, Colonel Herbert took occasion to say, "this is the second time in my long life of public service that recognition has been made of what I have endeavored to contribute to the good of my fellow men. The other instance being in connection with my service as a soldier in the Confederate Army."

A resolution was also adopted at this meeting of the Board expressive of the appreciation felt by the Board for the care with which the Rev. Dr. S. Scollay Moore, secretary of the Board, had kept the minutes during his long term of service.

Note is made of the death of Bishop Randolph, who, next to Colonel Herbert, had served longer on the Board of Trustees than any other of its members. The resolutions incident to the death of Bishop Randolph recite the influence exerted by him upon the Seminary by the eloquence of his preaching, by the breadth and depth of his scholarship and by the gracious charm of his personality.

Mention is made in the minutes of the Board of the fact that the Rev. Dr. W. Cosby Bell, professor of Theology in the Seminary, had accepted the position of Chaplain in the 42nd Division of the 117th Engineers, and that the Rev. H. Vankirk, D. D. resident near New York, had been secured to take temporary charge of Dr. Bell's classes during his absence. Dr. Bell, however, after a short period of service in France, was invalided home and was shortly after his return able to resume his work as Professor in the Institution.

Referring to the effects of war upon the Seminary, the Rev. Dr. Berryman Green reported to the Board at its meeting in June 15th, 1918, "That the student body of no other educational institution had felt the unsettled conditions of the times more than the young men here. Although exempt by act of Congress from Army service, the sense of duty to volunteer has been so compelling that several have gone into the War service during this session. Those remaining have just as conscientiously decided to serve the Church at home which is in greater need than the Army of our country at this time. The spirit of patriotism has been admirable, and has been equalled by the calmness and good judgment with which each man has decided as to his own course. The class work in all departments has been done as well as usual, in spite of the disquiet of the whole world around us. The students have mostly held themselves well in hand, and pursued their studies patiently and successfully. The Dean also reported having received the highest commendation from the physicians in charge of the Emergency Hospital in Alexandria, commending the students for their work done in the hospital during the influenza epidemic."

The Rev. Dr. C. Braxton Bryan reported that he had presented to the Library two manuscript sermons, one by Bishop Moore, and one by Dr. Sparrow. One of these, he said, had been given by the Rt. Rev. Dr. Arthur Selden Lloyd.

Mention is made of a bequest of about $20,000 to the Seminary in the will of Miss Catherine M. Haven of Portsmouth, New Hampshire.

A committee was appointed by the Board consisting of the Bishop of the Dioceses in Virginia and West Virginia to consider and investigate all nominations made for the degree of Doctor of Divinity. It was ordered that nominations for this degree might be received at any meeting of the Board except the regular meeting in November, and referred to the committee to be reported upon at the annual meeting of the Board.

At a meeting of the Board held in June 11, 1919, a resolution was adopted making it a regular order of the Board that the Dean of the Seminary and the Principal of the Episcopal High School should be invited in the future to present their reports to the Board in person, in order that opportunity might be given for explanation and enlargement of matters as presented by them in the report and for conference relating to any matters contained therein.

At this meeting of the Board the appropriation made to the Bishop Payne Divinity School was increased from $500 to $1000 a year. Provision was also made for making the grant to certain professors who were soon to retire from the Faculty of the Seminary, of such amount of money annually as would, together with the amount received by them from the Church Pension Fund, insure to them an annual appropriation of at least $2000. At this meeting the Rev. Dr. Crawford and the Rev. Dr. Wallis were voted the recipients of the Fund thus provided, at the close of the session 1919-1920, and the Rev. Thomas K. Nelson and the Rev. Beverley D. Tucker, Jr., were elected to the Faculty of the Seminary.

The minutes of July 11, 1919, contained resolutions incident to the death of Bishop Gibson and Colonel Herbert. Mention has been made of the appreciation of the Board of the services of Colonel Herbert. The resolutions adopted incident to the death of Bishop Gibson expressed the sense of gratitude felt by the Board for the ability and devotion with which, as President of the Seminary, the Bishop of Virginia had devoted himself to the interests of the Institution, and recited the sense of loss felt by the Board and friends of the Seminary throughout the state and throughout the Church, at his removal from the scenes of his earthly labor and influence.

Of all the alumni at the Virginia Seminary none was perhaps more loyal to her interests, and more thoroughly imbued with the spirit of her teaching than the Rev. Dr. Randolph H. McKim, alumni trustee, whose death was reported to the Board at its meeting in November 1919. His residence in Washington kept him in close touch with the Seminary and enabled him to render service which was both conspicuous and continuous.

Announcement was made in June, 1920, of the death of Judge Legh R. Watts, and a minute was offered appreciative of his long service upon the Board of Trustees.

In November of this year the Board suffered further loss through the death of Mr. Peter H. Mayo of Richmond, Virginia. Mr. Mayo's devotion to the interests of the Seminary was expressed by a generous donation of $10,000, left to the Institution in his will.

At the meeting of the Board held on June 7, 1922, the question of placing a limit upon the number of students to be received in Virginia Seminary was introduced and discussed. It was felt that it would be a mistake to allow the number of students to become so large as to run the risk of destroying, within the student body itself, the spirit of loyalty and devotion to the traditions and distinctive tenets of the Seminary. The conviction was expressed by many members of the Board that the number of students admitted should never be larger than the ability of the Seminary to assimilate them into the spirit of her life and teaching. It was resolved that this limit be fixed for the present at about sixty-five and that not over seventy-five should be provided for in all the dormitories, including the new dormitory which is contemplated.

At this meeting of the Board, the following proposition, dated June 6, 1922, of vital interest to both the Seminary and the High School was offered by Mr. Theodore S. Garnett:

"To the Rt. Rev. Dr. William Cabell Brown,

President of the Board of Trustees, Theological Seminary.

Dear Bishop Brown: At a meeting of the Old Boys' Association of the Episcopal High School, in the Virginias, the following was unanimously adopted:—Resolved That:—
If the Board of Trustees of the Protestant Episcopal Theo-

MISSIONARY CONFERENCE OF THE STUDENT BODY AT VIRGINIA
SEMINARY 1922-23

logical Seminary and High School in Virginia deem the time proper for the two Institutions to become individual entities, under separate Boards, this Association begs that it will take such action, and further begs to suggest for their consideration the following Board of Trustees for the High School." The names of those suggested as Trustees then follow, the communication being signed by J. M. Daniel, Jr., secretary of the Old Boys' Association of the Protestant Episcopal High School in the Virginias.

This matter was referred to a committee of five of which the president of the Board was made chairman, to investigate the legal and other questions which would naturally arise in the consideration of the proposition.

At a meeting of the Board of Trustees held on November 15th, 1922, this committee reported in favor of placing the two Institutions under separate and independent Boards of Trustees. The report as submitted contained so many and such important recommendations relative to the divisions of funds between the two Institutions and other matters of grave and far-reaching importance, that, while the majority of the Board seemed strongly in favor of consenting to the proposition suggested, it was unanimously resolved that the final determination of the Board be deferred to a subsequent meeting, pending which ample time would be given to each and every member of the Board to make careful study of the provisions outlined in the report of the Committee, which was ordered to be furnished, together with a copy of the Charter of the Seminary, to each member of the Board, for their perusal pending a special meeting of the Board to be called for the consideration of this question.

On November 22, 1922, a "Missionary Day" was observed at the Seminary concerning which the following interesting account was given in the "Living Church" of December 23rd.

MISSIONARY DAY AT VIRGINIA THEOLOGICAL SEMINARY

"The entire day, Thursday, November 23d, at the Virginia Theological Seminary, was devoted to the interest of Foreign Missions. The missionary spirit of the Institution, though always present and dynamic, was vividly apparent on this occasion. It is not possible at this writing to measure the value of this day, but it is evident the messages brought from the foreign field by missionaries, deeply stirred the students who formed the greater part of the audience, and we do not hesitate to say, the call was heard by many.

"A service of preparation, conducted by the Rev. Dr. Beverley D. Tucker, Jr., was held on Wednesday evening. The Missionary Day activities commenced with a corporate celebration of the Holy Communion, at which the Dean of the Seminary, the Rev. Dr. Berryman Green, was the celebrant, and was assisted by the Rev. W. M. M. Thomas, a missionary from Brazil.

"Two public meetings were held. In the morning, Dr. Green by way of introduction of, and in a word of welcome to, the speakers, said that no greater meeting in the interest of missions was held even at the recent General Convention. Dr. John W. Wood presided at the morning session. Dr. Wood, who is the Executive Secretary of the Department of Missions, said that a number of years ago it would have been impossible to accept every qualified applicant for the foreign field on account of the lack of funds, but that at the present time the Department of Missions had solemnly vowed, themselves, never to turn down a qualified applicant, despite what the financial situation might be. In the past it had often been necessary for applicants to raise their own expenses and to finance their work.

"The Rev. W. M. M. Thomas, representing the field of Brazil, related a fascinating story of the work in which he has shared for eighteen years. He asked for two men; men who were willing to bear hardships and inconveniences, and who were willing to serve Christ by forwarding the work of His Church in Brazil. One man is needed to relieve Dr. Morris at the Theological School in Brazil, and another to assist Mr. Thomas in his work at the boys' school. Mr. Thomas explained clearly the need of education in Latin America and the laying of a moral foundation as preliminary and necessary steps in the permanent Christianization of the people of this realm. He said, 'It is easy to arouse a superficial interest in Christianity among the people, but this will become nothing substantial without careful toil in developing a more reliable moral consciousness.'

"The Rev. Dr. Arthur R. Gray followed as the next speaker, representing the Latin Americas.   He very thoroughly reviewed the situation and great need for men in the Caribbean region, and in Central America and Mexico. He gave his hearers a deep insight into the political, industrial, and diplomatic condition in these sections.   He strongly emphasized the opportunity the Church has to give a better tone to the attitude of these countries to the United States.   Especially urgent, said Dr. Gray, is missionary enterprise in Mexico.

"The Rev. John A. Welbourn painted an interesting picture of Japan, including many phases of the life of that country.   He dwelt at some length on the need of Christianity among the Japanese, if they are to realize to the fullest their many different possibilities.   While the most influential men of Japan are very sympathetic to many occidental tendencies, yet they shrink from accepting Christianity whole-heartedly, and recommend the revival of Shintoism as a national religion.

"An interesting view of the situation in China was given by the Rev. Dr. A. M. Sherman, Dean of St. Paul's Divinity School at Boone University.   Dr. Sherman has been in China as a missionary for twenty-three years, and is well qualified to discuss the political situation there, and the tendencies that are prominent since the inception of the movement toward democracy.   The speaker emphasized the influence of Christianity in China and suggested its potentialities in giving scope, depth, and direction to the tide of democracy that is rising so rapidly in China.   The Chinese are rapidly taking on western civilization, and Dr. Sherman said it is highly important that this be accompanied by Christianity as an idealizing influence.

"The afternoon was given over to private conferences to those wishing the opportunity of talking personally with the missionaries and other speakers of the day.

"The second public meeting was held in the Seminary chapel in the evening.   The Rev. Dr. R. P. Wilder, general secretary of the Student Volunteer Movement, was the first speaker. The history and results of the organization he represents which was started more than thirty years ago, largely through the efforts of Dr. Wilder, who was then a student at Princeton, were given in brief detail by the speaker. This organization has been in a large measure responsible for the dedication and consecration of thousands of young lives to the work of the mission fields. Dr. Wilder's address was indicative of the spiritual enthusiasm that has always animated the movement.

"It was a happy thought of the program committee to have the Bishop of Brazil, the Rt. Rev. Lucien Lee Kinsolving, D. D., deliver the closing address of the day. Bishop Kinsolving's deep fervor for missionary work has been well substantiated by the result of thirty years' work in Brazil. He told in a graphic narrative of his decision, while a student at the Virginia Seminary, to go to Brazil. But the decision was the slightest of his difficulties, for he found very little encouragement in his purpose, and it was necessary for himself and others to raise funds to undertake the venture. Bishop Kinsolving's address was deeply inspirational and not only did he arouse enthusiasm in his listeners, but he also offered definite work for those who would decide to go to Brazil. Bishop Kinsolving won the hearts and minds of his student hearers when he declared: 'If one whom the Lord calls is not willing to go anywhere, he is not fit to stay at home. God will not call every man to the foreign field, but He wants every man to be willing to go.'"

THE PROGRAM OF THE SEMINARY CENTENNIAL

"The committee appointed at the meeting of the Board of Trustees in November, 1922, to arrange for the observance of the Centennial of the Seminary, met in the study of the Dean of the Seminary at three o'clock on Thursday, December 21st, 1922. There were present the Rt. Rev. Dr. William Cabell Brown, President of the Board and Bishop of Virginia; the Rev. Dr. W. A. R. Goodwin, of St. Paul's Church, Rochester, New York; the Rev. Dr. Berryman Green, Dean of the Seminary; and the Rev. G. Otis Mead, Rector of St. John's Church, Roanoke, Virginia. Bishop

Brown presided.   Mr. Mead was elected Secretary of the meeting."

The transcript of the minutes of the meeting is inserted in order that the History of the Seminary may thus preserve a permanent record of the proposed program of this event, so unique in the history of the Institution.

"Dr. Goodwin called attention to the fact that the Seminary was actually One Hundred Years Old in 1918, and that the celebration of the centennial of the Education Society in 1918 was, in reality, the observance of the centennial of the Seminary, by reason of the fact that the Seminary grew out of the Education Society and that the Education Society was, prior to 1823, in deed and fact doing the work of the Seminary in training men for the sacred ministry.   It was further pointed out that the date of the establishment of the Seminary in Alexandria, under the professorship of Dr. Keith, was October 15th, 1823.   This beginning was, however, pursuant to resolutions passed by the Virginia Convention in the preceding May.   It was, therefore, moved by Dr. Goodwin that the time of the celebration of the Centennial be in the month of June, and that the day be Wednesday, June 6th, of commencement week.

"Upon motion of Dr. Goodwin it was determined that all Church seminaries, colleges and secondary schools be invited to send representatives; and that William and Mary College, Williamsburg, where Dr. Keith was sent by the Church in Virginia in 1820 to be Professor of Theology, and where before this a Course in Divinity had been given for many years; The University of Virginia; Princeton University, where Bishop Johns and Bishop Meade were educated; and the Presbyterian Union Theological Seminary in Richmond, Virginia, be also invited to send representatives.

"It was moved by Mr. Mead that representatives of all accredited colleges in the State of Virginia be invited for the day.   The resolution was adopted.

"It was moved by Dr. Goodwin and Resolved that, in view of the cooperation of Maryland in the establishment of the Education Society in 1818, out of which the Seminary grew, the Bishops of Washington and Maryland be invited to represent their respective dioceses; and that the Vestry of Christ Church, Georgetown, of which Dr. Keith was rector, when elected to be professor of Theology in the College of William and Mary, and who was soon after called to teach in the Seminary when opened in Alexandria, be invited to send a representative.

"It was moved by Mr. Mead and Resolved that the clergy of the States of Virginia and West Virginia be requested to urge laymen of their respective parishes to attend the Centennial celebration for the day.

"Upon motion of Rev. Dr. Green it was Resolved that we invite the Rev. Carl E. Grammer, S. T. D. of St. Stephen's Church, Philadelphia, to make the missionary address on the occasion of the Centennial of the Seminary, the subject to be 'A Century of Missionary Life of the Seminary.' Bishop Brown moved that the Rev. Dr. Edward L. Goodwin, Historiographer of the Diocese of Virginia, be asked to make the historical address on the occasion of the Seminary Centennial celebration; and that the Dean of the Seminary, the Rev. Dr. Berryman Green, be his first alternate. Dr. Goodwin moved that Bishop Brown, be second alternate for this address.

"It was moved by Dr. Goodwin and Resolved that the Dean of the General Seminary be invited to speak in behalf of our sister seminaries.

"The committee decided that the Centennial occasion should commence with the celebration of the Holy Communion at seven o'clock Wednesday morning, in the Chapel. Dr. Goodwin moved that Bishop Brown, President of the Board of Trustees, make the opening address, and that the Dean of the Seminary make the closing address on 'The Future of the Seminary.' Upon motion made by Dr. Goodwin and carried, the Rt. Rev. Dr. Charles Henry Brent, Bishop of Western New York, was invited to preach the missionary sermon on Wednesday evening. It was decided that, as a feature of the Centennial program the hymn of Francis Scott Key, one of the founders of the Education Society, 'Lord, with Glowing Heart I'd praise Thee' be sung. It was ordered that if there is a missionary bishop, a graduate of the Seminary, available, he be asked to make the after dinner address.

"The Dean of the Seminary was authorized to form a local committee on arrangements, of which he shall be chairman, and of which the other members of the faculty should be members. And further, that the student body be requested to be present during the Centennial celebration and to aid in every way possible.

"The Dean was requested to invite Mr. A. R. Hoxton, the Principal of the Episcopal High School, to be chairman of the entertainment committee; and to appoint a committee of ushers from the student body of the Seminary; and a committee on transportation.

"It was moved by Dr. Goodwin and Resolved that the meeting of the Alumni Association on Thursday of commencement week be considered as a part of the Centennial celebration; and that the Rev. Dr. Wallace E. Rollins, in conference with other officers of the Association, be requested to arrange the program accordingly.

"It was resolved that this be considered the final program; which, however, is subject to amendment or correction as may be agreed upon by this committee.

(signed)   G. Otis Mead, Secretary."

The Latest Actions of the Board of Trustees

At the meeting of the Board of Trustees held at the Seminary on February 9th, 1923, the resignation of the Rev. Dr. Beverley D. Tucker as Professor in the Seminary was accepted, Dr. Tucker having decided to accept the call extended to him to the rectorship of St. Paul's Church, Richmond, Virginia, to succeed the Rev. Dr. W. Russell Bowie, also a graduate of the Virginia Seminary, who had resigned St. Paul's to become rector of Grace Church, New York.

The Rt. Rev. Dr. Henry St. George Tucker, Bishop of Kyoto, Japan, was elected a Professor in the Seminary, and has since accepted the election. The subjects to be taught by Bishop Tucker have not yet been assigned.

The Board reached the determination that it would be wise to place the management of the Seminary and Episcopal High School under separate Boards of Trustees. The general plan of separation was decided upon, but final action in this matter was deferred until the June meeting of the Board.

The pressing need for an increased Endowment was recognized by the Board and steps were taken looking to raising at least $500,000. to be added to the Endowment Fund of the Seminary. The growth of the Institution, the enlargment of the Faculty, and the increased cost of maintenance have all combined to make it absolutely necessary to secure larger available resources. It is confidently believed by the Board that the Church which has received so much from the Seminary will graciously and generously recognize and respond to this pressing need, and the Board faces this new responsibility with confident reliance upon the blessing of Him Whose Kingdom the Seminary is seeking to upbuild and extend.

In Conclusion

These broken fragments from the Minutes of the Board of Trustees and other records are like the fragments of glass picked up in a studio where some beautiful mosaic window is in process of creation. They reflect the colors of light and partly reveal the purpose of the master artist. Day by day, and year by year, this creative work goes on. In the family prayers in the homes of the faculty, in the devotions of the students in their class prayer meetings, in private prayer, and in the public services of the Chapel, as well as in the meditations in solitary places, the men upon "The Hill" are seeking, to see, with unclouded vision, the matchless beauty of the character of God as revealed in the face of Jesus Christ. They are seeking to make a picture of Him within their souls and in the souls of others, a picture whose beauty and perfection will satisfy the mind, illumine the imagination, and consecrate the will to service.

Every light is focused upon this picture of the Christ. From the class room of History there is thrown upon it the dim radiance of the past, and the many colored lights of revelation which gleam through the minds of those who in ages gone have seen Him and told of the wondrous beauty of His life. From the class room of History, there is also thrown upon the picture, the light reflected from the far fields where the heralds of the Christ have gone to proclaim the great Gospel of Redemption in Emmanuel's name.

From the class room of Theology there is thrown the light that shines from spirit-illumined thought, as, with reverence, it has come into His presence, to find the true interpretation of life and the many-colored beauty of the Divine Revelation.

From the class rooms where the Sacred Languages are taught, gleams of light are reflected upon the picture as the teachers unfold the mystery of the Divine purpose and the Divine Incarnation, wrapped in some meaning deeply hidden in the language of the prophets or in the writings of those who knew the Master in the days of His visible Incarnation.

From the class room of Polity and Liturgics there is thrown upon the picture the light which shines through the ordered sequence and beauty of the Church's life, and also the rich glow of revelation which shines refulgent through the liturgy used by saints and martyrs of old, and consecrated by the devotion of countless multitudes in the Church militant, who, through it, have passed into the presence of the King of Kings and Lord of Lords.

From the room where Homiletics and the English Bible are taught, there falls upon the picture the light of revelation which has come as the saints and prophets of the Church have unfolded the word of Truth, and, in Christ, found the meaning and purpose of life and seen that purpose worked out under the guidance of God's eternal Spirit in the lives of men and in the life of the nations.

From the class room where Pastoral Theology is taught, there shines upon the picture, the many-hued radiance which always follows the giving of the revelation of Eternal Love in terms of human sympathy. Here, as elsewhere, in the teaching of the Seminary, there come times when the gates are lifted up and light celestial falls through the open portals of Paradise upon this picture of the Crucified and Risen Lord of Life.

The record which has been given in this book, is, as we have said, nothing more than the reflection from the fragments of glass picked up from the floors of these halls, where, through the past century, consecrated workmen, called of God, have been seeking to make clear and beautiful this picture of the Christ, that men might see Him with unclouded vision and that they might go forth to reveal Him and to present Him to other men as Saviour, Lord, and Friend.

May God's continued benediction rest upon Seminary Hill, and consecrate and illumine this School of the Prophets, and inspire those who teach and those who learn, that they may see and know Him Whom to know and love and serve aright is life Eternal. May God's Holy Spirit ever prompt those who come to this place to learn of Him, to go forth to be His heralds to the uttermost parts of the earth, that all nations may come to see the glory of their Father as revealed in Jesus Christ, and that the time may be hastened when the "Kingdoms of this world shall become the Kingdoms of our Lord and His Christ."

SECTION IV

Special Monographs on the History

and

Life of the Seminary

THE RIGHT REVEREND DOCTOR WILLIAM CABELL BROWN

Seventh Bishop of Virginia and President of the Board of Trustees since 1919

SECTION IV

CHAPTER I

THE BOARD OF TRUSTEES

REV. S. SCOLLAY MOORE, D. D.

It has been thought best to preface this article by a list of the members of the Board of Trustees of the Theological Seminary in Virginia from 1821 to 1923.

The list is as follows:

TRUSTEES OF THE THEOLOGICAL SEMINARY IN VIRGINIA
from May 17th, 1821 to February 9th, 1923

RT. REV. R. C. MOORE, D. D.
* REV. JOHN S. RAVENSCROFT, D. D.
REV. WILLIAM H. WILMER, D. D.
* REV. WILLIAM MEADE, D. D.
REV. REUEL KEITH, D. D.
DR. AUGUSTINE SMITH
HON. BURWELL BASSETT
HON. BUSHROD WASHINGTON
COL. HUGH MERCER
MR. WILLIAM MAYO
REV. OLIVER NORRIS, D. D.
REV. EDWARD C. McGUIRE, D. D.
REV. ENOCH M. LOWE
MR. JOHN GRAY
MR. CARTER BERKELEY
MR. PHILIP NELSON
MR. JOHN NELSON, JR.
REV. JOHN WINGFIELD, D. D.
REV. JOHN GRAMMER, D. D.
REV. JOHN P. McGUIRE, D. D.
MR. ROBERT P. WARING
REV. ALEXANDER JONES
REV. CHARLES B. DANA, D. D.
MR. JOHN BRUCE
* REV. N. H. COBBS
REV. GEORGE ADIE, D. D.
MR. JAMES M. GARNETT
RT. REV. JOHN JOHNS, D. D.
MR. WILLIAM POLLOCK
MR. THOMAS F. NELSON
MR. CASSIUS F. LEE
GENERAL SAMUEL H. LEWIS
REV. GEORGE WOODBRIDGE, D. D.
MR. E. S. PEGRAM
DR. THOMAS H. CLAGETT
MR. SAMUEL H. SHELTON
MR. PIKE POWERS

REV. CHARLES W. ANDREWS, D. D.
MR. RICHARD H. CUNNINGHAM
MR. WILLIAM M. MacFARLAND
MR. JEREMIAH MORTON
MR. D. H. CONRAD
REV. CORNELIUS WALKER, D. D.
MR. DAVID FUNSTEN
REV. GEORGE H. NORTON, D. D.
REV. C. J. GIBSON, D. D.
COLONEL ARTHUR HERBERT
RT. REV. F. M. WHITTLE, D. D.
REV. J. A. LATANÉ
REV. W. C. MEREDITH
MR. DAVID H. MAY
MR. ROBERT PARKER
MR. ROBERT CRAIGHILL
REV. JAMES GRAMMER, D. D.
REV. HENDERSON SUTER, D. D.
REV. W. N. PENDLETON, D. D.
REV. JOSHUA PETERKIN, D. D.
REV. D. F. SPRIGG, D. D.
REV. RICHARD T. DAVIS, D. D.
REV. T. F. MARTIN
RT. REV. G. W. PETERKIN, D. D.
REV. WILLIAM H. MEADE, D. D.
MR. JOHN STEWART
MR. N. S. WHITE
RT. REV. A. M. RANDOLPH, D. D.
MR. EDMUND I. LEE
MR. JOSEPH BRYAN
MR. JULIAN T. BURKE
REV. S. SCOLLAY MOORE, D. D.
MR. THEODORE S. GARNETT
* REV. B. D. TUCKER, D. D.
RT. REV. JOHN B. NEWTON, D. D.
REV. P. P. PHILLIPS, D. D.
REV. JOHN J. LLOYD, D. D.

* Subsequently elected Bishop.

317

TRUSTEES OF THE THEOLOGICAL SEMINARY (Continued)

SECRETARIES OF THE BOARD

1821-1858   Rev. EDWARD C. McGUIRE

1859-1866   (RECORDS LOST)

1872-1878   REV. CORNELIUS WALKER, D. D.

1878-1879   REV. HENDERSON SUTER

1879-1907   REV. JAMES GRAMMER

1907-1923   REV. S. SCOLLAY MOORE, D. D.

TREASURERS OF THE BOARD

Editor's Note: It is distinctly remarkable that during the one hundred years of its history, the periods through which successive Treasurers have served have been of such long duration that the list of those who have served the Seminary in this capacity is so exceptionally short.

† 1822-1865 { MR. JOHN GRAY.
{ MR. WILLIAM POLLOCK.

1865-1890   MR. CASSIUS F. LEE.

1890-1911   COL. ARTHUR HERBERT.

1911-1916   MR. JULIAN T. BURKE.

1917-1923   MR. ARTHUR HERBERT, JR.

* Alumni Trustee.

† Mr. Gray continued as Treasurer up to and beyond 1840 to the time of his death. The minute book of the Board showing the date when his term expired is lost.

THE BOARD OF TRUSTEES

-1923-

THE BOARD OF TRUSTEES

REV. S. SCOLLAY MOORE, D. D.

Some one has said that "an institution is but the lengthening shadow of a man". As we study its growth, we trace back the shadow to its substance, the man who casts it. And, if its life be prolonged, we inevitably find in the shadow an interlacing tracery, the shadows of other men, who have left their impress, more or less clearly defined, upon the institution.

Two men stand conspicuous among the founders of the Virginia Seminary and their shadows lengthening blend in the creative forces out of which Virginia Theological Seminary grew. Those familiar with its history think first of all of Dr. William H. Wilmer and of Bishop Meade. Of them the present writer has little need to speak, since others will treat with power and knowledge surpassing his, of these men whose "lengthening shadows" fall across the lovely heights, which are crowned by the noble Institution of their foundation, and of their relation to this work.

And, perhaps, next to them in our thought comes the body of the teachers, who through the years have labored and prayed, and still today are laboring and praying, for the training and uplift of those young men, whose hearts God has touched for His great work. In the public eye the Faculty stands for the Seminary.

But back of the Faculty, selecting its membership, controlling its activities, themselves not conspicuously in evidence, but making up a body which has in some respects broadened the shadows of the founders, there has always stood this somewhat impersonal form, this shadowy substance, known to popular speech as "The Board". Of this the present writer is to tell the story, though he can do it only in a very imperfect way.

The first "Minute Book" of the Board lies before me as I write. It is a small book, somewhat defaced and mutilated, which possibly contained some two hundred pages, nearly half of which have been torn out. Its leather binding is unbroken, but much worn, showing signs of long and constant use. The paper is heavy and rough, without lines or margins, its edges stained by dampness and breaking away. There is, however, no difficulty in reading what is written on its pages. We handle the book with reverent care, for it undoubtedly contains the only record in existence of the proceedings of the Board for the period covered by it, which extends from 1821 to 1840.

There is some notation here of every meeting held during these years. And the record seems to be fairly complete, though many times the entries are tantalizing in their brevity, noting only, and that in very general terms, the substance, or possibly merely the subject of resolutions adopted without even the barest statement of their contents. The missing leaves were in the latter portion of the book, following almost the entire record of the meetings of the Board, and it is not difficult to conclude from an examination of the remaining pages that they contained no matter bearing upon its work. The first entry is, to one loving to pore over the manuscripts of old times, a picture. I could wish that it might be possible to provide a fac-simile for reproduction here. It is written in the beautiful lettering familiar to those accustomed to examine the ancient public records, especially of colonial days in Virginia, and it begins with this heading: "Proceedings of the Board of Trustees of the Theological School of Virginia, established at Williamsburg, by an act of the Convention held at Norfolk, May 17th, 1821."

The action of that convention was limited to the appointment of ten trustees: the Bishop, four other clergymen and five laymen, and the selection of a financial agent. It has seemed to the present writer appropriate that the names of these men, and of all others who have followed them in this most useful, but somewhat inconspicuous position, should be preserved in this record. In no other place have they ever been brought together, and it is now a difficult matter to collate them. A prolonged search in different directions has, at length, accomplished this, and the results are presented with this sketch in a list of names, believed to be complete, of all those who have served as Trustees of this Seminary, in the order of their selection. The ten names, which head this list, are those of the men chosen in 1821. In connection with this the present membership and organization of the Board are also set forth.

The first meeting of the Board appears to have been held at Charlottesville, in 1822, at which time a draft of a constitution for its government, prepared by a committee appointed at that meeting, was adopted, presented to the diocesan Convention then assembled there, and ratified by it. Among the several provisions contained in this brief paper were these; that the Bishop of the Diocese should be President of the Board; that there should be in addition thirteen members chosen by the Convention, which alone should have power to fill vacancies and to which annual reports of the proceedings of the Board should be made; that no changes in the constitution should become effective unless by a vote of two-thirds of the Convention. With the limitations indicated by these provisions, the Board was clothed with full powers of control by express enactment in the following terms: "The management of the Institution shall be vested in the Board of Trustees, who shall have power to choose a professor or professors, and to prescribe a course of study agreeable to the Canons of the Church, and in general to make rules and regulations for the government and good management of the Institution".

A committee was appointed to attend the next Maryland convention "to ascertain to what extent that Diocese will aid in the establishment of the School at Williamsburg".

A special meeting was held at Fredericksburg in July 1822, and at this time the first Professor, the Rev. Reuel Keith, was appointed by the Board. He was directed to "deliver his lectures in the College of William and Mary, where he had been sent under resolution of the Education Society adopted in 1820 to teach theology, provided the consent of the President, Professors, Governors and Visitors of the College be obtained". A resolution, significant of the spirit of the founders of the Institution, completed their action in this connection. It provided "that students of divinity of any Christian denomination be permitted to attend the said lectures gratuitously".

At this time the report of the committee, which visited the Maryland Convention, was presented, and this report appears to have marked the conclusion of the efforts to bring about such co-operation as had been sought between the two dioceses.

These records give no explanation of the difficulties in the way of the proposed union, but Bishop Meade, writing elsewhere at an earlier date than that of this report, gives the reasons alleged for opposition to it. He says, "The Convention of Virginia had appointed Col. Edward Colston and myself a committee to correspond with the Bishop of Maryland and some leading laymen in North Carolina, proposing a union with Virginia in the establishment and management of the Seminary at Williamsburg. From North Carolina we received no answer. From the Bishop of Maryland (Bishop Kemp) we received a prompt and decided refusal, accompanied with such severe strictures on the religion and morals of Virginia that we did not present it to the Convention, but only reported our failure. Williamsburg especially was objected to on account of its infidelity as altogether unfit to be the seat of such an institution. Those of us, who were engaged in the resuscitation of the Church, were also said to be extravagant in some of our notions, as is apt to be the case with those, who in flying from one extreme rush into the other."

The next matter of moment is noted in the record of the meeting of 1824, recounting the steps which were taken to establish the Seminary in Alexandria, Virginia. The resolutions passed by the Board in this and other instances are not quoted in this article in full as they appear in the chapters devoted to the history of the Seminary.

Details of the courses of instruction followed are given, and the "zeal, fidelity, and ability" of the Professors, now two in number, the Rev. William H. Wilmer having been added to the teaching force, are most highly commended.

The organization of the Institution may be said to have been completed, when an elaborate system of "Rules and Regulations" for its government was presented and adopted

at the annual meeting of the Board in 1825.   These prescribed the details of its operations, the courses of study,
division into classes, duties of the Faculty and students,
and other related matters.   It would not be within the scope
of the present article to dwell upon these, but we may call
attention to the spirit in which they were conceived, as
indicated in the emphasis laid upon "the duty of every student, with an humble reliance on divine grace, to be assiduous
in the cultivation of an evangelical faith and a sound practical piety".

As we turn the pages of this old "Minute Book" we are
constantly and increasingly impressed with the fostering
care of its fortunes and growth ever exercised by Bishop
Meade.   Many of the pages are covered with reports prepared by him, as a member of the Board, to be presented to
the convention of the diocese.   The longest and most carefully elaborated of these is that of 1826, in which with painstaking exactness and loving minuteness he discusses the
present condition and needs of the Seminary.   He dwells
with much detail upon the character and methods of its
work and speaks with deep and convinced earnestness of
results already accomplished.   He appeals with confidence
born of this conviction for interest and sympathy and aid.
His enthusiasm glows in every word.   "We rejoice over it
(the Institution, over which this Board is appointed to
preside) and call upon the friends of religion and our Church
to render thanks to God for that degree of prosperity which
it has pleased Him to grant to it.   We should never contemplate this school without the liveliest emotions of gratitude
to the great Head of the Church, who hath raised it up in
our time of need.   To what quarter can we look for a supply
of Preachers to repair our desolations but to this?   Whither
can our vacant parishes turn their eyes with the assured hope
of a certain and suitable supply, but to this?   Here it is
that our pious youths may equip themselves with the whole
armour of God and, being thoroughly furnished unto every
good work, become workmen, who need not be ashamed.
Here it is that, by mutual prayer and holy intercourse and
sacred studies, they may grow up in Christian love and form
a bond of union never to be broken.

"To this Institution will the hearts of our people be drawn: over it will the prayers of the pious be offered: to it will the alms of the generous be given, as to that which under God seems likely to prove such a blessing to His Church."

In 1827 a movement is initiated, the reasons for which are thus set forth:

"From the first opening of the school very serious inconveniences were found to attend the residence of the students and professors in Town. The expense of living is necessarily greater, and many interruptions to their studies are almost unavoidable. The want of a building exclusively devoted to their use, and where they may live in the most retired manner and in the simplest way, has been deeply felt, and often expressed, by the professors. It is believed that the Institution has already suffered, and may suffer still more, from the want of such an establishment."

Accordingly it had been decided to purchase property "in some healthy situation, near Alexandria, but within the State of Virginia", and in 1828 we find this decision carried into effect and the Seminary located upon the present site of which her sons love to think as like unto Mount Zion, "beautiful for situation, the joy of the whole earth".

We can picture to ourselves the simple life led by these faithful men, when we read that until this time the salary of each professor (not, of course, his sole support) had been $200 a year, and that in this very year, 1828, this resolution was adopted, "that the salary of the Rev. Dr. Keith as professor in the Seminary be $600 per annum subject to a deduction of $150 as a rent for the Seminary dwelling house and one-half of the farm, the proceeds of the other half to go into the funds of the School, the salary to be paid semi-annually." Moreover, while not expressly stated, it appears to be the case that the entire time of the Professor was to be devoted to the students. The entire farm owned by the Seminary at this time contained fifty-nine and a quarter acres.

So the record in this old "Minute Book" runs on continuously to, and including, the meeting of May, 1840. It is a story of struggle and of hope in the midst of great difficulties and serious limitations. It was still the day of small things, for at the close of the period the endowment amounted only to the sum of $27,500 in the hands of the Treasurer and a tract of land, about one hundred and seventy acres in extent, upon which stood a few small buildings.

When we reach this point in the annals of the Seminary, we find a gap in the records, which is explained by a memorandum in the handwriting of the Rev. Cornelius Walker, who was at a later date the secretary of the Board. This states that the next book of minutes, which recorded the business of more than twenty years through a meeting in May, 1861, was taken from his house, the rectory of Christ Church, Alexandria, during the war, and has never been recovered. The next entry bears the date of May, 1866. During these five years no meeting had been held. Bishop Meade had died, and more than four troubled years had passed since his death. It was appropriate that some note of the loss sustained by the Board should be made, and in the circumstances most appropriate that this note should be brief. The record of that meeting begins with such a note. The closing words are these: "We make this record simply that we may transmit to our successors the testimony of our reverence and love for our departed Father in God, to whose wisdom and devotion under the divine blessing this school of the prophets owes both its existence and the measures of prosperity and usefulness, with which it has been signally honored. We add our hope and prayer that it may be kept true to the great purpose for which it was founded and for which all its buildings and endowments were contributed, the Gospel as distinctly Protestant, Episcopal, and Evangelical."

It was during this period, the records of which are lost, that a change was made in the organization of the Board and in the manner of administering the affairs of the Seminary. For more than thirty years that organization was wholly inadequate and, in a business sense, ineffective. It had no recognized legal standing. It amounted to little more than a voluntary association of men, chosen by the convention of the diocese of Virginia for a definite purpose, to whose accomplishment they were held, indeed, by the highest of all obligations, those of a moral nature, but to these no legal authority attached and no legal restraints bound the men upon whom they rested. Even the funds, which they were slowly accumulating for their work, could not be invested with any sufficient security or protected by any adequate safeguards. There were difficulties in the way of securing a charter of incorporation. Under the law this could only be obtained by an act of the State Legislature. And so strong was the prejudice against the incorporation of religious societies that it was extremely difficult to obtain the passage of such an act.

During those years the Seminary was under the necessity, real or supposed, of conducting its business hampered by restrictions incident to such conditions.*

At length in 1854, a charter was obtained, which for the first time placed the Institution upon a good business foundation. By its provisions, as later amended, the mode of selection and organization of the Board of Trustees was radically changed.

That body was no longer subject in its composition to the choice of the Virginia convention, nor in any sense under its authority or control.

Sixteen men by name, the two Bishops of Virginia, eight other clergymen and six laymen, all then resident

---

Historical Note—Bishop Meade in his addresses, makes mention of the difficulties met in securing and safeguarding an endowment under former conditions. Every penny left by will (or given directly) to the Seminary had to be left or given to an *individual* by name, and he was not legally bound to account for it or to use it for the purpose desired. For many years the Journal gives a form to be used in making wills, drawn by the best lawyers, in which it was expressly recited, in order to make the legacy valid, that the legatee was not to be held accountable if he did not carry out the wishes of the devisee in regard to the legacy bequeathed to him. No one knows how many legacies Bishop Meade received under just those terms; but it is plain that under the conditions no large endowment could be gathered. It is noteworthy that the "Bruce Fund" was left to Bishop Johns by will "for the benefit of our destitute churches in Virginia;" but came also as "an honorable boon from the heirs at law, who, though under no legal obligations to comply with this provision of the will, promptly, and of their own accord, executed it as if really valid." The Virginia Convention besought the Legislature for a change in the law, but it was not secured until its necessity was so strongly felt in other quarters as to overcome the prejudice of three quarters of a century against Church endowments of any description.

References:—Journal of 1843, pp. 11-12, 21, 34; 1845, p. 11; 1846, p. 13 ff. 1847, p. 87; and subsequent Journals.—*Edward L. Goodwin.*

within the Diocese and State of Virginia, were constituted a body politic and corporate by the name and style of "The Trustees of the Protestant Episcopal Theological Seminary and High School in Virginia." This Board is clothed with the powers usually given in such charters and also with certain privileges somewhat unusual, such as a range of choice in filling vacancies, which is practically limited only by their own discretion. From the date of granting this charter to the present the work of the Board has been conducted in accordance with its provisions.

In the exercise of its discretion it has seen fit for the greater portion of this period to make residence within the limits of the State of Virginia, as those limits were defined in 1864, a condition of membership on the Board. But in 1904 it was deemed expedient to enlarge in some slight degree the field of selection, and provision was made for the possible choice of two members from the alumni under conditions determined by the Board of Trustees.

The gap in the records of the Board, to which allusion has been made, can in no way be filled. Doubtless many matters of interest could be gathered from those forgotten pages. They would show, at least, the considerations, which led to the change in the mode of organization, and the steps taken towards its consummation. And possibly we could trace in them some of the features that marked the disturbed history of the period leading up to the bitter conflict, which for a season divided the men of the North and of the South, in this our land. It has been remarked as a most singular peculiarity in Sir Thomas Browne that he, living in England through three-fourths of the seventeenth century, from its earliest almost to its latest decade, should have left in his writings no hint that he was conscious that his lot had fallen on troubled days. His stately prose seems to have stretched about him, like the aisles of a mighty forest, whose overshadowing trees gave shelter from the heat and storms beating and raging on every side. We can scarcely imagine that with like detachment from their immediate surroundings our Board of Trustees, living and laboring when and where they did, on heights devoted to lofty thought and holy calm, now resounding with the drums and tramplings of mighty armies, from whose eminence they could look across fields, once rich with corn and wine, now empurpled with the blood of many of the noblest of our country's sons lying still among the slain, could have failed to utter in some measure the emotions which stirred the hearts of men everywhere, as they looked upon the scenes that preceded such events as these.

Would not these lost records, sought but sought in vain, bear traces of the anguish which in those dark days oft wrung the hearts of men? But speculation as to their contents is idle. We can but lift the curtain a little way, here and there, upon the scene, and note that there are signs of constant growth and increasing influence, that the spirit which was in the wheels kept them in constant motion and their movement led them ever onward and upward. We can see enough to enable us to understand that in those days trustees, teachers and pupils alike "met the sturdy doubts and boisterous objections," as Sir Thomas Browne reminds us, "in divinity as in philosophy," and conquered theirs, as he conquered those that troubled him, "not in martial posture, but on their knees."

Within the compass of an article brief as this must be, it has seemed to the writer wise to confine attention almost entirely to the story of the early days of that body of which he treats. The men who were then its members are those who laid the foundations of the stately structure upon which we gaze today. The work they did, the record which they made, the story it tells, these are with us as living powers for good in our midst. They toiled, these, our fathers and leaders of the olden time, often amid the most baffling discouragements, with hopes buoyant in spite of all and with a faith that never faltered. And we are reaping now the fruits of their labors. The voice of the prophet rings through the pages of the old Minute Book. He speaks in no uncertain tone of his "conviction that the undertaking is acceptable to the great Head of the Church." And, as we listen, and look, and rejoice, shall we not also in this our day strive and pray that the same Spirit Who guided these men of old may direct and control us in all our efforts, so that the noble Institution which owes so much to them may continue to be for us and for our children a bulwark of the faith, pure, and simple, as it has been in the days that are gone.

We examine the list of names of those who have been members of this Board, and think with pardonable pride, I trust, of the high distinction achieved by many among them. It will not be thought invidious if we single out a few of these for special mention. Separate monographs in this work preserve the records of many of them.

We note in the list the names of fourteen Bishops in the Church. Ten are so designated there, having attained this high office before becoming members of the Board. Four are not thus indicated for the reason that their membership antedates their elevation to the episcopate. These are Dr. Ravenscroft, the first Bishop of North Carolina; Dr. Meade, the third Bishop of Virginia; Dr. Cobbs, the first Bishop of Alabama; and Dr. Tucker, the present Bishop of Southern Virginia. And among these Bishops is one, Rt. Rev. Dr. Arthur S. Lloyd, who, for many years, has held a leading position in the Church, first as Secretary of the Board of Missions and then as its President. We note the names of two men, Dr. William H. Wilmer, and Dr. Augustine Smith who, in succession, were Presidents of the College of William and Mary, the first college projected and the second founded within the limits of the United States. In several sessions of the General Convention Dr. Wilmer was President of the House of Clerical and Lay Deputies which distinction was also bestowed upon another and later member of the Board, Dr. R. H. McKim. Among the clergy there are the names of other men whose reputation has been more than local, but time would fail me to dwell upon the title of all to fame.

And of the lay members there are many who deserve more than a passing notice. It may suffice to make mention only of a few.

There is the Hon. Burwell Bassett, for some time a member of the House of Representatives and often called, it is said, to preside in its sessions, though never formally its speaker. And there also is the name of the Hon. Bushrod Washington, a nephew of "The Father of his Country" and for thirty-one years an Associate Justice of the Supreme Court of the United States.

And, coming down to later days, there is Judge Richard Parker, who in 1859 was a circuit Judge in Virginia, having among the counties in his circuit, Jefferson, whose county-seat is Charlestown and within whose bounds lies Harper's Ferry.   In the discharge of his official duty it became his painful task to preside at the trial of John Brown and his associates, and, when they were found guilty of crimes charged against them, to sentence them to death.

Passing by others, possibly of equal note, we may name two, who, for length of service upon the Board, for zeal in promoting the interests of the Institution, and for loyalty and devotion to its traditions and welfare, stand unsurpassed; Mr. Cassius F. Lee, who for about forty-seven years was an untiring toiler for its advancement, and Col. Arthur Herbert, who alone completed fifty years of service as a member of the Board and served for many years as its Treasurer.

"'Tis opportune to look back upon old times and contemplate our forefathers.'   We have sought, with whatever imperfection, to trace the outlines of 'past times' in such way as may serve in some measure for our instruction."

SECTION IV

CHAPTER II

THE PREPARATORY DEPARTMENT

REV. W. A. R. GOODWIN, D. D.

The need for a Preparatory Department connected with the Theological Seminary in Virginia had for sometime been felt by the faculty and the Board of Trustees, prior to the action of the Board in 1855 under which the Department was established. Young men seeking entrance into the Seminary who, through poverty or by reason of other circumstances, had been deprived of the advantages of a college education, were found in many instances unable to measure up to the entrance requirements. In other instances men having at a more advanced age determined to consecrate their lives to the ministry were found to have had no college experience, or else to have taken courses in college which did not cover all the subjects required under the canons for entrance upon a course of theological instruction.

As a result of these conditions it was found that many who otherwise would have entered the Seminary were forced to abandon the purpose, while others whose qualifications for entrance approached but did not measure up to standard were entered under conditions which imposed upon them the handicap of prosecuting their academic studies in connection with their theological work.

The Seminary course being arranged with a view to claiming the highest and best endeavor of the students in the mastery of this work alone, necessarily placed at a decided disadvantage students burdened with the necessity of doing extra academic work. It either prevented them from getting the full measure of benefit which otherwise would have been possible from the Seminary course, or made it necessary for the faculty to hold back the students who were prepared for the prosecution of their theological work in

332

order that the students unprepared might keep up with the class room work.

These conditions led the Board of Trustees in 1855 to establish the Preparatory Department. Their action in this matter was communicated to the Church through the following letter which appeared in "The Southern Churchman" of July 26th, 1855: "The Trustees of the Theological Seminary of Virginia would announce to the ministers and members of their communion, that they have been led by circumstances to think it their duty to connect with the Theological School under their care, another institution, which they trust with the blessing of providence, will render essential service to the cause of Christ and His Church, especially at this time when the demand for ministerial labors is so great and the supply so scattered. It is notorious that there are many young men in society of mature character, of good talents, and of the best spirit, who would gradually devote themselves to the work of the ministry and at once enter on a course of theological study if they possessed or could procure the needful preparation in classical and scientific knowledge. But this, under existing circumstances, seems impossible. They have not had a collegiate course and can not now, for various reasons, obtain one. Neither can they advantageously, if at all, supplement the deficiency at our common grammer schools and high schools. Their own age and settled habits of life and the form and associations under which instruction is imparted at these institutions has rendered them unsuitable and inconvenient places of study; consequently, they are impelled to surrender the first wish of their hearts and to forego to the great loss of the Church and Society, the privilege of preaching the ever-lasting gospel. To obviate this evil, the Trustees of the Theological Seminary and High School in Virginia have just made arrangements for the instruction of such young men in a department distinct from the Theological Seminary and also from the High School under their care.

"A building has been set apart for the purpose. Boarding has been procured close by and instruction will be given in part by teachers employed expressly for the purpose and in part by the members of the Theological Faculty. Such instructions will embrace all, and more than all, that is required by the Canons of the Church of those who wish to become candidates for orders.

"The government of this department will be in the hands of the Faculty of the Theological Seminary. Expenses: Board for the term of nine months, beginning with the last Wednesday of September and ending with the Thursday after the fourth Wednesday of June, $100. Tuition and rooms, without charge. Inquiries about this Institution may be directed to either of the professors, or the Theological Seminary, to whom also application for admission must be made, accompanied by a certificate of religious and moral character and of such dispositions and habits as may render the individual apt and meet to exercise the ministry. When circumstances require pecuniary aid it will be afforded by the Education Society as far as its funds will allow."

The Education Society, ever the faithful ally of the Seminary, quickly made response to the additional financial need created by this action on the part of the Board, and in 1858 announced that it had "assumed the expense of sustaining a professor in the Preparatory Department who will devote his whole time to this school." * The Rev. Dr. Cornelius Walker makes mention of the interesting fact that Phillips Brooks was the first teacher of the Preparatory Department and achieved here his first success as a teacher, he having failed in this vocation previous to his entrance upon his Seminary course.

When the shadows of war fell upon "The Hill" and the students dispersed, many to return to their northern homes and others to enter the military service either of the Federal or the Confederate Army, the Rev. Dr. Sparrow foresaw the conditions which would necessarily result in the life of the Seminary. He realized that many young men would have their college work permanently suspended, while others would be precluded from the possibility of entering college either during the war or in the years following. In 1861 he addressed a letter to the Board of Trustees in which, after speaking of the Seminary of the past, he says: "If I might

*Southern Churchman, August 13, 1858.

be permitted to say a word in regard to the future of the Seminary it would be this: Its hope of recovery from the tremendous blow which it has received lies with God's blessing in the Preparatory Department. It is only through this instrumentality that a sufficient number of indigenous students can be raised up to justify men in devoting their lives to their instruction in theology." *

Upon the conclusion of the war the Seminary made public announcement through the Church press of the reopening of the Institution, and included in the announcements which appear during this period a detailed statement of the opportunities offered through the Preparatory Department to those who desired to devote themselves to the ministry but who had been prevented by circumstances from acquiring a proper classical training for the study of theology.

In 1868 announcement is made of the election of Mr. Charles D. Lee as teacher of this Department at a salary of $600, the Education Society being asked to appropriate $200 so as to make the salary $800.

The Board of Trustees was not content to delegate to the elected teacher the entire responsibility of teaching and supervising the Preparatory Department. At the very outset they passed a resolution requesting the Dean "to attend as often as practicable the recitations of the preparatory teacher".

A mention is frequently made in connection with the proceedings of the Seminary commencement of the examinations of the students of this Department as well as those in the theological classes of the Seminary in the presence of the Board of Trustees.

In 1877 it was resolved by the Board, upon recommendation of Dr. Packard, "that no student be admitted into the Preparatory Department under nineteen years of age".

The following appreciation of the invaluable service rendered by the old Preparatory Department is taken from a letter from the Rev. Dr. Edward L. Goodwin, who was himself a student in this Department prior to his going to the University of Virginia for further academic work before entering the Virginia Seminary.

*Southern Churchman, May 24, 1861.

"There was an absolute necessity for this provision for preparatory study, which could have been supplied in no other way, during the greater part of the time the Department was in existence; especially from 1865 to 1885, the years of Virginia's poverty. Practically no provision was then made in our colleges, poor as they were, for students to work their way through; and there were no scholarships or State aid to speak of. For a period of about ten years I knew personally the men in that Department, and I am sure that one-half of them could never have gotten to College by any means then available. Moreover, the instruction given in this Department was quite equal, though not as extensive, as that afforded in most of our Colleges. It was the one way for young men, taken from the plow, to get the education they required for entering the Seminary proper. And with their previous lack of advantages it is surprising how well grounded they were after two years of intensive study in that Department.

"The old Preparatory students were not second-rate or third-rate men. Among them were R. S. Barrett, G. S. Gibbs, R. D. Roller, T. Spencer, E. A. Penick, L. W. Saltonstall, C. Grubb, W. B. Lee, C. E. Buck, R. R. Claiborne, M. P. Logan, W. G. McCready, C. J. S. Mayo, G. H. Edwards, John Moncure, J. Y. Downman, R. E. Jones, L. R. Combs, R. W. Forsyth, G. M. Funsten, Martin Johnson, N. F. Marshall, W. T. Roberts, A. J. Willis, E. B. Burwell, W. L. Gravatt, C. O. Pruden, L. W. Rose, W. R. Savage, J. W. Sykes, and later Bishops Jett, Tyler and Temple. Now all of these men were no doubt hampered by lack of a college education, but they made good. Of those I mentioned, sixteen became Doctors of Divinity, and for steady, effective work in the ministry few have excelled them.

"It was wise that the Department should have been abolished so soon as the Education Society could afford to help men at college and the University. It probably continued a few years longer than was necessary. This Department in the olden days was not a 'short cut' into the ministry or a 'side-door' for slackers. The best teacher I ever sat under, except Noah K. Davis and F. H. Smith, was Robert Jackson, who was then Preparatory teacher at the Seminary."

A committee of the Board of Trustees was appointed in 1878 to make a thorough examination of the Department and to report back to the Board the findings, especially with reference to the advisability of continuing this special Department of work in connection with the Seminary. This committee reported to the Trustees as follows: "After looking at the working of this Department, considering its advantages and disadvantages, it seemed best to the committee to continue it under the following regulations: No one shall be allowed to enter the Preparatory Department unless nineteen years of age, and well grounded in the ordinary branches of the English education, proficiency in which must be shown in an examination by the professors who will also test their capacity to write the English language correctly.

"Also, that this Department is not intended to encourage young men to give up a thorough collegiate education. The trustees and professors earnestly advise all who are looking forward to the ministry to graduate at college if possible.

"It was further resolved that the trustees make the same appropriation for the Preparatory Department as last year. (This appropriation had been running at $600 for a number of years.) "Resolved that Professor Nelson be requested to visit and examine the classes in the Preparatory Department except those taught by Seminary professors, at least once a month."

The teachers of the Department in 1890 were Robert K. Massie, who some years after his graduation was elected to the faculty of the Seminary, J. Addison Ingle, afterwards Bishop of the Church in China, and Ernest M. Stires, now rector of St. Thomas' Church, New York City.

Upon the minutes of the Board of Trustees there appears a resolution "appropriating $900 to the Preparatory Department, which is $300 more than was previously given."

The time, however, arrived when serious doubt arose in the minds of the Faculty and the Board of Trustees as to the wisdom of continuing the existence of this Department. There was a disposition to use it as a short-cut into the ministry, on the part of some students who would otherwise have taken advantage of the more adequate course of instruction offered in colleges and universities.

The time taken from Seminary work by the students employed to teach in this Department was also a consideration in the final determination of the Board in the matter. The most compelling conviction, however, which led the members of the faculty and the Board of Trustees in their consideration of the subject was their desire that those who entered the ministry through the Theological Seminary in Virginia might go forth fully and adequately prepared. It was realized that it was impossible for a student in this Department to gain the depth and breadth of culture which a college or university course would afford, and it was felt that the students were also deprived of the advantages which grew out of the associations and contacts of college life. In the faculty this conviction was most strongly felt and urged by the Rev. Dr. Carl E. Grammer, who in the Education Society sought to have all the beneficiaries sent to College; failing in this he secured scholarships to enable men to attend college. He also enlisted the cooperation of President Dreher of Roanoke College in this endeavor, and convinced some of the Trustees as to the wisdom of abolishing the Preparatory Department.

The matter was finally referred by the Board of Trustees to a committee of which the Rt. Rev. Dr. Alfred M. Randolph was chairman for a thorough investigation and report. The findings of this committee were submitted to a meeting of the Board of Trustees held on June 26th, 1894 and were as follows: "The committee deems it advisable to abolish the Department, First, because of the expense to the Seminary involved in continuing this Department, and secondly, because of the limited educational advantages offered by the Department as compared with the advantages of college education."

The report offered by Bishop Randolph is signed also by Bishop Whittle. Upon resolution of Rev. Dr. B. D. Tucker, the report was adopted and the Department abolished.

The standards of education which now prevail in the Seminary as to entrance requirements and the conditions under which the class room work is being carried on could never have been secured if the Preparatory Department had been allowed to continue in existence.

Deprived of the possibility of entering the Seminary through this smaller side door, students looking forward to entering the ministry through the Virginia Seminary turn to the colleges and universities, and from them have come to this Institution for their theological education with minds trained and disciplined for the prosecution of their work.

This has enabled the Faculty to pitch their work upon a much higher plane and to provide courses of study both more profound and more extensive than would have been possible had the Preparatory Department continued in existence.

The desire to become candidates for Holy Orders on the part of men who have entered business or professional life without having received the academic education qualifying them for admission into our Theological Seminaries, has led the Church to endorse the provisions made in such institutions as the DeLancey Divinity School in Western New York, and, more recently, the Du Bose School in Tennessee, where opportunity is given for academic and theological study while the men pursue their business or professional duties, thus providing support for themselves and their families. Such schools, working in cooperation with more elastic provisions recently made in the canons of the Church relative to the studies required of men seeking to enter the ministry under abnormal conditions, and making provision for electives and also for adequate substitutes for ancient languages for those who have had special scientific training, all point to a better way to meet these special conditions than could have been provided by continuing the Preparatory Department.

SECTION IV

Chapter III

Recollections Of The Old Chapel

REV. JOSEPH PACKARD, D. D.

A Discourse

delivered at

The Consecration of the New Chapel

of the

Theological Seminary of the Diocese of Virginia

on Thursday, June 23, 1881.

Preliminary Statement.

In the Spring of 1879, the Chapel of the Theological Seminary in Virginia was decided to be unsafe, and efforts were set on foot to collect funds to build a new one. These were so successful that the new building was begun in May, 1880, and mainly completed by the end of the year, although, in consequence of the severity of the weather, it was not occupied until the first Sunday in March, 1881.

The total cost of the building and furniture was about $11,000, of which the materials of the old building contributed about $1,500. The Trustees of the Seminary appropriated $1,500 more, and the remainder was made up by the gifts of Alumni and friends in all parts of the country, the larger portion coming from the cities north of the Potomac.

The new Chapel, which is in the decorated gothic style, stands nearly on the site of the old one, fronting east, and covers about the same area. It is built of dark red brick,

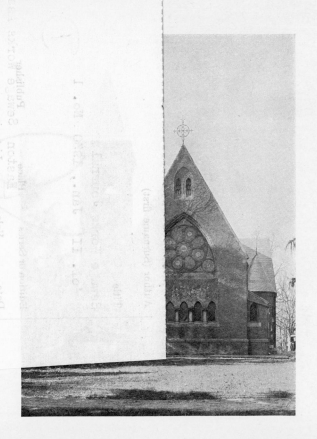

The Seminary Chapel

laid in red mortar, with brown-stone trimmings.   In plan it is cruciform, consisting of nave and aisles, transept, choir, and choir aisles.   The clerestory is supported by an arcade of columns, the clerestory windows being in the crown of the arches of the arcade.   At the southeast corner is a square tower, with pointed roof.   The Church is open roofed, the main timbers and purlins being of yellow pine, stained dark, and the interior sheathing of oiled pine, as the wainscoting also is.   The Chancel is in the west end, with an organ room occupying the choir aisle on one side, and a robing room occupying the other choir aisle.   There are spacious galleries in the transepts and in the east end, access to the transept galleries being from the aisles by corner turrets; from all of these galleries the view of the chancel is unobstructed.   The building will seat about three hundred persons on the ground floor, and two hundred in the galleries.   There is a three-light traceried window in the chancel.   In the front gable of the nave is a large equilateral window containing a wheel window, and the clerestory and transept galleries contain equilateral windows filled with tracery, with rows of smaller windows below.   The chancel window is of stained glass; the other windows are of rolled cathedral glass, in harmonizing tints.   The chancel furniture, and the panelling on the rear wall of the chancel are of walnut, with the exception of the chancel rail, which is of African rosewood, supported by polished brass standards.   The pews are of brown ash. The chandeliers and side lights are of polished brass.   The building is warmed by a furnace.   The architect was Mr. Charles E. Cassell, of Baltimore.

On Thursday, June 23, 1881, the new Chapel was consecrated to the service of Almighty God.   Besides those who took part in the services, there were present of the clergy the Rev. Doctors Pendleton, Peterkin, Wheat, Dame, Walker, McElhinney, and Hubard, and the Rev. Messrs. Grammer, Sharp, Johns, F. Stringfellow, Estill, G. W. Nelson, Phillips, Bryan, Page, S. S. Ware, Claiborne, Wellman, Clark, E. L. Goodwin, A. S. Lloyd, Logan, Mayo, Packard, and Winn, of the Diocese of Virginia; the Rev. Dr. Meade, and the Rev. Messrs. Leavell and Roller, of the Diocese of West Virginia; the Rev. Drs. Hutton, Dalrymple, Hoff, Williams,

Randolph, Mason, Forrest, Duncan, and the Rev. Messrs. Leakin, Harris, Hyland, O. Ingle, E. H. Ingle, Steele, Baker, Gardner, Lindsay, P. Wroth, W. M. Dame, N. P. Dame, Meade, Craighill, Andrews, Braddock, Barr, Schubert, Hipkins, and Fletcher, of the Diocese of Maryland; the Rev. Dr. Matlack, of the Diocese of Pennsylvania; and the Rev. Mr. Stone, of the Diocese of Delaware.

At the appointed hour, the Right Rev. Dr. Whittle, Bishop of the Diocese, accompanied by the Bishops of Delaware, Maryland, and West Virginia, and the Rev. Drs. Packard and Nelson, went from the robing room to the north door of the Chapel, where they were received by Mr. Cassius F. Lee and Colonel Arthur Herbert, and proceeded up the aisle to the chancel, followed by most of the clergy named above, who took seats reserved for them in the pews immediately in front of the chancel.

The Bishop of the Diocese then proceeded with the consecration services, the sentence of consecration being read by the Rev. Dr. Kinloch Nelson, Professor in the Seminary, and Chairman of the Building Committee. Morning Prayer was then said by the Right Rev. Dr. Peterkin, the Right Rev. Dr. Pinkney reading the Lessons. The Ante-Communion Office was said by the Right Rev. Dr. Lee. Then followed the sermon by the Rev. Dr. Packard, after which the congregation was dismissed with the Benediction by the Bishop of the Diocese.

DISCOURSE.

"Remember them who have spoken unto you the Word of God: whose faith follow."—HEBREWS, XIII, 7.

The consecration of a building for the service of Almighty God, for reading His Holy Word, for celebrating the Holy Sacraments, for offering the sacrifices of praise and thanksgiving, and for the performance of all other holy offices, is a solemn occasion at all times. It is so especially, when we consider the character of the congregation which assembles here; that hundreds of those who are to break the bread of life to others will kneel around this chancel, and will be hearers here of that Word which they are, in their turn, to preach.

We have, too, here, as regular attendants upon our worship, a large and interesting company of youth, trained at the High School for posts of usefulness, and who are destined to exert a great influence upon the community.

As we are thus assembled to consecrate this holy and beautiful house to the worship of Almighty God, we would bear in mind the kindness of numerous friends, by whose gifts this chapel has been built. Would that all who have aided in its erection, either by their own means, or by their influence over others, were here to-day to share our joy in its consecration, and to see with what taste and economy their contributions have been expended; how strength and beauty have met together in this sanctuary! The manner in which the contributions have been made has, in many cases, enhanced their value, and cheered our hearts. We have been assured by those who have contributed, of their unabated affection for the dear old Seminary. It gives us special pleasure to know that this Seminary has not been forgotten in Africa, as this chancel rail, brought from that dark continent by Bishop Penick, attests. It is a peculiarly appropriate memorial gift, since in the soil which nurtured it lies all that is mortal of Launcelot B. Minor, C. Colden Hoffman, Robert Smith, H. H. Holcomb, and E. Messenger, who were all prepared here for their holy work.

On this occasion I think it will be appropriate for us to turn aside to dwell upon some of the memories which gather around the old Chapel, and which make the place on which it stood, holy ground.

The Theological Seminary was moved out from Alexandria to this spot in 1827. For four years in town, it had no special buildings. From the year 1827 to 1840, the congregation here worshipped in two rooms in the old Seminary building, connected by folding doors, and occupied by the Library. The want of some distinct place of worship was greatly felt by this community, and Mrs. Keith, the wife of Rev. Dr. Keith, began to raise funds for the purpose, and obtained about four hundred dollars by means of a sewing society. To this sum was added a collection, taken up at the Norfolk convention in 1839, and with the aid of other contributions a plain building was put up.

In Bishop Meade's address to the convention in 1840, he says, "On the last week of April, I officiated on Sunday morning in the unfinished chapel to more than thirty theological students, and to more than sixty youths from the High School (then under the charge of Dr. Pendleton) and the Fairfax Institute (a school for boys, kept in the neighborhood by the Rev. George A. Smith). A more interesting congregation was never before my eyes. The fixed attention and expressive countenances indicated most clearly and strongly that the Spirit of God was within them, doing His holy work." Bishop Moore, in his address to the convention in 1841, speaks thus of the consecration of the chapel. "In July, 1840, my duties called me to Alexandria, at which time I consecrated the new chapel of our Theological Seminary." In Bishop Meade's address to the convention in the same year, he said, "On the 4th of July I addressed the students of the Seminary and the youth of the High School and Fairfax Institute, at the Chapel of the Theological Seminary. The morning of one of the days of the following week was introduced by the administration of the Rite of Confirmation to thirty-seven persons, twenty-seven of whom were youth from the two schools, who, during the session, had given such evidence of piety as justified their teachers in presenting them for this solemn ceremony." Two of the youth then confirmed, I may add, were sons of Dr. Keith; one of whom became a Missionary to China, and, returning thence, perished at sea, when the vessel, the "Golden Gate," caught on fire.

The next mention of the Chapel is in Bishop Johns' address to the convention in 1856. "The increased number of students in the Seminary, and of pupils in the High School, together with the growing population in the vicinity, has made it obvious that an enlargement of the Chapel was indispensable. The appeal made for this purpose to friends in the neighborhood and at a distance, was promptly and liberally responded to, and on the 19th of December, I had the satisfaction of consecrating the new building to the service of Almighty God. The Chapel has been enlarged to twice its former size, and much improved in its appearance at a cost of $4,000, raised for this special purpose, and not taken from the funds of the Institution."

A building devoted to religious services becomes sacred in our eyes when associated with the memory of those who have been preachers or hearers in it. A goodly company of such is even now looking down from the heights above. We have great cause to praise Almighty God for His favor manifested in the early history of this Seminary, in blessing it with three such professors in succession as Doctors Keith, Sparrow and May. The world and the Church are prone to forget those into whose labors they have entered, and who have enriched them by their deeds and their example. It is sad to think that the generation now entering upon the stage cannot know the ability and attainments, the gracious character and manners, of those who have gone from us. To some of us here to-day, the dead still live. They sit in this chancel; they stand at this desk; they fill these pews; they look down upon us with a look passing earthly love.

Doctor Keith is almost forgotten. Few men can do more than serve the generation in which they live, by doing faithfully the work God assigns them. To those who never knew him, I should despair of giving an adequate conception of his character. There was far more in him than could be transferred to paper. As you met him in the street he had an abstracted, dreamy air, as though he was looking at the things unseen; as though he was studying some deep point of doctrine; as through his life was deeply hidden with Christ, in God.

As a scholar, he was familiar with the original languages of Scripture, and had a very strong taste for exegetical research. We may truly say of him that God's law was his meditation day and night, and he frequently told his students that the best preparation for extempore preaching was a familiarity with the English version. He translated from the German language the great work of Hengstenberg on the Prophecies of Christ, a translation which showed his perfect familiarity with the idioms of both languages

As a teacher, he was remarkable for acuteness and clearness, and exerted a marked influence in moulding the opinions of his pupils. His theology was the theology of the Cross. Christ was the sun of his system, high and alone in the heavens, around which the whole system of doctrines revolved, attracted towards it, and borrowing light and warmth from it.

As a preacher, I have never heard one of such intense earnestness, and I was recently gratified in finding my own opinion confirmed by Bishop Wilmer, of Alabama. I have never known his equal in expatiating upon the themes on which he loved to dwell; the salvation of the gospel here and hereafter; the complete justification of the believer in Christ; the saint's everlasting rest. His mode of preaching, while I knew him, was without a manuscript. His voice was silvery and penetrating. No preacher of his day was so gladly heard by the common people.

I feel it my duty, and it gives me a sad pleasure, thus to revive the memory of Dr. Keith, to "scatter these withered flowers upon his grave," as he is in danger of being clean forgotten and out of mind. He stamped upon this Seminary much of the peculiar character and spirit it has since sustained. The spirit of an institution is determined very much by its first few years. "The childhood shows the man, as morning shows the day." Never should this Seminary forget what it owes to him, who, for the first nineteen years of its history, was its principal professor.

Dr. Sparrow was his successor, a man very unlike Dr. Keith, except in piety and ability. I need say less about him, as so many before me knew him and can never forget him. How well they remember his tall and erect, and slender figure, his countenance when lighted up by a smile, his sympathetic and loving heart, the charm of his conversation, his ripe scholarship, his wide and varied learning, rich with the spoils of ancient and modern times. His pupils remember well his love of the truth, his sturdy independence of all authority, save that of the Word of God, his intolerance of error, his felicity in the choice of words to express his ideas. Sometimes in the class he was kindled with his subject, his eye flashed, his face became radiant, his utterance strong; and his extemporaneous efforts there and in the Faculty meetings, surpassed his more studied performances. As a preacher, his clear and resonant voice was heard in the old chapel for more than thirty years, reasoning upon the deep things of God. He could not be heard without admiration, by anyone prepared to follow him in his clear and logical analysis of his subject. But though he was deep in thought he was clear in language. Muddy waters may appear deep, because we can not see the bottom; clear waters will always seem less deep than they are, because we can do so. He so presented the truth that it appeared to an attentive hearer as though it needed no explanation. He left behind him but little in print: the life of a laborious teacher, who has two or three lectures a day, affords little leisure and spirit to write and publish books. Yet Dr. Sparrow printed deep in the minds and hearts of his pupils the truth as he understood it.

Dr. May followed Dr. Sparrow, and was a professor here for twenty years. His Christian character was the most perfect one I have ever known. He was a living example of all that a minister of Christ ought to be. When we enter a Roman Catholic church we see a picture or statue of some saint; when a student entered this Seminary he saw before him in Dr. May, not a dead, but a living saint. He showed how much good can be done by being good. He was free from any of those little follies which detract from the usefulness of some of those had in reputation in the church. Baxter, in his old age, said, that he found as the result of his lifelong experience that good men were not as good as their admirers thought them. But it was not so with Dr. May; his character would bear the closest examination. What Bishop Burnet said of Archbishop Leighton might well be applied to him: "I never knew him to say an idle word that had not a direct tendency to edification; and I never once saw him in any other temper but that I wished to be in at the hour of death." As a preacher, he was gifted by nature with an excellent voice and fluency of speech. His sermons were variations of one theme. If it was sometimes thought and said, that the subjects of his sermons were too unvaried, it was because he had determined to know nothing among men save Jesus Christ, and Him crucified. In the Faculty meetings he was specially edifying. There his "tongue dropped manna." Not a few of his pupils feel that they owe to his example more than to that of any other man.

We are exhorted in Scripture to consider the end of the conversation, that is, the manner of the death, of those who have spoken to us the Word of God. Dr. Keith, for nearly two years before his death, was afflicted with bodily as well as mental disease, which left him no lucid interval. The veil which settled over his mind was not so rent that he had a full enjoyment of the beatific vision, a vision, not of earthly glory, but of the perfections of God. Dr. May passed unconsciously away, so that he gave no sign of loving farewell as he took his last look of earth, nor of joyful assurance as he looked up into heaven. Dr. Sparrow heard his recitations the day before his death, and stood to the last at his post of duty, with his loins girded about, and his lamp trimmed and burning, and doubtless he inherited the blessing pronounced upon that servant whom his Lord, when He cometh, shall find so doing.

These departed brethren were all fervent in spirit, single-minded in their aim in life. There are three stars in the belt of Orion which shine side by side with equal lustre; so these three men, that have gone into that world of light, shine down upon us in their bright example and sweet influences, as the brightness of the firmament, and as the stars, for ever and ever. Much of the tender love which the older Alumni cherish for this Seminary, as for a place in which they spent the happiest and most profitable hours of life, is owing to these men.

Nor should I omit to mention here Bishop Johns, who, though not a regular professor, was a frequent preacher in the old Chapel, and always, when here, sat in the chancel. No man in our Church has left so fragrant a memory behind him, not only in our own, but in other churches. He had uncommon gifts as a preacher, and might well have been called, as Chrysostom was, the golden mouthed. A well modulated voice, a graceful and earnest delivery, a memory which never seemed to fail him, and a rare fluency of speech, made him very popular as a preacher. On the fifty-fifth anniversary of his ordination he preached in the Chapel, and after expressing his gratitude to God that He had called him by His grace to the ministry of reconciliation, and granted him so long a continuance in it, he earnestly exhorted his young brethren to abound in the work of the Lord, and never to be weary in His service. He was as a man so warm in friendship that the Rev. Dr. Hodge, of Princeton, said of him, "I have no such friend on earth."

We turn now to speak briefly of the Alumni who have sat as hearers in the old Chapel. They form a great company of preachers. Some of them occupy high places in the centers of influence in our country; others are missionaries in heathen lands; the great majority are faithful laborers in country parishes.

We have been greatly blessed in the example of devoted piety of many of them while here. It has raised the standard of their fellow-students and made a deep and lasting impression upon them. There is no place where a Christ-like example does so much good as in a theological school. Without making mention of the living, my heart fondly turns to those who have finished their course and died in faith. Some of them have been taken away in the midst of their days, others before they even entered the ministry. As an instance of this last class was John Hulme Harrison, of Pennsylvania. He was obliged to leave the Seminary in consequence of ill health, and returned home to die. He said in his last days, "Oh, I had hoped to have preached the unsearchable riches of Christ, the fulness, the freeness of His grace, sovereign grace! What was I; what am I?" When after a wearisome night a friend said to him, "What a long and weary night!" "But it was pleasant," was his reply; "such delightful thoughts would pass through my mind. Eternal life! What is eternal life? Jesus is the watchword."

There were also Chisholm and Jackson, blessed martyrs during the yellow fever at Norfolk. There was Messenger, a missionary to Africa, who fell a victim to the climate a few months after his arrival, and who said, in his last moments, "I know that Jesus Christ died for me, and on this I rely." There was the lovely, the eloquent Dudley Tyng, whose last words were, "Stand up for Jesus." Time would fail me to tell of others whose life and death are recorded only in God's book of remembrance, which supplies the place of earthly fame and elegy.

The old Chapel had witnessed scenes of deep interest in the ordinations and farewell meetings of missionaries, in the addresses of Bishops Boone and Payne, and our other Missionary Alumni on their visits to this country. The circumstances of the ordination of Rev. E. W. Hening as Missionary to Africa were such as deeply to move many hearts. Four years after his ordination as Deacon he returned to be ordained Priest. In the meantime he had become blind from the African fever, and was led by the hand to the chancel, thus bearing about in his body, like Saint Paul, the marks of the Lord Jesus.

The old Chapel has also kept, for a brief hour, the forms of not a few on their passage to their long homes. Both the young and the old have been here. In the journal of the Virginia convention for 1857, Bishop Johns says; "My sad office was to conduct the services in the Seminary Chapel at the funeral of a daughter of our worthy brother (Rev. John P. McGuire), the Principal of the High School. She was so endeared to all who knew her, that the unexpected stroke came upon us with peculiar affliction. The decided Christian character of the lovely departed sister deprived the bereavement, as far as possible, of the sorrow of separation, and the event, to us so mysterious, was the occasion of deepening and disclosing the religious concern which for some weeks previous had prevailed among the pupils at Howard." Under date of June 29, of the same year, he says, "At night in the Seminary Chapel I preached, and confirmed twenty-three, twenty-one of whom were the fruits of the recent revival in the High School."

From this place devout men carried to their burial Dr. Sparrow and Bishop Johns, "nor was there wanting the costly tribute of tears, wrung from many a manly heart, to wash their way-worn feet for their burial."

We have thus revived some recollections of the old Chapel that were fast fading away. As we look back upon the history of the Seminary, with which it has been so identified, and ask the secret of its measure of success and favor with God and man, we may answer with Bishop Johns in his address at the dedication of Aspinwall Hall, that it is owing to the fact "that care has been taken that in this school the doctrines of the Protestant Reformation, which are the doctrines of the Scriptures, and of which justification by faith is the key-note, should be taught with distinctness and decision; that the ecclesiastical polity inculcated here has been that set forth in the Preface to the Ordination Service —so much, no more, no less, in a word, that the three orders have existed from the Apostles' times, and no other ministry to be recognized 'in this Church.'"

We may further say, that one thing which has distinguished the teaching of this Seminary, has been its firm and unshaken faith in the system of doctrine once delivered to the saints, and as held in the Articles of our Church. We have held fast the atoning work of our Lord as a satisfaction to the divine justice, as well as a revelation of the divine love; justification only by the righteousness of Christ; regeneration only by the power of the Holy Spirit; the Sacraments as signs and seals of spiritual grace.

We have neither gone to the right hand, nor to the left, nor gone beyond the Bible. We have never, to my knowledge, been charged with unsoundness in doctrine. The Seminary has never slipped the cable of its faith and drifted with the tide of thought of the day. It has discovered no new truths in Scripture, nor any new way of explaining away old truths. While it may, sometimes, have been charged with want of progress, with being behind the free thought of the day, with obsolete views of inspiration, it has never been charged with rationalism. We may, perhaps, too much have left the scientists to take care of themselves, remembering how, on one occasion, the enemies of Judah fought together and destroyed each other.

And what shall we say of the future of the Seminary? Will it be kept up to the point it has reached in time past, and will it go on to accomplish the end for which it was founded? We would not pry between the folded leaves of the future, which the only wise God has concealed from our sight. We might well rejoice with trembling, when we remember how other seminaries, founded in faith and prayer, have destroyed the faith of their founders. As rash and unhallowed speculation abounds, may not the foundations here be shaken?

But let us look forward with hope and trust in God that men even more devoted than those who have gone before, will fill this pulpit; that fervent prayer will continue to ascend here, as incense; that the Divine Spirit will continue to shed His choicest influences upon this hill of Zion, as the dew of Hermon, and as the dew that descended upon the mountains of Zion, where the Lord commanded his blessing, even life for ever more; that He who has the seven stars in His right hand will consecrate here those who shall minister before Him, and who shall pour out the holy oil into the ever-burning lamps; that this Seminary will flourish, the light and hope of ages to come; that many in our own and heathen lands will rise up and call it blessed.

NOW, THEREFORE, ARISE, O LORD GOD, INTO THY DWELLING PLACE, THOU AND THE ARK OF THY STRENGTH; LET THY PRIESTS, O LORD GOD, BE CLOTHED WITH SALVATION, AND MAKE THY PEOPLE JOYFUL IN THY HOUSE OF PRAYER. AMEN AND AMEN!

THE PACKARD-LAIRD MEMORIAL LIBRARY

THE INTERIOR OF THE NEW LIBRARY

SECTION IV

CHAPTER IV

THE LIBRARY

REV. SAMUEL A. WALLIS, D. D.

Standing conspicuous among the buildings of the Seminary Campus, a short distance west of the Chapel, is the handsome new building called the Packard-Laird Library. It was erected in 1921 as a memorial to the late venerable Rev. Joseph Packard, D. D., who lived in his home on "The Hill" for sixty-six years, as Professor of Biblical Learning, Librarian, Dean for a number of years, in succession to the Rev. Dr. Sparrow, and Professor Emeritus. In addition to this it is also a memorial to his grandson the Rev. William H. Laird, at the request of his brother, who was the largest personal contributor to the Library building fund. The Rev. Mr. Laird was the rector of Emmanuel Church, Wilmington, Delaware, an honored graduate of the Seminary, and prominent among the younger clergy of our Church. He died suddenly while on his vacation in Virginia in the summer of 1920. The Library was completed in June 1921, in time for the annual dinner of the Alumni Association which was held in the new building during Commencement Week, amidst ideal surroundings.

The new library is constructed of brick with stone dressings in the colonial style of architecture. It is a large and beautiful building of dignified appearance, having the front facing the North, being one story in height, but with the main floor well elevated above the ground, and approached by a handsome flight of stone steps, leading to a stately entrance. The whole interior is fine and well proportioned, satisfying the eye of the most critical observer. A cellar extending under the whole building forms an excellent place for storing old books, magazines and papers, which it is often most expedient to keep for reference. In its position on the grounds, the new Library harmonizes well with its surroundings. With the exception of the Chapel and the old Library, which, however, can not be seen from the new building, the rest of the buildings, although cherished for their sacred associations, are of rather a nondescript character, architecturally speaking. But the very sacredness of their associations has consecrated these halls as memorials from generation to generation. Even the old story we have heard concerning the origin of the unique cupola on Aspinwall Hall must give us one of the strongest arguments for its preservation; for it is said that it commemorates the establishment of the Seminary's mission in China, in its suggested resemblance to a pagoda. But if so, the conversion of China, as well as of all other heathen countries, is signified by the Cross which rises supreme in its beautiful proportions from the top of the cupola above all the buildings of the Seminary.

The former library, which, as every annual catalogue testifies, is now the oldest public building on the grounds, stands in a secluded spot immediately north of Bohlen Hall. This may give a wrong impression of the word "secluded", as we remember that on the other side is "Maywood" the residence of one of the professors. Yet the place, always quiet and full of repose, proves that the word "secluded" is singularly appropriate. The old Library building is a gem of collegiate Gothic architecture. It is of brick with the exterior mellowed by age. The approach to the main entrance through the east porch, embowered as it is by two noble Norway spruce trees, is truly romantic, suggestive of the presence of the genius of learning, beckoning to the hall of reading and study. This beautiful building was erected in 1855 from a gift received from John Bohlen and his sister of Philadelphia, amounting to $4000., and a legacy of $5000. from Mrs. Sophia Jones of Virginia. It has now been converted into a refectory which has been much needed for years. This takes the place of the antiquated one in the basement of Bohlen Hall, which is most inadequate and unworthy of the Seminary in these days of growing prosperity and general advancement. The new refectory has received the most appropriate name of "Wilmer Hall" as a memorial of the Rev. William H. Wilmer, D. D., one of the noted rectors of St. Paul's Church, Alexandria, Virginia, who was also one of the chief founders of the Seminary, acting as a professor in the beginnings of its history without any compensation for his services.   It was a very interesting coincidence that on the opening of Wilmer Hall as the refectory at the Commencement of 1922, the Rev. C. B. Wilmer, D. D., rector of St. Luke's Church, Atlanta, Georgia, was the guest of honor at the Alumni Dinner.   He delivered a very interesting and instructive address on the theological views and position of his grandfather.   Dr. Wilmer's address marked him as a man of learning and ability, possessing freshness and versatility of thought, and having a clear perception of the movements going on both in the Church and the world of to-day.

But having made this digression so as to give a short description of the old library building and its honorable place in the history of the Seminary, it is necessary to go back to the founding of the library itself.   It was first housed in two or three rooms of the old Seminary Building when books were few, and funds for their purchase were not in hand.   However, the alumni, seeing the great importance of making additions to the library, early united their efforts in raising a permanent fund for that purpose by levying regular contributions.   In the minutes of the Alumni Association for one year in the late fifties of the last century, five dollars appears to have been the annual levy for each member.   One of the most regular and liberal contributors to this fund was the Rev. William H. C. Robertson of the class of 1849.   He was originally a merchant and entered the Seminary in mature life.   He held a cure, at first in New York, and then took a parish in Connecticut, but a painful and distressing disease always interfered with the success of his ministry. Accordingly he was compelled to give up the active duties of his sacred office and then devoted himself chiefly to the education of his family.   He retired to the quaint and beautiful town of old Niagara now called Niagara-on-the-Lake, in Canada, not far from the mouth of the Niagara River as it enters Lake Ontario.   He died there on the fourth of August, 1873, the Semi-Centennial year of the Seminary.   He had a high appreciation of this Institution, and determined a short time before his death to make a substantial gift for the maintenance of the Library. His widow, knowing his desire, not only honored it by giving $5000 from his estate, but generously added $5000 herself, making the full amount $10,000, the annual income of which was to be expended in the purchase of books for the Seminary Library. It was to be considered and spoken of as "a donation from the Rev. W. H. C. Robertson and wife." Accordingly we find a printed slip, containing this statement, pasted in the front of all the volumes, now many in number, purchased under the terms of this wise benefaction. For fifty years the income has been the practical support of the Library. It is wonderful how judiciously the income has been spent by the professors, and what a fine selection of books they have to show for it. However, with this assured income it was observed that the annual contributions of the alumni ceased. We are indebted to the address of the Rev. A. Dalrymple, D. D., on the deceased Alumni, published in the proceedings of the Semi-Centennial Celebration of 1873, for the interesting account of this happy connection of the Rev. W. H. C. Robertson and his wife with the Library of the Seminary.

Additions have also been made from the beginning to the Library by gifts of libraries of deceased clergymen. Among the very earliest were the libraries of Bishop Griswold, presented by his widow, consisting of five hundred volumes. The Rev. James W. Cooke, the Rev. Malcolm MacFarland, the Rev. William H. Trapnell and the Rev. R. C. Moore, son of Bishop Moore, also gave their libraries, while the Rev. Edward Anthon, D. D., of New York, secured a legacy from Charles Betts of $1000, and gave a complete set of the Bampton Lectures and other valuable books. The Rev. Alexander Norris, when dying, bequeathed to the Seminary a magnificent copy of Bagster's Polyglot Bible in eight languages. These are, of course, of varying value, but it can be truly said that some of the finest books the Library possesses have been acquired in this way. It must be remembered, also, that in these olden days the life of theological books in general had a much longer term of existence, because there was comparatively little change in the development of theological and ecclesiastical thought, certainly so far as the old fashioned Evangelicals and High Churchmen were concerned. While criticism was beginning to feel its way on the continent of Europe, it was still unable to change the traditional faith of the majority there, but in Great Britain and the United States it met stern opposition on the part of the orthodox, who considered the old Reformed Confessions as the marks of an almost doctrinally infallible Church. Books studied by the fathers were studied by the sons and, we might say, in a number of cases by the grandsons. We can see this in the well known instance of "Pearson on the Creed" which was the recognized standard in its department for years. Butler's Analogy, Paley's Works and Horne's Introduction held sway for generations of students, couintng a student's generation as a period of three years in some cases, four years at the most. In this I can testify from personal experience, so far as a later generation is concerned. Butler has now been passed up, most honourably, indeed, from a necessary subject of study to the shelves as a book of reference and consultation, shedding much light on the religious conditions of his day. Paley, except for his invaluable Horae Paulinae is only a waymark in the history of evidences and moral theology. If we had time and space we could give other conspicuous examples, but this will suffice to show the conservatism of that age before "some heretics of yesterday" brought larger aspects of the eternal truth to light.

So today the movements of religious thought, brought about by criticism and the ever-enriching results of investigation, make many books old within a quinquennium, calling generally for a new and revised edition within that time. A decennium marks a very respectable age for many works which are reckoned as standards in fundamentals. So new books and new editions must be brought out to keep the libraries of Seminaries, Colleges and Universities up to date. For its income the Seminary is well supplied with books fully abreast of the time. It has a number of copies of the chief works of reference for the use of students and, in some few cases, for each member of the several classes.

On looking over books of universal value in the library, we should like to mention in the first place the Minge edition of the Greek and Latin Fathers of the Church. This was purchased through Dr. Packard in the early days of the Seminary. It has been said, on what appears to be good authority, that of all the Protestant Episcopal Seminaries in the country this was the first to have a complete set of the Church Fathers. The Minge edition was evidently issued in parts and afterwards strongly bound in cloth with leather backs. We have been told that Phillips Brooks gave many of his spare hours to the study of the Fathers during his Seminary course.

The library has had for years a good collection of works on history. The first noted enlargement was made during the professorship of the Rev. Cornelius Walker, fully seconded by the Rev. Dr. Grammer in his day. A wide range of books was added to the Hebrew department in the time of Professor Crawford. Likewise during Dr. Micou's professorship, the departments of Theology, Apologetics, and Ethics received a large accession of modern and standard works. In fact it can be most truly said that every department of study in the Seminary is well represented by its leading authorities now found on the shelves of the Library. The English National Library of Biography was purchased as the several volumes were issued by the wise forethought of Dr. Packard. Special notice should be made of the handsome Russian leather edition of the Encyclopaedia Britannica, with the latest volume issued on account of the great changes brought about by the World War of 1914 to 1918. This edition was presented, with many other valuable and interesting books, by Mrs. Anson G. Phelps Dodge, of Alexandria, Virginia. Among books presented to the Library during the last forty years is a complete set of Latin authors in the original, left by the late Rev. A. Dalrymple, D. D., of Baltimore, Maryland. The Rev. Dr. Giesey, former rector of the Church of the Epiphany, Washington, D. C., bequeathed his library to the Seminary as a memorial representing, as it does, an excellent average of a clergyman's working library of his day. Dr. Haslett McKim of New York City, also an alumnus, bequeathed a large part of his very valuable

library to his alma mater.   Other gifts of smaller size, such
as a number of books from the library of the late Rev. Frank
Page, D. D. and from that of the late Colonel Skinner, of
Staunton, Virginia, all containing most useful books, have
been received during late years.   The Rev. Dr. Tidball, a
well-known alumnus of the Seminary, now professor-emeri-
tus of the Theological Department of the University of the
South, has given his large and well-selected library to this
Institution.   We hope that he may still enjoy it for years,
but when it comes here in the order of time, it will be a treas-
ured memorial of his devotion to his old Divinity School.
It must not be forgotten that Mrs. Potter presented to the
Library a beautiful edition bound in leather of the collected
works of her husband, Bishop Henry C. Potter.

The Library was, until a short time ago, very deficient
in standard novels, and other works of a more literary character.   Undoubtedly the lack of funds for the general purchase
of books was the main reason for this, but it may have been
that there was just enough of the old Evangelical spirit to
cause the professors of that time to be thankful that the
students were guarded from the subtle temptations of too
much light reading.   However that may be, there was discovered in an old neglected corner of the Library, not so
many years ago, an old edition of the Waverley Novels, revealing the fact that Sir Walter Scott was a delightful companion in those days of the clergy, when in lighter mood they
relaxed from the deeper studies of their profession.   And
further that once famous novel "A Fool of Quality" by
Henry Brooke, was also found in another corner, but it is
well-known that John Wesley had a high opinion of it, and
published an abridgment of the same for more general reading.   By a singular oversight the works of Shakespeare were
not found in the Library until a handsome edition was placed
there twenty-five years ago.   Occasional copies of such poets
as Milton, Cowper, and Bishop Heber, with Keble's Christian Year in Bishop G. W. Doane's edition, the first published
in America were here from the olden days.   Now all this is
changed.   The standard works of fiction, together with the
standard English and American poets in the excellent River-
side Press edition, are on the Library shelves, and in addition

to these there are found the best novels, of the present day, with the leading poets and essayists as they are published from year to year. The library has a fine collection of biographies of men notable in Church and State. A good selection of theological magazines and reviews is found on the Library table, though a few years ago it was not thought possible to use a portion of the annual income for this purpose. These notes are given here, although some might count them out of place, to show the steady progress that has been made in adapting the library, with the funds that it has in hand, to the various requirements of study and culture that are needed to make a clergyman a full rounded man along these particular lines of his profession.

This library can not boast, like that of the General Theological Seminary, of any unique collection of old books, such as the latter's fine collection of ancient Bibles, for this requires the help of rich and generous friends. It possesses however an old and well-preserved copy of the Geneva New Testament, together with a good first edition of the Bishop's Bible, both given by the late Mr. Peter Mayo of Richmond, Virginia. A fine copy of the "editio princeps" of the Authorized Version of 1611 has been in the possession of the library for a number of years. There is also a copy of the "Bugges" Bible, so called because of the reading found in the fiftieth verse of the ninety-first Psalm. The oldest book in the Library is one volume of the "Speculum Historiale" dated 1474, said to have been found in a monastery during the Mexican War. Mutilated copies of the Bible and Prayer Book for the Reading Desk of Old Pohick Church, carefully preserved by the care of Dr. Packard and bound together in one volume, attract all visitors to the Library. These books, folios in size, were ordered by the vestry to be purchased by Washington from London for the "new Church upon the north side of Pohick Run" now called the Old Pohick Church. There are other old books and old editions to which we can only refer as a whole. A number of old registers and vestry books of the colonial parishes in Virginia are deposited here for safe-keeping. They are held by the authorities of the diocese, and are of untold value. The most important of them is the register of Christ Church,

Middlesex County, as it contains so many names of the "old families" whose descendants are now scattered throughout Virginia and the country at large.

But the great treasures of the Library are the three Assyrian tablets or slabs, secured for the Seminary when the noted English archaeologist, Henry Austen Layard, was excavating the ruins of Nineveh. The largest slab had to be broken into four parts so as carry it down the river Tigris, but after getting it to the Seminary, these were put together and set up against the wall. It is of hornblende, and is very hard, but the heroic figure and the old Assyrian characters are cut in the stone with wonderful clearness and precision. A translation has been made of this inscription.

We insert here an article written by Dr. Angus Crawford, Professor Emeritus of Hebrew, on the beginnings of the Biblical Museum, which he was so interested in starting at the Seminary.

"Soon after coming to the Seminary we felt that a Biblical Museum, however modest it might be, would be a great help in Biblical study and in illustrating to the students pages of history that were being opened by modern exploration. The Rev. T. A. Tidball very kindly became the medium of expending in the British Museum the sum of $100 for this purpose. He was on a visit to Europe at the time, and through the advice of Mr. Pinches, the large collection of Assyrian tablets in the Seminary Library and the obelisk of Shalmaneser came into our possession. The latter was the first of the kind imported to this country. The National Museum borrowed it for an exhibition they were holding at the time, and returned the favor by giving us the Canopic Inscription, or second Rosetta stone, and the case in which the tablets and other interesting curios are kept. In this collection students may see for themselves the Creation and Flood tablets; a case tablet (of Job XIV:17), the famous egg of Sargon, tablets of Babylonian and Assyrian kings, the Lachish tablet, and many other replicas, besides original tablets, one of which bears the name of Evil Merodak. The value of a such collection is not only great in itself, but it will stimulate the friends of the Seminary to add to it from time to time. It has been enriched already by an album of two hundred photographs from the Egyptian monuments and rare books and manuscripts. One may see here pictures of the Hittite and Philistine warriors and a king of Judah. We have a full collection of antique coins illustrating the Bible to be donated to the new library."

We might mention here that, in addition to the above, there is in this collection a fine tear bottle found by the Cesnola expedition to Cyprus, presented by Mrs. Kester, formerly of Gunston Hall, Fairfax County, Virginia.

The Library at present possesses only a few portraits, but they are valuable for their historic interest. Those of Bishop Meade in his gown and bands, of Dr. Packard and his grandson, the Rev. William Laird, presented by Mr. Winder W. Laird of Wilmington, Delaware, and of Mr. Reinicker of Baltimore, Maryland, the founder of the Reinicker Lectureship and the Reinicker Reading Prize, are especially worthy of mention on account of their artistic character. Besides these, there are portraits of Bishop Moore of Virginia and Bishop Randolph of Southern Virginia. Also hanging on the walls excellent likenesses are found in crayon of the Rev. George A. Smith, the first alumnus of the Seminary, who graduated in 1823, Bishop Meade in his old age, and Bishop Peterkin of West Virginia in middle life. An interesting photograph of Rev. Lawrence Mills, D. D., a graduate of the Seminary, late Professor of Sanskrit at the University of Oxford, England, is remarkable because it reminds us that the Virginia Seminary so far has the high honour, among all the Seminaries of our Church in this country, of giving a professor to that ancient seat of learning. Accompanying the photograph is a copy of the engrossed address presented to Professor Mills by East Indian students for his courteous relations with them when at the University, and their appreciation of the work accomplished by him in the study of their ancient languages. There is also a fine photograph of Bishop Henry C. Potter given by Mrs. Potter, who said that it was considered by his family to be the best likeness of all that had been taken of him. Two quaint silhouettes of Bishop White and Bishop Moore are also found in the Library with photographs of Bishops Gibson and Brown of Virginia, and of Bishop Kinsolving of Southern

Brazil.   There is also a small picture of the Seminary during the Civil War.   Two portraits, the one of Bishop Brooks in his robes, and the other of Bishop Potter, are on the east wall of Wilmer Hall, the new refectory.   There are two crayons of Bishop Meade and Bishop Whittle in the old refectory which we suppose will be removed to Wilmer Hall, also a number of photographs of graduating classes of the Seminary.   It is fully believed that in the years to come both the Library and Wilmer Hall will be adorned by portraits of Bishops, missionaries, and prominent clergymen of this country who are numbered among the alumni of the Seminary.   At present it is interesting to record that Prayer Hall has photographs of almost all the missionaries and bishops who are alumni, also of the professors with the exception of Dr. Reuel Keith, Dr. Wilmer, and the other professors of the Alexandria period.   In the students' reading room in Aspinwall Hall there is a portrait of Mr. Aspinwall of New York, the founder of that Hall.

We remember that in the old days the Library was open for the distribution and return of books only for one hour after dinner during the week, with a student as assistant librarian under Dr. Packard, but twenty-nine years ago it was determined by the Board of Trustees that it should be placed in the care of a permanent librarian, and that it should be open from ten o'clock in the morning to four o'clock in the afternoon   Accordingly Miss Maria B. Worthington, a resident of "The Hill", was appointed as the first incumbent, and still occupies the position very acceptably to the professors, students, and the visitors to the Library.

OLD PARISH VESTRY BOOKS AND PARISH REGISTERS IN SEMINARY LIBRARY

NOTE BY THE EDITOR

Through the kindness of Miss Worthington, librarian of the Seminary, we have been able to secure the following list of the old Parish Vestry Books and Parish Registers deposited for safekeeping and reference in that the Library of the Seminary. It is exceedingly fortunate these books of inestimable value were sent to the Seminary Library, as otherwise, many of them would probably have been lost or destroyed.

It would be well if some action could be taken by the conventions of the dioceses within the limits of the state of Virginia by which, in cooperation with the Board of Trustees and Parish authorities, the old Parish Record Books which have not been deposited in the Seminary Library and for which no absolutely fireproof protection has been provided, could be deposited and preserved in the fire proof Library of the Seminary. These records are of priceless value and through carelessness or by fire are liable to be lost or destroyed. This has happened in many instances and is liable to happen again. The new Seminary Library having been made fireproof and containing a vault, provides a convenient and adequate place where these records might be assembled for protection and for reference.

VESTRY BOOKS

County	Parish	Date
AMHERST	LEXINGTON	1779–1880
FREDERICK	FREDERICK	1764–1818
GOOCHLAND	ST. JAMES'	1744–1860
HANOVER	ST. PAUL'S	1705–1785
HALIFAX	ANTRIM	1752–1817
KING AND QUEEN	STRATTON MAJOR	1729–1783
KING GEORGE	HANOVER	1779–1796
LANCASTER	CHRIST CHURCH	1739–1797
LUNENBURG	CUMBERLAND	1746–1831
LOUDOUN	SHELBURNE	1771–1805
LOUISA	FREDERICKSVILLE	1742–1785
LOUISA	FREDERICKSVILLE	1742–1787
MATTHEWS	KINGSTON	1679–1796
MIDDLESEX	CHRIST CHURCH	1663–1767
NANSEMOND	UPPER	1744–1793
NEW KENT	ST. PETER'S	1685–1758
NEW KENT	BLISSLAND	1721–1786
NORTHUMBERLAND	WICOMICO	1703–1795
PRINCE EDWARD	ST. PATRICK	1755–1774
PRINCE WILLIAM	DETTINGEN	1745–1802
RICHMOND CITY	ST. JOHN'S	1730–1773
SUSSEX AND SURRY	ALBEMARLE	1742–1787

PARISH REGISTERS

County or City	Parish	Date
PETERSBURG	BRISTOL	1720–1789
WILLIAMSBURG	BRUTON	1739–1797
YORK	CHARLES CITY	1648–1800
MIDDLESEX	CHRIST CHURCH	1663–1812
FAIRFAX	DUMFRIES	1816–1824
RICHMOND	HENRICO AND ST. JOHN'S	1611–1904
MATTHEWS	KINGSTON	1755–1776
RICHMOND	LUNENBURG	1792–1799
NEW KENT	ST. PETER'S	1680–1750
NEW KENT	ST. PETER'S	1733–1778
STAFFORD	OVERWHARTON	1725–1758
PORTIONS OF THE RECORDS OF	OLD BRISTOL, NOTTOWAY, AND CUMBERLAND	1784–1815

SECTION IV

CHAPTER V

THE THEOLOGY AND TEACHING OF THE
REV. DR. WILLIAM HOLLAND WILMER

REV. C. B. WILMER, D. D.

Part of the address delivered before the Alumni Association of the Theological Seminary in Virginia, June, 1922, by the Rev. Dr. C. B. Wilmer, on the occasion of the Dedication of the old Library Building to the Memory of Reverend Doctor William Holland Wilmer, giving it the name "Wilmer Hall," and setting apart the building for use as the Seminary refectory.

The most appropriate use to make of this opportunity you have so graciously given me, is, I think, to present to you the leading ideas of my grandfather in religious and theological matters.

Dr. Wilmer's services in the cause of religious education and in helping to revive the fortunes of the Episcopal Church in this state have been sufficiently covered by Dr. Phillips. It seems to be in better taste for me, as well as more useful in itself, to confine myself to an exposition of his Religious Teaching.

As the means of doing that, I have in my possession two documents. One is a little book he wrote, called "The Episcopal Manual", and the other is a sermon delivered by Dr. Wilmer in May, 1814, in Monumental Church, Richmond, Virginia, the church that was built on the site of the theatre which had burned down causing the death of many of the most prominent people in the city. This was the first sermon preached in that Church, the Rev. William Meade, afterwards Bishop, preaching on the following Sunday. For the privilege of copying that sermon I am indebted to the vestry of Monumental Church who have it in pamphlet form. Taking the two documents together, it is interesting to note that the questions with which Dr. Wilmer dealt were fundamental and such as are still, more or less, discussed among us.

THE OLD LIBRARY NOW WILMER HALL

THE INTERIOR OF WILMER HALL

Taking up the Manual first, the sub-title is worth giving in full,—"An Attempt to Explain and Vindicate the Doctrine, Discipline and Worship of the Protestant Episcopal Church as taught in her Public Formularies, and the Writings of her Approved Divines. To which are added Observations on Family and Public Devotion, and Directions for a Devout and Decent Attendance on Public Worship with Prayers suitable to Several Occasions; the whole being intended to illustrate and enforce Evangelical Piety. By a Clergyman of the Protestant Episcopal Church." The manual was published in Philadelphia in 1815 (I do not know whether this was the first edition or not) and is advertised on the title page as being on sale with certain firms in that city and also in Baltimore, Georgetown, D. C., Alexandria, Richmond, Petersburg, and New York.

In the preface, Dr. Wilmer, after calling attention to the "great want of information" prevailing among members of the Episcopal Church "respecting their own peculiar principles," proceeds to pay an eloquent tribute to the heroes of the Reformation; men who "counted not their lives dear unto them." "It moved them not," he wrote, "though the torch with which they were to illuminate mankind was to light up their own funeral pile; but, having vindicated by their writings and illustrated by their lives the cause of evangelical truth, they joyfully sealed their last testimony for it at the stake."

He then proceeds to mention "four works of the reformers" which, in his estimation, "most clearly define the sense of the Church in all matters necessary to salvation, viz., the Catechism of King Edward VI; the Declaration of Doctrines in Jewell's Apology; the Catechism commonly called Dr. Nowell's; and the Homilies." "These documents, with the Liturgy and Articles, form the acknowledged standards of our Church;" and he quotes with approval the remark of a "great man", that "to the want of acquaintance with the writers in question is very principally to be attributed that diversity of sentiment on some of the most important points of theology, and even alarming departure from sound doctrine, which is too prominent a feature in modern divinity."

Next, he balances this position by saying, "There appear to be two prominent errors to which we are liable to be carried in regard to the principles of the Church, on one hand to prostrate or undervalue her order and institutions, and on the other to exhaust all our zeal in behalf of these external concerns and to permit the essence of religion to evaporate in this way.   It is the object of this work to guard against both these dangerous extremes, and, while it endeavors to maintain the dignity of our institutions and the excellence of our doctrine and worship it aims also to inculcate that power of godliness without which all our doings are nothing worth."

One other quotation, and we have the man before us as theologian and as Christian, concerns his mental attitude toward Christians of "other denominations".   He aimed to unite and not to separate and divide.   "Especially would the author entertain the hope that the work may tend by cherishing the unity of the faith, to cherish also the unity of the spirit, that heavenly charity, without which there is nothing left us worth contending for."

It is quite evident and worth calling attention to for its own sake, that Dr. Wilmer evidently used the word "charity" so as to include not only the common idea of refusing to condemn others for having their own contrary opinions, but also devotion to principle.   "Love", says the Apostle Paul, "rejoiceth in (or 'together with') the truth."   And so the author wrote, "The opinions entertained by him have been deliberately formed, and be they true or false, charity is bound to believe them sincere, and being sincere, that they require him who holds them to maintain them honestly and without fear.

Hanc veniam petimus
Dabimusque vicissim.

"He is ready to exercise freely the same candour towards others, which he claims for himself, in believing that they also are sincere and therefore justifiable in instructing their own members in their own peculiar principles . . . and happy would it be for the cause of charity and religion . . . if when occasions occur in which they (Christians) feel it their duty to support their particular opinions and in which they have to touch the chords of a powerful and often morbid sympathy, they would use the tenderness that becomes so delicate a task. 'For the time will come' says the excellent Hooker, 'when three words spoken with meekness and love shall obtain a far more blessed reward than three thousand volumes written with disdainful sharpness of wit.'"

So much for the author's preface. The volume itself is but an illustration of these principles of Churchmanship and character.

In treating of the ministry, he gets down to the root of the matter by first laying down this principle: "Without an external commission and the delegation to some specific authority to confer it, according to Christ's appointment, how could we know whether we have a valid ministry or not? If any one may rise up in the Church and claim the power of exercising or bestowing this commission merely by virtue of his being more holy than others, what limit can be assigned to the operation of the principle and to the confusion that must ensue?" This is appropriately followed by an argument for the Apostolic ministry.

Next in order follows a discussion of the doctrines of the Church, the Trinity, Original Sin, the Atonement, etc. But what I desire to call particular attention to is the manner in which the sacramental system of the Church is treated. Planting himself, as was his wont, squarely upon the words in which our Church teaches her own doctrines, he quotes the Articles and the Catechism, and then proceeds to comment. The sacraments are not only signs of grace, but "means by which we receive the same." "But", he adds, "they are not the only means of grace. For reading, and hearing, and meditating upon the Word of God, are part of the things which he hath appointed for this end, and prayer is another part, accompanied with an express promise that 'if we ask, we shall receive.'"

References to the dogmatic statements of Church teaching are in every case followed by quotations of relevant passages from Holy Writ which are studied with independence of judgment steadied by the opinions of others. I mention these things not merely as personal characteristics of the author, but as belonging to the true and typical Churchman. Also he had in mind, what seems to me is too often neglected today by exponents of our Church's position,—the way in which our doctrines are apt to be misunderstood by others. He would, if possible, obviate their objections and remove their difficulties. Thus, in treating the difficult subject of Baptismal regeneration, he not only steers between the Sylla and Charybdis of the *opus operatum* and that which reduces sacraments to mere symbols, but he also aims to make Church teaching acceptable to others as scriptural and at least not unreasonable. "If baptism", he says, "be a means appointed by our Lord Himself for our entering into that covenant to which belong the promises of remission of sin and the influences of the Holy Spirit, we are authorized to consider those who are baptized as being regenerate . . . We may with propriety consider the baptized person as regenerate by the Holy Spirit in another view. Supposing the change of relation produced by baptism to be merely external and to affect the *condition* and not the *character* of the recipient, still we are bound to thank God that this is done by the Holy Spirit, who is the Author of every good and perfect gift, and through whose agency all the means of grace and the administration of them derive their perpetuity and their effect." He then proceeds to push this home by quotations from the liturgy of the Dutch Church of the Netherlands, from Dr. Mosheim of the Lutheran Church, from Dr. Clark of the Methodists, and from Calvin. But so anxious was he to prevent the Church's doctrines from being misunderstood either within or without the Church, and so desirous was he to commend that teaching to others by scripture and reason, not by dogmatic dictation or any autocratic authority, that he goes back again, in the unfoldment of his theme, to say, "The Church understands baptism as descriptive of a new state rather than of a new nature; as implying a recovery from a state of guilt, and wrath to a state of pardon and acceptance, rather than as a recovery from a sinful disposition to holiness of heart. She nowhere authorizes the belief that baptism in the outward act supersedes, constitutes, or necessarily conveys that change of nature which the Scripture, under a variety of representations, makes necessary to salvation." The similarity of this statement to the Declaration put forth many years afterwards by the House of Bishops, having the same purpose in mind, will be noted.

And here let me re-enforce this with some quotations from the sermon to which I have referred as preached by Dr. Wilmer at the opening of Monumental Church in Richmond, Virginia, in 1814. With that respect for the opinions and even the words of others, joined to his own independence of judgment which characterized him, he first makes his own the language of "a pious divine" to this effect: "Regeneration is like the grafting of a tree; and if it takes place either before, at, or after, baptism, it will be shown by its fruits. But if it be fancy and delusion for a man on account of some inward feelings to think himself born again, newly created unto good works, while guilty of the grossest immoralities, we think it also fancy and mistake to suppose persons regenerate who are living in the practice of gross wickedness or of an ungodly life in any form, merely because they were baptized in infancy. If a nurseryman should be introduced into an enclosure planted with crab-trees, covered with their worthless fruit, and having not one apple or pear on any of them, and be told that all had been grafted when they were young and needed no other grafting, he would say, 'it is plain that the grafting did not take.'"

To this the preacher added, again illustrating his loyalty to the formularies of his Church, "Whosoever would indeed become a regular member of the Kingdom of God must be baptized; but as he desires to share in its spiritual and eternal blessing, he must experience the renewings and sanctifying influences of the Holy Ghost on his soul to cleanse it from the power of corruption and to animate and quicken it to spiritual and divine life. We have no objection to the term regeneration being applied in the sense of our Church to baptism. It is indeed a baptismal regeneration, a begetting again to new privileges and new hopes."

If we turn back now, in the manual, to the discussion of Confirmation, we find the same loyalty to the Church and the same effort to preserve true spirituality. He speaks of confirmation as "prayer and imposition of hands"; not as "laying on of hands merely"; and he speaks of it also as "communicating further measures of the Holy Ghost".

He quotes largely from Bishop Wilson, and in my judgment the three pages of "Address to those who are to be confirmed", drawn from that source, are far superior to anything contained in our modern manuals. Particularly noteworthy is the effort to make the confirmed understand the meaning of "I do" in the Confirmation service. "The two short words '*I do*' are soon said, but remember how much is contained in them. Whosoever uses them on this occasion says in effect as follows: *I do* heartily renounce, etc., etc. *I do* sincerely believe, etc. *I do* firmly resolve, etc. In a word, *I do* resolve to aim after that mind which was in my blessed Master, to follow His steps, to imitate His example, that with Him I may dwell in heaven."

I would also call especial attention to the opening sentence of the suggested "prayer that may be used by those that are to be confirmed"; (taken, apparently, from Bishop Wilson's Parochialia): "O Lord, graciously behold me thy unworthy servant, who, according to the appointment of thy Church, am going to dedicate myself to thee and thy service."

Here is the root of the present day suggestion to make of Confirmation (in addition to whatever else it may be), a service of Ordination of Laymen and Laywomen to Service.

In his treatment of "the Eucharist, commonly called the Lord's Supper," Dr. Wilmer, in marked contrast to many, not to say most modern writers of manuals of religious instruction, just as in the case of baptism and confirmation, emphasizes both the objective and the subjective sides. "Repentance towards God and faith in the Lord Jesus Christ are requisite to our salvation and consequently to our right use of the sacraments". And throughout he follows the really great writers of the Angelican communion, especially Hooker, in directing faith, not to some magical efficacy in the external means, but to the action of the Holy Spirit, received through faith in our Blessed Lord. As it has been more recently put by Bishop Hall of Vermont: "The grace of the sacraments is given in answer to prayer". This is scriptural and this alone, I undertake to say, can commend our sacramental system to intelligent and spiritually minded

Christians of every name or even save ourselves from super-stition.

THE PRESENT DAY OUTLOOK

If, now, in conclusion, we ask how stands this theological position in the light of present thought and problems, it seems to me that we need a broader statement of the Gospel than that given by Dr. Wilmer in his day, but that we do not need in any essential respects to correct what he wrote, but rather to re-affirm it.

We need today to bring to the front our Lord's endorse-ment of the Summary of the Law as current in his day, "Thou shalt love the Lord thy God with all thy heart and with all thy soul, and *with all thy mind* and with all thy strength", instead of the original Old Testament form, which omits "mind"; this to meet the intellectual questions of the age in which we live.

We need a broader statement of the Gospel so as to bring out the social, whereas Dr. Wilmer stressed the individual application of the teachings of Christ. We find what we need in our Lord's teaching concerning the Kingdom of God on earth. "The time is fulfilled; the Kingdom of Heaven is at hand; repent ye and believe the good news". According to this, the man who has not caught the vision of the kingdom of righteousness, peace and joy in the Spirit"; a kingdom social as well as individual; the man who has not adjusted himself in aim to the realization and actualization of this kingdom on earth, has not yet "repented" in the full sense of that much misunderstood word. But, and this is my main point, such a program waits for its fulfillment on the thorough conversion of individuals and their being filled with the Spirit of Christ. "The earnest expectation of creation waits for the revealing of the sons of God." And I believe that Dr. Wilmer's teaching, which lay at the foundation of this Seminary, needs no substantial modification; rather, I am suggesting, it needs re-affirmation. His position was what I should like to call Evangelical-Sacramentarianism. The two sides of the matter did not jostle each other in his mind, any more than they did in St. Paul's mind when he said: "Ye all are the children of God by faith in Jesus Christ because ye have in baptism put on Christ". We used to hear something of "Apostolical Order and Evangelical Truth". Today, the latter and more important half, if the two are to be separated, seems to have dropped out.

Dr. Wilmer's statements about the sacrament will not prove satisfactory in certain quarters today; but I make bold to suggest that if such teaching as his had received more of emphasis in the Church than it has had in the past or has now, the Cummins' Schism might have been prevented; and certainly our Church as a whole would today be on a much higher plane spiritually than it is.

In the year 1841, fifteen years after Dr. Wilmer's death, a new and revised edition of "The Episcopal Manual" was gotten out in Philadelphia and called "Wilmer's Episcopal Manual". From the Editor's Preface, I beg to quote the following words as confirming my own interpretation of the author's theological position and as showing the esteem in which that position was held in our Church at that time:

"We have many able works on the Constitution and external order of the Church, and numerous excellent treatises on doctrinal and practical religion; but a work devoted to the *united* interests of the *Gospel* and the *Church*, to the defence of both *Evangelical truth* and *Apostolic order;* as it had long been a desideratum before the appearance of the admirable compendium now presented to the public in a revised, and it is hoped, improved form; so it will probably not soon be superseded in general estimation by any similar publication. While its views of ecclesiastical polity are so sound and scriptural as to satisfy the most decided member of the Church, it at the same time so exhibits the spirituality of all her services, and the deep though sober piety required of her children, that the devout and humble Christian can not peruse it without blessing God for so rich a heritage, and that it is his privilege to enjoy communion and fellowship with such a holy and divinely constituted society".

You will note the prediction that "it will not soon be superseded in general estimation by any similar publication". This prediction, unfortunately, you will allow me to add, was not fulfilled. At the present time, the proponents of evangelical truth in our Church seem to have handed over the writing of books of instruction in Church doctrine to a class of people, as might be easily proved by quotations, who are stressing Apostolical Order but not Evangelical truth, and are not guarding sacramental teaching, as Dr. Wilmer did, against misunderstanding and abuse.   One can not, for example, even put emphasis on the necessity of candidates for Confirmation bringing real repentance and faith to the rail as they kneel before the Bishop, without being charged with minimizing or even denying the gift of the Indwelling Spirit.   So, too, the tendency is to lower faith to the acceptance of credal statements and submission to the authority of the Church.   Over and over again are we told that Baptism makes us branches of the vine; but seldom if ever are we warned that to be a branch of the vine is not necessarily to be a fruit-bearing branch.

I have called attention to the insertion, in the Summary of the Law, of the word "mind".   This grew out of the coming together in an ancient city, of the Jew and the Greek; the man of faith and the man of intellect; one result of which was the translation of the Hebrew scriptures into the Greek language, in which the Hebrew word for "heart", in the Summary, was rendered by the Greek word for "intellect."   May one discern a significance in the fact that the name of that city was Alexandria and find in it a prophecy that here in this Seminary Phillips Brooks' complaint that "you were strong on spirituality and weak on the Greek verb" would be met by that justice to modern scholarship, joined to spirituality, which now characterizes your faculty? And may not one also express the hope and the faith that this grand old Seminary, which has resolved on a splendid act of historical justice to the memory of one of her founders will also try, as he tried, to show how to combine in one truly catholic view, church history and religion; the external and the internal, the objective and the subjective; loyalty to the Church's formularies and the direct personal faith of every individual in the Lord Jesus Christ?

SECTION IV

CHAPTER VI

SEMINARY MAGAZINES

REV. KENSEY J. HAMMOND, D. D.

In its century of life this Seminary has given expression through various publications to the views taught on "The Hill". By them has been known the Truth for which the Seminary has stood. Through them it has exerted an influence for good among its Alumni and friends, and often far beyond these, among strangers. The printed page has provided permanent place for this instruction; and but for the obscurity of the library shelf, and changing tastes of readers, these publications would be known now, and exert a present-day influence for good.

Earliest among these stands "The Theological Repertory," its title "Repertory" representing its age, in the word now being supplanted by magazine. While antedating the Seminary, and under separate management, it was the official organ of the Education Society, and expressed the views of those in charge of that Institution. For it began its life in August, 1819; under the editorial care of the Rev. Drs. William H. Wilmer and William Hawley, and other clergymen of the District of Columbia, then including Alexandria, Virginia. The Professors of the Seminary were on the Editorial staff, and through "The Repertory" the business of the Seminary Trustees, as well as the needs of the Education Society, became more widely known.

A review of it shows the frequent publication of sermons, always evangelical in tone. A larger space is given to miscellaneous articles; and these deal with Church history, polity, biography, pastoral care, and some secular subjects. This Seminary's reputation for missionary zeal, so well founded, may be due in part to the "Repertory" and certainly to the influence of those in charge. Every month there is

376

given much and varied news from Foreign Mission fields, not only from Liberia, China, and Japan, which we should expect; but news of many other "uttermost parts of the earth". South Africa, Syria and India, the South Sea and Sandwich Islands, Brazil (Bible colportage) and Mexico, Canada, France and southeastern Europe, and even missions to the Jews are included. Domestic news covers the general work of the Church, Episcopal Ordinations and other services, proceedings of General and Diocesan Conventions, parochial events of general interest, the birth and infancy of this Seminary (November 1827, page 743) and also of "Kenyon Seminary and College" (page 194). Literary and Philosophical Intelligence is the chosen title of a department of book reviews and notices, with miscellaneous items of science, discovery, agriculture, and natural history. Contributions to the Education Society are carefully acknowledged and sometimes those to the Board of Missions. "The Repertory", as a magazine of broad usefulness, merited a wide circulation, and must have done a good work gratifying to its authors.

"The Southern Churchman" was originally established by the Rev. W. F. Lee as his private property. Published in Alexandria, Virginia, with the Rev. Edward R. Lippitt, D. D., Professor in the Seminary nearby as its Editor, its possible relation to the Seminary is manifest. In 1848 Dr. Lippitt gave up the editorship. "After his death the good-will, with the presses, was purchased by sundry gentlemen of the Church; and by them transferred to the Trustees of the Theological Seminary. The only connection the Diocese has with the paper, is through the Trustees." This report in the Journal of 1874, shows that "the Rev. D. F. Sprigg, D. D., took charge of the paper as editor; the type and presses were disposed of, and the proceeds accounted for to the Trustees:" the Editor providing himself with a new outfit. The Trustees owned the good-will of the paper, with the right to dispose of it, and appoint the editor. On June 22nd, 1881, the Seminary Board of Trustees passed this resolution: "The Trustees having no material property in 'The Southern Churchman,' for the sum of $600 do hereby transfer the name and good-will of said paper to the Rev. Dr. Sprigg."

When the present management bought the paper the good-will was included. The close relation ever existing between these two publications and the Seminary doubtless explains why for so many years the Seminary felt no need for any other special means of making known its needs, or expressing its views.

During the session of 1876-77 some students brought regularly to the Rhetorical Society a "paper" written to enliven the Society's meeting and amuse the audience, which includèd the public from "The Hill". This "Seminarian" was made up of fifteen or twenty pages of foolscap, containing occasionally a dignified article; but usually local allusions, humorous squibs, and jokes on the students. Messrs. N. P. Dame, Peter Boyden, "Willie" Walker, Frank Page, "Brax" Bryan, and Henry Thomas, were among its chief contributors. It well fulfilled their purpose, and even after its successor took the field, flourished for several years under the title of "Gasometer" or "The Rhetorical Budget".

In November, 1878, there appeared in print as an eight page monthly "The Seminarian," so welcomed by Alumni and students that it was self-supporting from the start. The first Board of Editors was T. J. Packard (chief), E. B. Rice, E. L. Goodwin (afterwards chief), S. A. Wallis, and W. H. Assheton. The next year Messrs. W. M. Clark and J. Fletcher succeeded Messrs. Packard and Rice. Members of the Faculty, particularly Dr. Walker, Dr. Blackford of the High School, and occasionally an Alumnus, contributed to its columns. Scholarly articles on saintly workers in the British Church appear from the pen of Mr. Wallis, and the Editors write on current topics. Other columns contain original essays of real merit in greatest variety from students' pens. The history of the Missionary and Rhetorical Societies and of the various neighborhood Missions is faithfully recorded among the local events; while the High School pages tell their story of athletics and give other items of interest. Jokes on the students of both Institutions find occasional place. "Several of the students are learning to sing by note. This method is said to be agreeable when learned. We are glad to hear this." "The Indian Club fever broke out and for three days swept all before it. Aspinwall Hall was filled with a promiscuous multitude exercising with anything from a club to a match. It reminded us of aboriginal times. We thought how nice it would be to have a Pocahontas rush in and rescue us. But no Pocahontas appeared, so we left." Poetry, sometimes original, occasionally passed the censorship of the editors. Editors graduated and left; so others served. Mr. Joseph Fletcher succeeded Mr. Goodwin in 1880, then Mr. Wallis. Messrs. A. B. and L. L. Kinsolving reported High School news. Messrs. J. T. Cole, J. G. Shackelford, and W. S. Campbell, assisted Mr. Wallis. With Volume IV other changes brought in Messrs. K. J. Hammond (chief), and J. B. Funsten later chief, with Messrs. B. M. Randolph, F. K. Leavell, W. T. Roberts, R. G. Noland, J. T. Cole, C. E. Grammer, and E. T. Lawrence on the editorial staff. Letters from the other Theological Seminaries now interest the readers, and some direct from the various fields fan the flames of zeal for Missions. As a students' publication, this magazine was thoroughly creditable to the Seminary, and superior in both purpose and contents to most college productions of its class.

The growth of "The Seminarian" into "The Seminary Magazine", yet retaining the student-editorial staff, shows that its editors hardly intended it to reach the proportions of a Review. Messrs. J. L. Patton and Ernest M. Stires were editors-in-chief of Volume 1, November 1887. Messrs. B. Green (afterwards chief), J. A. Ingle, C. F. Smith, W. D. Smith, W. C. Brown, and A. H. Mellen, assisted them. Messrs. Pannetti and J. R. Ellis were business managers. The need was felt of a periodical for discussion of living issues specially in the South, where conservative men could express themselves with largest freedom consistent with loyalty to this Church. Contributions from both the clergy and laity were desired, the faculty and editors not being responsible for any views expressed. The local news feature of "The Seminarian" was dropped, and four or five articles formed the body of the magazine, with brief editorial and missionary notes and book reviews. In this form, for five years, it gave the public valuable information from many of the Alumni and friends of the Seminary on up-to-date topics. Among its most constant supporters were the Bishop of

West Virginia, writing on Worship; Dr. C. Walker on Diocesan History; Dr. Crawford on Archaeology and Exegesis; and Dr. L. M. Blackford on Biography. Several Alumni essays and necrological notes were published. Dr. Winchester Donald said: "No one could dispute the scholarship of an Institution that could sustain a journal of such a character." The Business Manager reported to the stockholders in June 1891 eight hundred fifty-one subscribers, and a financial surplus which he suggested should be given to the contributors.

The sixth volume became "The Protestant Episcopal Review" in November 1892. The Seminary Faculty now took Editorial Management, Dr. Carl E. Grammer being chief. Under Dr. Grammer's able editorship the Manager reports a circulation of two thousand copies, and indulges in some friendly words: "Thank you for sending me the first number of "The Protestant Episcopal Review." "I like it very much. I enclose $5 for five subscriptions", wrote Rev. C. C. Tiffany, D. D. "The first number" said Bishop Dudley, "is worth the price of the year's subscription." "The first number interested me very much indeed", wrote Bishop Doane. Bishop Clark's Reminiscences now appear, followed after fourteen chapters by Dr. Packard's "Recollections of a Long Life" in seventeen numbers. Ancient and current history is contributed by various pens; archaeology and polity, missionary news, exegetical and theological essays, present-day problems and their solutions. The birth and infancy of the Mission in Brazil is recorded here, and the American Church Missionary Society is not forgotten. An occasional photograph with its owner's biography brings to mind some noted Church Leader. Virginia Church life is related by her devoted children. Opportunity was found in this Review to bring young writers before its readers. The Reinicker Lectures, delivered by experienced scholars, were printed in the magazine. Bishop Randolph's address on the Centennial of the Council of Virginia (June 1895) is a valuable contribution.

Drs. Foley and T. J. Packard were added as contributing editors for Volume XI. When Dr. Grammer resigned to take up pastoral work, Drs. Crawford and Wallis took chief charge, Drs. Micou and Massie assisting. For all these it was a work and labour of love, that there might circulate in the Church a Review "conservative yet progressive, liberal yet reverent, critical yet constructive," which was their declared purpose in beginning Volume XIII.

At the close of this volume, the Faculty felt that with the pressure of their regular duties, they could not continue to prepare and publish the Review. So, with all debts paid, at the Commencement in June 1900, it was offered to the Alumni, at their annual meeting. Since that time there has been no magazine continuously published by the Seminary.

SECTION IV

CHAPTER VII

THE SOCIAL LIFE OF THE HILL

REV. CARL E. GRAMMER, S. T. D.

Horace Bushnell has an illuminating discussion in which (with his own peculiar originality), he treats of the elements of ministerial success that are not sufficiently appreciated in the theological schools of New England, with their excessive emphasis upon scholarship, logical ability and gifts of speculation and analysis. Tact, liking for people, practical judgment, weight of personality were given their rightful importance by Bushnell. In the Seminary's Faculty Meeting talks, and in the lecture room of Pastoral Theology the necessity of the spirit of love and of a sound mind was frequently dwelt upon. These gifts, however, can never be developed by talking about them; they require the discipline of life, and the friction and stress of one personality against another. Many will agree with Dr. Edward Everett Hale that the best part of the training in every institution consists of the rubbing together of the students. Certainly in the Virginia Seminary, situated out in the country as it is, the association among the students, and also between the students and the professors and their families, was unusually close, and constituted an important element of the Seminary's power to mould and impress.

Before the Civil War this student-fellowship must have been peculiarly helpful. The General Seminary in New York and the Virginia Seminary were then the only seminaries in the Church of any size, and candidates for the ministry came to the Virginia School from the Evangelical Bishops, and the Evangelical parishes all over the East. In those days the industrial systems and social conditions of the North and South were so widely different that the gathering together of students of ethics and religion from these sections

382

"MAYWOOD"

The Home of Reverend Doctor Wallace E. Rollins
Former Home of Reverend Doctors Lippitt, May, Walker and Massie

"THE WILDERNESS"

The Home of Reverend Doctor W. Cosby Bell
Former Home of Reverend Doctors McElhinney and Crawford

in one Institution to study the will of God and the mind of Christ must have been a broadening and illuminating experience for all parties. Phillips Brooks of Massachusetts, with his Puritan forebears, and the son of Governor Henry A. Wise of Virginia, could not sit in the same lecture room, debate together in the debating society, or commune together about things of the Spirit and ideals of life without much mutual edification. In discussions of such a burning question as slavery, they must have exercised great tact, self-control and a large-minded appreciation of the extent to which each one was moulded by the environment in which he had grown up; for the students lived together in peace and good-will. The friction was lessened to a considerable extent by the Episcopal Church's aloofness from politics. Both High Churchmen and Low Churchmen were at one in this attitude. The Oxford Movement had increased the antagonism between these two schools of thought, but they were both in harmony in restricting the application of religion to the personal and family life, and in paying but little attention to the improvement of social conditions. The great Evangelical leaders in England like William Wilberforce and Clarkson had been the chief agents in the abolition of the slave trade; but the Evangelicals of America took another line. Their energies went into the Colonization Society, an organization for alleviating the evils of slavery and for Christianizing and civilizing Africa by exporting the colored people of America to that continent. They were also very assiduous in teaching religion to the slaves. But they regarded any political remedies as lying outside of the field of the Church. The result was that while the whole country was being convulsed by the throes of the approaching contest; while social intercourse was steadily diminishing between the North and the South; while the Methodist Episcopal Church was being torn in twain by contests over slave-holding; and societies were being formed and parties were arising whose very existence was as presageful of the approaching disaster as a warning bell in the night, the Episcopal Church, occupied with its rival theories of the Church and the Sacraments, and confident that the whole matter lay outside of the realm of religion, went on its way in comparative peace. The General Convention in Richmond in the autumn of 1859 was unusually pleasant and harmonious.

It has always been the policy of official leaders to ignore the problems they lack the courage to grapple with. The older men had become so accustomed to these mutterings of war that they had come to consider them as only a part of the game of politics, and a mere system of bluffing. So the obtuseness of the leaders is not surprising. The younger men, however, must have been more alive to conditions, and it must have required unusual Christian forbearance in them to live together and study together the principles of Christianity in holy union and concord, in days when close by in Washington such questions were being debated as the Wilmot Proviso and the Mexican War, and above all when Stephen A. Douglas, by his Kansas and Nebraska bill, and John Brown, by his raid, had heated the passions of both sections.

Doubtless the diversity of political views among the professors helped to appease strife. Dr. May was a Northern man by birth and conviction, and at the outbreak of the war withdrew to Pennsylvania. Dr. Sparrow's Irish parentage and early life in Ireland separated him somewhat from the natives of the South and North. He was an American without any special attachment to any state, and taught in his classroom that slavery was doomed by the spirit of the gospel: his chief ties, however, were with Virginia, and when the war broke out he "refugeed" to Staunton. Dr. Packard, who had come to Virginia early and married a Virginian, held the Southern views on the questions at issue. It was easier for the students to get along together when the Faculty differed among themselves in this way and yet worked together harmoniously. The zeal of the Seminary in the Evangelization of Africa must have contributed to lessen the prejudice of the Northern student against the slaveholders. A seminary that founded the mission in Liberia could not be regarded as indifferent to the welfare of the blacks. Northern and Southern men both laid down their lives upon that fever-smitten coast. Now that we have learned that the message of the gospel is social as well as individual, some may regret that our Church and Seminary did not speak out clearly on the moral issues involved. Yet we must not blame them for not being several generations ahead of their age. The Seminary of that day was a great religious power. It was the Antioch of the Church, an abode of the spirit, where men were stirred up to carry the message of salvation to the uttermost parts of the earth, a resort of missionaries to which Apostolic spirits like Boone and Payne returned with their reports, and from which they drew new recruits. Religion and morals were brought into the closest union in the personal life by Evangelical piety. The consecration of students and faculty made the Seminary's life glow with zeal. In the heat of its devotion many a shallow nature was fused and made over again into a new pattern. Many a man who afterwards departed from its theology confessed that in the Seminary's halls he had learned to pray.

Those ante-bellum days when the Virginia Seminary students founded the missions in China, Africa and Japan, and Evangelicalism was the dominant force in the Church in many ways, were great times. Even the dark shadow of slavery could not dim the brightness of the Seminary's life, or lessen the closeness of feeling among its students. Up until the outbreak of hostilities the number of students increased, and there was an unusually large body of students until the movements of the troops required the suspension of the Seminary's exercise.

These traditions of friendliness retained their power in the classes that re-assembled on "The Hill" after the fall of the Confederacy. By reason of the foundation of other Episcopal seminaries in the North, especially the Divinity Schools at Philadelphia and Cambridge, the northern contingent from that time diminished considerably; yet there were always students from north of the Potomac. They were warmly welcomed by the professors and students, who realized the value of these diverse elements, and did not wish to be a sectional institution. A theological seminary of an Evangelical character is bound to have something of a hothouse atmosphere. Probably this holds true of any institution where an earnest and persistent effort is made to hasten spiritual maturity, and impart moral zeal. The Rugby of Dr. Arnold's time was criticized on this score. Such a charge could undoubtedly have been made against Clair-vaux under St. Bernard, and against the club of Methodists at Oxford. Certainly under the Evangelical theology and type of piety, with its emphasis on motives and states of mind, this peculiarity of Seminaries was intensified. The more toughskinned students sometimes complained that their comrades were unduly sensitive. Some men lived regular monastic lives during their whole course. They were, however, the exception. Most of the students were wholesomely affected by the corporate life, learned valuable lessons from their fellows, endeavored to communicate those lessons to the people at their mission stations, and entered cordially into the life of the neighborhood. The religious crank was usually manifest by his inability to respond to his environment. The real religious genius, however, who every now and then appeared, such as young Ludwig, who died during his course, found his fellow-students quick to recognize his inspiration. It would be a great mistake to overlook the power in the Seminary's life of these rare spirits.

The class prayer meetings on Saturday nights and the custom of the hall prayers at ten o'clock, later on inaugurated, gave these ardent natures unusual opportunity to touch their fellows. As the prayer meeting by the cele-brated haystack at Williams College was the fountain head from which have flowed the missionary endeavors of America, so untold influences for good flowed into the lives of the Semi-nary students from these quiet seasons of devotion. No one can recall them without tender emotion. The tradition at class prayers was to open with a hymn. The General Con-fession in the Communion Office followed. There was usu-ally one extemporaneous prayer, and sometimes there were frank heart-to-heart talks about the class's duties and short-comings. Each senior class felt charged with the duty of conserving and transmitting these traditions of devotion and consecration. Once a year, on the Eve of St. Andrew's Day, there used to be a great service of consecration. Oc-casionally emotion was cultivated too much for its own sake, and some men abused such occasions; but the leaders were usually the men of the most consistent lives, and of the greatest spiritual gifts. The ideals upheld were the ideals that sent the missionaries to the foreign field, and have made the graduates of the Virginia Seminary irreproachable in their conduct. Some men, who were comparatively insignificant in the classroom, who never displayed anything but a vague comprehension of Christian theology, and exhibited only a languid interest in the history of Christian institutions, often proved themselves in the student life of the Seminary, and in their mission stations, real religious forces and true prophets of the Most High.

This phase of the life of a Seminary student is not usually comprehended by the phrase, "the social life of an institution." It has, however, seemed proper to emphasize it in this history, since it has always been one of the chief glories of the Seminary. In their constant association with one another in work and in play the students became thoroughly of one mind and one spirit on some of the great essentials of the religious life, and a certain type was created and made a creative and helpful tradition and ideal.

The Seminary's environment was a great assistance. The sterile soil of the surrounding country is unfit for farming and is covered chiefly by scrubby groves, in which are settled the humble folk who do the Seminary's chores and washing. There is no farming community with proprietors, tenants and laborers, representing the various grades of society. The Seminary and High School stand side by side with the homes of their faculties, and upon these families and some few residents, who have come to the neighborhood for suburban homes, and for the sake of educational facilities, depends the social life of the students.

Many of these were college graduates and came from homes of culture and refinement, but the call to the ministry has not since the Apostles' days been heard chiefly by these classes. Many came from remote rural districts and humble homes. To the task of aiding such young men to acquire social training and equip themselves for acceptable service in rectories, the households of the professors as a rule devoted themselves with great singleness of heart. The people of the community as a whole also did their part. The more gifted students usually heartily cooperated.

The influence of the Seminary's matrons ought not to be overlooked. Miss Mary Rhett, of the historic South Carolina family, was a remarkable woman. Her graceful and distinguished bearing, her vivacity, and unique ability to speak her mind without giving offence made her a valuable mentor and friend to a large group; and the efficiency, solid Christian work, and staunch kindliness of Miss Nannie Jacobs will never be forgotten by the students of her day. The chief social influences were of course the professorial families in which there were daughters. In the days before the Civil War, when Evangelical asceticism under the influence of Bishop Meade was at its height, these homes were marked by great plainness and an entire avoidance of anything that approached assumption or display in manner or apparel. It would, however, have been a mistake if the visitor from other sections had inferred from these indications that the Seminary was out of touch with the culture of the time.

Dr. Sparrow was a great traveler for that day. He visited Europe six or seven times, and traveled extensively throughout the United States. One of his brothers, Edward Sparrow, settled in Louisiana, where he married the niece of Jefferson Davis, and became the Senator from Louisiana in the Confederate Congress. He served on the Committee to draft the Constitution of the Confederacy, and part of the original is in his handwriting. Another brother, Thomas, was in Washington as a congressman from Ohio. Mrs. Sparrow was an Ingraham of Poughkeepsie, New York. She met Dr. Sparrow on a visit to her sister, the second wife of Bishop Chase of Ohio. Another sister was Mrs. Kip, the mother of Bishop Kip. On her mother's side Mrs. Sparrow was descended from the Greenleafs of Boston. The children of Noah Webster were her first cousins. Another near relation was Judge Cranch, the Chief Judge of the District of Columbia, a New England Unitarian whose son was the transcendental poet and artist, Christopher Cranch. He is still remembered by the oft quoted verse:

> "Thought is deeper than all speech,
> Feeling deeper than all thought.
> Soul to soul can never teach
> What unto itself is taught."

Dr. Packard came of a celebrated family of educators in New England. His college career at Bowdoin, and his theological studies under Moses Stuart, the great Andover scholar, had brought him in contact with the best scholarship of the day in his department. Mrs. Packard was the daughter of General Walter Jones, one of the legal giants of the day, when the bar of Maryland and the District had most of the cases before the Supreme Court of the United States. On her mother's side she was related to the Lees of Virginia. Dr. and Mrs. May were both connected with leading people in Philadelphia. They had no children, but they used to bring into the community their Philadelphia friends. A winter in Italy had made them both readers of Italian literature. These three families were especially charged with responsibility for the students. The household of Bishop Johns at "Malvern" was almost as closely bound up in their welfare. The Bishop was one of the most graceful speakers in the Church, and a person of great social charm, and his daughter, Miss Julia, was one of those consecrated women who are the chief pillars of religion and chief sources of kindliness in any community in which they find themselves.

At Clarens the Rev. George A. Smith, an Evangelical of the old school and a Christian gentleman of graceful dignity, had a girls' school. At "Manokim" lived Mr. Cassius Lee, a lineal descendant of Richard Henry Lee of Revolutionary fame. Mr. Lee was one of the most zealous of the Seminary's trustees, and was for many years the secretary and treasurer of the Education Society. Next door to Clarens, in the place afterwards the home of Mr. Charles Hooff, lived for a time that very remarkable woman, Miss Emily Mason, who became famous as a nurse in the Confederacy. She was one of those dominating women who might have been the foundress of some sisterhood if the times had favored. Among the number of young persons who lived with her on "The Hill" was her niece, Miss Kate Mason Rowland, who afterwards attained a high place in the literary world as the author of the standard life of her great ancestor, George Mason of Gunston Hall, Fairfax County, Virginia, who was called the "pen of the Revolutionary War". Miss Rowland also published the life of Charles Carroll of Carrollton, the signer from Maryland. Other families on "The Hill" in the ante-bellum days were the Misses Fairfax at Vaucluse, elegant ladies of the old school, and Mrs. Godwin and her high-spirited daughters.

The depth and reality of the religious life of this little community was undoubted. Their piety was not professional, but personal. Dr. Sparrow had a large family, but he could not resist the appeal of the helplessness of the motherless child of Mr. Hening, a missionary to Africa who lost his sight under the tropic heat of that coast, and adopted little Blanche Hening. Susan Sparrow, the second daughter, was a woman of unusual ability and earnestness of character, and went out with her husband, the Rev. Dudley D. Smith, as a missionary to China. Mrs. Packard's sister, Miss Katherine Jones, was a missionary to the same country. Many years after, in another generation, Miss Mary Packard went out as a missionary to Brazil. The home of Dr. May was a kind of Bethany, so genial and bright was the tone of its hospitality, and so deeply spiritual were all its interests. Incalculable were the influences for good that flowed out from these homes upon their student visitors.

Very often a permanent tie was formed by marriage. Thus Dr. Sparrow's daughters, all save one who was a great invalid, married graduates of the Seminary. One of Dr. Packard's daughters became a minister's wife, one of Mr. Smith's daughters, and two of Mr. Lee's daughters. The list might be lengthened.

After the fall of the Confederacy the life of the Seminary underwent a great change. The students were, many of them, seasoned soldiers, veterans of pitched battles, men who though young in years had borne their part with courage in great campaigns, and some of whom had served on the staff of great captains. A Seminary with such men as Thomas U. Dudley, George W. Peterkin, Charles C. Penick, Kinloch Nelson, William Dame, Robert A. Gibson, Landon R. Mason, and C. C. Randolph in its classrooms must have been a wonderful school. Their jovial fun was long remembered. How amusing it must have seemed to them to play baseball together, they who had played such deadly games of ball and cartridge. What reality and zest there must have been in the class talks and prayer meetings.   What a background of heroic deeds and sufferings lay behind all their thoughts and feelings.   Who would not wish to have been at a Faculty Meeting in these times, when the professors talked on eternal issues to such men.   All of them, professors and students alike, had come out of great afflictions, privations, destitutions and bereavements.   It is not surprising that the Institution was soon supplied with candidates for the ministry.   If the men who lived in portions of the country less scourged by war had appreciated the true values in a ministerial education, they would have crowded to the Virginia Seminary for special courses in the companionship of such manly men, under the instruction of such ripened Christian teachers.

In due time the vacancy in the faculty caused by the death of Dr. May was supplied by the election of Dr. Cornelius Walker to the chair of Ecclesiastical History and Homiletics, and "Maywood" was filled with young people.   Later on the failing strength of Dr. Sparrow led the Trustees to elect as a kind of assistant and understudy a learned Irishman, the Rev. Dr. J. J. McElhinney.   Other families also settled on "The Hill".   Col. Arthur Herbert, one of the trustees who passed his fiftieth year in that office, established himself at "Muckross".   Mr. Charles Hooff and his charming wife kept open house and made their home a social center. The widow of Col. Funsten with her children came to the neighborhood for the sake of the High School for her sons, with the result that three of her daughters became the mistresses of rectories.

When Senator James M. Mason made his home at Clarens, the presence of so great a personage in the community must have enlisted the loyal interest of every southern man, and touched the imagination of everyone who could appreciate the tragedy of his career.   After the fall of the Confederacy, Senator Mason had made his home for a season, like other Confederate leaders, in Canada.   But his heart was in Virginia, and he returned at last to his native state and settled himself with his daughters, Miss Virginia and Miss Ida Mason, at Clarens, where he could be in close touch with his daughter in Alexandria, and with his loyal

friend Mr. Corcoran in Washington.   Close by, at Cameron,
settled his brother-in-law, General Cooper, who had been
the military advisor of President Davis, and the chief of the
military bureau in Richmond.   He had been one of the highest officers in the army that went over to the Confederacy,
as Senator Mason had been one of the leaders in the Senate
in ante-bellum days.   Both had staked all and lost.   Both
were heart and soul believers in States Rights and the old
regime.   Senator Mason had been one of the most sanguine
of the Confederacy's leaders, one of the most deeply convinced of all the statesmen that John Brown's raid had shown
that the Union was no longer desirable.   The all-important
post of Envoy to England had been entrusted to him.   He
had been most cordially received by the nobility and society,
and had accomplished all that personal acceptability and
staunch courage could effect.   Behind the old statesman as
he sat on his porch and watched the steamers go down the
Potomac, lay stirring and tragic experiences.   He could recall great debates in the Senate in which he had upheld the
standard of Democracy, the rights of Virginia, as the followers
of Jefferson viewed them and the legal rights of the State's
peculiar institution against the assaults of such debaters as
Sumner, Seward and Chase.   He could recall the exciting
conventions when the adherents of the fiery Yancey broke
the Democratic party in two, the romantic episode of his
arrest together with Mr. Slidell of Louisiana on board an
English steamship by the American man-of-war, of their
restoration to the English government at a demand that was
backed up by a threat of war, of his reception by cordial
English friends and of the sickening alternations of hope
and despair of his long and trying mission in England.   As
he and his brother-in-law talked of these events and the sudden and complete collapse of their cause at the end, thoughts
of unspeakable sadness must have crowded upon them.
    Senator Mason's life and diplomatic correspondence have
been admirably written by his eldest daughter, Miss Virginia, and every line in the book, as well as in the Senator's
face, indicates that he was a man of high courage, who could
bear himself with dauntless fortitute; but it cannot be
doubted that the failure of the Confederacy shortened his

life and made death not unwelcome to him.   It is impossible that the students of the Seminary should not have been deeply touched by his presence in their neighborhood.   They must have felt like saying with Kent, at his funeral:

"He hates him
That would upon the rack of this tough world
Stretch him out longer."

Miss Virginia and Miss Ida continued to reside at Clarens for many years, where, following the precedent of Mr. Smith, they conducted a Home School for girls.   Their association with their father, and their descent from one of Virginia's great political families on the father's side and from the historic Chew family of Germantown on their mother's side, had given them the grand air of women accustomed to deference and high position.   Clarens, with its mistresses and their teachers and scholars, was one of the most delightful places which the students could visit.

One of Senator Mason's granddaughters, Miss Eliza Chew Ambler, made her home with her aunts.   After teaching a while in the school she married Mr. L. M. Blackford, and became the well-beloved mistress of the High School. The following reminiscences are from her pen.   They picture vividly the Seminary in the days shortly after the Civil War, and give that knowledge of dress and manners which John Richard Green has taught us are of such historical value:

"My recollections date back to 1869, just four years after the war, when we were all poor together, and economical simplicity was the order of the day, but when we were very happy in possession of what Thomas Nelson Page calls 'the kingdom of youth'.   From that time till the early eighties there was little change.   We girls dressed more in the fashion than some of the neighborhood ladies before the war, when, as Mrs. Douglass Corse, daughter of the Rev. George A. Smith of Clarens, told me, her father positively objected to her wearing a bonnet bought in Baltimore by her mother, because it was trimmed with an ostrich feather, which he thought too worldly for a clergyman's daughter. Mr. Grammer, afterwards the rector of St. Peter's Church of Balti-

more, earned her lasting gratitude by exerting all his eloquence in her favor, and persuading Mr. Smith to let her
keep it and wear it.

"In my day the girls generally possessed about three
dresses, a morning dress, a second-best, and a best dress,
the latter doing double duty as a walking suit, or a party
dress as needed. A cloth dress was simply turned in surplice
fashion at the neck and adorned with lace collar and cuffs,
also with flowers from our home supply, and we were ready
for grand occasions. Low-necked and short-sleeved dresses
were unheard of.

"Our parties were very delightful to us. Course dinners
were never thought of. Either a few friends were invited to
tea, or we had refreshments 'handed round' by the beaux.
Dancing and cards were out of the question, and rare flowers
from the florists were equally so, though for a different reason. We generally had a sort of Reading Club meeting at
different homes once in two weeks, with substantial refreshments always limited to two kinds.

"To the professors' houses all students of the Seminary
were admitted. To be a theological student was to have a
patent of nobility, to be introduced to a professor's house, to
his table, to the inner circle of his wife and children. What
a charming atmosphere of home those houses had! There
was such cordiality, such love pervading every look and tone.
When invited to tea, before we left the table we all knelt in
family prayers and rose feeling we were one in heart.

"Often we had games, music and songs, and generally
a few hearty hymns. The sweet singing of sentimental
ditties, or of merry ones, and the undercurrent of hearty
human interest roused tenderer feelings than the most musical victrola I have ever heard. What pleasant walks home,
often by moonlight, or over the snow, what pleasant confi-
dences, what heart to heart talks we had, often what fun as
we went over the evening's happenings together.

"Walking was one of our great pleasures. An engagement for Church Sunday night, missionary meeting Monday night, or the Rhetorical Society Friday night, was as
pleasant to the girl of our day as a well-filled dancing card,
and a promised automobile ride is to the present debutante.

How we loved to skate or coast in the cold clear winter weather, or to hunt for arbutus and Turkish violets in the spring!

"Our amusements were simple and inexpensive, but they made us very happy. All was bright for us young people because we were together and found each other attractive. We were so light-hearted and asked so little of life. And there was a constant succession of men waiting for our friendship who were to become known and widely loved as they went forth into the world. Such men as Bishop Gibson, Bishop Peterkin, Bishop Dudley, Bishop Penick and Bishop Beckwith had just left the Seminary when I first knew it. Bishop Jackson with his brilliant conversational powers, Bishop Tucker with his ready wit, Bishop Winchester, Bishop Lloyd, Bishop Gravatt, Bishop Funsten, Bishop Tyler— all men of ability, of most attractive personality and of noble character. Besides these were many gifted men, and almost all we knew have proved to be men of great worth, men of high ideals, whom it was a privilege to call friend.

"There were many attractive families on "The Hill". At Cameron we found General and Mrs. Cooper with their son and their daughter, a charming woman who had been a belle in Confederate days and now showed herself equally ready to flirt with a general, a bishop, or a Junior Prep. Always gracious and lovely, it might well have been said of her, 'Who though she oft rejects, yet ne'er offends'.

"At Clarens there were Mr. and Mrs. Mason, their two daughters, Virginia and Ida, a niece, Miss Marie Mason, a granddaughter, Miss Lucy Ambler, and almost always some lady visitor ready to entertain and be entertained by the neighborhood friends.

"At Mr. Charles Hooff's house he and his wife, with his daughter Carrie, just budding into a gracious woman, made their home most delightful to all comers. Across the road was Bishop Johns' beautiful house, 'Malvern,' with ever open doors, where the courtly old Bishop and Mrs. Johns, and his beloved daughter Julia frequently invited the young people for a merry evening, and where the Bishop's witty sayings were enjoyed and often quoted for years afterwards.

"Across the hill lay 'Muckross,' where Col. and Mrs. Herbert kept open house and often had young people to tea.

When they left Mrs. Herbert would point to a dark, narrow path through the woods, often telling a young couple, 'No one ever loses that path unless the heart has been lost first,' and it is strange how often that path was lost!

"At Dr. Packard's house were Dr. and Mrs. Packard, Miss Nannie, who died the next winter, Miss Nellie, with the younger daughter Mary, and her brother Tom, not yet grown. The hospitality of that house was boundless. The doctor told me that just after the war, when the Seminary reopened, he often asked the whole body of men to dine with him, because he feared they had poor fare. And this at a time when he himself was poor—his salary a pittance.

"Dr. Sparrow was a most interesting talker, and wherever he went all gathered around him, fearing to miss a word. We loved to hear of his experiences in travelling, and every subject gained by his charm and originality; but his wife and daughters were both invalids and not able to entertain when I knew them, though I constantly heard of his talks with the students.

"Dr. and Mrs. Walker had a large and interesting family, and a most sociable one. Their oldest son, Charles, and Miss Lizzie Walker kept their house gay with life, while Mary, Laura and Margie demurely waited for their turn to come, as come it did later, keeping up the bright atmosphere of their establishment. Their younger brothers, Willie, Baldwin, and John were delightful merry boys then, ready for anything, so full of life it seems strange to think of them as all turning to the serious professions of theology, and all dying so young, only Willie reaching the prime of life.

"At Mr. Cassius Lee's home, 'Manokim,' were three sons just growing into manhood, their little sister Annie giving promise of the beauty and brightness which were to make her such a favorite in years to come.

"At 'St. John's in the Wilderness' lived Mrs. Funsten (aunt of Bishop Funsten) with her pretty daughters Cary and Lizzie, and her sons Emmett and George. They were a lovely family and contributed to the ministry one son (George) and three daughters, Mrs. Reed, Mrs. Dame and Mrs. Hinks.

"Over the High School presided the Rev. William Gardner, lately married, and there he and his lovely young wife were always equally ready to give or accept an invitation. Great social favorites they!

"Time would fail me to tell of the church dressings where the greens were brought from the woods by the young men, and woven into wreaths by the ladies' own fair hands and festooned by the students, while bright eyes and smiling lips directed every motion. It was said that the best matches were made on these occasions."

These recollections, it will be noticed, relate to the days very near wartime, and the soldierly figure of Dr. Nelson has not yet appeared on the scene. Let us move the hands of the clock on some ten years. Mrs. Smith has built her home next to the Hooffs on the north, and Edward Goodwin and Robert Forsyth are especial frequenters of her porch; James Funsten and his sisters are spending the winter at "Malvern," and Dr. Kinloch Nelson, one of the soldier graduates, has taken up his residence in Dr. Sparrow's old house. Dr. Packard is now the dean.

Mrs. Nelson was very delicate, but the Doctor was as much in evidence in the general life of the community as in the class room. To his energy was largely due the new chapel that had taken the place of the ante-bellum chapel, and also a gymnasium. He had the gift of mingling freely and helpfully with young people, like a comrade.

Of unusual value to the neighborhood and students were Miss Annie and Miss Eliza Murdoch, who came to live about this time with their sister, Mrs. Jamison, at "Woodley." Of Scotch ancestry and Presbyterian faith, their father having been an elder in the influential First Church of Baltimore under the pastorate of Dr. Backus, these ladies brought into the community a new note, and exhibited the beauty of lives dominated by somewhat different traditions and theology. "Woodley" became a home of peculiar distinction. Miss Annie had the fervid temperament that has made the Scotch pulpit famous. Miss Eliza was always crowned with a sweet continual control. Both were fine conversationalists. They were of an age to be useful mentors and friends of the students, with whom they cooperated most wholeheartedly in the mission at West End. There was never the slightest friction in consequence of their Presbyterianism, which was staunchly Calvinistic. Their diversity in church membership simply enriched our social lives.

Through this household the attention of the Seminary was directed toward Brazil as a promising field for a new mission. The daughter of the pioneer missionary of the Presbyterians to Brazil, the Rev. Abel Simonton, was their niece, and made her home with her aunts. When the missionary leaders among the students were searching for a new field of missionary enterprise, the presence of Miss Helen Simonton on "The Hill" made the consideration of Brazil inevitable. By such unforeseen and subtle ways is the influence of a heroic life transmitted and diffused.

An entire chapter might be devoted to the reciprocal influences of the Seminary and High School. The religious life of the Seminary, and the devotional character of the chapel services were of great value to the school. Great deference was paid by the Headmasters to the Evangelical views on questions of conventional morality like card-playing and dancing, which were practically non-existent in the life of the whole neighborhood, and did not appear even at Commencement time at the school. And the High School contributed a goodly number of its students to the Seminary. Sometimes a teacher like William Cabell Brown was drawn over to the ministry. The Headmasters and their cultivated teachers were always valuable additions to any social gatherings.

These Headmasters were marked men in their day. Dr. Pendleton was an old West Pointer, like Bishop Polk of Louisiana. Both Pendleton and Polk had left the army for the ministry but took up arms again in the Civil War. Dr. Pendleton became General Lee's Chief of Artillery, and after the war resumed his ministry as rector of the Episcopal Church at Lexington, where his old General must have greatly enjoyed the association. His life has been most interestingly written by his daughter. He was a man of remarkable force and dignity, who impressed himself greatly upon his boys. The flogging schoolmaster of the School was Dr. Dalrymple, a clergyman, but above all a drill-master. A great raconteur, a wit, and frequent flogger, the neighborhood was long fond of telling of his sayings and doings. His contribution to the school was an increased zeal for accurate classical scholarship. His successor, the Rev. Dr. McGuire with his gifted wife restored the more wholesome atmosphere of the earlier days, and gave the High School its traditional character. Their daughter Fenton became the wife of Dr. Nelson. In their home grew up two ministers and two ministers' wives.

The most eminent of all these Headmasters by reason of the length of his headmastership and the great success of the school under his direction was undoubtedly Dr. L. M. Blackford. Adequate recognition has been given elsewhere to his career as a schoolmaster, and to his character as an earnest and consistent Christian. His social influence especially on the Seminary community is alone under consideration here. A great lover of the social amenities of life, he was a distinct power on "The Hill," for many years as an *arbiter elegantiarum,* a phrase sometimes heard from his lips. He had well grounded convictions on the close relation of manners and morals, *mores et moralia,* and had a native bias in favor of what I may call the English Public School standards on both subjects. Evangelicalism is more cosmic, more philosophical, more democratic in its morals and its whole body of concepts, than this aristocratic and provincial product of the right little, tight little Island. Accordingly there was often a good deal of merriment among the Seminary students and in the whole community over many of the pronunciamentos of Mr. Blackford, his devotion to conventional "form", his passionate partiality for England and things English, and the rigidity of his whole code. Yet the laugh need not have been all on one side. Through the periods we have been discussing, the Seminary came into contact with culture in only the most limited way. Evangelical religion could sympathize with philosophy, but it was afraid of art, and very distrustful of literature. The opportunities for hearing good music were meager, and the Chapel services, though uplifting by reason of their hearty responses, were not enriched by many fine anthems. Undoubtedly the function of beauty was imperfectly realized. This aesthetic poverty made Mr. Blackford's influence particularly valuable. Not that his musical or artistic taste was in any way preeminent. Where he excelled was in his realization of the importance of social culture, and the value of aesthetic gifts. To the beauty of a well-ordered social life and to gracious manners he was especially responsive. He loved all the observances, refinements, and conventionalities of a complete and well-ordered society. Though he spent so many years in the country, he was preeminently a city man. For many successive summers he travelled in Europe, journeying at one time as far East as St. Petersburg. But all the continent was a negligible influence in his life compared to England. The ordered beauty, the complex social life of that wonderful island, took captive his entire nature. It became the home of his imagination. He loved to say that he felt more at home in London than in New York.

He thought that Washington made a great mistake in not setting up a constitutional monarchy in this country, if we had to separate from England. His loyalty to the Confederacy, in which he had been a brave artillerist, was deep and unfaltering, but in any controversy between the United States and England, he always took the English view. Not even his great loyalty to President Cleveland could draw him from this attitude. He was in favor of letting England do as she pleased with Venezuela. Towards the end of his life he became a great admirer of President Roosevelt. But speaking of his career by and large, he was one of the pronounced admirers of things English in the country. In fact he was in mind and taste an English Headmaster conducting a school as far as possible on Rugby lines in Virginia.

These English proclivities and standards were much analyzed and discussed on "The Hill". They made themselves felt. Thought on social themes was keenly excited, and attention was called to living as an art, as well as a responsibility and a task. In short, Mr. Blackford gave tone to the social life of the whole community.

Col. Hoxton, his chief assistant and latterly his co-principal, was a man of unusual personal distinction. In face and figure he reminded one very much of the portraits of Charles the First. Mr. and Mrs. Hoxton were almost entirely absorbed by the High School, but their presence on "The Hill" was greatly valued by all who knew them.

After the coming of Dr. Crawford and Dr. Grammer as professors, a literary club was inaugurated, chiefly under the leadership of Miss Margie Walker and the Misses Worthington. Dr. Grammer was the president, and literary essays were read and recitations given. It was a most valuable feature in the life of the neighborhood, and did much for the Institution. But there were no such gatherings in the historic eras under review. The chief social events were meetings of the Debating Society and the Missionary Meetings. At the Commencements, however, there were great gatherings. The friends and relations of the graduating students were usually entertained in the neighborhood, and the grove was filled with couples. On graduation day the busses came out from Alexandria and the girls made all the lawns bright as they walked around, clad in simple white dresses and holding aloft their pretty pink-lined parasols. It used to be the custom to have an essay read by every member of the graduating class. No one except the faculty, the President of the Board and one or two remarkable trustees listened to all of them. The audience used to change constantly, as the speakers succeeded one another. As each reader had before him his special friends, he was sure of the most genial criticism. It was usually decided that the essays were quite remarkable. All these friends were invited to lunch in the dining room. What a scramble it used to be! How the boys were fluttered at seeing the girls in their old dining room, and how the girls were fluttered by meeting so many young knights of the Cross! Who that participated in the joy of those days can ever forget them? I shall not speak in this place of the solemn ordination service, for which we vested in the old Prayer Hall, marching on in a long reverent procession to the thronged chapel. How beneficently the sky seemed to overarch us and how approvingly the gentle summer breeze fanned our excited brows! None of us can ever forget those days.

Beautiful indeed is the Seminary as it stands on "The Hill", looking in one direction down upon the capital city of this great Republic, and in another upon the widening

reaches of the Potomac river; but there has been many a
man upon that Hill who has seen there a vision of a greater
city, the New Jerusalem that is slowly descending upon this
earth, and who has looked across wider reaches and caught a
vision of the sea of glass mingled with fire.   There are many
who never expect to find a purer society, until they enter by
the grace of God, into the General Assembly in Heaven.

SECTION IV

CHAPTER VIII

THE MATRONS OF THE SEMINARY

REV. W. A. R. GOODWIN, D. D.

A History of the Theological Seminary in Virginia would be incomplete, and those responsible for writing it most unappreciative, if no mention were made of those who had served the students and the Church as well as the blessed Christ as Matrons in this Institution. There are attributes in the character of God ineffably tender, attributes of gentleness, of sympathy, and of loving consideration, which have been revealed to us in Jesus Christ. It is the divine intention that these attributes in the character of God should be present also in the characters of men. But we men know full well that the continuous revelation of them comes to us through the heart and the loving ministry of womanhood.

In spite of the solicitude of the Board of Trustees and the watchful care and cordial interest of the faculty the indomitable tendency of men to revert at times to the instincts of barbarism would certainly have found expression and left an indelible impression of crude uncouthness in the life and character of the students, had it not been for the refining and gentle influences which constantly came to us from the Matron in our midst. She was as a mother in our Seminary home. The hospitality of her sitting room was always open to us. We saw her sitting upon the porch, or moving with grace and dignity through the quadrangle and about the Seminary grounds. In cases of serious sickness, there was the consciousness which came to men ill and far away from home, of a woman's presence and of a woman's solicitude and care, and the waiter which was brought by the servant to the sick student's room bore some token of a woman's thought and understanding.

403

It was, however, in the dining room that her restraining and refining influence was most strongly felt. The instincts of selfishness and even of animalism, and the forgetfulness of the amenities and decorum of good breeding, are not totally eradicated from a man's life upon his matriculation even in a Seminary. The consciousness of the presence of a lady in our midst and at our table, with her gentle thoughtfulness, instinctive courtesy and refined and delicate manner, tended to create or to keep alive and stimulate in the student the good manners and refinement indispensable to success in the ministerial office.

It is difficult to determine from the early records in just what capacity some of the women served who are first mentioned in connection with the care and the oversight of the students. The first mention which we find is of Miss Sally Griffith, at whose house at the corner of Washington and King Streets, Alexandria, Dr. Keith and the four first students of the Seminary lived. She was, as has been mentioned in the consecutive history of the Seminary, the daughter of the Rev. Dr. David Griffith, elected Bishop of Virginia in 1786, but unable for financial reasons to go to England for his consecration. He was the friend of Washington and Lafayette, and served as rector of Christ Church, Alexandria from 1780 to 1789. "Miss Sally, was a lovely character" says Dr. Packard, "and a devoted Christian. She was the aunt of Colonel Llewellyn and the Rev. William Hoxton, of Mrs. A. M. Randolph and Mrs. Buckner Randolph. She remembered General Washington dangling her on his knee when visiting her father. I buried her in Alexandria at the close of the Civil War."

The Rev. Dr. Clemson of the Class of 1826 speaks of the few students of his day having happy homes in the families of Miss Peggy Ashton and Miss Sally Griffith.

Record is made in the minutes of the Standing Committee of the Education Society, under date of October 27, 1825, of the increase of $20 a year to the amount paid Miss Peggy Ashton for boarding the Seminary students, and, in 1833 "order is given to pay Mrs. Jacobs $25 on account of salary" and a further order to "pay $70 to Miss Sally Campbell, for the hire of her servant at the Theological Seminary".

These two ladies rendered their helpful service during the stay of the Seminary in Alexandria.

The Rev. Dr. Packard mentions Miss Mary Dobson as the first Matron of the Seminary, * and quotes the Rev. G. T. Wilmer as remembering a trip out to the new site of the Seminary in a cart with some furniture. Mr. Wilmer says, "It was in the spring of 1828 when Miss Mary Dobson and I, a boy of nine years, took our seats in a cart with two horses hitched tandem, and journeyed out. Miss Mary would not let me return as it was a rainy evening, but put me in care of one of the students, who arrayed me for the night in one of his garments."

By 1843 it would appear that Miss Dobson had grown old in her service at the Seminary, for there appears a resolution in the minute book of the Standing Committee of the Education Society directing a correspondence with Mr. Jacob F. Mildela in relation to the removal "of Miss Mary Dobson from the Seminary, her advanced age and infirmities rendering her no longer a suitable person for housekeeper". Miss Mary, once having been congratulated by a friend on having such a pleasant life in her association with such holy men, replied very calmly, "There is a great deal of mortality even among theological students." She seems to have greatly endeared herself to the students of the Institution during her term of service, for among the records of the Society of the Alumni of the Seminary, under date of July 14, 1847, we note the following: "RESOLVED: that the Secretary of the Society of the Alumni be requested to communicate with the several alumni of the Theological Seminary who were with it up to the period of Miss Mary Dobson's connection with the Institution, and to request them, if agreeable to their wishes, to send to the treasurer of this Society annually during her life-time, $1.00, to be by him presented to Miss Dobson in token of the grateful remembrance with which we hold her unbought kindnesses and sympathies with us while members of the Institution."

The minute book of the Standing Committee of the Education Society under date December 23, 1843, contains a note to the effect that Miss Mary Stuart was appointed

* "Recollections of a Long Life", Dr. Packard, Page 237.

Seminary Housekeeper, but we have no record of the length of her term of service.

The Rt. Rev. T. U. Dudley gives the following record of the conditions under which the students lived and took their meals upon the reopening of the Seminary after the Civil War, and also of the selection of Miss Cornelia Jones to serve in the capacity of Matron of the Seminary. "The students took their meals in a room on the second floor of Aspinwall Hall, afterwards occupied by Bishop Peterkin, and these (*horresco referens!*) provided by Sam Williams, the devoted and self-denying manager, were cooked by an ignorant negro woman whose culinary experience was, to say the least, limited; and were spread upon a table of which I have tender recollection. It was an office table which had been left by some military officer, and became the companion of my student life upon my providing another better adapted for the use of our commons. Ah me! what melancholy viands were spread upon that table giving sure and speedy promise of dyspepsia. We were living as soldiers, while laboring as students, and there could be no doubt as to the end thereof. Quick and compelling was the impression made upon me that we could not go on after this fashion, and I took it upon myself to plead with Miss Cornelia Jones, then resident at Dr. Packard's, and who was his sister-in-law, that she would take pity on us and come and mother us. My effort proved successful, and in spite of the opposition of a few whose digestion was more vigorous than that of others, and who therefore preferred the larger freedom of the old order, she came, and a new and healthier condition straightway began. Her chief functionaries as I remember them were old Nathan and his wife, of whom the men of my day and of many years thereafter must cherish grateful remembrance."

In 1870 Miss Mary B. Rhett was elected Matron and continued to serve until 1892. Her term of service falls within the memory of many of the living alumni, and these memories are hallowed with the glow of affection and gratitude. Her very presence was a continuous source of blessing to the Institution. With grace and dignity and with all the charm and gentleness of refined womanhood, Miss Rhett radiated her influence into the life of all who knew her. There were, from time to time, those among the students who were unkindly critical as to the meals which were served, but there were others who remembered that the Matron was receiving only $300 a year for her services, that she was eating the same meals which were served to the students, and that the only money which she had with which to provide the Seminary table was the limited amount which was paid by the students, which had been reduced to the minimum in order to enable many of them to attend the Seminary at all. The faultfinders and grumblers soon found that they were speaking into an unsympathetic atmosphere, and something if not somebody generally reminded them that restraint in criticism under the circumstances was more befitting a Seminary student than to be able to fare sumptuously every day. In this connection the following communication from a Seminary student which appeared in The Southern Churchman of November 11, 1859, was of interest at the time of its publication and may be also of interest today: "I was much grieved to learn from your letter that there were several young men who would have entered this Seminary, provided they could be comfortable and have plain wholesome food. The report which has been circulated about our Seminary is without foundation. Our bread is light and made of fine white flour. Our meats are always fresh and very rarely any other than the choicest pieces; and our butter is fresh and sweet as can be bought in any city market. What more, I should like to know can we reasonably desire? None but the ungrateful and professional fault-finder will complain. I marvel that the table is so well provided, when I consider the moderate charge for board. There always have been grumblers at the Seminary as there are at other Seminaries, colleges, boarding houses, and hotels in the United States.

"The cost of board at the Seminary is $100 for the session of more than nine months. For this price the fare is most admirable. Good bread, good meat and vegetables. We do not see what more could be expected. We believe the fare at our Seminary is equal or superior to that of any institution of a similar kind in the country. More than this ought not to be desired. We do not want to be understood as wishing grumbling to cease. By no means! It aids digestion. It does good. The only idea we wish to inculcate is that there is no cause for grumbling!"

On the 23rd of June, 1890, the Board of Trustees increased the salary of Miss Rhett from $300 to $400.

The appreciation in which Miss Rhett was held by the students of the Seminary was voiced at a meeting of the Alumni held on the 22nd of June, 1892, when resolutions were presented and passed by rising vote, "in honor of Miss Rhett, the retiring Matron of this Institution, whose gentleness, refinement and Christian devotion in a most difficult position won the admiration of all and contributed so greatly to the refined tone of the Seminary life. She will be for a long time to come most gratefully and affectionately remembered". In the Seminary Chapel there has been placed a stained glass window as a memorial to her life, her character and the service which she rendered.

Upon the resignation of Miss Rhett, the Board of Trustees elected Miss Nannie Jacobs as her successor. Miss Jacobs served as Matron from 1892 to 1914. From the very outset she gave evidence of the executive ability and personal qualifications which gave assurance of the success of her administration. She soon won the confidence and affection of the students by her fidelity and kindness. By her unselfish devotion she won the lasting esteem and affectionate regard of the successive classes of students who passed through the Seminary during the twenty-two years of her loving and efficient administration. She resigned in 1914 and was succeeded by Mrs. Thomas Moss, who held the position and faithfully performed the duties of her office for two years, retiring in 1916.

Her successor was Mrs. R. B. Brooke, who acceptably served as Matron from 1916 to 1921. One who well knew Mrs. Brooke and the strength of her influence, writes "her regime was a perfect benediction to the students and to the whole Institution. Her long experience in Staunton and Harrisburg and her quiet dignity, her tact and her loving heart won for her many lasting and devoted friends".

Miss Jacobs, and Mrs. Brooke, lingered, as did Miss Rhett, long enough on "The Hill" to endear themselves not alone to the student body but to the whole community. They were ever thoughtful of the poor, both white and colored, and often gladdened their lives in times of sickness with flowers which grew under their care in the quadrangle of the Seminary.

The present efficient Matron, Mrs. Elizabeth Robins Lunn, was appointed in 1921. There will surely be those in years to come who will rise up and pronounce upon her the blessings which have been given by grateful students to her predecessors.

The writer feels fully conscious that this article is in no way an adequate expression of the gratitude of the students of the Seminary for the care and kindness of the Seminary Matrons, nor is it a worthy tribute to the self-sacrificing devotion which has characterized their loving ministry. What is here recorded is the history of service rendered. These noble women of God's Holy Church were not serving for the praise of man, but we feel very sure that their labor of love has been gratefully received and richly blessed by Him in Whose Name and for Whose sake it was rendered.

SECTION IV
CHAPTER IX
STUDENT ORGANIZATIONS
REV. W. A. R. GOODWIN, D. D.

The Student Organizations in the Theological Seminary in Virginia have been the spontaneous outcome of the disposition to fellowship in the fulfillment of a mutual purpose. The contagious power of an idea and the call to comradeship, which comes with the ideals inspiring devotion and service, naturally found their expression in the early life of the Institution in the association of the men together for the promotion of those ideals and aspirations which were dominant in the life of the student body. It is significant that the first corporate expression of the Seminary ideal was found in the coming together of the students in the home of Dr. Keith for mutual fellowship and prayer. Mention of these meetings is found among the reminiscences of the students who attended the Seminary in Alexandria during the first years of its existence.

The second expression of the disposition to comradeship for the promotion of a common ideal and purpose took form in the organization in 1824 of a Missionary Society which was called "The Society for Inquiry upon the Subject of Missions". In the Theological Repertory of July 1825 there appeared the following notice: "At a meeting of the Society for Inquiry upon the subject of Missions in the Theological Seminary, Alexandria, July 1, 1825, it was resolved that notice be given in the Theological Repertory of a Society in this Institution called a 'Society for Inquiry upon the Subject of Missions'. The design of which is to inquire generally into the state of Christ's Church militant and especially into that branch of it to which the Seminary is attached, with a further notice to the editors of the theological publications in the United States that a gratuitous supply of their papers addressed to the Society at Alexandria, D. C., will be gratefully received." (Signed) L. H. Johns, Recording Secretary.

Another article relative to this Missionary Association appeared in the Episcopal Recorder in May 1835: "The students of this Institution have been associated together as a missionary society, partly to collect funds for missionary objects, but more especially with a view to enlightening their own minds with respect to the subject of missions and particularly their duty in relation to them."

This article refers to a circular sent out by this society, expressing the need for a missionary library, periodicals and charts. It invites persons to become life members upon the payment of $10, or patrons upon contributing $25, and the hope is expressed that the appeal will be answered because of the fact that "to this School of the Prophets the Church must look for the missionaries so much needed to enable her to discharge her obligations to the unconverted world".

The diary of Bishop Payne makes frequent mention of informal services of prayer held in the room of Mr. Boone (afterward Bishop Boone of China). In these informal meetings and in the Spirit-guided meetings of the Society of Inquiry were born the Church's mission endeavor in China, Africa and Japan.

As the members went forth from the Seminary as pioneer missionaries to these far corners of the earth there was established a bond of fellowship between them and those who were left behind which was strengthened by constant letters written by the missionaries to the Missionary Society of Inquiry in the Seminary. Correspondence was also conducted with students of other seminaries relative to the work of Christian missions.

Mention is made of a letter from C. Colden Hoffman written from Liberia in 1849 glowing with enthusiasm and voicing the call "come over and help us". Among the correspondents whose letters served to give information and to stimulate the missionary spirit was the Rev. Horatio Southgate, writing from Constantinople descriptive of missionary endeavor throughout the Near East, especially in Persia.

On March 5, 1847, we find this Society using the columns of The Southern Churchman for the purpose of giving the following notice of appeal: "The Missionary Society of Inquiry of the Theological Seminary is desirous of sending early in the spring a box of various articles to the missionaries at Cape Palmas. An opportunity is thus offered to all who feel an interest in the Mission of making such contribution as their Christian love may dictate. The articles which would be most acceptable are cotton goods of all kinds, suitable for clothing and such as are required in house-keeping. Contributions may be sent to Messrs. Bell and Entwisle, Alexandria, directed to the Missionary Society of Inquiry, Theological Seminary, Virginia."

In 1878 the organization makes an appeal to the Church for contributions of books relating to missionary work in all parts of the world. The appeal is endorsed by Bishop Johns. The "Seminarian" published by the students of the Seminary under date July 22, 1880, gives an account of the annual meeting of the Missionary Society held in Prayer Hall on the evening of the 23rd of June. After a talk on missions and the missionary faith and love, the article goes on: "This Seminary has a priceless possession in her foreign missionaries, the living and the dead. We know them and love all whose names are on that roll of honor. They are far from our homes, but very near our hearts. They do the work committed to the whole Church, obey the commands given to the whole Church, help us in our private life, aid us in our public ministrations. We are joined together in one communion and fellowship. We think of them, we pray for them, we hold up their work before our people, asking their prayers and their alms. Today we hear a call that is wafted across land and sea from the shores of Africa. It comes from the lips of a dying son of this Seminary—the last cry of the expiring Hoffman to the Church in his native land, 'Tell them by the living Crucified One that they hold not back their hands.' This Church, this Seminary, sends back the answer, 'By the living Crucified One we will not hold back our hands.'"

This magazine also mentions the donation by Dr. Tyng of New York of fifty Prayer Books together with toys and other gifts appropriate to the season to be used by the Missionary Society at the Christmas celebration at the colored Sunday School.

The Missionary Society was reorganized after the War on November 26, 1866, and has continued in existence without interruption up to the present time. It holds its regular meetings the first Tuesday evening of each month during the session and the annual sermon is preached before the Society on the Wednesday night of Commencement Week.

At the time of the founding of the Brazilian mission when the endorsement and cooperation of the Church Missionary Society was withheld because of the opposition strongly voiced in some quarters of the Church and within this Society to the proposition of establishing a mission of the Church in a Roman Catholic country, the Seminary Missionary Society was the first organization which gave to this endeavor its sanction and its support.

When Kinsolving, Meem, and Morris offered to enter upon this work their decision was reached in the light of the encouragement given by the faculty of the Seminary and with the assurance of the support of the Seminary Missionary Society even before the American Church Missionary Society decided to give its backing and support to this endeavor. This determination on the part of the American Church Missionary Society was made after the Rev. Dr. Carl E. Grammer, representing the Seminary Missionary Society and the men who had offered themselves for this service, appeared before this organization and with compelling and persuasive power helped to formulate the purpose which resulted in the resolution giving the support of the American Church Missionary Society to the Brazilian Missionary endeavor.

"The Fairfax Brazilian Missionary Society" organized at this time embraced in its membership not alone the students of the Seminary, but also the interested Church people living on "The Hill" and in the neighborhood of the Institution.

Next in age among the student organizations of the Seminary was the "Rhetorical Society" established in 1830.

The Southern Churchman of April 22nd, 1842, gives an account of the objects for which this organization was founded followed by an appeal to the Church for books other than those theological. "This Society," says this article, "together with the 'Missionary Association', has always been deemed by the faculty of high importance. Its chair is filled ex officio, by the professor of Pulpit Eloquence, who decides each question after the debate. The Association is strictly speaking a debating society, having for its object the promotion among its members of logical habits of thought, facility of expression, a manly and efficient style of delivery, and a general acquaintance with subjects bearing a near or remote relation to theology. Its main object is to enable its members in their preparation for future usefulness to keep pace with the spirit of the age which seems to require of the clergy not only a strict acquaintance with their profession, but a large share of general knowledge.

"In behalf of this organization we ask for the contribution of books for a library on the ground that the books in the public library of the Seminary are almost wholly of a theological nature." (signed) M. P. Tillinghast, G. Wilmer, G. A. Leakin, J. Morsell, P. L. Franklin and A. P. McMurphy.

This organization has continued in existence and has proven of value in giving experience in speaking without the use of manuscript. A due and proper regard for the intelligence and feelings of the congregation is evidenced in the following article relative to Seminary "Reading Clubs" published in the "Seminarian" in 1878. Reading clubs seem to be a permanent institution in the Seminary. We now have three in successful operation, namely, 'The Eclectic,' Mr. Clark, president; 'The Philomathean,' Mr. MacCready, president; 'The Athenaeum,' Mr. Downman, president. These meet once a week. The members read in turn and all take part in the unsparing criticism which follows, extending to the minutest particulars of the reader's style and manner, such as position, voice, accent, pronunciation, etc. A marked improvement is sure to follow a course of such treatment and many a bad habit and mannerism has been corrected in these clubs which, if carried into the ministry by their unfortunate possessor, would have proved a source of annoyance to one congregation or another all the lifetime."

On October 11, 1890, Chapter No. 489 of the Brotherhood of St. Andrew was chartered and established at the Seminary and after being active for some years lapsed and was revived in October 1904. In addition to the two general rules, the Seminary Chapter of the Brotherhood has two additional objects:—First: "To be a transition period from lay membership in one chapter to a clerical headship in another." Second: "To instruct those of the students in Brotherhood work who have never been affiliated with the organization."

Next, perhaps in importance, in historic interest and in fame have been the baseball organizations which from time to time have enlivened the life of the student body. Among the students of the Seminary are to be found every year some men who, in college or university, had become proficient in this ancient sport, and who have stirred the enthusiasm to play the game. From time to time the High School nine would be challenged by the Seminary and would condescend to accept as it gave them opportunity for practice, but no disgrace could have fallen upon them which would have been more humiliating than to have been beaten by the Seminarians which however, sometimes happened. Even when the game was not played in ordered form the ball would be "batted up" in the afternoons and early evenings out in front of "the quadrangle." In Dr. Suter's day this was against the rule. We well remember one afternoon when J. R. Ellis (affectionately known as "Bishop" Ellis) was batting the ball for a numerous concourse of students, Dr. Suter suddenly appeared around the corner near the Chapel. "Why! Mr. Ellis," said the doctor, "don't you know it is against the rules to play ball in this place?" "Yes, Doctor," replied "Bishop" Ellis, "but I thought you were in Alexandria." On that same afternoon the Doctor having discovered a broken pane of glass in the bath-house window wrote the following admonition and pinned it on the bulletin-board:

"The man that threw the ball that broke the glass
That keeps the cold from him who bathes,
Will please restore *Instanter!*"

The most intimate and in many ways the most helpful student organizations were the informal prayer meetings held in the different halls at some quiet hour of the evening once each week. Extemporaneous prayers and silent intercessions were offered for God's blessing upon our work and for those who had gone out from the Seminary into the ministry of the Church and especially for those who were in the lonely and far away fields of the Church's Mission endeavor. We can not follow all the ways which are opened by prayer. They stretch into mystic realms of infinite life and power leading those who follow on to visions of Him "Who high and lifted up" yet bends to touch the heart of man with celestial glow and the tongue of man with live coals taken from the altar of sacrifice. They stretch into realms of sacrificial devotion calling souls into fellowship with human need and suffering, and into companionship with saints and martyrs who have given their lives that others might know the Life more abundant. From the "Hall Prayer Meetings" many paths have opened to vocation and some to martyrdom. Boone and Payne record the impress made by these meetings upon their lives. From these rooms, where two or three gathered together in His Name, streams of love and power and inspiration have flowed which have made many a desert place of earth to blossom as a rose. Forces have been generated there, as the divine and human have blended in prayer, which have resulted in the extension of His Kingdom through His Body, the Church, to the uttermost parts of the earth.

FRONT OF THE PRESENT SHARON MISSION CHAPEL WITH THE
CONGREGATION AND SUNDAY SCHOOL CHILDREN

SECTION IV

CHAPTER X

SEMINARY MISSION STATIONS

REV. SAMUEL A. WALLIS, D. D.

The Seminary Missions which form an important feature of the active life of this Institution had their beginning in the spiritual needs of the people living in its vicinity. For the most part the population consisted, as it does to a great extent today, of small farmers who were unable to provide more than a plain living for themselves and their families. They appear to have had no regular Church privileges of any kind, at least not in the immediate neighborhood, until the Seminary was removed from Alexandria to "The Hill" in the year 1827. So the students of that time had a great opportunity for religious work in this part of Fairfax county and they early consecrated themselves to it in the spirit of their Master Who went about doing good. They generally began by going about from house to house, on Sunday afternoons, holding short religious services wherever it was possible, chiefly in the form of modified prayer meetings, if we may use that expression, as it must be remembered there was very little education amongst the people in those days. The public school was not in existence and Mission Chapels were still in the future. However, the students endeavoured to have some central point where they could hold services and open a Sunday School in each district into which they gradually divided the country for their mission work.

At Sharon, for example, which is one of the oldest Missions situated about three miles southward from the Seminary, stood "Wilton", the hospitable home of Mr. and Mrs. Froebel, who were members of Old Christ Church, Alexandria, of which Mr. Froebel was organist for a number of years. It may be of interest to know that Mr. Froebel was a connection of Friedrich W. A. Froebel, the celebrated

417

German philosopher, philanthropist, and educational reformer.   Here at "Wilton" the students found a center for
their work, as Mr. and Mrs. Froebel were deeply interested
in the condition of the people dwelling around them, especially lamenting their lack of religious training.   So the foundations were then laid for what is still known as the truly successful mission of Sharon.   The Misses Froebel lived at the
old home until a few years ago, and delighted to tell of the
early days of this Mission so dear to them.   A chapel was
built about the years 1848-9 on a lot donated by their father.
It stands on a hill commanding a beautiful view of the surrounding country, with a fine prospect of Alexandria, and
glimpses of the noble Potomac.   As soon as the Chapel was
finished the services of the Church were established, an excellent Sunday School was carried on, and ever since Sharon
has been the religious centre of that community.   The first
chapel was destroyed during the Civil War.   In that sacred
building Phillips Brooks, Bishop of Massachusetts, and Bishop Randolph, of Southern Virginia, ministered as students to
this congregation.   A second chapel, very plain indeed, was
built immediately after the war, aided by contributions from
former students who came from the North and whose hearts
were true to their beloved people of Sharon.   In 1901 the
present attractive chapel was erected under the superintend-
ence of Messrs. John Robson and Robb White, Jr., students
in charge.   In its vestibule hang fine photographs of Bishop
Brooks and Trinity Church, Boston, donated by a member
of that congregation.   Sharon's Communion vessels date
from 1851.   It was the first Mission to have a cemetery.

Across the hills, three miles eastward from Sharon, we
find its daughter, Groveton Mission, founded nearly forty
years ago.   Among the earliest students who served at this
mission were Carl E. Grammer, Lucien L. Kinsolving, now
Bishop of Brazil, and E. L. Hinks.   From 1897 to 1900 D.
C. Mayers served the Mission.   He made the Communion
Table which has always been in the chancel.   Clinton S.
Quin, later Bishop Coadjutor of Texas, was a student here,
full of activity from 1906 to 1909.   Groveton Mission filled
a real need for that community as there was no Church of any
kind on the road from Alexandria to Woodlawn, a distance

of eight miles. At first and for some years afterward the congregation worshipped in the schoolhouse. But in 1903, through the earnest efforts of James L. Martin, assisted by Frank Whittle Hardy, then students at the mission, Christ Chapel, as it is called, was built on a lot donated by Mr. and Mrs. Frank Reid, who were Presbyterians. The communicants belonging to our Church are few in number, but at Groveton we find the true *Unitas Fratrum*, for Presbyterians, Methodists and Baptists all worship together with our people, and unite in keeping up the Sunday School and in supporting the chapel to which all are devoted.

St. John's, at West End, a mile and a half south-eastward from the Seminary on the Little River Turnpike, within the postal limits of Alexandria, has always been accounted one of the leading missions. We have been told there was a chapel dedicated to St. Mark near the Alexandria Reservoir, which was served by students, but however this may be, no trace of it remains. St. John's dates from the year 1866, when the first chapel of this name was built by Mr. James Williams, an earnest and consecrated student much beloved by the people. He is said to have remained with them a short time after his ordination. St. John's was noted for its large congregations and flourishing Sunday School, with a Young Men's Bible Class taught for a number of years by Mr. Charles R. Hooff, well known as the cashier of the First National Bank of Alexandria, a faithful Christian layman whose teaching of the Bible bore much fruit. A new chapel was erected in 1903 under Mr. Custis Fletcher, a student who won the love of the people of West End. The cornerstone was laid on Sunday the fifteenth of March, 1903. Seats for a surpliced choir were added by Mr. M. W. Riker in 1913. These were made by his own hands. This Mission was the first to have a parish hall. It was erected as a memorial to the Rev. J. G. Meem, D. D., now a missionary of our Church in the city of Rio de Janeiro, Brazil.

We pass now to the Chapel of the Holy Spirit, a mile west of the Seminary in the hamlet of Howardsville, erected in the year 1905, through the zealous efforts of Mrs. Marietta Minnegerode Andrews, on a corner lot presented by her husband, Mr. Eliphalet F. Andrews from their estate of "Vaucleuse". It succeeded a very poor and unsatisfactory chapel used sometimes as a school house. The new chapel is very attractive, especially for its beautiful windows, which were painted by Mrs. Andrews. Most of the people at Howardsville formerly attended the Seminary Chapel. But as the congregation at the Seminary increased in size, it was considered best to have a place of worship built at Howardsville to accommodate all the people there. So the Chapel of the Holy Spirit is practically a Chapel of Ease to the Seminary.

The next Mission in order, four miles west from the Seminary, is St. John's, at Glencarlyn, formerly called Carlin's Springs, a village pleasantly situated on the Old Dominion Electric Railway, chiefly inhabited by Government office-holders. This Mission has been established for at least thirty years. The services and Sunday School were held for a long time in the Town Hall, which proved to be a very convenient place until a chapel could be built. This was finally accomplished under the leadership of Mr. Herbert S. Osburn, the student-in-charge. The little chapel is very pretty and complete in its design, reflecting much credit upon its builders. The congregation is small, but the work is interesting and full of promise as this is the only place of worship in the village.

Passing southwest to the Little River Turnpike, six miles from Alexandria, we reach the village of Lincolnia, formerly called Lebanon, where a mission has been carried on for forty years. The people here are, as a rule, Methodists, but the Mission was mainly started on account of a few Church people who were too far away from any Episcopal place of worship to attend its services. The chapel dedicated to St. Paul was not built until 1894, when Mr. C. S. Davidson was the student-in-charge. As the people were poor, Mr. Davidson accepted the responsibility for whatever debt might be incurred, which was considerable. Eight years after his ordination, when he was in charge of a church in New York, he paid this off in full through the assistance of a number of friends who took an interest in his old mission. Mr. Davidson's faithfulness in this matter is worthy of record here. The people of this Mission, though few in number, form a devoted band of workers, and the results have been remarkable. With aid from the outside they have built a large parish hall, and by their own exertions have bought a piece of land for a cemetery, close to the chapel. This Mission has been a spiritual blessing to the whole community.

The last of the older Missions at present connected with the Seminary is the Chapel of the Good Shepherd for colored people, situated within its grounds. This chapel was built in 1883 under Mr. W. R. Savage, who received contributions from friends both in the North and in the South. As a student he was very much interested in this work, for his father had been a missionary in Africa, going out from the Seminary in 1836. This Mission has had varying fortunes, but it has never failed in possessing a band of earnest communicants who have maintained a good report among their neighbors, both white and colored, for their Christian character. The Sunday School is a great spiritual and educational influence among the colored population. But as a number of the children of this Mission grow up, they are drawn away to the large Baptist Church near the Seminary and High School grounds, on account of its wider social life. Notwithstanding all this, the teaching received at the Sunday School of the Good Shepherd is not forgotten. Above all, the chapel has given two men of excellent Christian character to the colored ministry of our Church, the Rev. E. E. Miller, rector of St. Stephen's Church, Petersburg, Virginia, and the Rev. Charles S. Somers, minister of the John Moncure Memorial Chapel, Stafford County, Virginia.

One great hindrance to the growth of this Mission is the fact that it is closed during the long vacation of the Seminary. It can be easily seen how such a condition must seriously affect the endeavor to build up its congregation. It may also be added that its present situation on the Seminary grounds does not make it a good center for the colored population.

Another Mission has lately been opened at Barcroft, a mile and a half east of Glencarlyn, on the Old Dominion Electric Line to Bluemont. It already has a large congregation and Sunday School, and is full of promise for the future.

We must now give a short account of the missions that have "graduated" from the Seminary.   Recently St. Paul's, Bailey's, united with Grace Chapel, Maywood, under the Rev. C. B. Sparks.   Some conditions have lately arisen which may bring it back to the status of a mission.   For some years past it has been the most flourishing of all the Seminary chapels, with a large attendance at the services and a prosperous Sunday School.   It is the only Protestant place of worship between the Seminary and Falls Church, a distance of six miles, and should, if possible, continue to hold its position as a Church.   Immediately after the Civil War St. Paul's was opened as a Mission by Horace B. Hayden and William M. Dame, later of Memorial Church, Baltimore, Maryland, students at the Seminary.   The present chapel was built under James M. Morris, D. D., now in Brazil, when he was a student at this Mission.   A large parish hall was added in the year 1903, as a very necessary equipment for church work, through the untiring efforts of A. P. Gray, Jr., student-in-charge at that time.

Trinity Chapel, Arlington, was united with St. George's Church, Clarendon, about two years ago, under the rectorship of the Rev. W. B. Everett, Jr.   This chapel was established as a Mission before the Civil War.   Bishop Henry C. Potter of New York was a student here.   On one occasion he related how General Robert E. Lee, then Colonel Lee, sometimes attended the chapel, when he came home to Arlington House on furlough.   He told with deep interest of Colonel Lee's reverence in Church, his earnest participation in the service, and careful attention to the words of the youthful speaker.

Old Pohick Church was under the Seminary from 1852 to 1881, the services, of course, being interrupted during the Civil War.   The first students-in-charge were T. Grayson Dashiell of Richmond, Virginia, and Charles R. Howard of Baltimore.   In 1866 services were resumed after the war by Messrs. William M. Dame and William J. Boone, afterwards Bishop of Shanghai, China.   The roof of the Church still remained in position, but the interior was dismantled, so these resourceful students made crude seats by placing undressed planks on blocks of wood standing on the earth floor for their congregation.   In the year 1874 the Church was put in good condition for services through the kind interest of a gentleman of New York City.   A succession of students continued until 1881 when a minister was appointed and Pohick has had a rector ever since.

Olivet Chapel, one of the old Missions, was built on "Bush Hill", Fairfax county, the owner, Mrs. Scott, being filled with the true missionary spirit for the people dwelling around her.   In 1883 this Mission was united with Pohick Church.   Bishop Lloyd, together with his friend, the late Rev. W. M. Clark, D. D., while students served here.

St. John's Church, McLean, now prospering under the efficient rectorship of the Rev. George C. Shears, was founded by S. S. Hepburn in 1867.   He was the first student to hold services in that part of Fairfax County.   As a Mission it was called St. John's Chapel, Langley, from a small village near which it was situated.   While a student at the Seminary W. A. R. Goodwin had charge of Langley for two years, holding service in Falls Church on Sunday afternoon on his way back to the Seminary.   In 1895 it was thought best to withdraw the students from this Mission, both on account of its distance from the Seminary and also to give it an opportunity to develop into a Church, which has been accomplished. A clerical supply was first secured from Washington and in due time St. John's was strong enough to call a rector.   It represents a cultivated and prosperous community earnest in good works.

The Falls Church was for some years connected with the Seminary until it was united with Zion Church, Fairfax Court House, under the Revs. John McGill and Frank Page. Afterwards it became an independent Church in Fairfax Parish.

St. Paul's Church Mission in Alexandria was founded by Edmund J. Lee as a student in 1898.   He is now a missionary in China.   The students are appointed from the Seminary, and work under the rector of St. Paul's.

Christ Church Mission, Emmanuel Chapel, Braddock, Alexandria, is now an independent mission Church, having acquired this status in June, 1922, under the charge of a minister.

The students formerly had Missions at the Alexandria Alms House, and in the hall of the Young Men's Christian Association of the Southern Railroad near its station in Alexandria.   In both these places the regular service of the Church was not used, but the order adopted consisted of the reading of a chapter of the Bible followed by prayer and an address with the singing of Hymns in the accustomed manner.   These missions after a conference with the full Executive Committee on Mission Work were discontinued some time ago, because it was agreed that the ministers and lay-workers of Alexandria should attend to them.

Meade Chapel, colored, under Christ Church, with its own minister and a good church building, was at its establishment and some years afterward, during the rectorship of the Rev. Henderson Suter, D. D., served by Seminary students.   It had a remarkably large Sunday School in which a number of the young ladies of Christ Church were teachers.

The Missions of the Seminary present a noble record of consecrated service on the part of the students which forms one of the glories of its history.   We recognize the supreme importance of the intellectual life and the training all the Seminaries furnish in connection with the classroom work during the traditional three years of their regular course, so that the students may be well instructed in the things both new and old of the mysteries of Christ.   But the practical preparation for the pastoral life reveals the great place the Missions hold.   They are superintended by the professor of Pastoral Theology, who administers the Sacraments, and exercises all necessary oversight.   The students are appointed by him to their several stations.   They then go forth to their work under the student-in-charge, who is a member of the Senior class familiarly known as "The Bishop".   In a full manned mission the member or members of the middle class have the designation of "priest" and in the case of the juniors that of "deacon".   Thus the three orders are found in the Missions, proving that this Seminary is an exponent of the historic ministry.

On one occasion a clergyman of our Church asked an alumnus of this Seminary, "How is it that your men make so few mistakes in entering upon their parochial work?" The answer at once came forth, "Because of the training received at the Missions". What a testimony is found in this reply to the high value of these Missions.

EDITOR'S NOTE

The following unsigned article relative to the Seminary Mission Stations was published in The Southern Churchman shortly after the close of the war between the States.—W. A. R. G.

"Presuming every item of news having reference to the Theological Seminary of Virginia, is a matter of interest to the Church, we desire to lay before your readers the history and condition of one important branch of Domestic Missions, immediately connected with this School of the Prophets.

"There have been for many years in the vicinity of the Seminary, a number of Mission Stations, at which the students have been accustomed to meet the people of the particular neighborhood, and instruct them in the word of life; thus exercising themselves somewhat in pastoral duties, and gathering souls into the Church of Christ.

"Before the war, these stations were kept open during the entire year, at the following places: Arlington, the Alms House, Bailey's Cross Roads, Lebanon, Mt. Olivet, Sharon, and West End. At each of these stations, buildings had been erected for Divine service, Sunday-schools had been organized, and the buildings with the exception of the Alms House, and the school-house at Bailey's Cross Roads, were entirely destroyed by the troops. Thus for nearly four years the citizens of these neighborhoods were deprived of all religious advantages and privileges.

"Since the reopening of the Seminary, the students have endeavored to re-establish these stations and rebuild the chapels destroyed. From the ravages of war, the surrounding country has become so impoverished, that very little aid can be given by the people themselves to effect this purpose. With what success the students have labored at this work, the following account will evidence:

"Arlington: This station has not been reopened, because the property is in the hands of the Government, whose chaplains officiate in the neighborhood, thus rendering other services there unnecessary.

"The Alms House: This building is the property of the corporation of Alexandria, and the number of inmates averages about fifty persons, male and female, of all colors. Services were held here at long intervals during the war by different clergymen.

"In 1865, the students of the Seminary revived the Sabbath afternoon services, and continue to visit there for this purpose. This station differs from all the others in having its congregation always present.

"Bailey's Cross Roads: The school house at this place is situated at the foot of Munson's Hill, was built by the neighborhood, and is used during the week by a school with an attendance of forty scholars. Divine service is held here every fourth Sunday by Rev. Mr. Dixon, the circuit preacher of the Methodist Episcopal Church. During three-fourths of the year, a flourishing Sunday-school is conducted under the auspices of the same church. On Sunday afternoon two of the students hold Divine service at this place whenever the roads are in such a condition as to allow the congregation to assemble. From the proximity of Falls Church, the attendance here averages only twelve persons.

"Lebanon: The building at this station was destroyed by the troops, and no effort has been made to rebuild it. Nothing can be effected before the Spring fully opens. A congregation could easily be gathered at this point if it had any building in which to assemble, but to effect such a plan the students will be obliged to depend almost entirely upon the kindness of the Church. Donations for this purpose are earnestly requested. A neat chapel or school house can be erected here for less than $200. Who will aid us in this matter?

"Mount Olivet Chapel: This station is situated near Bush Hill, and about three and a half miles south from the Seminary. It was originally established by the lamented H. H. Holcomb, who went from the Seminary as a missionary to Africa in 1856. After holding prayer meetings in the neighborhood for some time, Mr. Holcomb succeeded in arousing the interest of the people sufficiently to have erected a small school house, in which he opened a Sunday-school, and held divine service. This building was erected upon a tract of land generously donated and deeded to Trustees for the purpose by Mr. Scott of Bush Hill. Watered, doubtless, by many prayers from the beloved missionary, this station continued to flourish rapidly after his departure for his African field of labor, and when he passed away to his blessed reward, a neat little chapel was built near the school house upon the same tract of land at a cost of $1200. This chapel was consecrated shortly before the war, and named in honor of the deceased missionary, 'Holcomb Memorial Chapel'.

"When the Seminary closed in 1861, 'Holcomb Chapel' was left without its laborers. The troops were soon encamped about the site of the chapel and school house, excepting the Communion Service, everything disappeared with them. Thus all the fruits of several years of labor and patient toil, were destroyed in a few days. Since the opening of the Seminary, two of the students, Messrs. Hullihen and Lewis, have successfully endeavored to rebuild the chapel. By the terms of the deed, when the building was destroyed, and the property ceased to be used for religious purposes, the deed became invalid, and the property reverted to the estate of the donor. By the kindness of Mrs. Virginia Scott, a more eligible location was selected, and a new deed executed in 1866. Since then the two gentlemen aforementioned, aided by the people of the neighborhood, have had erected a neat weather-boarded chapel, capable of accommodating one hundred persons, at a cost of $600. This amount, through kindness of friends who have contributed readily of their means, has enabled the gentlemen to pay all but $250, which still remains due. The trustees earnestly appeal to the Church at large to aid in liquidating this indebtedness, until which time the chapel must remain unconsecrated. The attendance at the chapel averages forty persons. Divine service is held there every Sunday afternoon. A sewing society has been organized to assist the needy persons in the neighborhood and to collect funds to pay the debt. A Sunday-school will be opened in the ensuing Spring.

"Sharon: This station is located about one mile from Mount Olivet. A year or two before the war, a chapel was built by the neighboring people upon ground donated and deeded by Mr. Froebel. It was in successful operation,

under the care of the students, at the commencement of the
war.   The building, however, shared the fate of 'Holcomb
Memorial Chapel'.   During the past year, by the energetic
efforts of two of the students, Messrs. Hubard and Davis, in
conjunction with the members of the old congregation, a
plain and substantial chapel has been reared at a cost of a
few hundred dollars, upon the site of the one destroyed.   The
indebtedness upon the chapel has been paid, and it now awaits
consecration.   Its affairs are in a very flourishing condition,
and the station promises a rich harvest to the laborers.
The chapel accommodates one hundred persons.   The average
attendance of the congregation is about fifty.   A Sunday-
school has long been in operation, with an average attendance
of twenty-five scholars.   Divine service is held here, also,
every Sunday afternoon.

"West End: About eighteen years ago, a student from
the Seminary succeeded in organizing a small Sunday-school,
in that part of the suburbs of Alexandria called West End.
Most earnestly he labored there to win young souls to Christ,
and his efforts were richly blessed by the Master.   The
citizens of West End were not slow to appreciate the value
of the Christian instruction imparted to their children, and
they rewarded the laborer by erecting a small frame house
which would serve the double purpose of a school house
during the week and a chapel on Sunday.   Here Divine service was regularly held, and the Sunday-school gathered.
The tide of war which swept over the State reached even to
this little tenement, and it suffered the same fate as its sister
stations.

In 1865, two students from the re-opened Seminary,
Messrs. Williams and Reed, visited this neighborhood,
and succeeding in enlisting the interest of the people sufficiently to secure the use of a school house owned by Mr.
Lewis of West End.   In this place a small congregation was
gathered and here they have worshipped Sabbath after
Sabbath ever since, rapidly growing in strength and numbers
until it now averages an attendance of seventy-five persons.
Though unaccustomed to the services of the Church, this
assembly have already become so familiar with the Prayer
Book that it is always used in their worship.   The Sunday

school has also been revived and numbers fifty children. So rapid has been the growth of this congregation that the small house in which they now worship has long since been found too small to accommodate them.   And as the privilege of using the building is an act of Christian courtesy extended to them by the Methodist Church which has rented the building for their own services, there is a possibility that at any moment this little congregation will be left without a house of worship.   Every effort is, therefore, being made to purchase a lot of ground, and erect a suitable and commodious chapel for the purpose. This of course cannot be done without funds. The neighborhood is one pecuniarly poor, and can render but little aid to effect this end. The laborers are there, earnest and energetic. The harvest is ripe for reaping and they are already gathering in the grain, but where to garner it they know not. The simplest style of chapel cannot be built here for less than $600, a mere pittance when contrasted with the hundreds of thousands yearly expended in our land upon gorgeous temples of worship.   Of this little sum, thanks to kind friends in Alexandria and elsewhere, all has been subscribed but $250, an amount which many a church could treble and feel none the poorer. The chapel cannot be built until this amount is collected. Will not our friends abroad give of their little to this object. 'If thou hast much, give plenteously; if thou hast little, do thy diligence gladly to give of that little: for so gatherest thou thyself a good reward in the day of necessity.'"

SECTION IV

CHAPTER XI

NORTHERN INFLUENCES IN THE LIFE OF THE VIRGINIA SEMINARY

REV. W. A. R. GOODWIN, D. D.

From Puritan New England and other centers of theological thought in the North there came deep-colored and potent streams of influence, which entered into the life of the Virginia Seminary in the early period of its history and left upon the character of this Institution a strong and abiding impression. It is interesting to trace the circumstances which brought this influence to bear upon her life, and it is interesting, also, but much more difficult, to follow the fusing of these forces into the life and thought of the Seminary. Here Jamestown and Plymouth Rock met. The stern spirit of the puritan, cold, dark and severe, met the gentler spirit of the cavalier, warm, sunlit and pleasure-loving. The traditions of the old order of the English Church, and the iconoclastic, rigid, theological and ecclesiastical concepts of Calvinism and the Puritanism of the New England dissenters, met in the men who worked together in the founding and upbuilding of the Virginia Seminary. The conflict was not, primarily, so much between men of different convictions. It was inward and spiritual. It took place in the souls of Dr. Keith, Dr. Packard, Dr. Sparrow, Bishop Meade, and others who, in their search for truth, found it in the trial and conflict of heart and mind, in processes of reconciliation, and in the fusing of the iron sword and the jeweled scimiter into the keen two-edged sword of the Spirit.

Among those influential in the endeavor which resulted in founding the Education Society and the Virginia Seminary, Hawley, Henshaw, Henderson, Andrews, Dame, Woodbridge, Duchachet, Tyng, and Bishop Moore, consecrated Bishop of Virginia in 1814, were all Northern men, reared and educated, with the exception of Bishop Moore, amid the traditions of Puritanism, while Bishop Meade and Bishop Johns were educated under the Presbyterian influences of Princeton.

The influence of the North, was, however, much closer and far more potent as it entered the Seminary through her early professors. Dr. Reuel Keith, who in 1823 became the first professor in the Virginia Seminary, was born in Vermont, spent his boyhood in Troy, New York, and received his education at Hill's Classical School, St. Albans, at Middlebury College, and at Andover Theological Seminary.

The Rev. Oliver Norris, who was elected in 1825 and served only a year when his death occurred, was born in 1786 probably in Baltimore. The Rev. E. R. Lippitt, elected in 1826, was born in Rhode Island and received his education at Brown University. The Rev. Dr. Joseph Packard, who came to the Virginia Seminary as Professor in 1836, was born in Wiscasset, Maine. He received his education at Phillips Academy, Andover; Bowdoin College, Maine; graduated at Andover Theological Seminary, where he studied under Moses Stuart, and subsequently taught at Bristol College, Pennsylvania. The Rev. Dr. James May, born in Pennsylvania and graduated from Washington and Jefferson College, Pennsylvania, became Professor in the Seminary in 1842. The Rev. Dr. William Sparrow was born in Massachusetts and educated until sixteen years of age in Ireland, graduated from Kenyon College, Ohio, and came to the Virginia Seminary as Professor in 1841 from Gambier College, Ohio, of which he was President.

Thus it will be seen that the first six professors in the Virginia Seminary were all born and educated in the North, and, with the exception of Dr. Sparrow, were all trained in colleges and seminaries under the dominance of Puritan rather than Church influence. The debt which the Virginia Seminary owes to the North is not, however, confined to this early period of her history, for in later years the Rev. Dr. John J. McElhinney, who became professor in 1871, had been born in Pittsburgh, Pennsylvania, and educated at Washington and Jefferson College, Cannonsburg, Pennsylvania; the Rev. Dr. Angus Crawford, elected professor in 1887, and subsequently dean of the Seminary, was a Canadian by birth and a graduate of Trinity, Toronto. The Rev. Dr. Samuel A. Wallis, Professor from 1894 to 1920, was also a Canadian by birth.

This Northern influence, so pronounced in the early life of the Seminary, had its beginning in the search for health which led Dr. Keith to turn from bleak New England to the warmth and sunshine of Virginia. Subsequently Dr. Henderson went in search of Dr. Keith, who was on his way back to Vermont, "to fetch him to Georgetown" to start a Church School. He became rector of Christ Church, Georgetown, from which he was called to go to the College of William and Mary to become professor there in the Church School of Theology; from this position he was soon removed to take charge of the Seminary when established in Alexandria. Dr. Keith had come to know Dr. Packard at Andover and doubtless was partly responsible for his election as Professor in the Seminary. Thus through personal contact and fellowship the influence of Dr. Keith was continued through subsequent years. This, in brief, was the origin of the Northern influence in the life of the Seminary.

The nature of this influence was just what the student of theological thought, in the light of existing facts, would be led to expect. It placed upon the teaching given in the Seminary a marked and characteristic emphasis, and gave to the Seminary a character and tone as well as certain distinct tendencies which have continued, in greater or less degree, throughout the whole course of the history of this Institution. The natural trend of these influences was tempered and confined, first of all, by the controlling forces which had led these men out of Puritanism into the Episcopal Church. The same rigid, logical processes of Puritan thought, and the conclusions to which they led, were tempered and softened by the Southern influences into which they merged as the cold Arctic currents are tempered when merged into the sunlit waters of the gulf stream. There remained, however, the very distinct and pronounced Calvinistic and Puritan emphasis which produced, as is seen in the character of Dr. Keith, an austere type of personal piety.

Perhaps the most abiding contribution made by Puritanism to religious life and thought has been the influence of this system in the education of the human conscience. The disposition seen in modern education somewhat to over-emphasize the sense of delight and pleasure in the pursuit of knowledge and in the performance of duty, finds its needed corrective in the demands constantly made in the Puritan system that duty must be done whether it is pleasant or not, and that the right must be pursued regardless of the question of personal desire and personal pleasure.

With the Puritan the presumption was that if a thing was pleasant it was wrong, and that what tended to give happiness was to be regarded at least with deep suspicion.

It has been our privilege to read, not only a number of sermons and addresses which come out of this period and which were delivered by some of the men under consideration, but also the intimate personal journal of one of the earliest students in the Virginia Seminary. This journal is distinctly typical of the times. It reveals a morbid disposition to unrelenting and persistent introspection, and gives evidence on nearly every page of the fear of a great and sovereign God. Musty and yellow with age, the pages of this journal still retain the odor of the brimstone of Hell, and through it we catch the gleamings of an undying fire. The most painful solicitude is expressed for unrepentant members of the family who persist in lingering upon the dreadful verge of an eternal doom. The hope and the prayer that is breathed throughout these pages is for a personal salvation to be found only in and through the forgiving mercy of the personal Christ by the merits of His vicarious atonement.

The writer of this journal, after graduating in the Virginia Seminary, gave his life to the ministry in Virginia, and it is interesting to observe how Virginianized his Puritanism became under the softening influences of a changed environment. There breathes a larger hope and a sweeter tenderness, and the Church, first conceived of as a divinely appointed means for rescuing the perishing, merges into a congenial home for the mutual life and fellowship of the Father's children.

There was, however, contributed to the Seminary and to its students, as a result of this theological point of view, a dominating sense of the sovereignty of God and of the duty of man to subordinate his will to the divine purpose.

The theology taught by these early professors was unquestionably a modified form of Calvinism. The spirit of this theological and philosophical background had been instilled into these early teachers in the Seminary at Andover and other institutions in the North. Men of pronounced Puritan and Calvinistic convictions taught them the then prevalent theology of New England.

Among the means of grace preeminently emphasized by these early teachers was the preaching of God's great gospel of redemption. The Bible was presented as the final arbiter of thought, and its thorough mastery was demanded of the students. Here were to be found the eternal words of life. This was the message given for the salvation of mankind. These early professors had been taught to regard themselves as the prophets of God to their generation. In the Seminary they felt it to be their mission to raise up and train in the School of the Prophets those who would go forth to declare to men the whole counsel of God, and to preach the everlasting gospel as the chief means to salvation through Christ. It was this great passion of conviction, this compelling sense of prophetic mission, which, combined with the love of God and the passion for the saving of souls, made Dr. Reuel Keith the greatest preacher in Virginia during the long period of his residence here. This testimony is given concerning him by Dr. Philip Slaughter and others who knew him.

The place given in the teaching of that day and by these men to the atonement in God's plan of salvation was dominant and insistent. The traditional Puritan prejudice against the whole Roman system instinctively turned the attention of these early teachers away from any disposition to place a major emphasis upon the value of the sacramental system. The abuses which had gathered around the Roman Mass and the materialistic tendencies of sacerdotal teaching so dominated the minds of these early professors that to a large extent they obscured from their thought and attention the claims and benefits of the sacramental system of the Church. To them, other means of grace appeared to be supreme; and the fear lest the Church, and especially the students in the Seminary, might fall into the errors of the Roman system, hid from the vision of these men, and led them to hide from the vision of their students, the place and the importance of the sacraments in the divine economy of the Church. It therefore inevitably happened, as a result of the emphasis that was given to the Gospel and to preaching as the supreme means of salvation, and as a further result of the disposition to minimize the value of the sacramental system, that ritualism, especially as associated with the service of the Holy Communion, was deeply feared and earnestly protested against. The term "priest", because of its sacerdotal significance, was avoided, and the term "altar" was regarded as of dangerous significance, both being considered as savoring of popery.

Men and their systems must be judged in the light of the day in which they live. They move and have their being among the thought systems of their times. They are drawn by the larger luminaries, under whose orbits of influence they fall, and they, in turn, draw others whom circumstance and the providential movings of the Eternal Spirit bring within the circle of their impress. The American Church, regardless of the varied views of men of diverse schools of thought, has good reason to thank God that just at this time, and just in this way, there entered her life the convictions and the emphasis which were contributed by these sons of New England. They did not hold, nor did they teach, the whole truth. No man does. "We know in part and we prophesy in part". Elsewhere in the Church truth was being seen from other angles and taught with different emphasis. Had either view exclusively dominated the thought and life of the Church a narrow sectarian organization would have resulted, bearing within itself the seeds of schism and the certainty of ultimate extinction. A standardized Church, delimited by a one-sided conception of truth and a single, insistent, and exclusive emphasis, could never have won and preserved the marks of true catholicity. The emphasis placed in the early life of the Virginia Seminary upon the indispensable necessity of personal piety, upon the compelling claim of duty, upon the place and importance of the Holy Scriptures, upon the value, the dignity, and need of the prophetic office as a means of bringing men into God's Kingdom and extending that Kingdom everywhere, the fear of and warnings against the materialistic tendencies of sacerdotalism and of extreme ritual, were contributions needed to enrich and safeguard the life of the Church; and they have been given through the Virginia Seminary largely because of the influences which came from the North through the life and teaching of these early Puritan-trained professors.

They were, however, devoted Churchmen. The Church of their adoption was the Church of their convictions. They loved her and gave their lives for her upbuilding and extension. It is indeed remarkable, in the light of the known tendencies of men to swing from one extreme to another upon entering from outside the ministry of the Episcopal Church, that these men, nearly all of whom had been born and reared in the midst of non-conformity, should have remained upon the level on which they laid the foundations of the Theological Seminary in Virginia.

In their theological convictions they were strongly evangelical, and continued to think of the Church as Protestant against Rome, even when they became Episcopal in protest against the other extremes of non-conformity. They also continued non-ritualistic. It is true, good Dr. Packard even presumes to call Bishop Meade "narrow" because of the aversion to the Cross as a symbol, which the Bishop continued to cherish long after his Princeton training had ended. "For," says Dr. Packard, "he was in some respects narrow, as most strong men are apt to be. After the chapel was built at the Seminary, the pews, as designed by the architect, were finished with a cross at the top of the pew end. They stood so for some time, when on one of his visits they struck him unpleasantly, and he ordered them to be sawed off. This was done, and the chapel was a scene of direful destruction, with these crosses covering the floor. Strange to say, in the Psalter, (which was being read by William S. Perry, afterwards Bishop of Iowa) the Sunday after this was done, was the verse, Ps. lxxiv, 7: 'But now they break down all

the carved work thereof with axes and hammers'. Bishop
Meade mellowed very much in his later years, and I do not
think he would have done this fifteen years later."

It is somewhat remarkable, in the light of this incident,
that Mr. Meade survived the day of his ordination to become
a Bishop. He was ordained Presbyter in St. Paul's Church,
Alexandria, on January 10, 1814, by Bishop Claggett of
Maryland. On that occasion Bishop Claggett wore his
mitre, "which," says Dr. Packard, "he put on at a house
some distance from the Church and walked through the
streets". As he entered the Church his stentorian voice
and appearance so startled the quiet Virginia congregation
that one lady was overcome and had to be carried from the
Church. With the mitre gleaming across the Potomac
from the Maryland diocese, and with Bishop Ravenscroft
leading North Carolina to view the Holy Catholic Church
from the exalted heights of Valle Crucis and declaring that
Dr. Keith, "knew no more about the Church than the Bishop's horse", the Virginia Seminary felt convinced that *her*
mission was to give another emphasis and a contrary witness, and continued to do so.

It is interesting also to note that the witness which was
given in the early years of the Seminary (and which continues to be given) as to the unique and essential divinity
of our Lord and Saviour Jesus Christ was accentuated by
the fact that these early New England professors had come
in close contact with Unitarianism. Dr. Packard makes
mention of the impressions made upon his mind by Emerson
and the teachings of Channing, and remarks that "there is
something inexpressibly sad in the contemplation of a body
of men of high culture, generous human sympathies, refined
tastes, and disciplined characters, self-contained, calm,
serene, looking forth upon the world of struggling, suffering
men, from a lofty philosophic plane, and offering them
nothing better after nineteen Christian centuries, than the
speculations of Plato".

The review which Dr. Packard gives of the distinctive
tenets of the Congregational theology of his day as compared
with the teachings of the Episcopal Church gives evidence of
the careful processes of thought and investigation which led

him to his final convictions and into membership and the ministry of this Church.

A further influence which entered the Seminary from the North was the profound conviction which these men brought with them as to the duty of the Church to give the Gospel of Salvation to all mankind. Andover, which was the dominant theological institution in New England, sent out during the first fifty years one hundred and thirty-five foreign missionaries, "many of whom were eminent", says Dr. Packard, "as explorers, translators, and preachers, and as founders of great missionary enterprises". Both Dr. Keith and Dr. Packard, while students at Andover, had come under this strong missionary influence, and had been brought to share the conviction that the giving of the Gospel of Christ to others is an indispensable consequence of truly receiving that Gospel and the Christ of Whom the Gospel bears witness. This conviction found expression in the teaching of the Seminary from the very beginning. It led Dr. Keith to give his son to China and Dr. Packard his daughter to Brazil, and helped kindle the devotion which sent Boone to China, Payne to Africa, and Channing Moore Williams to Japan, and called many others to offer themselves as heralds of the Christ in the far lands to which they went to proclaim the Gospel of Salvation. "Those were the men and such were the dominant influences which they brought with them from Puritan New England into the Life of the Virginia Seminary. "What grand men," wrote Dr. Wilmer, "the North furnished us, and what good Southerners they became".

From the Rev. Dr. Edward L. Goodwin, Historiographer of the Diocese of Virginia, we have received the following historical note relative to the reason for the presence of the Puritan influence which was dominant in the life of the Virginia Seminary and in the Church in Virginia:

"Bishop Meade was indeed a Puritan, in the best and original meaning of that much abused word. But he did not derive his puritanism from Princeton—it was his by inheritance and was learned at his mother's knee. As far as we can gather from his letters and other writings he never attributed an ecclesiastical opinion and hardly a religious impression of his own to Princeton. After his graduation he returned for a short time to read theology, chiefly because of the advantages afforded by its library. He remained but about three months, most of which time he was desperately ill with typhoid fever. The Theological School had not then been established at Princeton.

"The origin of what is called Virginia Churchmanship has never been fully traced. To ascribe it to Wilberforce's tracts or Parson Jarrett's preaching is most inadequate. There was a deep undercurrent of evangelical piety, with its element of spiritual independence tempered by an inherited and invincible loyalty to the Church, which ran throughout our Colonial history. It was the Puritanism of Latimer and of Hooker and of the Books of Homilies, of Sandys and Ferrar, Hunt and Whitaker and, I take it, of the best of the early clergymen. But it was kept alive chiefly by godly women whose piety was fed on the Bible and Prayer Book almost exclusively but who handed down a religious tradition which was more potent than the Parsons' sermons. It shows itself again and again in our Colonial history and came out strongly in the Revolutionary period in such men as R. H. Lee and Mason, Washington and Pendleton. But when our old ecclesiastical system had fallen into ruins it came forth in its full strength in our Meades and Dunns and Grammers and McGuires, few of whom had ever been out of Virginia, but who were the pupils of their mothers and grandmothers. This Puritan tradition may be variously described. It had a touch of Calvinism and of stalwart resoluteness that lent itself to austerity, but its chief characteristic was that it produced saintliness; and its strength was shown when we recall the opposite tendencies with which it had to contend and which it finally so largely overcame.

"When Doctors Keith and Packard and Andrews and the rest came down from New England they found in Virginia, and elsewhere in the South, this purer type of Puritanism to which they had little to add by way of enrichment but from which they had something to learn, and they learned it gladly. Their personal influence was unbounded, but it is easy to ascribe to them too exclusive a part in determining the character of the theology and Churchmanship of the Seminary. That was preordained."

To the influences from the North introduced into the Seminary through the professors who have been mentioned must be added the further influence exerted by the large number of Northern students who entered the Seminary. Many of these were drawn to Virginia through the former acquaintance which they had enjoyed with the early professors in their homes, and in the colleges of the North. Two of the three men first aided by the Education Society were from the North. They continued to come. The presence in the Seminary of Phillips Brooks of Massachusetts, Henry C. Potter of New York, and many who preceded and followed them here have helped to save the Institution from becoming narrow and sectional in its tendencies and outlook.

Another chapter might be written on the influence of the Virginia Seminary upon the North. The Seminary recognizes her debt of gratitude to the North, and has ever sought to pay it. She has returned the Northern men who have come to her for instruction to their native dioceses imbued with her spirit and bearing the impress of her convictions, and has given many of her southern-born graduates to minister in the states and section of the country that furnished her with her early professors. The Virginia Seminary has also through her teaching and influence made contributions both constraining and constructive in the life of the American Church. Not alone in the South but also in the North and West her distinct influence has been felt and cordially recognized.

It may truly be said that she has trained these men in the large Catholic spirit which characterized the sympathies and comprehension of her early teachers, especially the great Dr. Sparrow. They have been men impressed, men convinced, but seldom men standardized. They have gone from Virginia to be leaders, prophets, priests, missionaries, and to become Bishops, bearing with them an impress which has made them fundamentally true to the Church and her teachings. The Seminary, however, has left them unbound in their freedom to express the truth as God gives them grace to see and know their duty, leaving them liberty to present and color it with the temperament, disposition and convictions of their varied personalties. She has followed her sons along their chosen paths through different schools of Churchmanship with an unfailing love, though at times she has looked upon them with perplexed and wondering gaze and marveled at the altitudes to which some of them have climbed and at the unbounded latitude which has sometimes characterized the teaching of others among her graduates.

This unstereotyped Churchmanship of the sons of the Virginia Seminary is due in large measure to the vision and faith and to the wide perspective of truth which characterized the founders and first teachers of the Seminary. They came down from the far North, at the call of Virginia, to help the students attending this Seminary of the whole Church located within her borders to seek the truth with open minds and consecrated hearts, and to teach them to be "Protestant against all error of man," whether of Romanism or rationalism, but "Catholic for every truth of God", "come whence it may and cost what it will".

SECTION IV

CHAPTER XII

THE FACULTY MEETINGS

REV. W. A. R. GOODWIN, D. D.

Faculty meetings in colleges and universities are not usually occasions of refreshment and delight to the students. They are ordinarily held behind closed doors and are generally devoted to the consideration of the problems of administration or of discipline. The earnest desire of every student is that he may remain as far away from them as possible. If, perchance, the student finds himself face to face with the faculty, the event may be long remembered but the memories are not apt to be the happiest of his academic experiences.

The term "Faculty Meeting" in the light and history of the Virginia Theological Seminary is of very different significance. It suggests memories which are, perhaps, the richest and most deeply cherished.

The bell rings, and we remember, if we had not remembered it before, that it is "Faculty Meeting" night. We gather in Prayer Hall. The place itself is holy ground. This room, though unconsecrated by the formal service of the Church, is consecrated by memories and associations which make their appeal to every man who is privileged to be a member of the Institution. From the walls there look down upon us the portraits of the men who have gone from the Seminary to the far-off and lonely places of the earth. Minor and Savage and Messenger and Holcomb and Colden Hoffman speak of the spirit of consecration to the Christ which led them to their martyrdom in Africa. Payne, Boone Williams, Hill of Greece, and many others, suggest the sacrifice and service of the far-gone years in the mission field of the Church; while Kinsolving and Meem, Morris, Brown and others recall the survival of this spirit as expressed in the light of the Seminary of later years.

PRAYER HALL

ST. GEORGE'S HALL
The Seminary Home of Phillips Brooks

And so now, as we meet in "Prayer Hall", where for many years the morning and evening services of the students were held, we seem to be in fellowship with the spirits of those who have once been in our place and are now calling us from higher places to a life of service, and of sacrifice.

And now it is Faculty Meeting night. The professors are sitting together facing the student body. There were not so many of them in the olden days as there are now. A hymn is sung and informal prayers are said. The spirit of devotion, deep and personal, pervades the meeting.

The Faculty Meetings were entirely different from the services of the Church. They were more personal, more informal, and more direct. They were different also from the meetings which the students had with the professors in the class room. There, the academic note predominated. The lectures, while they had reference to life and life's ministry, were related, also, to examinations at the end of the session and before the chaplains, and had to do with text books and the intellectual mastery of the subjects considere d We felt that we had come to the Seminary to attend the classes, but we felt in Faculty Meeting that the Seminary had come to us.

It was the custom then, and is doubtless so at present, for two of the professors to speak to us. This they did in a most direct, personal, and helpful way. The subjects presented were of a varied nature. The purpose seemed ever to be to spiritually relate us to some vital aspect of truth. The professors did not hold themselves at all to the subject matter of their Seminary course. They seemed to speak as the Spirit prompted, either of the deep thoughts of God in their relation to the practical problems of life, or of the various aspects of personal relationship to God and the personal religion which grew out of this relationship. They spoke of faith, of prayer, of the Cross, of consecration, and of the quality and kind of service which these inspired. Sometimes the older professors became reminiscent, and spoke to us of students of the by-gone days and of the sacrifices which they had made in after years in planting the Cross to mark the bounds between light and darkness and to point the way into the darkness for those who would go to enlarge the bounds of life and light. Sometimes they spoke to us of our student life and of our relationship with each other during our Seminary days; sometimes they led us by anticipation into the pulpit and the parish which lay ahead of us, visited with us at the bedsides of the sick and taught us how to bring consolation to those who mourned, gave us warnings of pitfalls which needed to be avoided, and ever pointed to the silent places where they told us we must go and go constantly to meet and hold communion with our risen Lord.

Long to be remembered were these Faculty Meeting nights. Out of them grew the closest bonds of fellowship between the faculty and the students, and a consciousness of comradeship in life's experiences as well as in life's noblest ideals.

The writer remembers the Faculty Meetings of the period of transition. Two of the older professors still remained as "Links among the days to knit the generations each to each". The dear old "Rab" was still with us,—the beloved Dr. Packard, rich and mellowed by life's long experiences and by his many years of close converse with God with Whom he walked as with a friend. And Dr. Cornelius Walker was also with us then. He was a man unhardened by the ripeness and fullness of accurate scholarship. Firm in his convictions, he was, of all men, the most tolerant and charitable. The stainless purity of his soul made his countenance, at times, appear almost transfigured by the light of the land whose portals lay so near after the long years of an earthly pilgrimage. These two professors spoke to us on these occasions as citizens of two worlds. They knew the world in which they had long lived, but they also knew the world invisible, spiritual, and eternal into which they were so soon to enter.

And then, there was Dr. Nelson, the friend, the pastor, the man not alone of scholarly learning, but of common sense. His talks were always practical, touched, as were Dr. Packard's, with a gentle sense of humor. Dr. Crawford, who had only recently come to the Seminary, was so different from the others, and yet with a difference welcomed and needed in the life of the Seminary. He had come from a different environment. His home had been in the North and his experiences had been colored by contact with men of affairs. He knew what the business world expected of the minister and the kind and quality of training essential to those called to minister to modern life. His devotion to the roots of Hebrew words which he loved to trace through underground ramifications stretching back to the patriarchal days had not chilled the genial current of his soul, and his talks, while practical, were also spiritual. Dr. Grammer had also been recently added to the Faculty. It was always a delight to hear him. Truth gleamed and sparkled from his mind like light from a diamond. His addresses in Faculty Meetings came to us with the passion and eloquence born of a supreme devotion to the truth. Some men absorb truth, some reflect truth, and some make truth contagious with the glow and light of Spirit-illumined personality. Dr. Grammer's Faculty Meeting talks seemed always to inspire in those who heard him a desire to "know the truth".

There was no roll call of students at the Faculty Meeting. Attendance was entirely voluntary, but there was always the will to be present and we never knew of a student who wilfully absented himself from these meetings.

The members of the Faculty seemed ever to have felt a deep sense of responsibility in the selection and preparation of the topics presented and the memory of the talks which had been previously given, and the anticipation, which was never disappointed, of hearing addresses which we could not afford to miss, prompted us always to be present.

Few students could, perhaps, after the lapse of many years write an outline of the subjects presented to us by the Faculty at these meetings. Truth transfigured by light celestial often transcends logical analysis and defies intellectual outlines. The appeal was not primarily to the intellect, but rather to the personality. The addresses passed into the very soul and spirit of our being. As the years have gone by outlines have vanished, but the memory of these meetings remains; and many a rough and rugged path, which sloped steep through the darkness, has been easier to climb, many trials and difficulties have been easier to face, many a Cross has been easier to bear, and full often stern duty has been lifted into the realm of privilege as a result of the something indefinable and yet ineradicable which came to us in these Faculty Meetings on the Thursday evenings of the long ago.

The Southern Churchman of June 4, 1846, quotes from the Washington correspondent of the "Witness" the following note relative to the Seminary Faculty Meeting: "On one evening of the week there is a meeting of the professors and students for prayer and exhortation conducted by the professors in which the duties and responsibilities of all in the present and future are the subjects under consideration, and many an individual now in the ministry testifies to the invaluable and blessed character of these services. In them the students have been so animated and encouraged and convinced in their purpose of faithful service for the Master as to have ever after looked back upon them with the greatest gratitude and interest. I remember upon being permitted to read the diary of the lamented Duy to have noticed his frequent and full references to these Faculty Meetings. His spirit seems to have been there more deeply stirred within him than under any other circumstances."

The Rev. Dr. Packard, writing of the Rev. Dr. May, says, "he was at his best at Faculty Meetings. There his 'tongue dropped manna'. He drew largely from his own experiences as a pastor, which were varied and fruitful. Many of the old students look back to these meetings as one of the greatest privileges of their lives, and, in the doctrinal, experimental, and spiritual addresses there delivered, found the most useful preparation for their ministry". Dr. Walker said, "With Dr. May it seemed to involve as little effort to extemporize as it did to converse; and he could upon very brief notice and without appearance of anxiety, be exceedingly profitable. It had indeed been with great effort, as his pupils afterwards ascertained from him, that he had attained this freedom."

Of these meetings Dr. Packard says, "The Faculty Meeting held every Thursday evening in Prayer Hall was a gathering of all the students with the three professors, when a few prayers were said, and each professor gave a short instruction or meditation. This was a practical searching appeal to young men preparing for the ministry, or a lofty monologue upon some great theme of Christian thought or life."

"With still deeper reverential feelings," says Bishop Bedell, "do I recall the Thursday evening Faculty Meetings, when our Professors met us in the basement to pray with and for us, and to remind us, week by week, to seek for higher attainments in the Christian life. They were greatly profitable hours."

Dr. Walker, speaking of the missionary spirit of the Seminary says, "that what perhaps most contributed to this, as to all spiritual life and effort in the Seminary, was the Faculty Meetings which have continued to the present time. No specific allusion is made to such meetings as having occurred during the first four years of Seminary life in Alexandria, though it is hardly possible that, with such men as Dr. Wilmer and Dr. Keith, something of the sort was not instituted. But its positive existence and influence during the second period of the first fourteen years on "The Hill" are undoubted. The peculiar function of these Faculty Meetings has ever been to bring out and emphasize the truth, not so much of the theological or ecclesiastical, as of the spiritual work of the Christian ministry. The students were taught that they were preparing for the ministry and must prepare themselves spiritually, continuing more and more to manifest God in their lives, as this was the supreme requirement without which the ministry of any man would be a failure. The personal consecration of the knowledge gained in the classroom not only to the Master's work, but to the spiritual upbuilding of the student as well, and the communication of his power and influence to others, were, and have been, urged and insisted upon at the Thursday night Faculty Meetings. It was thus an occasion of great inspiration to both teachers and students, one which reminded them of their most sacred obligations and privileges, and sent them forth uplifted and better fitted to realize their ideals. This Thursday night service generated the spiritual power of the Virginia Seminary. Its results can not be overestimated and it is to be hoped that its continuance may be permanent. The words of wisdom, of love and of power from the lips of Reuel Keith, of Joseph Packard, of

William Sparrow and of James May, spoken at these meetings, have fulfilled this high purpose in the past."*

In The Southern Churchman of March 5th, 1874, there is an unsigned communication, relative to a talk given by Dr. Sparrow at a Faculty Meeting, January 31st, 1867. The introductory letter and the notes of Dr. Sparrow's address are given as follows:

"Our beloved Dr. Sparrow 'being dead yet speaketh', and probably nothing that he said while living would have borne the stamp of having come warm and glowing from his heart more than his soul-stirring talks to the students of the Seminary in the Faculty Meeting, could they but have been preserved. The writer while a student took notes of some of these addresses of Dr. Sparrow. They are almost verbatim reports, made at the moment while the Doctor was speaking, and may therefore be relied upon as accurate. I find the following remark in my notebook, and add to it one of these reports of a talk by Dr. Sparrow.

"January 31, 1867. Dr. Sparrow was feeble, as he said after the meeting, but was earnest and exceedingly warmed up in the delivery of these remarks. His manner added much to their force and beauty and they were very impressive. The subject upon which the Doctor was speaking was 'The Uncertainty of Life'. He began thus;

"We are familiar with the remark that our religion is full of paradoxes. A paradox is a statement that runs contrary to received opinion, that contains an apparent condition. Yet the paradox may contain essential truth. The remark probably came from the ancient writers on Christianity. From the days of Horsely at least it has been customary to talk of the beatitudes as paradoxes.

"FIRST: In some of them the slightest explanation will enable us to catch the truth contained in them. SECOND: In others we find it by long induction from recognized truths. When they are thus received and understood, the mind counts them as no longer paradoxes. THIRD: But there is still another class which in order to be natural and congenial to our minds must become so by personal experience. They will always be 'a hard saying' until so understood.

* Dr. Walker's Manuscript Record.

One of the doctrines most commonly received might be put popularly under the second class, partly under the third, and that is that we are justified and saved by faith, and yet that good works are necessary to salvation, so there could be no salvation without them. It is by faith only and yet, 'without holiness no man shall see the Lord.' How are these two statements to be reconciled to each other, and dovetailed together so that there shall be no antagonism between them?

"The explanation lies, first, in the nature of faith, and secondly, in the necessity that our minds should receive these two truths simply as fact, stubborn fact. It began clear back in the days of the apostles, so far from making void the law, we 'establish the law' by faith. This is St. Paul's reasoning. This was shown in the Church which they established. The heathen had to acknowledge that the members of those Churches lived far better than they did, but still, I believe, that this paradox can not be cleared up as a logical thing until a man has experienced it. As soon as he has realized his lost and helpless condition and has cried 'nothing but Christ' then he begins to see that there is no paradox here, that all is perfectly natural and just as his highest intelligence would have it.

"I might give long lists of these paradoxes. Many have been enumerated, but I will mention only one, which concerns us in our peculiar position as having come out from the world and as having a peculiar spiritual object and end which the world knows nothing of. We come here (to the Seminary), under the impression that the eternal verities of the other world are the great realities, under the impression that we live under the care of our reconciled father in Jesus, under the impression that we have no lease on our life, no assurance that we shall see tomorrow, that it is with God and may never be ours, and if we allow ourselves to slide into the idea that we shall have tomorrow, we slide into an error that is contrary to the mind of God.

"It is remarkable that death has seldom entered the doors of this Institution. In my day, not at all. But there have been those who have died after they left here. This reminds me of one, a precious man he was, a wondrous man, such was the character of his mind, so mature, so well balanced.

I used to flatter myself that he would do great things, but after laboring one year he was cut down in three days. Oh, how that family mourned, even after twenty years. Those friends who were so bound up in him were anticipating what never came to pass. We, also, may be looking forward to usefulness, but remember that God does not have need of us. He can take us away at any time and he often takes the best one in the flock, just to teach us this fact, that he can do without us. This truth is that the present is ours, the future is not. How is it to be reconciled with the ordinary duties of life? Does it not seem inconsistent to call men to pursue long years of study, while at the same time they are told that they may not be alive tomorrow? This is something that would be foolishness to the natural man as a natural man, but Christians are not natural men. A different spirit actuates them. God tells us that we may die at any moment. He also tells us to be 'diligent in business'. It is the principle of faith that reconciled them and this principle submitting to His declaration, makes the whole thing plain. We can go forward without fear, brethren, I speak from experience. I think many err in not putting these two things together. We certainly are not living rightly without living in view of eternity every day, and at the same time, we are not living rightly if we do not live as if we were to live 'three score years and ten'. God requires us thus to view and thus to plan life, to cultivate ourselves for usefulness and yet as if we were to die the next day. This would be a paradox in natural things.

"But how are we to plan life? For honor and aggrandisement and a good station? Oh no! But as a term of service for God's glory. Then how consistent this will be with the thought that our life is hanging by a thread. This would enable us as ministers, to pass through life with the spirit of John the Baptist 'the voice of one crying in the wilderness,' but a voice soon to pass away. It becomes us, of all men, to take a proper view of life. Most of those at colleges lay their plans with reference to a future. We should ascend the mountain top and look out on life. We need the continual shining of truth upon our lives and this we can not have without much prayer and pains. God grant that we may be willing to pay the price for such a treasure."

From the midst of a busy life, and in the forty-seventh year of my ministry, I am calling up the time when I went to the Seminary, and the early days of my life there. For four years I had been a cannoneer in a fighting battery of artillery which was in the thick of all the campaigns of the army of Northern Virginia. After this very strenuous experience, the so different, quiet life on "The Hill" impressed me very deeply. All of its details and incidents took strong hold of me, so that they stand out in my memory as vivid and as clear cut as though they were of yesterday. Out of this material I may, perchance, make a picture which will interest and entertain my fellow Alumni, the sons of the old Seminary, who, wherever they are scattered through the world, love the dear old Mother. Everything of her history and life is dear to them. They have tender memories of their own times on "The Hill." The reminiscences of a time, other than their own, but, in the same well-remembered scenes, will appeal to them. They will understand, perhaps enjoy, —but to my story.

I went to the Seminary in September, 1866. I left my home in Danville, Virginia, in company with Charles Clifton Penick (in after years the Bishop of Cape Palmas, Africa), another candidate from my father's parish. We left at midnight, Monday, the 19th, to reach the Seminary the day before the opening of the session, on the following Thursday. We left Richmond the next afternoon, and caught the boat from Acquia Creek to Alexandria and Washington (the railroad from Alexandria to Quantico, now "The Washington Southern", had not as yet been built). As the boat passed Alexandria before day break we went on to Washington, to return to Alexandria by daylight. Arrived at Washington, we left the boat, and walked up into the City. Having large ideas of what the Capitol would be like we were much amazed by the sight of several hogs wallowing in a big mudhole in the middle of Seventh Street, almost in front of the Smithsonian Institute. We let them wallow, and went on with our sight-seeing. Later we took the boat back to Alexandria, and then met my father, Rev. George W. Dame, who had been to Baltimore, and had come to join us here, and to see us settled at the Seminary. After some purchases, we three started to walk to the Seminary carrying a lamp, a can of oil, a blacking brush, a box of blacking, two satchels, and other articles proper to new settlers. We climbed Shooter's Hill, took the short cut to the left, and came at last to the front door of Aspinwall Hall. Here, not seeing a soul anywhere, we stopped. My father said that if we would wait where we were, he would investigate. He went through the hall, out to the back door. Here he came upon Miss Cornelia Jones, the Matron, who asked him if he had come to be a student. He was a venerable looking man with very white hair and a white beard flowing down to his waist. He replied, "No, Madam, not yet, but I have two boys out here who want to be." He brought us out and introduced us to Miss Jones who received us graciously and said that she thought we were of a more suitable age for students. My father then left us to journey home.

We were assigned rooms in the third story of "Aspinwall". "Uncle Nathan," the good old darkey who cleaned the rooms and toted water to students for so many generations, soon fixed up our rooms with the simple furniture, proper to the time, and we moved in, filled our lamp, set up our "penates" and considered ourselves "located."

Advised that it was the correct thing, we first went to report to Dr. Packard, who received us kindly. He, however, drew such a picture of Seminary life and its requirements, that when we came out, we sat disconsolate on the hillside near by and debated whether we hadn't better go home and go to hoeing corn than to try to get into the ministry. However, after much discouraging talk our manhood came to our aid and more cheerful counsels prevailed. We agreed that other men "mostly humans" had got in. We could do what others had done! We determined to stick to the bitter end, and, to use Penick's strong rhetoric "to pull through or bust a trace." Well, we didn't "bust any traces" but we "pulled through" in the end. I reckon ours was a common experience. Many of the other fellows told me afterward, that they had many misgivings, and many downcast hours at the beginning of their Seminary life. Some of them said that they came near giving it up, leaving the Seminary in despair. The perils and difficulties of the service were, as in our case, rubbed in a little too hard for raw recruits, by the old veterans. Maybe, however, it made us humble, and put us on our mettle, and did us good. I know that I felt mighty "poor in spirit" at the time.

Well! Having decided to stick, we walked back over to the Seminary to meet our fellow students, who were coming in rapidly all this day, and the next morning, in time to matriculate at twelve o'clock Thursday, the opening day. The incoming men proved to be pleasant, companionable fellows and they met and greeted each other most cordially. We all quickly felt at home with one another, although nearly all of us had been utter strangers to each other to that hour. I think with pleasant memory of that gathering in which I met, for the first time, the men who were to be my daily associates for the next three years, and all of whom were destined to become my valued friends in after years, and some of them the closest friends of my life; friends whose loving brotherhood all through the passing years have been a source of inestimable pleasure and blessing to me. It was a noble band of men. Every man save one had served as a soldier, through the war in the Confederate Army, and each had come here consecrated of heart, strong of purpose, to train for a chosen life work in the Special Service of his Master Christ. Yes, deeply earnest was each and every one. Their work at the Seminary and later service in the Ministry fully proved that. Not one of those men has ever erred from the faith, or from righteousness of life as a Christian man and minister. Not one has forsaken the ministry until death or disability forced him. I think this a record worth recording. It meant a band of faithful hearts destined for faithful service to the end.

When we all had assembled, there were twenty-six students, these were as follows: William A. Alrich, Thomas U. Dudley, Horace Edwin Hayden, Walter Q. Hullihen, Nicholas H. Lewis, of the Senior Class; James B. Craighill, Edmund W. Hubard, Kinloch Nelson, George W. Peterkin, Benjamin E. Reed, James H. Williams, Edward Wooton of the Middle Class; William J. Boone, Pendleton Brooke, William Meade Dame, Otis A. Glazebrook, James E. Hammond, Sewell S. Hepburn, William H. Laird, Robert J. McBryde, Haslett McKim, Charles Clifton Penick, Henry T. Sharp, Charles Yancey Steptoe, William Hoxton, and George T. Fitzhugh, in the "Preparatory Department."

After we had matriculated, and after the classes had been organized, we got down to ordered work, and the regular routine of Seminary life began. The seniors and middles, "broken in" in the session before, knew the ropes, but we poor freshmen had a hard time getting down to study. We had led a disciplined life for years, but it had been in far different surroundings, and occupations from this. They rushed us at the Hebrew, then came the tug of war. In the other studies, where we could read about things in English, we thought we might do. But this! Well! For a time, we agreed that digging up Hebrew roots was harder work than digging entrenchments, or standing up in the firing line. But we toiled away, and, gradually, it grew easier, and finally we won distinction. I rather think that, in his heart, Professor Packard rated a man's worth by the way he took to Hebrew. It seems that the previous class had failed badly in this study. Our class worked at it hard, and so won the Doctor's heart. We came to be known as "The Synagogue" and we were very chesty over it!

After the way of all students we soon devised suitable names for the Faculty—Drs. Sparrow, Packard and Walker, it being Dr. Walker's first year. Dr. Packard had been named "The Rabbi" before our time, and we adopted this, as fit. For Dr. Sparrow, the dean, our military ideas suggested "The Captain". Dr. Walker, whose name was Cornelius, we promptly dubbed "The Centurion"; and thence-

forth, save in addressing them, these sages were never indicated except as "The Captain" or "The Rabbi" or "The
Centurion". One day a student meeting Dr. Sparrow
suddenly, in his confusion, called him "Captain" Sparrow to
his face. The student nearly had a fit, but the Doctor
laughed heartily. "Hah," he said, "that is what they call
me, is it?" Perhaps this was the occasion of the "Rab's"
complacent remark; "Mi-yah! I'm glad the students never
found a nick-name for me!"

We came to have a sincere reverence for these godly men.
Day by day we sat at their feet, and honestly tried to receive
what they had to give us. They taught us some Theology,
and Hebrew, and Church History, but they taught us something far more valuable. In our close association with them,
in and out of the class-room, they taught us the beauty of
holiness, inspired us with a sense of the solemnity of our calling, and impressed us with the strength of a sane and manly
type of religion. Above all they planted deeply in our
hearts and minds, never I trust to be uprooted, this thought,
that a personal Christian character is the highest preparation
and the vital necessity, for a truly successful ministry; that
he who preaches the Gospel must, above all things, live the
Gospel; he must be a good man if he will make men good.
These old saints have long ago "gone in to stand before their
Master," but they bore this clear, strong witness, and impressed this thought upon many generations of ministers.
And this was the greatest thing that we ever learned at the
Seminary! Because they learned this, and because they
took heed to it, the record of the sons of the Seminary is, what
it is, "almost stainless in the matter of moral character."
In the hearts of us to whom our teachers so faithfully taught
this truth, their memory is as "ointment poured forth." We
thank God for them!

Outside the regular work of the course we filled in our
spare time with such recreations, of various kinds, as were
within our reach. We got up a baseball club, and a good
one. Every suitable afternoon most of us indulged in this
strong exercise. Once we got the High School boys to
challenge a Washington Club with the private understanding
that our Club was to play the challenged team, for it was

not thought proper for a Theological Seminary to issue a
challenge. In this way we flanked that difficulty, and we
licked that Washington Club "out of their boots" and took
over the brand new ball they had brought with them as the
prize of victory. They were much humiliated because they
were "licked by a lot of preachers", as they put it. Nevertheless, it was a clear beat. The late Bishop of Cape Palmas,
Dr. Penick, Bishop Peterkin of West Virginia, and the writer
were the three "fielders" in that game, and the Washington
Club never once got a ball outside of the line. They found that
they were up against a "special brand" of preachers, and
they spread abroad our fame as players. It got too public and
it was thought that we had best not play any more match
games with outsiders. We received challenges from several
other clubs, but we saved them a licking by refusing to play.
We got great fun and good fun from our baseball.

Then we revived "The Rhetorical Society" which met
Friday nights. At the meetings of this society the students
strove for forensic honors, in debates, essays, recitations,
and the like, stimulated by the presence of the professors
and the ladies of the neighborhood. It gave us some good
fun and got the raw edge off the tongues of the greenhorns.

We also had Class Prayer Meetings every Saturday night
in which each class, to itself, met not only for prayer and meditation but also to discuss our work in general as well as to
throw light upon the peculiar difficulties of each member.
We helped one another all we could by sympathy and counsel.
These meetings drew very close the bond of brotherly affection between us, and were a strong force and help to us
all in our spiritual life.

And what shall I say of that institution so well remembered by all Seminary men,—the Faculty Meeting! The
purpose of this meeting was the spiritual uplift of the students in their personal religion. And what an inestimable
influence for good it was to us all! It was indeed an "instruction in righteousness." Every Thursday night we
assembled in Prayer Hall. The three professors, seated in
front, a brief service, then seated in their chairs they spoke
to us, in turn, first Dr. Walker, then Dr. Packard, and Dr.
Sparrow closing, this was the order. They had selected

some theme, bearing upon the personal Christian life, and all spoke on that, striving to bring out all that was profitable to us. Those three old Christian men, ripe in knowledge of the truth, and in experience of life spoke to us as to their younger brethren, simply, affectionately, earnestly, trying to show us clearly the power and beauty of truth, and to guide our inexperienced feet into the way of peace and of consecrated service to Christ. Those Faculty Meetings were the most solemn, impressive, and fruitful services in our Seminary life, and their blessed results went with those students through all their future ministry.

Only one interruption of the solemnity of the Faculty Meetings ever occurred. One night, one of the fellows, wearied by the toil of the day, went to sleep and had the night-mare. He leaped to his feet calling out aloud. I don't know what he thought had him, but he was much excited. It startled us all. I recall especially the look on Dr. Sparrow's face. His eye-brows were very mobile, and when that fellow yelled out, the Doctor's big bushy eye-brows went up nearly off his head, and he gazed with open-eyed astonishment. We pulled the sleeper down, woke him up, got him quiet, and the proceedings went on.

During this year, 1866, we revived the Missionary Society of the Seminary, which met once a fortnight. To these meetings all the people on "The Hill" were invited. Appointed men studied the mission field, and read papers on the various parts of the work, which we discussed. This kept us in interested and intelligent touch with the work of our Church in all parts of the world. We also collected such money as we could for their work. From time to time we heard returned foreign missionaries speak of their fields, notably Bishop Payne of Africa, who stirred a deep interest among the students. What was wrought by, and in connection with that Missionary Society, would be hard to estimate. It is a simple statement of facts, that from the first, the Seminary has founded all the foreign missions of our Church in China, in Japan, in Africa, in Greece, and in Brazil, and has to a large extent kept them manned to this day. The men who began and continued all this work went forth from our Seminary, and they got the impulse that sent them at the Seminary, and largely from what they heard at our Missionary Society. There they had forced strongly upon them, the Master's Word; "The field is the world;" and they accepted it, and many of them toiled and died on distant shores "for the testimony of Jesus". And what hath not God wrought by them for increase of His kingdom in the uttermost ends of the earth!

It was customary on Wednesday nights to have a sermon delivered by a member of the Senior Class to the students in Prayer Hall. The sermon was criticized by Dr. Walker, the Professor of "Pulpit Eloquence," for the benefit of the victim, and of us, his fellow sufferers. Once he called down Dudley, who had a voice like a trumpet, about a "nasal intonation" in his voice, and advised Dudley to cure himself of it, as he had done. At another time, a "Senior" very little of stature, whose head we could hardly see, as he stood behind the lecturn, rose on tiptoe and gave his text! "And there were giants in those days!" We remembered the fact more than the sermon. We thought the race had shrunk. That Wednesday night performance, because of the time it took from the student's work, and because of the weakening of our minds by hearing such preaching, and also because of the resentful consciousness of being "practiced on" by these fellows, who "had not got the shell off their heads," we thought "cost more than it came to." The preachers hated it, with more reason did the hearers. We survived, that is all.

The Mission Stations deserve special notice. The Mission Stations were intended to give services to the people in the surrounding country and also to give practical training in reading the service, in speaking, and in pastoral work to the students. They were located from two to six miles, in different directions, from the Seminary. Each Station was in special charge of two or three men, appointed, or volunteers, who were responsible for the services at their respective stations. After dinner on Sunday these men started off to walk to their respective stations, getting back to supper, and night service in the Chapel.

The Stations of "Sharon", "Olivet", and the County Almshouse had been established years before. The two first have each a chapel. The services were held in the Almshouse for the inmates, and employees and were in charge of George S. Fitzhugh, who said that he could always get a good congregation when it was raining too hard for the inmates to get outdoors.

In our time we started a station and built a chapel at "West End", Alexandria. Another station was started at Bailey's Cross Road, four miles off, where we held services in a schoolhouse. We also re-opened Old Pohick Church, which General Washington built near Mt. Vernon and which had been dismantled and used as a stable by Federal troops during the war. It had, thereafter, lain desolate until our time. We got a little money and fixed up the building somewhat, put in some benches, resumed the services, and gatherd quite a congregation from the neighborhood. Two of us began services at an old "Convalescent Camp" near Arlington where a large crowd of negroes had "squatted". We had very lively meetings and very large and enthusiastic congregations for a few months. When we returned to the Seminary after the summer holiday, Boone and I went over to the place to resume our work. Our Parish had disappeared. The buildings were all gone, and not a soul left on the spot. A neighbor told us that, during the summer, the Government had sold the buildings to be removed at once, and the negroes had scattered. This was a case where not the ministers but the *parish* resigned and moved to another field of labor.

This Station work was the cause of much suffering to the beginners in their first attempts at preaching. We are old veterans now, but what nervous anguish we had to bear in those early days! We all recall them. I well remember my own first experience. Being on the staff of "Bailey's Cross Road", the time came at last when I had to preach. I had dodged as long as I could with honor, now I had to stand up. So, with such outward cheerfulness as I could summon, but with great sinking of heart I accepted the appointment to speak the next Sunday. I was very low in mind that week, but got ready as well as I could. On Sunday I could not eat any dinner; I only chewed the cud of bitter reflection that my trial was just ahead and no escape. I wished I could be suddenly ill, or break my leg, or something, but none of these things happened to me. When Horace Hayden told me it was time to go I tried to smile, but it was a very sickly smile, and *outward only*. We started off for the four mile walk. It was a sorrowful way to me and every mile it got worse. The picture of myself standing up all by myself to preach to the people made me hot all over. I never was half so sacred in any battle of the war; a few bullets whizzing by my head would have been a relief. I thought I was the most miserable wretch in the country and it was the shortest four miles I ever knew. Dear old Hayden, seeing my misery, and kindly trying to cheer me up, said, "Old fellow, don't mind it so much, I am praying for you." This was too much! I said, "Hayden, for heaven's sake don't tell me that. I feel now, exactly as if I were going to be hanged and to know that anybody is praying for me makes it far worse. It seems like I am on the scaffold hearing the last offices." And I felt just that way! It was an awful strain. I don't know what I said in my sermon, or how I said it, but I know that I was happier on the walk back than on my way there. I was glad I was living.

Another incident of the Station work was not so sad, but on the contrary. It was customary, now and then, for the man in charge to invite one of his brethren to preach for him. George Fitzhugh had the Almshouse Station, about two miles toward the river, on the edge of Alexandria. Once he asked Penick to preach for him and Willie Hoxton to read the service. On Sunday as they were starting, "Fitz" said, "Brethren, on the lane this side of the Almshouse there are two pretty vicious dogs. Look out for those dogs." The injunction "Beware of dogs," had no meaning for Penick. He replied, "never mind about the dogs, come on Hoxton." The sequel was recounted by Hoxton, on their return. When, in due course, they struck the lane, which ran straight on to their goal with a high fence on either side, two large dogs with savage barks jumped into the lane, and came charging down upon them, showing every disposition to attack. The dogs were between them and the Almshouse. When they got near, Hoxton, who had been considered the bravest man in Jim Breathed's famous battery of Horse

Artillery, but who at present didn't relish being chewed up by a dog, said, "Penick, what shall we do?" "Never you mind, Brother Hoxton," replied Penick, "I will attend to the dogs." "Well," said Hoxton, "whatever you are going to do you had better do quickly. These dogs are about to rush in." Penick was a long slim fellow, with long legs and could bend over till his head almost touched his feet. He wore a very short sack coat. He had a large Bible under his arm with his notes, etc., for reference in his coming sermon. Suddenly Penick whirled round with his back to the dogs, bent far far over and looked at the dogs from between his own legs. The sight of Penick erect was one thing, the spectacle of Penick upside down was another. It was too much for the dogs. Instantly, with a yelp of terror, and with their tails tight between their legs, they turned around, and tore back up that lane as hard as they could run, yelping with fear, and expecting something to grab them at every jump. They leaped over the fence, ran out into the field, sat down, put up their heads and howled dismally in a tone of abject surrender. The instant the dogs started to run Penick rose erect and said, "Brother Hoxton, it is time for divine service, don't let us be late"; and perfectly serious, with his Bible under his arm, he walked on to the Almshouse, Hoxton following, nearly laughing himself into a fit. He said that Penick's unbroken solemnity, through all that scene, was the funniest thing he ever saw. Hoxton was a very sedate person, but the scene was too much for him and he never could refer to it without hearty laughter. He said it looked as if it were an every day thing for Penick to scare savage dogs with his face and especially when inverted.

Outside of the serious work of the Seminary course, and the various occupations already mentioned, we had many pleasant diversions to lighten our labors. There were many hospitable homes clustered about the Seminary which were open to the students in the kindliest fashion:—the homes of the Professors and of Mr. Cassius Lee, the "High School" of which Rev. William F. Gardner was the Principal, the home of Colonel David Funsten's family, who were then occupying the "Wilderness", the home of Mrs. Cazenove, "Malvern" the home of Bishop Johns, of Mr. Charles Hooff, of Colonel

Arthur Herbert, the last three down the hill, and the others grouped closely about the Seminary.

The dear, hospitable families in all these homes did all they could to make it pleasant for the students. From time to time they would give entertainments, at which all the neighbors and the students would assemble and have a royal time of social enjoyment. Between times we would be invited to tea or we would make social visits of our own motion. "The Hill" was one big family. We all felt that way, and treated each other that way. All were in it. "The old Bishop," the venerable Professors, the students, even the "Preps", we were all just a band of older and younger brothers. It was the sweetest and loveliest social life in the world, I think.

And besides there were, in nearly all these homes, young ladies whose society and conversation meant much for the pleasure of the students, some of them especially, "*quorum pars fui.*" The walks through the groves with these charming companions was the crowning touch of the social life of our time. Happy were the few of us who were able to beguile these dear girls to go on walking with us through the journey of life!

As part of our diversion we formed a "Reading Club" which met, in turn, at the different houses. It was composed of such of the students as chose to join, and the young ladies of "The Hill." We met, in the less crowded part of the session, once a week, and had readings and recitations, and essays and pleasant conversation, ending with refreshments. At one meeting a red-headed country boy from up on the Potomac river, who had just come to the Seminary, was present. It was his first time and he was very bashful. He sat uneasy in our midst. One of the ladies thinking to put him more at ease, said, "Mr. . . . . . . did you ever make a voyage?" With his face as red as his head and his hair standing up straight, he replied, "Yes, Marm, I have crossed the Potomick onct or twict in a skift." The Potomac was only half a mile wide where he crossed, but later on he made more voyages and longer than any of us present who chuckled over his funny answer. He became Missionary to Africa.

That Reading Club was the occasion of a piece of engineering which has been of great comfort to all the students, and people on "The Hill" since our time. I mean that "*walk*" from the "Wilderness" by St. George's Hall to Dr. Packard's, on down the hill to Clarens and General Cooper's gate. The soil all about the Seminary is very soft with clay and fuller's earth. When it rained the walking was abominable. There were no hard paths anywhere, except a narrow plank-way leading toward the High School. This was full of holes, and dangerous to walk on at night. From the "Wilderness" and Dr. Packard's, one had to wade in deep and slippery mud, and sometimes the young ladies from these two houses could not come out to the meetings of the Reading Club or other assemblies. So, some of us, to whom the presence of these ladies was especially desirable, resolved to fix a way by which they could come. We planned a hard path to connect these two houses with each other, and with the Seminary. We called the other students to our aid and they gallantly responded. We got some picks and shovels and then laid out a straight line, and rounded up a road bed. Then every man got his coal scuttle and we went hard to work, toting coal ashes from the piles, accummulated from our stoves during the winter. We went back and forth like a line of ants; we kept hard at it, and in a short while we had that path covered thick with coal ashes, which when well packed makes as firm a surface as bricks and our triumph of engineering was accomplished to the comfort of everybody around the Seminary. While we were working on the path to the "Wilderness" Dr. Packard came and watched us work. He chuckled and said, "Eh, a labor of love!" We were working without money pay, but the "Rab" didn't mean that. He had heard of the motive of that job. Three of us got our pay, all right, from the three nicest girls that ever walked on Seminary Hill!

After we had finished our task, we raised some money among the students, and with the financial aid of the Seminary Trustees and of the neighbors, we got Mr. Studds, with his teams and men, to carry a hard walk way on down to General Cooper's gate. We students started the improvement upon "The Hill" and did all the work with our own hands. The after generations of students owe us much. They ought to build a monument of coal ashes, anyhow, to the men of 1866.

Among the early experiences of that first session I may mention this, it is part of the picture of our life. We students were under pretty severe petticoat government. In fact we bachelors were "tormented before our time." The rule of our matron was very autocratic indeed. We had a fine opportunity to try the principle of plain living and high thinking. How high the thinking was I may not say, but the living was surely plain. Once for thirty days in succession we had veal for dinner, varied only once by mutton, and it was thought that that sheep was the twin to the ram that Abraham offered instead of Isaac. It could hardly have gotten as tough with any less age. But the rations were not all we were called to bear.

One night we were at our prayers in Prayer Hall. While yet on our knees the supper bell rang. Either prayers were late or the supper bell was ahead of time. We finished our prayers in about five minutes, then trooped out to the supper room. Arrived, the door was locked, and to our dismay we were told from the matron that because we did not come promptly at the ringing of the bell we could have no supper that night. As nothing to eat could be had nearer than Alexandria, three miles off, this was rather tough. There was some kicking and heated remarks on the situation but all the same that whole gang went away empty and afterwards went, supperless and sorrowful, to bed.

Upon another occasion at supper one night, a student at table No. 2. moved the one lamp a little way. The glass chimney had not been secured. It fell off and was broken. The penalty for this accident was that for four nights there was no light on table No. 2. The room was poorly lighted by one lamp on each table. So this left us in darkness. We considered this rather severe treatment for accidentally breaking a ten cent chimney, and there was much murmuring in our tents. But we did not like to complain of a lady and therefore thought it wise to turn it off as a joke. So on the fifth day of our obscuration we sent to town by Old Cleveland, and bought a pound of candles. These we cut in half making twelve short candles, one for each of the twelve men occupying our table. That night we gathered outside the door, lighted our candles, and marched in solemn procession into the room, and ranged around our table, each man setting his lighted candle in the tumbler at his place. Then we proceeded to take supper at a well lighted board. All this was to the delight of the fellows at the other tables, but not at all to that of the matron. She took our torch light procession and illumination very ill indeed, and said that we had insulted her. We meant it for a "counsel of peace" but it didn't work. The next morning at breakfast a note was handed which said: "the gentlemen at table No. 2 will make other arrangements for their dinner, as after this breakfast no more meals will be provided for them in the refectory." This was a little steep since there was nowhere else we could go for our meals. It was a practical dismissal from the Seminary. Shortly after breakfast while we were discussing the case we received a summons to the effect that the gentlemen of table 2 should meet the "Faculty" in Prayer Hall. We gathered, and went into "the presence." We knew that we had been reported as lawless and profane and were now to be called to account. As we filed in Dr. Packard was sitting with his eyes shut; Dr. Walker blest with the better sense of humor, than his colleague, sat smiling broadly. Dr. Sparrow was standing, tall, solemn and mournful. He opened up by saying "young gentlemen, what is all this about?" We asked, "What?" He said, "You have been reported as guilty of very disrespectful behaviour to the Matron." We replied, "In what particulars?" He then instanced our torch light procession at supper and our refusal at breakfast to eat butter which one fellow said was part of the butter which Jael offered to "Sisera" in a lordly dish. We thought so because it was evidently butter of very *high rank*. We then handed the Doctor the note received at breakfast which cut off all our hope of future nourishment, and asked him if the Faculty endorsed it. This was rather a stunner. They hadn't known about that note! He said, "The Faculty did not write it", which was plainly a dodge. The Doctor realized that the Faculty had acted in the dark and that the prosecution had not a leg to stand on. Then the conversation trailed off into a discussion of the respective merits and price of good butter and bad butter, etc. Finally the Doctor exhorted us to Christian behavior and then dismissed us. It was altogether as funny as could be. We were restored to the privileges of the refectory. The "Faculty" warned the Matron that she must not use such radical measures with the students and that such matters as dismissing men from the Seminary must be referred to them before action. She was pretty sore about it, but we finally got to be good friends. That afternoon, as a move toward peace, I offered to plant a vine that she was anxious to set out by the back porch. She accepted my offer and I planted the vine. It was the vine which in after years covered the back porch of Aspinwall Hall under whose shade many generations of students and Alumni sat and talked and smoked at Commencement times. I am sure many of the old boys remember that vine. This was the history of it.

One curious episode of that session I may record here. It might be entitled "Psalm Williams; his converts and their fall from grace." We pronounced his first name "Sam" but spelled it with a "P". This name which was not his baptismal name was given by the unregenerates who thought him rather unctuous. This student assumed the office of "Censor Morum", and proceeded to reform the manners of the boys and finally obtained a strong influence over some of them. To him they gave heed and did many things because of him. The secret of his influence I can only explain on the principle that "in the kingdom of the blind, the one-eyed is King." We were veterans as soldiers, but we were green at this business of being Theological Students. We didn't even think we knew. On general lines, we thought one ought to behave himself and get his lessons and say his prayers and be a good comrade with his brethren, but as to the particular "wrinkles", the special rules of conduct proper to our position, we did not know; nevertheless we wanted to do the correct thing. Now Sam set up to know it all and many of the fellows were willing to be guided by his superior knowledge. He was very strict with his converts, and cut off many of their pleasures and laid upon them burdens under which they were upheld only by the consciousness of virtue. They endured but for a time and then fell from grace. For instance one of our band, Edward W. Hubard, was a beautiful violinist and he brought his violin to the Seminary with him. He enjoyed it much and we delighted to listen to his superb playing. I recall how he could rattle off that foot-stirring old tune, "The Mississippi Sawyer", about which an old "Hard Shell" Baptist negro in whose eyes dancing was the deadly sin said, "Dat chune have drawd more poor souls to torment den any other invention of the devil, cause if you hear dat chune you can't help shaking your toes." Well, we did enjoy Hubard's sweet music very much. But Williams got hold of him. He gave him to understand that a fiddle (he scorned to call it a violin) in a Theological Seminary was intolerable, and that a fiddler was an abomination unto the Lord. He told Hubard that he was setting a snare for the feet of his brethren, and was risking his own soul by this ungodly practice. He so worked on dear old Ned that he sent his fiddle home and our music was gone. Ned, however, was not converted all through, he yearned after his fiddle. Once when his longing was on him very strong he said to me, "I'd give a thousand dollars if I had my violin, and a bow a *mile long*, and could just have *one full scrape*." But glancing at Williams who was standing near, added, "don't tell Psalm".

Another student, Benjamin E. Reed, had been induced to promise that he would not chew any more tobacco. He suffered and was sad under the privation, but held out for a time. Late afternoon three days after, Reed was coming along the hall stepping lively and with a cheerful face. He had a wad in his jaw half as big as your fist and was chewing like a goat. Unfortunately Williams met him, stopped in front of him and looked very sorrowful. He said, "Brother Reed, I am shocked and grieved. What does this mean?" Said Reed, "What are you talking about? Don't take that tone with me." "Brother Reed," replied Williams, "Didn't you promise me that you would not chew tobacco any more?" "Chewing tobacco! Why I am not chewing tobacco." "Oh Brother Reed how can you say that? What is that you have in your mouth?" "Oh that," cried Reed. "I'll explain about that. Yesterday morning a bee stung me and Uncle Nathan told me that if I would just moisten a little piece of tobacco and lay it on the place it would cure the bee sting. That is what I am doing." So he had a very large piece in his jaw and was chewing it hard, and he called this "moistening a little piece to lay on the bee sting thirty-six hours old." This was entirely too thin. It was too much for even Williams. He turned sadly away and said, "Brother Reed, I'll have to give you up", which Reed took as a release from his promise and thereafter became a much more cheerful person.

Yet another man, William H. Laird, had a thing which he fondly called a "musical instrument." It was in fact a producer of mournful noises. It was a sweezy old flageolet. Its notes attuned one's mind to thoughts serious enough to befit a Lenten exercise. But it was dear to Laird's heart and he would "pick" himself a little tune to "refresh his brain" when wearied with study. Psalm Williams took exception to it as a thing utterly inconsistent with a Theological Seminary and the spiritual pursuits of a Divinity student. Somehow or other he got out of Laird a promise that "he would not blow that thing in the Seminary any more." The flageolet was silent, and Laird was sad. Alas for poor human nature! Some days afterwards a group of us, including Williams, were standing by the steps at Bohlen Hall. Suddenly the faint sound of that flageolet was borne to our ears. Instantly Williams with stern face went striding up to Laird's room on the second floor back in Bohlen Hall. Some of us at once followed Psalm to see what he was going to do to Laird. When we came to Laird's door he threw it open and this is what he saw—Laird with one knee on the floor, bending over in a very constrained position blowing away for dear life at that flageolet, the front end of which was poked out of the window with the sash let down on it, to hold it firmly. As we entered without knocking, catching him in the act, Laird looked up rather shamefacedly and stood up. Williams, in a "Daniel come to judgment" tone, said, "Brother Laird, you have broken your vow. If anybody had told me this I would not have believed it. Didn't you promise me that you wouldn't blow that thing in the Seminary any more?" Laird, driven to bay, replied rather hotly, "Williams, that is a hard thing you have said. I have not broken any vow. I said that I wouldn't blow this thing in the Seminary any more, and I am not blowing it *in* the Seminary. I am blowing it *out*. Don't you see it is stuck out of the window. And now that the matter is up, I say, right here, that I take back that promise. I am going to blow this thing whenever I please! I've missed my music too much." Williams turned away sorrowful, without a word and left the room. Laird said, "Boys, I couldn't help it. I have been very lonesome without my flageolet." So, one by one, Psalm lost all of his converts, he pressed the boys too hard. After his failure with the students, Williams then directed his energies to building a chapel at "West End" which he accomplished and where he did a good work. He was better at that than being a reformer.

And so we lived our life at the Seminary. We had our fun, our pleasures, our recreations, and the students entered heartily into all that was going on. They were a manly and lively set. An old woman, who with her sister occupied two rooms in St. George's Hall and saw much of the students, was asked what she thought of them. Meaning to say that they were very much like other people in their enjoyment of life, she said, "there is a great deal of mortality in theological students." There was, the students were very natural and very happy. There was plenty of hard work and serious occupation, to which they gave themselves with their whole heart and soul and with all diligence. As the men, strangers before they came to the Seminary, learned to know one another better and to recognize in each other the earnest purpose, the upright life, and the pleasant spirit, they grew to love each other more and more. No wonder they formed friendships close and true which were to last all through life. They were a band of brothers and comrades and there was not a single one left out of the circle.

In closing this poor attempt to picture the Seminary life of our time, it only remains for me to speak of the Commencement. This was preceded by the examinations. The system of "Examining Chaplains" was not then instituted. Each professor examined the class in his own studies and his report to the Bishop was the credential of each student for his ordination.   Then, on Wednesday, Thursday and Friday, came the various exercises of the Commencement.   Wednesday, the visitors began to assemble for the finals of the High School, and for the Missionary Meeting in the Chapel at night.   On Thursday there was the Alumni Meeting and the Essays by the Graduating Class in the Chapel; on Friday, the Ordination.

To this great reunion the Alumni gathered from every quarter, far and near, old and young, men from different states, bishops from many dioceses, often missionaries from the Foreign Field at home on furlough, men from small country parishes, men from big churches in the big cities.   All were gathered there united by a common bond, love for the Old Seminary and for each other.   And in between the formal exercises they could be seen at all hours, day and night, standing or sitting on the porches or on the grass under the trees, talking and smoking, or strolling through the "grove," or going over to pay their respects to the Professors, and their families, or to Bishop Johns at "Malvern", or to the other old residents on "The Hill".   It was the most informal and the most delightful reunion of men I ever saw in my life.   They were men of every sort, every rank of ability and office in the Church and they mingled there on the most familiar and easy terms.   They gathered on the old "Hill" amid scenes and memories common to them all.   They were in heart and feeling to each other a big family gathered back under the old roof tree.   The old fellows would tell stories of the men, and experiences of their times, and the young fellows had their tales to tell.   Rev. George A. Smith, the first alumnus of the Seminary, was with us then, and for years after.   He could tell us of things at the very beginning and there were other old men who could carry on the story all along up to our time.   And it was all intensely interesting and very helpful to the younger men.   It was as if former victors in the races were talking to the young men who were training for the race just ahead of them, and inspiring them to run it well.   I do not believe that any Church assemblage in the American Church ever did as much good.   I know none was ever so delightful.   After all this pleasant converse and after the ordination, all would scatter to their homes, students and the guests, with good memories to carry with them, and love for the brethren and the dear old Seminary, and all that it stands for, stronger in their hearts.

When we, the students at the end of our course, separated after all we had heard and seen of the life there, we went our ways to our several posts of duty to begin our life work, thanking God with grateful hearts that He had given us the high privilege of training in that blessed School of the Prophets.

We pray that throughout all generations the sons of the old Mother may be worthy of her! As in the past, so in the years to come, may she send forth loyal sons, true heralds of the Cross, through whom "Her sound shall go out into all lands, and her words unto the end of the world."

God bless the Virginia Seminary!

SECTION IV

Chapter XIII—Part 2

Memories

Rev. Ernest M. Stires, D. D.

Rome on her seven hills was no more fortunate in location than our Seminary. Five miles to the north in direct line lies the nation's capital, her granite and marble buildings shining white in the sunlight. A few miles to the east, down the Potomac, is Mount Vernon, home of the great Washington; and three miles to the west stands Arlington, home of the immortal Lee. Every foot of the ground is historic and holy; a place where men may easily see visions and plan victories for the Kingdom of Christ.

One remembers how the tower of Aspinwall dominates the whole region, how the Cross surmounting it rises high above Washington and reminds men that except the Lord build the city their labor is but vain that build it.

The Druids never knew oaks more beautiful nor more eloquent than those in our Seminary wood. What memories those trees shared with the students! Memories of civil war days, when only the most supplicating pleading to the Federal government availed to save this little forest from destruction, the sole exception in the vicinity of the capital. Memories of saintly bishops and heroic missionaries walking here and planning conquest in the name of One Who was nailed to a tree. The oaks still hold themselves proudly, for a larger company than ever before walk beneath them, and in the company are young captains who offered their lives in France that humanity might live, and to fulfil this holy purpose they now seek commissions in the army of God. The memory of the oaks grows richer with the years.

Our class knew the glory of the old Spartan simplicity— it is a glory in retrospect, but at the time we indulged occasionally in less beatific description. Yet no man of us is

THE HOME OF REVEREND DOCTOR PACA KENNEDY

THE HOME OF REVEREND DOCTOR THOMAS K. NELSON
Former Home of Reverend Doctors Grammer, Micou and Bell

ungrateful for the truly constructive discipline of it all. However, modernism (*in plumbing*) was threatening through the zeal of Professor Crawford, who, while believing in plain living and high thinking, felt that mortification of the flesh could be carried too far even in a Theological Seminary where students made their fires, carried the coal often up three flights of stairs, and were forced to equally strenuous measures to obtain a bath.

We did not experience the new comforts, but we saw the new day dawn. We suspected the wide range of Dr. Crawford's iconoclasm and we prayed for his success. This, however, never prevented us from assuming a solemn pose when we revisited "The Hill," nor kept us from glorifying the old days and warning against the destructive influence of luxurious living, for today they have electric light, steam heat, bath-tubs, and other similar temptations.

It is the privilege of others to speak comprehensively of our great debt to Dr. Crawford. But one who records memories may be allowed to recall this genial Christian scholar and gentleman. No one can forget the cheerful welcome to his home; the rich voice almost shouting a greeting; the unfailing good-humor; the quick change to seriousness if you needed counsel, or if the conversation suggested a helpful thought; his pride in the Seminary, and his faith in the students and his boundless kindliness. Trained in the modern method of teaching Hebrew, his classes discovered that he could put life into a dead language. But Dr. Crawford put new life into everything he touched.

When memory recalls the faculty, the foreground of the picture is dominated by one who for more than half a century won the complete respect and affection of all the students. They did not love him less because they called him "the Rab." They did not respect him less because they never tired of telling stories which illustrated his ingenuousness or his absent-mindedness. Doubtless many of those stories were apocryphal, but we consumed them avidly and passed them on with glee. Every recital increased the hold "the dear old Rab" had upon the hearts of the students and alumni.

He was like no other man who ever lived, and the man who undertakes adequately to describe him is venturesome.

How many students recall the revelation of Dr. Packard's humor! One was unprepared for it. He was big and serious like a granite mountain, but the eyes could become wonderfully kind and there was a wry smile composed of equal parts of modesty, sympathy and fun.

A compliment from Dr. Packard was a heavy responsibility—one could not endure the thought of disappointing him. A student recalls a certain Ordination Day over thirty years ago when Dr. Packard met him on one of the walks, stopped him, looked at him earnestly for a moment and said; "My young friend, your class should render great service. I have been here many years and I recall only one other class which equalled it, and that class possessed a Brooks, a Potter and a Randolph."

Close to the beloved old Dean, in memory's picture, stands the saintly Cornelius Walker, gentle, patient, and with that kindly humor which the true saint must possess.

In strong contrast, yet not less saintly, stands Kinloch Nelson, whose personal influence and intellectual guidance made him the real ecclesiastical leader of the Seminary in our day. You could not fasten upon him the label of a school; he was not "Low" or "High," he was a Churchman, with definite convictions, sympathetic vision, and complete obedience to his divine Master. A grateful pupil is trying to thank him for his steadying, stimulating influence at a critical hour of development.

The faculty of our day was fortunate in another member who had graduated but a few years before, but possessed gifts inherited and acquired which made him a real force. Dr. Carl Grammer, grandson of the brilliant Dr. Sparrow, was a man of broad learning and strong convictions. We did not always agree with him, but that did not seem to disturb him; he was determined to compel us to think things out, and he succeeded to a degree for which we are increasingly grateful.

The faculty of today are a group of intellectual and spiritual leaders who stand comparison with any similar body of men in America. But we are loyal to the teachers of our earlier time, proud of their abilities, grateful for their teaching and their patience, and for their occasional approval; and our love and admiration for them has grown with the years.

When we entered in the autumn of 1888, Kinsolving and Morris were preparing to establish our Church in Brazil. The story of their immediate success thrilled us, and our class felt honored when Brown and Meem answered the call for reinforcements and volunteered for service in Brazil.

China had long attracted some of us. The Student Volunteer Movement had reached the University of Virginia in 1887 and under its influence Ingle and Massie were seriously considering foreign service. The visit to the Seminary of Archdeacon Thomson (father of the present Bishop Coadjutor of Southern Virginia) was memorable. He had journeyed from China to tell of the campaign in the front line trenches. He recounted the victories of the Cross; he pictured the multitudes no longer hostile, but listening, receptive. He described the opportunities and their far-reaching importance. He had come to appeal for recruits, for men needed at once. And then, in a tone low and desperately earnest he asked, "Must I go back alone?" Ingle and Massie walked out of old Prayer Hall arm-in-arm repeating those last words, "Must I go back alone?" and immediately they volunteered for China.

Some other memories of Ingle will interest those who loved him. In 1884 his saintly father, the Reverend Osborne Ingle, rector of the Church in Frederick, Maryland, visited the Episcopal High School to see his son, and took occasion to seek out a near friend of his boy. "You are very close to Addison," said Dr. Ingle, "and I am hoping you can help in a matter very dear to my heart. I understand that you have decided to study for the ministry, and I wonder if he has shown any disposition to do likewise. I do not wish to urge him, and I have refrained from doing so, but it has been my prayer for years that he would enter the ministry and become a missionary."

Dr. Ingle was assured that the boy friends had frequently taken long walks for the discussion of their vocation, and there was every likelihood that Addison would feel called to the ministry. How could it be otherwise, reared in such a home, educated deeply and wisely, and consecrated by the prayers of one of Christ's purest servants!

Those boy friends were close through life; they roomed together at college, joined the same fraternity, graduated together at college and seminary, and they would have gone to China together had not the apparent order from headquarters kept one of them at home. But the friends were lovers and helpers of each other through the years, rich with memories, even to the exchange of cablegrams in the last illness, an illness resulting from Ingle's characteristic pouring out of mind and heart, of spirit and body in sacrificial service of the "other sheep" to whom his Lord had looked with wistful eyes.

The mind goes back to the Preparatory Department in which Ingle, Massie and the writer largely constituted the faculty for a short while. Doubtless the present rules and methods are wiser, but take it all in all, the "Prep. Department" of our day seems to be justified. The "Faculty" were just out of college, young, enthusiastic, in deep sympathy with their comrades in the service, very proud of the achievements of their brother-pupils, and glad to work early and late to give their best.

One recalls the progress of a pupil who had graduated from a western college without taking Greek. Under the guidance of a member of the "Prep. Faculty" he began with the Greek alphabet, in six weeks was translating Xenophon with ease, and in a year wrote a thesis in Greek which he sent to his Alma Mater which promptly conferred an M. A. upon him. That man has for many years been rector of a strong parish in one of our largest dioceses. One remembers, too, that there are three bishops who were in that "Prep. Department" of our day.

A memory of one of these bishops should be recorded. In 1894 or 1895 Archdeacon Crook, working in Colorado and Nevada, stopped in Chicago on his way from the East to his field. He called on the rector of a Chicago parish in search of brotherly sympathy. "We are in serious need of men," he said. "It is a glorious work among the men of the mountains and the plains, the mines and the lumber-camps, in the towns, villages, and little settlements which must soon become cities, and which can be won for Christ now if I can find men with His spirit in them. I have visited three seminaries, have told the story, and am returning without a recruit or the slightest encouragment. In one Seminary the students told me that the only man interested in missions was one who lately wrote an essay on the subject for a prize. At another Seminary a student asked me whether there was any society out there!"

The bitterness and sorrow in the missionary's voice recalled Vibert's picture. He was asked if he had visited Virginia. He replied, "No, my hope and money were gone and it was time for me to return to my work." He was offered the necessary money if he would go to Virginia and repeat this story. He accepted; in a week he was back with radiant face and exclaiming, "Virginia did not fail me. I have one man surely and perhaps two." When asked who had definitely answered the call, he said, "A splendid fellow named Hunting," now the beloved missionary Bishop of Nevada.

Few cathedrals have received such consecration as our old Prayer Hall,—may it long be preserved in its utter simplicity. It has something of the character and atmosphere of a certain "upper room" in Jerusalem. How often have heroes of the mission field told their story in that room, how often have they appealed in Christ's name for recruits, how seldom if ever have they appealed in vain! Here the student made their first attempt at preaching, to a congregation composed of their teachers and fellow-students, and here they assembled daily for morning and evening prayer, led by one of their own number. There was an unforgettable charm in that evening prayer, just before supper. They were a wholesome, normal lot of men coming at the call of the prayer bell from studies, from tennis-court, baseball or football field; many kneeling in garments of their sports, men who kept strong and responsive "the temple of the spirit." One felt that all the reasonable activities of man were here consecrated to the Master of life. Religion was natural and inevitable.

It is unusual to emphasize an athletic element in the life and history of a theological institution, but many of the students had been conspicuous in college sports and brought this quality into their later school. Three members of our class, among them Ingle and Massie, had been on the football eleven at the University of Virginia; another had been winner of the hundred yard dash, the two hundred and twenty yard dash, and the hurdle race at the same college. Some of these men had received their first athletic training at the Episcopal High School, and the contests between the boys and "the students" have for many years contributed to a bond of affection and respect between the two schools. Memory recalls many an amusing or dramatic incident of these contests in which appear figures of those who later became distinguished bishops, famous missionaries, or, able statesmen, leaders in learned professions or captains of industry.   The motto over the High School gymnasium had a message for them all,—*Ut sit mens sana in corpore sano.*

One cannot turn from memory of the High School without comment upon its contribution to the Seminary. Intimate contact with the boys always helped the theologues to keep their feet on the ground. Contact with the Seminary students helped the boys to get a companionable touch with genuine, practical and manly religion.

The headmasters of the High School did much to strengthen a real and vital relationship between the two groups. Memory recalls Dr. Blackford so vividly and so gratefully that it is hard to turn away without an effort to record his nobility and far-reaching influence, though it would be almost impossible to do this in a manner worthy of one who ranks with Arnold of Rugby.

Nor can we leave the School without a salute to Dr. Blackford's longtime associate, Colonel Llewellyn Hoxton, a modern Bayard, without fear and without reproach; a very perfect gentle knight whose influence upon the boys and students is life-lasting. Fortunate it is, that a son, every whit worthy of him, is Headmaster of that school today.

The voice of memory calls the writer on but one must recognize limitations imposed and begin to stop. Three closing pictures can be but briefly stated.

How often we recall the class-prayers, as we met on a week-night in the rooms of successive members of the class for a brief, intensive, very personal, spiritual exercise. The short selection from holy scripture, indicating something of the reader's study or aspiration at the moment; the extemporaneous prayers which instantly related the men more intimately to each other and to their Lord; the quiet "goodnight" afterward, with a light in the face revealing increased gentleness and increased determination. That picture abides.

When we think of our "Mission Station" many emotions are excited, among them amusement, as we reflect upon the awkwardness, sometimes the elephantine ponderosity, of some of our well-meant attempts at preaching under the guise of "addresses." We recall also the story of the student coming to us from another body and insufficiently instructed in the proprieties of reading the service, who in a mission-station not only read the Absolution but followed it at once by saying,"Or this," and read the second form of Absolution also. How great must have been the peace of Israel that day!

The work at the mission stations was an education in itself,—the visiting of one's first parishioners, the intimate revelation of their qualities and their needs, and the inspiration of the traditions. "Here, at Sharon Mission, Phillips Brooks preached his first sermons." It was here the student really found people, his people, and therefore more truly found himself and God.

Many will write of the spirit of the Seminary, of the love of adventure for God and the fire of sacrifice kindled in the hearts of her sons. It is the spirit of service in the love of Christ, manifested in a hundred forms, and one of those forms memory presents. It was an August night in Fere-en-Tardennois in 1918. In the ruins of the rear garden of a Frenchman's home a son of the Seminary lay in his blanket-roll, trying to sleep despite the enemy planes overhead dropping bombs which shook to the earth the few cracked walls still standing in that thrice captured town. The red triangle on the sleeve of his blouse indicated that he was in the "Y" service. In fact he was a sort of "Y" chaplain, sent along the front to make brief talks to the lads on whom at the moment the critical responsibility rested. He often made six or more such talks in the late afternoon of a single day, and he received more than he gave.

To this man, trying to sleep, a comrade came at 2 A.M. asking help for another. "Can you come quickly with your first-aid kit? There's a 'Y' man here badly wounded." They ran to the door of a kitchen on which the enemy's injunction "Durchgang Verboten" had been permitted to remain. It was a wreck of a kitchen, but it still afforded a little shelter, and at a strong oak table, marvellously intact, were gathered four men ministering to a fifth whose head rested flat upon his hands on the table. The head was badly cut and much blood had been lost. A telegraph pole, cracked by shell-fire but still standing, had been jarred by the backing-up of a "Y" camion, driven by this man. The pole fell, striking his head with a glancing blow. It was a very close call, and one wondered whether already too much blood had been lost. It was a matter of five minutes only to give a restorative, to clip away the hair from the long, jagged cut, to draw the edges together and hold them with "adhesive" and bandages. Then the amateur surgeon said, as he saw the color coming back to his patient, "I hope you are feeling better." The wounded man lifted his head, glanced at the speaker, called him by name and asked, "Old man, where did you come from?" It was Frank Ridout. We had not met since the Seminary days nearly thirty years before. He had obtained leave from his parish, offered his service to the "Y", had been promised the charge of a "hut" near the front in France, had arrived when camion drivers in sufficient number could not be obtained, had consented to drive for a week that the boys might have their tobacco and other supplies, had been kept on this job, day and night for over six weeks, and was now worn-out and wounded. He said he was not worn-out, and that the wound was nothing. Despite his physical weakness, on his face was still the victorious smile of the old Mother on "The Hill".

The old Mother on "The Hill": what a goodly company of sons she has trained, inspired, sent forth! Memory treasures the record of their service, but joins them in laying the laurels at her feet. At every thought of her our hearts are brave again; our arms are strong.

SECTION IV

Chapter XIII—Part 3

Later Memories

REV. MIDDLETON S. BARNWELL, B. D.

The year was nineteen hundred and five, the month September, and the day hot beyond belief, when Clingman, Quin and I disembarked from an east-bound C. & O. train at Alexandria. An old negro slept on the front seat of an ancient chariot, in which Phillips Brooks had doubtless often ridden. Ahead of us rose the long sweep of Shooter's Hill, red and dusty as it had been for a century before it became a bitulithic suburb of Washington. That there were four miles of it, we knew, and our bags were heavy, but our purses exceedingly light, so we left the old negro asleep and set our faces toward the "Wilderness". An hour later we threw the remains of a box of cigarettes into a clump of golden-rod, passed through the great iron gates, climbed the hill and gravely knocked at the front door of Aspinwall. Naturally, nothing happened. We pushed on in, and through, and came at last to a group of students lounging on the grass around the sacred pump. Munsey Gill was clamoring for a cigarette. I went back down the hill to the clump of golden-rod and brought him one. It appeared that this strange place was not to be a monastery after all, but the abode of strong, clean men whose religion and humanness went hand in hand. In that little incident I saw the first sign of what I have come to feel is a prevailing characteristic of the Seminary and Seminary men; a religion whose concern is with the eternal verities rather than the accidents of life; men utterly devoid of cant and professionalism, not so much self-conscious members of a sacerdotal priesthood, as men whose hearts and lives were God's. One could write a book on this, but it is unnecessary. These words are for Virginia Seminary men, and they understand.

481

It did not take one long to realize that the vague, yet vital thing which we called the "spirit of 'The Hill', was but the active, outward expression of the spirit of the men who made up the permanent life of "The Hill". There was Dean Angus Crawford, who had seen service with Packard, Walker and McElhinney, and who brought the traditions of those splendid days over into a new and forward-looking era through Green and Wallis and Massie and Micou to Tucker and Rollins and Kennedy and Bell. Dean Crawford never for one instant forgot the stern old Evangelical truth which had characterized those earlier days, nor did he ever for one moment close his eyes to the needs which a new age was continually revealing. On the strong foundations of that faith of his youth he built enduringly for the year which is and the years which are to come. Under him the Seminary felt the first stirrings of that new and forward-looking life which opens out today into wider fields of service than men had dreamed of forty years ago.

Then there was Samuel A. Wallis! Dare I call him, here to his face in these printed pages, by that old, familiar name we knew him by and which we loved so well? To us he was, and ever shall be "Buckie". Why we called him that, I never knew. I never knew anyone who did know. It seemed to be one of the traditions which we inherited. It was just as natural to call him "Buckie" as it was to call the Seminary "The Hill". But I do know this, that when that mysterious name fell from the lips of a student through thirty generations of student life, it carried with it all the loving admiration of which loving men were capable. Whatever, in our boyish wilfulness, we may have failed to take of Greek and Polity and Liturgics from the boundless store of knowledge he so gladly spread before us, the poorest student of us all was immeasurably strengthened by basking in the spirit of loving Christliness which glorified him continually. I wonder how many of his old students have ever told him this. I have not, but I am telling him now for myself and for all who knew him. Wherever a man is at work in the vineyard of our Father who was blest with this man's friendship for three glorious years, there, through him, the shining

soul of Dr. Wallis is lighting the feet of weary men toward
God.

And so one might write of all the men who made the life
of "The Hill" what it was.   Dr. Green was doing some of his
best work, and was already known by us to be the outstanding leader which the whole Church has now discovered him
to be.   Dr. Micou was lecturing with unfailing brilliance
and regularity, speaking of the things of God as one with
authority, and with a few, well-chosen words, opening for
us new and wondrous worlds of thought of which we had
never dreamed.   Dr. Micou was more than a teacher of
truth.   He was an inspiration and a challenge to us to seek
the truth ourselves.   More than this, a man could not be.
Dr. Massie was laying for us the foundations of historical
knowledge which gave continuity and meaning to all that
we learned elsewhere.   His personality was strong, his lectures clear and concise.   He had a real gift for interpreting
history and for pointing out the significance of events and
the obscure drift of world-thought.   He made us see history
not as a secular thing, but as the shaping of men and nations
by the Guiding Spirit.   Speaking for myself, my debt to
him cannot be measured, and I feel sure this is true of us all.
Nor can we forget Willoughby Reade.   He was a splendid
type of Christian layman, a member of the High School
faculty, who came to us and taught us the rudiments of
elocution.   I am afraid some of the men thought they had
passed the "elocutionary" stage of life, and did not take Mr.
Reade's course as seriously as it deserved.   These overlooked
a great opportunity.   To those of us who remembered the
things he said and tried to practice them, he was a blessing
indeed.   Through his Seminary work, he has made a large
contribution to the students by teaching them how to deliver
sermons and how to render the services of the Church.

It was during our term, 1905 - 1908, that the new chancel
was built to the chapel through the generosity of Bishop
Potter.   I remember how we shivered through the winter
months when a thin board partition was supposed to fill one
end of the place, and how eagerly we awaited the coming of
the dignitaries of the Church at the time of the consecration
of the addition.   Dr. Micou was a member of the building

committee, and so thorough was he in his investigating of the heating appartus that on one occasion, while peering down a warm air pipe, he fell through a register and had to be rescued by passing students. And the old chancel furniture, strained by long years of service, gave way one evening and precipitated Dr. Wallis to the floor. The furniture was repaired, and after being forcibly removed several times by students who cherished the traditions which had gathered around the old pine desk in Prayer Hall, was permanently placed in that room of sacred associations, where I believe it abides unto this day.

A sketch of this kind would be incomplete without reference to the social life of our time. The homes of the members of the faculty were ever our homes, and in them we found that delightful social intercourse without which a man is less than he should be. It was almost predestined that a girl raised on "The Hill" should "enter the ministry", and in addition to these a never-ending stream of the fairest daughters of Virginia visited the Greens and the Massies, the Crawfords, the Wallisses and the Micous. Ah! what tales of dreams and hopes, realized and sometimes blasted, the old "Bouly" could tell; what tales of eager youth calling to youth sometimes not so eager, to come and serve the Master in crowded city street or across the far-flung sea! What triumphs and what tragedies those silent groves have seen! No man may write of these, but they had their powerful part in shaping and strengthening the men who were about their Father's business. From that Hill have gone noble women as well as noble men to build Christian homes in un-Christian places. These, the world knows well, but only the Recording Angel knows of the men who were disappointed; who went forth broken-hearted and alone to distant fields of sacrifice. The Spirit which hovers above those moon-lit groves knows the price these had to pay.

And then there were the Hooffs and the Andrews and the Dawsons, the Rusts and the Worthingtons, and a dozen others in whose homes the students were ever welcome. Walking home from Groveton through driving storms of sleet and snow and rain, we would sight the shining lamps of "Cranford" as mariners sight a light-house upon a storm-bound coast.   Never a Sunday night, when we came in tired from a day of labor, but that light was shining a welcome, and within was ever the refreshment and the warmth of food and drink, and the gracious, Christian hospitality which the Worthingtons gave to all.   Such were the things which made the Seminary what it was, a happy, God-blest place where men could grow in wisdom and stature and in favor with God and man.

Gone are those days, and gone back to God are some of those of whom I write, and we who studied there are scattered the wide world over.   The days are flying as a weaver's shuttle and more and more those distant years are haloed by the mists of sweet remembrance.   Those years have passed, but they have not died.   In memory we live them through again and again, and day by day we find in them the strength for present labor and the courage to meet life's pressing problems unafraid.

SECTION IV

CHAPTER XIII—PART 4

REMINISCENCES OF SOME OF THE OLDER ALUMNI

Prefatory Note

The Memories recorded in this section of the History constitute a veritable treasury of devotion. In addition to those given in this chapter, there are a number of most interesting reminiscences of the older alumni, recorded in Chapter V. of the current history. The reminiscences in Chapter V. were secured and preserved by the Rev. Dr. Cornelius Walker and were found in his manuscript record.

It was the intention of the editor to include a chapter on the memories of the Rev. Dr. Joseph Packard. This thought, however, was abandoned, in view of the fact that his recollections are fully recorded in the book which he wrote entitled "The Recollections of a Long Life". This volume has been largely quoted in the current history, where many of the priceless memories of this old beloved professor and dean are to be found.

It will be noted that in the memories contained in this section many repetitions are to be found of material used in the current history and in the special articles; it was thought best in many instances to allow these repetitions to remain as they are so richly and so beautifully colored by the soul and personality and the tenderness and devotion of these older alumni of the Seminary.—W. A. R. G.

Memories

REV. G. THURSTON BEDELL, D. D.
(Subsequently Bishop of Ohio)
Class 1840

BEING PART OF AN ADDRESS DELIVERED AT THE
DEDICATION OF ASPINWALL HALL, ON
TUESDAY OCTOBER 5TH, 1859

I remember with deep affection and gratitude the instructions received in the venerable hall behind us. Never can I forget the logical, discriminating, systematic, teaching of that father in theology, the honored Keith; nor how invariably every statement of doctrine was tested by the infallible Word; by what an accurately balanced mind we were led constantly to preserve the analogy of faith, whilst studying its particular doctrines; and as constantly directed to Holy Scriptures as the witness for the whole range of truth, maintaining all parts in their integrity and proportion . . . With deep reverential feelings do I recall the hours spent while at the Seminary in the Sanctuary on the Lord's Day, the Thursday evening Faculty Meetings, the Tuesday evening sectional prayer meetings, the monthly meetings of the Missionary Society of Inquiry, and in practical efforts for "improving the religious and moral condition of the neighborhood". I do not hesitate to say, as the result of my experience, that the system here pursued in cultivating the religious character of students, and giving them knowledge of their public work by opportunities for practicing whilst they are studying its principles, is worth more to the future pastor than any amount of mere theological instruction. If either must be neglected, give me, for efficient labor, a man who will carry with him an unction of the spirit, and be reasonably secure of a heavenly benediction; one whose theoretical training has suffered rather than his experimental and practical training. Little as I may have profited by them, I rejoice to think of those happy days, when, we were here taught to put the principles of the recitation room and chapel into immediate practice in neighboring Sunday schools, in the alms-house, in tract distribution, and in visiting among the poor, from house to house, with prayer and exhortations. And among my most grateful recollections of early life are the hours of social communion enjoyed in our circles for prayer, each hall by itself; and those greatly profitable hours, when our three beloved professors met us in the basement chapel, to pray with and for us, and to remind us, week by week, to seek for high attainments in the Christian's life. That lesson of the Seminary, how valuable for every day of our ministry! Mere professional and perfunctory discharge of its duties, how vain and unprofitable a service! The minister of Christ needs a lively faith in, and an experimental appreciation of, the Gospel which he attempts to preach; a love for souls which springs only out of a knowledge of the depth of ruin from which his own soul, as one of a ransomed race of sinners, has been rescued; and a love for Christ, offspring of a sense that he is himself, through the grace of Christ, an adopted heir of immortality. If the student in theology be also a student at the foot of the Cross, gaining knowledge of scripture truth *pari passu* with knowledge of himself, and having doctrines impressed upon his understanding only as they are wrought, in their practical and personal meaning, within his own soul by the blessed influences of the Holy Ghost, he has the prospect of entering on his noble office as an able minister of the New Testament."

MEMORIES

REV. JOHN MCGILL

Class 1861

I well recall the dilapidated chapel at the Seminary when I entered there in 1858. I noticed that the pew ends next to the aisles, were roughly finished at the top, differing from the finish of the body of the pews. When I asked how this had happened, I was told that each pew-end next to the aisles had been finished in an ornament formed in the shape of a cross. When Bishop Meade entered the Chapel, upon his first visit, after its completion, he at once noticed the crosses on the pew-ends and gave instructions to have them removed. The quickest and least expensive way was to saw them off, which was done, and the carpenter, possibly offended by the action of the Bishop, took scant pains in finishing the disfiguration of his work and so left the roughness which had attracted my attention. It was during Lent that this took place. It happened to be the 14th day of the month and in the Psalter read in the afternoon service occurred the words: "But now they break down all the carved work thereof with axes and hammers".

That noble "Roman" declined to use carpets on his floors, walked when necessary between the plough handles, and on Sunday preached the Gospel to his neighbors. Men won by his whole-souled devotion to the Saviour and His great salvation could not resist the call to go preach the glad tidings to their fellows.

MEMORIES

REV. BENJAMIN E. REED

Class 1868

On my arrival at the Seminary in the early autumn of 1865, I found but three students, Messrs. Lewis, Williams and Hubard. The Seminary had not been opened for formal work. A good old colored man, Uncle Nathan, acted as a kind of general director. The first night I spent in the room with Williams, and the next day we prepared a room adjoining his with such furniture as we could find, a bed, one chair, washstand, and a small table. Bare, but luxurious to one who had been a Confederate soldier from April, '61, and in the past winter had shared in the hard experiences of war. The next morning I reported to Dr. Sparrow, who placed me in the Juniors, with a short period to be passed in the Preparatory Class.

The three Professors, Dr. Sparrow, Dr. Packard, and Dr. Walker, were high types of thoughtful, spiritual, and practical men; they balanced and harmoniously worked out the great problems of that desperate period in the Seminary. Dr. Sparrow, the profound student was not without a fine sense of humor. One day a member of the Preparatory Class translated after infinite labor, a Greek sentence thus, "When relations meet they kick each other." "What?" cried the Doctor, and after a moment's pause, "Perhaps, Mr. Barr, you are right about the way they feel; but the Greek says 'they kiss each other.'"

The Doctor had wonderful patience with us. Hubard, Williams and myself met in the recitation room, his own study. We each had to read a paper on Mondays *seriatim*. Mr. Hubard's subject, when his turn came, was "Heathenism". At that time the Church at large was too little interested in the heathen, and it was natural that Mr. Hubard and the others of us should have practically no interest. For six weeks, Hubard had said, when "'Heathenism', Mr. Hubard", was called in the class room, "Doctor, please excuse me. I am not quite prepared." The Doctor went on with the lesson as usual. But after class was dismissed, we got around our brother and plead with him to be ready next Monday, as he valued his life. We had him sick with worry. Next Monday he was ready. He told us "the mountain had groaned and brought forth a mouse," that he was the mountain and we would soon see the mouse running around in the Doctor's study. We were in the highest glee at what was about to happen. After the prayer, the Doctor opened his Paley, leaned back, closed his eyes, and said "'Heathenism', Mr. Hubard." Hubard lifted his six feet length in the air, flushed, fumbled his paper, announced in most unnatural voice "Heathenism", and burst out laughing. We thought, "Surely the Doctor will slay him now," but no, he only opened wide his eyes, looking, one said kindly, the other said quizzically, at Mr. Hubard, and said, "Lesson, gentlemen." It has not been confirmed, but it is whispered around, that whenever "Heathenism" is mentioned the Doctor's eyes twinkle.

Another side of the Doctor's character is shown in this incident. One of the students in the winter of '66, finding himself in great money-trouble, asked me if I thought Dr. Sparrow would him help out. I advised him to try. He told me that when he made known his situation, Dr. Sparrow broke out, "How wonderful is God's way of helping. If you had come yesterday I could not have helped you; but now I have the money. By mail just received, fifty dollars is enclosed. I don't know who sent it. I am so grateful to our Heavenly Father for the gift that I may help you. Take it!" The student returned it, of course.

At the Faculty Meetings, the professors revealed their personality in their talks to us. Dr. Sparrow suggested St. Paul in the intellectualities; Dr. Packard, St. John in the sympathies; and Dr. Walker, St. James in the practicalities. Faith in God, love for man, and "the how" in application, made a happy trinity in the blending of their heart to heart utterances. Rarely did we leave Prayer Hall without feeling an increase of faith, love, and the urge of service.

As a child may laugh over the oddities of a parent, with no disrespect, so we at times laughed over the peculiarities of our honored professors. Each supplied us at times with "a jolly laugh". As an instance, Dr. Walker had fallen in the way of using the word "fact" in sermons and class lec-

tures to the great amusement of the students. One morning
in a class held in Williams' room, the Doctor was dealing out
"facts" with his usual generous flow; and one of the class,
inattentive to the lecture, was absorbed in keeping the score.
Peterkin, looking over his shoulder, saw what he was doing,
and secretly signalled to the others. As the tabulator scored
the forty-fifth "fact", Peterkin signalled the score, and a
panic of amusement seized the class, and shook out of every
one an uncontrollable burst of laughter. In vain they tried
to disguise and to suppress the giggles. The Doctor paused,
stared, and said, taking the defeat like a man, "Gentlemen,
you are dismissed. Go!" and we went, shamed, but laughing still.

Our Prayer meetings were held weekly in the rooms, by
the different classes; and as our numbers had increased, the
"meetings" formed quite a little congregation. These meetings were impressive and inspiring; yet at times little in-
congruities would appear, not altogether without innocent
humor. One evening an embarrassed leader prayed "Give
us a hateful (grateful) sense of all Thy goodness." Another,
the youngest of the class "gave out" "The Hymn for Baptism of Infants". The old soldiers didn't have presence of
mind enough to call for a change; but, led by Hayden, rash-
ly plunged in, and strained hard to follow on. One by one
they broke down, till the leader was left all alone, to sing
the last verse. It was too much for him; he broke on the
second line, and the leader called in most unnatural voice
"Let us pray". We knelt, shoulders shaking, unnatural
sounds heard over the room, till the "amen" was jerked out
from the leader; then, contrary to custom, every student
bolted for his room, whence issued loud and uncontrollable
laughter. We were all shamed, and grieved, but we could
no more help it than Father Philip in the Monastery could
help singing "Swim we Merrily" before his indignant Abbot.

If I remember aright Uncle Nathan was at the the Seminary at its opening after the Civil War, our quarter master,
cook, room cleaner, and general factotum, for the first few
weeks. Then Miss Cornelia Jones graciously and efficiently
turned our camp life into the comforts of a home. If there
were hardships in the first days, we didn't know it; we were

too full of gladness and hope at the thought of serving Him Who died for us and of serving our fellow men.

We were wont to go out Sundays, two by two to establish missions. My room-mate, James H. Williams, and I took the "West End Mission" As many know Williams as "Sam", this explanation of the fact may be in order. One morning he went into Mr. Hubard's room, and asked him, spelling the word "What is the *P S A L M* (pronouncing it "Sam") for the day?" Henceforth Hubard called him Sam Williams (he never knew why) and through his Seminary life he was so called. I think I began West-End mission, but I know Williams did far more to its ultimate success. The beginning was on this wise. We got, in centre of West End, a school room right down on the street, and on a Sunday afternoon, opened a mission school. Many children passed by, not one came in. Getting desperate, I said "Sam, you get on that platform. Strike up, and sing at the top of your voice. I'll get the children." Taking a black gum switch from the teacher's desk, I went out and stood on the street before the door. To the children coming by I held my rod cross-wise, and said, "You go in there!" And they went. From small acorns great oaks grow. The West End Church was born that day. We kidnapped the kids.

The social features of "The Hill" were charming. By inheritance, association, culture, and above all by the surrounding religious atmosphere, they were the F. F. V's indeed. Among them, were the families of Bishop Johns, General Cooper, Colonel Funsten, Cassius Lee, Mr. Cazenove, Colonel Herbert, Mr. Hooff, and the professors. They formed a delightful circle, and made a home for the students.

> "Memories may come and memories may go—
> But the memories of these dear days will flow on forever."

MEMORIES

REV. EDWARD WOOTEN

Class 1868

I was born October 6, 1837. Educated at poor schools until I entered Trinity College, Hartford, Connecticut, January 1, 1859. Freshman class half advanced. I left Trinity May 12, 1861.

Entered as private in the Confederate Army in 1861, in December of that year. I was at the last Battle of the Civil War, when General Robert E. Lee surrendered, April 9, 1865, Captain, Company B. 5th N. C. Cavalry, J. E. B. Stuart's corps.

I began the study of law, but entered the Virginia Theological Seminary in 1867, and left said Seminary 1868.

Bishop Peterkin, Kinloch Nelson, Edmund Hubard, J. B. Craighill, Mr. Williams, Benjamin E. Reed, and Bishop Boone were my classmates. They are all in Paradise now, save Reed and myself.

The Faculty Meetings were held on Thursday nights. Dr. William Sparrow and Dr. Packard and Dr. Walker spoke. Dr. Sparrow was a learned preacher and a godly man. Dr. Walker was a very good elocutionist.

I think the Theological Seminary of Virginia the best of its day. Faculty and students being good and true. I wish I could recall all the meetings, services and good deeds done, but I write this propped up in bed and am too old and feeble to write more.

MEMORIES

REV. OTIS A. GLAZEBROOK, D. D.

Class 1869

The class of which I had the privilege of being a member was exceptional in some respects. The formative period of the lives of most of its members was spent in the Confederate Army. This was both a gain and a loss. By it we gained knowledge of men, the loss was educational opportunity. I say the experience with men was a distinct gain. I recall that Bishop Johns in his pastoral lectures to our class once said, "Young gentlemen, be much with men". I have always remembered this saying of the witty and good Bishop as one of the most profitable of his lecture course. I think, too, the history of the class justifies this statement, for it was with commendable pride I observed the manly career of my colleagues, most of them commanding the attention and influence of congregations in which the man element was conspicuous. They were all men of marked personality; Steptoe with his dignified gentleness; Will Dame, the prince of good fellows and incomparable raconteur; Boone of the class of '68 and Penick, differing widely temperamentally, but one in fervid consecration as missionary Bishops; McBryde, tender but strong; Pendleton Brooke, the genial humorist; Sharp, serious but not sanctimonious; Hoxton, the perfect gentleman; Laird, with his modest thoughtfulness; Hepburn, characteristically true; Haslett McKim, pre-eminently the scholar of the class and as unfailing in his loyalty as gifted in his mentality. John S. Lindsey, distinguished in the Church as a preacher and prominent and influential in his leadership in General Convention. Besides these, James E. Hammond, L. Carroll McAfee, and Albert R. Stuart, were afterwards faithful and devoted in the exercise of their ministry. Truly it was a rare group and the sweetest memories of my life cluster round its delightful comradeship.

I was obsessed, after my graduation at the Virginia Military Institute, with the intention of studying law. In the leisure afforded by freedom from business restraint I was influenced by a devoted clergyman, an Alumnus of our

Seminary, to take part in Missionary work both as vestryman and lay-reader of his parish, and frequently accompanied him in his calls upon the poor. This experience resulted in turning me from the University of Virginia to the
Theological Seminary. As I reported for the examination
required for the middle class, I met a strikingly distinguished
looking young man in "top hat", something unusual in
Dixie in those days, fresh from Harvard, who was to be my
companion in this examination. The closest friendship of
my life dates from that meeting.

As I think over the moulding influences of the past I
believe the Faculty Meetings of the Seminary have been the
most satisfactorily enduring. The spiritual atmosphere of
the Institution was the direct product of these meetings, and
the old Faculty was at its best in those never-to-be-forgotten
and prized Thursday night intimate talks. The inspiration
of contact with such men as Dr. Sparrow, Dr. Packard and
Dr. Walker has never failed me in the many years of a varied
and active life.

No memory of Seminary days can exclude Miss Cornelia
Jones, the godly matron, a very angel of comfort to us all.
Being the only *pater familias* in the Seminary, in the absence
of my family at times, I availed myself of the Seminary board.
I recall it was a special pleasure to be placed at her right hand.

The home life of such a "Hill" could not be other than
exalted. The refinement of the hospitality of the Professors'
families; Mrs. Cazenove, of the open house; the ever-cordial
household of Mr. Cassius Lee; the attractive environment
of the Bishop's home illumined by the kindly welcome of
Miss Julia and Bishop Johns himself—all conspired to create
a social life, the beauty of which must still linger in the memory of all who came under its charm. I could especially
emphasize the home life of Mrs. Funsten, and I speak from
an intimate experience, for she made her home a very real
one for Mrs. Glazebrook and me, including babies and nurse.
Verily that "Wilderness" home blossomed as the rose.

In a final word, I wish to testify that the spirit of the
Seminary bestowed upon me a priceless boon, and as I approach nearer to the time of my departure, I more and more
gratefully recognize the debt I owe to the hallowing influence
of those old Seminary days.

MEMORIES

REV. S. S. HEPBURN

Class 1869

You have asked me for some reminiscences of the Seminary in my day, I am glad to give them, for there is no period of my life upon which I am more fond of dwelling than that which found me a student on the dear old Hill.

In September 1866, at the opening of the first session after the Civil War, I was among the first students to arrive there. I hailed from the Eastern shore of Maryland, then in the diocese of Maryland. I had just passed my twenty-first birthday and was one of three students from North of the Potomac. Twenty-five matriculated that year, all old Confederate Soldiers but two, one other and myself. This one other had been in some one of the departments in Washington, and had been for a few days in the trenches to defend that city when threatened. I, alone, had not been in either army, though a most ardent Southern sympathizer.

The Seminary and surrounding country of that day was very different from the place and section of today. The country had been denuded of its forests, every hilltop was crowned with a fortification, and these were connected by trenches. The country was almost depopulated and those who were left were very poor. The Seminary had been used by the Army and the bare buildings had been left. These were in bad condition. The provison for taking care of students was poor indeed. Miss Cornelia Jones, our then matron, fed us simply, but abundantly, at sixteen dollars a month. Our rooms were furnished in the plainest way, bedstead, shuck mattress, bureau, blanket, and wood stove, washstand, bowl and bucket. The rest we furnished ourselves. Those who used wood paid for it, cut and carried it up to their rooms, or paid the old negro janitor to do it for them. We were a hardy set, just off the farm, or who for four years had lived in the open and had been used to roughing it. The life was no hardship to any of us. To not a few it was luxury. Not a few of the students wore home-spun and homemade clothes. I was looked upon as a dude, as I had one store bought suit, the rest of my clothing, from socks up to hat, were home-made. From September to Christmas I had no sheets on my bed or case on my straw pillow. Those things could not be bought ready made at that time. After Christmas my mother saw to it that I was supplied with these *luxuries*.

The session of sixty-six and seven was not only noted as the most remarkable in the history of the Seminary because of its student body, made up almost entirely of old and tried men who had four years endured the soldier's life, but because of the three striking men who occupied the professors' chairs—Dr. Sparrow, Dr. Packard and Dr. Walker, familiarly known among the students as the *Captain*, the *Rab*, and the *Centurion*. They would have been remarkable men in any age, perhaps more remarkable because of this special period. To us, they were giants. To my mind each of them had those special gifts which fitted him for the position which he occupied.

Having an unbounded admiration for Dr. Sparrow I often went to his study and was a frequent guest at his supper table.   Perhaps my first visit to his study was the cause of this. I knocked at the door; from the inside came the hearty "Come in", as he only could say it. I entered most timidly. I was going into the presence of the King. Looking up over his spectacles he said, "Ah, Mr. Hepburn. Take a seat." He opened conversation with "I see that you are from the Eastern Shore of Maryland. I have often desired to go there, but have not done so. What sort of country is it? What do the people do for a living?" With Eastern shore pride I told him of the beauty of the country, of our wild fowl, fish and oysters. Growing eloquent I launched out into an account of our peach industry (then in its prime) and told of our great orchards and the numbers of boxes of fruit shipped. I made quite a wonderful and attractive story of it. The old gentleman was greatly interested and said, "All that is news to me." After some talk about my studies I left him. Getting back to my room I began to rehearse in my mind what I had told him about the peach crop. My conscience accused me of exaggeration. I picked up my hat and went straight back and knocked at his door again. At his "come in" I entered very shamefacedly and refused to sit down until I had eased my conscience. I began most haltingly "Doctor, in talking to you just now about peaches on the Eastern shore and the size of orchards, did I say hundreds or thousands of trees?" "You said thousands." "Well, sir, I wish to correct that, and say hundreds." "Well", said he, "I *swallowed* it all." In his innocence he would have swallowed the most marvelous story.

I heard one evening that the old gentleman was celebrating his sixty-ninth birthday. I went over to congratulate him. He was in good spirits. When I expressed my good wishes, he said, "Yes, Yes. When I was twenty I never expected to see twenty-five. I was then teaching school in Ohio, a tall, slender, delicate man. One Saturday I wished to take a horse-back ride. The horse was brought to the door. When I had mounted him, my landlady said, 'Mr. Sparrow don't let that horse throw you, for you will break like a pipe-stem.'"

One other story about this grand old man. He made frequent visits North to gather funds for the Seminary. On one of his visits to New York or some city, he lost fifty dollars by having his pocket picked. The news of his misfortune preceded his return. When he came back I went over to express my sympathy and hear his story. "Mrs. Sparrow," said he, "wanted to deepen my pocket before I left home. I told her it was not necessary for I am so ticklish I thought no man could put his hand in my pocket without my knowing it. I was getting on a street car. The platform was crowded and, in the jam, my pocket was picked. Good friends more than made up to me the loss. My pocket has now been deepened."

My admiration for this among the purest and greatest men of the Church in his period, has I fear made me dwell so long upon my reminiscences of him that I can say but little about Dr. Packard and Dr. Walker. Both men were greatly loved by us all, and we were most fortunate to be under their wise leadership.

I have one story of Dr. Packard that has never been told. It has influenced me for fifty-five years. I had charge of Lebanon Station. In my senior year a young man named

Terrett was to be married. I got Dr. Packard to go with me up to Langley (near where the bride's home was) to perform the ceremony. Cake and wine were served. I determined to be guided by the Doctor as to whether I would drink the wine or not. I was, by habit, a teetotaller. He took the glass handed him. I did the same. Soon I saw him edging his way nearer the mantel upon which he placed the untouched glass. Mine was immediately placed on the table also untouched. It was a striking force of example. On my first visit to that community afterwards, a mother said, "I want to thank you for not drinking that wine on the day of the wedding, for my son and others were watching you and had bragged what they were going to do if you drank it." I owe Dr. Packard a debt which I will never be able to repay. His example has been the unfailing rule of my long ministry.

I can not close without a word about the student body of 1866-'67. It was a period which can never be duplicated in the history of Church and State. After the drastic experiences of four years of Civil war, twenty-five men of this Church, wounded in body and pauperized by the loss of property, enrolled themselves as candidates for the ministry. All of them matured men, with fixed purposes, ready to fight as determinedly for the cause of the Church as they had fought for that of State. It was a rare body of men. They were bound to be heard from. After the lapse of fifty-six years, their history has been written. It is a history to be proud of. It tells of the revival of impoverished and broken down country parishes in Virginia, West Virginia, and Maryland, and the opening up of new fields in all these dioceses. It tells of strong city Churches in Baltimore, Elizabeth City, Pennsylvania, Staunton, Richmond, and Louisville, presided over by these men. It tells of splendid work done in the Mission field by Boone and Penick, and of strong dioceses built up by Dudley and Peterkin. Well do I remember the last day of that session when we gathered for the last time in old Prayer Hall for family worship. A hymn was sung as such men only can sing. Dudley read the Scripture lesson, made a few tender farewell remarks—his class was to be ordained—we knelt in prayer. It was the last time we would ever meet under the old conditions.   Strong men, who had faced all manner of hardship and death, arose to fall upon each other's necks and weep tears of love.   Even now, after the lapse of more than half a century, my heart swells with tender emotion as I think of that scene.

MEMORIES

REV. J. G. MINNIGERODE, D. D.

Class 1871

I went to the Seminary in the Fall of 1867. I look back to my stay there with the most grateful recollection.   I have never known any place where the spiritual amd moral tone was so high and pure.   Nor have I ever been associated with a better, nobler body of men than those who were gathered there.   Most of us had but lately come from the service of the Confederacy.   Afterwards several of us were together in the Piedmont Convocation—Peterkin, Nelson, Dame, Lindsey, Laird, Steptoe, Powers and others—all but one of them now gone to their reward.   We travelled two and two together, on horseback, and there are but few places in those six counties where we failed to preach the Gospel. We made it our boast that no Parish, Church or Mission in the Convocation should receive aid from the Diocesan Missionary Society.

The most vivid recollection I have of the Seminary and what impressed me most deeply, were the Faculty Meetings, held each Thursday evening in Prayer Hall.   Dr. Sparrow was then at his best.   He would speak sitting in his chair, his face all illumined, and his words of wisdom and deep spiritual truth went straight to the heart of each one.

I feel that I owe much to the Seminary.   I pray that the work may go on ever-increasing and that it will be a blessing to the Church and to the world.

MEMORIES

REV. LANDON R. MASON, D. D.

Class 1873

The chief organizations among the students of the Seminary were the Debating Society and the Missionary Society. I belonged to both, but always preserved a judicious silence. I had concluded in early youth that public speaking was one of the things, not that I would never do well, but that I could *never* do at all, and did not mean to *try* to do. At school I always paid my fine in the Debating Society and did my part by listening with more or less patience. At the Seminary I followed the same practice in the Debating Society and listened with more interest in the Missionary Meetings, but abstained from vocal expression. Like all my contemporaries, I felt that the Faculty Meetings were helps and inspirations to all who wished to speak in the Master's Cause.

During my years of service in General Conventions at the Seminary Alumni Meetings held during the sessions, I heard Dr. Phillips Brooks three or four times declare, with more emphasis than courtesy, that Dr. Sparrow was the whole team that made the Virginia Seminary worth while, and now Dr. Sparrow was dead, so he left his hearers to draw their own inference as to what that Seminary stood for. At about the third General Convention where he made that statement, Dr. Kinloch Nelson took him up and said he had heard the learned Doctor and prince of preachers give utterance to the same view of the value and status of the Virginia Seminary three or four times. But, he said, the "Doctor had forgotten that things *grew*." He ought to remember, Nelson said, that "He—Brooks—had grown himself." He touched on the fact that the Doctor's avoirdupois was greater (he weighed somewhat over three hundred pounds) than in his Seminary days, and no doubt his intellectual and spiritual powers had likewise increased. Otherwise he would hardly now be considered the "Master of the American Pulpit, and be able on occasion to set English Churches on fire." Seeing then, that these facts were not to be controverted, Dr. Brooks "ought in fairness to concede the possibility of growth in the Virginia Seminary."

I do not remember hearing Dr. Brooks sit down so hard on the Virginia Seminary at subsequent General Conventions.

Dr. Sparrow was a great teacher, with a massive mind, and high spiritual vision, and these gifts came out much more effectively in the class room and Faculty Meetings than in the pulpit, where he shot rather over the heads of those who listened.

For myself, I am free to confess that I was of small enough caliber to learn a great deal from the other professors. The dear "Old Rab" (Dr. Packard), and "Dr. Facts" (Dr. Walker) were godly and faithful men, who conscientiously and prayerfully labored to teach the ideas of the embryo theologs how to shoot upward toward the light that shines in the face of the living Master and Teacher of us all. No doubt the Seminary has grown since then, as all living things and opinions must, or rot, but, for a weak vessel, I am glad I had their help.

They were patient, too, with the infirmities of their students. *e. g.:* One day one of them expressed a very decided view on a matter about which the good "Old Rab" had put a question to his class. When he got through, the Doctor expounded the matter in a very different light. The student at once apologized, and declared that it was his "honest opinion, but he saw he would *have* to *change* his *opinion*", and quickly followed the request "Doctor, can I go to my room?" Of course, for weeks afterwards the class-mates were inquiring, "Did you find your new opinion in your wardrobe, bureau, or in a book? How near did it correspond to 'the Rab's' opinion, and which opinion do you hold now?"

Miss Mary Rhett was matron, and was *fine*. We all liked her.

MEMORIES

RT. REV. G. H. KINSOLVING, D. D.

Class 1874

In what I am about to write, of course, there can be no elaborate evoking of memories; one can only hope to turn back in thought for a moment into the Hall of Reminiscence and listen to the echoes of the receding footsteps of that ghostly company passing further and further away into the mystery and silence of the years that have gone.

In the autumn of 1871, I entered the Theological Seminary in Virginia, and was admitted as a member of the Junior Class. There were fourteen regular members of the Class, only two of whom are now living, the Rev. Dr. Frank G. Scott and myself. We were an aggressive and pugnacious set of novices and introduced many innovations into the traditional management of student affairs in the Institution. We formed an alliance, offensive and defensive, with the Preparatory students and exerting a seductive influence over several of the middle-class men; we quite easily caused the Seniors to know their places, and to beware putting on airs in our presence, or arrogating to themselves rights and privileges which up to that time were supposed to belong to the Seniors by virtue of priority of occupancy of the buildings and to the operation of various unwritten laws transmitted from the past by a kind of primogeniture inheritance. As an illustration of our revolutionary methods in our Junior year, I was nominated to make a missionary address before the Missionary Society; the President of the Society, who was a Senior, ruled the nomination out of order on the ground that Juniors had never been elected to that privilege; the honor was reserved for Seniors and occasionally a middleman. There was no written law to that effect and upon an appeal from the ruling of the chair made by Charles J. Holt, the appeal was sustained and amidst a great uproar of triumph and confusion, I was declared elected. It was my first experience in practical Church politics.

F. G. Scott was the scholar of our class and one of the best prepared Grecians we have ever had in the Seminary.

He was my Fidus Achates.   "Wash" Nelson was also one
of my intimates.   He had commanded a company of artillery
in our war for Southern Independence and was a fine fighter
for the right in all the relationships in life.   It is a suggestive
commentary on the shortness and uncertainty of human life
when I recall how rapidly the different members of that class
crossed over the Great Divide into the "Stille Land", only
three of us, I believe, filled out our three-score years and ten,
and at present, as I have already said, only two of us remain.

Dr. William Sparrow was our instructor in Theology and
Christian Ethics.   As a teacher, the Doctor was indeed a
Prince in Israel; a preacher for preachers and one of the
profound thinkers of the American Church.   His power
resided largely in his personality; the way he said things;
the meaning imparted to a word or sentiment; the flash of his
eye; the uplift of his brows, which arched high on his noble
forehead; the intellectual glow which would suffuse his
face and the magnetic gestures of his body.   I was always
entranced in his presence in the classroom and in his study.
I have never known anyone in the Church whom I would
place by his side as his intellectual superior.   Possibly I was
the last student who had a conversation with him before his
death.

Late in the session of our Senior year, our class work
having been interrupted by the illness of the Doctor, the
class deputed me to see the Doctor and ask for exemption
from writing certain essays; it was my turn to read the next
essay; I went to the Doctor's study, Friday evening I think
it was, and plead my cause and that of my classmates as
best I could and when I had finished, the Doctor looked at me
with that sweet ineffable smile which often played over his
countenance, and these were almost literally his words as I
can now recall them: "My young friend, had you not felt
a call to the Ministry, I would have suggested the law for you
excel as a special pleader, but you must write your essays."
On the Saturday morning following, while busy with the
essay on a chapter of Butler's Analogy, Harry Lee rushed
into my room and exclaimed, "Dr. Sparrow fell dead in the
Burke and Herbert Bank in Alexandria, an hour ago."   A
few days later, I acted as one of the pallbearers when we

placed all that was mortal of this transcendently great man in its resting place in the hallowed God's Acre near the Seminary.

Dr. Cornelius Walker taught us Church History. It has been said that perhaps the best test of a man's intelligence is his capacity for making a summary. Both as a teacher and preacher, Dr. Walker possessed this power to a very marked degree. At a public meeting when other men were speaking, or at a close of a series of Convocational Services, if the Doctor was allowed to sum up what had been said by other speakers, he was then at his best and few men could equal him in the exercise of this splendid gift. As a teacher, the Doctor did not indulge much in theories or speculation; he was almost an idolater of facts, and we used to call him "Old Facts." He might have been more interesting at times had he philosophized or allowed his imagination to give us his interpretations of facts. He preferred rather to insist upon our learning the facts of Church History, and you could not evade this requirement in the classroom or on examination days by glittering generalities or erroneous guesses. He demanded that you should know exactly what was said and done at the General Councils and the dates of their assembling and the characteristics of the great epochs in the development of the Church's life.

Dr. John J. McElhinney was the Professor of New Testament Greek. He had the reputation of being one of the most accurate and learned scholars of his day; his health was delicate and he seldom left his house without consulting the thermometer and barometer and dressing according to the temperature and arming himself with gum shoes and an umbrella if it threatened rain. He possessed a gentle and modest disposition and all of his class was impressed by his vast fund of reference and quotations. His private library contained a number of rare and valuable books and many years after my Seminary days, when a rector in Philadelphia, the library was sent to that city to be sold at auction. I begged the Doctor not to risk it, but he was in need of money and though I made an earnest appeal to the clergy of Philadelphia to buy some of the books, I know it grieved to the heart the dear old bibliophile to see his valuable treasures sacrificed for the most paltry prices.

Dr. Joseph Packard was our Professor of Hebrew and Old Testament Literature; the Doctor lived to an advanced age and was well-known to the present generation. The one lesson above all others which I learned from Dr. Packard was to reverence the Bible as a Holy Book, as being indeed the Word of God. His very manner in the classroom breathed forth an atmosphere of solemnity and at times even of awe. Now and then a scintillation of humor, subtle and quaint, would flash out spontaneously, but in the main, the ground whereon we trod was holy ground and with shoes from off our feet, we moved softly before the Ark of the Covenant, and that spirit has remained with me as a blessed heritage all during my Ministry.

May the loving recollection of those mighty men of God who taught me in my youth abide until the end and influence and steady my thoughts and conduct in the midst of an age of innate skepticism, of unseemly levity, and which handles with "an icy and disintegrating touch" all those questions around which clustered the generous fervor and massive piety of the past.

MEMORIES

RT. REV. JAMES A. WINCHESTER, D. D.

Class 1877

It has been my privilege to travel much on land and sea, to gaze upon the snow-capped mountains and wonderful glaciers of Alaska and the sunken gardens of Mexico, and the vine-clad fields of Italy, to study the historic Cathedrals of England, to visit the sacred places of Egypt and the Holy Land: but, in my memory, today, there is no spot so enwrapped with sentiment as the dear old Seminary Hill, where fresh inspiration comes into my heart and mind as from a sparkling fountain. Nothing like it except the beautiful home of my childhood, where at a sainted mother's knees, I knelt with folded hands and said after her "Our Father."

The Civil War had just closed, when the Rev. William F. Gardner, as Principal, assisted by the Rev. Edward Ingle, Mr. George W. Peterkin, a member of the middle class of the Seminary, afterwards the first Bishop of West Virginia, and Mr. Pinckney Mason (officer in the War on the Merrimac) taught the dozen or more day pupils of the country neighborhood and the four boarding boys of the High School. I was one of that quartette, and we had our beds in the four corners of what became the Chapel of the High School, a room used during the Civil War as the morgue when the buildings on "The Hill" were turned into a hospital for Federal soldiers. It is now included as a part of the great auditorium where the students of the High School gather for addresses and services. All other rooms in that immense brick building were vacant, and I can almost hear the falling plaster reverberating in my memory, as the rain beat upon the decayed roof, leaking down to the second floor. Our teachers (except Mr. Peterkin) had their domicile in the original front part of the High School, and the falling of plaster at midnight and the scampering of myriad rats in the vacant rooms made us realize "change and decay in all around I see".

George Peterkin took our Latin class through the Gallic Wars and in doing so, left on our minds the impression that he was himself an ideal soldier of the Cross. The Rev. Mr.

Gardner, one of the most princely Christian gentlemen I ever knew, got into the hearts of those boys, as a sympathetic friend and loving father in God.   Under him we came to confirmation in our boyhood days, for he was indeed a "good man and full of the Holy Ghost," and he bore in his wounded leg the mark of a brave soldier.   Under Mr. Gardner, "The E. H. S." rose Phoenix-like from the ashes of War. Through his unflagging energy the necessary repairs were made.   All honor to the Trustees of the Seminary and High School, of whom Mr. Cassius F. Lee was one of the most active, for the raising of funds in those days of poverty to restore the wrecked buildings, making them habitable for men and boys.

Through such heroism the great Dr. Launcelot Blackford and the eminent Archibald Hoxton, son of the grand old teacher, Col. Llewellyn Hoxton, came into a goodly heritage and have developed the High School into the greatest School for boys (in my judgment), in the country.   They have built upon a spiritual foundation.

Down the vista of years, I see a picture, embodying an inspiration that still moves my soul.   Miss Julia Johns, daughter of "the beloved John Johns" (Bishop of Virginia), was one of the teachers in the Sunday School that gathered in the Seminary building.   She had nine boys in her class. During the summer her nephew, Henry Peyton died.   He was a manly Christian boy.   His death affected us as no other event.   Four of us entered the Holy Ministry, John J. Lloyd, Francis Dupont Lee, Thomas J. Packard, and I. Two of the class graduated in Medicine, Edmund Jennings Lee and Louis Cazenove, one became attorney at law, C. G. Lee, and one launched out upon business, A. Emmett Funsten, who was my senior warden and vestryman during my ministry in St. Louis.

Is it strange when I visit the Seminary Hill that I should go to the sacred little Cemetery and fall on my knees at Miss Julia Johns' grave and thank God for her abiding influence upon my life?   In these days of agitation about "Church Schools" I see nothing equal to the work that holy woman accomplished upon the nine boys, drawing them by chords of love to that Blessed Saviour Whom we knew she consistently served. I get a glimpse of the vanished doubts, driven away by her loving counsel, and there comes a thrill that inspired my college course in subsequent years. It was my spiritual privilege to be a member of her household after I had the high honor of acting as pall bearer at her father's funeral. My dear room-mate there in her home was C. Braxton Bryan, an encyclopaedia of knowledge and a spiritual giant. We felt that the shadows of the great Bishop, who had laid his hands on my head in confirmation, rested upon us. I entered the Episcopal High School, as it were, through the door of the Seminary and then the Seminary through the High School. My first acquaintance and friend made on Virginia soil was Mr. Edmund Hubard, a member of the middle class of the Seminary that year 1866-'67. I found myself at the door of Aspinwall Hall, having been guided on foot from Alexandria by a little negro boy. The Rev. Mr. Gardner missed me at the boat landing, and also at the old "Mansion House Hotel", and I paid my little Ethiopian guide, whom I picked up in the street, thirty-five cents to show me the way to the Seminary Hill. He it was, a little boy faithfully discharging his duty, who left me with the tall man of God, Mr. Hubard, whom I discovered was a warm friend of my uncle, the Rev. Dr. Ridout, who had been "the beloved Physician" at the Seminary during his Theological course of three years. I needed no other introduction in Virginia than that of this dear uncle, who had selected the High School for me. Through Mr. Hubard I found my way that afternoon to the ballgrounds of the High School, and was immediately at home.

I discovered that the Theological Seminary had a set of men, the like of whom I had not seen before and perhaps have not seen since. Some of them wore the Confederate uniform and it was commonly reported that among the student body there were only three or four dress coats, suitable for calling upon young ladies in the evening. Consequently visiting was somewhat abridged. Yet those few dress suits did their work, judging from the happy marriages that came about. Bishop Peterkin married Miss Constance Lee, daughter of Mr. Cassius Lee. The Rev. William Laird married Miss Rose Packard, daughter of the Professor of

Hebrew, Dr. Packard.   The Rev. Benjamin E. Reed, married Miss Mary Funsten, and Dr. William M. Dame married Miss Susie Funsten.   I think of these couples as brave men and fair women.

Among those students was Thomas U. Dudley, whose valedictory address at the end of the session impressed me as the most eloquent piece of oratory I ever heard.   He became the silver-tongued orator of the House of Bishops. I see in memory, William Boone, with a far-away look toward China, where he became Bishop, following his father, who had also dedicated himself to Missionary work at the Seminary and became the first Bishop of China.   And there rises up dear Bishop Clifton Penick, whom the boys loved, with his great heart of sympathy.   It was not strange that the Church saw in him a soul that took in Africa and sent him to carry the Gospel to those benighted people.

Of that splendid student body at the Seminary during my first year at the High School, there are only seven left— Drs. W. Q. Hullihen, William M. Dame, James Minnigerode, and Revs. Messrs. Henry T. Sharpe, Edward Wooten and Benjamin E. Reed.   The High School boys admired and loved the Theological students.   It was the type of manhood a boy delights to see.   They joined us in baseball, told us war stories, and advised us about becoming good men.   In our first match game of baseball, we had Dame as our pitcher, and Minnigerode as fielder, and we took the game from Alexandria's crack amateur club, "The Young America."   That game erected a pennant that has waved many years, and it has been fair and honest ball.   I am still proud of the fact that I was third baseman on that nine. The cordial relationship between the boys of the Episcopal High School and the students of the Seminary began in those early days and continues to the present.   The influences were strong factors in bringing boys to the conviction of the holy ministry.

The Seminary overlooks Arlington, the historic home of Gen. Robert E. Lee, whose name was associated with "The Hill"; our dear friend, Mr. Cassius Lee, his first cousin, being a resident at "Manokin" up to his death.   Having been prepared for college it was natural that our eyes should turn to General Lee, who had become President of Washington College at Lexington, and numbers of the boys in those early days decided upon General Lee's college, rather than the "University of Virginia". Going to Lexington I found my rector, Brigadier-General William N. Pendleton, D. D. had been Principal of the Episcopal High School before the Civil War, and it was a wonderful link with the Seminary Hill, as I lived in his rectory two years, and had my warm High School friends as chums in college and all under the greatest Christian heroes of any age. I touched a wonderful honor system that General Lee had erected in Washington College. It was nothing less than the continuation of the Seminary Hill life I had received. One of the proudest moments of my college life was the announcement that I was selected as one of the guard to watch by the casket of the beloved President of our College. Washington and Lee University seems a part of the very Seminary in my affection.

When College work was over Bishop Johns saw to it that I could return to the Seminary Hill as a Theological student, and I had three years of blessed experience, full of spiritual uplift. The Faculty Meetings were benedictions. I see Dr. McElhinney with his hand on his forehead, bringing out quotations and teachings of the Fathers and Reformers; Dr. Packard holding up for our examples the Missionaries like Hoffman and Payne, and showing how they made the very Seminary walls sacred by their prayers as students; Dr. Walker with incisive sentences of wisdom; and Dr. Kinloch Nelson telling of Christian experiences in the great world.

We got sermonettes out of those Faculty Meetings which we delivered in the adjacent Missions connected with the Seminary. We did not find in the Faculty Meetings anything that justified the words regarding the sermons of one of our Theological Professors that,—"He went down deeper, stayed under longer, and came up drier than anyone". Volumes of inspiration came from those men of God.

How could anyone ever forget Miss Mary Rhett, our matron, and her dear aged mother? It was my honor one year to occupy the room just above her apartment, and which she had the right to assign to a student. I look into that window from these far away days and see my predecessors and most helpful fellow students.   The year previous, Robert A. Goodwin was living there as a beautiful Christian example to all of us.   During one period of Spiritual doubt in my Junior Year, it was Robert Goodwin who brought comfort and light.   I think of him as an Enoch, who "walked with God."

Miss Mary Rhett was a mother in Israel to the students of my day.   A Southern lady, with the most delicate refinement, it was a privilege to have her at our table, day by day, because Theological students can not afford to be away from the true woman's influence, and now, as Bishop of Arkansas, I see the influence of the Seminary.

Bishop Leonidas Polk was the first of the alumni of the Seminary to be made a Bishop.   He went to the South West, and Arkansas was included in the scope of his great Missionary field.   I have had a number of his family in my parishes in Tennessee and now have members of his family in my diocese.   He was a wonderful Bishop, as also military commander, having had the West Point training as well as the Seminary instruction.   Then I see Bishop Lay, as the third Bishop of Arkansas, a distinguished scholar and one who has left an impression upon Arkansas that will live on forever.

It seems strange indeed that I should have been the only student of my day at the Seminary to be called to the Episcopate.   Why were John K. Mason, Robert S. Barrett, Henry B. Lee, Braxton Bryan, or some others, not called instead of me?   Of the forty students in the three classes of my Junior year, there are left now Messrs. Edward Wroth, William H. Barnwell of the Senior Class, and Roller, John Gantt and Charles Randolph of the Middle, and Rev. Messrs. John Gravatt, Nelson P. Dame, Peter M. Boyden, and the writer of the Juniors; six of us in the active work of the ministry.

Thinking of the Seminary I call to mind "The Reformed Episcopal Church Movement".   It was predicted that our students were in peril of "deserting the old ship."   Out of our band only one man of the Middle class felt that he should join that movement.   We felt almost as though a death had occurred, when Reynolds left us.   We met as a body and declared our allegiance and I realized that we were true to the "faith once delivered to the Saints". "The Higher criticism", which was in its infancy at that time, did not disturb us in any way. The Hebrew and Greek texts were studied as the inspired word of God, and it did not occur to me to doubt the canonical books of Holy Scripture or the interpretation which had come down through the Historic Church from Apostolic days.

The Virginia Seminary has stood for two great principles, Religion and Patriotism. Two of its special founders were Bishop William Meade and Francis Scott Key. The one carried the standard of the Cross over his vast Mission field, distributing religious tracts through the mountains of the State as well as over the country districts. Such distribution became the seed corn of the Church, and houses of worship have sprung up over that great area. It was Bishop Meade who earnestly upheld the Cross in his day, to whom we are indebted for the consecrated Churchmanship of Virginia, which her successors, Johns and Whittle, consistently pursued—in which the students of the Theological Seminary, class after class, have co-operated, driving away all erroneous and strange doctrine.

Francis Scott Key, as one of the promoters of the Education Society of Virginia, which gave birth to the Seminary, may be regarded as one of the lay founders of our Seminary. Out of his consecrated heart burst the beautiful hymn so dear to myriad souls "Lord with glowing heart I'd praise Thee", and equally fervent is "The Star Spangled Banner", the finest embodiment of patriotism in our literature.

Why not, in front of Aspinwall Hall, erect two granite memorial statues, one to Bishop Meade and the other to the poet Key, with "The Stars and Stripes" daily waving its morning greeting to the Capital of our country across the Potomac? And above the Stars and Stripes keep the Cross upon the cupola of the building that has taught the world the Brotherhood of Man?

MEMORIES

REV. CARL E. GRAMMER, S. T. D.

Class 1884

It is not so easy for one to give his impressions of the Seminary in his student days as it would be, if he had had no other associations with the Institution. The later experiences have rather blurred the outlines of the earlier picture, and the mind is like a palimpsest, which only by the most judicious treatment gives up the incompletely erased record over which a new history has been written. The worst of it is, that when one begins this stripping away of the last impressions, he finds himself always prone to pass beyond matriculation, and to return to the days of boyhood. For there have been three distinct eras in my Seminary life: the first when I visited my grandfather, Dr. Sparrow; the second, my three years as a student; and the third, my eleven years as a member of the Faculty. My effort will be to write about the second; but like an ignorant witness, who can omit nothing, if I am to disentangle these recollections, I must begin at the very beginning.

I can recall distinctly the first time that I ever came near the Seminary's pagoda-like cupola, called by many of the country folk, who live within the sound of its bell, "the cupalo". My mother was taking her children to visit the home of her girlhood; and an uncle who was accompanying us, suddenly called out, "Here we are, close to the Seminary," whereupon my brother, next to myself in age, suddenly and most mysteriously fell asleep. His slumber was so profound that it was impossible to awake him, and to the amusement of all, he had to be carried, in this deep sleep, by my uncle into the room prepared for my mother, and laid upon the bed; when, the coast being clear of aunts with possible tendencies towards kissing chubby nephews, he suddenly awoke. This visit was very shortly after the close of the Civil War; and the grounds still bore the marks of the camp fires; and we children, every now and then, kicked up out of the grass in corners dilapidated canteens and other cast-aside paraphernalia of war.

The mail-carrier was Cleveland, who lived for many years on "The Hill," to bind together the present and the past, by his memories. He was pointed out to me as a man who had been "a guerilla." I was more familiar with gorillas, than with this new designation of warriors; and while I knew that a gorilla and a guerilla must be quite different, and in fact, soon gathered a correct enough idea of a guerilla, still something of the fierce associations of the gorilla long lingered in my mind as a lad, when I saw the carrier.

None of the professors was at home, that first summer, except Dr. Packard. I can see now his tall figure, dressed in black, with something of the New Englander about him, in spite of his long years of residence in the South, and his strong Southern sympathies. At this first glimpse of him, he was, characteristically enough, going to the library, and with childish attention to insignificant details, I noticed that the right leg of his trousers was hitched up by the hind strap of his gaiter. Years after, when I came to the Seminary, as a student, I saw the same strap, holding up behind the trousers of the same leg.

On Sunday, we went to the old Chapel and I dimly recall its solemn gloom. My recollection of the exterior, however, is more distinct; for the front door was our favorite base, in a game of "Honey, Honey, Peep-Po." I wonder whether little boys play it to-day. The fleetness of foot, and prompt decisions of my playmate, Baldwin Walker, linger in my memory. That very summer, the flower beds in front of the matron's rooms were laid out, if I remember rightly, by a man who was completing his work, during our visit, by fencing off my grandfather's grounds. My brother and I greatly marveled at the leisurely manner, in which he used to work, and the long intermissions of rest. It was explained to us, by a knowing older lad, that the man was working by the day. It was my first experience of that kind of work. Few institutions have suffered more from it than the Seminary. But with the able and conscientious administration of Dr. Henderson Suter, a new efficiency was brought into the care of the grounds and the general oversight of labor.

A board walk, in those days, ran between the houses of the professors, and went part of the way through the woods

towards the High School.   At this famous Academy, Mr.
Blackford was then but a recent arrival, and I heard much
about his new ideals, and especially about his encouragement of athletics.   He was very popular with the boys of the
neighborhood who attended his school.   As my visit was
made during the holidays, I came in contact with no others.
One day, we were over on the school ground looking at the
horizontal bar, which was out of doors; for this was before
the day of the Gymnasium; and the boys told me that Mr.
Blackford favored exercise upon the bar.   Indeed, to be
exact, my memory runs, that they said that he himself would
do a turn on the bar; and for years, I always associated Mr.
Blackford with "skinning the cat."   During my long and
intimate intercourse with him, when I was his neighbor on
"The Hill", I saw him in many different relations, and under
various circumstances, but some how or other, I never once
saw him on the bar; and in some way or other, I neglected
to ask him, whether my early recollection was correct, and
had he ever "skinned the cat".   And this, when all the great
masters of history are continually reminding us of the duty
of verifying our facts.

But I am afraid that these are not the kind of reminiscences wanted.   There are, indeed, other and sacred associations
of my boyhood days; but I doubt if they would be of general
interest.   I recall still the solemn awe with which I went into
my grandfather's study, where all the books neatly covered
with brown paper, with their titles clearly written on their
backs in his scholarly hand, told of his learning and system.
My grandmother's portly figure, also, rises before me, and I
can see her seated on the front porch of shady Oakwood,
with her grown sons and daughters around her; while her
grandchildren had a mimic warfare in the grove with those
full large acorns for missiles.   It seems to me that there are
no such large acorns, now-a-days.

She was a great Shakesperean.   I remember that not
one of her children, all fond of books and poetry, could catch
her as to the play, in which a quotation was found.   Dr.
Albert Tayloe Bledsoe, the eminent metaphysician, who was
at one time the professor of Mathematics at the University
of Virginia, was a great friend of Dr. Sparrow's, and I recall

seeing him at Oakwood. He was full of quip and jest; and loved to turn away in conversation from the deep problems that filled his working hours. Dr. Andrews, also, came to "The Hill;" and even as a boy, I realized that there was something broad and statesmanlike about the old Evangelical leader and debater in the General Convention.

Behind these recollections there move dim shades, as it were in penumbra that deepens into total darkness, visions called up by anecdotes of my parents. In this dim land I see the figures of saintly Dr. May, and many a student, some grotesque in their ignorance, some gently radiant like Colden Hoffman, with the holy light of self-sacrificing devotion. But there are others who can speak of these earlier days from personal knowledge, and I will forbear.

I entered the Seminary as a Theological student, in the fall of 1881. Brought up and educated in a city, I can never forget the charm of those student years, amidst such beautiful surroundings. It was a perpetual delight to watch the white sails of the distant schooners upon the broad bosom of the Potomac, with the soft hills of Maryland, "My Maryland", in the background; to mark the slow progress of the tall shaft, dedicated to Washington, which after a long rest, like the sleepers of Ephesus, had waked up to activity, in very different days from those in which it had been born; and to walk in the leafy grove beneath those stately oaks.

At night, we could see part of the horizon, bright with the lights of the nation's capital, and were reminded of Wordsworth's fine lines:

> "The river glideth at his own sweet will
> And all that mighty heart is lying still;"

or recalled that splendid description of a sleeping city, in Sartor Resartus. I doubt not, that many a student has climbed at night into the cupola, and looked down upon the dim landscape below him, the thick gloom of the woods, the solitary lights of scattered homes, and the general brightness in the direction of the cities, and echoed Teufeldsdroch's praise of his sky-parlor: "Ach, mein lieber, it is true sublimity to dwell here. These fringes of lamplight struggling up, through smoke, and thousandfold exhalation, some fathoms into the ancient reign of Night, what thinks Bootes of them, as he leads his Hunting Dogs over the zenith, in their leash of sidereal fire?" and so on to the last words: "But I, mein Werther, sit above it all, I am alone with the stars."

I had spent many summers at the seaside, or in the Virginia mountains, but this was my first Autumn, Winter and Spring in the country. What glorious months they were: how musical the rustle of the fallen leaves: how exquisite the parti-colored woods: how entrancing the clear outlines of a winter scene in the grove: what witchery there was in the Spring's tender tints, its films over the landscape, its first flowers. What a glory in those June days, which so often brought to mind Lowell's verse, in praise of this queen among months:

> "What is so rare as a day in June?
> Ah then, if ever, the earth is in tune."

One day, out on the baseball field an eagle was seen slowly winging its way across our grounds. At the sight, a great shout went up, which caused the eagle to ascend directly upwards by a series of spirals. A buzzard was, at the time, wheeling through the air on its tireless wings; but the eagle's ascent was in much smaller circles, and its movement was much more energetic. Upward it climbed on its viewless spiral stair, till it was more than a thousand feet above the boisterous crowd, when it stretched its wings and glided away into the sunset, bound for the distant Alleghanies, Such sights and influences, I count among the most valued possessions of my life.

> "One impulse from a vernal wood
> Can teach us more of man,
> Of moral evil and of good,
> Than all the sages can."

Through large donations secured by Dr. Crawford, soon after he came to the Seminary, a number of valuable improvements were made under his intelligent direction, in the grounds and general arrangement. The grove became more like a park, and the scenery gained very much in refinement and cultivation. But the law of compensation is ever

at work; and with the coming of the new bridge, the broad
roads, the pump-house and the tank, much of the wild wood
charm departed.   The walks are better kept, but the autumn
leaves do not rustle so musically upon them.   The lawns are
now finer, but they are not so starred with forget-me-nots.

One of my pleasantest recollections relates to the society
of the neighborhood. The Seminary never could have
moulded the students with the power that it exercised upon
all who entered its halls, without the aid of the kind and loyal
friends in these Christian homes.   They came with wonderful regularity to our Missionary meetings, and listened with
unfailing interest and appreciation to the untrained speaking
of the students, and to their academic debates.   They entertained our friends during the Commencement, and on
special occasions of Missionary Conventions.   Their generosity aided the students to send delegates away, and furthered
the interests of the Seminary in countless ways.   Never
have I known a community that made a greater sacrifice of
time and pleasure, to foster the life of an institution.   Not
only the professors and their families, but the whole neighborhood, lived for the Seminary's interest with a unique
devotion.

Of my fellow-students and class-mates, it is too soon to
speak individually.   But the general impression must be
given, if recollections are to have any value.   The Senior
class, when I entered, contained a number of fine men, like
H. D. Page, Kensey Hammond, Francis Leavell, James B.
Funsten, Buckner Randolph and Yates Downman; and
they gave a high tone of feeling and spiritual aspiration to
the whole undergraduate body.   Taken as a whole, the
students were marked by singular unworldliness.   No one
ever heard them talk of big parishes or prominent places,
or worldly signs of success.   Their standards were all high
and spiritual.   This was, of course, largely due to the Professors, who never failed to remind us, in their helpful Faculty meeting talks, that the ministry was not a profession, but
a calling; and who exemplified their teaching in their own
walk and conversation.

I should not be frank, if I did not add that I thought the
students, as a whole, inclined to cultivate the negative rather

than the positive graces; and more anxious to pull up weeds, than to bear fruit. Well do I recall an experience on the night of my first St. Andrew's meeting. I was going directly to my room after supper, when I was asked the reason for my haste. I replied, that as we had a meeting that night, I found it necessary to save time by beginning at once upon the lessons for tomorrow. "It's clear you have never been to one of these meetings," cried my interrogator, "for there is no room for lessons to-night." He evidently intended to let his preparation go by the board. I suppose that it will always be the case, that there will be many men attracted to the ministry by the desire to help their fellow-men, and serve Christ in ministering to His flock, who have an inadequate grasp upon the vital importance of Truth, as the proper food for the mind and heart, and the ordained guide of our life. But I came from a great University, that had as its motto "Veritas vos liberabit," where zeal for knowledge was intense; and I was often painfully impressed by a lack of intellectual aspiration, on the part of some of my fellow-students. Yet they were rare men, and I am proud to belong to a class, whose members have done such excellent work.

The brotherly feeling was remarkable. My heart glows as I recall the hours of earnest converse with my special friend Carter Page; our simple class prayers; our reading clubs for improvement in articulation and pronunciation; our debating society, which did so much for those who earnestly tried to learn to debate and speak without their paper; our Missionary meetings; our morning and evening prayers conducted by the seniors. The whole Institution was governed with a minimum of rules, and a most inspiring confidence in the trustworthiness of the students.

How valuable, how precious were the ministrations at the Mission Stations. My mission was Groveton, and I love every stone on the road, and know every rise and fall of the way. How solemnly the old earthworks frown upon the traveler at one point; how the snow packed at times in that deep gully; how faithfully the people came out to attend the services and listen to our addresses! Every now and then Dr. Nelson used to be very stringent that we should not use our texts for our discourses, for fear that we should preach sermons; but as "themes for meditations" or "subjects for remarks," the text would slip back. It may have stretched the canons, but a definite text certainly curtailed the "address", and gave it point and direction.

When Dr. Nelson came to Groveton in my student days, he used to give the people a little correction of my lax churchmanship, by preaching about the value of Episcopacy, as part of the seamless robe of Christ, which only impious hands would rend. He was always a little more "churchly" on such lines than usual. The best friends of the Mission, Miss Pierson and Miss Harrison, who although Presbyterians, played on the organ and taught classes, took it very sweetly, though I remember they once hesitated a little afterwards, when the Doctor had been especially pronounced as to the "seamless robe", about assisting in folding his surplice. Miss Susie Pierson, my own Sunday School scholar, is now doing a noble Christian work among the colored people. Among the best influences of my life, I put Groveton Mission and its dear people. All of my fellow-students felt the deepest interest in their missions. In fact, some of us gave them too much time and thought.

Something ought to be said of our Matron, Miss Mary Rhett, though she was only slightly known to me, when I was a student. She presided in our dining room with a singular charm, and had a delightful and original personality that will always be held in affectionate remembrance by her "boys".

The members of the Faculty afterwards became my colleagues; but as they are no longer with us, I may be permitted to write a few words about my impressions of them as a student. Dr. McElhinney was the most bookish man I ever knew. His health was very delicate, and he met his classes very irregularly. We all respected his learning. Under pressure he could make a good repartee. One day a presumptuous student began a discussion, on some topic of Ecclesiastical Polity,—the Doctor's own particular field of study, where his monograph is still invaluable for reference, —by saying quite aggressively "My opinion is"—"But are you entitled to an opinion on this subject?" queried the Doctor. Dear man! his own standard of qualification was so high that it was often difficult to get any opinion out of him. He read with facility unpointed Hebrew, and abbreviated Greek, and the Latin of the old chroniclers. He was a perfect repository of information about books and authors; but he balked when it came to a definite view. He was too deeply impressed with the weight of learning, on both sides, and with the clouds and darkness that lie round about us, "to speak dogmatically." Yet I must make some qualification to this, for he was very pronounced in his opposition as to Farrar's "Eternal Hope". On this, seemingly the obscurest and deepest of all subjects, he had a clear cut view. He was also very precise about the Intermediate State; and advanced for his theory subtle arguments, drawn from critical particles and prepositions. He was not at home at the Faculty meeting; but was at his best, reading one of his beautifully written sermons: where the divisions were all according to the best models and the style was of classical purity, and all the adjectives were used in the conventional manner of the writers of the 18th Century.

Dr. Nelson was our comrade among the professors, and played ball with us, and mingled with us around the pump, whose railings served the same purpose as the historic fence at Yale. He made no claim to profound scholarship; but won the respect of all by his manly reality and freedom from pretense of any kind. He had the gift of making his classes work hard at the text-book. Educated at the University of Virginia, he was a great believer in its method. His natural turn of mind was for debate; and by nature conservative and a strict constructionist, he had many elements of a great Church lawyer. His notes upon the Oxford Movement, and upon the famous Ecclesiastical trials were particularly good. I made copious use of them, when I succeeded to his chair. He was an example of a man who does a valuable work for God, in a position to which he was not drawn by natural aptitude. With his moderation of temper, strong sense, vigor of character, piety and reality, he would have made an admirable bishop. He was, by nature, a pastor and friend of souls. He did much to foster the spiritual life of the Institution.

Of Dr. Packard so much has been written that I need not add any special recollections. He became very dear to me, especially during my professorship; and his family contain some of my most valued friends. He was a scholar and theologian of the old school; but his interest in learning was always more literary than theological. He had no turn for controversy or argument. His sermons and conversations were replete with good things. His faculty meeting talks and prayers were always helpful, and his patience in pain, his dignity of character, and his unworldliness of life made him a kind of Christian Patriarch among us. He had a rare gift for friendship, and a strong and loyal personality. One of his attractions was "the patient deep disdain", with which he viewed all so called improvements in the Seminary grounds, or in religious thought. For him, the view of the old Church Father was the orthodox one: "Whatever is true is not new, and whatever is new is not true." The story used to be told, that he came to a meeting of the students on one occasion, when some suggestions to the Faculty were being considered, and simply said "The old is better—Resolve that there be no change". Matthew Arnold's fine lines, in which at the conclusion of The Scholar-Gipsy, he describes the spirit in which "some grave Tyrian trader from the sea" faced "the merry Grecian coaster, the intruders in his ancient home" always brings to my mind the undaunted spirit with which Dr. Packard faced new methods and modes of thought.

To these I add a few recollections of the class room of Dr. Walker. If Dr. Packard was our Patriarch, Dr. McElhinney our Encyclopaedia, Dr. Nelson our comrade and faithful exacter of honest work, Dr. Walker was our thinker; and both as Professor of Systematic Divinity and by reason of native gifts, he chiefly helped us to make our faith self-consistent and congruent with reason and the Scriptures.

I came to the Seminary much embued with the theology of Calvin, which I had been reading, and convinced that the Epistle to the Romans was only rightly interpreted by the School of Augustine and Calvin, which I then thought to be in agreement on these subjects. In the class room of Systematic Divinity, I abandoned such unethical views of God, and such a degrading view of man. I can still hear the question —"But, Mr. Grammer, you speak of God's omnipotence; let me ask, will you deny that he could make a free agent?"

I recall the luminous explanation, that the language about baptism in the Scripture was to be referred to adult baptism; and that in the case of infants, the changed conditions must be borne in mind. But it is needless to specify. Taking up an article, lately published by my old Professor, in Bibliotheca Sacra, and kindly sent me, I thought that a professor was to be envied, who could make so lasting an impression; for I am sure that I remembered hearing him read the substance of it, in the class room twenty years ago.

None of the dangerous leaven, which has worked so powerfully in our Church of recent years, and is now trying to obliterate some of her distinctive features, and eventually narrow, in the name of Catholicism, the very platform upon which she stands, was ever put into our minds in that class room.

I might go further, and speak of our indebtedness to our teacher for the unselfish life he led in our midst. Still, this much I must say, I should count myself blessed indeed, if those who knew me as a Professor could thank me for a moiety of what our class owes to him. His consistent Christian life will ever be one of the Seminary's precious possessions.

To the Seminary Alumnus "The Hill" will always be a sacred spot. It is the Antioch of our Church, from which the missionaries go out and to which they return. I shall always be grateful for the privilege of having been both a student and a professor within those sacred walls. May God ever keep it an exponent of a spiritual conception of Christ's religion; and make it an ever increasing power for good to His children. I hope that the length of these recollections will be pardoned, but as Bunyan says, "As I drew, it came, and so I wrote."

MEMORIES

RT. REV. W. T. CAPERS, D. D.

Class 1894

My Seminary days were out of the ordinary in that I was married (had been for three years) and had my wife with me throughout my entire course, 1891-1894. For this reason I had to find quarters outside the dormitories and take the rank of a "Day Student." In this way I was deprived of some of the privileges of the Seminary, but even in spite of this handicap of outside residence I experienced enough of the student life to realize what a priceless endowment it had for every man who entered its sacred walls.

As I think back over those blessed days they come to me with the impression of days during which I was shut out of the world and shut in with God, as was Noah in his ark. And again they impress me as being filled with a wonderful fellowship which was shared by the whole student body and faculty alike. It is difficult for me to think of those days without seeming to idealize them: but they were to me just as I now describe them.

I think of the Seminary Hill as a veritable "Mount of Transfiguration". Moses and Elias were not with us, but the Master was with us, and so were His prophets: Dean Packard, Dr. Nelson and Dr. Walker, who have long since entered into the presence of their Lord and have received the reward of their labors in training us for His ministry. Dean Crawford and Dr. Grammer were, also, members of the faculty at that time and they, too, were peculiarly gifted in setting the mind of the student to the mind of the Master.

While the scholarship of the faculty was deep and broad and the classes were most ably conducted, yet the Seminary made its largest contribution to the student through what might be called its social and religious life, which was expressed through the monthly missionary meeting, the weekly Faculty Meeting, and the Class Meeting. These were the outward and visible signs of an inward and spiritual grace of which the spirit of the Seminary was the source.

I suppose that every student recalls the Faculty Meeting as having been the most definite religious influence in his student life. But, on the other hand, possibly, he may not have thought of the Faculty Meeting as having been related to all the other religious gatherings and meetings of "The Hill." I am inclined to think, however, that the Faculty Meeting was and is so positively related to the whole community as to make it the very key-note of the spiritual life of "The Hill."

We must remember that of necessity the professors and their families have always been the religious leaders of the community life of the Seminary. Now at the Faculty Meeting the professor always speaks to the student out of his own religious experience: it may be a subjective experience, or a practical one that comes to him out of the duties of the week. But whatever may be the source of his experience, it is sure to bear upon the life of the student as well as upon his own life. The secret, then, of the pervasive power of the Faculty Meeting lies in the fact that teacher and student alike are brought into a common experience which always leads them together to the feet of the great Master Teacher, the Lord of the Seminary. No report of a Faculty Meeting is ever given out except as each student and teacher reports it in his daily conduct. Now, in turn, the weekly Class Meeting has always been the student's opportunity to reveal to his fellow classmate the inner battle of his soul. And, understand, it is the Faculty Meeting that has definitely prepared him for this self-revelation, and has furnished him with the courage and the hope to "March breast forward." These two weekly meetings, so inseparably related, undoubtedly deepened the religious life of the student and prepared his mind and heart for the real work of the Church, which we describe as missionary work. How logically, then, the monthly missionary meetings grew out of this state of mind and heart. And here we have the secret of the enthusiasm and spiritual power of these meetings.

Nowhere have I ever witnessed such a striking co-ordination of the spiritual and intellectual faculties as was always manifested at these missionary gatherings. The very highest order of mind was generally leading the discussion and giving the detailed information concerning the country or nation that was under investigation. It is not at all surprising, then, to find that the missionaries who have been sent out from our dear old Seminary have had always an unusually deep and comprehensive understanding of their respective missionary fields. Think for a moment of the sainted Ingle, of Kinsolving, of Brown, of Meem, of Tucker, and of Miss Packard. I only mention a few of those whom I personally know. I honestly believe that the very foundation upon which these noble souls have built their life's work is that of the Faculty Meeting where the heart and soul of the teacher and student met in common religious experience and then passed out into the daily walks of life aflame with the presence of Christ.

But before the student went out from the Seminary upon his sacred mission, whether it happened to be in the foreign or home field, he had had a wonderful training in practical missionary work by serving on one of the various Missions which were under the supervision of the Seminary. Here he was trained in the principles of the ministry of Christ by being given the opportunity of serving without the thought of financial consideration: three years of service with only the reward of the joy that comes to all who serve was the student's full compensation. I am of the opinion that this was one of the greatest lessons that I personally learned while serving on my Mission. And now that I have come into such close, practical relations with the ministry of others, I am inclined to believe that the greatest lesson that any student can possibly learn is that he has not entered the ministry to follow the dollar mark. This is not a very gracious statement for me to make, but my experience as a Bishop in the Church of God leads me to believe that it is a very necessary one to make. I had the privilege of serving on the staff of Sharon Mission. It is, I believe, about four miles from the Seminary. My associates and I walked this distance every Sunday afternoon, and during the winter we often went through snow half way up to our knees. Oftentimes we paid pastoral calls which added two or three more miles to our walk. And this work, to us all, was the real event of the week; for we felt that it was just this experience that made real all that we had studied the week preceding. The text that comes to me now as possibly expressing more definitely the idea (for us) of the Mission is this challenge of Christ: "If any man willeth to do His will, he shall know of the teaching."

Many very amusing incidents occurred during my service at the Mission, but I fear space will not permit the telling of any. I will, however, try to slip in this one. We students found that there were many children and adults near Sharon Mission that had never been baptized, and accordingly we began like faithful shepherds to round up the stray sheep. I think that we gathered up about twenty-five children and adults. We found one little man with quite a family to be baptized. He had possibly about six children for baptism. The Rev. Dr. Nelson was asked to come over and officiate for us at this most important and strikingly beautiful service. Each little, or big, family, as the case may have been, grouped themselves around the Font. My little friend was there with his six or seven children. At last the Doctor began on his family and started down the line, but for some reason was diverted and it looked to my friend as though he was going to get into another family before he finished the remainder of his children. This was a most exciting thought to my friend, and so, acting upon his fears, he caught Dr. Nelson by the surplice and at the same time handed him his little baby with the statement; "Now is the time to switch in 'Buena Vista.'" And so my friend saved to his children the unbroken continuity of their baptism, but at the same time came mighty near breaking up the meeting.

Now we were not a morbid set of students by any means. No body of men ever had a healthier attitude toward the whole of life than we did. Many of the men were prize winners in all sorts of out-of-doors sports. I had the honor of being on my class football team, and it was never defeated by any team of the Seminary. But I think that the highest evidence of the normality of our student body was the absence of those vices which are truly indicative of abnormal moral and physical conditions: such as jealousy, selfish ambition, censoriousness and the like. During my three years at the Seminary, I saw no evidence of unfriendly rivalry among

the students, and the faculty always presented an absolutely
united front. It is true that at great intervals of time something like this would happen: it came Dr. Nelson's turn to
preach the Thanksgiving Sermon at a time when Grover
Cleveland was our President. The Doctor began his sermon
by recalling the origin of Thanksgiving Day, but gradually
his thoughts drifted toward the South and back to the days
of the Confederacy, (I think the G. A. R.'S had just had a
reunion in Washington), until at last the whole reason for
thankfulness seemed to be centered around these two facts;
namely, that Robert E. Lee, the greatest of Americans, was
a Confederate General, and that the incomparable Grover
Cleveland, the President of our nation, was a Democrat.
During the course of the Doctor's sermon his brethren of the
faculty who were of the other political persuasion, showed
much uneasiness while sitting in their stalls, and the opposing
students expressed their disagreement by shuffling their feet.
The moment was tense, and yet after the service the students
who gathered on the grounds contented themselves with
such a comment as this: "The Doctor evidently thinks
that if any man can not devoutly give thanks for Robert E.
Lee and Grover Cleveland he really has no place in the government."

MEMORIES

RT. REV. DR. EDWARD A. TEMPLE

Class 1895

As my memory goes back to the days I spent at the Seminary, I realize now that the thing that has meant most to
me was the spiritual atmosphere of "The Hill". The simple
genuineness of the high standard of Christian living has
remained an inspiration to me.

The Senior Class, 1923

SECTION IV

CHAPTER XIII—PART 5

STUDENT LIFE OF TODAY

ROLAND J. MONCURE

Member of the Senior Class of 1923

It is night on "The Hill". From almost every window the light streams forth. All is silent except for the constant click of a typewriter here and there, or the occasional conversation of two students studying together. In this room a student is reading his history assignment, in the next two students are translating Greek. The bell sounds across the campus. Some one calls out "Prayers in six". The men in each Hall issue from their rooms in various stages of dress and undress, discussing some assignment as they gather in room "six" for the ten o'clock prayers. For a brief period earnest, devout, but informal prayer and thanksgiving are offered to the Heavenly Father. For a few moments after the benediction they kneel in silent prayer. They rise from their knees and stand about the room discussing a recent student body meeting or a baseball game. Someone pushes a fellow through the doorway; a scuffle ensues, into which everyone is drawn. The hall is in an uproar. The noise gradually stops as one man after another drops out to return to his room to resume his studying or to retire. This period at night best shows the general spirit of the student body. Here we have the boyish play of young men, the study of an educational Institution, and the earnest prayers of those planning to spend their lives in leading men closer to God.

The Seminary looks back with pride upon its one hundred years of service; and yet it could hardly be said that we have allowed our traditions to hinder our progress. Our attempt is rather to make our traditions live in spirit. One custom of tremendous value in keeping alive the loftiest traditions

531

of the Seminary is that of frequent "meetings". These
"meetings" are sometimes irksome when "exams" are drawing near and we realize that "we have left undone those things
which we ought to have done"; but there is no question of
their value. Weekly Class Meetings bind the members of a
class closer together. The custom of having some member of
the class make an informal talk at each of these meetings
brings to our attention serious subjects to which some of our
members have given thought.

The "Faculty Meetings" are the medium for a relationship between faculty and student somewhat different from
that gained in the class room. Here the professor turns "big
brother" and gives us advice on the use of our time at the
Seminary or in the ministry. Many a good resolution has
been made at a "Faculty Meeting". Frequently the regular
order is set aside at these meetings so that we might hear the
message of a celebrated visitor.

Most important, probably, of all, is the monthly meeting
of the Missionary Society. Stirring accounts of the Church's
work and the Church's needs are brought to us here, direct
from the field. Frequent contact with the men actively
engaged in mission work keeps our zeal for missions ever
alive thus forwarding the loftiest traditions of the Seminary.
As we listen to the speaker we have before our eyes the pictures looking down upon us from the walls of that long line of
our alumni who have gone into the foreign field to preach
the Gospel.

One of the most important portions of "The Hill" is
Crawford Field. A practised eye might discover that the
brand of baseball played here is a bit different from that
played on the Polo Grounds; but it is just as much exercise
and much more fun. Inter-class games or games by "choosing
up" sides are always in order in baseball, basketball or anything else. Tournaments furnish an added incentive in
tennis. The curious array of costumes seen on the field are
an index to the mixture in ability. Here and there is a sweater
with a university letter, added to these are a few uniforms
with the name of a local team across the chest, but by far the
greater number play in old clothes.

The social life, like all else on "The Hill", is most informal. Twice a year, it is true, the students try to remove the academic air from Aspinwall Hall and give to it the air of the drawing room; once to welcome the Juniors and again to bid farewell to the Seniors. One or two of the professors usually entertain these classes too. But the most conspicuous part of the social life is the free camaraderie between student and student, and between faculty and student. It is through this that we learn to enlarge our vision by discussion in our rooms or in a professor's study. Communication with the outside world is constantly becoming easier, as the automobile comes into wider use and as good roads slowly, yes, very slowly, approach "The Hill". This, of course, is having its effect; but still the center of our social life remains on "The Hill".

The religious life of the Seminary cannot be said to center in any one place. It is in the Chapel, the class room, and the dormitory. It seeks after the same ideals that have characterized Virginia for the past hundred years; and its expression has not materially changed. Once each day we meet in the Chapel for public worship; here Morning Prayer is simply and informally read. This order is varied twice a week; on Thursdays there is a celebration of the Holy Communion, on Fridays the Litany is read. The only other week day service is on Wednesday afternoons, when some senior quakes in his boots as he delivers his sermon before the faculty and student-body. The prayers in the different Halls at ten o'clock, the prayers with which Faculty Meeting is opened, and the prayers before classes, all form a very important part in our religious life.

Sunday is a busy day on "The Hill". After the Morning Service comes dinner, and immediately after dinner we start for our various Missions. The program is about the same for them all. There is the hike to the Mission, or Sunday School, those glorious suppers, Evening Prayer, and the hike back to the Seminary. Many of our number are not connected with the Seminary Missions; these may be seen leaving "The Hill" Saturday afternoon for services or Sunday School work at various points in Maryland or Virginia.

Little has been said about our classes or our study, yet they, of course, take up by far the greatest portion of our time. May it suffice to say that in the class room we endeavor to carry out Dr. Sparrow's injunction: "Seek the truth; come whence it may; cost what it will." A word, too, might be added about our professors. "B." Green is our spiritual father. "Pip" Kennedy extracts meanings from St. Paul where, to us, no meaning was. "Cosby" Bell finds living theology in the tree outside his window. "Skinny" Rollins gives us a personal contact with Augustus and Francis of Assissi. "Bev." Tucker shows that the spirit and not the form of the Prayer Book is most important. Dr. Nelson tenderly suggests to Juniors that possibly Jonah didn't swallow the whale.

SECTION IV
Chapter XIV
The Virginia Seminary—An Appreciation
REV. FLOYD W. TOMKINS, D. D.

My first knowledge of the Theological Seminary in Virginia came when I was a lad, and my brother went from New York to Alexandria to pursue his studies in Divinity. It was in the War Time when the South and the North were striving together, and my brother's course of study was cut short by the closing of the Seminary and the use of the buildings for the wounded. But his frequent and sometimes amusing accounts of his life on "The Hill" made a profound impression on my youthful mind.

The Seminary was filled at that time with stories associated with the life there of the Rev. Phillips Brooks, already a great preacher. The atmosphere then, as now, was deeply religious with the happy association of Faculty and students, and the Faculty Meetings were a power for good. The missionary spirit was strong, and many were preparing for the Mission Field. The simplicity of the life, and the service rendered by the men in the little missions about Alexandria, which are so important a part of the education to prepare men for great usefulness, made the Seminary then, and have kept it since, a model School of the Prophets.

There were great leaders in those days. Dr. Sparrow, Dr. May and Dr. Packard, and others, were men whose guidance their students never forgot. There are still great men who have succeeded their worthy predecessors in the dear old Seminary and we can rejoice in the work which has continued with ever increasing strength; yet it is well for us to consider the noble men who laid the foundations, and who gave reputation to this Virginia School. As a graduate of another Seminary, I may be permitted to give expression to my thoughts as to the spirit which has always animated the Seminary on "The Hill".

And the first is the truly Evangelical spirit which has ever marked the School and sent men out to preach the Gospel with hearts full of love for Christ and for man. It is a spirit sorely needed in the Church today, and the influence of Alexandria will largely help in supplying the need. The English Bible is studied in the Virginia Seminary with splendid results. A Seminary course should not only fill a man's mind and guide him in theological truth, but it should also, and chiefly, enlarge his heart and bring him nearer to God.

Again the happy spiritual and social relationship between the students and the Faculty brings an influence to bear upon the future Minister, the importance of which can not be over estimated. It is not merely the teaching and the books that are needed to fit men to be Ministers of the Gospel. It is that personal guidance of consecrated leaders who, out of the fulness of their own service, are glad to bring inspiration to the younger brethren.

I know of no college or seminary in the country where there is such a beautiful family ideal made real as at Alexandria.

Again there is the missionary spirit which has sent so many wonderful missionaries to all parts of the world. We can well rejoice that this altruistic spirit from the very first has guided the Seminary in her work. Not only do her sons rise up and call her blessed, but the multitudes who have been led to God through the service of her sons sing her praises and thank God for her.

And then there is one thing more which has always impressed me greatly about this Seminary of Virginia. It is the happy brotherhood which makes it almost a kind of "Associate Mission" without any of the unnatural restrictions sometimes associated with such missions. The students feel their privilege even as they recognize the atmosphere, both physically and spiritually. No one who is sensitive can visit the old Seminary without being conscious of this atmosphere. It is a benediction just to stay on the grounds for a few days. It calms the soul, it fills one with hope and it opens the way towards the coming of the Kingdom of God.

Long may this old Seminary live and do its work! God has given His blessing; may He continue to give it as the years roll by.

SECTION IV

CHAPTER XV

AN APPRECIATION

THE CHURCH'S GREAT SEMINARY IN VIRGINIA*

GUY EMERY SHIPLER

It may be true that "pigs is pigs", but seminaries is not necessarily seminaries. To those in the Church and out of it who have been depressed as they thought of the ministry of the future, I have to offer a cure. Let them dare the red clay mud holes of Virginia roads and visit "the old Seminary," where it sits aloft on Seminary Hill, as it has for nearly a century now, a symbol of all that is finest in the Master's service.

Even a former Seminarian does not look forward to a trip to a theological seminary as a source of shock; certainly not the sort of shock that I received. Now that I look back upon the experience I am not quite sure that it was not a dream; for, frankly, I was among those who, as they studied the type of man going into the ministry in these latter years, had been inclined to fear that the line of the prophets was tapering out into thin air. My lack of faith has been rebuked.

I saw at Virginia Seminary as fine a lot of men as I have seen at any educational institution. As I talked with them and heard of their records in scholarship, in athletics, and in the war, and felt the virility of their personalties, it seemed to me that a new day for the Church was dawning before my eyes. I am quite conscious that what I am writing will sound like exaggeration or bad judgment or both to some who may read this article. But I am recording a conviction, and recording it with the knowledge that it is backed by men better qualified than I to judge.

*From "The Churchman."

There are certain facts about the men at Virginia that are heartening, quite apart from the individual personalities. The average age of the sixty students there is twenty-eight years. This means that some of the men are well above this age and have had years of experience in professional or business life. In the case of Virginia men it has been successful experience. They have not undertaken preparation for the ministry because, in the popular phrase, they have failed at everything else. I was told, though I could not positively verify it, that all but two of the sixty men have had experience either in the war, or business, or some profession. To those who know something of the tragic immaturity, from the point of view of the practical ministry, of so many men who go to our seminaries having had only school and college experience, this is in itself a fact of no means significance.

I am not unconscious of the great heritage of Virginia. She has sent men into the ministry whose names are written imperishably upon her records of high achievement. But the glorious fact is that that heritage is now in full flower. Lest someone challenge what I have here written, let me give a sample "who's who" of the student body.

Captain P. J. Jensen was in command of a company of the Black Watch in the late war. He was gassed at the second battle of Ypres, wounded in the spine, cut off from his company, and buried by shell fire. Having dug himself out he crossed no man's land in a hail of machine gun bullets, was caught on the wire of his own lines and finally brought in by a British Tommy. Out of a very remarkable religious experience coincident with these events, of which I do not feel at liberty to speak in detail, Captain Jensen determined to give himself to the ministry. I shall long remember the few moments' talk I had with this man of outstanding personality, who is somewhere around six feet three or four in height. And most of all I shall remember the fervor with which he said, "Of all the places I know of in the world I love this place best."

Then there is Captain Francis H. Ball, hailing originally from somewhere in South Africa, who is one of the three surviving officers of the Princess Pat's; who fought through the various campaigns of that famous outfit, and who was severely wounded in several battles.

Dennis Whittle, a distant relative of Bishop Whittle, was graduated from Cambridge University with first honors. He went through the Gallipoli campaign—which ought to give any chap a wholesome background for the work of a parson—and later served in France. I was informed that, in common with other Englishmen, he possesses a total incapacity to talk about himself, but the few who have succeeded in smashing through tradition have heard tales of stirring adventure.

George A. Trowbridge is a graduate of Princeton and spent a year at Oxford. He was Princeton's champion hurdler, and represented Oxford and Cambridge against Yale and Harvard as champion hurdler of those universities. Arthur B. Kinsolving, son of Bishop Lucien Kinsolving, was a University of Virginia football man who served in the ambulance corps of France and later with the American forces. Richard H. Baker, of Norfolk, is a University of Virginia man who won the Croix de Guerre in the late war, with exceptional citations. William St. John Blackshears, LL.B., University of Texas, was for several years a successful practicing lawyer. Dr. Albert C. Tebeau was a practicing physician of notable success for several years in North Carolina. Joseph M. Waterman, B. A., of Harvard, came to the Seminary after two years' experience in settlement work in New York.

That is a cross-section of the student personnel. It would seem that the heritage of Virginia is in safe hands.

When a northerner enters the gate of Virginia Seminary he may as well know in advance that he is to be swept off his feet and straight into the heart of Virginia hospitality. I know what Captain Jensen meant when he put all that fervor into his words of love for the Seminary. No normal person could resist the charm of this place where the very air sparkles with wholesome good fellowship. We had motored down from Washington with no idea of staying for luncheon, but when Virginia folk want you to stay, you stay. I can't recall just how many persons, not knowing how we had come, offered to drive us back to town. And when I expressed a desire to see the room where Henry Potter took Phillips

Brooks in on the night the latter arrived at the Seminary we were taken over to Dr. Bell's house—it was a dormitory in Brooks' day—and there was no hesitation in routing Dr. Bell out of a mid-day siesta to take us up to the attic floor and the famous room. And he came down all smiles—and offered to take us back to Washington when we were ready to go!

I had always heard that the students and professors at Virginia lived a family life that reflected the best Virginia traditions. Yet I was delightfully surprised when Dr. Tucker took us into the common room of that architectural curiosity, Aspinwall Hall, to find a large group of students loafing between lectures, and three professors smoking with them. There was a sound of merriment, and the sight of laughing faces, and certainly a very Episcopal fragrance of tobacco. I thought of some Seminary professors I had known and was appalled at the chance these teachers were taking of becoming really good fellows—until by closer contact I discovered that these "profs" had either been born good fellows, or had acquired the habit long enough to have it sit naturally upon them.

Dr. Tucker and Dr. Rollins took us to luncheon in the refectory, where again we had an opportunity of sensing the family atmosphere. We had not been long at table when Miss Maria came to talk with us. Be it known that Miss M'ria is Miss Maria Worthington, librarian of the Seminary and mother confessor to all the students. Miss M'ria has also a certain pride in Seminary's historic data. Dr. Tucker had several times launched into a recital of bits of history, keeping, I noted, a weather eye on Miss M'ria. And with good reason, for Miss M'ria applied all the canons of modern criticism to Dr. Tucker's stories. One dispute arose when he was telling of that occasion when three great future bishops of the Seminary were on their way to Brooks's mission at Sharon. It was necessary to cross a run which was swollen with recent rains. Phillips Brooks being large of stature, waded in carrying first Henry Potter and then Alfred Randolph across on his back. Dr. Tucker and Miss M'ria got into a blood-curdling discussion over some such question as to which was carried first, or who carried who.

The boys of the famous old Episcopal High School adjoining the Seminary have an important part in keeping the life of the Seminary wholesome. In the afternoon we saw some of them out on the football field playing soccer with the seminarians—and socker football isn't a bad foil for lectures in theology. When Dr. Tucker showed us the chapel, where the high school boys sing in the choir and make up a large part of the congregation, he told us that their critical gifts had a steadying influence on the man who happened to be preaching. On the fly leaves of the Prayer Books and Hymnals one found after service such comments as this. "Dr. Blank is in the box. His delivery is slow and his curves are ineffective."

Ever since the day when in college I read Dr. Allen's life on Phillips Brooks, I had longed to see the room where Brooks lived the greater part of the time he was at the Seminary. It was the room to which he moved after leaving his attic. There it was, quite as it must have been in his day; a plain, simple room in a plain, simple old building. But the chap who lives there now keeps warm from a modern central heating plant, instead of from the stove for which Brooks had to lug his own wood. It was in this room, Dr. Rollins said, that Phillips Brooks compiled those stacks of notebooks which played so great a part in his preaching.

There is a charm about the environs of the Seminary that is impossible to put into words. One feels a sense of expansion as one walks about in the spacious grounds, and looks off to lovely vistas of Washington, across the Potomac, catching through the oak trees glimpses of the dome of the Capitol and the Washington monument. The Seminary buildings and faculty houses, some of them a hundred years old, are scattered about in seeming abandon, with a sort of self-assurance of joy in long existence. During the Civil War the buildings were used as a hospital for the Union troops, after they had cut away, for the purpose of defense, the old trees that covered Seminary Hill. It is said that Dr. Sparrow, then dean of the Seminary, persuaded Secretary Stanton, a friend of many years, to save the oak grove that lends to the Seminary so much of its beauty. Captain Jensen is right. It is a place to love.

SECTION V

Biographical Sketches
of the
Virginia Seminary Professors

SECTION V

CHAPTER I

REV. DR. REUEL KEITH

REV. W. A. R. GOODWIN, D. D.

Special interest clusters about the life of the man chosen to be the first professor in this Institution. His personality, his character, his theology, the point of view from which he taught the truth, and the content of his teaching all combined to create the ideals and to place the emphasis which predominated in the early life of the Seminary. It is true that prior to the election of the Rev. Dr. Reuel Keith the Rev. Dr. William H. Wilmer had been for some time teaching a number of young men in his home in Alexandria and in the Sunday School room of St. Paul's Church, preparing them for Holy Orders. But this work was under the supervision of the Education Society or was done by him under the stress of necessity prior to the formation of the Education Society. The Board of Trustees of the Seminary had not then been constituted.

The Rev. Dr. Keith, was, however, the first officially elected professor of the Theological Seminary in Virginia, serving first as professor of theology in the College of William and Mary. When it was finally determined by the Board of Trustees to locate the Seminary in Alexandria, he was called to give his full time to the work of teaching in this Institution, and entered upon his duties on the 15th of October, 1823.

Dr. Keith was born in Vermont. During his boyhood he served for awhile as a clerk in a store in Troy, New York, where he first became acquainted with the Episcopal Church. He prepared himself for college at St. Albans and entered Middlebury College in 1811, graduating with the highest honors. He was baptized by the Rev. Dr. Henshaw and became a most earnest and devoted Christian.

543

His slender constitution and delicate health constrained him to seek the milder climate of the southern country and he came to Virginia, where he secured the position of private tutor in one of the most respectable and ancient families in Prince George County. While acting in this capacity he served as lay-reader in the Parish and pursued his studies preparatory to entering the ministry of the Church. He returned to Vermont and became a tutor in Middlebury College. He then entered systematically upon a course of study in preparation for the Holy Ministry under the Rev. Dr. Henshaw of Brooklyn, New York, "and later pursued his studies as a resident graduate of Andover". He was ordained by Bishop Moore in Alexandria in 1817.

Upon receiving orders, he was invited to become the assistant of the Rev. Dr. Addison, at that time rector of St. John's Parish, Georgetown, D. C. His removal to Washington was largely due to the desire of Dr. Thomas Henderson to establish a school which he hoped would grow into a college in the District of Columbia. Dr. Henderson tells of having pursued Dr. Keith on his way to Vermont hoping to find him at the General Convention which was then in session in Philadelphia. Under the zealous and popular ministry of Dr. Keith in Georgetown, a new congregation was formed and Christ Church, Georgetown, was built, largely through the influence of Dr. Henderson and Mr. Francis Scott Key. The Vestry Book of this Parish under date November, 1817, contains the record of the call extended to Dr. Keith and also the copy of the letter addressed to him by the Vestry.

Dr. Keith served in this parish most acceptably for three years until January, 1820, when, under a compelling sense of duty, he resigned to accept the professorship of Theology in the College of William and Mary. The Vestry Book of Christ Church contains the record of the letter written by Dr. Keith expressing his profound regret in leaving his Parish. He says in this letter, "I have been brought to the consciousness that it is my indispensable duty to go."

During his residence in Williamsburg, Dr. Keith served also as the rector of Bruton Parish Church. The pastoral work in the parish could not have been very exacting, as he reported to the Convention which met in Norfolk on the

17th of May, 1821 that there were only twenty-five communicants at that time in Bruton Parish Church.

The experiment of establishing a Theological Professorship in the College of William and Mary proved a complete failure. This was not due to any lack of ability on the part of Dr. Keith, but doubtless to the deep-set prejudices which existed against Williamsburg and the College of William and Mary on account of the reported prevalence of skepticism and infidelity in that locality. During his two years residence in the College, only one student offered himself for the course in Theology. Upon the formal establishment of a Theological Seminary in Alexandria by action of the diocese of Virginia, Dr. Keith removed from Williamsburg and entered upon his successful career as professor of Old and New Testament Literature, Biblical Criticism and Evidences in the newly established Seminary, continuing as professor in the Institution until his death in 1842.

He became deeply interested in Hengstenberg's Christology and learned the German language thoroughly in order that he might translate it. A book-seller in Alexandria undertook the publication of this volume, but being unable to carry it through, it had to be printed in Andover. Dr. Packard says, "I saw it through the press for him there in 1836, just before I came to the Seminary." It is said of this book that it was one of the most admirable translations ever made into the English language.

Dr. Packard, who was the close and intimate friend of Dr. Keith said: "I boarded with him for a year, having my room in the Seminary, and derived great profit from my association with him. He had the power of abstraction in a very high degree, the highest of all mental powers, and would become so absorbed in his subject as to forget everything else. Thus he was very strong intellectually and was a master of what he had studied. Everything he read and saw and heard he put into his own crucible, tested it, and laid it away for future use. This was the secret of his wonderful command of all his resources.

"He was a many-sided man, great in the lecture room, and in the pulpit, and there were other sides of his character equally pleasing. He was an excellent and accurate scholar and thoroughly understood the Hebrew, Greek, Latin and German languages, as his translation of Hengstenberg's Christology shows. He was a man of tall but stooping figure, with a noble forehead and piercing eye. Bishop Meade says, 'he was a most eloquent preacher, and the most earnest one I have ever heard.' He made a great impression on the students with his 'blood earnestness,' as Chalmers says. There was a glowing sense of the Divine Presence on him which moved others. He was much sought after to preach at associations; at conventions he was often heard with delight, and was thought the best preacher in the state. His manner of reading the Psalter and the Prayers, especially the Litany, was remarkably fervent and impassioned. He prayed the service throughout as I have never heard any one else do.

"His voice was very good, silvery, penetrating and awe-inspiring. His mode of preparation for the pulpit, when I knew him, was to look over one of his old sermons and then to give its substance, with any new thought he had, without notes. I never knew him to write a new sermon on the six years of our association."

Bishop Smith bears witness to the impression made on him by the solemn earnestness and deep piety of Dr. Keith. "The solidity of his argument and the force of delivery of his sermons riveted the attention of all who heard him and produced powerful effects."

Dr. Keith brought with him to the Seminary the impress of Andover and a theological system colored by the prevalent Calvinism of Protestant New England. When a student on one occasion, after Dr. Keith had presented the Calvinistic view of the subject, said to him, "When, Dr. Keith, are we to have the other side?" He answered, "There is no other side." This answer was very different from the answer which would later have been given to any such question addressed to Dr. Sparrow, who saw truth as many-sided and gleaming from many and varied angles.

Dr. Keith is said to have been very fond of horses, and was given at times to horse-trading, in which he generally got the worst of the bargain. He was wont to spend his vacation driving around through New England in a yellow "carryall" with two horses, one of which is described as a large bony gray horse and the other a small sorrel one. He seemed never to have paid much attention to appearances. "He was of nervous temperament, moody, and subject," says Dr. Packard, "to spells of deep depression and from time to time would sit days together in his house without saying a word, leaning his head upon the back of his chair." Emerging from these spells of depression, Dr. Keith would frequently pass into periods of high exaltation, at which time his humor was often most engaging. A student visiting across the Potomac had become so absorbed by his fascination for a young lady that his mind had become completely diverted from his studies. On one occasion he called on Dr. Keith and asked if the doctor could explain how mind could be affected by matter. The doctor replied that he could not, but added, "there seems to be a little matter over in Maryland that affects your mind very much."

On another occasion when a discussion arose in the doctor's class room about the deluge and the ark, one of the students asked "What became of the fish?" to which the doctor replied, "It was a fine time for the fish."

"The Southern Churchman" of February 19, 1880, contains a long letter written by J. H. Morrison, addressed to the Rev. Dr. Philip Slaughter, urging him to write a worthy appreciation of the life and service of the Rev. Dr. Reuel Keith. This request having been urged, the writer proceeds to analyze the life and teaching of Dr. Keith, comparing him, after the manner of treatment followed in Plutarch's "Lives", with the Rt. Rev. Nicholas H. Cobbs. Dr. Keith is portrayed "as the lowest of low Churchmen" and Bishop Cobbs as being "a Churchman decidedly high". "Dr. Keith," says the writer, "seemed to be profoundly impressed as he preached with the holiness of God's character, and his own immeasurable distance from the infinite purities. This consciousness gave a powerful impressiveness to his words. Though the doctor's life was that of a student, mixing little with the world, yet he had a keen insight into human character. He had no narrow views and drew men to his heart, no matter how widely he differed from them either in question of ecclesiastical polity or in doctrinal views. He was a decided Calvinist and his views of the sacramental side of religion were very low, but no man lost the doctor's esteem or love because he differed from him in these matters. What a grand Bishop this American Leighton would have made; a Bishop whose massive intellect and width of view would have been a powerful brake on the narrowness and weaker minds running headlong into reformed Episcopalianism on the one side, and Romanising ritualism on the other."

Dr. Keith engaged in a somewhat bitter controversy with Bishop Ravenscroft with reference to certain matters regarding the position and teaching of the Church. On one occasion when Dr. Keith was the subject of conversation, Bishop Ravenscroft remarked, "If there is a man in the world who lives close to God, it is Reuel Keith, but he knows no more of the Church than my horse." The editor of "The Southern Churchman," commenting on this controversy and the remark of the Bishop, observes that, "If the Bishop's horse knows as much of the Church as Professor Keith, he is an ecclesiastical prodigy, worthy of a choice stall in the Cathedral." "To those," says Dr. Packard, "who knew Dr. Keith, I could not give an adequate conception of his character, without taking more time than can be allowed me here, and without infringing upon the duty assigned to one who was his pupil, and knew him well.

"I seem to see again, his tall and stooping figure, his piercing eye, his noble forehead, a dome of thought, and to hear again his silvery voice. Who that has heard him pray our service, or in social and family prayer, can ever forget his lowly reverence, like that of the Seraphim, who veil their faces, as they bow before the Holy Majesty of Heaven. The clothing of humility covered him, as it did no other man I ever knew. Bishop Meade said of him that he was the most eloquent preacher, and one of the most impressive readers of the service he had ever heard.

'His look
Drew audience, and attention still as night.'

"His intense earnestness was that of a soul fired with the Glory of the Gospel. As a teacher he was distinguished for clearness and positiveness. His theology was that of the Cross, his learning was exact and extensive. The Hebrew

Bible and Greek Testament were always before him. His translation of Hengstenberg's Christology is the best translation of any book I know of."

The Rev. Dr. Woodbridge, another of his pupils, says: "Dr. Keith's influence upon the Seminary was remarkable for the high standard of holiness which it cherished. There was the secret of his power. His personal piety was so great that it more than atoned for all other defects. That influence is felt now; in that respect he liveth and will live, as long as the Seminary shall live." Bishop Bedell after narrating many interesting incidents of the lecture room, says, "the greenest spot in his remembrance of Seminary life was the social prayer meeting of the Professors and students. The Faculty were a unit in their expression of spiritual communion by faith with the Lord; and the insensible influence upon their instructions, on these occasions, was irresistible." He describes Dr. Keith, sometimes as sitting with his eyes closed, and his meditations seemed a heavenly conversation. Sometimes with a flashing gaze, as if he were standing in the midst of heavenly visions, his speech was affluent of sacred wisdom, as though the rivers of life overflowed in our midst.

On the first of January, 1841, Dr. Keith suffered the stunning loss of his accomplished and devoted wife. Mrs. Keith had been the constant and companionable co-laborer with Dr. Keith during the whole period of his professorship in the Seminary. In order that she might help him with his work, she learned every language which the doctor had occasion to use in connection with his work, and assisted him in his work of translation. She was a woman of exquisite charm and grace of manner. Her culture and refinement won for her, not only upon the Seminary Hill, but throughout the state, a wide circle of devoted and admiring friends. To the students of the Seminary her life and presence was a constant benediction, and she made the professor's home a welcome retreat for them in their hours of loneliness, contributing to their training the inspiration which flows from the heart and mind of refined and sympathetic womanhood. Her loss was a crushing blow to Dr. Keith. His mind, already somewhat under a cloud of periodic depression, passed into the darkness of a deep despondency from which it never emerged until he

was called on the 3rd of September, 1842, by the God whom
he had so faithfully served, into higher realms of service and
into the light and peace perpetual of Paradise.

Dr. Keith was buried in the cemetery of Grace Church,
Sheldon, Vermont. The Rev. Walter W. Reid, now Rector
of Christ Church, Tarrytown, New York, writes that "while
Rector of Sheldon Parish, Vermont; I rescued his grave from
the oblivion of weeds and put it in good order."

SECTION V

Chapter II

Rev. Oliver Norris

REV. SAMUEL A. WALLIS, D. D.

The Rev. Oliver Norris, who was the rector of Christ Church, Alexandria, Virginia, for nearly twelve years, was appointed the first Professor of Pastoral Theology at the Theological Seminary then located in Alexandria in the year 1825. He succeeded the Rev. William Meade, afterwards the third Bishop of Virginia, as rector of Christ Church, in the year 1813.

Mr. Norris was born on the 7th day of November, 1786, we should judge, in the City of Baltimore, for in the very short sketch of his life and work, given by Bishop Meade in the "Old Churches, Ministers and Families of Virginia" we are told that he was of Quaker descent, but occasionally attended services at St. Peter's Church in that city during the godly ministry of the Rev. Mr. Dashiell. There he was brought under the power of the Gospel, "and first became convinced of sin, then of his need of a Saviour, and then of the excellency of our service to build up a convert to the true faith and practice of a Christian."

We can find no record anywhere of how he prepared himself for entering the ministry, but it must be supposed that he studied under some clergyman. Nor is there any statement made by Bishop Meade with reference to his ordination. In the Funeral Sermon preached by the Rev. William Meade in memory of the Rev. Mr. Norris, at the request of the Vestry, in Christ Church, on Sunday, September 18, 1825, (for the loan of which we are indebted to the present rector of Christ Church, Alexandria, Virginia, the Rev. W. J. Morton, D. D.), he says, "Together did we enter upon the hallowed duties of the sanctuary", but whatever that may mean, it cannot refer to ordination, for in the "Old Churches, Ministers and Families of Virginia," already referred to, Bishop Meade gives an account of his own ordination by Bishop Madison in Old Bruton Church in Williamsburg, and he alone was ordained at that time. He also relates that after his ordination he was sent into the pulpit to preach the sermon as no special preacher had been appointed. Mr. Norris was, of course, ordained in Maryland where his first charge was at Elk Ridge, near Bladensburg. There he remained for four years, where, as Bishop Meade writes, "his affectionate manner, laborious services, and faithful preaching so endeared him to a faithful people, that it was with the utmost difficulty that he could be torn from their embrace, and where he will ever be remembered and loved, while any survive who once sat beneath the sound of his voice."

He then received a call to Christ Church, Alexandria, Virginia, and accepted it, succeeding the Rev. William Meade, who had been in charge for eighteen months. Mr. Meade had commenced his ministry in the year 1811 as assistant to the Rev. Mr. Balmaine in Frederick County. But in the fall of that year he was urgently solicited to take charge of old Christ Church, Alexandria, by the vestry, so he concluded to do so, with the privilege of spending a part of the year in Frederick, so as not to give up all his engagements there. The circumstances of the congregation of old Christ Church were very peculiar at that time and the appeal very strong, else he would not have gone. As soon as he felt he could relinquish this charge, he returned to the Valley of Virginia, and as we have seen, the Rev. Mr. Norris, a minister of like spirit with Mr. Meade, became rector of Christ Church.

The Rev. William Wilmer assumed the charge of St. Paul's Church during Mr. Meade's short stay in Alexandria. He pays the following tribute to these two exemplary ministers. "These beloved brethren coming from Maryland with the views of the Gospel and the Church, which the Evangelical clergy and laity of England were then so zealously and successfully propagating there, contributed most effectually to the promotion of the same in Virginia, and to them is justly due much of the subsequent character and success of the Church in Virginia, as is well known to all of their day."

Bishop Meade was devoted to Mr. Norris as these words from his sermon show, "I take a sacred delight in saying that I knew him well, and have known him long. We loved each other with the affection of brothers." Mr. Norris excelled in pastoral relations with his people. He was indeed the good shepherd who knew his sheep and was known by them. Few equalled him in this respect. He was eminently fitted for the chair of pastoral theology at the Seminary, but his work was soon accomplished there, for God took him. Dr. Clemson of Delaware said of the Rev. Mr. Norris, "he was a lovely man of the sweetest piety, he always reminded me of the Apostle John." For the short time that they were together Dr. Wilmer and Mr. Norris had services of a social nature for the students in the evenings of the week, in which the students were also invited to exercise their gifts.

Mr. Norris was seized with a fever in the month of August, 1825, and from the very first commencement of his sickness, he felt that he would never recover. There is an account of his last illness appended to the Rev. Mr. Meade's sermon written by Mr. Cairns, one of the students. It is characterized by that fullness of description which the old Evangelicals loved, and which no doubt has brought comfort to many Christians as they looked forward to their own departure hence in the faith of Christ. To the students gathered around him, he would often with emphasis exclaim, "My young friends, be faithful. If you wish to die in peace, be faithful." His dear people were ever in his heart and prayers and he commended them to God. He left three little children of his own, already motherless, and now about to be fatherless. For their future he was truly solicitous, but he knew that his God and the God of his fathers would be their God. To an intimate acquaintance, he said, a short time before his death, "You have been my friend, do now be a friend to my dear, dear children." They had kind relations, as Mr. Meade said in his sermon, who would provide for their earthly comfort, but he asked the congregation to remember them in their prayers, and also do for them what they could, for their father's sake. On the day before he died the Rev. Lemuel Wilmer had the Holy Communion with him, which gave him much comfort and peace. On the next day while the bell of the old Church was ringing for evening prayer, he caught its sweet tones, and the last words he was heard to utter were "Go to Church". He lingered until a short time after midnight, and passed away to the life of the world invisible on the morning of the 19th day of August, 1825.

His remains rest beside those of his wife in that portion of the Alexandria cemetery belonging to Christ Church.

On the marble slab resting upon six plain pillars above his grave is this inscription:

IN
MEMORY
OF
THE REV. OLIVER NORRIS
FOR MORE THAN ELEVEN YEARS
RECTOR OF CHRIST CHURCH, ALEXANDRIA, VIRGINIA
FAIRFAX PARISH
HE WAS BORN THE 7TH OF
NOVEMBER, 1786
AND FULFILLED HIS EARTHLY COURSE
THE 18TH OF AUGUST
1825, IN THE 16TH YEAR OF HIS MINISTRY
AS DEEPLY LAMENTED AS HE HAD BEEN ARDENTLY
LOVED BY ALL WHO KNEW HIS WORTH
IN THE JOYFUL HOPE OF A BLESSED IMMORTALITY
THROUGH CHRIST JESUS.
HIS LIFE WAS CONSECRATED TO THE GLORY OF GOD AND
THE BEST INTERESTS OF MANKIND.
UNIFORMLY EXHIBITING A RARE EXAMPLE OF EVERY
VIRTUE THAT CAN ADORN THE CHARACTER OF A
GENTLEMAN, A CHRISTIAN, AND A MINISTER OF THE GOSPEL.
HIS DEVOTED AND BEREAVED CONGREGATION HAVE
ERECTED THIS MONUMENTAL STONE TO EXPRESS THEIR
GRATITUDE FOR HIS BENEVOLENT AND UNWEARIED
EFFORT TO PROMOTE THEIR SPIRITUAL WELFARE AND TO
PERPETUATE THEIR HIGHEST ESTEEM FOR THE UNCOMMON
EXCELLENCE OF HIS CHARACTER.

NOTE:—The discrepancy between the date of the death of Mr. Norris on his monument, and that in Mr. Cairn's account is no doubt owing to the fact that he died a short time after midnight.

SECTION V
CHAPTER III
REV. DR. EDWARD RUSSELL LIPPITT
REV. SAMUEL A. WALLIS, D. D.

The Reverend Edward Russell Lippitt, D. D., was born in the city of Providence, Rhode Island, on the 23rd day of April, 1798. He came of distinguished Rhode Island lineage, the family having been settled in the Colony from an early period of its history. Dr. Lippitt was also, as Dr. Philip Slaughter reminds us, an hereditary Churchman, descended from a long line of Episcopal ancestors. Dr. Slaughter further states that, in going back to the first charter of the Colony of Rhode Island, he remembers that in reading Updike's History of the Narragansett Church some years ago, he noted the following entry in the diary of Dr. McSparran, the pastor of the family, under the date 1745, viz;—"Buried Moses Lippitt in his own grounds at Warwick, where the Lippitts had great possessions." Thus we see that they were people of large wealth for those days. They were also loyal members of the Church of England, the overwhelming proportion of the population of New England being Congregationalists. Of course the Church of England as the Established Church of the Mother Land was the Church of the vice-regal court. We see this in the city of Boston, where King's Chapel, rich in historic interest, was the old vice-regal church in which was placed the Governor's pew.

Although the Church of England fell under the ecclesiastical ban of the Puritan Established Church on account of its acceptance of prelatical bishops as its chief rulers, still, its connection with the colonial government kept it from overt persecution so long as it had no bishops over here. But the Puritan Church was not forgetful of the persecutions it had received at the hands of the Established Church in England and often placed many difficulties in the way of its growth, especially outside of the influence of the colonial capitals.

On account of the well-known reasons which brought the Pilgrims and the Puritans to this country, the genial and truly Christian Dr. Cheverus, the first Roman Catholic Bishop of Boston, had a sly way of reminding his Protestant friends that their forefathers had fled to these shores not to escape the persecutions of Popery, but that of a Protestant Prelatical Church. However, what did these Protestant forefathers do in their turn? They undertook to persecute all people and religious bodies, like the Quakers, who rose up in opposition to the organization and doctrines of their own establishment. So, as the Puritan came from England in search of religious liberty, the persecuted people of Massachusetts Bay followed the banished Roger Williams into the wilds of Rhode Island and upheld the great principal of freedom to worship God according to the dictates of the conscience of each man first set forth by him in founding the Colony of Rhode Island, and the city of Providence. There the Church of England established herself as one of the Churches enjoying the spirit of liberty, and in this free colony the Lippitts and other Church of England people settled in the midst of the followers of Roger Williams and the Quakers who found a refuge there.

When the Revolutionary War broke out two of the sons of Moses Lippitt, to whom reference has been made, were officers in the American Army and fought by the side of Dr. Slaughter's father on the field of New Jersey. Dr. Edward Lippitt studied at Brown University, Providence, Rhode Island, where he graduated and received his degree in 1817. He was then appointed Master of the Latin School of his Alma Mater, which was a great tribute to his classical attainments. He, however, determined to study for the sacred ministry, and as was the custom in many cases in those days, studied theology privately under the venerable Rev. Dr. Croker. He was ordered deacon by Bishop Griswold in the year 1819. During the period of his diaconate he officiated as minister at Quincy, Massachusetts. Receiving a call to Virginia he was ordained to the Priesthood by Bishop Moore at

Walker's Church, Albemarle County, in the year 1822. He became rector of Norborne Parish in Berkeley County, representing that parish in the diocesan convention of 1822-23. He then removed to Germantown, Pennsylvania, and after two years was elected Professor at the Virginia Seminary, entering upon the duties of his office in 1826.

After serving the Seminary as professor for seventeen years he resigned this position and became editor of "The Southern Churchman", still regarding himself, according to Dr. Slaughter, in the service of the Seminary, as "The Southern Churchman" was especially devoted to its interests. During his management of this paper Dr. Lippitt steadfastly maintained the evangelical principles which from its first foundation to the present time have distinguished it, in accordance with what we believe is the best expression of the position of the doctrines of the Anglican Communion and its authorized services in the Book of Common Prayer as the noblest result of the English Reformation. Dr. Lippitt at the time of his retirement from the editorship of this paper stated the guiding principles to which he adhered during the period that he held this office: "It has been, however, our chief aim to make "The Southern Churchman" a plain, practical, family Church paper, especially suitable for reading on Sundays, and as little a vehicle of controversy either within or without our own Church as was consistent with such an acquaintance with the topics of discussion of the day as might be desirable to our pious and intelligent lay-men." As a family Church paper we can say without any hesitation it stands supreme to the present day.

The chief reason which led Dr. Lippitt to the determination of giving up the management of "The Southern Churchman" was that which has been the reef on which many Church papers, to say nothing of others, have gone down, namely the large deficit due on unpaid subscriptions, causing financial embarrassment which made it impossible for him to continue its publication. Happily another was able to take it up so that "The Southern Churchman" has never failed in its mission to the Virginia Church and evangelical Churchmen everywhere throughout the land.

After his resignation from "The Southern Churchman" in 1848, Dr. Lippitt for a time became Master of a Young Ladies' Institute in the City of Washington. On giving this up he retired into private life and lived with his sons in Clarke and Jefferson counties in the Valley of Virginia. In the latter part of his life, as Dr. Slaughter relates, he passed through a series of distressing providences which he bore with uncomplaining meekness, until at last he departed this life at his son's residence in Charlestown, Jefferson County, on Wednesday, the ninth of March, in the seventy-second year of his age, "in the communion of the Catholic Church, in the confidence of a certain faith, in the comfort of a reasonable, religious, and holy hope, in favour with his God and in perfect charity with the world."

One of his most intimate friends was Bishop Smith of Kentucky. They had roomed together for a short time when students at Brown University. The Bishop had a high regard for his learning and character, speaking of him as a refined gentleman, an accurate scholar, and exemplary Christian. In an obituary notice published in "The Southern Churchman" on the 17th of March, 1870, the author of which was undoubtedly Dr. Sparrow, he is described as a man of "highly cultivated mind, of sound judgment, and kindly disposition, of gentle and gentlemanly manners, and of uniformly elevated Christian sentiment. To have intercourse with him was to be drawn towards him. His estimate of himself indeed was very humble, altogether too much so, and largely interfered with the proper exercise of his abilities; though when forced to put forth his strength, he exhibited as the writer once witnessed, a power previously unexpected." Among his last utterances was the expression of his firm and cloudless confidence in the Divinity and Grace of Jesus Christ.

Dr. Packard's testimony comes from the heart as he writes that "the older alumni will never cease to remember with affection his pious and amiable character, which did much to sustain the religious spirit of the Seminary."

THE REVEREND DOCTOR JOSEPH PACKARD

Professor 1836-1902

SECTION V

Chapter IV

Rev. Dr. Joseph Packard

REV. CARL E. GRAMMER, S. T. D.

No name is more closely associated with the Virginia Seminary than "Packard". Dr. Packard lived so long on "The Hill", and always carried about with him so much of the tradition of a former era, that he seemed to belong to the same category as the great oaks of the Seminary's splendid grove, and to be as permanently associated with the Institution. In the last third of his life, that is, for some thirty years, he stood like a great peak on the horizon, which springing from the earth many miles away, looks down upon the fields about the observer; all its outlines softened by the distance, and its very foliage of a more heavenly color than the verdure close at hand. If the Doctor were to be described without a certain amount of idealization and without certain clouds of legend, he would no more be the Dr. Packard of our memory, than Saturn would be the same planet without its enclosing rings.

It is no wonder that he often spoke of his past; for it was full of interesting associations. His father had borne a musket in the Revolutionary War, and the son had sat as a scholar in the class of Longfellow, when the poet was a teacher of modern languages at Bowdoin. Dr. Packard loved to recall that Hawthorne had preceded him by not many years as a student in the same college. Many of his relations were prominent educators or ministers. Through his marriage to the daughter of the famous lawyer, General Walter Jones, he was connected with the Lees of Virginia, from whom his wife was descended on her mother's side. By these numerous ties Doctor Packard early became acquainted with many noteworthy and interesting people. Authors, educators, prominent ministers, great missionaries, bishops, famous public men, he had met in great numbers. About them all he had something interesting to tell. His father-in-law, General Walter Jones, remembered Washington and Jefferson. He, himself, knew well General Robert E. Lee, who was a cousin of his wife. He had talked with General Stonewall Jackson, and beheld the great Puritan soldier of Cavalier Virginia reading his Bible at sunrise, standing by a fire out of doors. Information which other people have to glean from books, he had derived from personal observation, or from conversation with eye-witnesses. "How do you know that?" he would sometimes abruptly ask. When a book would be mentioned as the source, he would smile indulgently and remark, "It's true; I was there," or, "I heard it from an eye-witness."

His memory was exceedingly exact and tenacious, as is often amusingly manifest in his entertaining "Recollections of a Long Life." Facts with him did not come under the influence of that subtle rationalizing process whereby most people recast and remould their crude experiences, so as to make them fit in with the general philosophy of the observer. His mind was entirely unmetaphysical, and he had none of the French gift of generalization. He was quite content to consume his experiences raw, so to speak, and never cooked them over and made them more digestible by mingling philosophy with them. If he could not find a place for an incident on the numerous shelves of his capacious memory; if it was either too high or too broad for his shelf room, or too cumbersome, or too revolutionary, he simply rejected it. For him it was henceforth as if it had not been. He would not multilate it, or alter it, or modify it in the slightest degree. He simply ignored it. For him it was non-existent. Sometimes it excited merriment that he did not exhibit more dexterity in pruning reminiscences. Nobody but the Doctor, we felt, would include in the mention of a student whose diary was published, that one of its entries ran that he had spent an unprofitable evening at Professor Packard's. His incapacity for such an excision, however, was deep-seated. If he reproduced, he must do it exactly. He would have made an admirable witness.

This tenacious hold on the past, combined as it was with a great veneration for ancient days and ways, fitted Dr. Packard for his special function in the life of the Seminary, namely to be the preserver until another era of the Evangelical type of piety as it existed in its great days. For this, I take it, was Dr. Packard's great contribution to the Seminary. Others might endeavor to trace Christianity's profound relation to human thought and the cosmic scheme; others might essay the perilous toils of the theological pioneer and seek to open up new fields of Christian thought or experience; these tasks were not for Dr. Packard's conservative and home-loving nature. For him the type of religion which had revived the Episcopal Church in Massachusetts under Griswold, and awakened the torpor of Virginia under Moore and Meade, was sufficient. The Evangelical Fathers filled his ideal of what men of God should be, and the Evangelical missionaries Boone, Payne, and Minor had thrilled his soul by their consecrated heroism. This religious life and this theology satisfied him entirely. As in the case of Dr. Charles Hodge of Princeton, there can be no history of his theological opinions, after the beginning of his professorship, for there was never any subsequent change of any importance. His days were linked each to each not merely by natural piety, according to Wordsworth's wish, but also by his whole system of theology. At the end he was among us like an outcropping of an earlier geological era. Our difficulties seemed to him unnecessary, and our problems were to him incomprehensible or preposterous. Moderately Calvinistic, a believer in the highest views of Inspiration, he was an Evangelical Churchman of the type of Bishop Johns.

As such he was recognized throughout the whole Church. When new theories or customs were broached that seemed inconsistent with Christian traditions, or irreconcilable with the Christian tone which our forefathers had set, people would say, "What would Dr. Packard think of it?" He stood up like some tower on a distant hill, which the traveler knew was situated on the right road. It was a comfort to know that if the path were lost, he could make his way back to that point, and starting at the tower again make another cast for the trail. In his last days at the Seminary, Dr.

Packard was such a landmark, known throughout our whole Church. The following incident is quite typical:

On one of the Sundays during the session of the General Convention in Baltimore in 1892, ten years before his death, an eloquent young bishop preached to an immense congregation for nearly an hour, a remarkable compound of philosophy and Christianity. A master of long, involved and carefully balanced sentences, the graceful orator sought to combine in an indissoluble union concepts of a somewhat Hegelian character, and the faith of the Gospels. Only a few of his listeners could appreciate the true nature of the problem he was endeavoring to solve. The foe that he was attacking was clearly not sin, but some rival philosophy, and the faculty to which he appealed was not the conscience but the speculative reason. The interest of the congregation was manifestly not in the message, but in the marvelous word-skill and sentence-building of the speaker. As the dazed and dazzled people poured down the aisle after the benediction, the Rev. Arthur Lawrence, a clerical deputy from Massachusetts leaned over and whispered to a Virginia deputy, "I wonder what Dr. Packard would think of such preaching?"

Certainly there were few people equally equipped to tell us what the Evangelicals believed in their great days. None of our professors ever enjoyed greater advantages (for their time) than Dr. Packard. His father was a Harvard graduate, a school teacher of ability, and a Congregational minister of approved usefulness and enduring influence. His collegiate training was received under the most inspiring and helpful conditions at Bowdoin, a small new college, where his elder brother Alpheus had set the younger brother an excellent precedent of high scholarship, and a gifted young faculty was making its mark in many fields. His theological instruction was received at Andover, in the best theological school in America. His professor of Exegesis, the celebrated Moses Stuart, was as fine a teacher of that department as the English speaking world could show. So far ahead of Oxford was he as a Hebraist, that his Hebrew grammer and reader were used as text-books in that University. As a preacher, controversialist, linguist, and commentator, he was a giant.

Upon young Joseph Packard was poured forth the best Evangelical influences and learning of New England, where Evangelical religion was compelled by the presence of Unitarianism to examine with care its Biblical and philosophical foundations, and was not allowed to rest content with the heart's eager response to the Evangelical message. To all these influences he was heartily responsive. At Bowdoin he was Salutatarian of his class, and Moses Stuart certified the Virginia Seminary's trustees that he was competent to fill the chair of sacred literature in any institution.

During his course at Andover he had become attracted to the Episcopal Church, and had regularly attended the services conducted by the Rev. John S. Stone, the eminent Evangelical theologian who closed his career as Dean of the Cambridge Divinity School. The chief attraction of the Episcopal Church for young Packard was its beautiful liturgy. As the Episcopal Church in New England under Bishop Griswold was Evangelical in tone, the doctrinal transition was easy. He was doubtless drawn to our Church in some degree by the primitive character of our polity. He was always glad, staunch conservator that he was, that we had the ancient order. At times he would intimate that in some way our view of the Sacraments as seals was more Biblical and satisfying than the current Protestant theories. But this was not often. The real bond that drew him to our Church was his liking for our tone and form of worship. He would have nothing to do with the theory that his father's congregations had been without a valid ministry or sacraments. "Irregular, but not invalid," expressed his mind. But he shrank from the subject. He never was a controversialist; his turn of mind was neither legal nor metaphysical, but literary and poetical. In these questions he was not on his native heath, and he stepped carefully in the footprints of Bishop Johns, for whose gifts of definition he had a profound admiration, and with whose Princetonian views of man and of the Fall, and of grace, he was in close accord.

After graduating from Andover he taught awhile. Though he wished to be a minister, for some reason he never seems to have thought of taking a parish. While he was teaching at Bristol, Pennsylvania, in an Episcopal Academy or College, as it was ambitiously called, founded and managed by the Evangelical leaders, with Dr. Milnor and Dr. Tyng at their head, for the training of young men for the ministry, he was elected to the chair of Biblical Literature in the Virginia Seminary. Thereupon he took orders, being ordained to the diaconate by Bishop Griswold, and the session of 1836 found him at his post in the Virginia Seminary. Dr. Reuel Keith and Dr. Lippitt, both like himself New Englanders, were his first colleagues.

At the time the Seminary was in a great glow of missionary enthusiasm. The elder Boone had returned from China, and delivered some thrilling missionary addresses, made doubly potent by his inspiring example. Payne, Minor and Savage were all in the Seminary, and were determined to inaugurate a mission on one of the most dangerous coasts of the world, the deadly West Coast of Africa, among the natives about Liberia. Their heroism, fervor and consecration made a profound impression upon Dr. Packard. Many of the Seminary students eventually laid down their lives in that fever-smitten coast. They were always ranked by Dr. Packard among the noble army of martyrs, and he loved, as he used to phrase it, "to strew flowers on their graves," by recalling their names in his public addresses. From that first year he was a steadfast upholder of foreign missions, and when, towards the close of his life, his youngest daughter, Miss Mary, offered herself for the new mission to Brazil, he gave her willingly to that distant field.

Phillips Brooks doubted whether any theological professor is ever much of a preacher. He probably thought that a professor is apt to be too much interested in theology, and too little acquainted with the modes of thought and needs of the people. Certainly Dr. Packard was not open to the criticism of being too much of a builder or defender of systems. In his "Recollections" he praises Dr. McElhinney as a practical preacher. And so Dr. McElhinney was at times, though always too bookish, and conventional in his language, after the pattern of Pope's diction in his celebrated translation of the Iliad, which the scholars tell us did so much to conventionalize the language of English poetry in the days before Cowper and Wordsworth. I can never forget Dr.

McElhinney's description of the widow of Nain and the way in which he rang the changes on the word "widow," and amplified upon her desolation. "Raven locks," and "marble" or "alabaster brows" were frequent in his descriptive passages. At times Dr. McElhinney would preach a controversial sermon, and set up some theory, which those who held it usually claimed was incorrectly represented by his men of straw, and then would proceed to trip it up by any number of subtle arguments. He scorned the brutality of knock-down blows, or the obvious and banal arguments of common sense. Few men could phrase more elegantly and exactly a subtle objection; the subtler, the more satisfactory.

On other occasions he would vindicate some antiquated translation, such as "charity" instead of "love" in the thirteenth chapter of I Corinthians.

Nothing of this kind, however, was ever heard from Dr. Packard. His sermons were as a rule devout meditations. Martineau has claimed that all other preaching falls short of its proper function, and is better fitted for the expositions of the lecture room or the casuistry of the confessional. As he puts it, "in virtue of the close affinity, perhaps ultimate identity of Religion and Poetry, preaching is essentially a lyric expression of the soul, an utterance of meditation in sorrow, hope, love and joy from a representative of the human heart in its divine relations." Along these lines Dr. Packard's sermons were as a rule laid. He abounded in excellent quotations; a literary flavor was always evident, and he had the gift of rising to meet the requirements of special occasions, being particularly good at anniversaries and celebrations.

There was a certain quiet distinction in his reading of the lessons. By his well-placed emphasis he would often throw fresh light on the passage. At times he would take the privilege of a lifelong student of the original languages and alter the translation. All of his old students will recall the great improvements he made by the simple device of rearranging the punctuation in the lesson in the Burial Office, and how he would change the Gospel taken from St. John VIII, and read it according to the best authorities: "I am the good shepherd; and I know mine own, and mine own know me, even as the Father knoweth me, and I know the Father; and I lay down my life for the sheep."

In his Faculty Meeting talks he was under the great disadvantage of never having been the rector of a Church. On a large class of ministerial problems he was consequently unable to speak with the authority and force of Dr. May, Dr. Walker and Dr. Nelson. His own life had been so blameless, and I may say cloistral in its unworldly detachment from secular affairs, that he was unaware of certain aspects of life. Yet he was not the descendant of many generations of thrifty, shrewd New Englanders without inheriting some of their "gumption". He often exhibited a keen insight into the sources of worldly power and success. One of his greatest charms was this commingling of childlike innocence and worldly shrewdness. It made him full of surprises. Sometimes, the wonder was that he was so ignorant, and the next moment the surprise was that he was so keen-sighted. A certain Oxford College Head was famous for his ability to pick out rising men. Dr. Packard had a good deal of the gift. Being poetical, rather than legal or logical, he attached little importance to powers of argument, and gave great weight to personal traits like tact, amiability, a fine voice, a good presence, general friendliness, and rhetorical gifts. His best Faculty Meeting addresses were made on devotional topics. As Dean he made an excellent opening address for the session.

His scholarship was literary rather than philological or critical. His judgment was good, but he had not the gift of laying bare the processes whereby he reached his conclusions. He often used to say, "Don't you feel it?" This unanalytic method has its own effectiveness. It was employed by Webster himself, great debater though he was, in a case against that subtle logician Rufus Choate. Webster's client claimed that Choate's client had infringed his patent of a machine with a certain kind of wheels. Choate in defense argued that the wheels of his client were constructed on different principles. He supported his thesis by profound mathematical and mechanical arguments. Webster's rejoinder was to bring out the wheels, and setting them up before the jury, to exclaim in his weighty way, "Gentlemen, look at the wheels!"

Such was the Doctor's usual method. I distinctly recall an instance. One of my classmates somewhat impetuously declared in class that John's baptism must have been the same as Christian baptism, since we had no record of the baptism of the disciples. The Doctor differed, and, as the student wished to debate the question, disposed of the matter by assigning him the nature of John's baptism as an essay. The student called in some helpers, and they went diligently to work to make out a strong argument for the substantial identity of the two rites. They consistently ignored everything on the other side, and treated the question as counsel retained for the defense of the dignity of John's baptism, resolved that the Doctor, who had waived that theory aside so summarily, should have a different argument to answer. At the close, they said they took their stand on the great text, "One Lord, one Faith, one Baptism." The Doctor listened composedly to the essay and complimented the author upon the ability with which he had defended his views. However, he added, the nineteenth chapter of Acts is conclusive, whereupon he read the passage in which St. Paul clearly distinguishes the two baptisms. As for all the cobwebs that the essayist had carefully spun, he simply ignored them.

He knew how to dispose, with a good deal of humorous dexterity, of the students who would quote against his exegesis a long catena of authorities. "You see, Doctor," some ambitious and argumentative student would conclude, "the majority of commentators is on the other side." "But, Mr. Blank," the Doctor would rejoin, "do we count authorities, or weigh them? I am glad to know that Meyer takes the view that I have given." He always had a high and correct estimate of the great ability of Meyer as an exact grammarian, and a thorough exegete. After a while the Doctor would give some interpretation opposed to his favorite commentator, and the student would announce triumphantly that Meyer held the opposite view. The Doctor was, however, always too dexterous to be unhorsed by such an assault. He would calmly transfer the question to another realm by saying sententiously, "Let us cease from man, whose breath is in his nostrils and his foundations in the clay: Let us fix our attention on the text." We never could ascertain whether or not he tasted the fun of this, for his countenance was in such cases absolutely inscrutable. This inscrutability was one of his marked characteristics. We could never tell by his expression what he thought of us, and he always seemed supremely indifferent about what we thought of him.

His interpretations might be at times too literal, but he was always guided by a sound literary instinct. He never allowed himself to be drawn into far-fetched and tenuous deductions from slender premises, and not being a systematic theologian, did not try to force a vast and complicated theology into the text. He used to pour quiet contempt on the Churchly exegetes, who are always trying to force their system into the Bible, who interpreted the regular word in Greek for giving thanks, (ε'υχαριστεῖν) in the story of St. Paul's shipwreck, in the technical sense of a much later age, as indicating a celebration of the Eucharist, or rendered the Greek verb for serving, "diaconein," (διακονεῖν) wherever it was possible as "serve as deacon." He had a great dislike of ponderous discussion on matters that could be settled by a little common sense in interpretation. He would call such argumentation "shooting a cannon-ball at a fly."

Of course he followed the scholars of his day in finding Messianic references everywhere in the Old Testament, even in such an epithalamium as the Forty-fifth Psalm. What else could be expected of a scholar who had helped his revered leader, Dr. Keith, to get through the press his translation of Hengstenberg's Christology? He had too much sound literary taste to endeavor to carry the imagery of a sheep and shepherd all through the Twenty-third Psalm, after the fashion of a very popular modern tract by an Orientalist on this Psalm.

The importance of grammar as a key to the interpretation of literature he never fully appreciated, and he never sought to strengthen the grasp of his students on Greek or Hebrew by requiring them to turn English into these languages.

But this is no reflection on him; it is only another way of stating that he was educated before Hadley came to Yale, or Goodwin taught at Harvard, or Gildersleeve was at the University of Virginia. He had the full equipment of the men of his generation, and when the greatest honor of his life came to him, in the shape of an invitation to be one of the American Revisers, and a member of the Old Testament committee, he was able to do his part with credit to himself and the Seminary, and with benefit to the Church. Dr. Schaff, the head of the whole committee, was so well pleased with him that he engaged him to write the commentary on Malachi in his edition of Lange's Commentary.

The hospitality of his home is one of the cherished traditions of the Seminary. With the cordial cooperation of his wife and daughters he used to keep open house. All the classes were invited to his home and entertained in due order. No stranger could visit the Seminary without an invitation to his bountiful board. The Commencement season used to throw heavy burdens of entertainment upon the faculty; but the Packards always bore a generous portion of the load. He kept up this hospitable custom till the very end.

A critic of the various manifestations of the religious life declares that the library of Evangelical biographies shows that the Evangelical saints were of a somewhat querulous and despondent type. There is probably a measure of truth in this criticism, for Evangelical religion was too introspective, took too much to diaries and records of self-examination, and did not permit its votaries sufficient relaxation or variety. But whether it was true of Evangelicals as a school or not, this criticism could never be justly attached to Dr. Packard. While he was not by nature buoyant or expansive, he was always stout-hearted and uncomplaining. He suffered much in the vicissitudes of the Civil War, when he had to live without any fixed income, an exile from his home, and a resident of the border country where the battles were most frequent, and passion ran highest. Two promising sons fell in that conflict. Later on in life he had some long and very distressing illnesses in his family. He himself suffered much pain from his right arm, which eventually had to be taken off. But he kept his troubles to

himself and never made his pain or trials an excuse for failure
to discharge his full measure of duty.   After enduring
much suffering he finally had his right shoulder opened up
to eradicate that troublesome cyst.   The operation was
pronounced by the surgeon, Dr. Frederick May, more painful than cutting off an arm.   He underwent it without any
anaesthetic, and with great fortitude.   No man consumed
his own smoke more completely in the great things of life.
This staunchness under suffering, together with his tenacious
hold of ancient traditions, and his ability to transmit them
unchanged and unphilosophized made Dr. Packard an admirable example of the kind of man the ancient Church possessed
in the martyr Polycarp, the faithful transmitter of primitive
traditions, and the loyal and uncomplaining sufferer for
the sake of his Master.   One felt that Dr. Packard would
have won the same martyr crown under the same circumstances.   Loyalty was his most distinctive grace, loyalty to
his traditions, to his family, to his friends, to his Church.

As for the Seminary, he felt as assured of the Divine
blessing upon it as a Hebrew prophet was confident that God
would build up Zion.   Oxford might have its Bampton lectures and its great traditions, and Andover might have been
in Moses Stuart's day, a great Seminary, but in his heart of
hearts the Doctor thought that there was no Seminary on
earth comparable to the Virginia Seminary, where the religion
of Jesus, he was convinced, was more truly interpreted than
anywhere else; where the ancient missionary zeal was fostered and the ancient and dignified rites of Early Church
Order and Worship were observed.   It was true that he
was inclined to hold at times that even this elect Institution
had passed the meridian of its glory; that its *anni mirabiles*
had been in the days when Keith, Sparrow and May were
associated with him, and Brooks and Potter, Randolph and
Dudley, and the early African missionaries had studied in
its halls.

On one occasion, when the students were projecting
some change in their customs, Dr. Packard came into their
conference and put an end to the whole matter by remarking
"The old is better."   This was peculiarly his feeling with
regard to the alumni.   Any alumnus was sure of a cordial

welcome, however recent his graduation, but let him be a student of ante-bellum days, and the Doctor's eloquent and characteristic notes of pleasure were greatly increased in number and loudness; and if he was one of the oldest group of all, he would break into a kind of chant of joy as he welcomed him with cordial, inarticulate noises.

Though the old was better, and the older alumni were the most cherished, all of us felt that he set great store by us. Everyone realized that he was the kind of man "to tie to." I had a signal proof of his staunchness. When I became a member of the Faculty, Dr. Packard turned over to me, as the junior professor, the publication of the catalogue. I employed a new printer who made a frightful mess of the job. In taking out the type to correct one error, he made a number of new mistakes. The result was a catalogue in which the stars that indicate death fell in the most disastrous fashion, resurrecting the dead, and consigning to the tomb the living. We had a lively time at the annual meeting of the Alumni that session. Alumnus after alumnus rose to remonstrate against being stricken out from the land of the living in this fashion. One aged and distinguished alumnus made much merriment by accepting the record and appearing as a re-surrected spirit. I can never forget how my cheeks burned. I took it for granted that Dr. Packard would entrust the catalogue to other hands next year. But he did nothing of the kind. He gave me another trial, as a matter of course, and stood by me staunchly through the whole episode. The next catalogue was not open to this criticism, and by successive improvements I was able eventually to show that the Doctor had made no mistake in giving me another chance. I mention the story to show the staunchness of his friendship. He did not guide his steps by the judgments of critics.

This indifference to criticism, when he thought it ill-founded, often left people under a false impression. There was an immense number of jokes current among the students about "the Rab" as he used to be called, an abbreviation of Rabbi. Many of them arose from misunderstandings, and many others were fathered upon him. But he let them pass and refused to spoil a good story by explaining. Gratefully do I recall his advice to me to follow this policy. We had all

been over to the meeting of the Evangelical Alliance at
Washington, and had listened to an eloquent address by
Bishop Harris of Michigan. Some not very discreet remark of mine was slightly twisted, and then handed around
among the students. In its proper form, it was nearly as
stupid as old Nick Bottom, but as altered by the students, it
was Bottom with the ass's head, and I was about to deny
indignantly the paternity of such a monstrosity. We were
all coming over in the train together when I heard the joke.
Before I could speak, the Doctor gently checked me, and
advised me not to contradict. I recognized the wisdom of
his counsel and by following it, took all the life out of the
story.

Some of these anecdotes about Dr. Packard should be
preserved. They do not signify any disesteem; often they
reveal him in a most amiable light. As, for instance, in
the tale of his preaching from a chair. It was in the early
days of his professorship, so the story came to me, and Dr.
Packard was journeying with friends by carriage to the
White Sulphur Springs. Finding themselves at a village
on a Saturday night, they made their arrangements for
resting over Sunday, after the excellent usage of those days.
When it came to the ears of the worthies of the little town
that a minister was in their midst, a delegation was sent to
request him to preach. This Dr. Packard was reluctant
to do, as he had no sermon with him, and he was not accustomed to preach *ex tempore*. They were, however, so insistent, that he finally agreed to deliver such an address as he
was in the habit of giving at the Seminary's faculty meetings.
All that he exacted was that he should be allowed the privilege of sitting in a chair, at the head of the aisle, according
to the usage of the professors in their conferences with the
students. This privilege was freely granted. For many
years the people of that village would say, "We have had
many ministers spend the night here, and preach for us on
their way to the Springs. Some of them were famous and
eloquent preachers. One of the best was a settin' preacher.
We have never had another of his sort."

One of the Doctor's sayings most frequently quoted was
"Take one—take two." The origin of this saying was the

Doctor's hospitable insistence that a guest, some old student doubtless, upon whom he was showering attentions, should take two buckwheat cakes, on the excellent principle that one would keep the other warm.   This was distorted in course of time, till the Doctor was made to insist that his guest should take two rolls at one helping, and then it was applied to two of anything and everything.   Doctor Packard once explained to me the origin of this oft-quoted saying. Doubtless year after year through the Seminary's future, some alumnus will say to another at the annual banquet, "Mi-yah, take one, take two."   Never will it be heard or repeated by one of the Doctor's old scholars without recalling his characteristic manner of speech or the generous hospitality, which produced that historic saying.

He had the distinction of having more stories told about him than any of the other professors.   These tales no more interfered with the veneration for his sterling piety and manly fortitude than the gargoyles on a cathedral detract from the dignity of its soaring architecture.   He had in an unusual degree the gift of sententious utterance, and his sayings were much tasted and handed about, as Ian MacLaren would express it.   In conversation with him, a clergyman of marked business ability and considerable property once remarked to the Doctor that he could have made a great deal of money if he had invested in some vacant lots in Washington City when he first came to the Seminary.   "Imagine the Apostle Paul," exclaimed the Doctor impulsively, "looking around for good corner lots on his visit to Athens!"

When his daughter, Miss Mary Packard, was embarking for the first time for Brazil, with Mr. Brown and Mr. Meem, the Doctor went down to Newport News to see her off.   It was naturally a time of deep feeling, and the captain of the ship did not exactly strike the right note, when he began to run on about the fearful storms that he expected to encounter with so many Jonahs on board.   "I know of a case," said the Doctor, regarding him fixedly, "where a missionary saved two hundred and seventy-six people from shipwreck." "Indeed," said the captain, and the subject was dropped. "I rather shut him up," said the Doctor to me, afterwards; "You recognized, I suppose, the instance to which I referred." "No," I answered, "What was it?" "St. Paul," was the reply. It was characteristic of him to remember the exact number of souls on board St. Paul's ship, and also to leave the matter unexplained to the incurious sea-captain.

I once attended a theological meeting of some kind in Washington, which he thought was hardly of our kind. His comment was that I must have been like to a speckled bird among them. He had a healthy contempt for successful time-servers, and remarked of a rising clergyman of this class, that the higher he climbed the more he exposed himself.

His sense of humor, and of the grotesque, is correctly mirrored in his "Recollections." When I joined the faculty I always accompanied him to his own front door after the faculty meeting on Thursday night, a little attention against which he never failed to demur on the ground that it was really unnecessary. After this preliminary protestation we would set out together very sociably, for he liked companionship. When neither of us had taken part, he would occasionally remark, "As the deacon said after the meeting in which he had not spoken, 'we had rather a dry time to-night.'"

He was very fond of a good quotation, and often used to quote from Young's Night Thoughts:

"Talk they of morals! Oh, thou bleeding Lamb,
    The great morality is love of Thee."

I see from his "Recollections" that he derived this from Bishop Meade.

He loved to quote the poets, especially Young, Cowper and Vaughan. Verses from hymns were often on his lips. Occasionally he would quote Keble's Christian Year, but his chief favorites were the hymns of the Evangelicals, like Newton, Cowper, Toplady, Montgomery, and Charlotte Elliott.

Ecclesiastical History occupied only a subordinate place in the theological studies of his youth, and he never made any systematic study of the development of doctrine. As he expressed himself in one of the most elaborate of his addresses, Christianity is in his view, a documentary religion, a religion to be learned by interpretation of the Bible, and as once for all given to the saints, is not to be improved. He belonged to the pre-Darwinian era, and never grasped the idea of evolution. He thought that the system of religion as he held it, was the exact teaching of the Apostles, and that Christian dogma issued forth, fully developed from the College of the Apostles, as the St. Lawrence is a full grown river at its outflow from Lake Ontario. His theory of inspiration barred the way to any analysis of the growth of the Canon, and closed his eyes to any indications of the composite authorship of the books as we have them. He believed in the historical accuracy of the first chapters of Genesis, of the Book of Job, and of the prophecy of Jonah.

Having an aversion to metaphysics, he never realized how large a part of our thinking in Christianity, as well as in all other departments, is colored and conditioned by our metaphysical theories. It would have been a great shock to him, if he could have been made to see how many of our dogmas which are supposed to be drawn from the Sacred Scriptures, are really read into them, and have as their real source either Greek speculation, or Roman Law, or the philosophy of some great thinker like Augustine, or Anselm, or the experience of some religious genius like Eckhart, or Luther, or Spinoza, or Wesley, or grow out of some great historic occurrences. But such studies were not in his line. He was an interpreter of Biblical literature first and last. He knew that the Divine Spirit spoke through the Bible. A progressive revelation through the utilization by the Divine Spirit of the experience of the race, and the individual, was too elusive for him. He had too long been an interpreter of written documents to think of Christianity as revealing itself by any other process. I believe there is more of wisdom, as there is certainly more of faith, in a more teachable attitude toward Divine Providence than was taken by these venerable men. A Seminary for college graduates ought to rise above the timid Normal School standard and seek to be a group of searchers after truth. Only in such a way can it continue to be a School of the Prophets. It is good to know that Horace Bushnell thought it more important to liberalize theological students than to fit them out with a rigid system. The question is of great importance. The Seminary has since made this transition and now under younger men has more of the modern spirit, is more liberal than of old. There are many who thank God that such is the case.

On one point all the Seminary's alumni and friends will agree, and that is that religion itself is more important than any system of theology. We want our professors to be men of sound learning, and of up-to-date knowledge, but we desire them above all to be men of real piety; and the great majority of us, the overwhelming majority, I believe, wish the Evangelical emphasis upon the witness of the Spirit and personal piety to be continued in the supreme place in our Seminary's teaching and life. We do not want our theology taught by men of lukewarm religion. We are profoundly grateful to Dr. Packard, whatever we may think of his Biblical theories and theology, because we recognize that his piety was vital, living and transforming. In a conceit of knowledge he never lost the vision that is vouchsafed unto babes. Life buffeted and tried him, but it was powerless to break or embitter his spirit. The general verdict was that his nature grew tenderer as he grew older. The light that guided his youth cheered his declining years. He saw the theories dominant in his early life professed by diminishing numbers, and his old masters no longer revered as safe guides, but the everlasting gospel that was, we know, enshrined in his old theology, ever refreshed his soul, and kept his faith strong. He took his stand on the Bible, as the word of God, on the work of Christ, on the proven efficacy of prayer, on the enduring witness of the Spirit, and found that he had builded on the Rock. As a man of faith and prayer, he will always be held in reverent affection by his old students.

As I write, I become once more a student, and find myself sitting in Dr. Packard's study. His arm has pained him so much that he has felt unable to go over to his classroom, and has requested the class to come to him. Our chairs are ranged around the wall of the room, and the Doctor is seated at his table. The French window that served for a door is open, as it is a mild Spring day, and outside we hear the birds busy at their nest-building. We are reading in Greek St. Paul's great chapter on the Resurrection, and I can hear the Doctor in his sententious way, explaining that the sentence,

"There is one glory of the sun, and another glory of the moon, and another glory of the stars, for one star differeth from another star in glory," was not intended to teach that there are different degrees of glory in heaven, but simply indicates the infinite variety of the Divine operations. What an honor it is for any man to be thus closely associated with the sacred literature of our faith, so that his remarks will come in this way to the minds of his old scholars, and be handed on to countless numbers through the generations to come. Such was Dr. Packard's great privilege. In the constellation of the Seminary's teachers his star will always shine with a light of peculiar softness.

SECTION V

CHAPTER V

REV. DR. WILLIAM SPARROW

Dean and Professor of Theology

BY HIS GRANDSON, REV. CARL E. GRAMMER, S. T. D.

The earliest description of Dr. Sparrow is afforded by his sometime colleague in Gambier, the Rev. Dr. McElroy. "On a Sunday morning in September 1828," he writes, "I reached Mount Vernon from Sandusky, and having taken a room in the principal tavern of the pleasant village and nascent city in the woods, I soon learned that Professor Sparrow from Gambier would that afternoon at three o'clock officiate and preach in the Court Room. The information was peculiarly grateful, for I had a letter to him from the Rector of St. Mary's, Kilkenny, Ireland, the Rev. Peter Roe, his mother's brother, with whom I had become acquainted at my home, a few miles distant from his residence, and through whose instrumentality I had come to cast in my lot with Bishop Chase in his great work. I was very anxious to see Professor Sparrow. His uncle was a leading man in the Church of Ireland, and very decidedly of the school of Venn and Simeon, and had shown me Professor Sparrow's last letter to him and impressed me with his very exalted views of the capacity and excellence of his nephew. I expected therefore to meet no ordinary man.

When I entered the Court Room, the service had already commenced. I was somewhat distracted by the novelty of appearances. The room was dingy, the clergyman was in his plain citizen's dress, the congregation with few exceptions wore a very unkempt look; few had prayer books and the responses were feebly rendered. But the earnestness of the clergyman soon arrested my attention and brought me under the influence of his fervor. From the moment the text was announced to the close of the sermon, the attention was breath-

578

THE REVEREND DOCTOR WILLIAM SPARROW

Professor 1841-1874

less and riveted. I had seldom or never heard before such a sermon; so able, so full of truth, so clear, transparent, beautiful and impressive. At this long distance of time the whole scene is vividly before me; the preacher with his sweet and distinct voice, his modest yet commanding mien, his soft, yet brilliant and penetrating eye, his gleaming and expressive features, and his whole countenance, betimes, one brilliant blaze of light. The congregation were enchained, enrapt, and I cannot describe my own delight, surprise and astonishment and gratitude to the Great Head of the Church, that among the pioneers in the wilderness for Christ and His work there was one so profound, eloquent and evangelical." Dr. Sparrow was at this time in his twenty-eighth year.

Though he was born in Charlestown, Massachusetts, March 12, 1801, William Sparrow was of Irish birth. His father, Samuel Sparrow, left Ireland a few years before the birth of his eldest son, on account of his participation in the rebellion of 1798. In 1805 he was permitted to return, probably through the intercession of his father, William Sparrow, who had some influential friends. The Sparrows originally came over to Ireland in the time of Cromwell, and settled in Wexford. Many of them became Quakers. The same Dr. McElroy whom we have quoted, gives us the contemporary Irish opinion of the family. "Mr. Sparrow's father belonged to the class styled gentry in Ireland, and was very respectably connected. He was a gentleman of vigorous intellect, of extensive reading, particularly in the department of human rights, popular and national interests and political economy. Mrs. Sparrow was a lady of great refinement, of exquisite grace and polish, and of most lovely and winning character." She was by birth a Roe, an English Irish family that came over, like the Sparrows, in the Protectorate of Cromwell, and also settled in the pale in Wexford, but in the time of his father, Dr. Henry Roe, moved to Dublin to avoid the disturbances of an Irish rebellion. To this side of the house William Sparrow owed his religious disposition, and his earliest religious impressions. All the indications are that his father lacked the practical ability to get on in life.

As long as the elder William Sparrow lived, the family were in comfortable circumstances in Ireland. It was generally understood that William Sparrow, the eldest grandson, was to be his grandfather's heir, and the lad was prepared for college, young as he was, in the best public school in the vicinity, a boarding school, under the principalship of a clergyman, whom Dr. Sparrow characterized in after years as "a scholar and gentleman, though too much sought after by the neighboring gentry on account of his social qualities to leave him devoted as he should have been to the interests of the school." The instruction was very thorough. Dr. Sparrow used often to refer to the teacher in mathematics, who would never accept an imperfect recitation. "Sit down, honey, sit down, honey," was his standing order at anything like hesitation, confusion or haziness. In 1817 William Sparrow, the grandfather, died, just when the grandson was ready to enter Trinity College, Dublin. For some unknown reason no special provision was made for his grandson William, according to the general expectation, and the family emigrated back to America.

Those years from the age of five to sixteen in Ireland, made an ineffaceable impression upon Dr. Sparrow. They taught him by personal experience the evils of the secularization of the Church by union with the State, for it was the unworthy character of a Rector that made his upright grandfather give up churchgoing entirely. The boy's sensitive nature realized keenly the difference between the easy-going, worldly-minded ministers of the old school, and the zealous, spiritually minded Evangelical pioneers. He had experience of house-searchings by the military, and the evils of civil war in poor storm-tossed Ireland, that was rocked with special violence in those Napoleonic days. Waterloo was an unforgettable memory. He would tell his grandchildren stories that he heard in Ireland of the great Duke, how, for example, he was said to have ridden twenty miles the day before the Battle of Waterloo on his great horse Copenhagen for a private interview with Blucher to make sure that the Field Marshal would not fail him next day. "What was the difference between Napoleon and Wellington?" he asked one of his little grandsons who was known to be devoted to military biography. The lad had come to the Seminary with his parents to attend the funeral of his grandmother, and was taken into the room, where his grandfather lay too ill to attend the funeral service. "The one followed glory, and the other duty," answered the boy, and his grandfather, ever the teacher, beamed at the reply, even at that sad hour.

All his life long he felt a special tenderness for Ireland. He often revisited it, and kept up his intercourse with his Irish relations, the Roes of Dublin in particular. He said that he never passed an Irish laborer on the street without feeling an outgoing of affection to him. He often enlivened his conversation by anecdotes of Irish experiences.

The first home of the family in America was in Utica, New York, where by the advice of his mother William Sparrow became a competitor, youthful stranger though he was, in an examination for the position of classical teacher in the principal academy. His thorough mastery of the extensive preparatory courses in Latin and Greek required by Trinity College won him the position. His unique power as a teacher disclosed itself at once. One of his pupils, afterwards the greatly revered Dr. Burr of Portsmouth, Ohio, testified of him, "He was very exacting, and yet it was easier to prepare for him, and I felt happier in preparing for his recitations, than for those of any other. There was no let off, no chance of shirking, and the good hard work he demanded brought its own reward."

The young teacher, however, felt the need of a college education, and in 1819 entered Columbia College, where he seems to have remained during the sessions of 1819-1820 and 1820-21. Of the professors at Columbia, that enthusiastic classicist, and prolific editor of Latin texts, Dr. Charles Anthon, made the strongest impression upon him, and gave him an enduring love for the Greek language and literature. In these studies and in mathematics, Dr. Sparrow was a true modern in his zeal for thoroughness. He held with Plato, the greatest of idealists, that the imperfect is the measure of nothing. Quality, he always insisted, is more important than quantity. If the first is properly insisted on, he held, the latter will in the end not be deficient. It was indeed one of his fundamental principles as a teacher, that the student

must be made to realize the difference between merely understanding and thoroughly possessing a subject.

His early Evangelical training carried him to St. George's
Church, New York. Its rector, Dr. James Milnor, was a
remarkable man. He had begun life as a lawyer, and had
been elected Congressman from New York. During the
leisure of his evenings in Washington, where he boarded in a
hotel, he began a course of serious readings in the evidences of
Christianity, which caused him to abandon politics and enter
the ministry. As this incident indicates, he was a man of
unusual force, and made St. George's one of the strongest
churches in the country. He was one of the chief Evangelical leaders. Dr. Sparrow always spoke with gratitude of
his teaching, and particularly of his Wednesday evening
lectures. His great church, St. George's, was one of the
bulwarks of sound theological education in the Episcopal
Church. Later on it founded at Gambier the Milnor Professorship, of which Dr. Sparrow was the first holder, and
still later erected a dormitory for students at the Theological
Seminary of Virginia, the well known St. George's Hall, in
which Phillips Brooks roomed during his Seminary course.

When William was studying in Columbia, the family
moved to Huron County, Ohio, where his mother died in
1821. "She endured with great fortitude and resignation,"
writes Dr. McElroy, "the deprivations of the wilderness and
pioneer life, but at last her health failed under its hardships,"
and she died beloved and lamented by the whole community.
Her son ever spoke of her with reverent tenderness. It was
from her, undoubtedly, that he derived his distinguishing
characteristics. He at once resumed his profession of teaching, when he rejoined the family in Ohio; at first in the classical school of Bishop Chase's son, the Rev. Philander Chase,
Jr., and afterwards in Cincinnati College, of which Bishop
Chase had been elected President. When Bishop Chase
went to England on his courageous trip to collect funds for
educational institutions in Ohio under the Episcopal Church,
Mr. Sparrow accepted a tutorship in Miami University,
which at the end of six months became a full professorship
in Latin and Greek. From this well-established and growing college he was summoned by Bishop Chase to assist him

in organizing the educational institutions that afterwards
developed into Kenyon College and Gambier Theological
Seminary. The stout-hearted Bishop had prospered in
his strenuous undertaking. The English nobility, as the
names of Gambier, Kenyon and Bexley fittingly commem
rate, were particularly impressed by his appeals. No one
but a man of unusual forcefulness could have achieved such
a success so shortly after the War of 1812, while the Protestant Episcopal Church in the United States had not yet
been fully recognized by the Established Church of
England. The Bishop was greatly aided by his splendid
presence. "He was," said Dr. Sparrow, "when I first saw
him, the most majestic looking man I had ever seen. He
filled the whole doorway." All the force of this impressive
personality was brought to bear upon the youthful professor
to leave Miami and cast in his lot with an educational institution under Episcopal auspices, that was too poor to call
a professor from the East. The Bishop pleaded that the
young professor, who was at the time a candidate for orders,
owed his services to the Church. This argument prevailed,
and Mr. Sparrow became "professor of languages and also
for the present of mathematics" in the nascent College and
Seminary, at one third less than his salary at Miami. This
was in 1825. In the following year he was ordained to the
ministry.

He was rewarded for his loyalty and self-sacrifice by
finding in the home of Bishop Chase his future wife. She
was Frances Greenleaf Ingraham, the daughter of Duncan
Ingraham and Susannah Greenleaf of Poughkeepsie, New
York. Mrs. Chase was her eldest sister. Her family seemed
to have a special inclination to the ministry. Another
sister, Mrs. Kip, being the mother of Bishop William Ingraham Kip, and of the wife of Bishop Burgess of Maine. The
marriage was in 1827. Mrs. Sparrow at once took upon her
shoulders the burden of financial management to an unusual
degree, that her husband might devote his entire time to
study, teaching and preaching. As a girl she had been a
great reader, having been brought up on the principle that
all that an intelligent girl needed after learning the rudiments of knowledge was the society of cultivated people

and the freedom of a fine library. She retained this enjoyment of literature through life, being a persistent reader of good books and making herself quite a proficient in Shakespeare. But the care of a large family, to which they added by adoption Blanche Hening, the daughter of the blind missionary to Africa, absorbed her entirely, and she was but little known in general society. For her critical ability her husband had the greatest respect. "If there is a fly in the ointment," he used to say of his own compositions, which he read aloud to her, "Mrs. Sparrow is sure to detect it." Her name calls for grateful remembrance, not only for the Christian influence of her home, but also because she always gave her influence and counsel in favor of his continuance as a teacher. At times, under the pressure of anxiety for the future of his young family, he would seriously question whether he ought not to accept some of the calls, which offered him a larger salary and greater advantages for his children, and would also lighten the heavy burdens of his wife. In all these cases she resolutely sacrificed herself and family to the interests of the cause, and what she felt was her husband's proper task in life.

In 1828 the chair of mathematics was taken by Mr. Preston, who shows the enthusiastic admiration that Professor Sparrow awoke in his colleagues, in the following description of those days:

"There were fifty or sixty students, about half of them in college classes. There were no theological students, so Mr. Sparrow taught the classics in the college. He was a very warm friend and supporter of the bishop, and stood very high as a preacher. I found him one of the best friends I ever had, alike in his capacity as a scholar and advisor and also in the warmth and cordiality of his friendship. He was one of the most faultless men I ever knew; ever seemed to feel the deepest interest in the success of the bishop and the welfare of the college. I graduated at Yale, and I confidently say that I found no officer there whom I thought his equal, in his capacity to teach and govern young men and in the good influence he acquired over them." This is the period at which Dr. McElroy joined the college. It was a strenuous era.   Dr. Fitch, the professor of ancient languages, thus described it a little later: "The Bishop confined himself to the financial interests of the College, soliciting funds, clearing ground and putting up the buildings.   Mrs. Chase kept the books and attended to the College commons and the personal wants and comfort of the younger students.   Dr. Sparrow devoted himself assiduously to the duties of the Theological Seminary and of the Vice-President of the College.   His preaching was greatly sought after.   Till Bishop McIlvaine came no one could hold the breathless attention of an audience for a whole hour but Dr. Sparrow.   All who came under his training believed him the most competent of professors, having a giant intellect, and richly stored mind and pure heart.   Bishop Chase (while at Gambier) was absolutely head, but took no part nor seeming interest in the college as an institution of learning, did not know what students were taught nor definitely who taught them.   Dr. Sparrow as a senior professor presided at the faculty meetings and was to the students what they looked for in the head of the College.   They had confidence in him and revered him."

The number of students steadily increased, and some of them subsequently became national leaders.   One of these was Edwin M. Stanton, Lincoln's great Secretary of War, who always gratefully referred to the wholesome and stimulating influence of Dr. Sparrow, and in his last hours summoned his old professor from the Seminary Hill to his bedside in Washington.   Another notable student, whom Dr. Sparrow always ranked as one of the brightest minds he ever taught, was Henry Winter Davis, the brilliant Maryland radical, who made such a profound impression upon the House of Representatives.   Rutherford B. Hayes graduated from Kenyon after Dr. Sparrow left, and was only under his influence for a short period, but often referred to the professor's power to mould and govern young men.

Dr. Sparrow was at this period working far beyond his strength.   Though his height, about six feet two inches, and his erect carriage made him an impressive figure, he was of a slender build, and lacked robustness.   His over-exertions brought on severe nervous headaches, that were a great handicap all the rest of his life.   Indeed his energy at this time outran all discretion: not content with his theological classes, his practical headship of the College, he also assumed the editing of a diocesan weekly, "The Diocesan Observer;" was the secretary of the Convention of the diocese; a member of the Standing Committee; and delegate to the General Convention. He also preached at the neighboring stations. Moreover, it is to be borne in mind that he never attended any theological seminary, and was obliged to educate himself in theology, as he taught his classes.

He was clearly overworked; but the College and Seminary were prospering, and he was happy in his congenial occupations till a question of authority arose between the faculty and the bishop. Dr. Sparrow had always believed that the Episcopate could only be naturalized in America by bringing it under law. He felt that the personal rule of the Bishop unlimited by law meant tyranny for the clergy. Though Bishop Chase was not by any means an extreme churchman, still he claimed vast and vague prerogatives, looking on the young men whom he had ordained as his children who ought to submit their judgment to his. As for Kenyon, he was its creator and sustainer. His frequent absences necessarily threw much responsibility on the Faculty, and they claimed power adequate to their responsibility. "When Bishop Chase claimed as bishop a veto upon the acts of the faculty," Dr. McElroy writes, "it produced a painful estrangement. Professor Sparrow was ready to grant to the bishop for his own life all that was demanded, if it could be arranged that his successor should not inherit the veto power; but the bishop was honest in his conviction and the alienation continued." As the Vice-President of the College Dr. Sparrow had to bear the brunt of the conflict, which was made peculiarly painful by his wife's close relation to Mrs. Chase. Ultimately the question came before the Diocesan Convention, and the Bishop, unsupported to the extent that he desired, resigned his jurisdiction. Of course there were pamphlets on both sides, and the whole controversy was most distressing. Bishop Chase was soon elected Bishop of Illinois, and zealous pioneer that he was, resumed his work of college-building, founding Jubilee College, near Chicago, as he put it in homely vigorous phrase, "planting a mignonette under a pumpkin vine." Later on he became the Presiding Bishop of the Church. It is pleasant to record that in subsequent years the brothers-in-law and co-founders of Kenyon met and lived as friends.

This spectre of the undefined rights of the Episcopate, however, proved a Banquo's ghost, that would not down. Hardly had the gifted and admired Bishop McIlvaine, the great Evangelical bishop, appeared on the scene when the old question returned. Dr. Sparrow who was by nature sensitive and retiring, who all his life struggled with shyness, and used to lament that he had not more brass in his composition, saying whimsically, "no bell sounds far unless it contains much brass," could not bear to go through another such contest. But neither could he accept the position that he must ask the permission of the Bishop to leave the hill. It was at this juncture, in the spring of 1841, that a call reached him from the Theological Seminary in Virginia. It was a fearful wrench to his affectionate nature to leave Gambier; but the situation was unbearable; it was clear that he was looked on suspiciously as the man who had cost Bishop Chase his diocese, and he accepted the call. This episode has been told at some length because it was the most trying experience of Dr. Sparrow's life, and shows his moral courage, as his whole nature shrank from such strife. It is also profitable for instruction, for these undefined rights of the Episcopate have been a stone of stumblings in the way of our Church colleges, not to speak of other relations.

History has a great way of playing into the hands of the Tories, the historian Green, of Short History fame, used to point out in his letters to his brother historian Freeman; it places too great emphasis on official leaders, the title-bearers and office-holders, and does not sufficiently bring out the part played by less highly placed, but often more active agents. It seems to many that this has happened in Kenyon. Bishop Chase, it is true, was more than titular leader; he was the creator of the College, but surely Dr. Sparrow, who came to his assistance at a great financial sacrifice, and organized and built up the teaching of the Institution, was also one of the founders. If the Bishop's work was the necessary prerequisite, Dr. Sparrow's work was the essential end and object

which gave the Bishop the plea that secured the funds. The
foundation of the College ought to be ascribed in justice to
the firm of Chase and Sparrow.

In Ohio Dr. Sparrow was chiefly known as the head of a
college. In Virginia he gave his whole life to Theology. For
a brief season he held the chair of Church History. He had
no special taste for this department, and was glad to move
over, on the resignation of Dr. Keith, to the chair of Theology
and Christian Evidences. Perhaps it may be permitted to a
lover of history to count it as a misfortune that he did not
remain longer in his first chair. It is true that his special gift
lay in the realm of abstract thought, but for that very reason
it would have been helpful to have spent some years in studying those non-rational elements, those circumstances, secular
influences and great personalties that have affected so profoundly not merely the life, but also the doctrines of the
Church. The systematic theologian is far too apt to ascribe
changes in doctrine to logic, or new interpretations of texts,
without due recognition of the vital experiences or the altered
conditions that are incessantly bringing to light new problems, or new solutions. That Dr. Sparrow was somewhat
open to this reproach as a theologian may be inferred from
his habit of referring the ills of his beloved Ireland to the
superstition and oppression of the Roman Catholic Church.
That the son of an Irish revolutionary should ignore in this
way the oppressive and disgraceful legislation of the Protestant Irish Parliament and the tariff laws and Navigation Acts
of the English Parliament was extraordinary. But perhaps
we must not ask too much of a descendant of the dominant
Protestant class in Ireland. Moreover this aloofness from
secular concerns was common to all the Evangelicals. With
their intense spirituality they were loth to admit the reflex
influence of secular life upon the spiritual nature. With
them, spirit, truth, morals were the dominating and all controlling considerations.

Theoretically no student of Ecclesiastical institutions
pointed out more clearly than Dr. Sparrow that the State
was a divine institution, as truly as the Church. He was
fond of pointing out that as changes in the forms of State
governments did not invalidate its authority, the Church,

an assembly of freemen, must be conceived of as enjoying the same power of adjustment, unless clear and definite proofs to the contrary can be alleged. But his Evangelical training, and his native bias drew him away from the study of the non-rational elements, that make themselves felt in such countless and subtle ways in our intellectual life. As a lover of truth, his great aim was to bring reason to its rightful predominance over custom and circumstance. In practical matters he was an eminently wise man, and knew the season when to take occasion by the hand; but as a philosopher and theologian he realized that his chief concern lay in the stressing of ultimate ends, and the pointing out of the great highways that lead up to them. It may be that any gain from a longer study of history would have been offset by a loss in the singular clarity of his abstract reasoning.

The Church has had a surfeit of teachers who emphasize the non-rational elements in our belief, with the result in some cases that some of their pupils cannot distinguish between the ore and the gold; between the scaffold and the building; between the things that are shaken and must be removed and the things that cannot be shaken and must remain; while in other and more numerous instances the student in despair relinquishes the difficult task of discrimination, and takes refuge in an Infallible Guide, either of Inerrant Scripture, or the Infallible Church.

No such distrust of reason was inculcated in Dr. Sparrow's classroom. "Seek the truth; come whence it may, cost what it will," the closing words of a classroom discussion, were chosen by Dr. Norton as the most fitting inscription for his teacher's monument. "He taught us," said Bishop Brooks, in an address in the Seminary dining room, "that however far thought might travel it would still find God."

To his eye the universe was the abode of reason, and he loved to point out its sequences and to justify the ways of God to men. In the chair of Theo'ogy, he found his proper sphere.

With Virginia, both ecclesiastical and social, he was enraptured. Though he had borne the hardships of pioneer-life in Ohio with fortitude, it was none the less a great delight to live in the more cultured East. The church life of Virginia was entirely congenial to him. He found in Bishop Meade, the President of the Board of Trustees, a wise and considerate leader, and a theologian after his own heart. His colleagues were like-minded men, particularly Dr. May, who soon joined him at the Seminary, to become at once the special friend of everyone. The famous Virginia Conventions and Convocations charmed him with their spiritual fervor. The social warmth of Virginia, and its abundant and cordial hospitality delighted his warm Irish heart. The students were young men of promise from the chief parishes of the Protestant section of the Church in the East.

Under these pleasant conditions his health improved, and he threw himself with ardor into the duties of his congenial sphere. His fame and influence spread through the Church. He was invited to Trinity Church, Boston, as an associate of Bishop Eastburn, who in addition to his diocesan responsibilities, was rector of Trinity Church. It was believed that Dr. Sparrow's intellectual presentation of the gospel would be particularly helpful in Unitarian Boston. He was called to be rector of Christ Church, Cincinnati, of St. Paul's, Richmond, and of Emmanuel Church, Baltimore. He was twice urged to return to Gambier. He was generally recognized to be what Dr. Tiffany subsequently pronounced him in his History of the Protestant Episcopal Church, the profoundest theological mind among the Evangelical leaders. He was early made Dean of the Seminary, and deputy to the General Convention. His constant re-election to this legislative body was a great proof of the value placed upon his counsel, for he was too shy for its somewhat vociferous debates, and never opened his lips on the Convention's floor. Through the generosity of friends and alumni, he made several trips to Europe, revisiting the scenes of his boyhood, and re-establishing relations with his Irish kin. Like Socrates he preferred the society of men to the beauties of nature. He traveled widely to make up as much as possible for the isolation of his life on "The Hill".

One of his most interesting trips was down the Mississippi to Louisiana, returning by way of Georgia. Forty years afterwards one of his grandsons met a leading citizen of Georgia, who spoke of the great impression made on him by a sermon preached by Dr. Sparrow on this tour. On board the Mississippi steamboat, he was drawn into a controversy with a Roman Catholic priest, which showed that while he had no liking for a rough-and-tumble fight, he could hold his own like a man, if necessary. It was the fashion in the West in those days, for ministers of different churches to debate their differences when they met, as knights in the story-books invite one another to a tilt. It so happened that a Methodist minister and a Roman Catholic priest in the train of Bishop Spaulding, a scholarly prelate of that Church, fell into an argument of this kind on the boat, Bishop Spaulding and Dr. Sparrow being among the listeners. Dr. Sparrow's vivid interest was manifest in his face, and caused the priest to ask him in a rude tone, what he thought about it. The Doctor rebuked his tone, but answered his argument, and was thus drawn into the discussion. Bishop Spaulding also took a hand. The controversy eventually narrowed down to the issue, whether the Roman Catholic Church was supported in its claims by the Bible. "If that be true," said Dr. Sparrow, "why does not your Church distribute the Bible in the language of the people? Here is my Bible," and he drew out King James' Version, "show me yours." The priest had only the Vulgate, and the discussion closed.

Dr. Sparrow spoke highly of Bishop Spaulding's controversial skill, and thought him superior to himself in the art of winning the crowd. The conclusion of the argument however shows that this opinion was due to that spirit of self-depreciation which was so much regretted and marveled at by his pupils in their admired professor.

Such for twenty years was the even tenor of his life till the outbreak of the Civil War. That contest was in his case a divider of households. One of his brothers, Thomas, who remained in Ohio, entered the Congress of the United States; his youngest brother, Edward, who had gone as a youth to Louisiana, and married Minerva Parker, the niece of Jefferson Davis, took an active share in the secession, part of the Constitution of the Confederacy being in his handwriting, and became Senator from Louisiana in the Confederate Senate. Dr. Sparrow's sons entered the Southern Army.

He himself endeavored as much as possible to stand aloof. He was a good deal of a pacifist, and had lost some property rather than engage in a family law suit. He abhorred war as a method of settling a constitutional question. But he could not sympathize with the South in her sympathy for the institution of slavery which he regarded as doomed by the progress of civilization and the spirit of the gospel. In Staunton, where he refugeed, he never went to the prayer-meetings for the success of the Confederacy. He always taught in his classroom that Christianity was bound to put an end to slavery. His position was understood, and so exalted was his standing, that the people of Staunton, even amid the fierce passions of war, made an exception in his case, and in spite of his opinions, accepted his spiritual ministrations and provided as best they could for his needs, a proceeding as creditable for their large-mindedness as his aloofness was to his consistency.

His pastoral ministrations were only occasional. The parish had a rector, and Dr. Sparrow's time was occupied with the few theological students who followed him to his retreat. They were only a small band. But as Williams College men held that Mark Hopkins at one end of a log and a student at the other was enough to make a college, so these theological students felt that as long as they had Dr. Sparrow, they had the essential elements of a theological Seminary. The member of this company who became most widely known in the Church was Randolph H. McKim, for two General Conventions President of the House of Deputies, and a pronounced champion of the Protestant features of our Church's life and teaching. In his book, "A Soldier's Recollections", he calls Dr. Sparrow "a host in himself, a fine Greek and Hebrew scholar, a theologian of great learning and a profound and original thinker." It shows the unusual gifts of Dr. Sparrow, as a teacher, that he should have impressed with his Hebrew scholarship this gifted student but recently from the University of Virginia, for the Professor had never enjoyed any advantages for the study of this language, and must have qualified himself by special study for that emergency. It is worth recording, that under these conditions, with their limited facilities in books, the Professor used to make the students rack their brains, by requiring of each of them an essay in an assigned topic every two weeks.

At the close of the war, while the Seminary grounds were still strewn with canteens, and scarred by camp-fires, Dr. Sparrow was called back to Gambier. Twice before invitations back to that loved Institution had shaken him to the depths, but this last call made no appeal. "Immediately on the receipt of the proposition from Ohio, I declined it," he wrote his intimate friend, Mr. Cassius F. Lee. "I have no disposition to leave Virginia while she thinks my services worth having. Her being in distress is a reason with me, if I can live at all, to abide with her and share her lot."

In spite of his constitutional shyness, he went North and solicited aid for the stricken Institution. The lines of the poet,

"Pity the sorrows of a poor old man,
Whose trembling steps have borne him to your door,"

he confessed were often in his mind as he went his weary rounds. He was most generously received, and his efforts were speedily crowned with success. Five thousand dollars a year were pledged for five years, and overpaid. Another pledge of the same nature for seven thousand dollars a year for five years was arranged shortly before his death. The extent of his influence in securing these pledges was shown by the fact that only one-fourth of these last pledges was paid. The subscribers evidently felt that the money was pledged to a Seminary where Dr. Sparrow taught.

One of his Philadelphia friends, Mr. Powers, insisted on bearing the entire expense of publishing his biography. Years after, Dr. Crawford in raising funds for the substantial improvements that were made by him, found that Dr. Sparrow's name was an open sesame to the treasure house of generous Philadelphia.

At the re-organization after the War, Dr. Walker, a former pupil, took his place by Dr. Sparrow's side, and was as a friend and also a sharer of the same philosophical and theological interests, the great comfort and companion of his final years. Never had a teacher a more loyal and devoted follower. "I thank my God upon every remembrance of him," Dr. Walker would say. Not only did he continue the teaching of theology in the same spirit, but he also wrote the thoughtful and judicious biography from which much of the material of this brief memoir is taken.

It is a pity that Dr. Sparrow left no adequate records of his teaching. His sermons show intellectual power, and sweep of thought, but from the nature of the case, do not contain any profound analysis.

As a teacher he was admittedly preeminent. The testimony of Dr. Albert Tayloe Bledsoe is of unusual weight. He was a student under Dr. Sparrow at Kenyon; but declined to be ordained by Bishop McIlvaine on account of his objection to the Baptismal Office, and some of the Thirty-Nine Articles. He entered the Methodist ministry. He found his proper vocation however as a teacher, becoming Professor of Mathematics in the University of Virginia some years before the Civil War. His metaphysical and mathematical gifts were widely recognized. His Theodicy was a reply to the theology of Jonathan Edwards and was much praised. He was also the author of "Was Davis a Traitor?" He closed his career as editor of "The Southern Review." Through all these changes he kept up his close intercourse with Dr. Sparrow and his family. In an article on Dr. Walker's memorial of Dr. Sparrow in "The Southern Review," July, 1876, he calls Dr. Sparrow a "model teacher".

Dr. Bledsoe held that the secret of his power lay not so much in his learning or his intellectual gifts, highly as he valued these, as in his love for his scholars and the way in which he sympathized with them and encouraged them to think for themselves. "He never made his pupils feel his superiority except in open, free and fair discussion with them, which he welcomed as the best means for the development of their intellectual powers. He could enter into such discussions with them, with the unaffected simplicity of a little child or a great man, and on perfectly equal terms. But more than this, unspeakably more, if one of his pupils happened to be right, as was sometimes the case, the great Doctor was no sooner made to see than to acknowledged his error."

Dr. Walker's description of his teaching, in an address after his colleague's death, should be quoted here: "Need I describe to those who so well have known, that rare power of impartation, that aptness not only to teach but to quicken thought in the recipient, to set men to thinking and investigating, so as to enable them to reach conclusions really their own, and therefore of permanent value. Whatever may be said of William Sparrow in other respects, this was peculiarly his gift, preeminently his power. It was not merely that he was endowed by nature with the regal prerogative of a superb intellect, an imagination adequate to all the demands of that intellect to vivify its conceptions to others, an emotional structure promptly and thoroughly responsive. With all this there was something more, the power of living communication, of stimulating thought, of quickening intellectual activity."

Bishop Phillips Brooks wrote of him years afterwards: "It is easy to say of men who have not much accurate knowledge to impart, that they are men of suggestion and inspiration. But with the Doctor, clear thought and real learning only made the suggestion and inspiration of his teaching more vivid. I have never looked at Knapp since he taught us out of it; my impression of it is that it is a very dull and dreary book, but it served as a glass for Dr. Sparrow's spirit to shine through, and perhaps from its own insignificance, I remember him in connection with it more than in connection with Butler. His simplicity and ignorance of the world seemed always to let me get directly at the clearness of his abstract thought, and while I always felt that he had not comprehended the importance of the speculative questions which were just rising in those days, and which ever since had occupied men's minds, he unconsciously did much to prepare his student's minds to meet them. His intellectual and spiritual life, seem to me as I look back upon him, to have mingled in singular harmony and to have made but one nature as they do in but few men. The best result of his work in influence on any student's life and ministry must have been to save him from the hardness on the one hand, or the weakness on the other, which purely intellectual or purely spiritual training would have produced. His very presence on "The Hill" was rich and salutary. He held his opinions and was not held by them. His personality impressed young men, who

were just at that point of life when a thinker is more to them
than the results of thought, because it is of the utmost
importance that they should learn to think and not that they
should merely fortify their adherence to their inherited
creed.

"With all his great influence I fancy that he did not make
young men his imitators. There has been no crop of little
Dr. Sparrows. That shows, I think, the reality and healthiness of his power. The Church since his day has had its
host of little dogmatists, who thought that God had given
His truth to them to keep, and of little Ritualists, who
thought that God had bidden them save the world by drill.
Certainly Dr. Sparrow is not responsible for any of them.
He did all that he could to enlarge and enlighten both. He
loved ideas and did all that he could to make his students
love them. As to his preaching I have not very clear impressions. I remember that his sermons sometimes seemed
to us remarkable, but I imagine that a theological student is
one of the poorest judges of sermons and that the Doctor
had preached too much to students to allow him to be the
most successful preacher to men. On the whole he is one
of the three or four men whom I have known whom I look
upon with perpetual gratitude for the help and direction
which they have given to my life, and whose power I feel
in forms of action and kinds of thought very different from
those in which I had specifically to do with them. I am
sure that very many students would say the same of Dr.
Sparrow."

There were, indeed, different opinions about Dr. Sparrow
as a preacher. In Ohio, he was considered a great preacher.
All the ablest Episcopal ministers in Ohio thought his Chil-
lecothe Convention sermon the greatest they had ever heard,
and they were men accustomed to listen to the eloquence of
Bishop McIlvaine, who was recognized as a prince among
pulpit orators. Dr. Bledsoe ranked one of Dr. Sparrow's
addresses to the Kenyon students as the most eloquent
extemporaneous address he ever heard, and said that in his
sermons "his logic appeared to be all feeling and his feeling
all logic". In Virginia, however, there was less unanimity.
The witticism of the eminent lawyer the Hon. John Baldwin,

that "Dr. Sparrow can dive down deeper, stay under longer and come up drier than any man I have ever known" has been much quoted, but must not be taken too seriously. This is shown by his frequent calls to prominent parishes. But still he evidently gave less thought to sermonizing in his later years and doubtless Dr. Bledsoe is right in saying that "In later life he was a preacher for the few rather than the many".

An uneducated woman said of him in his Virginia Seminary days, "Dr. Sparrow put the fodder too high in the rack for me". His addresses on special occasions were always strong, clear and eloquent.

In his class room he had no difficulty in extemporizing, amplifying, illustrating, explaining with great freedom and ease. "How often," says one of the students of his later years, "how often have we seen his eyes dilate and his countenance shine and his whole mien take on a certain majesty, as the very oracle of truth, as he sat in the class room and spoke to us of the things of God. By what a subtle, irresistible magnestism, have we sometimes listened to his fervent words."

"No man," adds Dr. Bledsoe, in quoting the above, "no king of thinkers, ever wielded, from such a throne with more majestic mien of unconscious greatness, or with more genuine meekness, the golden sceptre of truth and love."

But it was different with his "talks" in the Faculty Meeting. He found it exceedingly difficult to manage there without his papers, and only at a great cost did he attain the power that marked these addresses. In extemporaneous prayer, on the other hand, he enjoyed great freedom and uplifted the hearts of all his fellow worshippers.

An admirable illustration of his method of teaching is afforded by an anecdote told by his son Leonard, who inherited much of his father's gifts of teaching, though he never exercised them in any adequate field. As a boy he was much pleased by the subtile distinction made by the schoolmen between essence and accidents in the doctrine of Transubstantiation, and one day on a walk, asked his father to explain the philosophical objection to the doctrine.

"Let us imagine," said the Doctor, "that I take a lump of mud and give it the shape of an apple, the weight of an apple of that size, the smell and taste of an apple, the color of an apple, the feel of an apple, the chemical and nutritive properties of an apple, so that by no possible test could it be distinguished from an apple—what would I be holding in my hand?" The boy stood dumbfounded. "Don't you see that I would be holding an apple? We only know matter by its properties, and a substance that has all the properties of an apple, and none others, would be an apple."

Perhaps the best proof of Dr. Sparrow's power of analysis is the paper that was published a few years back in the "Chronicle" on the meaning of the Lord's Supper as determined by the words of institution. It reminds me of Wycliffe's treatise on Transubstantiation, in the manner in which it vindicates the judgment of common sense by subtle processes of logical analysis.

The best indication afforded in Dr. Walker's biography of his intellectual breadth, apart from the testimony of his pupils and contemporaries, of the impression their teacher made upon them, is his discussion in that volume of the trial of Dr. Cheney who was condemned for the omission of the word "regenerate" from the service after the actual baptism. This was the Dr. Cheney who afterwards became a bishop of the Reformed Episcopal Church. Dr. Sparrow argued that the form of clerical subscription gave our clergy greater liberty in doctrine than was enjoyed by the clergy of the Church of England. This he easily proved. But he went further; he held that there was nothing to show that the same relaxation did not extend to worship. Indeed he felt it to be unworthy of the moral earnestness of the Church to grant larger liberty in belief, and refuse to allow a similar liberty in expressing that belief in worship. Where the life of the clergyman making minor changes in the service showed that he was an earnest-minded man, and the departure from the prescribed order was alleged to be made on conscientious grounds and was such that under no theory did it invalidate the rite, he held that the accused should be acquitted of transgression. The argument is most statesmanlike. The other Evangelicals did not agree with him in this matter, holding that the forms of the Prayer Book must be rigidly adhered to.

Nothing shows Dr. Sparrow's courage and vision more clearly than his resolute refusal to be frightened by the secession of Dr. Cummins and his followers and the creation of the Reformed Episcopal Church. He took a more liberal view than the seceders of subscription and the teaching of the Prayer Book, but he believed that troubled consciences were entitled to relief, and felt that it little became any servant of the Truth to condemn men for following their consciences. He held that the Church erred in insisting on such rigid uniformity.

In breadth of view, and confidence in the power of truth Dr. Sparrow showed himself in sympathy with the Broad Churchmen. As a theologian he was practically self-taught. Though he was a diligent student, thought rather than reading had played the chief part in moulding his beliefs. This is probably one explanation of his unusual lucidity. His early Evangelical experience had been broadened by his studies in Butler and Paley, by his reading of Coleridge and Isaac Taylor, by the teachings of Whately and Arnold, not to speak of the sanity and moderation of the excellent though uninspiring Knapp, whose theology he used as a textbook. His liberal tendencies were manifest in his theory of the Will, in his views on the elevation of woman, and questions of that character, and in general by his reliance upon the spirit-illumined reason.

If he had been connected with a college, or thrown much in contact with men of science, he would undoubtedly have given a larger place in his thought to the development of science, and the rising methods of historical research, but hardly had he come to Virginia when the influence of the Oxford movement began to be felt in America. In Dr. Sparrow's early days Evangelicalism was the new and rising school, which a High Churchman like Bishop Hobart did all that he could to suppress, antagonizing with all his authority its prayer-meetings of the Clergy and other manifestations.

But it continued to make converts and managed to carry such leaders as McIlvaine, Johns and Henshaw into the Episcopate. Not long after it was strong enough to pull down the mighty from their seats in the trials of the Bishops, that so convulsed our Church in the middle of the century, trials which can only be rightly understood as expressions of the Evangelical determination to require of our bishops the same ethical strenuousness that the Evangelicals themselves exhibited. By this time, however, the new views of authority and indefectibility of Orders had come in, and caused the more Churchly school to become passionate defenders of the accused as representatives of the principle of authority.

Against these Tractarian views Dr. Sparrow set his face like a flint. He knew how these exclusive claims appealed to pride and self-love. "There is no soil so poor that it will not readily produce this weed of exclusiveness," he said. He called the bishopric "a social Apotheosis". He saw in Tractarianism an old foe with a new face. Cardinal Newman was in his opinion, incomparably the greatest mind in the new school, and had followed its premises to their logical conclusion, when he entered the Church of Rome.

The exclusive doctrine of Apostolical Succession he regarded as the tap-root from which all the other peculiar views of this school drew their strength and vitality. As a thinker he shrank with profound repugnance from binding the grace of God to one form of Church government, or one method of administering the rites of religion. He held that the Truth made us free, and that the Church was a fellowship of freedmen.

His gift as a teacher seemed to suffer no diminution with age. It is indeed a remarkable proof of his vigor, that instead of degenerating in time, his fine handwriting even improved towards the end. He had a forward-looking mind, and loved to scan the intellectual horizon, and learn what was going on in the world. Satisfied with his task, eagerly interested in his pupils and delighting in the exercises of worship and teaching, his whole heart was in his work. In 1873, after a brief illness Mrs. Sparrow was taken from him; but he bore the loss wonderfully. He had a hope full of immortality. On a Thursday in February, 1874, he made the chief address at the Faculty Meeting. His text was St. Paul's injunction, "not slothful in business, fervent in spirit,

serving the Lord." By this time all that strange nervous-
ness about extemporaneous speaking seems to have left him
at the Faculty Meetings. He made a fairly full skeleton
beforehand, but he clothed it with the flesh of words on the
spur of the moment. Particularly moving was his exhortation that evening and characteristically fervent and exalted
was his closing prayer. The next Saturday he drove into
Alexandria on business, was taken sick, and died suddenly
in the First National Bank.

At his funeral there was a great gathering of clergy and
friends, and Bishop Johns, and Dr. Andrews of Shepherdstown, spoke in heartfelt tones of the irreparable loss which
the Seminary had sustained. The School of the Prophets
felt that an Elijah had been taken away.

His tablet in the Seminary chapel bears beneath his name
the text of his last Faculty Meeting talk, and on his tomb-
stone are his own glowing words: "Seek the truth; come
whence it may, cost what it will."

SECTION V

CHAPTER VI

THE THEOLOGY OF DR. SPARROW*

RT. REV. ROBERT A. GIBSON, D. D.

In response to your invitation I am here to-day to speak to you as graduates of the Virginia Seminary. The task is a pleasant one. Whether known to me personally or not, you have trodden the paths familiar to my feet in years gone by, have looked upon the scenes which feasted my eyes, and have followed the lead of many-hued wisdom through the same intricacies which perplexed me during my stay on this Hill.

Of the men who have graduated here since my time, I have met many whose feelings were just those of the earlier days, whose principles were the principles always inculcated by this Seminary, whose purposes in life and whose outlook on the world could not be distinguished from the purposes and views which gave a solid basis of character to my own old companions. There could be no difficulty in talking to *them* as Seminary men. And the old comrades aforesaid! Thankful am I to think they are not all gone. Representatives of the noble body of men, tried on many fields and true everywhere, who studied with me in these halls, are still to be counted on as attendants on Alumni meetings. It can never be anything but a *pleasure* to talk to them.

Nor could I expect to take up my parable on an occasion like this without having as auditors some, at least, of those who had made the reputation of the Seminary in the great Episcopal Church of America when my contemporaries yet filled the ranks of callow youth. The older men are here, with recollections of days simpler and sterner even than

*This address, which was delivered before the Alumni of the Theological Seminary in Virginia, was published by the special request of the Alumni who heard it.—Editor

mine, bearing on their minds and hearts marks of conflict waged for principles theological and churchly which have characterized this Institution through its whole career. They are the fathers, and there must be much which every loyal son of the Seminary has in common with them.

But what must the theme be? The field is large. The choice is wide. Only this guide seems safe. The theme must be something connected with the Seminary itself. Something which will have an interest from its associations, whether it carries with it value of its own or not.

With these feelings I have chosen as my subject: "Recollections of the Teaching of Dr. William Sparrow."

It is a bold venture I am aware—one to which many objections immediately appear. The time has been long since I sat in these class rooms. Theological discussion has in recent years passed through many phases. Even to our wind-sheltered nook the ripples on the surface of religious thought have been borne. Men indebted to this place for the determining principles of their lives have developed in very different directions; a fact suggesting diverse interpretations of the basic truths here taught. And above all, there must always be recognized the danger of mistaking for the true logical growth of the germs implanted by the teacher, the inference of the pupil; which may on the one hand be dwarfed by the poverty of the soil receiving it, or, on the other, forced by a too free admission of the light of modern ideas to an expansion of which its author never dreamt. These considerations have compelled me to hesitate long in finally deciding on my theme.

But when I think of the value the instruction of Dr. Sparrow has had for me personally, of the impression it made at the time it was delivered in class, of the wonder expressed by students of other theological schools on hearing of the teaching given so many years ago at the Virginia Seminary, of the urgency of friends in whose intellectual processes I have most confidence demanding my reminiscences, of the interest I have seen arise whenever my view of Dr. Sparrow's views has been stated, and especially when I think of the breadth and strength of the foundation laid for every one believing as he believed, on which to build a

philosophy of Christianity as well as a stable and lofty Christian character, I feel that I am obliged to take this opportunity to put on record my recollections of the utterances
on Theology of the master of sentences on that theme for
me and my contemporaries of the Alumni—our Berkeley
and Butler, our Plato and Aristotle all in one.

During the General Convention of 1883 it was my good
fortune to meet Bishop Brooks when we were both returning
to Philadelphia from places in the neighborhood.   Naturally
we talked about Dr. Sparrow.   In all Dr. Brooks' public
speeches on his Seminary life, his admiration for Dr. Sparrow
had been freely expressed.

Among other things, I said I thought it a great pity and a
great loss to the age that Dr. Sparrow had not left some connected view of the Theology he taught in the Seminary—
something in the nature of a systematic treatise on Divinity.
To my surprise Dr. Brooks dissented emphatically.   He said
he was *glad* Dr. Sparrow had not left any system of Divinity.
The work for which Dr. Sparrow's pupils had reason to be
grateful was, in his opinion, that Dr. Sparrow made men
think for themselves.   Dr. Sparrow was a great spiritual
power and had stimulated thought on spiritual subjects.

Here was a marked diversity of sentiment.   To the positive part of Dr. Brooks' statement, viz: that Dr. Sparrow
was a great spiritual power and stimulated thought, I assented heartily.   For the rest I could not but retain the
opinion I had expressed.   Dr. Sparrow gave to Bishop
Brooks' magnificent intellectual and spiritual faculties in
their blossoming period the needed stimulus and direction,
and Bishop Brooks went on his appointed way through the
world as a preacher of the Word with a glorious vision of
God and humanity before him, and with an impatience in his
soul of obstacles to man's progress towards God so strenuous
and intense as almost to amount to denial of their existence.
But the vast majority of useful preachers and even philosophical optimistic Christian thinkers have not the idealism
nor the remote prophetic foresight which belonged to Bishop
Brooks.

To sustain them under the shocks their faith receives from
the hard facts of life, much more to elevate them to a plane

of feeling so exalted that religious difficulties, mental and moral, are no longer felt, both ministers and people need something else. They must have the results of grave study, profound reflection and careful exegesis, not only illuminating certain difficult points but giving consistency and solidity to their religious beliefs. Because, in the case of most of us, detached views of great subjects are like separated columns—lofty it may be and graceful, but exposed to disintegration and easy overthrow, while a system of thought in which each such view has its place and its connections is like a buttressed wall.

Dr. Sparrow had a system—as the state of the case appeared to me—a system which I have never seen in any one book—a system different in many important particulars from those of our text-books—a reverent, learned, philosophical, common-sense scriptural method of stating his beliefs about God, man, the world, the Bible, and the relation of Jesus Christ our Lord to each and all of these, which not only ensured harmony between the several statements but put each one into the position to support and corroborate the others.

This system I wish briefly to outline, or rather to touch on some of its salient points, again guarding myself by insisting that I speak only my own memories, that I am open to correction from any one who remembers better, and especially that I make no claim to an exhaustive acquaintance with the sources of theological thought, either past or present, and am therefore privileged to say perfectly trite things.

Man has an idea of God. It is one of the most interesting questions in the world how that idea has its origin. If communicated to the first man supernaturally, how was it ever lost? How did it ever come to break up into the fragmentary deification of the several powers of nature, as among some of the highest races of men, or degenerate into the worship of ancestors, as with the Chinese? If it was constituted a part of man's mental furniture in the original creation, how was it lost, as seems almost certain in the case of some degraded tribes? Was the worship of one God prior in time to the worship of many gods or was the reverse the order?

Dr. Sparrow taught that while the knowledge of God is not inborn in such a sense that every man brings it into the world with him, yet that we are so framed as to receive it with the utmost readiness when brought to us from without, either through instruction or the process of reflection.

"If by innate knowledge of God," said he, "we understand that the mind in normal circumstances readily accepts the idea of God, just as it accepts the idea of true or false, there is no objection to it." Thus he occupied a position on this question not contradicted by the facts known then or discovered since; he left room for the Divine initiative in the communication of God to man, whether in revelation or in providence, and he retained the word "innate" as applied to this idea in the human mind! The last point is of special importance, because to recognize that the idea of God is in any sense innate takes it back of all speculations on the subject and affords ground for reasoning from it for those who accept neither the old teleology of Paley, the new teleology of evolutionary theists, the ontology of Anselm, the moral argument of Kant nor the basis for knowledge of God in self-consciousness claimed by Hegel. The position seems to me practically equivalent to that which is held to-day by Professor Bruce in his Apologetics.

On the subject of the Trinity, Dr. Sparrow's views were illuminating. He taught that the *mode* of subsistence in the Godhead was no part of the doctrine. The doctrine was simply the spirit of Holy Scripture concentrated in the Baptismal Formula or the Apostolic Benediction. It was not irrational, because while it transcends reason it does not antagonize reason. It was not self-contradictory, because the numerals three and one are applied to different subjects. "No more self-contradictory," said he, "than to say there are three persons in this room and one in the other."

It was not incomprehensible, because when the mode is excluded the doctrine is simply the language of Holy Scripture, ascribing divinity to our Lord and personality to the Holy Spirit, which language is perfectly plain and simple.

"Person" he thought, with Archbishop Whately, an unfortunate term; because the person with us is a unit, the unit of the human race, whereas the unit of the Godhead is

God. "Three hypostases or subsistences in one essence" was the statement which he thought best for us in our studies, though we could not, of course, import scholastic terms, like these, into common use. "I would rather incline to Sabellianism," said the Doctor, "than to Tritheism," and the sentence draws a line of demarcation for the theological student better than any number of definitions.

As an illustration of the strength of his hold on the Divine Unity, and the consistency of his feelings, he said in class that when, after reciting the Litany with its repeated address to our Blessed Lord, he came to the prayer "We humbly beseech thee, O Father, mercifully to look upon our infirmities," etc., he was careful not to emphasize the words "Thee, O Father," nor to allow in his mind the feeling which would make such emphasis natural, "because," said he, "we must avoid the error of turning, as we would do with human beings, from one individual to whom we *have* prayed to another to whom we are just going to pray." Rather the emphasis should be adjusted so as to indicate that, as it was God to whom our prayers had been addressed up to that time, it was the same God to whom we would offer the petition on our lips, only called by a different name.

The doctrine and the illustration make unnecessary many of the taking emendations to Church Theology offered by Swedenborgians, and, on the other hand, remove some of the difficulties in the way of persons having a bias towards Unitarianism.

Accept this contribution as to Dr. Sparrow's teaching about God, and turn with me to his views about men. As to man, Dr. Sparrow believed that the original condition of the race, though innocent, was simple; thus discarding the Rabbinical notions sometimes called traditions. He believed that man fell through wrong choice, referring constantly to the story of the Fall, and never giving the slightest opening for the belief that the account in Genesis is allegorical, as does even so conservative a writer as Dean Vaughan, late Master of the Temple.

He believed that the seat of sin was not the body only, as the deists and the old philosophers claimed, but the soul especially, and that original sin is, as the Ninth Article says, the "fault and corruption of the nature of every man that naturally is engendered of the offspring of Adam; whereby man is very far gone from original righteousness and is of his own nature inclined to evil," etc. But he was very careful not to say that human beings are in a state of condemnation on *account* of this fault. The Article declares that in every person born into this world it, *i. e.*, *original sin*, deserveth God's wrath and damnation. Dr. Sparrow stood by the Article. What the people deserved he did not say; but that they were under damnation prior to actual sin of their own he did not believe.

The distinction between Natural and Revealed Religion, as used by Butler, Dr. Sparrow accepted, though no man ever held more strongly that "*every* good and perfect gift is from above," and he told us that in his efforts to attain clear ideas in connection with the words "nature" and "natural" he had looked up and tabulated seventeen or nineteen words used constantly in opposition to one phase or another of their meaning. Natural Religion meant with him the relation of God's sentient creatures to Himself, sustained "always, everywhere and by all;" nor does it seem to admit of serious doubt that he held Bishop Butler's sentiment, which, with its terms transposed, is this: "Though natural religion is *not* in any sense the *whole* of Christianity, it is the foundation and principal part of it." Still, I have no recollection of any reference to this sentence in lecture or sermon. It is introduced here simply because it would have been very natural for Dr. Sparrow, in briefly defining the position which I think he held, to have used the language of that great work "The Analogy", which he taught for thirty consecutive years, and understood as probably no man has done since Joseph Butler—not even its latest editor, Mr. Gladstone.

But, after all, it was as the foundation of Christianity that Dr. Sparrow valued Natural Religion, for himself, his world and the world of future ages, and it was in teaching Christianity, as such, that he imparted the greatest delight and stimulus to his pupils. His thought was that Christ was the Lamb slain before the foundation of the world, that every transaction on the face of the earth had taken place in view of Bethlehem and Calvary, that the history of the race, nay the possibility of such history, had been the result of the Atonement.

But the Atonement was not, in his view, the payment of blood for sin. The text in Hebrews "Without shedding of blood is no remission" was the statement of a fact of the Jewish Ritual economy—not the proclamation of an eternal theological principle. Christ was the Atonement. His incarnation, life, death and resurrection were to be taken together. The crucifixion was the climax of the life. The blood was to be freely spoken of, after the Scripture example, as marking the whole work of Redemption and setting to it a seal. The blood poured out was the most impressive exhibition of the love which hesitated not to give life for its enemies, and the effect upon the world of the sacrifice of the death of Christ would be to draw those who should behold the sight, and those who should hear of it, for all time, to Him who was lifted up on the Cross; but as to the result on God's government, it was inexplicable. Real it was; necessary doubtless, but—"This thing angels desire to look into."

Such was Dr. Sparrow's conception, as I received it, of the world-wide objective effect of the work of Christ. The Atonement was not Regeneration, as William Law said right out and as many now think. It was vicarious; it was "for men." Christ rendered our repentance and our faith, too, of the efficacy of which they now are. So much was made known in Scripture, and reason had no ground of dissent; but the mode of the operation in the Divine plan, of what Christ did and suffered for us, was no more revealed than the mode of the Divine existence! With the acceptance of this view were dismissed, as with the wand of a dispeller of illusions, those ultra pietistic statements which have caused the Christians' God to be compared to Moloch, the refinements of scriptural interpretation which ascribe one portion of salvation to the life of the Lord and another to His death, and all possible grounds for belief in the ownership by the Church of a treasury of merit based chiefly on the superfluous blood shed upon the Cross from which pardons could be drawn and indulgences granted. All these tumbled together into ruins, and in their place arose a glorious conception of the faith that saves.

All students of the Virginia Seminary know that Dr. Sparrow taught as earnestly as Luther ever did the doctrine of justification by faith. With him, as strongly as with any one who ever lived, it was the doctrine of a standing or a falling Church. His view of faith and its effect was as broad and as high as his conception of the object of faith made requisite. "Have faith in God," he said, in this connection, quoting the Master. "Faith! the instrumental cause of salvation in the case of every man who finds or has found acceptance with God." Faith! the empty hand of the soul; a work indeed, inasmuch as it is the operation of the soul itself, but the only conceivable work which lays no claim to merit! Faith! the gift of God, not specially or partially, but as a part of the salvation which comes entirely and altogether from Him! Faith! the open eye of the soul, whereby the child of God discerns the Father, whom to know is everlasting life.

This was the doctrine, the touching, often pleading presentation of which has left echoes in the souls of many who hear me to-day.

The essence of religion, said the Doctor, referring to Schleiermacher, is trust. The Bible—Old Testament and New—is full of it. Trust in God is the basis of repentance, the ground of pardon, the implantation of the seed of a new life. Trust in Christ is trust in God. Trust in God has *always been* trust in Christ. Let *any* man come with empty hands and uplifted eye, suing the Author of his spirit for mercy! Mercy is his; under whatever dispensation— Christian, Mosaic, Patriarchal, Natural. It was always so; it is so everywhere. No need of special conditions for the Antediluvians or the Patriarchs. Away with all limbos. Faith saves, and salvation by faith is the condition of the permission of moral evil by a God who is not only just, as men count justice, but a Father. This was Dr. Sparrow's conception of faith—not assent to a creed, nor even the formal acceptance of promises, but an attitude of the soul. It is connected with revelation, of course, but every man has a revelation of some sort, to some degree. The revelation in Christ and in the Gospels is beyond comparison most favorable to its birth in the heart of man, but it is not confined to the sphere of any one *mode* of revelation. It is possible wherever there is a spiritual being who discerns his true relations to the universe, and it is accepted wherever found.

How well do I remember, and doubtless there are those here who remember with me, that when this more than world-wide—this cosmic—conception of faith had been reached in class-room, Dr. Sparrow looked up, and with the air of conviction of one who, foreseeing possible unpleasant consequences, had finally taken his place among the contending parties, exclaimed, "Gentlemen, I could not have a hole-and-corner theology!" I might shape the words to suit better what some might think required by the dignity of the subject and the occasion, but, as I recollect the circumstances, that is what he said. His purpose, no doubt, in using a phrase so derogatory to prevalent opinions, was to inspire his pupils with the distaste he felt himself for ideas which were small and shifty, and, as a consequence, necessarily on the defensive.

One cannot but think of the Andover Controversy and the discussions all through the history of the Church, on the question of the salvability of the heathen; of the mistakes recorded of some missionaries; and, by contrast, of the idea of missions which animates those who go out from these walls to-day—a far higher and nobler idea, surely, than that they go merely to give some poor soul in distant lands the one chance of salvation from which his Heavenly Father has, without the compassionate intervention of some man, cut him completely off.

Dr. Sparrow was a Trichotomist. He believed that the distinction of body, soul and spirit was very probably true. His word on that subject was, "there are phenomena of the spiritual nature which seem to demand a substance distinct from what we call the soul, in which they may inhere."

The subject was never fully entered upon in class, but I remember taking the Doctor the first sermon I ever wrote; one, namely, on the text "Blessed are the poor in spirit," and receiving his approbation, in general, of the theology contained therein. The sermon, without elaborating any theory, treated the spirit of man mentioned in the text as

the special presence-chamber of God, closed before regeneration, glorious with the effulgence of the Shekinah when the
new birth had taken place. Dr. Sparrow was pleased to
express, as I say, a qualified approval of my effort at eluci-
dating religious experience in the light of Trichotomy, and
I have wished ever since that I had in mind or at hand the
conclusions to which he had come on the whole subject. It
was easy to see, however, from what he said and taught, why
he expressed a sentiment which at first struck me with surprise. This was, that of the five points of Calvinism the
most attractive to his mind was "The final perserverance of
the saints." He did not believe it, because he thought the
record of Scripture precluded it; but it was tempting to one
who believed that the birth or awakening of the human
spirit made man "partaker of the Divine nature."

Speaking of the new birth, this illustration comes back to
me, showing Dr. Sparrow's view of the co-operation of human
agency and divine grace in the renewal of the soul. "In
the infant," said he, "who knows which is first—the action
of the lungs, to inhale the air, or the contact of the air, to
give the lungs their initial movement?"

But, my dear friends, I detain you too long. The theme
is so full of fascination to me that I know not when to have
done. Had time allowed, I should have been glad to take
up the divisions of theology, as it was taught in my day, and
to state in connection with each one any sententious expression or illustration of it from Dr. Sparrow's lips which has
found lodgment in my memory, that as little as possible of
the wisdom of the great teacher whom I praise might escape
imprisonment on the written page. But the task is too great
for an occasion like this.

I feel like apologizing for every sentiment of my own
which has crept into this paper. My wish has been simply
to tell the Alumni, who never knew Dr. Sparrow, some of
the great truths we, in our day, heard him utter, and to the
older men—those who were Dr. Sparrow's pupils—to recall
the scenes of the class-room and the words on which hung so
much for us all.

A convert myself from a mild system of Calvinism, it was
natural that I should watch eagerly every argument by

which this wonderful system, as it appeared to me, was supported—the shaping of every stone put into a place from which I had been obliged to remove one. Many of Dr. Sparrow's sayings have remained in my mind because they expressed opinions which superseded in my formulated thought opinions just as clearly defined. I have given them to you to-day because I was impelled to do so. Let me express the hope that others, possibly many, may be impelled, either in speech or in print, to bring out the points of Dr. Sparrow's teaching which have impressed *them*.

This teaching was not mere cut and dried Arminianism. It followed nobody's Institutes. Towards Calvinism it was thoroughly irenical. Some one has lately said that every one's views about God and man are important. Dr. Sparrow was evidently of that opinion. He was eclectic; yet he was logical. To a reader of theology he seems to have swept the field from Origen, Swedenborg and Schleiermacher to Channing, Parker and Socinus. Yet he quoted little. What he gave us was the result of his own intellectual processes, touched with a certain gracious mysticism which suggested not a hard and fast horizon of thought but star-strewn depths of ever-expanding contemplation.

Nothing would please me better than to go on now to tell, at such length as would be necessary for clearness, Dr. Sparrow's views about grace prevenient and assisting; about the sacrament of the Lord's Supper as an occasion for the exercise of a living, apprehensive faith in Christ; about the action of the Spirit of God on the soul through the truth and through the truth alone; about the Church, the sacraments, and many other matters on which I have definite recollections. But with the mention of two points—one general, the other specific, connected with his teaching—I shall close.

The prayers with which our recitations were invariably commenced were the most wonderful productions of sanctified culture that one would hear in a lifetime. Three times a day, with different classes, these devotions would be repeated; but while there was repetition of the act of prayer, there was none of the subjects nor of the language. In apparently endless variety, from day to day and from hour to hour, and yet in words as simple as a child would use, the most profound thoughts and the loftiest aspirations of the Christian soul were addressed to Him in whom we live and move and have our being. Those who listened and strove to follow felt themselves very near the gates of heaven.

The other point is the lectures, as they came in course, on the Attributes of God. To one easily moved by a combination of grandeur and pathos in thought with eloquence in expression, they were overwhelming. Men sat and heard these modestly-expressed, intensely but quietly-delivered descriptions of the glories of God in His works and Word, as in an ecstasy, sometimes with tears coursing silently down their cheeks.

The room was uncarpeted, the wooden chairs were the only furniture, but it was the vestibule of the ineffable Presence itself.

> Round the Lord in glory seated,
>   Cherubim and Seraphim,
> Filled his temple and repeated
>   Each to each the alternate hymn.
> Lord, Thy glory fills the heaven,
>   Earth is with thy fulness stored;
> Unto Thee be glory given,
>   Holy, holy, holy Lord.

Whenever I think now of these occasions, these and words like them throng to my mind.

THE REVEREND DOCTOR JAMES MAY

Professor 1842-1863

SECTION V

CHAPTER VII

REV. DR. JAMES MAY

REV. SAMUEL A. WALLIS, D. D.

The Rev. James May, D. D. was born in Chester County, Pennsylvania, on October 1, 1805, and received his earlier education at Norristown, Pennsylvania, and at Campbell's Academy in Maryland. He then returned to his native state, and studied at Washington and Jefferson College, Cannonsburg, where he took the degree of Bachelor of Arts in 1823. During a revival at the College, he was converted and became an earnest follower of the Lord Jesus Christ. At first he decided to enter the legal profession and for this purpose he went to the home of his brother-in-law, ex-Governor Stevens, who resided near Easton, Maryland; but, as he relates, he went out to walk while there one Sunday afternoon, and beheld God with the eye of faith as a reconciled Father. "At no former period," he continues, "had I enjoyed such joy and peace in believing."

Accordingly he resolved to study for the Holy Ministry, and entered the Middle Class of the Virginia Seminary in the fall of 1825. He remained there until the close of that session in 1826, as appears from the list of the Alumni in the Seminary Catalogues. While there he was a teacher in the Sunday School of Christ Church, Alexandria, Virginia. He then returned to Philadelphia, finished his studies under the Rev. Dr. Boyd, and received ordination at the hands of Bishop White in old Christ Church, Philadelphia, on December 24, 1826. He said at that solemn hour that he desired to make the grand subject of his preaching, "Salvation by Faith in Jesus Christ".

He entered upon his duties as a clergyman in St. Stephen's Church, Wilkes-Barre, Pennsylvania, in the historic Wyoming Valley. At that time it was the missionary centre of that district, and he entered most heartily upon his work, blessing

and being blessed through his faithful ministry. It is stated
that one day as many as seventy persons came to him earnestly inquiring about the way to salvation. He remained there
for two years, when he received a call to St. Paul's Church,
Philadelphia, Pennsylvania, which he accepted. At that
time "The Episcopal Recorder" of Philadelphia was a leading paper in our Church. Like "The Southern Churchman"
it was strongly Evangelical in its tone. In addition to his
pastoral duties he became associated with the Rev. Drs.
Tyng, Clark and Suddards, on its editorial board.

His health now began to give way under the strain of work
he was doing, so it was judged best by his friends that he should
take a rest by going on a trip to Europe. The vestry of St.
Paul's Church granted him leave of absence for one year,
but Dr. May's high sense of honor would not permit him to
accept this offer. He felt that he must resign his charge, as
he thought the time given him for his trip was too long a
period for him to be away from his people, in the event of
his salary being kept up. But his resignation was not laid
before the Vestry until he reached Europe. However his
vestry would not agree to it until he sent it in for the third
time before he left Europe for his voyage home, and then it
was accepted with great reluctance on their part. One of
his fellow students affirmed of him "May is the soul of honor."
While in Europe he became proficient in Italian and French,
and pursued his historical studies amid surroundings both
suggestive and inspiring.

Dr. Philip Slaughter, to whose eloquent address on the deceased professors found in the Semi-Centennial Memorial
pamphlet of the Seminary we are so much indebted and whose
general description and language we have followed, has a beautiful sentence on his visit to Europe. "The scenes which had
most attraction for him in Greece were not the Acropolis but
the Rev. Dr. Hill's School; in Germany, not so much the
castle-cragged Rhine, as the memorials of Huss and
Melancthon and Luther; in Rome, not the Palace of the Vati-
can, but the Mamertine prison where Paul was imprisoned."

After his return from Europe, Dr. May was invited to
take the chair of Ecclesiastical History in this Seminary,
which he accepted in July, 1842. He filled this position for

nineteen years with the spirit of true learning and understanding of the great issues that were involved in the movements of central periods. He ever recognized the presence and guiding power of the Holy Spirit in human history. Dr. Slaughter reminds us that Dr. May's intellectual and moral constitution was so symmetrical that there were but few salient points for criticism to seize upon and emphasize, and his friend Dr. Riddle, quoted by Dr. Slaughter, says that "intellectually May seemed to me to have breadth and a capacity for large views, a fondness for principles rather than details." He was a man of even temper and sound judgment, which made him the trusted counsellor of the students and the adviser of all who were in doubt or difficulty, even as his successor, Dr. Walker, was in his day and generation.

Trained in the school of suffering and affliction he was able to comfort and sustain others who themselves were passing through the deep waters of sorrow and trouble. After the death of his beloved wife who was a woman of uncommon personal and moral loveliness, "he seemed to have garnered up the fragments of his shattered earthly affections in this Seminary". Soon the storm of War came on and at its commencement he bade the Seminary farewell.

Just as the tie with it was about to be broken he took a last walk and with a last lingering look at the new buildings, the beautiful green lawn, the grove bursting out in the new leaves of spring, and the birds filling the air with song, he exclaimed, "Who knows how soon everything here may be destroyed". With this feeling in his heart he took his leave and returned to Philadelphia and after a short term of service at the Divinity School of our Church there, he passed, on the 18th day of December, 1863, to his eternal rest.

"The Southern Churchman" of January 29, 1864, stated that among the resolutions in regard to Dr. May's death was one passed by the Faculty of the Divinity School to the effect that "further examinations in that School be suspended until after the funeral of the Rev. Dr. May, professor of Ecclesiastical History".

A high tribute is given to Dr. May in succeeding resolutions which state that "in his death the Church has lost one of its most loyal citizens, and all who have known him a beautiful and most consistent exemplar of all the gentle graces and all the stern and high virtues of an humble follower of Jesus Christ". The Rev. Dr. Stone was requested at a proper time to deliver a discourse commemorative of the life and service of Dr. May. These resolutions were signed by Bishop Potter, William B. Stevens, M. A. de W. Howe, William Welsh, Charles R. King, Lemuel Coffin, and George L. Harrison, Secretary.

Dr. Packard who loved and revered Dr. May said of him: "Dr. May was the most perfect Christian character I have ever known, and after long and intimate intercourse with him, I count my knowledge of him among my greatest blessings." Dr. Dalrymple in his address on the deceased Alumni at the Semi-Centennial Celebration of the Seminary said: "Who can worthily tell of Dr. May? Who can convey to those who knew him not, a proper idea of his wonderful equanimity of temper, his touching gentleness, his ready and inspiring sympathy with all who went to him for counsel or for comfort? How can we, as is meet, make known to others the earnestness and plainness with which he always in every sermon failed not to display the Saviour in all the fulness of His love? Dr. May was a model of punctuality, method, and fidelity in his discharge of duty. Dr. May never seemed to be without a sense of God's constant presence and companionship: and now, after many years, the memory of his perfect peace comes back with great impressiveness."

"Truly we can say of Dr. May that he was an example unto all the Seminary, and in every place where he served Christ in word, in conversation, in love, in spirit, in faith, and in purity." The verse on the tablet to his memory in the Seminary Chapel tells the secret of his life—"The disciple whom Jesus loved."

THE REVEREND DOCTOR CORNELIUS WALKER

Professor 1866-1898

SECTION V

CHAPTER VIII

REV. DR. CORNELIUS WALKER

Together with an Historical Review of the Theology Taught by Him and His Predecessors in the Virginia Seminary

REV. CARL E. GRAMMER, S. T. D.

I appreciate very highly the privilege of writing this chapter on Dr. Walker. As one of the scholars in the days of his vigor, and a colleague in the Faculty for over ten years, I had the opportunity of knowing him in various relations. In the early days of my professorship, while the theological agreement between us was close, and I still abode with Terah in Haran, he intimated at times that he looked to me to render him some such service when he was gone. Later on, there were indications that he had become uncertain whether I was just the man for the task, and it was evident at times in his sermons and Faculty Meeting talks, that he was trying to keep me in the well-trodden path of my Evangelical fore-fathers and teachers.

It is pleasant to recall that in the years after we both left the Seminary (I to a parish and he to the well-earned rest of his retirement), he reverted to the earlier attitude. The diversity in theology grew less important in his eyes, and the union in spirit, which I trust always existed, as-serted its power. Once more he thought of me as his former scholar and associate, united to him by many bonds, and the natural person to aid him in the recollections he began to write, and to tell of his work as a teacher of theology. Much that is here written is taken from a memorial address that I delivered at the annual Alumni meeting in June, 1907, which was printed by the Alumni, and may be said to have been accepted by them, as expressive of their sentiments about their old professor.

Cornelius Walker, the first Virginian by birth to become a professor in the Virginia Seminary, was born June 12, 1819, near Richmond. His father was what was then called a "master builder," or contractor. He was prospering in his business, and had bought a home near Richmond, going in and out on horseback, when he was thrown from his horse and killed at the age of thirty-four. His widow was left with four young sons in great poverty. Dr. Walker, the second son, rarely referred to this period, as his boyhood was very sad. He remembered his parents always with the greatest reverence. His mother was a brave and strong woman, who kept her little family together and educated them herself until she was able to send them to school. Cornelius early showed a deeply religious nature, and was sent to the Episcopal High School in 1839, to be trained for the ministry. Dr. Pendleton, of whom he always spoke with the greatest admiration, was the principal. Milo Mahan, who afterward became the rector of St. Paul's Church, Baltimore, and one of the most aggressive Oxford Churchmen in the United States, was the teacher of the classics, and Dr. Walker often referred to his enthusiastic and accurate scholarship. In 1842 he entered the Seminary, and found in Dr. William Sparrow his ideal of a religious thinker and Christian preacher. Among his classmates was the gifted Albert Duy, whose early death was so widely lamented, and of whom a brief biography was written. Dr. Walker always regarded him as a young man of extraordinary promise, and evidently found much stimulus in his society.

On his graduation and ordination to the diaconate in 1845 Dr. Walker went to Amherst Court House. In 1847 he became assistant to the Rev. Dr. Norwood at St. Paul's Church, Richmond, where he married in that same year Margaret J. Fisher, daughter of James Fisher, Jr., and Elizabeth Montgomery McKim. In February, 1848, he became rector of Christ Church, Winchester. His wisdom as a counselor, his fidelity as a pastor, and his helpfulness as a preacher were long held in grateful remembrance in this parish. This was his longest rectorate. He remained in this chief emporium of the lower Valley over twelve years, till December 12, 1860, when he accepted a call to Christ Church, Alexandria.

After six months in Alexandria the Civil War broke out and he was obliged to leave that distracted town. He and his family refugeed in the country near Winchester. In this exigency he was invited to take charge of the Lutheran Church in Winchester, with liberty to use his vestments and the Episcopal service. This invitation he thought it wise to decline, and in November, 1861, accepted a professorship in a college at Camden, South Carolina. When he reached Richmond on his way to the College, he learned that owing to war conditions, it had closed. Thereupon he accepted the rectorship of Emmanuel Church, Henrico County, Virginia, where he remained till he became the professor of Ecclesiastical History in the Seminary, in September, 1866. His pastorate at Henrico covered almost the entire period of the Civil War. His resignation in bereavement, his contentment amid privations, his indefatigable industry both in the study and in the parish, his thoughtful and loving sermons made a profound impression on the congregation. He kept up this hallowed friendship by frequent visits, and on his death forty-one years afterwards the Vestry of Emmanuel, Henrico, recorded in words full of gratitude and veneration the deep impression that his life and teaching had made upon that parish.

During this parochial ministry he had made good use of his time, and grown greatly in scholarship and ability. He was never content to preach emotional sermons, but always brought to his congregations a well thought-out discourse. The intellectual discipline of a carefully written sermon was a favorite topic with him as a professor of homiletics. He undoubtedly spoke out of his own experience. He studied solid books and able reviews with an eager and analytic mind. He read Latin easily, and carried on his studies in Hebrew. He also took up Syriac, and wrote articles for the reviews. By this discipline his profiting appeared unto all. The eminent leader of the Alexandria bar, Mr. Beach, who had such a large practice at the Court of Appeals of Virginia, was of the opinion that Dr. Walker was one of the ablest preachers who was ever rector of Christ Church in that city.

This judgment, which was pronounced after the rectorship of such eminent pulpit orators as Alfred M. Randolph and Randolph H. McKim, showed how acceptable Dr. Walker's logical discourses were to an eminent debater. General William Craighill, the distinguished Chief Engineer of the Army, also had an exceedingly high opinion of Dr. Walker's power of analysis.

The high esteem that he enjoyed in the diocese was shown by his membership on the Board of Trustees of the Seminary, a position which has always been a kind of blue ribbon for a parish minister in Virginia. He was Dr. Sparrow's choice for Dr. May's vacant chair, and was the first full graduate of the Seminary to enter the faculty. Since his time almost all the vacancies have been filled by alumni, —Dr. Nelson, Dr. Grammer, Dr. Wallis, Dr. Massie, Dr. Green, Dr. Kennedy, Dr. Bell, Dr. Thomas Nelson, and Dr. Tucker, all being the Seminary's own graduates. In this way the Seminary has followed the example of most colleges and theological schools, and sought to perpetuate the helpful traditions and influences of its own past. It has not, however, restricted itself to this class, and wisely, went outside to bring in new ideas and methods in the election of Dr. Crawford, Dr. Micou and Dr. Rollins.

Dr. Walker, as we have seen, was both alumnus and trustee. At that time there was no rule excluding a professor from membership on the Board, and he took counsel with Dr. Sparrow, his Dean and close friend, whether he should retain his seat. Dr. Sparrow strongly urged him to remain on the Board, on the ground that it would be very helpful to the Faculty if they could have their point of view presented in the deliberations of the Board, by one of their number. Dr. Walker consequently did not resign his membership, and was subjected to the mortification of being virtually expelled by the passage of a resolution that no member of the Board could also be a professor. Absolutely free as he was from any trace of self-seeking, this experience made a deep impression upon him, and gave him the enduring conviction that a Vestry was a more considerate body than a Board of Trustees. As my own experience is also greatly in favor of the Vestry, it may be expedient to point out the

wisdom of an improvement here. In my time the faculty
was never officially consulted by the Board in any way. We
handed in our individual reports on the year's work, and had
to wait till the secretary's letter arrived, after his return home,
to learn what action the Board had taken. Sometimes it
leaked out through other parties. The most impossible
regulations were laid down, or perhaps I should say, remained
unrepealed, as for example that the roll must be called before
every class. Another rule ran that no text-book should be
used without the approval of the Trustees. The Dean was
not present, even in a consultative capacity, at the sessions
of the Board.* Dr. Packard had been under Boards all his
life, and knew of nothing else and was accustomed to their
ways. But Dr. Walker had been associated with Vestries
in the government of parishes, and had himself been on
governing boards, and he was never entirely happy in his
relation to the Seminary's trustees. He felt that they
should confer with the professors more frequently. To this
Dr. Nelson would have said "amen" most heartily.

Dr. Walker taught Church History only six years, and
was then transferred on the death of Dr. Sparrow to the
chair of Systematic Divinity. The latter department was
much more congenial to him, and it is as a theologian rather
than as a historian, that he will be remembered.

It is so much the habit, since the wide spread of the Oxford theology, to speak of Evangelicalism as if it were merely
the crude conception of Christianity by uncultured minds,
unable to take in the more complicated Catholic theology,
that it may be worth while considering briefly the place
that Evangelical religion occupies in the history of English
religious thought before we endeavor to estimate Dr. Walker
as a theologian. When all of Western Europe, the most
civilized portion of the world, belonged to one Church, and
acquiesced in one interpretation of Christianity, this universal agreement supplied a sufficient foundation for belief.
Just as people to-day do not take the trouble to examine
the arguments in favor of slavery, or monarchy, or oligarchy,

---

*In recent years this isolation between the faculty and the Board has been
abolished. The Dean is now always invited into the Board meeting to make
his report and recommendations in person.—Editor.

but are content to ground their lives and conduct on the principles of freedom and democracy, as the results of the experience of the race, so in the days before the Renaissance and the Reformation there was a general acquiescence in the teaching of the Church.

After Europe was divided by the Reformation into two camps, however, this basis of belief was no longer possible. Something more than acquiescence in the authoritative teaching of the Church was demanded, and men had to acquire another basis for their convictions. In England, where the doctrinal standards of the Church varied for a number of years, according to the personal convictions of the Sovereign, men were largely influenced by national feeling, and stood by the nation: under Henry VIII breaking with the Pope but holding on to much of the Romish dogma; under Edward accepting an out and out Protestantism; under Mary going back to the Roman obedience without returning to the Church its temporalities; and under Elizabeth swinging back to Protestantism, with a distinction. This procedure was subsequently justified by that gifted philosopher, Thomas Hobbes, who was born in the year of the Spanish Armada, 1588, and entered upon conditions that had been created by this process. According to his theory the seat of authority in religion is in the government. It is the duty of the individual to accept the religion of his sovereign.

Such a solution, however, could never be accepted by the truly religious portion of a nation. Accordingly, in one section of the Church of England, the claim was set up that the true seat of authority is the Church, organized according to the primitive model, its officers derived in unbroken succession from early times, and its doctrine derived from the sacred Scriptures. With this school the emphasis was laid on the Church and early usage as the interpreter of the records. The Puritans, however, deeply impressed with the corruptibility of the Church as was manifest on the Continent, laid greater emphasis on the Bible as the uncorrupted source of our knowledge of our religion. The two schools thus had different first principles. As the one party associated itself with the crown, and the other with popular rights, the breach steadily widened and the debate extended into many fields. All England became a great debating society: Romanist against Protestant, High Churchman against Puritan, believer in Divine Right against believer in popular rights. Out of this welter of confusion George Fox and the Quakers sought to find a way of escape by appealing to the light that lighteneth every man that cometh into the world. This great and fruitful principle was, however, brought into contempt by the half-crazy fanatics that associated themselves with it and justified their extravagant follies as Divine revelations. It was too mystical for the practical English race, and seemed to be too much the parent of confusion for a nation of rulers.

Wearied by the hard literalness of Puritanism's Biblical interpretation and its legalistic spirit, England tried awhile the High Church theory. The entire inadequacy of its Divine right theory of government in the face of the despotic conduct of the Roman Catholic James II, disgusted the nation with such narrow conceptions. Neither in the Episcopally governed Church, nor in the Bible as interpreted by the Puritans, nor in the inner Light of the Quakers could a satisfying basis for religious belief be found.

The next recourse was to common sense. Christianity was defended as a scheme analogical to nature and the constitution of society, and authenticated by miracles that have been vouched for by competent and disinterested witnesses. Butler and Paley were the two great defenders of the faith, and the dominant philosopher was John Locke. There was a great dread of enthusiasm, and a man was expected to select his religion or church in the same prudential and calculating spirit in which he chose a bank for his deposits. The resultant barrenness and coldness of the moral tone of the whole nation is well known.

In this brief outline it is not intended to imply that these various schools of thought made no contribution of value to English life. Few people would deny that each brought its own gift. The High Churchman acted as a conservative element theologically, and kept religion in a friendly relation with the Arts and with History. The Puritans gave England its Sunday, its moral strenuousness, its liberal government. The Quaker brought to light neglected elements of the Christian life, and showed the beauty of meekness and quietness. The doctrine of the inner light was a needful announcement of the great truth, that God has not left himself without witness in any heart. And as for the school of Locke, it is well known that to it in large measure we owe the noblest gift that the eighteenth century handed on to the nineteenth, the prevalence of toleration in religion or, as it is better expressed in the language of our own day, the prevalence of religious liberty.

But each basis of belief had proven to be of only temporary and partial use. The credentials of the Church, the interpretation of the Scripture, the inner light, the evidence for miracles were sources too recondite for the unlettered day-laborer. The cold, argumentative discourses upon such premises were not suited to awake the indifferent, to arouse the callous. The great masses of English people in the mines and in the rural districts were without God. The Church had lost its hold on the nation, and belonged only to a class. Such was the condition when the Wesleys and Whitefield, with their associates, revived religion in England and the Colonies. They appealed neither to Church nor to written documents, nor to the light of nature, but to the response of the human heart to the doctrines of the Cross. Under their preaching a vivid type of religious experience was produced, which was felt by all who went through it to be a sufficient credential for faith. According to this school the doctrines of Christianity were proven by their power to convert the sinner and build up the saint, rather than by their literary or ecclesiastical credentials. It is unnecessary to dwell on the great work of these men. Unfortunately many of them were obliged to go out of the Church of England to exercise their gifts with freedom. A great number, however, remained in the Establishment, and became, as Sir James Stephen has well called them, the second founders of the Church of England.

This new type of religious experience had been undergone in America by Jonathan Edwards and his gifted wife even before the days of Wesley, and the preachers of this Evangelical message were cordially received everywhere in the colonies. The Methodists grew in such great numbers that they soon became the largest Protestant Church in the land. The Episcopal Church, under its first leaders, White and Seabury, was a reflex of the English Church of the days before the Great Awakening, White being of Lockian type, and Seabury of the Divine Right school. Unless the Church had responded to the new enthusiasm for souls, and to the doctrines of repentance and faith, the Methodists would have swept into their fold the great majority of America's earnest people. This happened, indeed, to a great extent in the far South.

A number of clergymen and laymen of evangelical convictions arose in the Episcopal Church, and gave to it a new vitality. In Virginia the great leaders were Bishop Moore and Bishop Meade, especially the latter, who was closely identified with the State by birth, and touched its life in numerous ways. Of this Evangelical school were the Seminary's founders and first professors.

Under the Evangelical Dr. Stone, Dr. Packard entered the Episcopal Church. Dr. Sparrow was from his birth a member of the Church of England, but he sat as a student at Columbia College, New York, under Dr. Milner of St. George's, and had passed through the Evangelical experience in his prayer meeting. His maternal uncle, the Rev. Peter Roe, was a great Evangelical leader and did a great work in reviving the Church in Ireland. Dr. May was distinguished in a preeminent degree by the characteristic marks of Evangelical piety. Out of a parish church of this type Cornelius Walker came to the Seminary. By training and personal experience he was admirably qualified to carry on the more liberal Evangelical tradition.

The common mark of all Evangelicals, as we have seen, was their insistence upon a personal experience of the power of Christian truth. They were one in their exaltation of the Scriptures as a means of grace, in their valuation of preaching, in their Gospel of repentance and faith. But when it came to the philosophy of religion, and the more abstruse doctrines, they were divided into the two schools of Calvinists and Arminians. In the Calvinistic division were found the large majority of the Evangelicals in the Church of England, Toplady, Grimshaw, Romaine, and their fellows. According to their reading, the Thirty-nine

Articles had an Augustinian character, and they felt that they were in their rightful place in a Church with such standards, and that there was no proper place for them among the Arminian followers of Wesley, even if their staunch loyalty to the English Church had permitted the thought of defection to enter their minds.

The men of this school were equipped for their great work by their profound sense of human depravity and the necessity of conversion. If they depressed man, they exalted God, and when they had brought their hearer to believe that he was the object of the Spirit's operations, the sense of God's elective love gave him strength and courage. Faber's hymn,

> "Oh, grace of grace! Oh, gift of faith!
> My God and can it be,
> That Thou who hast discerning love
> Shouldst give that gift to me!"

shows us the humble gratitude such a theology in some of its aspects is well calculated to inspire. In these days when we are slow to believe that God can ever be finally bereaved of a spirit created in his image; when we dwell more and more on the thought that what began best can't end worst, or what God blessed once prove finally accurst; when we trust the larger hope; when we cling to the text that the gifts and calling of God are without repentance; it is not fit that we should make any animadversions upon Calvinism without expressing our immense indebtedness to its great affirmations, to the way in which it brought God and man close together, to its insistence that humanity is an organism, not a mere collection of individuals, to its moral strenuousness, to its confidence that the Universe is a government, and that God reigns as well as lives and loves, both rules and overrules. But if Calvinism shed a great light in some directions, it is undeniable that in others it threw a deep shadow, and over some natures cast a horror of great darkness. As long as its system was not fully explored, and its consequences not logically drawn out, it proved a source of mental development. But, when this had been accomplished, it disclosed that it was a tree that could not bear the

richest intellectual fruitage, since it had a principle of decay
at its root in its doctrine of total depravity.   For if man's
nature is corrupt throughout its entire extent, and so corrupt
that his sense of justice can be no guide to the nature of
Divine Justice, then it follows that man can have but little
confidence in the operations of human reason.   In the case
of Augustine, this doctrine of depravity led to exaltation of
the Church, and made that great restorer of the Pauline
religious experience also the father of the Sacramental System.   The early Evangelicals, in their distrust of reason,
fled for refuge not to the Sacraments, but to the Inspired
Word.   No theory of inspiration could have claimed too
much for them.   Before the Book which contained the Word
of God, which they asserted was the Word of God, reason pros-
strated itself.   Exegesis became a mere question of grammar
and dictionary.   With the later Evangelicals, this abasement
of the reason before revelation went so far that the Calvinism
which had created this mental attitude was itself destroyed,
as having too much of the character of a logic-wrought system of thought.   Charles Simeon, who was an effective
Evangelical leader, professed that he was a Calvinist on the
Calvinistic proof-texts, and an Arminian on Arminian proof-
texts.   He had many followers, who felt no necessity of
harmonizing their beliefs or constructing a self-consistent
theory.   Such was the theological result of excessive reliance
on feeling and distrust of reason.

To this Calvinistic wing of Evangelicalism, in one of the
other of these stages, belonged the early Evangelicals in
Virginia.   The first Dean and Professor of Systematic Divinity in the Seminary, Dr. Reuel Keith, was a consistent
Calvinist.   After hearing him preach for the first time, Dr.
Sparrow writes: "I suspect he brings the strong meat of
Calvinism in huge joints and sirloins on the table."   Bishop
Johns, who had been trained for the ministry by Dr. Archibald Alexander at Presbyterian Princeton, belonged to the
same school, though he used its great affirmations with the
tact and discretion of a popular preacher and wise adminis-
trator.   He used to chafe somewhat against Dr. Sparrow's
use of Knapp's Theology, on the ground that the German
theologian was deficient in depth and solidity in his views of

sin and grace. Dr. Andrews, of Shepherdstown, who was recognized by the whole Church as one of the Evangelical leaders in the General Convention, was in entire sympathy with Bishop Johns in his theology and his criticism of Knapp. Dr. May, who took the chair of Church History after Dr. Sparrow became Professor of Systematic Divinity, was a theologian of the same stripe, although his gentle spirit shrank from dwelling on the harsher side of the system. "He is a sweet man, of good sense, of Evangelical principles, and moderate in his Church views," writes Dr. Sparrow to his old Gambier colleague, Dr. Wing. "He is a little more Calvinistic than you or I should like, perhaps, but it is not brought out offensively." Dr. Packard, who had been trained in New England under Moses Stuart, came from a center of Calvinistic theology, and interpreted the Pauline Epistles in the Calvinistic sense. In the life of Colden Hoffman we read how much he was impressed by the Calvinism of Professor Packard's exegesis. The Doctor adhered to this school to the end, though with an inclination towards the unsystematic stage of Simeon.

Whatever were Bishop Meade's opinions upon this fundamental question of Christian Philosophy, and they do not appear to have been very pronounced, it was into the hands of the theologians of this type that he confided the training of his candidates for the ministry. Unless some other influence had been brought into the Seminary, the Arminian side of Evangelicalism would have made little progress in Virginia, or gained merely by the unwholesome process of the simple disintegration of Calvinism instead of by the vivifying influence of a more living system of thought. Yet Arminianism was a school of Evangelical thought that had an important part to play. Its kindlier views of human nature, and its more generous recognition of the will's unique power, put it in a friendly attitude towards the reason. Many of its exponents sat at the feet of Coleridge in his acute analysis of determinism and drank in along with his philosophy of the Will many of his liberal principles.

Such was the Evangelicalism that was brought into Virginia by William Sparrow. It was rightly named Evangelicalism, on account of its emphasis upon personal experience, its message of repentance and faith, and its insistence upon the value of the Christian consciousness, *Pectus theologum facit* being one of its great key words, but it also had, by reason of its psychology and appeal to primal self-evidencing verities, a general connection with the so-called Latitudinarians of the eighteenth century.   Dr. Sparrow first gained his hold upon his scholars by his exposition of Butler's Analogy.   He was also a great admirer of Whately and Arnold, and the early Broad Churchmen.   Like them, he was profoundly antagonistic to the Tractarians.   His opposition was not due to a conservative repugnance to new views, but to a profound opposition to their philosophical first principles, as well as to their specific dogmas.   They feared the dissolving force of the intellect; he trusted that the soul was naturally Christian.   They looked backward; he looked forward. They turned to the authority of the Church; he appealed to the authority of the Truth.   "He taught us," said Bishop Brooks, "that however far thought might travel it would still find God."   The teaching of his last years has been ably set forth by Bishop Gibson in an address of permanent value for the history of religious thought in Virginia, an exposition that makes it easy to see how this Arminian type of Evangelicalism naturally led on to the hopefulness and trust in humanity that find such glowing expression in the great sermons of Phillips Brooks, and to the alliance of religion and philosophy which marked the sermons and Paddock lectures of the eloquent Bishop Randolph.

I have spoken at some length upon Dr. Sparrow's theology, because, unless we bear it closely in mind that with him Evangelicalism in Virginia entered on a new phase and was being prepared for new developments, we shall not be in the right position to understand Dr. Walker.   He was one of the students of Dr. Sparrow's earliest days at this Seminary, and was his close friend, his biographer, and successor in his chair.   Although he had received his earliest religious impressions in the old-fashioned Evangelicalism of Virginia, he was in thorough sympathy with Dr. Sparrow's more genial attitude toward the reason, and came to the Seminary after the Civil War as Dr. Sparrow's preference among the Virginia clergy.   By that time Calvinism as a complete system had been badly shattered, and no longer dominated the Protestant world. Dr. Andrews had sought to strengthen its hold on the Seminary by securing the election of Dr. McElhinney as an assistant to Dr. Sparrow; but in spite of his learning, Dr. McElhinney was not equal to such a task. A scholar who reminds one of the immortal Dominie Sampson in his love of erudition and ignorance of the world, his spirit was not fitted for controversy, and the system as held by him had so many qualifications and limitations, and, like his view of baptismal regeneration and the Lord's Supper, was so exceedingly vague in outline and difficult of statement, that it lacked all value as a working hypothesis, belonging rather to the category of ingenious puzzles or toys for the amusement of a speculative hour. Dr. Packard, whose cast of mind was literary rather than argumentative, had no turn for religious speculation, and realized that the times did not seem to need the specially Calvinistic truths, though he faithfully exegeted the Scriptural passages in the old-fashioned way. Dr. Hanckel, who belonged to the old school, came to the Seminary, and examined the candidates for the ministry on the old lines, and showed in various ways the distrust that the less closely-knit system of the Arminian Evangelical created in his logical mind. But, on the whole, Dr. Walker had little trouble with predestination and fatalistic theories of the Will. When Calvinism came up in class, he made short work of it, and was usually able to eradicate it thoroughly. I remember this with special vividness, because I came to the Seminary much under the influence of Calvin's teaching, and can never forget how skillfully he pointed out the inadequacy of its theory of the Will.

The Evangelicals as a body gave up the Calvinistic doctrines of predestination and reprobation without any great struggle, and on this side of his teaching, Dr. Walker had the pleasure of being in thorough accord with Bishop Whittle and Dr. Nelson. What separated him from them, and made him the continuer of the more liberal traditions, was his friendly attitude toward the reason, and his desire to bring his religious views into harmony with themselves and with his other knowledge. He absolutely rejected the Calvinistic and Augustinian theory that we are by birth of such a depraved nature that we justly deserve the punishments of Hell. His loving heart shrank back from the appalling theory that unregenerate infants are akin to devils. "Little angels," he said, "was much nearer the truth." He believed that not alone Adam, but all men are created in God's image, though the lineaments are blurred by sin. With this theory of humanity, he linked its logical consequence, a quiet confidence that the mind would eventually find the truth. He was not afraid of progress, and looked hopefully into the future. In this he stood almost alone. The great majority of the Evangelicals had not abandoned their distrust of the reason when they threw away the theory of total depravity that nourished it. On the whole, they dreaded Neology, as they called it, or Latitudinarianism, even more than Puseyism, to use the old terms. To this school belonged Bishop Whittle who lived his brave consistent Christian life under the shadow of great distrust of progress.

Dr. Nelson, was more afraid of Essays and Reviews, than he was opposed to Tracts for the Times, though his opposition to Tractarianism was neither superficial nor lacking in earnestness and force. It was from no passing impulse or chance reason that the speeches of Dr. Nelson in opposition to the amendments of Dr. Huntington, which aimed to broaden our Church, gave so much comfort and assistance to the conservatives and ritualists who opposed that endeavor. Conservative by nature, with a fine loyalty to his traditions and inheritance, Dr. Nelson had this strongly marked characteristic intensified by his distrust of the reason. His practical temper inclined him to turn for guidance to the *Via Media*, both in theology and Churchmanship. While a thorough Protestant in theory, in practice he leaned heavily upon the authority of the Church, and thought that the next step forward, or (as he would not have cared for that term), I should say, the duty of the hour, was the rounding out of the Seminary's teaching by placing greater emphasis upon the function of the Church. Except in opposition to some such extreme dogma as predestination or transubstantiation, he rarely appealed to the reason. He had been a soldier, and always bore himself in a frank soldierly fashion of his own, and he turned naturally to authority as his guide.

Loyalty and obedience were his favorite virtues, and were illustrated in his Christian character and example, which will ever be valuable heritages of this Seminary.

With such colleagues, it can be seen that Dr. Walker stood alone in his mental attitude. They were all so much united by the similarity of their religious experience and training and their deep spirituality, that they worked harmoniously together. All of them disliked any efforts to bring our Church closer to Roman Catholic forms of worship and life. None of them was a worshipper of system. They were closely united in the great essentials. In gifts and tastes they supplemented one another. But Dr. Walker stood alone among them in his frank trust in the operations of the reason. His was the only class-room where Science was looked on with a friendly eye, and his the only mind that was seriously at work coordinating, systematizing, and scrutinizing its own operations and store of facts. I cannot say that he was always willing to enter every field that his scholars invited him to explore for their benefit. At times he would say, "This question ought not to be raised," whereas it had been raised and could not be exorcised by any criticism upon the legitimacy of its origin. But this was not often. He was a man of real intellectual courage. While he was naturally opposed to the assumptions of the Higher Criticism, he never fled to the arms of the Church for refuge, and was willing to see the battle of the scholars joined. He had a calm confidence that the Truth would win. He read Cheyne largely, and with considerable appreciation of his earlier Commentaries. In days when the unending nature of the punishment of the wicked was one of the chief doctrines of Evangelicalism, it required no common courage in a professor to ask scholars in his class-room, whether it was not conceivable and credible that God could combine punishment with reformatory measures, inasmuch as human ingenuity had been able to effect this union in our penitentiaries and reformatories. I remember distinctly such an utterance in Dr. Walker's class-room, five years before a stormy council in Fredericksburg, and a futile resolution in reprehension of a speculative sermon on such a theme, showed the strength of the opposition to any speculation on this subject.

He had been a scholar of Dr. Sparrow's earlier days, and when I sat under him had not attained the liberality that marked Dr. Sparrow's latest theology as expounded by Bishop Gibson. But he was remarkable for his steady growth and broadening out, up to the end of his professorship. An indefatigable reader, he carefully digested all that he took in, and was fond of talking about the books he had on hand. He was not one of those scholars whose reading precipitates itself upon his thinking and clogs all the mental processes. Moreover, he read great books. Late in life he read with avidity and admiration Lotze's *Microcomos*. While he naturally clung to the Evangelicalism that had trained him, and produced the great leaders who had revived the spiritual life of Virginia, he was never quite happy in any attack upon liberal thought. A thinker himself, he loved a man whose mind dwelt on the high themes of God's nature and man's destiny. His chief theological opposition was directed against legal and pagan elements in religion. He had no sympathy with exclusive claims for one form of ecclesiastical organization and scant sympathy for any theory of the Sacraments that had any magical or nonmoral elements. With his Christlike view of children, as of the Kingdom of Heaven, he felt no need for certain theories of Infant Baptism. The language of the Bible about Baptism he held only referred to the baptism of adult converts, and could not be transferred to the baptism of a new born babe without many qualifications, In his eyes, the Sacraments were efficacious "through the Word and Spirit," which he interpreted to mean through the truth as the instrument, and the Spirit as the agent. To some his theory may appear rationalistic, but it has the great merit that it can be stated and grasped, which is more than can be said of the theories that try to avoid his simplicity and yet keep away from the materialism of Rome's dogmas.

In his discussion of the Sacraments, Dr. Walker was at his best, for it brought out in high relief his entire sanity, which was in my eyes his chief mental distinction. He had been a careful student of Kant's Critique of the Pure Reason, and gained from it a profound distrust of the mind's power to solve by speculation the problems with which theology is confronted. His method was inductive. He declined to subordinate the certain teachings of reason or experience to the requirements of a metaphysical or ecclesiastical system. Against the theories that held a soul is given to an infant in Baptism or a special gift of the Holy Ghost, he appealed to our observation, to the fact that such endowments would surely manifest themselves so plainly that the children of Baptists and Quakers would be plainly inferior to baptized children. He appealed to "facts" so constantly that it became a by-word among the students, and I take it that this cannot be said of many professors of Systematic Theology.

His emphasis upon "the necessity of differentiation and definition of terms" will not be easily forgotten by his old scholars. He held his facts and doctrines in a systematic way, and linked them together by "unifying principles," but he was no wire-drawer. No man knew better the distinction between a cable and a cobweb. He cared not for cobwebs even if strung along with the dewy gems of glittering rhetoric. He was not afraid to confess on some deep subjects that he was without the materials for an opinion. Though he taught Church History for some years, as we have seen, he never entered the modern idea of the development of dogma, not at least to any fruitful extent. Evangelicalism in his hands insensibly became less emotional. While he held, of course, to the Nicene theology, like a true Evangelical, his chief theological interest was in the Atonement, and the doctrines of grace. He was always able to give a reason for the hope that was in him, with meekness and yet with decision, and was a truly conscientious thinker as well as believer. This moderation he doubtless owed as much to his study of Bishop Butler as to Emmanuel Kant.

I have dwelt at length upon Dr. Walker as a theologian because in his last years the failure of his vocal powers prevented the students from appreciating him at his real worth. He loved to write, and excelled all his colleagues in the number of his publications, but his philosophical reading had an injurious influence on his style. He was better at analysis than at exposition. In his biographies his style is

better than in his later works. In his little handbooks of
Ethics and Doctrines, he did not, in my judgment, do himself justice. A handbook requires condensation, and intensified his fault of too great compression. The nature of his
theological thinking is shown much better in the articles that
he published from time to time in the *Bibliotheca Sacra*.

In addition to theology he also taught Homiletics, and
none of his old students will ever forget his interest in this
department. Although his efficiency was impaired by his
weak voice, as we have seen, he had been a very successful
parish preacher in his day, as well as a wise and tender shepherd of souls. Later on in life his love of analysis mastered
him, and he would at times think a congregation sufficiently
edified if he analyzed a text and its implications in their hearing. But he always had a sound theory of preaching, and
made many helpful suggestions to his scholars. Some of his
sermons still linger in my memory, particularly one which
opened up the meaning of the phrase, "in Christ." He was
at his best, however, in his admirable Faculty Meeting
addresses, where the wisdom of his fatherly counsels was the
fruit of his rich Christian experience. Dr. Blackford often
spoke of the interesting and helpful character of his talks to
the High School boys in their chapel.

He never gave up the pastoral habit. During his long
professorship he was the chief pastor of the neighborhood.
For miles around he was a faithful visitor to the poor, and
his charity was disseminated almost as widely as his pastoral
care. "The poor ye have always with you," was as true of
his thoughts as of the Church. In the administration of the
Seminary, his colleagues always looked upon him as a wise
counsellor. There was no one to whom a student in distress
of any kind turned more naturally for sympathy or direction.
There was no visitor more certain to inquire at a sick man's
door.

His Christian character was marked by great reality
and simplicity. He was absolutely free from any professionalism in manner, and hated any treatment of the
ministry as a profession. In his eyes, it was a high and holy
calling only to be entered on in obedience to a summons
from God. He never gauged a minister's success by the

size or wealth of his congregation. All his weights and measures were taken from the sanctuary. The key-note of his teaching in the Faculty Meeting was that the Christian character is the norm and basis of the ministerial character; and that only a faithful Christian can be a good minister of Jesus Christ. This note was resonant in his whole life. He went up and down among us in such meekness, fidelity and godly sincerity that we all recognized in him a true man of God, and realized that he spent much of his time in mystic communion with Christ.

Never have I known a more preeminent example of Christian conscientiousness. His whole life was dominated by a sensitive Christian conscience. Take him in whatever relation you would, this was his outstanding characteristic. He was a very pattern and model in the use of time—careful of the moments, an early riser and retirer, with a systematic arrangement of duties and a well-considered change of occupations. His conscientious economy showed itself in the noble proofs of his wide liberality. No one was ever more regardful of the rights of others, or more careful to guard his lips from idle words. Naturally far from robust, he made a conscience of observing the laws of health and kept himself in fine condition by his regular exercises and wise regimen. There was nothing sour or ascetic about him; he had an aversion to radical and fanatical types of religion; but his conscientiousness was so pervasive that self-indulgence never seemed to come near him. He was ever in his great Taskmaster's eye. A man of marked devotional spirit, he watched as well as prayed.

This close attention to the inner voice made him singularly independent, for such an affectionate man, of the support of the praise of his fellow men. He must have known that he was considered by many as deficient in Churchly temper, and dogma; but he never showed the slightest sign of any craving for recognition or sympathy. With him it was a small matter to be judged of man's judgment. He was ever bringing himself in thought before a higher tribunal. His constant dwelling in this higher region gave his character a saintliness and simplicity that was recognized by all who came in contact with him. Many little pettinesses could not bear to show themselves in his presence. His whole life was a rebuke to vanity, self-will, and self-seeking. No one can measure the power of such an example. As a student and I were driving to a funeral, and saw Dr. Walker ahead waiting for us at the appointed place, his blue overcoat buttoned to protect him from the cold, in serene unconsciousness of any lack of clerical appearance, the student turned to me and said, "When I look in the face of Dr. Walker, I can see that he is under the influence of heavenly powers." All of us felt that. The whole neighborhood would rise up, if occasion offered, and bear the same testimony. The more closely one knew him, the more clearly was this manifest. It is not proper that the manly reserve and fortitude with which he bore his burdens should be permitted to obscure the brightness of his example. During all the years that I knew him, Mrs. Walker was a great invalid, and in spite of her indomitable spirit many additional cares and anxieties fell upon the Doctor's shoulders. But no one ever heard him refer to this. On one occasion a blundering person endeavored to sympathize with him in the troubles which so much domestic sickness must give him; he put the subject aside gently but firmly, simply remarking it was a pleasure to him to be of service in that way. The air of such low levels of selfishness was stifling to him, and he carried the conversation into others regions.

We owe him respect, and we owe him gratitude. Among all the Seminary's professors, Dr. Walker was the one who suffered the most in his loyalty to this Institution. He accepted his election to the Chair of Church History, and came to the Seminary's assistance shortly after the Civil War, in the hour of its greatest poverty and distress. He told me once that when the call came, he drew Mrs. Walker aside and foretold that if he accepted the position they would be obliged, in the impoverished condition of the Institution, to endure such privations as they had never known. She saw that the call appealed to him and urged him to go on; although, as the result proved, her own loss of health was the price that had to be paid for his larger career. Dr. Walker was not the man to forget her heroism, nor should this Seminary ever forget it of either of them.

It was regrettable that his meek and brave spirit should not have enjoyed more recognition. During his whole connection with the Seminary, Dr. Packard was always beside him to enjoy the honors of greater age and longer service. Towards the end, while he was steadily growing in learning and breadth, his weak voice greatly impaired his efficiency. When Dr. Packard resigned the Deanship, Dr. Walker was clearly too old to assume its duties for any length of time. It is good, however, to remember that he was the Seminary's Dean for a year. In June, 1898, he was retired. A standard of munificence in dealing with retired professors had been set in the case of Dr. Packard that the Trustees were not able to continue, and Dr. Walker was not able to live out the close of his life on the beloved Hill. This was a great disappointment to him, but he bore it with his customary gentle fortitude. He withdrew to the home of his youngest daughter, Mrs. J. D. La Mothe, and remained with her till his death, June 23rd, 1907.

His lot was cast in days when the good ship Evangelicalism had grounded in a place where the two seas of advanced Churchmanship and Liberal Thought meet, and he saw many of his scholars drift off in either direction. I often regretted this during his lifetime, and wished that more public honor could have been bestowed on him. But he never needed it. He dwelt in heavenly places with Christ Jesus, and to him it was supreme happiness to have been counted worthy to preach the Gospel of the grace of God, and to train young men for their high office as Ambassadors of Christ.

I can see now that his life is of more value to us, just as it was. With some obvious changes, the lines that Matthew Arnold wrote on the death of Edward Quillinan express my later thought:

"I wished him health, success and fame;
    I do not wish it now.

"For these are all their own reward,
        And leave no good behind;
    They try us, oftenest make us hard,
        Less modest, pure, and kind.

"But he is now by fortune foiled
No more; and we retain
The memory of a man unspoiled,
Sweet, generous and humane.

"With all the fortunate have not,
With gentle voice and brow.
Alive, we would have changed his lot;
We would not change it now."

With how many different scenes he is associated in our minds. We see him equipped for his regular morning walk before class, a walk that was apt to be turned to the bedside of some sick cottager, and one that was hallowed in our eyes by the tradition among the students that the Doctor's favorite sanctuary for private prayer was in the recesses of some thick copse. Again, he comes before me as he used to sit beside the desk and listen to the student's sermon on Wednesday afternoon, never appearing in his bearing quite so much the professor and minister of the Gospel as in that congenial commingling of the duties of devotion and analysis. We can see him standing by some open grave, reading the great words of unquenchable hope and triumphant faith, or he is making his little semi-circular gesture with his hands as he expounds some truth in class, and gathers his thought round some ultimate or "unifying principle," or he beams upon us from the head of his hospitable board, where the students were so thoughtfully entertained; or he is out in the garden among his flowers, bees and fruit trees, the best gardener of the neighborhood. We have seen him in the chapel, in class, in home, in company, and marked him for years; but we never saw him when it was not plain that he was seeking another city, that is, an heavenly, and that he was freed from earth's slaveries by the great deliverance of fellowship with Jesus Christ and devotion to His cause.

Now we can appreciate at its true worth such a life and such a character. "The longer that I live," wrote Dr. Sparrow, "the more I fall back upon a few great principles." Dr. Walker trod the same path. It was always a striking characteristic of his phraseology, Professor of Systematic

Theology and expounder of the Nicene Christology though he was, that his favorite and almost unvarying name for Jesus was "The Master." He accepted the mysteries of the Divine Nature as revealed, but he knew by personal experience that Jesus of Nazareth was his Master. His strict views of inspiration made him disapprove any quotations of Scripture that did not use the passage in the original sense; yet I can but think that an appropriate inscription for his tablet would be the word's of the ancient record, "He went in and stood before his Master." In that Presence he walked by faith, and into that Presence he has assuredly entered, and his joy is fulfilled.

THE REVEREND DOCTOR JOHN J. MCELHINNEY

Professor 1871-1887

SECTION V

CHAPTER IX

REV. DR. JOHN J. McELHINNEY

REV. SAMUEL A. WALLIS, D. D.

The Rev. John J. McElhinney, D. D., was born in the city of Pittsburgh, Pennsylvania, in the month of March, 1815. He attended Washington and Jefferson College, Cannonsburgh, Pennsylvania, and we have no doubt that he graduated there.

Dr. McElhinney appears on the Clergy Lists as a "Deacon in Alleghany City," Pennsylvania in 1841; as "Missionary at Connellsville, Fayette county, and parts adjacent" in 1844; as "Residing in Pittsburgh" in 1847; as "Rector of St. James' Church, Wooster, (Ohio) and missionary" in 1850; as "Rector of St. Paul's Church, Pittsburgh," (Penn.) in 1853; and "Professor in Theological Seminary, Gambier," (Ohio) in 1856, where he served for fifteen years. In 1872 he became professor in The Virginia Seminary, holding the position until the year 1887, when he resigned on account of old age and infirmity. A moderate pension was granted him by the Seminary authorities and he retired to the home of his son, near Fall's Church, Fairfax County, Virginia. He died there in the month of August, 1895, and after a short service conducted by his old friend, the Rev. Professor Walker, his remains were taken to Pittsburgh and interred in one of the cemeteries of the city where he was born. Dr. McElhinney was a clergyman of most venerable appearance, and with his white hair flowing almost down to his shoulders, he reminded one of an Oxford or Cambridge professor of the olden days. In the reading desk and in the pulpit he brought to mind the immortal description of the village pastor in Goldsmith's "Deserted Village".

Dr. McElhinney was a man of wide culture and great learning. Dr. Packard considered him the most learned professor that had ever been on the faculty of the Seminary up to his time, and we are satisfied that no one since has ever been his equal in what is generally known as ecclesiastical learning in the full Anglican conception of that subject. He was well versed in Hebrew, Latin and Greek. We remember on one occasion he said that he had committed to memory some of the Psalms in Hebrew, with an especial desire to know the twenty-third psalm in that language, that he might be able to repeat it on his dying bed. In Churchmanship he was a fine Evangelical without that tone of partisanship which was so opposed to the spirit of his character and the breadth of his historic learning. His library was a very large one. At that day it was considered to be the largest private theological library in the South. It was filled with theological and other works of great value, a number of them being old editions. It was very interesting to see the old doctor with his cane in one hand, and a newly purchased ancient volume under his arm, walking at times through the Seminary grove, reverently carrying it to his study and carefully depositing it there among the books of his library. Nor must it be forgotten that Dr. McElhinney was not only well read in ancient and mediaeval as well as reformed theological and ecclesiastical literature, but also kept up fully with the theological thought and writing of his day.

As a teacher Dr. McElhinney was not always interesting to the careless student. But those whose minds were open to the fact that in him the treasures of theological knowledge were clearly manifest, could derive great benefit from his lectures. Like the late Professor Sanday of Oxford University, Dr. McElhinney always gave a summary of all possible conclusions which the various writers deduced from any particular subject, without ever definitely stating his own. Perhaps this was done to allow each student the pleasure of working one out for himself, and thereby strengthening his own mental powers.

Dr. McElhinney published a work entitled "The Doctrine of the Church" which is a valuable contribution to the historical treatment of the subject. The method pursued is to discuss the notes of the Church which may be called vest-pocket definitions, then to give the definitions of

the great leaders from Clement of Rome down to the date
of issuing the work, and lastly, beginning with the Reformation, to state the definitions of the Church found in all the
confessions of Faith, Roman, Greek, and Protestant, with
historic and doctrinal discussions explaining their meaning
and the reasons that led them to take their several positions.
It is well known that there were no official definitions of the
Church until the Reformation compelled each national
division to draw up a Confession of Faith to explain what it
believed, and the reason for its existence before the world.

In the retirement of his study he delighted to talk
with friends on subjects of mutual interest, upon which
he never failed to cast some new light from the full range of
his study and reading. It must not be imagined that his
reading was restricted to the dry tones of deep theological
lore. He was familiar with the best novels of the day, and
among the numbers had a great regard for the works of
Anthony Trollope, both for their style and for their portrait-
ure of English clerical life.

To a large majority of the students of his time, Dr.
McElhinney was a venerable form, passing in and out among
them, from his study to his lecture room untouched by the
more practical spirit of modern times. Yet as we remember
that God reveals Himself in many types of sanctified human
nature, we cannot but feel that the Faculty and the Seminary
were enriched by his saintly life and high scholarship. His
was a spirit which instinctively breathed the prayer of "*Il
Penseroso*,"

> "But let my due feet never fail,
> To walk the studious cloister's pale.
> And love the high embowed roof,
> With antique pillars massy-proof,
> And storied windows richly dight,
> Casting a dim religious light."

SECTION V

CHAPTER X

REV. DR. KINLOCH NELSON

REV. JAMES W. MORRIS, D. D.

Sprung from a race of Statesmen and Churchmen, Dr. Kinloch Nelson received by inheritance a noble legacy of patriotism and of piety. The fine ideals of the Virginia gentleman were his by nature, and an ardent devotion to his state and his Church beat with his very blood.

Through both father and mother, he was descended from the celebrated Governor Nelson of revolutionary times. As is well known, the devotion of this great man to his country brought upon him very severe financial distress, so that his last years were passed in considerable embarrassment. At the same time his devotion to the then established Church was as conspicuous and as sacrificial as that to the state. This unselfish spirit survives in the descendants of the famous governor, and was eminently manifest in the subject of this sketch.

Born in 1839, Dr. Nelson had just reached young manhood when the fateful war between the States began. By that mighty struggle, as by a vast flood, life for men of his generation is divided. Those who buffetted its furious waves and came through in safety, left far behind in the process the bright shores of youth. With strenuous activity and with swift decision, they donned the *toga virilis*. As boys they entered the conflict; they came out of it as men. The rigorous experience of that dire time brought quite abruptly the putting away of childish things and the manly facing of the stern verities of life. As in the case of most high-spirited men of his age, the war left its invisible marks upon young Nelson's character and fixed in great measure its distinctive qualities.

It was at the Episcopal High School, near Alexandria, then under the able management of the Rev. Dr. John Pey-

THE REVEREND DOCTOR KINLOCH NELSON

Professor 1876-1894

ton McGuire, that Dr. Nelson was prepared for the University of Virginia. Here he was a diligent student, and an eager participant in all the happy life of the school. It was here that he formed many of those warm friendships, which were the joy of his life. It was characteristic of the man to attract the love and affection of his associates. He bound his friends to him with hooks of steel.

His decision for Christ by a public profession of His name, was made at this time. Together with a large number of his schoolmates, he received the rite of confirmation at the hands of Bishop Johns. The number of boys confirmed was unusually large. A beautiful daughter of Dr. McGuire, lovely in person and saintly in character, and a great favorite with the boys of the school, suddenly sickened and died. The glory and triumph of her death so impressed the whole school, that a great many boys came forward for confirmation.

At the outbreak of the war, Dr. Nelson was a student at the University of Virginia. Like most of his friends, he was earnestly opposed to armed conflict. But when President Lincoln's proclamation forced the secession of Virginia, there was no hesitation on his part as to what must be done.

He enlisted first in the Albemarle Light Horse under Captain Eugene Davis, serving in that command at the first battle of Manassas. Later he transferred to the Rockbridge Artillery, whose first captain, the Rev. W. N. Pendleton, became later General Lee's chief of artillery. In this command, he served as a private, in warm comradeship with many of his dearest friends, until the last year of the war. At the last, he received a commission as second lieutenant, surrendering in that rank at Appomattox.

These four years of war were a great school for the formation and discipline of character. They had much to do in the making of the firm and decisive character of this exceptional man. One of his intimate friends, Mr. Joseph Packard, Jr., who served with him in the same battery, has this to say of his life as a soldier: "Nelson was assigned as cannoneer, to the same piece at which I served. I had, therefore, constant opportunity of observing him in the closest way, and I can say with the strictest truth that I never saw in him the least shortcoming of his duty as a soldier and as a Christian gentleman.   In the spring of 1862 I discharged temporarily the duties of chief of the piece, and was thus in an humble way in immediate command of him.   In the assignments of tasks that fell to my lot to impose, I had perhaps more occasion than others to remark the fine spirit in which he discharged them.   Sometimes these tasks were of a disagreeable and onerous kind, such as care of horses, cleaning and oiling of harness, and the like.   Whatever he had to do, he did it well, with the cheerfulness, faithfulness and steadiness that were characteristic of him.   At the Battle of Port Republic, our gun team was driven by Nelson and R. E. Lee, Jr., and it was their care and skilful driving that saved the gun from capture during the charge of the enemy."

He never lost his interest in guns.   He loved to talk of cannon.   He had planned with his intimate friend Bishop Peterkin of West Virginia, whenever the chance should be given, to visit Waterloo, and to study the location of artillery on that famous field.   The Bishop tells of an occasion when he and the doctor were walking together deep in the discussion of some Church problem, when suddenly Dr. Nelson stopped and exclaimed; "Look, George, at that hill.   What a splendid position for a battery!"

An incident, vouched for by a dignitary of the Church, though declared by himself to be apochyphal, is most characteristic of him.   Early in the war, in the midst of a particularly hot engagement, Nelson was standing by his gun then out of action, waiting with nerves on edge, shot and shell falling around him, when a reckless young officer passing by and observing his nervous state, cried to him, "Hello, Nelson, what's the matter?   You look scared to death!" "Yes," was the reply, "and if you were as scared as I am you would run away!"

That is the spirit of the normal, yet faithful man.   Heroism is not so much reckless insensibility to danger, as it is facing peril with full knowledge of its meaning.

The war ended, Lieutenant Nelson, like most of his gallant comrades, refused to give way to despair.   He bowed to the evident ruling of divine Providence, and took up life again with cheerful courage and dauntless hopefulness.

He taught school for a short time, but at once began preparing for ordination to the sacred ministry. He attended the Seminary of Virginia near Alexandria, for one session, and immediately thereafter in June of 1868, was made deacon by Bishop Johns, and sent by him to Leeds Parish in Fauquier County. Shortly after his ordination, he was married to Miss Grace Fenton McGuire, a daughter of his old principal at the High School. He then settled down to a happy and most active six years' pastorate of his delightful country parish. He constantly referred to those years as perhaps the happiest of his life. He dearly loved people, and especially the people of the old Virginia stock, and so he gloried in this hard, yet joyous work. He was advanced to the priesthood by Bishop Whittle in 1869. From Leeds Parish, he was called to Grace Church in Richmond, at that time one of the smaller churches in the west end of the city. Here he served in his accustomed strenuous way for two years and then was chosen to the position of Professor at the Theological Seminary in Virginia in 1876.

Surely no man chosen to such a post had received for the task before him so unusual a preparation. It is not the approved way of fitting a professor for a school of theology, to cut short his college course, to throw him into a strenuous military service of four years, and to follow that with the busy life of a country parson. And yet Dr. Nelson was a successful teacher. He never pretended to profound learning or extensive reading; but as a man of action and decision, with definite ends of a practical kind held steadily in view, he did teaching in a down right and indubitable fashion that was of tremendous value to men beginning the study of theology. Theology, which is truth about God, is so vast a subject and touches so vitally all branches of learning, philosophy and culture, that the young student may easily become desperately mystified and confused. It is apt to seem too high for him to attain unto, and indeed so full of speculative dubieties as to make the attaining unto it a mere mental exercise. It is well for a class of young men, who have thought little about systematic divinity and whose first contact with it is somewhat forbidding and chilling, as well as vague and doubtful, to be faced by a man who saw always the doctrine of religion from the angle of plain, common, every day living. He had no patience with any sort of mystical or speculative thinking unconnected with downright living in the world.   With him it was always a "Standing on earth, not wrapped above the poles". It is that sort of teacher, a man with not so much a theory as a message, who had left behind doubtful disputations, that most young divinity students need.

Dr. Nelson was a favorite with the students. There were, of course, some men with great notions of culture and learning who complained of a lack of intellectualism in his teaching. "We do not go to a lecture to hear a sermon" they would say. But such men were not many. It was a great comfort to sit under a man, who, however thought to fall short of profoundness, was ever so clear, so definite, so thoroughly honest to himself and to his class. In all matters of moment, in the prime truths of salvation and life, in the place to be given to the written word, in the doctrine of sin, of judgment to come, he had very clear and entirely definite views. There never was any doubt of where he stood in any vital matters concerning the Church and her teaching. If his peculiarly sane and logical mind could not grasp satisfactorily, so as to express plainly any matter of doubtful or speculative sort, he hesitated not to say in his bluff way, "I do not know."

He was all for definiteness in his teaching. It was a worry to him to have a subject left in vagueness. One man, who had attended another seminary, was no little surprised and a bit nettled at the keen, careful manner of his quizzing. He demanded a very precise knowledge of the text book. The student referred to thought this method decidedly primary; he felt that the subject should be taught by lectures, requiring wide reading and giving a chance for independent thought. Men should come to take notes on the great matters prepared for them, rather than be closely questioned on an assigned lesson. Whatever may be said of such freer methods, they were not Dr. Nelson's way. He wanted a frontal attack on any question of history or exegesis; he had no taste for any feinting or flanking. He was quite determined that the men should know and fully understand one approved and accepted view, whatever else they might think. "You may read all you please; the more the better," he would say, giving at the same time appropriate references, "But before you start on all that, I want you to read and weigh carefully the text assigned." He was convinced that young students should fully master some sensible, well-established, and generally accepted view of a difficult or very important subject, and then having done that, they might expatiate more largely if they saw fit. There is a great deal to be said for his view. Theoretically a good way to teach a boy to swim is to throw him at once into water much over his head, but practically the chances are that you will drown the boy.

As a short and reliable aid in New Testament exegesis, he used Ellicott's Handy Commentary. All of his old students have a fond remembrance of his constant demand, "Well, now suppose you tell me what Ellicott says." He firmly insisted upon that view, whatever else was said. It was amusing after some man had given an extended exegesis of a difficult passage, to note the doctor's attitude of interest, to hear him express his appreciation of the exposition, and then to have him come out with his inevitable request: "Yes, Yes, very good indeed, but would you mind telling after all what Ellicott has to say on the subject?"

Whatever the limitations of such teaching, it is without doubt quite effective with immature and withal, conceited young theologs; for it insists upon concentrating attention upon some one accredited view of each important matter of interest or of controversy.

Dr. Nelson delighted in the weekly Thursday night "Faculty Meetings". There his hard, common sense in dealing with the practical matters of the ministry, his rich experiences as pastor, and his love of human nature, made him immensely interesting and helpful. In these delightful and informal addresses to the students, "His favorite themes," says his colleague, Dr. Carl Grammer, "were the value of fidelity to obligation and the supreme importance of character. He never spoke of success in the ministry as betokened by large charges and elevated position. His influence was steadily against holding out such things as

incentives and in favor of unworldliness. His appeal was
ever to duty, sense of responsibility, and the greatness of the
work."

He was a distinctly higher churchman than his colleagues
in the Seminary. He could not get away from the view that
the rejection of episcopacy was a rending in a real way of the
divine order of the Church. He held, however, that our
Church had made no statement in regard to non-episcopal
orders. He regarded them as valid, though irregular. On
the great matters of justification and grace, of faith and
works, he was a staunch and convinced evangelical. He,
therefore, had a horror of the romanizing tendencies of the
Church. He thought the whole Oxford movement tainted
with dishonesty and deceit. His lectures on the movement
are a very vivacious and forceful presentation of that point
of view. He loved the Bible, and accepted it with whole-
hearted devotion as God's word written, needing exposition,
of course, but not susceptible of modification or reversal.
There was, therefore, nothing that he more profoundly dis-
trusted as the modern free criticism of the sacred writings.

Dr. Nelson was not and never tried to be a brilliant
preacher. What he had to say, he strove to say in the
simplest way possible. He aimed at the average man, and
thought out his themes along the lines of the practical issues
of the ordinary man's life. For heroics of any kind he had
no taste, being too dead in earnest to try any tricks of rhetoric. His message was very direct, and was so delivered as to
convince his hearers that he himself had first taken it to
heart. Emotionalism or sentimental excitement in the solemn
matters of the soul, were to him particularly distasteful. He
persistently appealed to reason and calm judgment; and in
full dependence upon the Holy Spirit, he confidently looked
for best results from such appeals.

The missions in the country around the Seminary conducted by the students, were for many years in charge of Dr.
Nelson. He gave a great deal of time and thought to these
little congregations, being ever ready with counsel and help
for the students in charge. He did much pastoral work in
this connection, associating himself with the young men in

this service.   In this business, he was in his element, exempli-
fying his own theory of "sanctified common sense".   While
dealing very kindly and lovingly with people, he was noted
for his courageous frankness.   He despised any temporizing
with sin, and believed in attacking it boldly in frontal style.
He earnestly believed that he had the cure for spiritual disease in the free grace of God through Christ's redemption,
and so was not afraid to probe any wounds that Satan's darts
had made.   His students learned invaluable lessons from
the association of this forceful and earnest man with them
in the cure of souls.   The paid, sensational revivalist was his
abomination.   Once when one of his favorite missions was
threatened with a visitation from a belligerent exhorter
of the violent type, the student in charge came to him in
great distress as to what must be done.   "Well," said he,
"all we have to do is to *out-pray* them, to *out-preach* them,
and to *out-work* them."   There spoke the artillery-man, planting his battery and getting the range.

His intimate friend and former comrade in arms, the
late Dr. Launcelot Blackford, then principal of the Episcopal
High School, tells of his delightful influence among the boys
of the School.   The School until the coming of Dr. Blackford had always had a clergyman at its head; but when Dr.
Blackford became principal he requested Dr. Nelson to take
the spiritual oversight of the boys.   Says Dr. Blackford,
"The fact that Dr. Nelson was himself a distinguished old
High School boy and an experienced teacher of boys, that he
was a friend of the principal, that he was in the prime of
life and keenly sympathetic with the young, at once designated him for the office of pastor of the School.   His stated
ministrations included a monthly Sunday night service and
sermon in the School chapel, a noon meeting on Friday preceding the first Sunday with the boy communicants, a weekly
night service during Lent, and the examination and admission of candidates for confirmation.   His informal care of
the spiritual interests of his charge was of value scarce inferi-
or to his regular offices, though less readily described.   It is
not easy to imagine a man better fitted for such a position.
His feeling toward boys, and his knowledge of them were extraordinary and the mingled tenderness and dignity of his

nature were at once recognized by them.   He was an expert
in baseball and football, a frequent umpire and referee, and
such a lover of these and kindred sports that interest on his
part in this   important element in boys' life was always
secure, and the fact very greatly increased his influence.
For fourteen years he was senior judge in the annual athletic
sports of the School, and discharged the arduous duties of the
post with admirable zeal, patience and efficiency.   Nothing
that he could do to evince his regard for the boys or to
strengthen the firm hold he had on their confidence and affection, was deemed by him too much to do.   A modest
testimonial of their love in the shape of a tablet in the School
Chapel where he so long ministered has been erected."

It was the opinion of Dr. Blackford that no man of his
generation wielded so great an influence in the Diocesan
Council as did Dr. Nelson.   He never spoke except when he
had something really worth while to say.   He spoke rather
infrequently, but always with a cautious consideration of the
statements he was making.   He was therefore a redoubtable
arbiter, whose calm and earnest presentation of matters in
hand was a great factor in many important decisions of the
Council.   He served on many important committees, but the
most important perhaps, was that in which acting as chairman, he made the final report on the division of the diocese.

He was also a member of three General Conventions,
as a representative from Virginia.   On that wider field, he
quickly became conspicuous, rapidly growing in influence
and leadership, when his sudden illness and subsequent
death cut short his distinguished career.   He enjoyed the
friendship of such men as Dr. W. R. Huntington of New York,
and held his own with them in many forward debates in the
Convention.   Some of his sayings became known throughout
the church.   Once in opposing changes in the Prayer Book,
advocated by Dr. Huntington and others, he declared they
meant virtually "Side-tracking the Thirty-nine Articles".
This was a phrase which caught the attention of everybody.

On another occasion, he brought down the amused applause of the house when, replying to a brother, who insisted that we should "trust our bishops" and not be so
careful about making restraining canons, he cried, "I trust

the bishops of this Church, I trust the priests of this Church, I trust the deacons of this Church; but I trust them all under law!" Dr. Nelson was twice urged for the position of assistant bishop of Virginia; in 1883 when Dr. A. M. Randolph was chosen for that office, and again in 1894 when Dr. John B. Newton was elected to the same office. On both occasions he received a strong vote. He was elected in 1886 to the position of Bishop of Easton; but after due consideration, declined. Once again in 1888, he was chosen bishop by the clergy of Southern Ohio, but the laity failed to confirm.

Up to May 30, 1894, not long after the Council in which he had been a prominent candidate for assistant Bishop of Virginia, no one had suspected that the health of Dr. Nelson was at all impaired. He was not yet fifty-six years of age and seemed to be full of youthful enthusiasm, and tireless vigor. But on the date mentioned above, he suffered a sudden and severe attack of what seemed to be apoplexy. He rallied from this illness, however, much to the joy of his hosts of friends; and after a restful summer, he was able to take up his work at the Seminary in the autumn. But alas, the improvement was but brief and temporary, and he succumbed to another attack of the disease on October 25th, 1894.

He lies buried in the cemetery of the Seminary that he loved so devotedly and served so well.

The translation of this brave, true, simple-hearted man was felt as a loss not only by Virginia and her Seminary, but by the whole Church. Dr. Nelson had arrived at the full ripeness of his powers and seemed fitted for years of fruitful leadership in the Church. His sane, practical evangelicalism attracted to him men who loved the old paths. He gave, indeed, no uncertain sound; he knew Him in whom he had believed, and where that holy authority was present, he yielded without question. But he steadily refused to be certain on matters that the Lord had left uncertain; he abhorred the modern so-called science, with its cock-sureness above and beyond what was written. To put human philosophizing on a par with revealed truth was to him abominable. And many rejoiced in his fearless challenging of

such endeavors, whether coming from rationalists or roman-
ists. The deep reverence for the word of God in such a
strong practical mind was most inspiring. Taking true wisdom to be founded on the fear of God, we should unhesitatingly maintain that whoever might be considered more learned,
there have been few wiser teachers than Dr. Kinloch Nelson.

THE REVEREND DOCTOR ANGUS CRAWFORD

Professor 1887-1920

SECTION V

CHAPTER XI

REV. DR. ANGUS CRAWFORD

REV. W. A. R. GOODWIN, D. D.

A carriage drawn by two beautiful horses swept into
the grounds of the Seminary over the road by Whittle Hall.
A student was standing with Dr. Packard in the quadrangle
and the Doctor turned to him and said, "Mi-yah, Mr.
——, who is that?" To which the student replied: "Doctor that is our new professor of Hebrew." With a smile
"the old Rab" said, "Well, they can never call this a one-
horse place any more."

This incident occurred shortly after the arrival of the
Rev. Dr. Angus Crawford with his charming family on the
Seminary Hill in 1887. The great difficulty of finding a scholar
thoroughly versed in the Hebrew and cognate languages was
realized and a committee of the Board of Trustees, of which
Bishop Randolph was chairman, was appointed to look
the whole country over in search for a man who possessed
the qualifications needed to enable him to fill this chair.
Upon the recommendation of Dr. Harper, of Yale University,
seconded by a number of other testimonials, Dr. Crawford
was nominated by the committee to the Board of Trustees,
and elected to the Faculty.

Dr. Crawford entered upon his work with unbounded
enthusiasm. Thoroughly versed in his subject, he taught
not only with vigor, but with a passionate devotion to his
subject. It was a revelation, as it doubtless had never
occurred to any student in the Virginia Seminary that any
man on earth could be as enthusiastic about Hebrew as
was Dr. Crawford. He made exacting demands upon the
time and application of the students. Indeed there were
many who felt that if they succeeded in learning Hebrew as it
had been learned by Dr. Crawford, or as Dr. Crawford insisted that it should be learned at the Seminary, it would

be the only examination which they would be able to pass at the end of the session.

Combined, however, with his scholarly attainments, Dr. Crawford possessed a genial disposition and a kindly heart which did much to soften the rigor of his demands upon the students in preparation for his recitations. His influence in the Seminary was, however, not confined in any way to the classroom. Possessed of inexhaustible energy and of a practical disposition of mind, he soon set about to improve the grounds and buildings of the Seminary. His wide circle of acquaintanceship in the North gave him access to many persons of means and influence whom he was able to interest in the welfare of the Institution. The chapter by Dr. Crawford on "The Benefactors of the Seminary" printed elsewhere in this history, will give some conception of the extent and the success with which Dr. Crawford secured the sympathy and the help of others for the Seminary. He was the originator of the Class Contribution Plan, through which the various classes of the Seminary were enlisted in the effort which he was leading for the improvements of the grounds and the betterment of the buildings. The records of the Alumni Association give evidence of his success in this special endeavor. The trees in the Seminary grove were trimmed and treated, and many of them rescued from decay and destruction. In place of the walks of cinder and mud through the Seminary grounds, concrete walks were built, electric lights were installed in the buildings to replace the oil lamps, and an artesian well, successfully drilled and linked to a power plant, gave to the Seminary for the first time a reasonable protection against fire and provided a convenient water supply. The improvement which, perhaps, was most welcomed by the students, who until then had been obliged to carry up their wood and coal from the basement of Aspinwall Hall, was the installation of the Seminary heating plant. An electric motor was secured for the Seminary organ and an adequate reading room opened in Aspinwall Hall for the use of the students. Much of this work was begun by Dr. Crawford before he was elected Dean in 1900, which position he continued to hold until 1916.

It was through Dr. Crawford's aid and instrumentality that the Biblical Museum, mentioned in the article on the Seminary Library, was secured for the Institution. He brought to the life of the Seminary through his example and precept an emphasis which was unquestionably needed in the interest of neatness, decorum and order.

It is doubtful whether any man ever entered an Institution from the far outside, who came to love it and to serve it more devotedly than Dr. Crawford. The resolutions passed by the Alumni Association when his retirement was announced, expressing appreciation of his scholarship, of his untiring and successful efforts for the betterment of the Institution, and of the kind and constant interest of Dr. and Mrs. Crawford in the students shown in the welcome always given to them at "The Wilderness", give evidence of the deep and heart-felt appreciation of the Alumni for the services rendered by him to the Seminary.

He was standing one day with the venerable Dr. Packard on the steps of the Seminary overlooking Alexandria, Washington, and the far stretches of the valley of the Potomac. As they stood there with the dome of the Capitol and the Washington monument rising in the distance, Dr. Crawford called attention to the way in which Washington had extended across the Potomac, and was already stretching its suburbs down in the direction of Alexandria. He said to the old Dean, "Dr. Packard, it seems to me that you would have realized when you first came to the Seminary that the country around Washington would necessarily increase in value as the years passed on, and that you would have invested either for yourself or for the Seminary in some of the real estate adjoining the city." To which the old Dean replied, "Mi-yah, Crawford, can you imagine St. Paul investing in corner lots on Mars Hill?"

The grove, the silence and the beauty of the scene, and the nearness of "The Hill" to God, with the opportunity that it gave to teach successive classes of students the deep and hidden truths of the spiritual world, had all through the years absorbed and satisfied the old Dean. Dr. Crawford felt that better lights in the Seminary with which to pursue the paths leading to truth, easier access to fresh, pure water,

the possibility of reaching the Chapel and St. George's Hall
without getting mired on the way, the preservation of the
trees which the old Dean loved, and which, as he said, "He
loved because he had seen them grow", the painting and
the improvement of the homes of the professors, were all
acts which also showed a consecrated devotion to the Institution. The chances are that Dr. Crawford would have
invested in corner lots in the interest of the Institution,
while at the same time he would have been no less enthusiastic in giving to men the revelation of God through the better
understanding of some hidden Hebrew root.

Upon the retirement of the Rev. Dr. Crawford in July,
1919, the following appreciative notice appeared in "The
Southern Churchman" of date July 12, 1919, from the pen of
the Rev. Dr. Wallace E. Rollins: "Dr. Crawford will have been
a professor in the Seminary at the time of his retirement for
thirty-three years, and has thus helped to train a whole
generation of ministers. For sixteen years, from 1900 to
1916, he was the able and energetic dean of the Institution.
Dr. Crawford's active service will, happily, not cease until
July 1, 1920. I shall, therefore, not undertake at this time
and this brief space to estimate his long and valuable services
to the Seminary and to the Church. This will doubtless be
done at a more fitting time by those who are fully competent
to speak. Suffice it to say here that in the judgment of
many of his former students, and of other competent judges,
Dr. Crawford has not, in his day, had a superior in the
Church as a teacher of the Hebrew language. His never-
failing enthusiasm for his subject, due to his profound conviction of the value of the knowledge of the original Bible
languages, his high standards of Christian scholarship, and
the thoroughness of his methods of teaching have made him
a teacher not soon to be forgotten.

As dean of the Seminary Dr. Crawford did much to
improve the buildings and to beautify the grounds. He
has always been deeply interested in the material side of the
Seminary and has been the means of raising various funds
for the Institution, and of adding considerably to the endowment fund."

THE REVEREND DOCTOR CARL E. GRAMMER

Professor 1887-1898

SECTION V
CHAPTER XII
REV. DR. CARL E. GRAMMER
REV. W. A. R. GOODWIN, D. D.

The Rev. Dr. Carl E. Grammer was elected to the Faculty of the Theological Seminary in Virginia in February, 1887, and entered upon his duties at the Seminary in the autumn of 1887. He was educated in Baltimore City College and at Johns Hopkins University, from which he graduated in February, 1880 with the degree of A. B. but continued his studies in the University till the summer, attending the Greek classes of Professor Gildersleeve. He spent a year in the law school of the University of Maryland. He then entered the Theological Seminary in Virginia, graduating in June, 1884. The degree of S. T. D. was conferred upon him in 1895 by Trinity College, Connecticut. Dr. Grammer was ordained deacon in 1884 and priest in 1885. He served as deacon and rector in charge of St. Thomas' Church, Hancock, Maryland, from 1884 to 1886, and of Epiphany Church, Cincinnati, until his election in February, 1887, to a professorship in the Virginia Seminary.

Dr. Grammer was first elected assistant professor of Hebrew and Greek, whereupon he went to Yale University and took a special course in Hebrew under Dr. Harper, in order to prepare himself to do the teaching in Hebrew. At the June meeting of the Board of Trustees, the Rev. Dr. Angus Crawford, was elected professor of Hebrew and Dr. Grammer was elected professor of Greek, subsequently exchanging this work, with the approval of the Board, for the Professorship of Church History and Canon Law. Dr. Grammer was the son of the Rev. Dr. Julius E. Grammer, for many years the distinguished rector of St. Peter's Church, Baltimore, and was the grandson of the Rev. Dr. William Sparrow of the Theological Seminary in Virginia. He thus possessed a clear title to an exceptionally rich heritage of talent and mental endowment, to which he added the attainments of comprehensive and accurate scholarship.

As a thinker and teacher, Dr. Grammer was distinctly brilliant. He loved the truth and the truth seemed to love him in return, and sparkled from his mind like sun from the burnished diamond. Through studious application and a wide range of reading, his mind had become enriched with the knowledge of truth and with literary culture, which seemed always to be at his disposal for illustrative use and application in his class room work. Dr. Grammer possessed in a rare degree the power of stimulating the minds of his students. He was a militant Protestant and came to the Seminary as a profound Evangelical. As he taught the truth and pursued it further, his mind broke through traditional limitations and he came to be recognized by those who followed the trend of his thought as distinctly progressive and later still as distinctly broad in his theology and in his churchmanship.

The teaching of Church History gives to the versatile and comprehensive mind fascinating invitations as well as frequent opportunities for the expression of conviction upon many points. Dr. Grammer accepted the challenge which his course offered and entered as a fearless antagonist into various realms of speculative thought and dogmatic theology. There were doubtless more books taken from the library as a result of Dr. Grammer's brilliant excursions into the realm of Church Polity and Theology than were asked for as a result of all the other courses of the Seminary combined. The books were sought for and read to see "whether these things were so." Sometimes the students concluded that they were, and others concluded that they were not, but, in both cases, Dr. Grammer was producing the stimulus which he desired and leading the students through investigation and study to reach conclusions upon the basis of accurate knowledge.

The distinct and outspoken Protestant tendencies of Dr. Grammer's mind often found cogent and timely expression in the protests which he uttered in his classroom against intellectual laziness. He refused to consider costless piety as a substitute for intellectual earnestness. Though he, himself, was Evangelical in his theology in the highest sense of the term, he clearly saw the temptations which this system offered to lazy men and to lazy thinkers, to lie down on the kindly graces and infinite mercy of a benevolent God.

Not alone in his classroom, but also in his talks at the Faculty Meetings and in his sermons in the Chapel, Dr. Grammer contributed to the development and enrichment of the heart and mind of the student body. Some men go through college and through the Seminary with only a thin surface soil of mentality offered to the seeds of truth. Beneath this surface soil there lies a sub-soil, rich in possibilities, but often hardened by selfishness, selfish indulgence and indomitable laziness. When Dr. Grammer's penetrating mind struck this complacent and hardened surface, he drilled straight through and broke it up, and there is no question but that many men who were privileged to sit in his classroom have acknowledged in after years their debt of gratitude to him for taking the trouble to do it.

While there were those in authority in the high places of Seminary life who sympathized somewhat cautiously with Dr. Grammer in his progressive philosophical thought, they were not then prepared for the extension of the rights of reason so far into the realm of Biblical criticism and historical interpretation as Dr. Grammer's mind fearlessly followed. Dr. Grammer doubtless recognized that he had come to think in advance of the views long held and then still cherished by the Seminary, and in search for the fuller freedom which his mind demanded in its pursuit of truth, he resigned his professorship in 1898, much to the regret of the students and many friends of the Institution, and accepted the call to the rectorship of Christ Church, Norfolk, in which he continued to serve until he was elected to the rectorship of St. Stephen's Church, Philadelphia, where, until the present time, he has continued to exercise a faithful and devoted ministry.

A good many years have passed since Dr. Grammer took his official departure from "The Hill". He is still, however, and will long be remembered not alone as a scholarly and brilliant teacher, but as one who contributed, in association with his charming wife, to the enrichment of the social life upon "The Hill" and to the lifting of the whole Seminary to a higher and nobler plane of spiritual and intellectual devotion.

SECTION V

CHAPTER XIII

REV. DR. SAMUEL A. WALLIS

Professor Emeritus

REV. W. A. R. GOODWIN, D. D.

Dr. Wallis was born at Woodbridge, a village eighteen miles north of Toronto, Canada, and received his early education in the public schools of Toronto and at the Toronto Grammer School. In 1870 the family moved to Stafford County, Virginia. After teaching school for awhile, Dr. Wallis studied at the University of Virginia and in 1878 entered the Virginia Theological Seminary graduating in 1881. He was ordered Deacon in 1881 and ordained Priest in 1882 by Bishop Whittle, and was appointed to serve in Pohick Church, Truro Parish, Fairfax County, Virginia. Olivet Church, formerly a Mission of the Seminary, was united with Pohick in 1883, and Dr. Wallis continued to serve both churches until elected Professor in the Seminary in November, 1894, to succeed the Rev. Dr. Kinloch Nelson. His course embraced the Greek New Testament, Church Polity, Liturgics and Religious Pedagogy, and also Pastoral Theology. He succeeded the Rev. Dr. Cornelius Walker as Secretary of the Faculty, and has for many years been the faithful and efficient Secretary of the Alumni Association, which position he still occupies. Dr. Wallis served as Examining Chaplain of the Diocese of Virginia from 1888 until 1904. Hampden-Sidney College in 1906 conferred upon him the degree of Doctor of Divinity.

In 1890 Dr. Wallis married Miss Mary Snowden, daughter of the late Edgar Snowden, editor of "The Alexandria Gazette."

In addition to his heavy course in the Seminary, where he worked with constant devotion, Dr. Wallis was the pastor of the Seminary Mission Stations and rendered a service in this capacity which endeared him to the hearts of the people. He possessed marked ability as a pastor, and in and out of the

THE REVEREND DOCTOR SAMUEL A. WALLIS

Professor 1894-1920

THEOLOGICAL SEMINARY IN VIRGINIA

Seminary was beloved because of his gentleness and exceeding goodness. With the gracious assistance of Mrs. Wallis, his home became noted upon "The Hill" and among the Alumni for its ever kind and beautiful hospitality. He continued in the Faculty until 1920 when he was made Professor Emeritus. Since his retirement from the Seminary Dr. Wallis has been in charge of the Church in the suburbs of Alexandria where he is doing faithful and devoted service.

The following appreciation of Dr. Wallis written by Rev. Dr. Wallace E. Rollins appeared in "The Southern Churchman" of July 12th, 1919; "Dr. Wallis at the time of his retirement on July 1, 1920, will have been a professor at the Seminary for more than twenty years. His earnestness and piety, which always remind one of the old evangelicalism at its best, and his faithful work as a pastor have made him universally beloved. His knowledge of liturgical history and of the intricacies of rubrical and canon law made him a court of appeal in such matters among both students and faculty. His love for the Seminary and his loyalty to its traditions have been unfailing. His home has always been a haven of rest and delight to students and alumni, and his abundant hospitality has been of the ideal sort typified by the word 'Virginian.'"

SECTION V

CHAPTER XIV

REV. DR. ROBERT K. MASSIE

REV. W. A. R. GOODWIN, D. D.

Dr. Massie was elected Professor of Church History and Canon Law in the Virginia Seminary in 1898 to fill the vacancy caused by the resignation of the Rev. Dr. Carl E. Grammer. He was born in Charlottesville, Virginia, on February 4, 1864, where he was educated at a private school and subsequently at the University of Virginia from which he graduated in 1888. In 1902 he received the degree of M. A. from George Washington University, D. C., and in 1906 was honored with the degree of Doctor of Divinity by Washington and Lee University. He was ordered Deacon by Bishop Whittle in 1891 at the Virginia Seminary and ordained Priest by Bishop Whittle in Berryville, Virginia in 1891. Immediately upon his hastened ordination to the Priesthood, he left for China, where he served from 1891 to 1895, being compelled by the ill effect of the climate upon his family to return to America. He became Rector of Meade Parish, Virginia, where he served from 1896 to 1898, when his election to the Faculty of the Seminary took place. He remained in the Virginia Seminary from 1898 to 1912, when he resigned to become Dean of Christ Church Cathedral, Lexington, Kentucky, where he continues to exercise an acceptable and devoted ministry.

Dr. Massie graduated in the class of 1891 with J. Addison Ingle, William Cabell Brown, John G. Meem, and William D. Smith, all of whom volunteered, as he did, for foreign service. As Professor in the Seminary he helped keep alive the missionary spirit which sent him to China and which dominated his class. He carried into his classroom work the enthusiasm which characterized his nature and by his fidelity to duty and his spirit of good comradeship won the respect and devotion of the students. During the period of his

666

THE REVEREND DOCTOR ROBERT K. MASSIE

Professor 1898-1912

Professorship, Dr. Massie served for some years as Treasurer of the Alumni Association, and lent himself to every endeavor for promoting the welfare of the Institution.

SECTION V

CHAPTER XV

REV. DR. RICHARD W. MICOU

REV. PAUL MICOU, B. D.

The Rev. Richard Wilde Micou, D. D. was born in New Orleans, Louisiana, June 12th, 1848. The family was of Huguenot extraction, being descended from Paul Micou, a lawyer of Nantes, France, who settled in Essex County, Virginia, soon after the revocation of the Edict of Nantes. The father of Dr. Micou was William Chatfield Micou, a lawyer of eminence in New Orleans and the partner of Judah P. Benjamin. His mother was Anna Davenport Thompson, whose Scotch-Irish ancestor, Rev. John Thompson, came to America in 1730 and became rector of St. Mark's Parish, Culpeper County, Virginia, in 1739.

In 1863 Dr. Micou entered the University of Georgia, but the following year changed to the University of Alabama. He was in the cadet corps when it marched out of the buildings April 3rd and 4th, 1865, in an endeavor to repel the advance of the Federal soldiers. After the disbanding of the corps, he enlisted as a private in the Confederate Army for the remaining days of the War. Years later the University of Alabama conferred on him as a "war-time student", prevented from finishing his course, the honorary degree of Bachelor of Arts. At the conclusion of the War he went to the University of Erlangen, Bavaria, where he studied for a year under the noted faculty of the time, which held such professors as Herzog, Ebrard, Hofmann, Thomasius and Delitzsch. Next he spent two years at the University of Edinburgh, Scotland, where in 1868, he took the prize in English and the Philologus and Junior Humanity Medals, the highest honors in the classics, under Professor John Stuart Blackie. Returning to America, he taught Greek for a few months at the University of the South, Sewanee, Tennessee, and then continued his theological studies for a

THE REVEREND DOCTOR RICHARD W. MICOU

Professor 1898-1912

year (1869-70) at the General Theological Seminary, New York. The honorary degree of Master of Arts was conferred on him in 1893 by Trinity College, Connecticut. Kenyon College, Ohio, honored him with the Doctor of Divinity degree in 1896.

On June 12th, 1870, he was ordered Deacon by the Rt. Rev. William M. Green, D. D., of Mississippi, at Sewanee, Tennessee and served for a year as assistant minister of St. John's Church, Montgomery, Alabama. He then took charge of his first parish, St. Mary's Church, Franklin, Louisiana. On May 16th, 1872, he was married to Mary Dunnica of New Orleans. Her father was Granville Price Dunnica, a merchant in Covington, Louisiana, and her mother was Mary Ann Bagley. He was advanced to the Priesthood November 15th, 1872, by the Rt. Rev. Joseph Wilmer, D. D., Bishop of Louisiana. In 1874 he took charge of St. Paul's Church at Kittanning, Pennsylvania, and in July, 1877, accepted the call to the rectorship of Trinity Church at Waterbury, Connecticut, taking charge of the parish seven weeks after its organization.

"The Waterbury American" in an editorial at the time of his death said of him: "Dr. Micou was a man first, a citizen next, and a clergyman last. Of scholarly mind and of wide attainments, he was never academic. In his thinking and conduct he was sincerity itself. . . . Never a sensationalist, never stirring up doubt for the sake of challenging attention, Dr. Micou was always frank and open in the pulpit and out of it, ready to face any problems of our modern life with the serene confidence of assured faith. Beloved as a rector, respected as a citizen, admired as a scholar and thinker, he for a long time held a unique place of influence and regard in Waterbury, and his friends have watched with pride his widening sphere of influence and recognition."

He was known as one of the most studious clergymen in the diocese, and took the lead in discussions at clerical gatherings. The Rt. Rev. Edwin Stevens Lines, D. D., bore testimony to this. "He belonged to a company of clergymen who met together regularly through many years for study . . I think we would all say that he was the first among us, the most widely read in history and theology, and an inspiration to us all. The books which he read both in number and in solid character on a great variety of subjects were an astonishment to us all. How he found time to read so much in connection with well performed church duties, we could not understand."

When he was suggested for the professorship in the Philadelphia Divinity School, the Rev. Francis T. Russell, D. D., who was later a professor in the General Theological Seminary, wrote of him, "If you can name anything of note that he might be expected to have read for the last twenty years, he has read it. He is an intensely active man intellectually, and squarely abreast of the times, and will keep so." In similar vein the Rev. Charles H. Hall, D. D., of Holy Trinity Church, Brooklyn, wrote, "He is, and I emphasize this, the *best read* man of his age in the Church, and has at his tongue's end the stores of acquisition in theology and literature which have been gained by years of faithful and unremitting study."

He was called to the professorship of Systematic Theology and Apologetics in the Philadelphia Divinity School, where he remained for six years, going thence to take the similar chair in the Theological Seminary in Virginia, to which he was elected on February 10th, 1898, where he taught until his death fourteen years later.

His scholars and friends hoped he could find time to publish the results of his labors. In 1900 the venerable Professor John S. Kedney, D. D., wrote to him, "I know of no one, now in our Church, more likely to carry on a theological advance, so make use of your mid-age before declining days come." But it was not until the fall of 1911 that opportunity was given him to prepare the books he had in contemplation. A temporary breakdown in health led the Board of Trustees to give him an eighteen months' vacation, stating that "in the opinion of this Board it is eminently desirable that the Rev. Dr. Micou should embody in literary form for publication the results of his long and valuable course of teaching in the Virginia Seminary."

He was not spared to do this. In February, 1912, he sailed for England and, after some months of leisurely preparation for the task in the southwestern counties went to

Oxford, expecting to find there congenial atmosphere for work. On June 4th he succumbed to sudden heart failure, and was buried during the Commencement of the Virginia Seminary two weeks later.

At that time the President of the Seminary, the Rt. Rev. Robert A. Gibson, D. D., Bishop of Virginia, thus described his work: "Class after class of students have known Dr. Micou as teacher and friend, and have appreciated him at the high value which was his due. A man of rare acquirements, of rapid intuitions, of intellectual courage and of the most profound reverence for the great themes with which he dealt, many of his pupils will carry his name and his words ever in their memories, and will think of him in the depth of their hearts as the person who to them was 'the master'."

His former students paid their tribute to him in the following words: "As a scholar his learning was as profound as it was varied and extensive. The wide range of his information did not seem to limit the thoroughness with which he investigated every problem of philosophy, or obscure his great critical gift in drawing the nice distinctions so necessary in theological definition. It was his task to teach Apologetics at the most difficult period of the century, the period when Christianity had to fight for its life with materialism. All his students during the last twenty years know how well and successfully he defended the spiritual explanation of Life and the Universe. With the wisdom of a true seer he saw the triumph of idealism of the next generation, while most philosophical teachers were becoming resigned to the fact that materialism was final, and that the conflict must be waged along that line until the end. So while Professor Eucken in Germany is being hailed as a new and inspiring interpreter of the spiritual view of life, the younger alumni of the Virginia Seminary would like to acknowledge gratefully the very similar, though less conspicuous, teaching of their lamented professor.

"An able thinker, a thorough student of science, and a great theologian, he was yet a man of the clearest, simplest and most childlike faith. Every one who knew him realized what a deeply pious man he was, and that his was indeed a life of prayer. His quick and generous impulses, his affectionate interest in his neighbors and pupils and his genuine sympathy for all in need and trouble, made him a friend who can never be forgotten."

Dr. Micou was a member of the Church Congress, and served on its Executive Committee. He was also a member of the Society of Biblical Literature and Exegesis. He addressed the Congress three times. During his residence in Waterbury he was prominently identified with educational work, serving as a member of the Board of Education, with the exception of one year, from 1883 to 1891. He was also a trustee of Cheshire Academy, Cheshire, Connecticut. He belonged to the Independent Order of Odd Fellows.

His publications comprise several essays in "The Protestant Episcopal Review", two lecture syllabi, and two manuals of his lectures, published privately by his students from their class room notes. His work in the field of Apologetics has been published by his son, Rev. Paul Micou, in "Basic Ideas in Religion, or Apologetic Theism" (Association Press, January, 1916), who edited the lectures delivered to the students in the Middle Class at the Virginia Theological Seminary. This book met with immediate acceptance on the part of those best qualified to judge, namely the professors of Apologetics in the leading theological seminaries of the country. Their comments were uniformly of high praise. The consensus of opinion is that it is scholarly, vital, exceedingly clear, and the most complete treatment on the field it covers that had yet appeared.

The Present Faculty

Seated (*Left to Right*): Rev. Dr. Paca Kennedy; Rev. Dr. Berryman Green, Dean; Rev. Dr. W. Cosby Bell.
Standing: Rev. Dr. Thomas K. Nelson; Rev. Dr. Wallace E. Rollins; Rev. Dr. Beverley D. Tucker.

SECTION V

Chapter XVI

The Present Faculty

REV. W. A. R. GOODWIN, D. D.

We envy the satisfaction and pleasure with which some future historian of the Virginia Seminary will face the task of saying what can then be said, but which now can not, in honor of the Present Faculty of the Institution. He will have no apologies to offer. There will be no lack of inspiration. The personalities and the work of those concerning whom he will be privileged to write will make his task both easy and delightful. If he should be a gracious as well as a gifted writer, he will also have high words of commendation for the Board of Trustees which exercised the wisdom displayed in choosing the men who now constitute the Faculty of the Seminary.

The one who regretfully relegates this pleasant task to the more worthy historian of the future, confesses to a real sense of reluctance in being compelled to place restraint upon his natural disposition to say what he thinks. He, however, knows that the members of the Present Faculty are not only worthy men, but modest men also; indeed one of them took the precaution to urge that when we came to speak of the Present Faculty the writing should be confined to chronological data and the barest possible statement of essential facts. The students, however, know the professors, respect, admire and love them, and the Church knows them through their scholarship and their students.

In spite of preliminary warnings, one can not refrain, however, from speaking of the satisfaction with which all who know and love the Seminary have viewed the administration of the present Dean. He has proved a worthy successor of worthy predecessors. With the other members of the Faculty, we must, of necessity, keep faith and insert the very brief sketches which indicate the preparation through which these men have passed previous to their election and the brief notes of the nature of the service which they are now rendering to the Institution.

Rev. Berryman Green, D. D.
Dean and Professor

The Rev. Dr. Berryman Green, the present Dean of the Seminary, was born in Charlotte County, Virginia, July 25, 1865. He was the son of Colonel William E. Green and Jeonie Elliot Boylon Green. His father served with distinction in the Confederate Army and was Colonel of the 56th Virginia regiment. Dr. Green graduated from the Virginia Theological Seminary in 1890, and subsequently received the degree of B. D. from this Institution. The degree of Doctor of Divinity was conferred upon him by Washington and Lee University. Dr. Green married Miss Nina D. Bouldin, daughter of Judge Wood Bouldin, Judge of the Supreme Court of Virginia. Dr. Green served the term of his Diaconate at Emmanuel Church, Bristol. From 1891 to 1893, he served as Rector of South Farnham Parish in the diocese of Virginia, from 1893 to 1895 as Rector of St. James' Church, Leesburg, Virginia, and from 1896 to 1902 he was the rector of Christ Church, Alexandria, Virginia. While rector of Christ Church he was called by the Board to do emergency teaching in the Seminary when Dr. Packard and Dr. Grammer were both ill. In 1902 he was elected full professor in the Seminary and assigned to the chair of the English Bible and Homiletics.

When in 1916 Dr. Crawford retired as Dean, Dr. Green was elected to succeed him and has since with fidelity and conspicuous ability continued to serve as Dean of and Professor in the Seminary. Since 1896 Dr. Green has been a member, and since 1902 the President, of the Standing Committee of the Diocese of Virginia, and has for several sessions represented the diocese in General Convention. He was

THE REVEREND DOCTOR BERRYMAN GREEN

Dean of the Seminary

twice elected Bishop Coadjutor of the diocese of Virginia, first on December 16, 1908, and again, upon the resignation of Bishop Coadjutor Lloyd, on February 1, 1911, but declined both elections because of his conviction that a somewhat weakened constitution resulting from an illness which had then but recently occurred, would make him, at the time, unequal, in full justice to the Diocese, to perform the many duties which would be required in the exercise of the Episcopal office. By this declination he was saved for the need which the Seminary turned to him to supply and for duties and a position of influence as vital and as far reaching as could have come to him as a Bishop in the Church of God. Some of his students who have been elected to the Episcopate now rejoice and others who will in course of time be called to this high office, will rejoice also, that Dr. Green was called of God to train Bishops rather than to be one himself.

In recognition of the Centennial anniversary of the Theological Seminary in Virginia and of the scholarship and literary culture of Dr. Green, the Board of Visitors of the College of William and Mary, (where the first effort was made in 1820 to establish the Seminary), has invited Dr. Green to appear at the College in June 1923 to receive the honorary degree of Learned Doctor of Laws.

Dr. Green lives at "Melrose", the former home of Dr. Lippitt and Dr. Packard, now called "The Abbey" and it is hoped by the living alumni that he will continue there for many years to come.

Rev. Wilbur Cosby Bell, D. D.

The Rev. Dr. W. Cosby Bell, was elected professor of Systematic Divinity in December 1911. Dr. Bell was born in Augusta County, Virginia, on the first of April, 1881, and graduated with the degree of A. B. from Hampden-Sidney College in 1900. In June, 1905, having graduated from the Theological Seminary in Virginia, he was ordained to the diaconate in the Seminary Chapel by the Rt. Rev. Dr. A. M. Randolph and assigned to Trinity Church, Onancock, Virginia, where he served from 1905 to 1906. He was ordained to the priesthood by Bishop Randolph in St. Paul's Church, Norfolk, Virginia, in 1906. Having been called to the rectorship of the Robert E. Lee Memorial Church, Lexington, Virginia, he entered upon his work in that important center of Church influence, where he served from 1906 to 1911, exerting a strong spiritual and personal influence, not alone upon the local congregation, but also upon the students of Washington and Lee University and the Virginia Military Institute.

In 1911 Dr. Bell accepted the call to the rectorship of St. Andrew's Church, Louisville, Kentucky, and in December of that year was elected professor in the Virginia Seminary to succeed the Rev. Dr. Micou.

Offering himself to the service of his country during the World War, he was appointed Chaplain of the 117th Engineers, A. E. F., in which capacity he served in 1917 and in 1918.

Dr. Bell, since he became professor in the Seminary, has built his course in Theology upon the great fundamental and essential truths of the gospel of redemption. His teaching has been distinctively Christocentric and he has placed the historic and ever living Christ as the center and soul of all theology, and of all truth. He has stimulated the minds of the students to candid and careful investigation, and has brought the course committed to his care thoroughly abreast with modern thought in so far as modern thought is in accord with the ancient and eternal truth.

Until the election of Dr. Thomas Nelson to the Faculty Dr. Bell lived in the house adjoining the High School property formerly occupied by Dr. Grammer and Dr. Micou. In 1919 Dr. Bell moved to "The Wilderness", the former home of the Rev. Dr. Angus Crawford.

Rev. Wallace E. Rollins, D. D.

The Rev. Dr. Wallace E. Rollins was elected "Ely Professor" of Ecclesiastical History and Christian Missions in January, 1913. Dr. Rollins was born in Marshall, North Carolina, January 26, 1870. He received his early education in the public schools of Raleigh, North Carolina, and the Bingham School, and graduated at the University of North Carolina in 1892 with the degree of A. B. He entered Yale Divinity School, graduating with the degree of B. D. in 1895. The Theological Seminary in Virginia in 1916 conferred upon him the degree of Doctor of Divinity. Dr. Rollins was ordered Deacon by Bishop Randolph in Covington, Virginia, in 1897 and Priest by Bishop Randolph in 1898. He served as Deacon in and as Rector of Emmanuel Church, Covington, from 1897 to 1905, and as Rector of St. Thomas' Church, Christiansburg, Virginia, from 1906 to 1908, when he was called to be chaplain in Sweet Briar College, Virginia, where he served from 1908 to 1913 when called to the Seminary. Dr. Rollins married Miss Helen Collens of Asheville, North Carolina.

During the nine years of his professorship in the Seminary Dr. Rollins has developed and extended the course in Ecclesiastical History, and in recent years, by reason of the high standards of scholarship which have marked the men entering the Seminary, he has been able to do intensive work in his department which has been most helpful to the students and most gratifying to the friends of the Institution. Dr. Rollins lives in the home adjacent to Wilmer Hall previously occupied by Dr. Lippitt, Dr. May, Dr. Walker and Dr. Massie.

The section in this volume devoted to the Contributions of the Seminary to the Foreign Missionary Work of the Church was prepared under the editorship of Dr. Rollins, he himself writing the illuminating chapter on the Mission of the Church in Greece.

REV. PACA KENNEDY, D. D.

The Rev. Dr. Paca Kennedy was called to the chair of New Testament Language and Literature in the Seminary in November, 1907, beginning his work in February, 1908.

Dr. Kennedy was born in Charles Town, West Virginia, August 2nd, 1878. He was educated at Roanoke College, Salem, Virginia, where he was graduated in 1899 with the degree of B. A., receiving the degree of M. A. in 1902. He pursued his theological studies in the Virginia Theological Seminary, graduating in 1902 and receiving the degree of B. D. in 1904. The Board of Trustees of the Seminary conferred upon him the degree of Doctor of Divinity in 1910.

Dr. Kennedy was ordered Deacon by Bishop Peterkin in the Seminary Chapel in June, 1902, and was ordained Priest by Bishop Gravatt in Zion Church, Charles Town, West Virginia, in August, 1904. He served in the mission field of West Virginia at St. Mary's and Ravenswood from 1904 to 1908. Dr. Kennedy was elected by the Faculty of the Seminary to receive the benefits of the Sparrow Fellowship and studied from 1902 to 1904 in Oxford University, England. He is married and lives in one of the newer homes of the Seminary adjacent to "Melrose", the home of the Dean. Dr. Kennedy, in addition to his scholarly work as Professor in the Seminary, is also secretary of the Faculty.

The work of Dr. Kennedy among the students of the Episcopal High School has been far-reaching in its influence, and has won for him the affection and esteem of the High School boys and the high appreciation of the principal and masters of that Institution.

REV. BEVERLEY DANDRIDGE TUCKER, JR., D. D.

The Rev. Dr. Beverley Dandridge Tucker, Jr., was elected Professor of Practical Theology in the Seminary, July 1, 1920. He is the son of the Rt. Rev. Dr. Beverley D. Tucker, Bishop of Southern Virginia and Maria Washington Tucker, and the brother of Rt. Rev. Dr. Henry St. George Tucker of Japan. His education was received at Norfolk Academy, where he studied from 1892 to 1899. In 1899 he entered the University of Virginia, graduating with the degree of B. A. in 1902. In September, 1902, he entered the Virginia Theological Seminary, graduating in 1905 and receiving from the Seminary the degree of B. D. in 1915. He was appointed Virginia Rhodes Scholar in 1905 and from 1905 to 1908 studied at Christ Church, Oxford, England, receiving B. A. (Oxon) in 1908 and M. A. (Oxon) in 1912. In 1920 the degree of Doctor of Divinity was conferred upon him by the Board of Trustees of the Virginia Theological Seminary.

Dr. Tucker was ordered Deacon by his father, the Bishop of Southern Virginia, in St. Paul's Church, Norfolk, September 6, 1908, and was ordained Priest by Rt. Rev. Dr. A. M. Randolph in St. James' Church, Boydton, Virginia, on March 12th, 1909. He served as rector of St. James' and St. Luke's Parishes, Mecklenburg County, Diocese of Southern Virginia, from 1908 to 1911; as rector of St. Paul's Memorial Church, University of Virginia, from 1911 to 1920; and as Red Cross Chaplain attached to the University of Virginia Base Hospital 41 at Camp Sevier, Greenville, South Carolina, May and June, 1918; was commissioned chaplain, United States Army, on June 24th, 1918; 1st. Lt. Chaplain United States Army 1918 to 1919; and served with 17th Engineers (Ry.) A. E. F., Base Hospital 41, A. E. F.

Dr. Tucker brought to the Seminary a devotion to the Church inherited from a long line of ancestors distinguished in the Church and in the civic, military, and political life of Virginia; a devotion which has been enriched by the exceptional services which he has been privileged to render. His experience as rector of St. Paul's Memorial Church, adjoining the Campus of the University of Virginia, and his service in the Army gave him rare opportunities for cultivating that knowledge of men which enables the teacher to establish vital points of contact with the minds of his students. Dr. Tucker's home was the house near the Chapel formerly occupied by Dr. Keith, Dr. Sparrow, Dr. Nelson, and Dr. Wallis.

In the spring of 1923 Dr. Tucker resigned his professorship at the Theological Seminary to become rector of St.
Paul's Church, Richmond, Virginia.

The Board of Trustees elected to succeed him his brother,
the Rt. Rev. Henry St. George Tucker, D. D., LL. D., Bishop of Kyoto, Japan. Bishop Tucker's splendid scholarship,
the experience gained by him as President of St. Paul's
University, Tokyo, and in the work of his missionary jurisdiction, will enable him to bring to the Seminary rare
and varied gifts and qualifications for this new work to
which he has been called.

REV. THOMAS KINLOCH NELSON, D. D.

The Rev. Dr. Nelson was born into the Seminary. His
father was Professor of Greek and New Testament Literature
and was living in the home next to the Chapel when in April
11, 1879, Thomas Kinloch Nelson arrived to begin his life
in the Seminary. He received his education at the Episcopal
High School and McGuire's University School in Richmond,
Virginia. He was graduated from the University of Virginia
with the degrees of B. A. and M. A. in 1907, and from the
Theological Seminary in Virginia in 1910, receiving the degree of B. D. in 1911, and the degree of Doctor of Divinity
in 1920. He was ordered Deacon by Bishop Gibson in the
Chapel of the Seminary in 1910 and ordained Priest by Bishop Graves of China in 1911.

Upon his graduation Dr. Nelson went as Missionary to
China and from 1910 to 1913 was Professor in St. John's
University, Shanghai. Compelled, because of ill health to
return home, Dr. Nelson became Rector of St. Paul's Church,
Salem, Virginia, where he served from 1914 to 1916, being
called from Salem to become Professor in and Vice-Rector
of the Virginia Episcopal School in Lynchburg, Virginia,
which position he held from 1916 to 1919, when called back
to the Seminary to take the Chair of Old Testament Language and Literature.

Dr. Nelson's exceptional gifts as a teacher, tested and proved in St. John's, Shanghai, and in the boys' school in Lynchburg, and his scholarly training marked him as learned and well qualified for the position to which he was elected. It is a source of great satisfaction to the Alumni that the son of their former beloved Professor is in the Faculty of their Alma Mater.

Dr. Nelson is married and lives in the home adjoining the High School grounds formerly occupied by Dr. Grammer, Dr. Micou and, before he moved to "The Wilderness", by Dr. Bell.

IN RETROSPECT

Through the pages of this volume we have sought to trace and follow the ascending and ever widening path along which the Theological Seminary in Virginia has passed from its birth to its Centennial. All along the way the path is illumined by the radiance of transcendent faith and by the light of the Divine benediction. It is marked by the footprints of saints and scholars who walked with God and talked with Him in silent places of the hidden meaning of the truth eternal which they were seeking to unfold to the students committed to their guidance and care.

We have seen the buildings rise along the way, and with the passing years have seen them enshrined in affection and hallowed by rich and beautiful associations. Thus from the treasure chambers of the heart's devotion the Seminary has been enriched by the beautiful gifts of God which could never have been purchased with silver and gold.

We have marked the stay in this place amid changing conditions, and yet ever in the presence of abiding faith and conviction, of successive generations of those who had been called here of God and who, having been furnished for their work, went forth to be the ministers of Christ and heralds of the great Gospel of redemption. We have seen them seeking the truth in the class room and "Faculty Meetings" under the instruction and inspiration of consecrated and learned men of God. In "Prayer Hall," in Chapel, in "hall prayer services" and in the silent places we have seen them in companionship with the risen Christ. We have heard them asking, "Lord, what wilt Thou have me to do?" We have seen them rise as men who had seen a heavenly vision and, obedient to the Master's call, go forth to the uttermost parts of the earth. All through the years we have seen and felt them coming back, as they come today, from Greece and China and Africa and Japan and Brazil and from Domestic wildernesses and the towns and cities whither they had gone;

—coming back through prayers of intercession and through the inspiration of example to bring an added blessing to this Heaven-blessed Hill.

The contributions which have been made to the Seminary and by the Seminary for the enrichment of the life of the Church will be set forth in Volume II together with the presentation of the life and influence of those devoted Fathers in God who as Presidents of the Board of Trustees and in other capacities have helped to guide the Seminary in the fulfilment of her high mission.

From this Centennial stage in the History of the Seminary we look back with profound gratitude to God for the goodness and mercy which have surely followed this Institution all the days of her life. With sure confidence we look also to the future believing that He will give to those to whom the care of this School of the Prophets is now committed and to those who shall come after, the full measure of blessing which will insure the further fulfilment of the mission committed by God to the Virginia Seminary.